HAUNTED SKIES

Preserving the Social History of UFO Research

HAUNTED SKIES VOLUME 10 1987-1988

Copyright © 2014 John Hanson & Dawn Holloway. All rights reserved.

First paperback edition printed 2014 in the United Kingdom.

A catalogue record for this book is available from the British Library.

ISBN 978-0-957-4944-3-5

No part of this book shall be reproduced or transmitted in any form or by any means, electronic or mechanical, including photocopying, recording, or by any information retrieval system without written permission of the publisher.

Published by
Haunted Skies Publishing

For more copies of this book, please email: johndawn1@sky.com

Telephone: 0121 445 0340

Designed and typeset by Bob Tibbitts ~ (iSET)

Printed in Great Britain

Although every precaution has been taken in the preparation of this book, the publisher and author assume no responsibility for errors or omissions. Neither is any liability assumed for damages resulting from the use of this information contained herein.

FOREWORD
By NICK POPE

THIS is the tenth in a multi-volume series of *Haunted Skies* – a series that is set to become the definitive reference work on UFO sightings in the United Kingdom.

While many classic cases are featured, as one would expect, much of the material is being published for the first time. Volume 10 covers the period 1987-1988.

This is a particularly fascinating period for a number of reasons because I have a personal interest in all of this. I used to work for the Ministry of Defence and between 1991 and 1994. I worked in a division called Secretariat (Air Staff), where my duties included investigating UFO sightings reported to the MOD and evaluating whether or not there was evidence that UFOs posed any sort of threat, or were of any defence significance.

While I was able to explain most UFOs as misidentifications of ordinary objects and phenomena, a small percentage defied explanation and did seem to be of Defence interest.

Examples of such cases included those where reliable witnesses such as police officers or pilots who witnessed structured craft performing speeds and manoeuvres that seemed to go beyond the capabilities of our most advanced aircraft. They also included cases where UFO sightings were backed up by radar evidence. With the above in mind, it is fascinating to delve into the already published previous volumes and read about UFO sightings that occurred all over the country involving a large number of sightings from members of the public, police officers and military personnel, from the early 1940s to the early to mid-1980s.

As with the previous volumes, while UFOs are at the heart of the book, other strange phenomena are featured. Entity reports, men in black, strange markings on the ground; these are just some of the areas covered. The book is data rich and will demonstrate – whatever people's beliefs – that we live in a weird and wonderful world where not everything can be labelled, pigeonholed and explained.

The authors are a formidable double act. John Hanson is a retired CID officer, who gathers and sifts the evidence in the methodical and critical manner that one would expect from an experienced police officer.

Dawn Holloway is a meticulous researcher, whose quest for the truth has involved countless hours of hard work. Witnesses have been tracked down and interviewed. Sources have been checked. Photographs and films have been collected.

It is noteworthy that the authors are consultants for *Flying Saucer Review*, a publication that dates from 1955 and was once edited by the late Gordon Creighton, a career diplomat in the British Government. *Haunted Skies* is a project of monumental significance and, when complete, will be an authoritative, chronological guide to the UFO phenomenon in the UK. It will serve as a resource for the UFO community, journalists and all those with an interest in the UFO mystery. The depth and breadth of the research is extraordinary and demonstrates that when drawn together, the evidence that underpins the UFO mystery is compelling. The authors are to be congratulated on a phenomenal piece of work that now also includes both American and Australian accounts which will make a major contribution to our knowledge about the UFO phenomena.

Nick Pope and wife, Dr Elizabeth Weiss, pictured at the BUFORA Conference 2012

INTRODUCTION

The Ron West UFO archives

THANKS to the assistance of Brenda Butler and her colleague, who wishes to remain nameless, we are now able to provide details in this and other subsequent volumes of hundreds of previously unseen UFO reports archived by BUFORA representative Ron West and Brenda Butler, who were responsible for running the *East Anglian UFO & Paranormal Research Association*.

If those records had been lost, British UFO research history – never mind the public's knowledge of reported UFO activity for this period – would have been a great deal worse off. As a token of our appreciation for the help of Brenda's colleague, who was custodian of the UFO files following Ron's death, some years ago, at her request we have included a photo of her dog 'Bailey'.

Assessment of the Volumes so far

Although covering a different period of time, each Volume of *Haunted Skies* is uniquely, individually different. For example, Volume 7 was the beginning of a new era as we were now publishing our own books. Because of the enormous amount of information collected over the years, we decided to increase the pagination to over 400 pages, as we had always promised ourselves that nothing was going to be left out – not forgetting what all of those sightings meant to the persons concerned, some of whom are now no longer with us.

Of course, we could have gone down the easy road and kept the books to 320 pages. Unfortunately, this would have meant publishing volumes of possibly just one year, which was going to take us forever, so we were forced to increase the size of the book to 600 pages plus.

With Volume 8 we finally produced our first book in colour, but underestimated how long this volume was going to take to complete, as it covered the events that took place at RAF Woodbridge. In December 2013 we received this email from Colonel Charles Halt after a copy of the book was sent to him.

> *"Just received Volume 8; I skipped back to the Rendlesham part. I'll go back later to read the first part. You did a great job and uncovered many things that were not made public before. Probably best you withheld any final conclusion – a lot to digest. It will be interesting to see any reaction and I'd be interested in hearing about it."*

Haunted Skies Volume Eight

Volume 9 covers the period from 1981-1986 and includes many accounts of vehicle interference, our investigation into the now famous case at Birmingham, when a street in Thornton Road was bombarded by stones by an unknown assailant, and so much more, in fact without the books we would struggle to remember it all!

During the course of publication of the books, we received a number of enquiries from readers, asking us if we were going to include details of American and Australian/New Zealand sightings.

We decided that it would beneficial to publish those sightings in order to contrast, wherever possible, the events that had taken place in England. However, during subsequent research, we realised how prolific that activity had been and felt it was now appropriate to include matters of such interest.

Accordingly we were only able to include details relating to 1940-1962 within the framework of this book, but will extend this facility in future volumes – if only to recognise the commitment made, by so many, to document a number of fascinating UFO sightings that paralleled what had taken place many thousands of miles away in the United Kingdom.

Australian Events

We were also fascinated by the events that took place at Nullarbor, in Australia, involving members of the Knowles family, during January 1988, who – after having encountered a UFO while travelling through the early hours of the morning – were subjected to ridicule by the media after reporting the matter to the authorities. We shall be outlining this fascinating case in a future volume of *Haunted Skies*.

1987

At the beginning of the year, the Archbishop of Canterbury's envoy – Terry Waite – was kidnapped in Lebanon and remained a hostage until 1991. The major political event of this year was the re-election of Margaret Thatcher, in June, making her the longest continuously serving Prime Minister since Lord Liverpool in the early 19th century. The year was also marked by a number of disasters: The sinking of the ferry *Herald of Free Enterprise*; the Hungerford massacre; the 'Great Storm of 1987'; the 'Remembrance Day Bombing' in Northern Ireland and the 'King's Cross fire'.

The *Haunted Skies* dogs

Over the years, many people have assisted us by contributing their time and resources for free. We thank them for that.

All they have ever asked for is the chance to show their much loved animals. This is the least we can do. The first photo is of the evergreen *Maude,* now passed away some years ago but never forgotten. The second one shows the two dogs belonging to Doncaster-based David Sankey and his partner Erica. David provided much assistance with computer generated illustrations, and encouragement with the series of books. We would also like to thank Robert Townshend, Wayne Mason and Steven Franklin, for their assistance with some of the illustrations.

In John Keel's book, *The Eighth Tower* (now long out of print), John tells us the following, which seems very appropriate to what has been going on for a very long time now on the planet.

"In the end, all paranormal manifestations may seem utterly meaningless. However, all of these weird events and games do have a subtle underlying purpose. They very efficiently provide a cover-up camouflaging the presence of the real phenomenon and its purpose. Penetrating that camouflage and correctly interpreting the true nature of the phenomenon could well be the final stage of man's evolution."

Mr Matt Lyons – formerly with BUFORA

This Volume is dedicated to Mr Matt Lyons, previously head of BUFORA, for his advice and support for the *Haunted Skies* project.

Matt Lyons was interested in the UFO concepts from an early age, and enjoyed watching the now classic Gerry Anderson *UFO* series, Spielberg *Close Encounters* film, Jeff Wayne, and the *War Of The Worlds* musical to name just a few. He is a talented musician by profession, and during his investigation into reported UFO activity has applied a factual, scientifically evaluated approach to UFO reports brought to his attention, without committing himself to one particular belief system.

Matt is currently very much involved with researching the role of music as a reflection of the UFO phenomenon, with emphasis on belief systems and the psychology involved in the subject. Matt resigned from the BUFORA organisation due to work and family commitments, in November 2013, while this book was in the process of being completed. Matt has always been very supportive of the publication of the *Haunted Skies* series of books, and we wish him every success for the future. We are proud to call Matt a friend and wish John Wickham, who is taking over his role within the organisation, the best of success.

Haunted Skies Volume Ten

CHAPTER 1

JANUARY TO AUGUST 1987

JANUARY 1987

5th January 1987 – UFO over Essex

AT 5pm on the 5th January 1987, Canvey Island, Essex, resident – Shaun Roy Williams – sighted something unusual and called his mother. As a result of this, he later contacted the Essex-based *East Anglian UFO & Paranormal Research Association* and was asked to fill in one of their sighting forms.

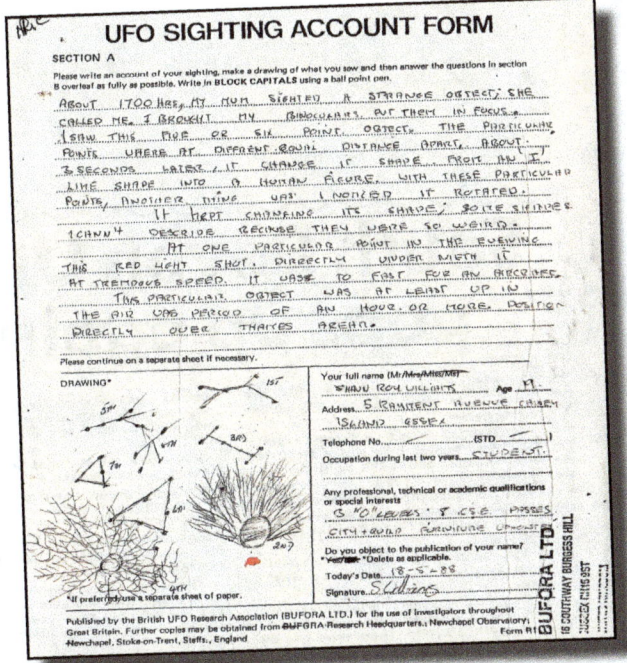

FEBRUARY 1987

20th February 1987 – UFO seen inside house, Kent

Cliftonville, Margate, Kent, resident – Mrs June Taylor – wrote to Gordon Creighton, head of *FSR*, telling him what she had observed, one evening, while in the comfort of her house. Incidents involving strange objects seen inside rather than outside are uncommon, but not rare. The object described by June is very odd indeed. What it was and where it came from we cannot say.

June:

> "Between midnight and 1.30am, my husband and I had been watching the TV and had fallen asleep. I was lying stretched out on the sofa; he was nearby. I opened my eyes and saw an oblong-shaped blur on the other side of the room, about two and half feet long. It was spinning silently as it moved. It looked solid – as though made of a light grey metal, and had a body shaped like an old threepenny bit – and had five or six arms, all the same length, coming from the centre. Each of these 'arms' had a box-shaped piece at its tip. Within seconds it was gone from view."

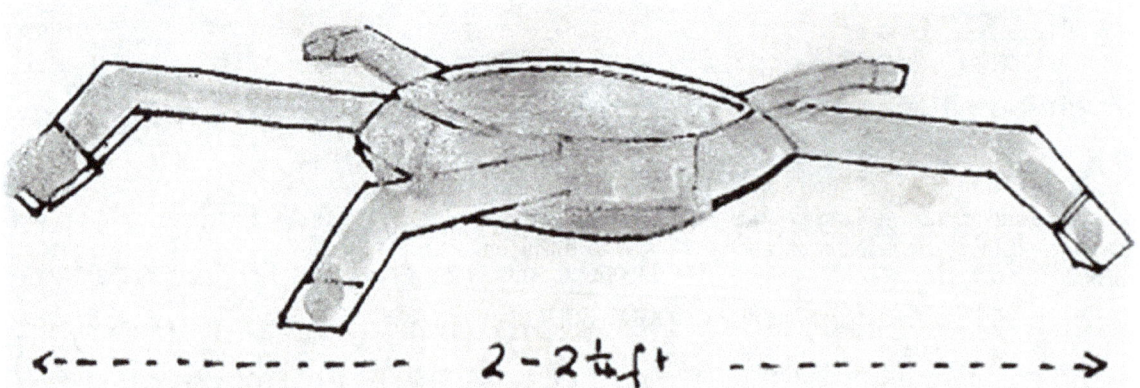

Image from FSR Volume 36 No. 2, Summer 1991

MARCH 1987

6th March 1987 – Glowing lights over Newcastle

Declassified MOD records tell of three Gosforth residents, who made separate reports of a green object they saw in the sky above Newcastle. It was reported to Northumbria Police and then to Newcastle Airport.

On 7th March, an object described as resembling a straw hat was seen in China. Was there any connection?

South Devon UFO pops up again

2374

SPACESHIP suspense is hovering over South Devon after a second UFO sighting within a week.

On Tuesday the Herald Express reported that two Paignton men saw a mysterious object floating across the night sky of the resort.

The story prompted Joe Burrows, of Newton Abbot, to ring in about the strange craft he saw exactly 24 hours after the Paignton sighting.

Joe, secretary of Newton Abbot Athletic Club, says he's totally baffled by what he saw.

"It passed very slowly across the sky without making a sound. I thought it could be some sort of airship. There were two disc-shaped objects with vaguely coloured lights. They were very bright. I've never seen anything like it before," said Joe, who lives at Mile End Road.

He first saw the object as he was driving in his car towards his home.

The phenomenon was also witnessed by his son and daughter before it disappeared in a northerly direction.

Hugh Merrick, one of the Paignton witnesses, said the object looked like a cruise liner illuminated at night.

"There were about ten rows of parallel lights with about 80 lights in each row. It was much bigger than any aircraft could possibly have been," said Hugh, of Penwill Way.

8th March 1987 – 'Sail like' UFO seen over Lancashire

Harold Hill – a long-standing member of the British Astronomical Association – wrote to us with an account of what he saw, while looking through his telescope, at 6am, on 8th March 1987.

> "I was surprised to see what appeared to be a stellar object north preceding the moon and thought it was a high flying aircraft, reflecting the Sun's rays, until I noticed it was showing regular fluctuations in brightness. Looking through the telescope – an 8 and a half inch Schmidt reflector – I was unprepared for the image under the magnification of x245, which is the power I normally use for the Moon. It consisted of a bright central object, on each side of which were irregular-shaped sails or vanes, similar to solar panel appendages seen on our spacecraft, except these 'sails' were constantly changing shape in a totally unpredictable manner, like a yacht sail which had broken lose and were flapping in the wind. They were attached to the principal object by slender filaments of lesser brightness."

Chinese spot a 'straw hat' UFO

MORE than 20 people in central China reported seeing an unidentified flying object shaped like a straw hat, the official China Daily newspaper said today.

The newspaper reported that the witnesses in Sichuan province said they saw the object in the sky about 40 miles south of Chengdu at around midnight (1600 GMT) on March 7.

The object "looked like a straw hat and was reddish-orange in colour. It was about 1000 metres (3000ft) high and disappeared in half an hour," the paper said.

It quoted a 17-year-old high school student, Luo Jincheng, as saying he heard the object make a noise unlike that of aircraft. He added that he felt dizzy and upset for some time after the sighting.

The paper gave no further details.

EVENING STANDARD 19 MARCH 1987

In discussions with him about the event, Harold accepts he sought a rational and logical explanation for what he saw, such as a collapsed large balloon satellite of the 'Echo' type, tumbling over and over in the sky, but felt this would not have explained the change of direction (at least twice) during the general drift of the object.

Harold sent a full report to the *Astronomy Magazine*, who published the article. As a result of this he was contacted by a reader from Lancashire, who confirmed from his research into the time and date given, that there were no spacecraft or other such objects in the sky which could have explained away what was seen, but did suggest one possible explanation – *'a flock of several migrating geese flying from Martine Mere, west of Penwortham, to the South of England'* – an attractive hypothesis, according to Harold, who firmly rejected this as the answer!

APRIL 1987

22nd April 1987 – BA Jumbo Jet sights UFO over Russia

A British Airways Jumbo Jet was on its way from Heathrow to Bangkok and over Russia, when First Officer Anthony Colin, along with four other crew members, sighted a UFO while flying over the Russian *Hinterland.

> "We were changing over duties on the flight deck, and all five of us were together, when suddenly we saw what we took to be the lights of another aircraft. It was displaying two white lights as it should do. We watched it carefully and then saw a green light instead of red port side navigation light. It was clear. It was coming towards us at the same flight level, so we turned towards it, to ensure that we passed behind it. As we did so it accelerated across our nose, displaying a long line of small lights – vaguely phosphorescent – and vanished off to our left, at high speed. It was not an aircraft and none of us had ever seen anything like it before."

---

*The hinterland is the land or district behind a coast or the shoreline of a river. Specifically, by the doctrine of the hinterland, the word is applied to the inland region lying behind a port, claimed by the state that owns the coast. The area from which products are delivered to a port for shipping elsewhere is that port's hinterland. The term is also used to refer to the area around a city or town.

Haunted Skies Volume Ten

Howard Miles, of the British Astronomical Association, suggested they had seen a satellite, re-entering the Earth's atmosphere. (Source: *The Times* 27.6.1987 – 'Jet dodges mystery flying object over Russia'/*News on Sunday*, 28.6.1987 – 'No Probe on UFO Jet Drama')

24th April 1988 – UFO Meeting, London

On this day, the *Aetherius Society held its open day at Kensington Central Library. Spokeswoman Christine Aubry said:

> "A lot of people see UFOs but don't know how to report them. We will get a few cranks, I'm sure, so we have to discriminate carefully."

She was asked about the founder of the society, former cab driver, 'Sir' George King, who claims that Martians have twice saved Earth from attacks by the fish men.

> "He's in America in the middle of a UFO campaign; we believe there are beings both outside and inside the solar system from Mars, Jupiter, and Venus, to name but three planets."

WESTERN MORNING NEWS, Plymouth, England – April 21, 1987

Hotline link for UFO spotters

by PHILIP SHERWELL

THE Tibetans call them pearls in the sky and the Bible talks of chariots of fire. We know them by the somewhat less prosaic name of flying saucers.

The name itself implies a certain degree of scepticism in their existence and it is this attitude that the Aetherius Society is battling to overcome.

The latest move by these flying saucer lobbyists is the installation of a UFO telephone hotline — the number is 01 731 1094.

"For years people reporting sightings to the authorities have been made to feel foolish by the totally ludicrous explanations they have been given," says Dr. Richard Lawrence, the full-time secretary of the society in Europe.

"The hotline offers these people the chance of being taken seriously."

The Westcountry has always been a good source of sightings and two UFO reports from Devon and Cornwall have already come in since the hotline service was introduced earlier this month.

One couple spotted two UFOs at Seaton. One of the objects was a very bright orange light which appeared immense and hovered low in the sky for about five minutes before blinking out. Then a red light flew past at an estimated 300-400 mph.

At St. Breock an Essex holidaymaker saw a cigar-shaped UFO shoot past at a "phenomenal" speed before suddenly disappearing. The Aetherians believe the cigar-shaped craft are the mother ships from which the saucers emerge.

It is the ability of extraterrestrial objects to "blink out," travel faster than the speed of light, in flight paths that no known phenomena can repeat, that Dr. Lawrence says makes standard Ministry of Defence explanations ridiculous.

The Aetherians travel to Devon each year to visit Holdstone Down, near Combe Martin, which they regard as a holy mountain. This annual pilgrimage attracts enthusiasts from all over the world.

Dr. Lawrence, who has had sightings himself at Holdstone Down and Bude, believes flying saucer activity in the region ties in with its history of mysticism.

"Significant magnetic forces are at play in certain parts of the earth and the Westcountry is one of them. These forces are of great importance," he claims.

But that's another story.

---

*The Aetherius Society is a UFO religion and was founded by George King, in 1954, combining yoga, and ideas from various world religions, notably Hinduism, Buddhism, Christianity, and Theosophy. The religion's stated goal is to prevent the annihilation of the Earth by improving cooperation between humanity and various alien species, and by improving the spiritual lives of the world. The society has claimed that various disasters may be prevented by prayer, often aided by "Spiritual Energy Batteries" meant to store healing psychic energy. The society also believes that it is to make the way for the "Next Master", a messianic figure who will descend upon Earth in a 'flying saucer', possessing magic more powerful than all the world's armies. The society is named after Aetherius – a being King claims to have telepathically contacted and channelled. Aetherius is believed to be a "Cosmic Master" from Venus, along with Buddha and Jesus. The society's membership, although international in composition, is not very large, consisting of approximately 650 members as of 1993. (**Source:** Wikipedia)

Haunted Skies Volume Ten

EVENING NEWS, London, England – June 8, 1987

Is anybody there?

Six out of ten believe we are visited by UFOs says expert

MARIE AYNES 'We can't know'

KATE ADAMS 'There can't be'

IAN LYNSEY 'Who knows?'

MURVYN BERGIN 'Someone there'

ROBERT HICKS 'Several sitings'

VERNE LANDSBERG 'I believe'

LITTLE GREEN MEN: We tracked these typical visitors down and they told us it must be true...

MARIA LAURA 'Must be true'

By OWEN HUGHES

UFOs – little green men from Mars or beings from distant civilisations? The products of a fevered imagination or a real phenomenon backed up by facts and photographs?

Over the weekend sceptics and believers alike gathered in a London hotel for a UFO symposium organised by the Aetherius Society to debate and discuss the extra-terrestrial issues.

We did a little space-travelling through London's streets to find out what people thought of UFOs.

Kate Adams, 25, a computer operator from Chelmsford wasn't sure. "I don't know. I have not seen one and nobody I know has either. There might be something out there but I think if there was we would have caught one by now."

Ian Lynsey, 25, from Beckenham, said he would give UFOs the benefit of the doubt. "I don't think they exist but if I saw one perhaps I would change my mind.

"Lots of people have taken photographs of what they say are flying saucers, so who knows?"

But Verne Landsberg, 76, a visitor to London from Australia, thinks there are spacecraft visiting the earth.

"I believe in them; I went to a display in Sydney where there were lots of people speaking who said they had seen them."

Post Office worker Murvyn Bergin, 24, of Clapton believes the trackless wastes of space have to contain something more than uninhabited asteroids.

"It is such a big universe and I don't think human beings are the only things living in it. There is something or someone else out there."

It is a theory that 50 year-old Brian Bailey of Ealing would agree with. Although he has not spotted a UFO himself he believes others who say they have.

"Yes, it is a strong possibility. Our world is far too small to be the only planet with life on it in the universe."

Italian journalist Maria Laura who lives in South London is another convert to the belief that UFOs exist. "There are so many sitings and photographs that people cannot have invented everything.

"I am convinced this is not the only world. I have not seen a UFO but I wish I had!"

Robert Hicks 24, who works in a business machinery firm said: "Quite a lot of people including pilots have made sitings."

Robert, from Dartford, added: "There is quite a lot of space out there and it seems to be sensible to think that we are not alone."

Marie Ayres 37, who comes from Bermondsey and works in a publishing company, reckons UFOs may or may not exist.

"I have not seen any but I suppose there are some about or at least things that are different to us. I think it is wrong to say they don't exist when we can't know they don't."

The last word should go to the man who *knows* there are UFOs visiting earth.

Mr Richard Lawrence, secretary of the Aetherius Society said: "You just cannot dismiss us as a lot of cranks. We have thousands of members across the world."

The Aetherius Society's telephone is 01-736 4187.

TODAY, SATURDAY, APRIL 11, 1987

Britons who believe we've got visitors

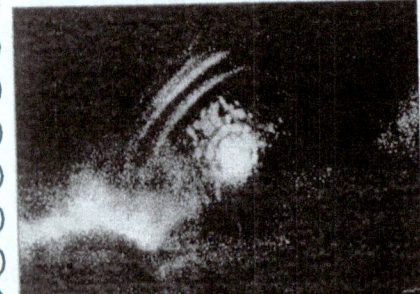

SOURCE FACT: It's either a swirling star formation or an alien visitor to Rochdale, where this picture was taken in 1976

It came from outer space

---

by FLEUR BRENNAN

(OR DID IT?)

SCIENCE FICTION: How they saw it in Close Encounters

ONE hot July night last year, Neil Gardner saw something "out of this world" in the sky over Bisley rifle range, where he had spent a day's shooting.

Struck by the vivid colours streaking from the object, he looked through his marksman's telescope.

"I saw a craft about four times the size of a jumbo jet. It was changing shape as I watched, from bell-shaped to saucer-shaped and back again."

He stood spellbound for more than an hour while smaller saucer-shaped craft constantly left and returned to the "mother ship".

"It was like watching a kaleidoscope with brilliant laser lights of different colours," he said.

A former crew member with British Airways, Mr Gardner, 61, is convinced they were not aircraft.

Eventually the objects disappeared into the clouds and Mr Gardner and his companions, who also saw them, went home.

PUZZLE

Mr Gardner, of Iver Heath, Bucks, is one of a growing number of people who are fascinated by Unidentified Flying Objects. They present a puzzle that seems to defy solution unless life from other planets really has, at last, decided to visit Earth.

A survey by the Aetherius Society — an international pressure group which promotes and researches the idea of inter-galactic travel — has shown that 61 percent of people in Britain (but only 14 percent in London) believe they have seen UFOs.

Are they cranks and ballucinators, or do they know something that the rest of us don't?

A call to the press office revealed that the RAF does not keep check on sightings unless they appear over military installations. Most sightings are explained away as the red, green and white lights of aircraft or the searchlights of helicopters on practice landings, or by natural phenomena.

Surely that must mean the RAF is sceptical? "Oh no I have seen one myself," said the duty officer.

Although he did not want to be identified, he described the mysterious, round metallic object he and fellow officers came across when flying in formation over Cyprus some years ago. "All 24 of us saw it and it had to be a UFO because it was moving at a speed no earthly craft could achieve."

He was not frightened, but just wished he could go with them on a flight.

He is one of a growing number of people who believe in beings on other planets. Seventy two per cent of Britons think there is life elsewhere in the universe.

The survey also found that three quarters of the population would like more UFO information.

The authorities are noticeably coy about spilling the beans — in 1982 Lord Clancarty in the House of Lords asked the Ministry of Defence to give an explanation of 600 sightings. He is still waiting for an answer.

SIGHTING

The Aetherius Society in London this month obtained from America 200 documents which show an attempt by the Federal Aviation Administration to cover up a sighting of a UFO reported by Japanese Air line Pilot Kenju Terauchi when he was flying across Alaska last November.

At first, the FAA confirmed radar tracking of the UFO, but when they later claimed it was an error, a public outcry led to them releasing all their documents. Copies clearly show reports of UFO sightings on the radar screens of air traffic controllers in Alaska.

Captain Terauchi and his crew say they watched three UFOs flying with them for more than 40 miles above the Arctic, for 32 minutes. The captain tried to photograph them, but his camera would not work. He said the objects moved with amazing speed and abrupt stops. "We did not feel threatened by the space ships."

John Holder of the Aetherius Society says the documents vindicate their campaign for more information about UFOs.

If you have seen lights in the sky, call the Aetherius Society's hot-line (01 731 1094) between 10am and 10pm any day.

Nick Mockler, of Chiswick, saw the lights last year when he was driving to Wales along the A60 at Shipton and stopped to take a look. "I was just about to fall asleep, when I heard a noise like hundreds of jets and looked up to see a strange object with red lights and a yellow glowing beam above my head. It was in the shape of a cross." Nick was not

21st April 1987 – UFO over Cheltenham

A metallic 'disc'-shaped unidentified flying object was seen moving through the sky over Leckhampton Hill, on the outskirts of Cheltenham, by members of the Vernon family. Through binoculars, a second object was seen. Someone else who saw UFOs around the Cheltenham area was retired PC Trent Davis, whose previous sighting of a triangular object, hovering over the GCHQ Transmitter mast, over Cleeve Hill has already been outlined. Trent recently sent us another 'period' photo which we felt should be included.

29th April 1987 – UFO seen over Swansea

At 10.30pm, an oval-shaped object, described as being the size of a dining room table, showing four green lights, was seen hovering silently, 50ft up in the air, over a house in Upper Killay, Swansea, according to Mr and Mrs Nick Bates and their four year-old daughter, Hannah. (**Source:** *South Wales Evening Post*, 30.4.87 – 'UFO buzzed us, says family')

MAY 1987

May 1987 – UFO reported over Essex

This sighting was the subject of attention by the local newspaper, after the witness – an MOD workman – contacted them. Ron West wrote to the MOD, asking if he could visit the site and was refused permission.

Whitley Strieber and his books

In this month considerable publicity was given to the publication of Texas Lawyer, Whitley Strieber's new book – *Communion*, which was sold to the American Publisher, *Morrow*, for $1 million dollars. According to the *Birmingham Evening Mail*, who interviewed him during a visit to the Midlands City, the book was selling at 100,000 copies a week!

Strieber asserts that he was abducted from his cabin in upstate New York on the evening of December 26, 1985 by non-human beings. He wrote about this experience and related experiences in *Communion* (1987), his first non-fiction book. Although the book is perceived generally as an account of alien abduction, Strieber draws no conclusions about the identity of alleged abductors. He refers to the beings as "the visitors," a name chosen

Haunted Skies Volume Ten

to be as neutral as possible to entertain the possibility that they are not extraterrestrials and may instead exist in his mind.

Both the hardcover and paperback edition of *Communion* reached the number 1 position on the *New York Times* Best Seller list (non-fiction), with more than 2 million copies collectively sold. With *Communion*, an esoteric subject had reached the cultural mainstream, and Strieber found himself, perhaps unexpectedly, as its representative.

Following the popularity of the book, the author's account was subject to intense scrutiny and even derision. Some disparagement came from within the publishing world itself. Although published as non-fiction, the book editor of the *Los Angeles Times* pronounced the follow-up title, *Transformation* (1988), to be fiction and removed it from the non-fiction best-seller list (it nonetheless made the top 10 on the fiction side of the chart). *"It's a reprehensible thing,"* Strieber responded. *"My book is a true story . . . Placing this book on the fiction list is an ugly example of exactly the kind of blind prejudice that has hurt human progress for many generations."* Criticism noting the similarity between the non-human beings in Strieber's autobiographical accounts and the non-human beings in his initial horror novels were typically acknowledged by the author as a fair observation, but not indicative of his autobiographical works being fictional: *"The mysterious small beings that figure prominently in* Catmagic *seem to be an unconscious rendering of [the visitors], created before I was aware that they may be real."*

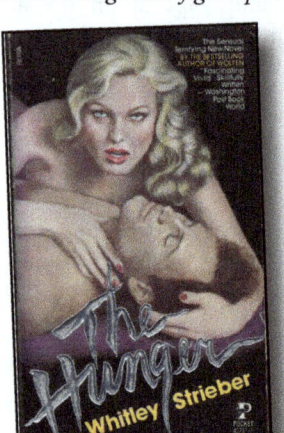

Over the next 24 years (since the 1987 publication of Communion), Strieber wrote four additional autobiographies detailing his experiences with the visitors: *Transformation* (1988), a direct follow-up; *Breakthrough* (1995), a reflection on the original events and accounts of the sporadic contact he'd subsequently experienced; *The Secret School* (1996), in which he examines strange memories from his childhood; and lastly, *Solving the Communion Enigma: What Is to Come* (2011).

In *Solving the Communion Enigma*, Strieber reflects on how advances in scientific understanding since his 1987 publication may shed light on what he perceived, noting, *"Among other things, since I wrote* Communion, *science has determined that parallel universes may be physically real and that time travel may in some way be possible"*. This latest work is a consolidation of UFO sightings and related phenomena, including crop circles, alien abductions, mutilations and deaths in an attempt to discern any kind of meaningful overall pattern. Strieber concludes that we as a species are being shepherded to a higher level of understanding and being within an endless "multi universe" of matter, energy, space and time. He also writes more candidly about the deleterious effects his initial experiences had upon him while staying at his upstate New York cabin in the 1980s, noting *"I was regularly drinking myself to sleep when we were there. I would listen to the radio until late hours, drinking vodka . . ."*

Other visitor-themed books of Strieber's include *Majestic* (1989), a novel about the Roswell UFO incident; *The Communion Letters* (1997, reissued in 2003), a collection of letters from readers reporting experiences similar to Strieber's; *Confirmation* (1998), in which Strieber reviews a variety of evidence that is suggestive of alien contact, and considers what more would be required to provide 'confirmation'; *The Grays* (2006) a novel in which his impressions of alien contact are presented through a fictional thriller/espionage narrative, and; *Hybrids* (2011) a fictional narrative that imagines human/alien hybrids being born into the modern world.

Additional visitor-themed writings include a screenplay for the 1989 film *Communion*, directed by Philippe Mora and starring Christopher Walken as Strieber. The movie covers material from the novel *Communion* and a sequel *Transformation*. Strieber has stated that he was dissatisfied with the film, which utilized scenes of improvised dialogue and includes themes not present in his books. Strieber also wrote a screenplay for his novel *Majestic*, which has not been filmed. Whitley Strieber has repeatedly expressed frustration that his experiences have been taken as "alien contact" when he does not actually know what they were. Strieber has reported anomalous childhood experiences and suggested that he may have suffered some sort of early interference by intelligence and/or military agencies. He was extensively tested for Temporal Lobe Epilepsy and other brain abnormalities at his own request, but his brain was found to be functioning normally. The results of these tests were reported in his book *Transformation*. **(Source: Wikipedia)**

Also in this month were reports of slow moving orange spheres seen over Farnworth, Cheshire, by four people, a disc-shaped object sighted for several minutes over Salford, and a bright *'light'* seen *'corkscrewing'* in the sky over Fallowfield, near Manchester. **(Source:** *Evening News,* **Manchester, 14.5.1987)**

30th May 1987 – Yorkshire UFO Society Conference Leeds

JUNE 1987

12th June 1987 – UFO over Buckinghamshire

On this late evening, Aylesbury resident Sidney Coomber, and his wife, Nancy, were on their way home to Bishopstone, Wiltshire. While driving along the A418, near Stone, they noticed a curious red glow in the sky.

Sidney:

> "It was as plain as the nose on your face, and very red like the sun. It looked like a mushroom on top of another. Suddenly, it disappeared from view. We estimated it was moving at thousands of miles an hour."

(Source: *Bucks. Herald,* **18.6.1987** – 'Was Glowing object a UFO?')

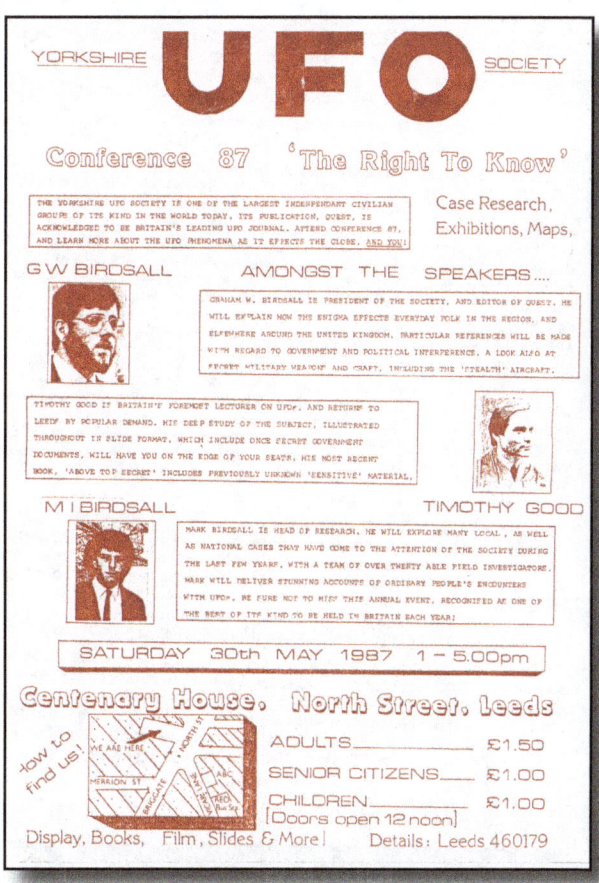

21st June 1987 – Solstice UFO Display

At 3am on 21st June 1987, a number of Police Officers on duty at Stonehenge, Wiltshire, including Police Constable Philip Hutchings, sighted a bright object, carrying out a number of right-angled turns across the sky. (**Source:** The PRUFOS Police Database)

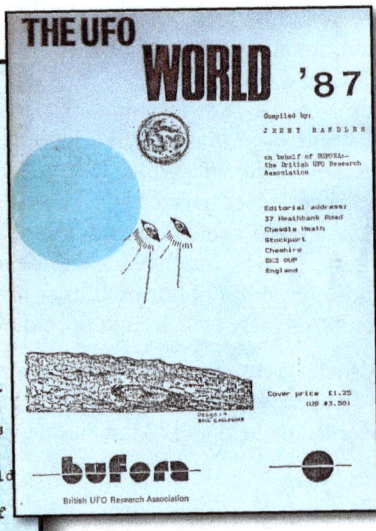

30th June 1987 – UFO Display over Newcastle

A night security guard in Newcastle sighted white lights hovering over the city in 1987, and contacted RAF Boulmer, after watching them for 15 to 20 minutes. The former member of the Armed Forces wrote:

> "A large white light was travelling west to east. The other five lights travelled in various directions."

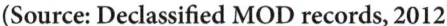

He described the weather conditions as clear, but said it was too high to estimate the distance of the lights. Although we do not appear to have a response from the MOD or the RAF with regard to this sighting, it is of interest to note what an unnamed Squadron Leader had to say about previous reports of UFOs, seen during April 1987:

> "We have checked our records covering the period April 2 to 22, 1987, and are unable to confirm or deny that your reports of unknown targets originated from aircraft taking part in exercises being carried out at the time . . . I can inform you that our day-to-day practice sorties are carried out over the North Sea and would not normally be visible from the coast . . . However, between April 6 and 10, 1987, we were involved in Exercise Mallet Blow and from April 13 to April 15, Exercise Priory took place in a similar area. Both of these events did include a number of low-flying target aircraft, which would have flown inland from the North Sea toward firing ranges in the Otterburn area . . . ..Unfortunately, I am unable to tie any particular aircraft to any given UFO sighting."

(Source: Declassified MOD records, 2012)

JULY 1987

4th July 1987 – UFO seen over Wiltshire

At 8.10pm, Mark Robinson, and his wife, Jean, from Gifford Hall Farmhouse, Broughton Gifford, Wiltshire, were in their garden, when they saw something odd in the sky. After fetching binoculars they looked through and saw:

> "... three or four creamy coloured globules, linked together, like flying frogspawn, moving across the sky."

(Source: *Wiltshire Times*, 10.7.1987 – 'Flying Frogspawn?)

12th July 1987 – UFO Conference . . .

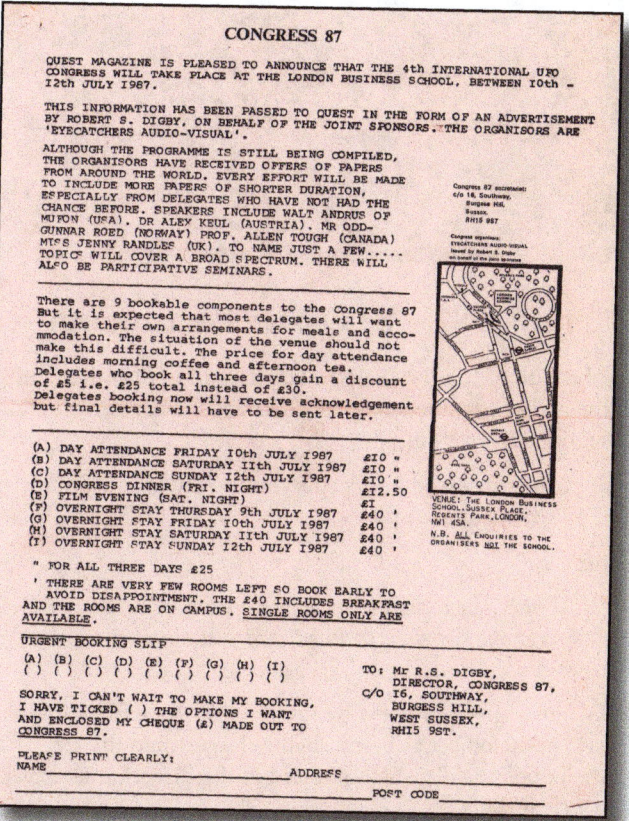

22nd July 1987 – UFO seen over Lancashire

The Accrington Observer (26.7.1987 – '3rd Green UFO riddle') told of being contacted by a motorist, who was driving near Baxenden Golf Course, Accrington, when he sighted a UFO, followed by his lights dimming and the car moving with great difficulty. The matter was brought to the attention of UFO enthusiast Mr Raymond Broderick, of the Hyndburn Sky Watchers, after it was revealed that early morning golfers had discovered five impressions left in the ground near the 3rd Green. He said:

> "I have been to the golf course. There is a half inch indentation in the ground, which would not have been there if fuel had been spilt and set alight. There is a definite framework visible with the markings and the centre has been blasted away. I can't see anyone going up there in the middle of the night. If it is a hoax, someone has gone to a great deal of trouble."

Mr Alan Gilberston – secretary of the Course – who was one of the group of the men who had discovered the markings said,

> "If it's a hoax, it's a very elaborate one."

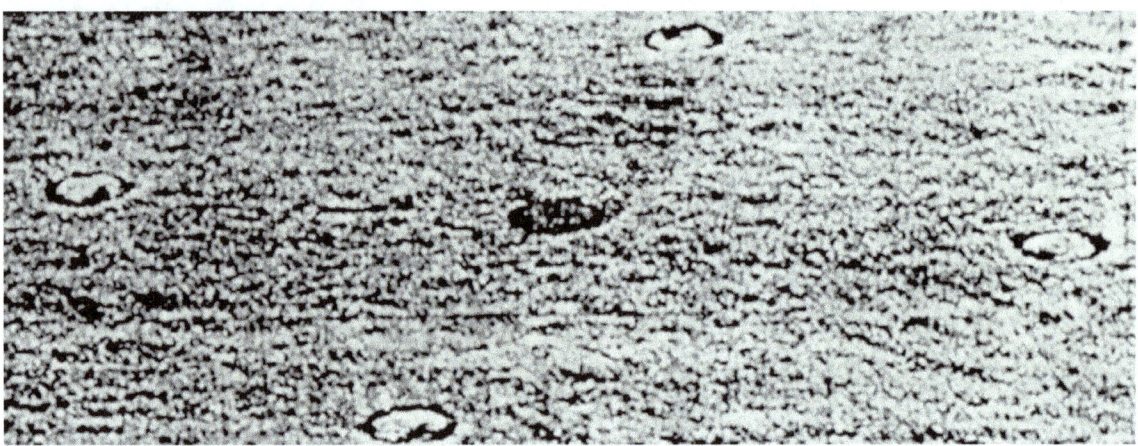

27th July 1987 – UFO over Portsmouth

On the 27th of July 1987, Anne Hayter and her brother, Philip, from Portsmouth, had been out job hunting. At the end of a fruitless day they climbed up Portsdown Hill, overlooking the City, and sat down on a bench close to the *George Inn*.

At 6pm, they observed a dark speck in the sky, at an elevation of some 70°, moving towards their position from the Foulness Island area.

Anne:

> "Within ten minutes, an object appeared in the sky overhead; it resembled an upturned rusty red saucepan. We were stunned and just stood there watching, as it headed silently towards the west direction."

Following a later interview by Portsmouth-based UFO researcher Nick Maloret, and Stan Pitt, they further described the object as being slightly larger than the size of a house, and that several protrusions were seen on the opposite side, which pointed in the direction of travel. The weather at the time of sighting was warm, with a clear sky.

Coincidently, this was not the only occasion when Foulness Island and its associations with UFO activity were to be brought to our notice, as the reader will see for themselves.

[Drawing labeled "PORTS DOWN HILL"]

AUGUST 1987

2nd August 1987 – UFO over Kettering

A number of people telephoned the police after sighting what looked like a huge airship, hovering under cloud cover, making a droning noise.

5th August 1987 – UFO over Barnsley

At 5am, Peter Beard (35) from Barnsley – a trainee computer operator by employment, living in Sheffield Road with his wife, Angie – was disturbed by a buzzing sound. Thinking it was a fly, trapped in the room, he got up and went to the window and saw the incredible sight of:

> " . . . an aluminium disc-like object, spinning through the sky, with flashing lights and making a buzzing noise."

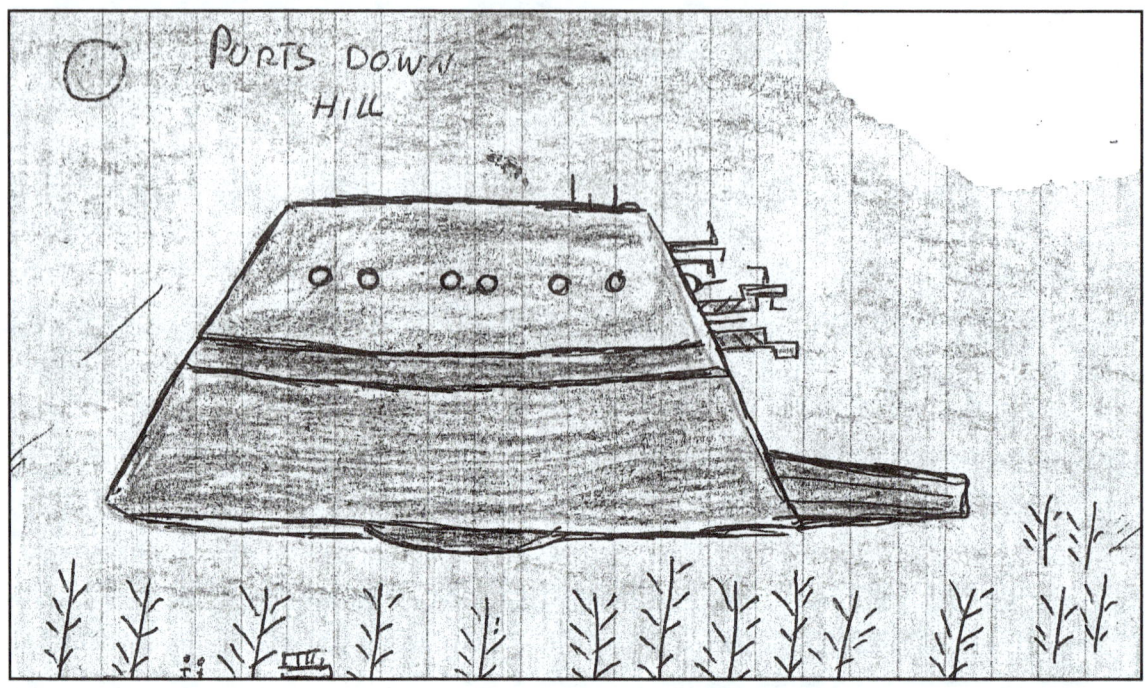

EVENING TELEGRAPH, Northamptonshire, England – Aug. 4, 1987

Lights in sky baffle police

Mystery of UFO sightings

A MYSTERY object with flashing lights has been spotted hovering over Kettering, but police are baffled as to what it might be.

The unidentified flying object was sighted by several people on Sunday night including Neel Ginna, from Federation Avenue, Desborough, and his wife Jose.

He told the ET: "It was nine minutes past ten when my wife spotted flashing lights in the sky to the west of Kettering. It couldn't have been an aeroplane as they were stationary.

"Ten minutes later I rang Kettering police to report it and they said they'd already had a number of calls about it and were trying to find out what it was."

Mr Ginna' neighbour, John Marlow, also saw it and said: "I thought it could have been a large airship."

After about 15 minutes the UFO began to move slowly towards Desborough, said Mr Ginna, who by this time was watching through his binoculars. "There was a dark blur, a white flashing light underneath and what appeared to be cabin lights on the left hand side. I could hear an engine which wasn't very loud. It sounded like a propeller-driven thing."

The object disappeared from view in the direction of Market Harborough at about 11pm, said Mr Ginna.

Rothwell couple Clive and Teresa Austin spotted the UFO above the town at about 10pm.

Mrs Austin, of Magellan Close, said: "It really was amazing. I have never seen anything like it.

"It was massive, hovering just under the clouds. It was making a droning noise."

Kettering police said they had no record of any calls about the UFO and they did not know what it was.

Peter had been on a fishing trip, the previous weekend, and had taken a loaded camera with him, which was still in the room. Thinking quickly, he picked it up and took four shots of the UFO before the camera jammed. The photos were sent to Philip Mantle, of the Yorkshire UFO Society, who conducted a number of interviews held with Peter about the circumstances in which they were taken. Philip then later submitted the photographs to Ground Saucer Watch in the United States – a now defunct highly respectable organisation, founded in 1957, whose members included scientists, engineers, professionals, and educated laymen. Following analysis of the photos, it was concluded they were likely to be a hoax. (**Source: Personal interview**)

Peter Beard

Haunted Skies Volume Ten

Haunted Skies Volume Ten

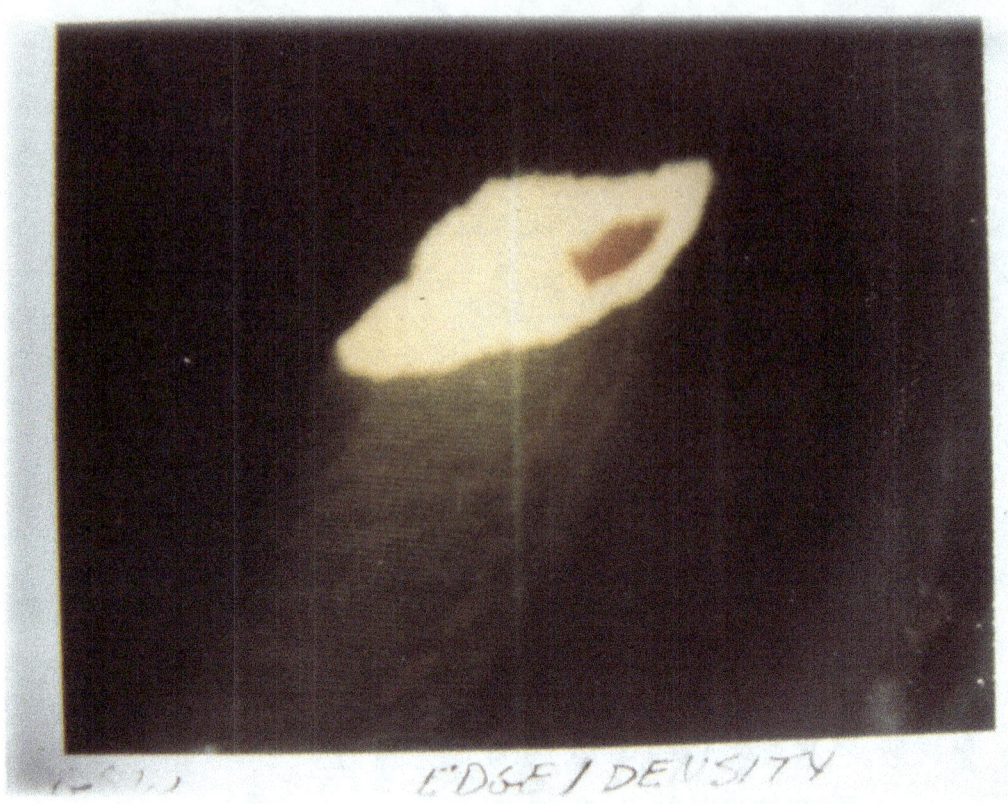

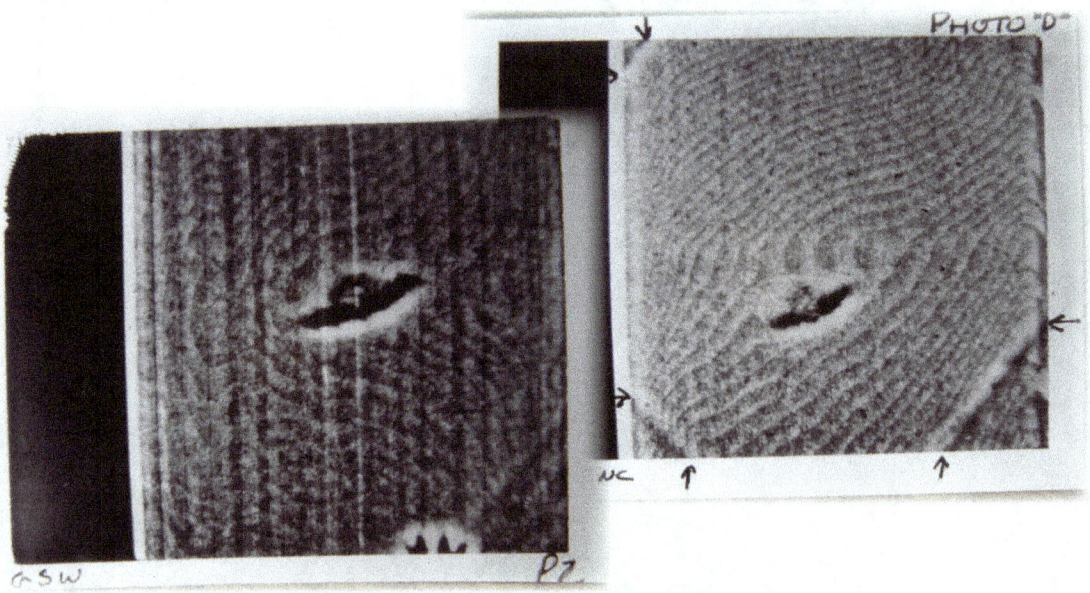

Photo analysis images by Ground Saucer Watch

8th August 1987 – Kite-shaped UFO over Nottinghamshire

At 10.55pm on this date, Mrs Jennifer Clement was sat outside the *White House* Public House, at Kegworth, with a group of other friends, when she noticed an unusual kite-shaped object to the left of a cluster of stars, in what was a clear sky. A friend pointed out a glowing object at high altitude, at an elevation of some 45°. The object was seen to descend slowly and head away towards the north-west. It then stopped again, glowed, and shot out of sight at speed. In addition to these two witnesses, around 20-30 other people also witnessed the movement of the object.

Approximately 40 miles to the north of Kegworth is situated *Bolsover Castle. At about the same time, a woman resident of Bolsover, employed as a tax inspector, was driving along a lane below the Bolsover Castle ruins, known as Limekiln Fields. On reaching the junction with Hilltop Road, which leads to the castle ruins, the woman looked to her right, in the process of turning left, when she noticed:

> "…something with a white light on it, about the size of a double-decker bus, at ground level, in the shape of a flat square, showing 10-12 white lights around its perimeter. The lights were bright and looked like car headlights, and may have gone across the middle of the object as well as the sides. I couldn't see any shape, unless the other half of, whatever it was, was around the bend."

After ensuring the object was not moving, she turned left and drove home feeling quite frightened. She told her husband and son what she had seen. They made their way to the area, but found nothing of any significance.
(Source: David Kelly/Philip Mantle/David Clarke)

14th August 1987 – UFO over Derby

At 11.30pm, Mr Allan Holden was stood outside his house, talking to a friend in Chaddesden Park Road, when he happened to look up into the sky and see a gold-orange coloured object, moving rapidly in an east to west direction.

---

*The castle was built by the Peverel Family in the 12th century. It became crown property after William Peveral fled to exile in 1155. A stone keep was built in 1173 surrounded by a curtain wall, this was breached in 1216 during the reign of King John, it was then left to ruin. The castle was bought by Sir George Talbot in 1553 it was sold on again in 1608 to Charles Cavendish and he set about re building it. It was finished in 1621. During the Civil War it was taken over by the Parliamentarians and once again left to get in a ruinous state. William Cavendish then built a new hall and staterooms; by the time of his death in 1676 the castle was once again in good order. The castle was left uninhabited from 1883 until it was given to the nation by the Duke of Portland in 1945. English Heritage now takes care of the castle.

There are a few ghosts that haunt the castle including a woman carrying a baby and a man and a woman who are seen together, also strange noises are heard, and smells appear for no reason, also one part is said to be so active by a nasty spirit that it has been cordoned off for safety. **(Source: Paranormal Events UK)**

Haunted Skies Volume Ten

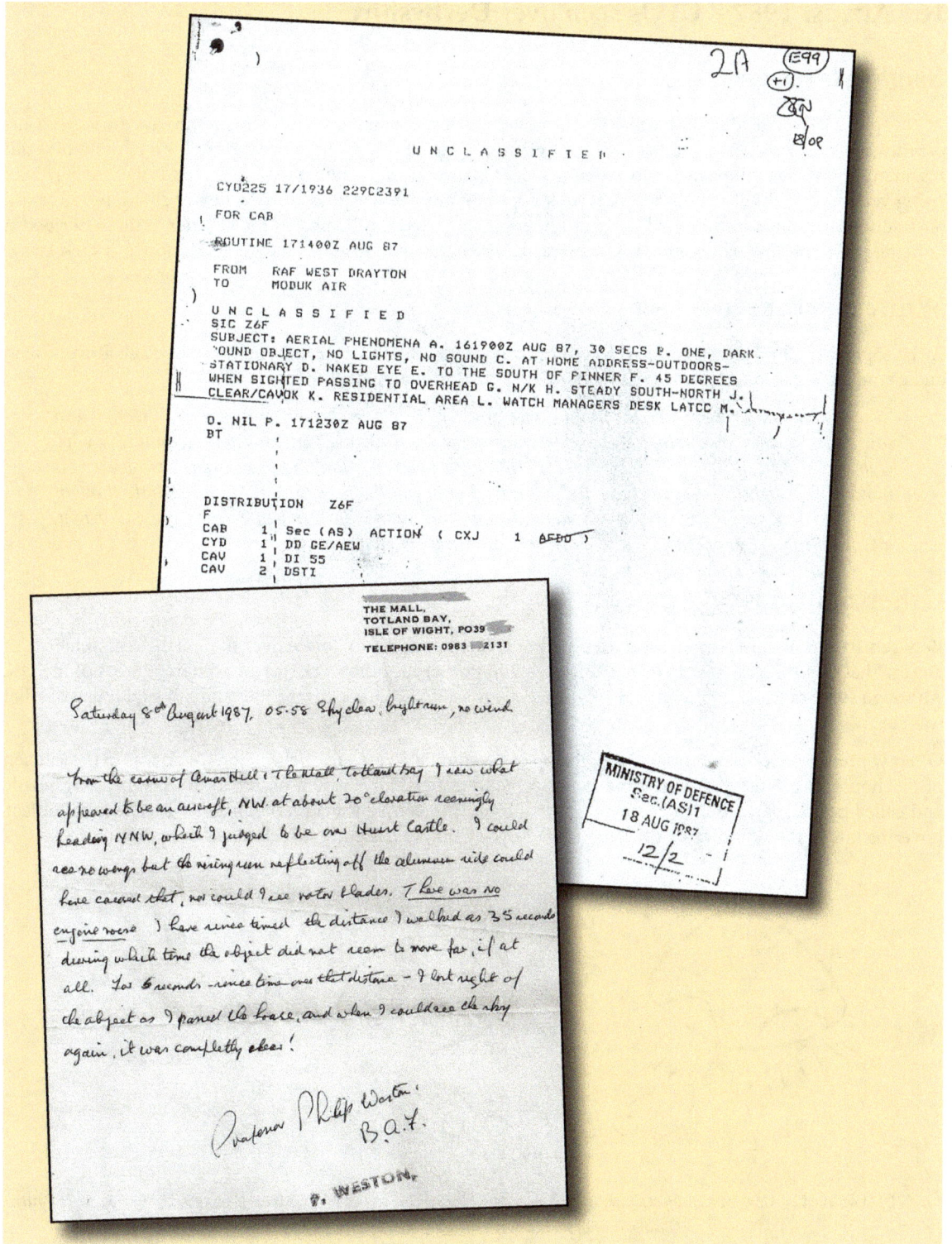

Haunted Skies Volume Ten

16th August 1987 – UFOs seen over Derbyshire

Bright Star seen . . .

At 9.45pm, Mr Kevin Meredith, aged 31 – an engineer by occupation – was in the process of leaving his parent's house, at Pinxton, accompanied by his girlfriend. As he was about to drive away, his girlfriend brought his attention to something she could see in the sky in front of them. Kevin looked out and saw a bright *'star'* rising vertically, at about 80° elevation. It took approximately five seconds to rise, before changing direction on a southerly course, and headed away at phenomenal speed. According to his girlfriend, she described it as being similar to that of a bonfire night sparkler, which dimmed when it changed direction and sped away.

White object seen . . .

At 10.15pm, Mr Christopher Lewis of New Inn Lane, Duffield Road, Derby – employed by Rolls Royce Fuels, and a student of Astronomy – had just got out of his car, after arriving home.

> *"The sky was very clear, when I noticed something very bright in the corner of my eye. I looked and saw a bright white object, high in the sky, towards the south-west – gone in a few seconds. My wife, who was still in the car, got out to have a look – but there was nothing to be seen. The object was moving in a slightly downward arc and left a trail of bright blobs behind it. My immediate thought was that I had seen a meteor, but the way it disappeared suddenly, from being very large and bright, and from the size of particles in the 'tail', were not what I would expect."*

Other sightings take place . . .

Between 10.55pm and 11.15pm, over 20 separate UFO sightings took place over the north-west outskirts of Derby. These sightings appear to have coincided with numerous other reports from different areas of the UK. Although some of these sightings were explained away as NATO manoeuvres, it would not explain all of what was seen.

Other witnesses included pensioner Joan Hislop of Weston Park Avenue, Shelton Lock, who was in the kitchen of her house, at around the same time as above. Joan noticed an unusual object in the sky, heading north, and called her husband, Bill, to come and have a look. The couple watched the brightly-lit, spherical object, hovering low in the sky, towards the large Rolls Royce Computer Centre, which backs onto Sinfin Moor.

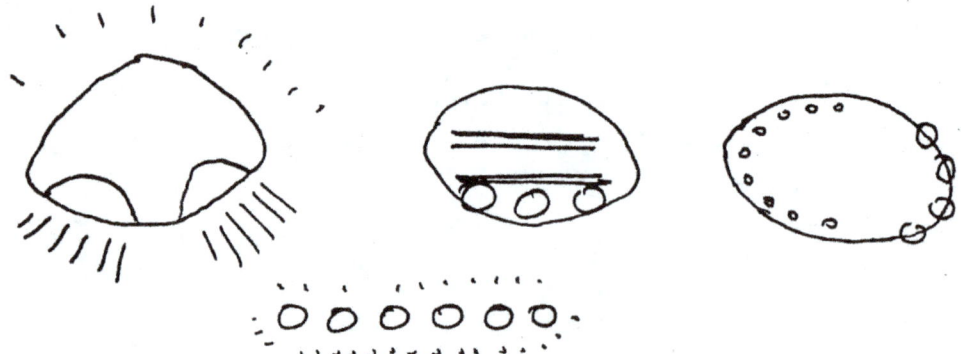

Left: UFO watched by Mr & Mrs Hislop. Centre: UFO sketched by Mrs Sandra Bryan. Right: Same object sketched by Mrs Joyce Potter. Below: Row of manoeuvring lights drawn by Dennis Read.

Joan:

> "It was travelling very slowly. We thought it was a helicopter, because it was about that size. It had green lights, as big as a football. There were also two lights, resembling car headlights, in front of the object, and a sparkling effect at the rear."

After observing the object for approximately 10 minutes, it was seen to turn to the right, before disappearing behind houses and then finally flying away towards the direction of Chaddesden.

Massive UFO seen by motorist

At 10.57pm, Mr and Mrs Boon of Spencer Road, Belper, Derby, had just driven onto the A608 and were coming down to the island onto the A61, heading towards Little Heaton, North of Derby.

> "As we went underneath the bridge I saw this thing in the sky, which I thought was a plane but very bright. I remarked that it was getting very low and, if landing, it would be on the racecourse at the back of us.
>
> At this point I realised it wasn't a plane and wondered if it was a UFO. It was massive. The lights were brilliant and situated either side of it; there was a red glow underneath. I could also see many more lights looking like big cabins, resembling a double-decker bus in the sky. At one point, I thought it looked like it had a metal thing on top, but due to the brightness, I was unable to make out any definite outline. I estimated it to be about 100yds away from us and 100ft high. Oddly, we did not see another car on the road – which was strange, as normally there is traffic on this road."

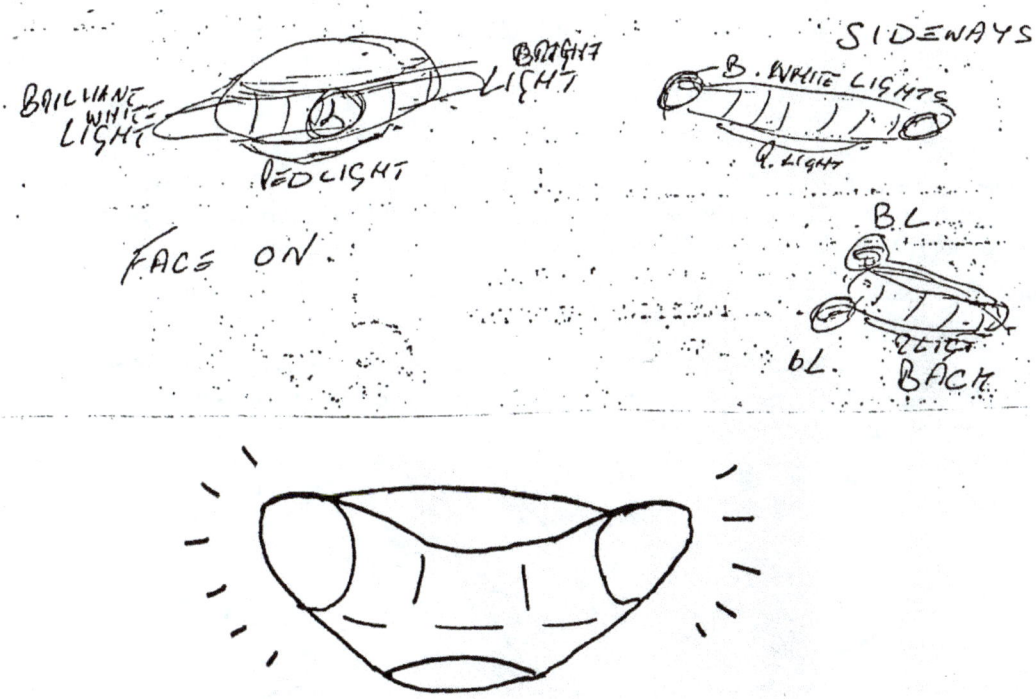

Sketch of UFO seen at Breadsall Hilltop, Derby, August 16, 1987, drawn by Mrs Audrey Boon. Also, sketch below this drawn by Dr David Clarke under direction from Mr & Mrs Boon, in September 1987

Haunted Skies Volume Ten

Fishermen sight strange lights . . . .

Minutes later, at 11pm, Dennis Read, David Forman, and Tony Barlow – a group of men out fishing on the River Derwent, North of Derby City Centre – noticed a number of peculiar *'lights'* that appeared horizontally in the eastern sky, towards the direction of Chaddesden, at an angel of 45° off the horizon. These *'lights'* moved towards the City Centre and then stopped for a short time, before moving back towards where they had originally been seen. The men described these *'lights'* as:

> "... of different colours, appearing to throb or pulsate, before they disappeared behind trees over the direction of Chaddesden, five minutes later."

Three photographs were taken but, when developed, showed nothing – probably due to the distance involved.

UFO splits into two . . .

At about the same time, Joyce Potter from Devon Close, Chaddesden, was with her three-year-old son, Jason, when their attention was caught by some women screaming and shouting, a short distance away.

> "I went to have a look and saw a round object, as big as a car, with glass windows, pass through the sky over the Estate; it had red, green, orange and yellow, lights on it. I watched it for about twenty minutes, until it suddenly split apart before disappearing from view."

'V'-shaped UFO formation

Fifteen minutes later, Chaddesden estate resident – Mr Holmes – was awoken by his wife, who told him about a brilliant *'light'* seen in the sky. The couple then got out of bed and watched the object, which was stationary and circular in appearance, for about ten minutes.

Mr Holmes:

> "It seemed to be one bright *'light'*, but when my eyes became accustomed to it there were probably about eight of them. They seemed to be arranged in a semicircle. The lights then started to move slowly, going between the Church and a house."

The couple continued to observe the object for about 15 minutes before it finally went out of sight. They heard a slight whining sound:

> "... like an electric motor. It then 'opened out' into an arrow or delta-shaped object, and headed away towards Sponden. The lights came into a 'V'-shaped formation, one down each side of whatever it was, and that was the last we saw of it."

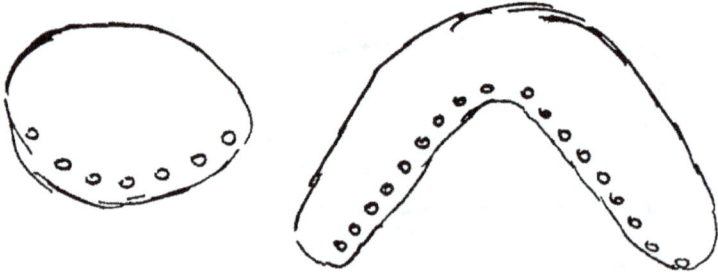

Sketches by Mr Holmes, of object seen at Chaddesden on 16th August, 1987. On left, the object as it appeared from front bedroom window; on the right of this, object as it "opened out" from rear bedroom window.

UFOs seen over Derby

The story does not quite end there. At 11.55pm, Patrick Lavelle – a 35 year-old charge nurse of Westbourne Park, Derby – had just opened the back door to let the dog out, when he noticed a white glow, at a distance, in the night sky.

"I was able to discern two bright spheres of light at 10 and 12 o'clock positions, in the easterly part of the sky. Beneath each was a concentric ring of eight smaller spheres. The objects were stationary and gave off an intense white light, illuminating the sky around them. I ran upstairs and awoke my wife. My wife and I then watched what was now one object, which faded away leaving an afterglow; this then too faded away."

On the left: Lights in the sky watched by Mr Chris Lewis, at 10.15pm, August 16th, 1987. Right of this: Lights in the sky drawn by Mr Patrick Lavelle, which were seen at 10.55pm, August 16th, 1987 – Mackworth, in Derbyshire.

UFO seen over Batley, Yorkshire

An elderly couple (who declined to be named) were in the process of retiring to bed, when they saw an orange glowing object moving across the night sky. As it approached closer they saw a cigar shape, which was visible for 2-3 minutes over the Howley and Woodkirk area of West Yorkshire. They telephoned Philip Mantle on the UFO 'hotline' number, who then contacted Yeadon Airport. They confirmed that flights in and out of the airport had finished by 10pm and that it could not have been one of their aircraft. (Source: Philip Mantle/*Batley News*, 20.8.1987 – 'UFO team hot on trail of shooting cigar')

Strange sightings on the UFO watch

STRANGE objects have been spotted in the skies over North Derbyshire, say Unidentified Flying Object watchers who have set up a 24-hour telephone hotline to receive reports of sightings.

UFO Hotline was established earlier this summer in Batley, and the organisers have received reports of sightings from as far afield as Blackburn and Birmingham.

A couple holidaying near Matlock saw a large, triangular object, covered in small lights, moving slowly and silently above Bonsall Moor. And a couple from Hasland, Chesterfield, saw a bright object behind their house, displaying eight glittering lights. They took three photographs, which are now being analysed in America.

17th August 1987 – UFO over Uttoxeter

Between 9.20pm and 10pm, Mr and Mrs Richard Roberts were driving home to Uttoxeter, after having been to see relatives in the Rocester area.

As they neared the small village of Crakemarsh, Mrs Roberts brought her husband's attention to something unusual in the sky over Eaton Wood, about a quarter of a mile away from them. Mr Roberts slowed the car, wondering if it was a helicopter in trouble and about to crash. He said:

> "It looked like a ring of rotating white lights, with coloured lights inside it; one a pale green in colour, the other an orange-brown. It reminded me of a pie-shaped object, which had a funnel-shaped searchlight beam coming from its underside, and appeared to be looking for something."

The couple got out of the vehicle and watched the silent object for 20 minutes, before it moved away and out of sight.

On 20th September, Mr Roberts returned to the scene with David Clarke and Andy Roberts, and pointed out where he had observed the UFO, which was estimated to have been near to Patonhall Farm, just below Doveridge Ridge and Eaton Wood. (**Source: Declassified MOD 2009 records/Andy Roberts, David Clarke and Philip Mantle**)

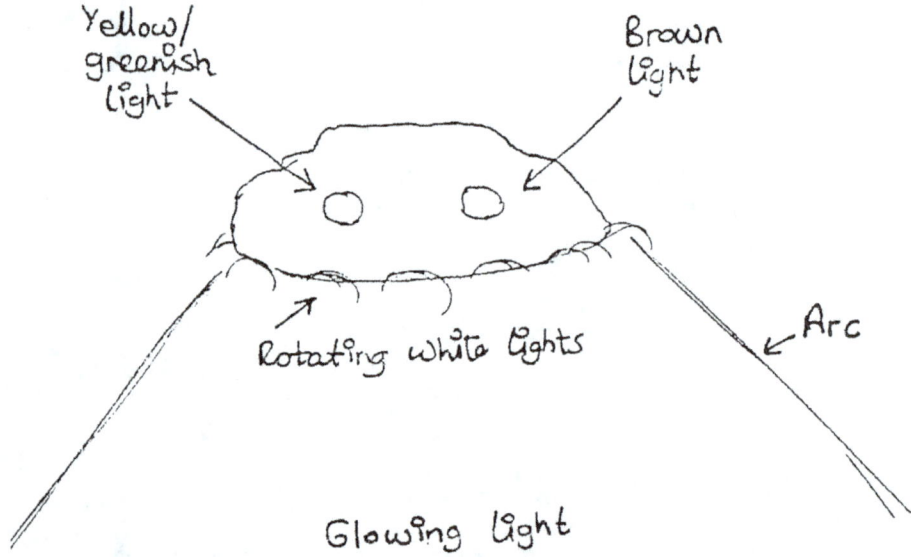

18th August 1987 – UFO over Northants

Martin Millar of Ashchurch Crescent, Corby – a bus driver by occupation – was stood in his kitchen, smoking a cigarette, unable to sleep.

> "The time was 1.35am, as I looked at the clock on the window. The sky was clear, cloud free, with no moon, or wind, when I noticed a bright object in the sky, surrounded by a sort of fuzzy cloud, approximately a mile away from the house. I watched it slowly move towards the south-west and upwards into the sky. That was the last I saw of it."

(**Source: Ron West, Brenda Butler**)

18th August 1987 – UFOs seen over Stone Circle

Musician/Therapist Sally Hope told of an event that took place, while visiting *Mitchells Fold Stone Circle, in Old Churchstoke, accompanied by her then husband, Stewart, and two friends, during a four-day visit as part of a †harmonic convergence.

Sally Hope

> "The first day I noticed some faint lights that I attributed to the haziness of the day, and a buzzing noise that appeared to emanate from a large stone in the Circle, but put it to the back of my mind. On the fourth evening, just before midnight, we were sat almost level to the largest stone, and were discussing a strange light having been seen in the sky by Stewart, when suddenly, we saw what looked like a 'runway of lights' on the ground coming towards us. The clouds then appeared to open up and a beam of light shot upwards, followed by four of five dark shadowy shapes seen moving across the sky. We shouted out in excitement, fear turning to wonder as they moved across the sky in what looked like some sort of display. Ahead of us appeared strobing pillars of light, forming an arc, followed by what looked like 'a fiery sun' and thousands of little lights travelling across the top of a nearby larger hill. Suddenly the display 'blinked out' or stopped, as a military jet fighter flew overhead, but as soon as the plane had gone the 'lights' returned. This happened, we understand, on at least three occasions, almost creating an impression the lights were playing with the aircraft."

The view opposite Mitchells Fold

How many times had we come across similar reports, involving the 'scramble' of RAF jets on an intercept mission, and their occasional attempts to catch up with something or someone, who appears to show some form of intelligence, judging from their unwillingness to show themselves? However, we should exercise great care in forming any conclusions based on limited information, although the tabloids would no doubt depict a scenario which seems more in keeping with an episode of *X Files*!

Sally:

> "Two hundred yards away from us, a single light hovered in the sky before descending earthwards, and split into three. Tom and Stewart wanted to go over and stand in the lights, but Annette and I urged them not to, feeling that something may happen to them. The lights then extinguished and darkness returned – the whole episode over in an hour."

The next morning the group met a man in a white boiler suit, carrying a Geiger counter, who told them he was writing about the paranormal for a magazine, and expressed an interest in hearing what had taken place – which seems an extraordinary coincidence. The incident and what it meant personally was to inspire the production of a music track found in an album of music, some years later, entitled *Squanasie 'Sky People'* from Squanasie Recordings, produced by her, and partner, Jezz Woodroffe, who has worked with Black Sabbath, inspiring and haunting in melody.

Haunted Skies Volume Ten

Left: Mitchells Fold Stone Circle. Right: Sally Hope

Our Visit

Dawn Holloway with daughter, Marie

In November 2013, in company with Dawn and her daughter, Marie, we travelled to Mitchell's Fold on a cold, damp afternoon, to take some photographs. While we were there Marie checked for energy levels by using a **Gauss meter held close to some of the stones but only obtained a high reading (nearly off the scale, on two or three occasions) at the large one, alongside some smaller 'spikes', one of which we captured on camera.

All was quiet, apart from one or two people out walking and exercising

their dogs, the solitary cry of a crow circling the nearby area, and the croak of a pheasant. The sun was now beginning to drop down in the sky, although the rain kept off.

As darkness threatened we left, but couldn't help wondering poignantly what it must have been like to have existed in that long gone civilisation all those years ago, when the stone circle was young, and what lay behind the construction of so many others that now litter the landscape of the British Isles. (**Sources:** *Ovni*, **July/August 2003/ Personal interview/***County Times*, **9.5.2003 – 'We were faced with the unknown')**

---

*Mitchell's Fold (sometimes called Medgel's Fold or Madges Pinfold) is a stone circle in south-west Shropshire, located near the small village of White Grit on dry heath land at the south-west end of Stapeley Hill in the Chirbury with Brompton, at a height of 1083 ft (330m). It is a Scheduled Ancient Monument (number 107448) in the guardianship of English Heritage.

†A planetary alignment which occurred on August 16th to 17th 1987, and of importance to the Mayan Calendar, which prophecies a time of renaissance and planetary quickening, linked to the completion of our Sun's 26,000 year orbital cycle around the Pleiades star system and the alignment of our winter solstice with the Galactic Centre, said to be complete by 21st December 2012, and the stimulus for people to gather at sacred sites around the World.

**Karl Friedrich Gauss was a German mathematician, who lived from 1777 to 1785. He helped to invent the Gauss meter, which measures the magnetic field at any point. It uses a measurement called Gauss. A Gauss is centimetre-gram-second unit of magnetic flux density.

1987 August – Three UFOs over Rochdale, Lancashire

At 10pm one evening, towards the end of August 1987, Mr John Doherty (43) – a professional artist from Marland (a place which is situated on the edge of the moors, near Rochdale) – was out walking his dog. He had this to say:

> "There was a bright moon casting light onto scattered milky-grey clouds, at a ceiling of 5-6,000ft. It is a regular walk for me and I take pleasure in observing aircraft navigation lights in the distance on planes heading into Manchester Airport. I was looking towards the North when I saw a group of shimmering lights in the distance, which became bright, dull, and then bright again. I first thought I was seeing a number of fireflies directly in front of my face. I actually took my hand out of my pocket to wave them away, but realised they were flying directly above me. Four of them broke cloud as they passed. They were circular in shape, brightly lit, which made them appear to shimmer. On the underside of each of the objects were three bight lights; these did not shimmer and appeared almost still. They glowed fiercely through cloud on the two that were hidden, before disappearing southwards. I have observed wide bodied jet liners at height, and am convinced that one of the UFOs could have accommodated, quite comfortably, four Boeing 747s."

1987 – UFO over Bristol

Bristol resident Miss Julie Wall, from Stockwood Road, wrote to us in 2006 about what she witnessed, while aged 21 in 1987.

> "I have only confided in two people my viewing of a low flying craft, in 1987. It is hard to hold a conversation with some people that think you a storyteller, so I have kept the information to myself for a long time. I was living on the main road, at the time, and was awoken at 2am by strong headlights, shining through the window. They were impossible to look at. I shielded my eyes – then I realised they could not be a vehicle's headlights, as they were shining some 20ft off the ground through the bedroom. I was astounded to see a UFO appear 10ft away from where I was standing. The 'nose' of the object faced the house. I looked at it and then it turned to my right and moved away, following the line of houses. I opened the window and actually shouted 'Hey where are you going', but it carried on until out of sight."

After the incident Julie spoke to her then boyfriend, who was in the Armed Forces. She described what happened and asked him if he thought it was military. He denied this could have been the case, as it was so low off the ground. She told her son about it and he constructed a model, using cardboard, at the school.

1987 – UFO over Essex

In late August, receptionist Wendy Copleton (23) was in the garden of her house in Western Road, Rayleigh, Essex, with friend, Rachel Nolan, when they sighted a silver coloured egg-shaped object, moving slowly across the sky in a westerly direction.

(Source: Ron West/Brenda Butler)

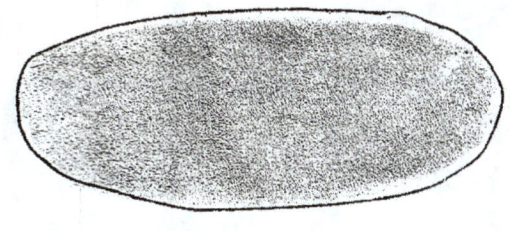
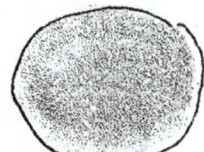

CHAPTER 2

SEPTEMBER & OCTOBER 1987

SEPTEMBER 1987

9th September, 1987 – 'Red parachute flare' seen over Derbyshire

AT 10.15pm on the above date, the Derbyshire Police received two separate calls from members of the public, reporting what looked like a 'red parachute flare' hovering low in the sky over Big Moor, Baslow, Derbyshire.

The Mountain Rescue team were called out but, despite a search, nothing was found.

(Source: Phillip Shaw, Glossop Mountain Rescue Team)

In Dudley, West Midlands, people contacted the police after sighting green lights in the sky. On this occasion it turned out to be laser lights, operated from a local nightclub.

Stocksbridge, near Sheffield

The valley in which Stocksbridge is situated lies between the Pennine hills of Hunshelf and Waldershelf and was, in former times, thickly forested. Wharncliffe is mentioned in the opening paragraph of Sir Walter Scott's *Ivanhoe*. Remains have been found there, dating back to Roman times, and a Mesolithic campsite was discovered on its edge, overlooking the ancient crossing place of the River *Don* at Deepcar.

Stocksbridge grew from a tiny hamlet at the crossing place of the *Little Don* River into a thriving industrial centre, during

---

Sandwell Mail, West Midlands – 9 SEP 1987

UFO alert as disco launched

A new space-age disco and cafe bar in Dudley has been inundated with telephone calls from people who believe they have seen UFOs.

People living as far as eight miles away from the £1 million Goldsmith's Complex in Martin Hill Street have been reporting seeing green lights in the sky.

But they have been assured that all they have encountered is a green laser beam from the futuristic club's powerful lighting system.

General manager of the Goldsmith's Complex Mr Martyn Raybould said: "We were given permission by the Civil Aviation Authority to test the powerful laser in the sky.

"We have been inundated with calls from people who claim they have seen UFOs and other strange lights in the sky.

"One woman telephoned us thinking it

STAFF REPORTER

was the after-effects of the Chernobyl disaster.

"All they have been seeing is a strong green light from a lighting unit which we have been shining into the air.

"It is so powerful it can be spotted eight miles away."

The club opening was delayed for a week, until tomorrow, after a delay in delivery of specially toughened glass which is to be positioned above the dance floor.

The club is owned by Birmingham-based Fantasy Clubs Ltd.

the Industrial Revolution. Although this development began on the north of the river in Hunshelf Township, Penistone Parish, it eventually extended onto the south side, which was more accessible.

September 1987, *Sheffield Star* – 'Ghost sightings on a new road'

On the front page edition of 21st September 1987, the *Sheffield Star* newspaper told about *'Ghost sightings on a new road'*. This was one of a number of other strange happenings which had been reported during the construction of the Stocksbridge bypass, to the north-west of Sheffield, by the *McAlpine* Company whom we wrote to in December 2013 asking if we could obtain a copy of the original plans showing the original route taken by the 'New Bypass' but never received any answer.

One of the incidents involved two Police Officers – PC Dick Ellis and Special Constable John Beet – who were later interviewed by members of the 'Sheffield Society for Researching into the Paranormal', at Deepcar Police Station, on 1st October 1987.

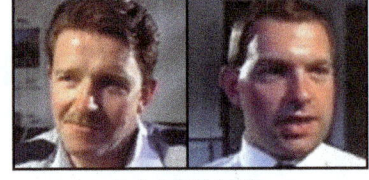
Left: PC Dick Ellis
Right: Special Constable John Beet

The matter was also brought to the attention of UFOIN researchers – David Clarke and Ralph Knutt – of the Independent UFO Network (IUFON), who discussed the incident with the Police Superintendent in charge of the Ecclesfield Division, at Hammerton Road, Sheffield, following his concern about how media publicity would reflect on the Force.

The Stocksbridge Bypass as it appears recently

Children heard singing

Another incident involved Hillsborough man – John Holmes. He was working in a lorry depot immediately below the bypass. During an interview, conducted by David and Ralph, he told them:

> "When construction work was going on, we often heard kids singing late at night and it was very frightening. It started on freezing cold nights and would continue on and off until the early hours on a few nights. We could not work out what the song was, but it sounded like a group of small voices and it seemed to be coming from the woods. It was really spooky and we had a strong feeling that someone was watching us all the time."

[**Authors:** USAF Officers reported that while on guard duty at RAF Alconbury, they heard children's voices on a number of occasions, apparently emanating from a nearby wood, which was suggested to be connected with a Victorian train disaster, in 1899 when a number of young children lost their lives. In addition to this several of the airmen reported having sighted a very tall person covered in hair, who was shot at by one of the security men at the base.]

Children seen dancing

One night, early in September 1987, security guards Steven Brookes and David Goldthorpe, employed by Rotherham-based *Constant Security*, were on patrol near Pearoyd Bridge, which carried a narrow flyover above the route of the then unfinished bypass into the town's steelworks. The two men saw what they later described as:

> "... a group of young children in medieval clothing, playing and dancing in a ring around a pylon beside the road near the bridge."

The men drove past the children and stopped their vehicle – only to find the group had vanished, leaving no sign of footprints in the soft mud.

Headless 'figure' seen

Shortly afterwards the two security men were to experience an even closer encounter with the unknown, which was to have a dramatic effect upon both their lives. Brookes later told police how they had spotted what appeared to be the figure of a man, standing on the newly-constructed Pearoyd Bridge, which could not be reached directly from the road below. Initially believing they were the victims of a joke, Brookes stayed at the base of the bridge while his colleague drove around behind the 'figure' and directed the full beam of the vehicle's headlights upon it. They were shocked to see:

> "... a 'figure', enveloped in a long cloak that appeared to have no head; the beam of the headlights shone straight through its body. Within seconds, it had gone."

Constant Security's Director – Mike Lee – confirmed having been called out by the two frightened men.

> "In all my experience I have never seen or heard anything remotely weird, but this sighting was definitely peculiar. I was called out at 4.30am and saw these two hysterical men, who were totally out of it. I always think policemen and security guards are very unimaginative people, but when something like this happens to them it makes you scratch your head. My two former employees were fit, down-to-earth South Yorkshire lads; one was a rugby player and weight-lifter, but 24 hours after the sighting they were both still shaking with shock and their nerves had gone. We understand one of them now lives in Canada and the other still lives locally, but neither have worked since this happened. You can usually tell if people are kidding or winding you up, but this was unique in my experience."

Haunted Skies Volume Ten

The police are called in to investigate

The two security men unsurprisingly did not relish the thought of returning to the construction site. Extremely disturbed by what they had witnessed, they visited the local Vicar – Stuart Brindley, at Stockbridge – asking if it was possible to have the bypass exorcised, as they believed the road builders may have disturbed a graveyard. Eventually, the two men contacted the police who, after being satisfied they were dealing with a genuine complaint, decided to send some officers to carry out an investigation.

Just after midnight on 12th September 1987, Police Constable Dick Ellis, accompanied by Special Constable John Beet, made their way to the bypass and parked the police car onto the unfinished stretch of the road – on what was a clear sky, with a full moon. A couple of minutes later, they both noticed a shadow moving around a large painted pallet box, left by workmen, near *Pea Royd* Bridge. They flashed the headlights of their car at the box, several times, in an effort to identify the shadow, before concluding that it was caused by a piece of plastic, flapping around in the wind.

Apparition appears next to police car!

By now the bypass was pitch black – the lights from the steelworks, below, reflecting upon the bridge and the box in front of their car.

> "We'd been sat there for about twenty minutes"…

PC Ellis told David Clarke and Ralph Knutt, in an interview conducted a fortnight after the events.

> "It was a nice night and I put my window down. Suddenly I had a peculiar feeling – not like I'd ever had before, because we have been working nights for a long time – just as if someone had walked over my grave, because I just froze. What was so odd, I went cold without knowing what the matter was. Then, a few seconds after, I had another feeling that someone was stood at the side of me and I turned my head slowly and could see that there was something stood by the side of the car, but as I turned quickly around there was nothing to be seen. At that very moment, John let out such a scream and hit me with his arm; I looked around and saw somebody stood next to the car."

Special Constable John Beet:

> "As Dick was looking out of his window, I was just gazing up onto the banking; I just turned to Dick and shouted, and there was this chap, just stood there, next to the car. It was really weird. To me, from what I saw of him, it sort of connected to the 1820s – that sort of era. I just looked at its face, which I presumed was that of a man, and it was just literally staring at me. I only saw the face for a split second. It looked as if he had got some kind of cravat on, and a waistcoat. It looked like something out of Dickens' time, but as I looked again and tried to focus, it was gone."

Both men leapt out of the car and searched the local area, but found no trace of anything untoward. The officers then drove further along the bridge itself and parked up. Knowing this was a bad spot to use the police radio, they shouted out to Don (a fellow officer) – and his colleague – to join them, so they could explain what they had just experienced. A few seconds later, the Vauxhall Astra patrol car they were sitting in was jolted by a series of loud thumps – as if something was impacting upon the boot. They looked out, but there was nothing to be seen. Now understandably shaken, the officers drove down to where their colleagues were. After explaining what had transpired, they drove back and parked up for a few minutes, but all was now quiet. [According to Dick Ellis, his cat died the same night. Was there a connection? We wrote to the police, hoping that we might be able to speak to PC Ellis, but were unsuccessful in being able to contact him.]

The following day PC Ellis made an official report to his superiors, describing 'inexplicable phenomena' on the Stocksbridge bypass. Soon the story reached the Press and appeared on the front page of the local evening newspaper – the *Sheffield Star*. Despite the dose of light-hearted ribbing they received from friends and colleagues in the build-up to Halloween, both men stuck with their story – which has never changed. Six years later, when a TV company visited the area to film a documentary on the experience, PC Ellis said:

> "There was definitely something there, but I can't explain it. I might have dismissed it as my imagination, but my partner saw it and had the identical eerie feeling at the same time. It was definitely unnerving and it wasn't a publicity stunt, as was claimed at the time. We don't do that sort of thing in the Police Force."

'Ghost' sightings on new road

EXCLUSIVE By Bob Westerdale

TERRIFIED security guards called in police and a clergyman after spotting "ghosts" on a £14m bypass being built near Sheffield.

A sergeant and Pc sent to the scene — near Stocksbridge — later said they "felt a presence" as they patrolled.

But South Yorkshire Police have refused to comment on the incident, or on reports that the Panda car was jolted by mysterious thuds.

Police were brought in after experienced security men Steven Brookes and David Goldthorpe spotted a hooded figure on Pearoyd bridge.

The pair drove closer and claim the beam from their car shone straight through the figure.

Two days earlier, Mr Goldthorpe allegedly spotted three young children dancing round a nearby tree ... in the middle of the night.

After the second sighting, the security men went to the home of a Stocksbridge clergyman, waking him at 7am. They wanted to know if the area had once been a graveyard and whether an exorcism was possible.

One of them later burst into tears and was in deep shock, but both agreed to return to work there.

Deepcar Pc Dick Ellis and a supervisory officer were both said to be disturbed by their visit, and reported back to their bosses, sources confirmed today.

Other sightings in the locality

Nigel Brooke

In late summer 1987, Graham and Nigel Brooke from Sheffield were out jogging on the Stocksbridge Bypass during its construction, one evening, when they noticed ahead of them a *'figure'* walking with its back towards the traffic in the middle of the road. As they drew nearer they noticed that it had no discernible features except for the nose and eye sockets. Accompanying this figure was a *'fusty, rotten, smell'*, but more bizarrely, the figure was walking in the road from the knee down, as if on a different level to the tarmac. When they were closer still the *'figure'* disappeared, leaving father and son very frightened.

Graham Brooke

Other witnesses to strange things seen along this stretch of road during autumn 1987 were Judy and David Simpson, who were driving over the bypass on a bridge, one day, when out to their left, over the fields, they noticed something odd and distinctly unsettling; a *'figure'* was floating above the field. They described it as having no face, but it did have arms and legs which were flaying around. The *'figure'* was then seen to move up the embankment and disappear into the car, leaving them terrified.

Ghostly woman seen near Stocksbridge

Another report from an unidentified male from an internet-based Sheffield Forum, dated 2004, tells of the following:

> *"I was riding my motorcycle just outside of Stocksbridge, some years ago. It was about 3am and very cold. As I rode along the road I saw what looked like a woman, walking in the verge, coming towards me. When she got close, I slowed down. She seemed to be wearing a long white gown, and she was looking at the floor as she walked.*

Her hair looked long and white, but I couldn't see any facial features. I rode past her and looked back over my shoulder; there wasn't anyone there when I looked back. Needless to say I opened up the throttle and away I went, only to be stopped by the police about five minutes later. I asked if they had seen anyone on the road but they said no, politely issued me with a producer, and away they went."

We were also told of a spate of sightings of ghostly children near 227, Manchester Road, Stocksbridge which is alleged to have been an old butcher's shop, although we have not been able to obtain any evidence supporting this currently.

Ghosts of two boys reported

A van driver was travelling along the Stocksbridge Bypass, at 3am, on his way home from work. After discovering gas bottles in the back of the van had come loose, he stopped the vehicle to secure them. As he pulled over, he saw two little boys in front of his van.

"They were about 8 years old, and I wondered why on earth they were out so late. I thought they must be lost or something. They were both wearing grey shirts and one had a cap in his hand, and it was as though he was waving it at me. One lad looked quite happy, and the other didn't look unhappy but he wasn't smiling like the other one. I couldn't see below their waists because I was in a transit van and the dashboard stopped any more of a view. When I got out they had gone. I was a total non-believer until I saw this. I have only ever told family, but it's true. I don't do drugs and hadn't had a drink. I was wide awake. The funniest thing about it was that I had used my gas bottles that night, and they had never come loose in 15 years. I know I would never forget to secure them. I used that road thousands of times and never seen anything before or since but I would never stop again either. I know what I saw. I have tried to come up with an excuse or explanation, but I can't. They were there and I saw them."

Red light on the dash and 'something' in the car

Millie wrote on a BBC *South Yorkshire* website, in 2002, the following version of events that befell her aunt and uncle, who were driving past Pea Royd Bridge, on the way back from Cleethorpes, at around 10pm, on an unspecified year.

"My auntie noticed a red light on the dashboard. She asked my uncle, who was driving, what the red light on the dashboard was. He said he didn't know. All of a sudden there was this really horrible fusty smell; it smelt like a rotten body – my auntie saw this long black cloak, sat in the back of the car behind the driver. She ducked down and said to my uncle 'there is someone behind us in the back seat' – it all went freezing, like in a freezer, then everything went back to normal."

Children dancing around the pylon

Matt Pearson tells of walking along the Stocksbridge Bypass with a friend, after the bus failed to turn up at the appointed time.

"I looked into a field with a pylon in it, and saw something circling it. It looked like fog but I wasn't too sure. At the same time I heard a screech behind me. My friend was pointing into a field and we saw a man with a cape on, walking around the field. I looked back and saw about ten children dancing around the pylon. We ran home and I have never felt the same when driving along that road again."

Figure of a monk

In 2003, Vicky and her partner, Paul, were driving back from Manchester, after watching a Sheffield Steelers game (Ice Hockey), and made the Langsett side of the bypass at about 11pm.

> "We knew of its reputation and right up until a few months ago had never witnessed anything unusual. Neither of us had consumed any alcohol, and we were not overly tired – in actual fact, due to the fact the Steelers had won their game, we were quite awake and in a jubilant mood. As we headed up the bypass, towards Pea Royd Bridge, I noticed a distinctive fusty smell fill the car, only faint at first, but it grew stronger. I felt the temperature start to drop. I didn't mention this to my partner, who was concentrating on the road ahead. The hair on the back of my neck started to prickle and I noticed that my partner, who in normal circumstances was a careful driver, had put his foot down. The smell stayed with us until the Wortley turn-off, where it disappeared as fast as it had appeared. It wasn't until we arrived home that my partner asked me if I'd noticed anything unusual about the drive home. I told him what I had experienced, and he told me that he had felt the same, but for one thing ... just before we had reached Pea Royd Bridge, my partner had looked in his rear view mirror and had seen what had appeared to be the figure of a monk, 'walking' at the side of the road. What had frightened him the most was the fact that he hadn't seen the figure at all through the windscreen. 'It was like he appeared out of thin air', he told me."

Strange man sighted

A man was driving back from Manchester to Sheffield, at 1am one Sunday morning, in October 2003, accompanied by four others – two females and a man in the rear seat, with a male friend in the passenger seat.

> "None of us had been drinking, as we had all been working. As we approached the end of Stocksbridge Bypass, we pulled up at the roundabout, where the 'Brewsters' pub is. As I pulled out to go right at the roundabout, to lead us down to the M1, two of the five people in the car saw a man stood in between the lanes on the triangle verge, slightly bent over, peering into the car right next to me! The front male passenger saw him and the female in the back far left saw him, although I didn't. They both described him exactly the same. As I pulled out they both said 'What was he looking at? What a weirdo!' The rest of us said, 'What are you on about?' They both described him exactly the same too! They said he had a hat on that came down around the ears. (Those old fashioned ones that would tie to keep the ears warm, or you could tie the straps above the hat on the top of the head). They also said he had a handle bar moustache and beard and had a long coat on. This really freaked all of us. We all knew Stocksbridge Bypass was haunted, but we have all travelled this route a lot but have never seen anything. Why did only two of the five of us see it? And why was a person (if it was!) stood on the small triangle of grass between lanes, in the morning, looking in my car? I do try to be sceptical, but this incident was strange to all of us."

According to another source, who wishes to remain anonymous, we were told that following a crash on the bypass, a motorist told the police he had swerved out of the way, after seeing a young family crossing the road dressed in Victorian clothing!

Ghostly visitor

Another story found on the internet tells of a Stocksbridge man, who worked at Samuel Fox Steelworks well before the bypass was built. He and his wife and family were in the process of clearing out a smallholding on the hill that looked down on the steelworks, with a view to living in the property. One day a man knocked on the door of their house. When his wife opened it, he spoke to her briefly before leaving, at which point she realised that the man was soaking wet from head to toe, which was thought very strange as it was a warm evening with no sign of rain. Enquiries made later revealed that, a few years earlier, a man was repairing a water tank in the area and had fallen in and drowned. The woman also claimed that a few days later, while pulling out an old staircase, a little boy dressed in old style clothes, with a ruffle collar, appeared in front of her. She said hello to him (presuming he was in fancy dress and had walked into the house) and, suddenly, he disappeared from view.

1960s

Yet another story tells of a couple who were out driving, on their way over the hill (known as Pea Royd Hill at the turn of the Century) to Pea Royd Farm around the 1960s, near to Briary Busk Farm, close to Hunshelf Bank, when they saw a woman in the middle of the road. The driver braked hard and the *'woman'* simply disappeared in front of them. If, in fact, these accounts are true, they would negate a theory that manifestations along this stretch of road were caused following construction of the bypass. We tend to favour the possibilities that something, or someone, was disturbed during the construction process. Was it an ancient burial site, or the grave of a more recent death? We shall probably never know.

The problem with these stories is that while they certainly appear genuine, without interviewing the people personally we were unable to form any conclusions other than there was, no doubt, more accounts than we shall know – we left email details for them but never received an answer.

Deaths along the bypass

Many people allege this bypass is one of the most dangerous roads in Britain, and that the road is unlucky through association with the date of its opening. Others claim a number of accidents which have occurred along the bypass (many of which have been fatal) can be attributed to ghostly apparitions, which jump out into the front of cars.

In the 1980s, Stocksbridge lay on the main route from Sheffield to Manchester centre. Throughout the day and night the narrow high street became choked with trucks heading to and from Manchester Airport, and the docks at Liverpool, beyond. It was decided that a bypass was necessary, and original plans were drawn-up for a dual carriageway with a central crash barrier. Shortly before work was due to begin it was downgraded to a single carriageway. The only concession was a passing lane on uphill stretches so that drivers of cars could get around the trucks, which would be limited to 40mph on the otherwise 60mph route.

Bypass opens on Friday, 13th May 1988

The bypass was opened by the Transport Minister – *Paul Channon – on Friday 13th May 1988. Just after he cut the ribbon, the then Mayor of Stocksbridge – the late Malcolm Brelsford – handed Channon a letter, which contained, it is said, his personal expressed opinion that this stretch of road was very dangerous.

On the 24th August 1988, the first person to die was Maurice Reed. He was followed by Daniel Considine on 22nd March 1989. A year to the day after the first fatality came Leslie Starkey. Three months later, on the 1st November 1989, a Mr Mohammed Miah was killed.

---

*Channon was appointed Secretary of State for Transport on 13th June 1987. His tenure as Transport Secretary was blighted by several major transport disasters: 31 died in the King's Cross fire on 18th November 1987; 35 were killed when three trains crashed near Britain's busiest railway station in the Clapham Junction rail crash on 12th December 1988; 270 died when Pan Am Flight 103 was brought down by a bomb over Scottish town of Lockerbie in the Lockerbie Disaster on 21st December 1988; and 44 died when a British Midland plane crashed beside the M1 motorway in the Kegworth air disaster on 8th January 1989.

Police meeting held in July 1987

On the 13th July 1987, at a police meeting held at Stocksbridge to discuss community issues, Chief Inspector Sumner told its members that

> *"On the new A616 many motorists were ignoring the double white lines, as a result of which over 400 motorists had been issued with a fixed penalty ticket fine of £24 and three penalty points. In addition to this, numerous motorists had been prosecuted for exceeding the 60mph speed limit."*

Also during this period Police Sergeant Farrell mentioned that an investigation had been conducted into the road safety record for a stretch of the A6135, running from Chapel Town roundabout to Mill Lane, during the last five years, when it was established that there had been 38 injury accidents. However, this statistic according to him was below the national average (then) compared to other stretches of similar roads.

In 1991, along the stretch of the A616, one person died as a result of an accident.

In 1992, one person sustained fatal injures.

Two persons died in 1993; four persons in 1996, and three in 1998.

November 2001 (surnames omitted)

In November 2001, shortly after passing his driving test, John an 18-year-old apprentice carpenter, from Barnsley – lost control of his mother's Fiat close to the access gates to the Corus steelworks on the Stocksbridge bypass. He drifted across the central 'no overtaking' white lines and straight into the path of a motorcyclist – Jean (48) and his pillion passenger, Catherine (47) – who were killed instantly. On the 14th January 2002, John appeared at Sheffield Crown Court to be sentenced on two charges of causing death by dangerous driving, and was sentenced to 200 hours community service. Judge Robert Moore described the A616 as *"an important trunk road built on the cheap but quite inadequate for the traffic on it."*

January 2002

At 5pm on Monday, 7th January 2002, an HGV Dutch truck driver was driving towards the M1 from Manchester, via the A616. He approached the Tankersley roundabout marking the eastern end of the A616, known as the Stocksbridge Bypass, where the road narrows. He ignored the 50mph warning signs, advising drivers to slow down for the junction situated around the bend, and continued at speed, where his HGV crashed into the back of a car transporter queuing at the junction, the top platform of which crashed through his windscreen and into his head, killing him instantly. When the inquest was opened, three days later, the coroner was told that because of the extent of his injuries, it had not been possible to identify the man save by a passport and driving licence found in the cab. He was the twenty-second person to die on the Stocksbridge Bypass.

March 2002

At 8.30am on 24th March 2002, Joanne was on her way to work in the family BMW. In the back of the car were her twin four-year-old sons, whom she was going to drop off at her mother's house nearby. She was seen to pull onto the Stocksbridge bypass, at Deepcar, just as the road heads uphill. According to witnesses, she appeared to lose control of the BMW. The vehicle first 'fishtails', its back wheels fanning from side to side, and then spins out of control, sending its rear end into the opposite carriageway, where it is hit by a 38-tonne truck coming the other way. Joanne is seriously injured by the impact. The twins are flung from their car seats and onto the road, killing them instantly. They will become the twenty-third and twenty-fourth people to die on the bypass.

The death of the twins has dominated debate about the Stocksbridge bypass ever since, blowing open the argument between those who blame the drivers and those who blame the road. The local newspaper, the *Sheffield Star,* launched a massive campaign for change on the back of the tragedy and, with the people of Stocksbridge, raised a 46,000-name petition demanding it be turned into a dual carriageway.

Petition to Tony Blair

Ken the grandfather of the twins – delivered the 46,000-name petition on the Stocksbridge bypass to John Spellar then Transport Minister. Ken also wrote a letter to Prime Minister Tony Blair:

> *"For 24 lives to have been lost on a bypass that is barely five miles long is unacceptable. I am asking you now ... to do something before it becomes number 25 and 26."*

May 2002

At 8.45pm on 28th May 2002 Leigh (28) was driving his partner and their four-year-old twin children in the family Skoda, eastbound, along the Stocksbridge bypass. Some 200 metres from where the twins died, he collided head-on with an Isuzu Trooper going in the opposite direction. The driver and two passengers in the Isuzu are unhurt. One of the passengers, Grace, was taken to hospital with severe head injuries, where she died a few days later. She was the twenty-fifth person to be killed on the Stocksbridge bypass.

July 2002

On 22nd July 2002, after first announcing that the Stocksbridge bypass is safe, and then rejecting calls for a public inquiry into the road, Transport Minister – John Spellar – announces an investment of £400,000 in speed cameras for the A616.

> *"I hope that the cameras [in place by November 2002] will reinforce to motorists the need to keep to the speed limit and drive safely."*

It appears that these cameras were actually installed on the stretch of road in 2003.

September 2002

At 9.55pm on 8th September 2002, two women aged 39 and 35, were driving towards each other on the Stocksbridge bypass. About 200 metres from the junction with the A61, the westbound driver's car drifted inexplicably into the eastbound lane. The cars collide head-on, but miraculously neither driver suffers more than whiplash. According to police statistics, in 1999, there were 16 slight injuries. In 2000, there were two serious injuries, 15 slight ones but no fatalities.

December 2002

On 21st December 2002, car driver Leigh (27) crossed a double white line before crashing head-on into an Isuzu Trooper. His daughter, Grace, died and her twin brother, Jamie, was seriously injured in the crash on the A616 Stocksbridge Bypass, near Sheffield. Leigh was jailed for three years at Sheffield Crown Court after admitting causing death by dangerous driving, and other matters.

Haunted Skies Volume Ten

May 2010

On 6th May 2010, June and Sam of Mottram, died when their Rover collided with an Audi at the junction of the A616 Whams Road and Bents Road, Barnsley. Sam (76) suffered multiple injuries and was pronounced dead at the scene of the crash, close to the Stocksbridge bypass. June (71) died later the same day, at Leeds Royal Infirmary. Relatives were to later call for better safety measures at the accident black spot, which was investigated by local councils, in 2009, following several smashes including two more deaths in 2005.

A Sheffield inquest heard how the couple were at a stop sign at the junction from Bents Road, when they were thought to have edged out into Whams Road to see if it was clear to cross; police estimated that they were travelling at just two or three miles per hour.

June 2011

On June 22nd 2012, Daniel (aged 27) from Langold, near Worksop, and 47-year-old Mark, of Hoyland, Barnsley, died at the scene of a collision, which happened on the A616 between Tankersley roundabout and the junction with the A629, near Wortley. The smash happened at 6.12am when Daniel, who was driving a white Vauxhall Astra van downhill, towards Sheffield, tried to overtake several other vehicles and crashed head-on into Mark's blue Ford Transit, travelling in the opposite direction. A passenger in the Ford – a 23 year-old Hoyland man – had to be treated at Barnsley Hospital for a broken right hand and whiplash. Following the initial collision, a red Rover car crashed into the rear underside of the Transit van; the 42 year-old male driver from Gleadless, Sheffield, suffered bruising and whiplash. These are believed to be the 27th and 28th fatalities on the A616, known as an accident black spot. Sgt. Andy Noble, of South Yorkshire Police, said:

> *"From what we understand at this time, a light-coloured Vauxhall Astra van has travelled down the incline on the wrong side of the double-white lines that has been in a head-on collision with a blue, or a light blue Transit van, that has been going in the opposite direction."*

December 2013

In this year an unlicensed motorcyclist from Thurcroft was jailed for six-and-a-half years for a drink drive accident, which killed his teenage girlfriend. Stephen (25), admitted causing death by dangerous driving and over the limit drink-driving at Sheffield Crown Court. He was travelling along the notorious Stocksbridge bypass when the accident happened, which resulted in the death of his 19-year-old girlfriend – Joanne. Prosecuting, Kath Goddard said the crash happened when he went to overtake a Ford Focus during the rush hour, close to Tankersley Manor, on the A616.

(Sources: *Sheffield Star* and *Worksop Guardian*/WWW Internet, 2013)

FOI request, 2013

In December 2013 we emailed the West Yorkshire Police under the FOI asking them for an up to date list of Road Traffic casualties along this stretch of road covering the last ten years. They very kindly obliged and following are the details that they supplied (oddly, the dates of fatal accidents have been omitted):

Haunted Skies **Volume Ten**

SEVERITY	DATE	LOCATION
Damage	07-Jan-03	A616 BYPASS WORTLEY
Slight	15-Feb-03	A616 WORTLEY J/W A629
Damage	06-Mar-03	STOCKSBRIDGE BYPASS LANGSETT
Slight	27-Mar-03	MANCHESTER RD MIDHOPESTONE
Slight	28-Mar-03	A 616 TANKERSLEY AT J/W A 61
Slight	10-Apr-03	STOCKSBRIDGE BYPASS WORTLEY BARNSLEY AT JCT A629
Slight	25-Apr-03	MANCHESTER RD LANGSETT 800 MTS FROM J/W GILBERT HILL
Slight	02-Jun-03	A616 TANKERSLEY 500 MTS FROM A61 ROUNDABOUT
Damage	06-Jun-03	STOCKSBRIDGE BY PASS STOCKSBRIDGE
Slight	02-Jul-03	A616T MIDHOPESTONES J/W MORTIMER RD
Damage	07-Jul-03	STOCKSBRIDGE BYPASS TANKERSLEY AT J/W A61
Damage	10-Jul-03	A616 STOCKSBRIDGE BYPASS J/W SLIP RD TOWARDS TANKERSLEY
Damage	12-Jul-03	STOCKSBRIDGE BYPASS TANKERSLEY 1/2 MILE FROM
Fatal	14-Aug-03	STOCKSBRIDGE BY PASS TANKERSLEY 1/2 FROM ML A61
Slight	21-Aug-03	A616T TANKERSLEY 350 MTS FROM J/W WESTWOOD NEW RD
Slight	29-Aug-03	STOCKSBRIDGE BY PASS STOCKSBRIDGE AT J/W CORUS ACCESS RD
Slight	31-Aug-03	A616 STOCKSBRIDGE J/W MANCHESTER RD
Slight	16-Sep-03	A616 MIDHOPESTONES 50 MTS FROM MORTIMER RD
Slight	23-Sep-03	A616 STOCKSBRIDGE BY PASS STOCKSBRIDGE
Damage	29-Sep-03	A616 TANKERSLEY 400 YDS FROM J/W TANKERSLEY ROUNDABOUT
Slight	29-Sep-03	A616T STOCKSBRIDGE 30 MTS FROM J/W MANCHESTER RD
Damage	07-Oct-03	STOCKSBRIDGE BY PASS STOCKSBRIDGE 40 MTS MOTORWAY JCT 35A
Damage	29-Oct-03	STOCKSBRIDGE BYPASS STOCKSBRIDGE
Serious	31-Oct-03	A616T TANKERSLEY 400 YRDS FROM PARK LN
Slight	18-Nov-03	A616T TANKETSLEY 500 MTS FROM J/W WESTWOOD NEW RD
Slight	20-Nov-03	A616T TANKERSLEY 500 YDS FROM J/W A61
Slight	09-Dec-03	ROUNDABOUT ON A616 TANKERSLEY 20 MTS FROM A61
Serious	17-Dec-03	STOCKSBRIDGE BY PASS STOCKSBRIDGE 1/4 ML MANCHESTER RD
Damage	12-Jan-04	A616 WORTLEY
Damage	17-Mar-04	A616 STOCKSSBRIDGE BYPASS WORTLEY 200 MTS FROM J/W A629
Slight	16-Apr-04	A616 STOCKSBRIDGE 1 MILE FROM J/W MANCHESTER RD
Damage	16-May-04	A616 BARNSLEY AT JCT A628
Damage	03-Jul-04	A616 BARNSLEY
Slight	31-Oct-04	A616T WORTLEY BARNSLEY AT JCT A629
Slight	11-Dec-04	STOCKSBRIDGE BY PASS, DEEPCAR, SHEFFIELD .
Slight	19-Jan-05	A616T STOCKSBRIDGE BYPASS 100 MTS HALIFAX RD
Slight	28-Jan-05	A616 WORTLEY 200 MTS EAST OF A629
Damage	15-Feb-05	A616 STOCKSBRIDGE BYPASS 1200 MTS TO STEEL WKS SERVICE RD
Slight	17-Feb-05	A616T STOCKSBRIDGE BYPASS 100 MTS FROM J/W A629
Slight	21-Feb-05	STOCKSBRIDGE BY PASS STOCKSBRIDGE 900 MTS FROM WORTLEY RD
Slight	12-Mar-05	A616T CHAPELTOWN THORNCLIFFE ROAD
Damage	07-Apr-05	STOCKSBRIDGE BY PASS STOCKSBRIDGE AT J/W TANKERSLEY RDBT
Damage	04-May-05	STOCKSBRIDGE BYPASS, SHEFFIELD
Damage	07-Jun-05	A616 JNCT, STOCKSBRIDGE, SHEFFIELD, AT J/W MANCHESTER RD.
Slight	21-Jun-05	A616 LANGSETT
Damage	29-Jun-05	STOCKSBRIDGE BYPASS STOCKSBRIDGE AT J/W CORUS EAST ACCESS
Slight	12-Jul-05	STOCKSBRIDGE BYPASS STOCKSBRIDGE 60 MTS FROM WESTWOOD NEW RD
Slight	22-Sep-05	A616 MIDHOPESTONES
Damage	03-Oct-05	A616 ROUNDABOUT TANKERSLEY
Damage	12-Oct-05	A616 T STOCKSBRIDGE BY PASS BARNSLEY
Damage	12-Oct-05	A616 T STOCKSBRIDGE BY PASS BARNSLEY
Damage	30-Oct-05	A616T NEAR JCT 35A BARNSLEY J/W THORNCLIFFE RD
Damage	10-Nov-05	STOCKSBRIDGE BYPASS, SHEFFIELD
Slight	15-Dec-05	STOCKSBRIDGE BYPASS WORTLEY 70 MTS FROM J/W HALIFAX RD
Slight	09-Jan-06	STOCKSBRIDGE BYPASS STOCKSBRIDGE AT J/W HALIFAX RD
Slight	11-Jan-06	A616T BARNSLEY 30M LANGSET BARN
Damage	14-Jan-06	STOCKSBRIDGE BY PASS SLIP ROAD, SHEFFIELD.
Damage	20-Jan-06	STOCKSBRIDGE BYPASS TANKERSLEY AT J/W A 61
Slight	11-Mar-06	.A616 TANKERSLEY
Slight	11-Jul-06	STOCKSBRIDGE BYPASS TANKERSLEY 200 MTSFROM J/W NEW RD
Damage	18-Jul-06	STOCKSBRIDGE BY PASS STOCKSBRIDGE
Damage	26-Jul-06	STOCKSBRIDGE BY PASS, SHEFFIELD.
Slight	31-Aug-06	STOCKSBRIDGE BY PASS STOCKSBRIDGE
Slight	08-Sep-06	STOCKSBRIDGE BY PASS STOCKSBRIDGE 300 MTS FROM WORTLEY RD

Haunted Skies Volume Ten

Severity	Date	Location
Damage	12-Sep-06	STOCKSBRIDGE BYPASS BARNSLEY 100 MTS MANCHESTER ROAD
Slight	04-Oct-06	STOCKSBRIDGE BY PASS STOCKSBRIDGE AT J/W WORTLEY RD
Serious	05-Oct-06	A616 SHEFFIELD, 100M J/W MIDDLECLIFFE DRIVE.
Slight	06-Oct-06	STOCKSBRIDGE BYPASS WORTLEY 20 MTSFROM J/W WOODHEAD RD
Slight	01-Dec-06	A616 TANKERSLEY
Slight	07-Jan-07	A616 TANKERSLEY 500 YDS W THORNCLIFFE ROAD
Slight	15-Jan-07	A616 TANKERSLEY 50 MTS FROM J/W A61
Slight	31-Jan-07	STOCKSBRIDGE BY PASS STOCKSBRIDGE 100 MTS WESTWOOD NEW RD
Damage	08-Feb-07	STOCKSBRIDGE BYPASS BARNSLEY
Slight	24-Feb-07	A616 TANKERSLEY
Slight	21-Mar-07	STOCKSBRIDGE BY PASS STOCKSBRIDGE 85M WEST M1
Damage	05-May-07	A616T STOCKSBRIDGE BYPASS
Slight	11-May-07	STOCKSBRIDGE BY PASS TANKERSLEY 980M WEST WESTWOOD LANE
Damage	03-Jul-07	A616 STOCKSBRIDGE BYPASS
Damage	03-Jul-07	A616 STOCKSBRIDGE BYPASS
Serious	02-Aug-07	STOCKSBRIDGE BYPASS BARNSLEY AT JCT SHEFFIELD ROAD
Slight	12-Aug-07	STOCKSBRIDGE BY PASS BARNSLEY 50MTS WORTLEY ROAD
Slight	23-Aug-07	A616 MIDHOPESTONES
Damage	12-Oct-07	STOCKSBRIDGE BY PASS, SHEFFIELD.
Slight	20-Oct-07	A616T TANKERSLEY
Damage	22-Oct-07	A616 STOCKSBRIDGE BY PASS PENISTONE
Serious	19-Nov-07	A616T BARNSLEY 240M WEST GILBERT HILL
Damage	21-Dec-07	STOCKSBRIDGE BYPASS TANKERSLEY
Damage	07-Feb-08	STOCKSBRIDGE BY PASS STOCKSBRIDGE
Serious	28-Feb-08	STOCKSBRIDGE BYPASS WORTLEY
Slight	04-Mar-08	STOCKSBRIDGE BYPASS STOCKSBRIDGE J/W MANCHESTER RD
Slight	05-Mar-08	STOCKSBRIDGE BYPASS STOCKSBRIDGE J/W MANCHESTER RD
Slight	08-Mar-08	STOCKSBRIDGE BY PASS TANKERSLEY 10 MTS FROM A 61
Damage	21-May-08	STOCKSBRIDGE BY PASS STOCKSBRIDGE AT J./W ROUNDABOUT
Slight	01-Jun-08	STOCKSBRIDGE BYPASS STOCKSBRIDGE 500 MTS FROM HALIFAX RD
Slight	19-Jul-08	STOCKSBRIDGE BY-PASS SHEFFIELD
Damage	14-Sep-08	STOCKSBRIDGE BYPASS LANGSETT TO FLOUCH
Slight	21-Sep-08	STOCKSBRIDGE BYPASS TANKERSLEY 200 MTS FROM TANKERSLEY RDBT
Slight	23-Sep-08	A616 STOCKSBRIDGE BYPASS
Damage	30-Sep-08	A616 TANKERSLEY
Slight	10-Oct-08	STOCKSBRIDGE BYPASS TANKERSLEY
Slight	28-Nov-08	A616 TANKERSLEY 200 MTS FROM J/W A61
Slight	28-Nov-08	STOCKSBRIDGE BYPASS WORTLEY
Slight	29-Jan-09	A616 TANKERSLEY 100 MTS FROM J/W WESTWOOD NEW RD
Damage	15-Feb-09	STOCKSBRIDGE BYPASS STOCKSBRIDGE
Damage	22-Apr-09	STOCKSBRIDGE BY PASS, SHEFFIELD.
Damage	01-May-09	STOCKSBRIDGE BY PASS STOCKSBRIDGE
Slight	24-May-09	STOCKSBRIDGE BY PASS, SHEFFIELD, 1000M J/W MANCHESTER ROAD.
Slight	22-Jun-09	A616 SHEFFIELD WARREN LANE
Slight	23-Jun-09	STOCKSBRIDGE BY PASS TANKERSLEY
Slight	15-Aug-09	STOCKSBRIDGE BY PASS TANKERSLEY
Serious	08-Sep-09	STOCKSBRIDGE BYPASS TANKERSLEY J/W WESTWOOD NEW RD
Slight	05-Dec-09	STOCKSBRIDGE BY PASS TANKERSLEY 200 MTS FROM TANKERSLEY RDBT
Slight	09-Dec-09	STOCKSBRIDGE BYPASS TANKERSLEY 300 MTS FROM MANCHESTER RD
Damage	05-Jan-10	STOCKSBRIDGE BYPASS TANKERSLEY
Slight	01-Feb-10	STOCKSBRIDGE BYPASS WORTLEY
Slight	05-Mar-10	A616 TANKERSLEY 400 MTSFROM J/W A61
Slight	22-Mar-10	A616 SLIP RD WORTLEY J/W STOCKSBRIDGE BYPASS
Serious	21-Apr-10	STOCKSBRIDGE BYPASS TANKERSLEY
Slight	10-May-10	STOCKSBRIDGE BY-PASS SHEFFIELD J/W CORUS STEELS ACCESS RD
Damage	18-Jun-10	A616, SHEFFIELD, 10M J/W THORNCLIFFE ROAD.
Serious	06-Aug-10	STOCKSBRIDGE BYPASS STOCKSBRIDGE
Damage	25-Aug-10	STOCKSBRIDGE BYPASS TANKERSLEY 1500 MTS FROM WETSWOOD NEW RD
Slight	23-Oct-10	STOCKSBRIDGE BYPASS TANKERSLEY
Slight	31-Oct-10	STOCKSBRIDGE BY PASS WORTLEY
Damage	07-Nov-10	STOCKSBRIDGE BY PASS STOCKSBRIDGE
Slight	10-Dec-10	STOCKSBRIDGE BY PASS, SHEFFIELD, AT J/W MANCHESTER ROAD
Damage	27-Jan-11	STOCKSBRIDGE BYPASS TANKERSLEY
Damage	18-Mar-11	STOCKSBRIDGE BY-PASS SHEFFIELD J/W MANCHESTER ROAD
Slight	20-Mar-11	A616T TANKERSLEY 300 MTS FROM WESTWOOD NEW RD

Slight	03-May-11	STOCKSBRIDGE BYPASS TANKERSLEY 200 MTS FROM A61
Slight	07-May-11	STOCKSBRIDGE BYPASS TANKERSLEY 300 MTS FROM A 61
Damage	07-Jun-11	STOCKSBRIDGE BYPASS TANKERSLEY
Serious	09-Jun-11	STOCKSBRIDGE BYPASS TANKERSLEY AT J/W TANKERSLEY RDBT
Fatal	22-Jun-11	STOCKSBRIDGE BYPASS TANKERSLEY 1 ML FROM TANKERSLEY RDBT
Slight	24-Jun-11	STOCKSBRIDGE BY PASS SLIP RD WORTLEY J/W WOODHEAD RD
Damage	06-Jul-11	A616 LANGSETT
Slight	11-Aug-11	STOCKSBRIDGE BY-PASS SHEFFIELD
Damage	19-Aug-11	A616 SHEFFIELD 200M J/W THORNCLIFFE ROAD
Slight	25-Aug-11	A616 TANKERSLEY 700 MTS FROM J/W WESTWOOD NEW RD
Slight	28-Aug-11	A616T LANGSETT J/W GILBERT HILL
Serious	03-Sep-11	A616 TANKERSLEY J/W PARK LN
Slight	16-Oct-11	STOCKSBRIDGE BY-PASS SHEFFIELD
Damage	07-Nov-11	STOCKSBRIDGE BYPASS BARNSLEY AT J/W MAPLE RD
Damage	16-Nov-11	STOCKSBRIDGE BYPASS WORTLEY
Damage	23-Nov-11	A616 TANKERSLEY
Slight	26-Nov-11	STOCKSBRIDGE BY PASS TANKERSLEY
Slight	13-Jan-12	A616 FLOUGH R/ABOUT BULLHOUSE J/W A628
Damage	15-Jan-12	STOCKSBRIDGE BYPASS BARNSLEY
Slight	18-Jan-12	A616 TANKERSLEY
Slight	24-Jan-12	STOCKSBRIDGE BY PASS SHEFFIELD 1/4M PRIOR TO STEELWORKS
Slight	07-Mar-12	A616 SHEFFIELD 100 METRES WESTWOOD NEW ROAD
Slight	08-Apr-12	STOCKSBRIDGE BYPASS SHEFFIELD AT J/W MORTIMER RD
Slight	30-Apr-12	A616 TANKERSLEY
Damage	10-May-12	STOCKSBRIDGE BYPASS SHEFFIELD
Slight	20-May-12	A616 LANGSETT 50MTRS GILBERT HILL
Slight	26-May-12	STOCKSBRIDGE BY-PASS SHEFFIELD
Damage	01-Jun-12	A616 TANKERSLEY
Slight	15-Jun-12	A616 TANKERSLEY J/W WARREN LN
Damage	21-Jun-12	STOCKSBRIDGE BY PASS STOCKSBRIDGE
Slight	24-Jun-12	STOCKSBRIDGE BY PASS BARNSLEY 300MTRS HALIFAX RD
Slight	08-Jul-12	STOCKSBRIDGE BY PASS SHEFFIELD
Slight	12-Jul-12	STOCKSBRIDGE BY PASS SHEFFIELD
Serious	21-Aug-12	STOCKSBRIDGE BYPASS TANLKERSLEY 100 MTS FROM TANKERSLEY RDBT
Slight	18-Nov-12	STOCKSBRIDGE BYPASS SHEFFIELD 400M J/W M1
Damage	29-Nov-12	STOCKSBRIDGE BY PASS STOCKSBRIDGE M1 JUNCTION 35A
Slight	03-Dec-12	STOCKSBRIDGE BYPASS MIDHOPESTONES, SHEFFIELD
Slight	18-Mar-13	STOCKSBRIDGE BY PASS SHEFFIELD AT J/W STEELWORKS ACCESS
Damage	04-Apr-13	STOCKSBRIDGE BY PASS TANKERSLEY 150MTRS WESTWOOD NEW RD
Slight	05-May-13	A616 TANKERSLEY BARNSLEY
Damage	21-May-13	A616 SLIP RD DEEPCAR J/W WORTLEY RD
Damage	07-Jun-13	STOCKSBRIDGE BYPASS BARNSLEY
Damage	22-Jun-13	A616 LANGSETT
Damage	18-Jul-13	A616 SHEFFIELD NR PREMIER INN
Slight	28-Jul-13	A616 HIGH GREEN 100MTRS M1 ENTRY SLIP RD J.35A
Damage	19-Aug-13	A616 BARNSLEY J/W A628
Damage	23-Aug-13	STOCKSBRIDGE BY-PASS SHEFFIELD AT JUNC WORTLEY ROAD
Slight	10-Dec-13	STOCKSBRIDGE BYPASS SHEFFIELD J/W MORTIMER RD
Damage	18-Dec-13	A616 ROUNDABOUT SHEFFIELD J/W THORNCLIFFE ROAD

Our visit to Stocksbridge

In November 2013 we travelled to the location and took a number of photographs from Pea Royd Bridge, overlooking the bypass. We were surprised to discover, when pointing a Gauss meter towards the 400kv pylon, situated approximately 25ft away from the top left-hand side of the bridge, a marked increase was showed on the dial. To our astonishment, the needle on the dial moved over rapidly from 1milligauss 50/670Hz to 10 maximum, when some 8ft away. This enormous surge in electromagnetic field energy was sustained up to a point of approximately 50ft away up the hill before it tapered off. (At the top of the hill was a microwave tower, which would not have been there in 1988). Interestingly this high reading, as seen on the meter, was not duplicated in a 'downwards' motion – suggesting some flowing action, perhaps, rather than a circular field of electrical energy, as the layman may have expected.

Whether long-term exposure to the electromagnetic current found at Stocksbridge would be detrimental to health, or as some people allege would cause hallucinations, we cannot say, because we don't know. Despite procrastinations by those that maintain exposure to microwave/electromagnetic radiation, particularity around pylons, is not harmful to health, we believe otherwise.

Some people have speculated the reported paranormal activity could be connected with the accidental deaths of local children in the area and that their spirits continue to haunt the locality.

We searched through many journals and newspapers covering this area. While we found a number of tragic accidents, involving miners and people in the Stockbridge area around the late Victorian era and more recent years, as to be expected during part of everyday life, we discovered nothing of significance.

Sobering in its implications

This is a frightening list of fatalities. Our hearts go out not only to the victims – some of them children – but those that were left behind. Until a central crash barrier is installed, the accidents will continue to mount up. We take into consideration that a number of motorists have reported seeing ghostly forms crossing the road in front of them, while driving along the bypass – not forgetting the evidence given of the previous witnesses who have been on foot. If one accepts the validity of what these people have said then there must also be a distinct probability, on some occasions that a proportion of these accidents *were caused by manifestations* appearing in front of the drivers or worse – entering their vehicles. If this is correct then this is not acceptable. We appreciate from the details made available with regard to the circumstances of the accidents as outlined above that the majority of the accidents were caused by recklessness and dangerous drivers ignoring the double white lines along this stretch of road. These facts speak for themselves, but one cannot discount the distinct possibility, small as it may be, that accidents have been triggered by the appearance of something inexplicable in the path of the motorist.

On 7th June 1968, the *Sheffield Star* newspaper reported on a number of blue lights seen rushing over the town of Stocksbridge, during the previous three weeks, which were brought to the attention of the police – who were unable to offer any explanation.

One should also bear in mind that the pylon under which the children were seen dancing around would be the next one lower down, situated on the left-hand side of the bypass. Whether the same effects would be found there, with some sort of electromagnetic energy 'spillage' onto the bypass, is a matter we can only speculate on at this stage, as we did not find time to go and have a look at this pylon, but take note of numerous claims from other motorists, over the years, who tell of interference caused to their vehicle's electrics and lights when passing this location.

If we accept the possibility that interference to motor vehicles may have been caused by electromagnetic fields spilling out onto the road from the pylon, then what would be the effect on the human brain? It is common knowledge that shock treatment is used on certain areas of the brain, to pacify people. Prolonged exposure to electromagnetic fields can cause a number of far more serious effects. Studies have shown it can alter the flow of blood in the brain, and turn off neuron groups. It can also cause violent seizures, loss of consciousness, comas, and ultimately death. It is also suggested that this is one of the reasons why houses under high electromagnetic fields report claims of ghosts being seen inside the property.

Electric shocks have induced specific hallucinations in people. Those exposed to them, even in laboratory settings, have caused people to complain about a feeling of people following them, talking to them, or watching them. This is not always an uncomfortable sensation. Some interpret this presence as a malevolent presence, especially if it is coupled with a feeling of unease, while others say they felt an inspiring or comforting presence.

Members of paranormal research organisations will reject this explanation and claim ghostly manifestations create high electromagnetic fields, which sometimes allow ghosts to appear. We cannot say that any of this is proven; it is up to the reader to form their own conclusion. Personally, we believe one should judge every case on its individual merits. Is it possible this explanation could explain the Stocksbridge 'manifestations'? However, there are other incidents involving paranormal behaviour brought to our notice, over the years, where it is highly unlikely one could attribute the phenomena to this cause – not forgetting that incidents of high strangeness have been occurring over the landscape long before pylons were erected.

An identical reading, as shown on the meter close to the pylons, was observed after placing the instrument against the flat screen of the television/computer console used at our home address. One accepts that this is a normal reading when placed close to an electrical field, but the effect at Pea Royd Lane were felt up to 50ft away!

Digging up the past

An example of what may occur when objects are removed from their original resting places, followed by unsettling things that happen, took place during 1970 – according to Ian Barham who was working in a bunker at Aldeburgh Golf Club, in 1970, when he dug up a Bronze Age burial urn, containing cremated bones. The urn was later dated as being 1400BC and contained the bones of a woman. Ian took the burial urn to Ipswich Museum, which is where it is currently housed but decided to keep a few bones as a souvenir, which were kept in a small box in his room.

Mrs Barham (69) takes up the story . . .

> "Several months later we were sitting in the lounge when my husband and I heard the back door open and shut, followed by footsteps on the stairs. We thought our son had returned home, but later discovered it was not him. This happened once again. In September 1970, a loud banging was heard from the lounge door – so loud our next door neighbour came around to investigate. We checked the garden, wondering if anyone was causing this; there was nothing to be seen. These mysterious disturbances began to increase and we speculated if they could be connected with the human remains, as they appeared to occur around the anniversary of the remains being brought home. When we took the bones back to where they had come from, and reburied them, the noises stopped."

In a letter sent to Brenda Butler, in September 1988, Mrs Barham tells of another incident, which may well be connected to the presence of bones in the house. She had this to say:

> *"Being a collector of dolls, after making the beds in the morning, I would leave a doll lying on my bed next to the pillow. One afternoon, while sitting in the lounge, I heard a loud noise coming from upstairs. I went to investigate and was amazed to find the clay doll had been moved off the bed and had finished up on the other side of the room, several yards away.*
>
> *One Easter Sunday, my family and I were sitting down, after lunch, when we heard a noise. I looked around and believed it was coming from the window sill area, close to a cardboard Easter egg. Suddenly the Easter egg began to spin like a top.*
>
> *As it did so, gathering speed, the lid came off and flew right across the room."*

We contacted Philip Wise, Collections and Curatorial Manager of the Colchester and Ipswich Museums, regarding the whereabouts of the funerary urn, dated 1500 BC.

Philip:

> *"I have done some research on the Internet and this find would appear to be the same as that referenced as ADB 011 in a desk-based assessment, dated 2009, on the Red House, Aldeburgh. Here it is described as: 'In 1970 a collared urn, containing burnt bone, was discovered in the north-western area of the golf course.' Unfortunately, no information is given as to the current location of the urn. Please could you therefore let me know if you have any published information which states that the urn was donated to Ipswich Museum? This will be most helpful in establishing whether or not the urn is actually here in Ipswich."*

(Sources: As above/ITV *Strange but True: The Haunted Bypass*, 2.12.1994, From IUN Report *'Fly by Night'* prepared by David Clarke (1988) following investigations made by IUN members David Kelly, Andy Roberts, Gary Anthony, Clive Potter, Philip Mantle, Albert Budden, Andy Walmsley and Rodney Howarth, South Yorkshire *Spooky Tales* BBC website, 2013)

14th September 1987 – UFO over West Midlands

John Hurley, Chairman of The British Aerospace Organisation and member of UFOSIS (UFO Studies Investigation Society) – a Birmingham based UFO group, run by the late ex-Police Officer Margaret Westwood – told of a number of UFO sightings, which took place during this evening at around midnight. They included a report from a woman travelling to Bromsgrove from Birmingham along the A46. She sighted an orange object, showing a green light on top. Some 30 minutes later, a couple from Stone was retiring to bed when they saw a bright *'light'* in the sky. Although one may feel that these are just examples of space debris or a fireball, according to some of the witnesses, the object was seen to halt in the sky for a short period of time before continuing its flight. (**Source: Margaret Westwood UFOSIS**)

18th September 1987 – UFO over Langsett Hill, South Yorkshire

At 9.30pm, a motorist was driving home to Manchester, after having visited relatives in Stocksbridge. As he travelled along the A616 Manchester Road, at the top of Langsett Hill towards the direction of *Flouch Inn*, he noticed that inside a clearing alongside pine plantation were several strips of alternate red and white pulsating lights, which appeared to be attached to a circular object, hovering some 50ft off the ground. He also had an impression of something dirty black/grey in colour beneath the lights, illuminating the tips of nearby fir trees. Enquiries made later revealed the possibility of some missing time, reported by the witness.

(Source: Peter Hough – MUFORA Manchester UFO Research Association)

22nd September 1987 – UFO seen over West Yorkshire

In the early hours of this morning, a woman resident from East Street, Newton Abbot, Cornwall, contacted the police after sighting an object, displaying six lights, hovering over her house. Other sightings of what appear to have been the same UFO were reported by several people living in the Torquay area, a short time later.

At 7.45pm, Mrs J. Sugden was walking on Railway Bank above Firths Mill, at Bailiff Bridge, near Brighouse, with her husband and 8-year-old son, when they noticed an object travelling across the clear evening sky from west to north-east.

"It appeared to be a bright ball-shaped object and was moving quite fast. We saw three smaller yellow orange flashing lights on it, before it disappeared over the horizon."

Later the same evening, at 10.18pm, a triangular or 'V'-shaped object was sighted over Abbots Bromley, Staffordshire, by Tony and Josie Goodwin of Mosley Drive, Uttoxeter, who, with their son, Dominic (21) and friend Steven Asbridge (18), were driving home at the time.

Dominic Goodwin (22):

"My family and I were driving back from Walsall Illuminations and had just passed through Bagots Wood, when my father shouted, 'Look up'. I did, and saw the underneath of what looked a triangular-shaped craft in the sky. It was moving very slowly, almost stationary. I wound down the window but couldn't hear anything. The craft slowly banked over, allowing me a glimpse of the top of the object which was slightly raised on one side; its underneath showed pulsating lights in sequence. Down the middle of the 'undercarriage' was a red cross, very dimly lit. On each side of the 'body' were large strobe lights. It then headed away towards Abbots Bromley, and stopped over the woods, at which point all I could see was a long thin red stripe in the sky over the trees."

Tony:

"All of a sudden it stopped and hovered in front us. I had never seen anything like it before. It was like something out of a Spielberg movie. It was huge, about 5-100ft long, triangular in shape, surrounded by about 30 coloured lights, flashing in sequence and only about 100ft above, illuminating the ground."

(Source: Clive Potter and Tony Pace)

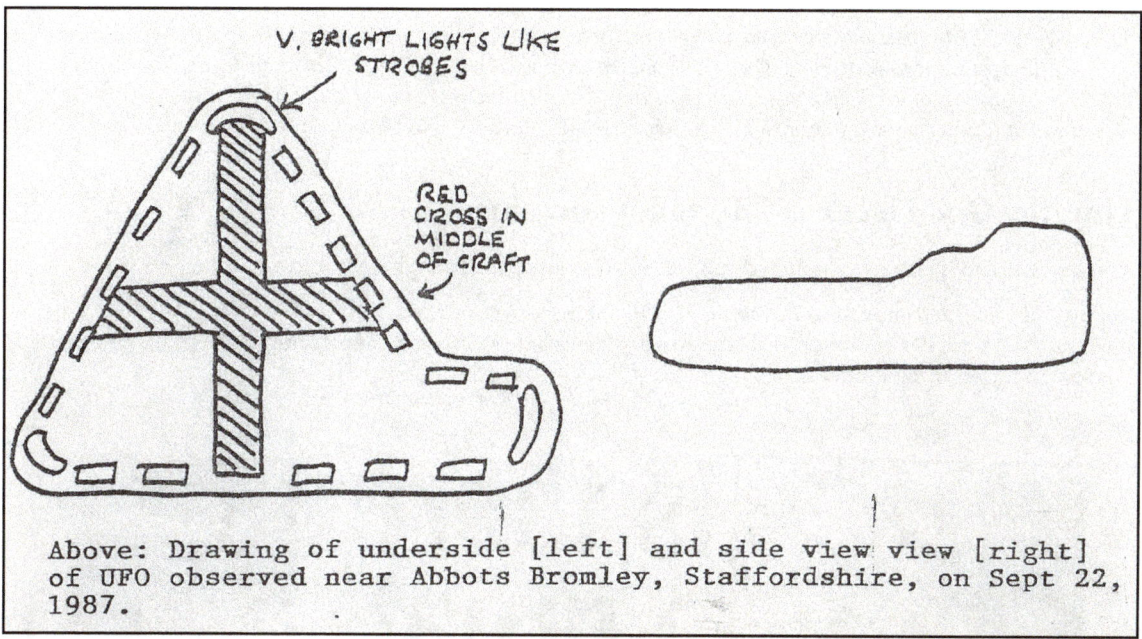

Above: Drawing of underside [left] and side view view [right] of UFO observed near Abbots Bromley, Staffordshire, on Sept 22, 1987.

25th September 1987 – Triangular UFO, South Yorkshire

At Houghton – near Thurnscoe, Barnsley, South Yorkshire – Sandra Taylor was stood outside her house with her daughter, at 12.15am, when they saw an object in the sky, *"as big as a dustbin lid in size"*, moving towards their position.

Sandra:

"We watched it pass overhead, at a height of about a 100ft. It was triangular in shape, showing three white lights and four orange lights. As it passed over we were unable to make out its outline, due to the brightness of the lights. It glided very slowly through the sky, toward some fields at the end of the road, and disappeared out of sight." **(Source: David Clarke, Clive Potter)**

Timothy Good lecture – Bolton, Lancashire

Also on this date, Timothy Good made a visit to Bolton, Lancashire, where he gave a talk on UFOs.

In an unprecedented move the *Police Review* in their edition of the 25th of September 1987 showed what appeared to be a UFO endorsed with the words *'Identified Objects'* on their front page, which related to an article written by Jenny Randles.

Haunted Skies **Volume Ten**

Police Review

25 September 1987 50p

Identified Flying Objects

September 1987 – Cured by a UFO!

In September 1987, Michael Perkins from Tamworth, Staffordshire, was driving past Thoresby Hall, towards Sherwood Forest, Nottingham, when he noticed a *'light'* in his rear window, which he took to be the headlights of a vehicle approaching him from behind. After no attempt was made to overtake, he increased his speed, trying to outrun the vehicle, but the situation remained unchanged. Frightened, he slammed on the brakes, and jumped out of the car, taking shelter under a nearby railway bridge, and watched with astonishment and fear as the glowing *'light'* shot past him and continued its travel along the road, until out of sight.

> *"I can't say if there was a connection but, shortly afterwards, I was helping a friend with his car, when I happened to touch the metal body and received a shock – powerful enough to knock me off my feet. The most amazing thing was that following a visit to my Hospital Consultant, who was treating me for a nervous incurable disorder, which I was told would eventually confine me to a wheelchair, I was surprised to find that the condition had cleared up completely. I've never had any problems since."*

Michael believes his miraculous cure was brought about as a result of his encounter with the UFO. Whether this was the case we cannot say, but we would not be surprised if it was, accepting those many occasions when people's lives were to inexorably change out of all context, following a close encounter like that described.

(Source: Personal interview)

September 1987 – UFO over Staffordshire

Paul Simcox from Tamworth, Staffordshire – then aged 18 and employed as a Bank official – had this to say:

> *"I was driving along Camp Lane, in the direction of Sutton Coldfield, during September 1987, when a short distance away from the junction of Hill Wood Road with Black Wood Forest to my right, I saw a 'tube-like' object, resembling a petrol tanker, without any wheels, passing overhead, just before dusk, with the sun catching its highly polished surface.*
>
> *I was frightened by the appearance of this 'thing', seemingly only a couple of hundred feet above me, enabling me to see a saucer-shaped craft, with a dome and base. The car ignition lights came on and the vehicle slowed to a stop. I jumped out of the car and stood mesmerised, looking at the UFO shimmering and vibrating slightly, showing a rainbow effect of colours, like a prism. Within seconds, it accelerated away, made a perfect right-angle, and disappeared from view. I tried the ignition on the car – a Vauxhall Chevette – the engine burst into life.*
>
> *When I got home, I told my father what had happened. We went outside to have a look at the car, as dusk was now falling, and discovered that none of the lights on the car would work. When we examined the bulbs, we discovered that, while the filaments had not been broken, the bulbs refused to work and that the glass on each bulb – normally clear glass – was now yellow and opaque . . . frosty in appearance. We took the car to a local garage, who suggested that the damage to the bulbs and electrical wiring had been caused by an overload of energy. Subsequently, we had to scrap the car."*

(Source: Personal interview)

September 1987 – Police sight cigar-shaped UFO

During the same month, Police Constable Stanley Osbourne and PC Douglas were driving along the M6, between Leyland and Shevington, at Charnock Richard, when they were astonished to see a cigar-shaped object race past them on a parallel course across the sky, a mere 30-50ft off the ground, and then out of sight within five seconds.

(Source: *Windsor Slough and Eton Express.* 23.12.1987/*4th Annual Police Report,* 2005, Gary Heseltine)

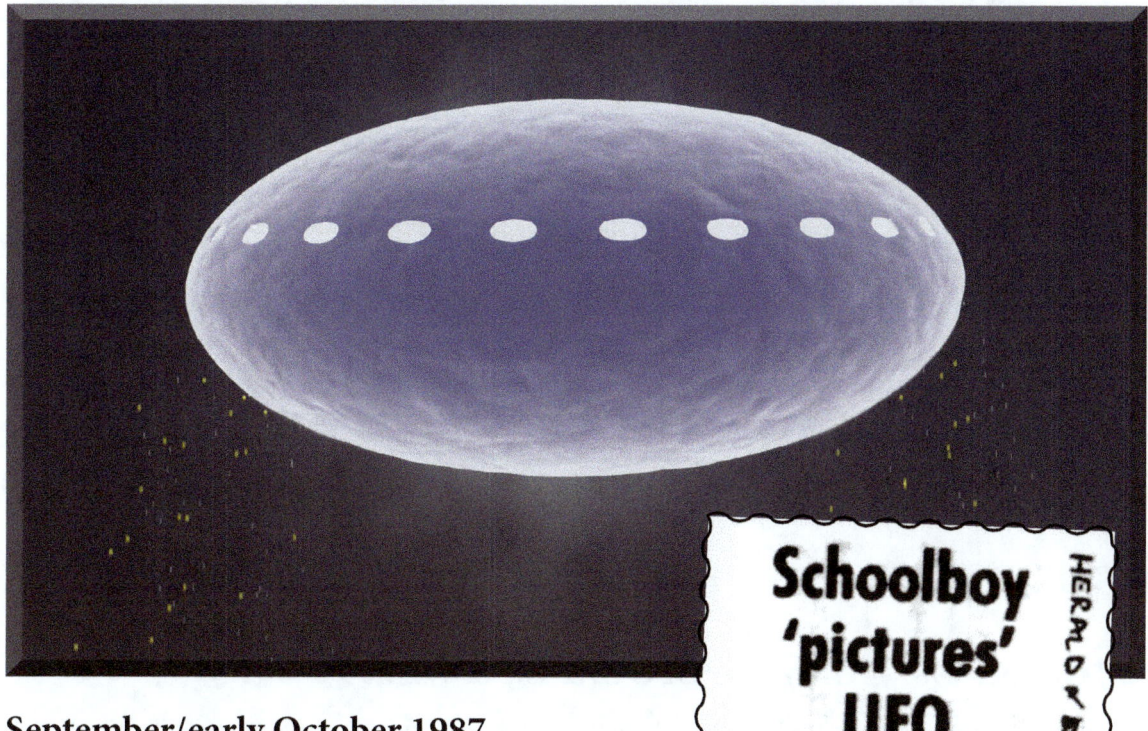

September/early October 1987, 'V'-shaped UFO, Sheffield

Ms. Sharon Lindsay – holder of a Degree in Psychology and Sociology, from Sheffield University – was walking along Holgate Crescent on the Longley Estate, North Sheffield. As she turned onto a street (running across a narrow valley of wasteland) at Parsons Cross, she noticed on object with red lights on its side and rear, passing through the sky in an east to west direction.

> "The lights were in a 'V' shape, with the point going downwards. I couldn't make out if the object was a different shape from the pattern of lights. It was moving very slowly at about 30mph and twice the height of rooftops. It sounded like a very noisy low flying RAF jet. I ran down to the bottom of the valley and watched it for a few minutes, before walking away." (**Source:** David Clarke/Andy Roberts)

Schoolboy 'pictures' UFO

SCHOOLBOY Clifford Doney of Torquay is the latest to report a sighting of a UFO over South Devon — and has even drawn a picture of the mysterious "spaceship."

Clifford, 11, depicts a circular brightly coloured object, but says it made no sound.

"I was coming home from St. Johns, almost outside Lower Westlands School when I looked up in the sky and saw a circular object, surrounded with very bright coloured lights which lit up all the area around it."

HERALD & EXPRESS (TORQUAY) 30 SEPT. 1987

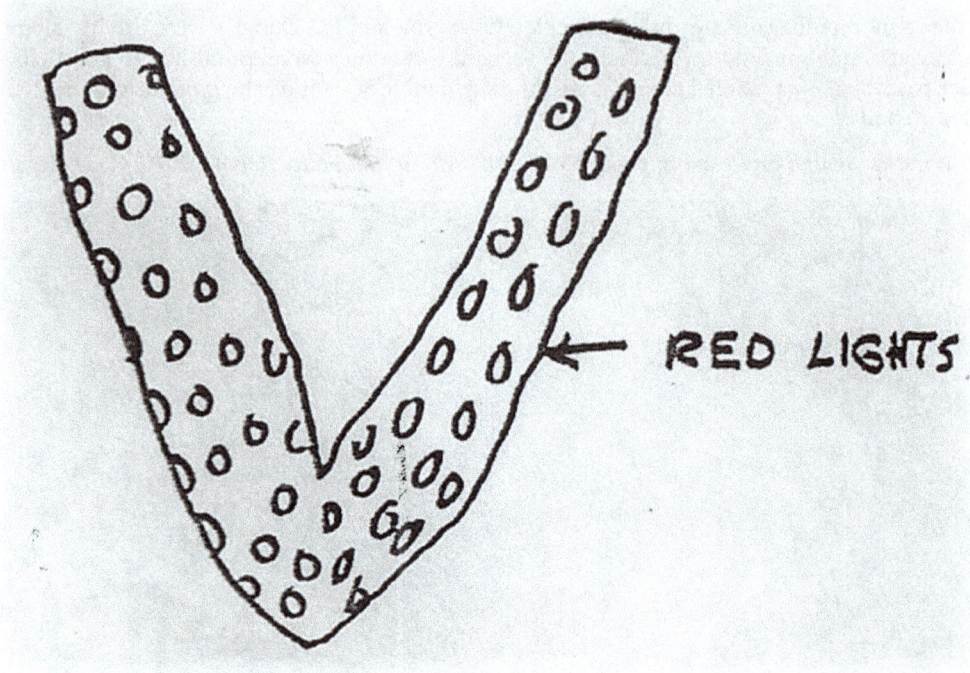

OCTOBER 1987

2nd October 1987 – Triangular UFO over Isle of Wight

Clifford Roper, from Niton on the Isle of Wight, contacted us in 2008, describing what he saw at 6.45pm, while outside his house in Trinity Road.

> "I looked up and was stunned to see an object, motionless in the sky above my head, at a height I estimated to be only 40ft. I stood rigid with disbelief as it slowly moved a few feet at a time through the air, heading towards the direction of some bungalows on the adjacent side of the road. I ran over to the bungalows. As I did so, two white lights appeared on the body of the object but they did not produce any beams – just plain lights. Whatever it was rose up slightly, to presumably avoid striking the tops of the buildings, enabling me to burn to memory what I was seeing. The craft was about 80-100ft from corner to corner, with massive glass or plastic domes hanging down, with lights inside them, spear-shaped and thin, but there was nothing to hold the lights in place. These were 6-8ft wide and 10-12ft long, with a bulge just down the sides, fitted inside the craft at a 45° angle. The lights comprised a first white light; the second, two yellow or green, third – three were red, the fourth royal blue. The craft had a groove running around the middle of its side, approximately a foot wide by a foot deep; the body of the UFO being about 4ft in depth. The side skin was one piece, no joins, although underneath the metal or skin did not join and was held together with what looked like two inch rivets. I estimated the whole object must have weighed 50-60 ton; it was a perfect triangle, with really sharp edges."

Haunted Skies Volume Ten

We eventually met up with Cliff and found him to be a most helpful man. We cannot thank him enough for his kindness and generosity and are indebted to him for driving us around the Island to meet former members of the now defunct Isle of Wight UFO Society, one of whom was Kath Smith, married to Tom – a retired Police Officer. We thoroughly enjoyed talking to Kath and her colleague, Pat, who handed over to us a great quantity of documents, personal letters, and many copies of *UFOLOG*.

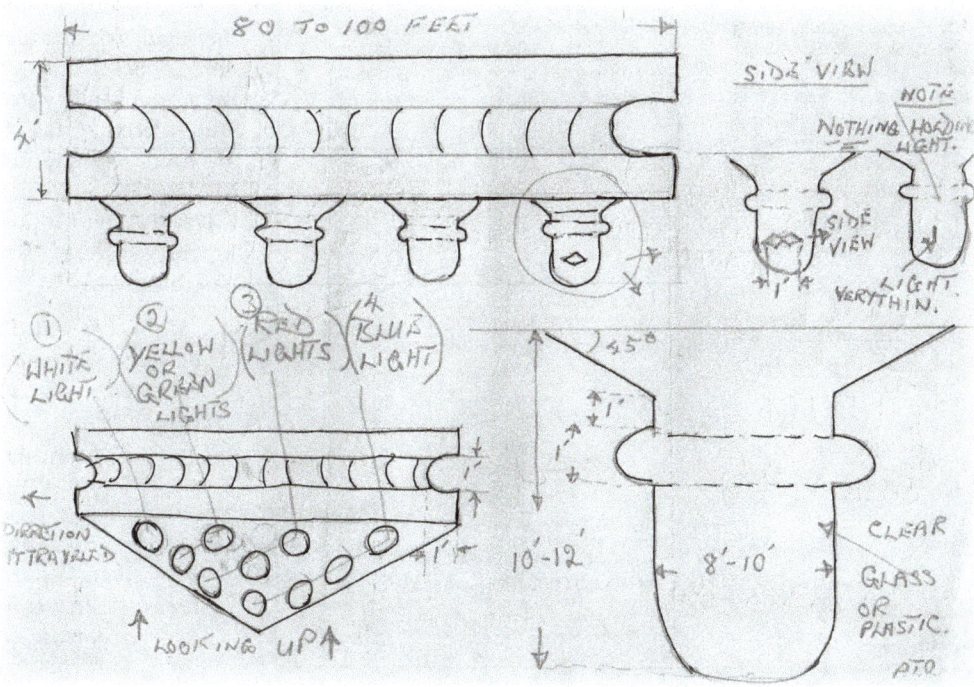

Haunted Skies Volume Ten

In addition to this incident were reports of UFOs seen over the Midlands on the 2nd October 1987, according to UFO researcher John Hurley, following sightings of an oval orange object, showing a green band, hovering above the ground over Stone and other parts of Staffordshire.

> "We received 130 calls from the public about this UFO. Incredibly, someone suggested it might have been an expended fuel tank from a Russian satellite!"

9th October 1987 – UFO display over Basildon

At 7.10pm, keen fisherman Peter Wray, from Southend-on-Sea, was sat in his car after working on his boat at Leigh Wharf, Old Leigh, near Leigh-on-Sea. He noticed four large round red/orange *'lights'* appear in the sky over Canvey Point, which then began to move towards his position. A few minutes later, six more of these *'lights'* appeared in the sky over the direction of Hadleigh, and met up with each other over the direction of Hadleigh Castle, at an estimated height of 300-500ft. Peter continued watching. Thirty minutes later, the two separate formations of lights joined up and headed away towards the Basildon area.

At 7.45pm, Ellen Gibbs (aged 77) of Braybroke Road, Basildon, was putting the milk bottles outside, when she noticed a dozen or so, red, white, mauve/purple lights, moving about erratically in the night sky. She alerted the next door neighbours, who came out and watched the UFOs 'playing tag' for over an hour. Neighbour Jaclyn McCoy (37) and her husband – David Allen McCoy (38) of Braybrooke Road, Basildon – had this to say:

> "Mrs Gibbs called us outside. I was amazed to see red, orange, and white lights, flying around in the sky. I couldn't believe what I was seeing. It was like fireworks night, but these weren't fireworks. They looked like coloured eggs; some were hovering,

while others were racing around all over the sky. When the police arrived my daughter was crying and clutching the cat, saying 'I won't let the aliens take him away'. At this point I took her inside, as she was now very frightened. People have tried to explain them away as being fireworks or flares, which is rubbish."

Another witness was Arthur Fielding (27) – a fireman on duty at Basildon Fire Station, at 9.45pm.

"One minute the sky was clear, except for a few stars, and then these red, white, and orange lights, about the size of a cricket ball, appeared. They seemed to be playing tag – hovering, shooting off, going around in circles, zigzagging across the sky."

He, and a number of colleagues, watched the strange *'lights'* for over an hour, until they moved silently away and out of sight. (**Source: Brenda Butler & Ron West**)

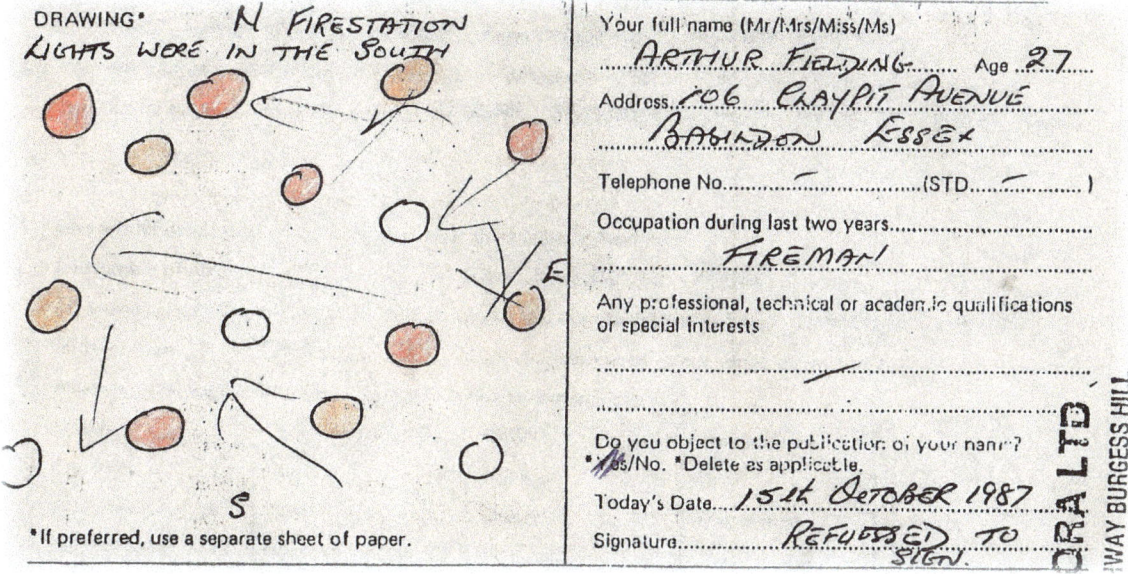

13th October 1987 – Lancashire UFOs

At midday, a silver and red bright glowing globe-shaped object, with a small dome on top, was seen by over twenty pupils from year ten class, at St. Joseph's Junior School, Leigh, Lancashire, apparently 'buzzing' a helicopter above the school. (Source: *The Sun*, 14.10.87 – 'No kidding Sir, we did see a flying saucer')

15th October 1987 – UFO sighted over school

Teenagers at a youth club, next door, witnessed a similar object hovering over the school, projecting red and white beams of light onto the playground, before heading off across the sky at a phenomenal speed.

JAS INE

After reading your article in the South Wales Evening Post referring to "UFO" sightings including the Cox family in 1993, I've put pen to paper and would like to share with you an incident which took place on an early morning in 1987. At this point I would like to point out that only my immediate family know about the incident and have always regarded it as a family secret.

As most young teenagers growing up I had a weekend job which would see me walking around 5a.m. in the morning to the local Dairy to load up a friends milk van, and then start to deliver at 6.30am. On this particular Saturday morning I walked my usual route towards the Dairy. I remember it was a very cold morning and also very clear. As I approached a railway viaduct I remember looking toward the top of the bridge. I could see the outline of the bridge in the morning light but above the bridge I could see a darker shadow. I remember thinking it was a strange place to put a sign, over a railway bridge. As I came to within 100ft of the bridge I could hear a dull sound coming from above the bridge. As I walked within 50ft I could see the dark shadow was above the bridge but seemed to be suspended in mid air. I continued to look and saw the outline slowly changing shape. I stopped for a second and became fixed onto the object. I remember seeing two lights green in colour, but these lights seemed to move around the object and dissapear. I walked under the bridge and came out the other side. On turning around I looked up and saw the shape move up into the air vertically, and finally vanishing. I know that I am to this day 100% certain that what I saw was a U.F.O. of some kind. Since my teenage years ive taken a keen interest in this subject, and always had an open mind into this subject. Its not something that can be spoken about openly and fact many people are very sceptical about the matter. I've studied local sightings and found that this area seems to be very active in the way of sightings. I remember reading about the "Fox incident" at the time but little about it. I've heard of other sightings since and have always kept an open mind. I hope you find more information on the subject and find what you are looking for. As a grown up proffesional adult there are not many people you can discuss this subject.

Yours faithfully

[signature]. 7-3-00.

16th, 17th October 1987 – UFO seen over East Sussex

On this date a severe storm struck the south-east of England, the worst since 1703 – powerful enough to topple some 15 million trees, decimating buildings and causing severe damage to ships, some of which were driven onto shore – and sixteen people died as a direct result of the storm damage.

At 4pm the following day (17th October 1987) a resident of Peacehaven, East Sussex, was surveying the damage to his house, when he noticed an enormous circular object through a break in the grey clouds, just above cloud base.

> "It had a completely flat underneath and I estimated it to be 100-150ft across and 15-20ft in height. It had a circular mushroomed-shaped dome, with what appeared to be square-shaped windows, sloping inwards at the bottom, resembling a sheet of reflective glass, mounted on base wall of some 4ft high. The 'body' seemed to be made of chrome steel, or aluminium, and a low swishing noise could be heard."

(Source: *Sky Search*)

19th October 1987 – Strange lights seen in the sky, Kent

At 8pm, Roger Ford – a part-time fireman from East Malling – was contacted by his father, Gordon, from Larkfield, who brought his attention to some strange lights in the sky. When Roger went outside to have a look, he saw:

> " . . . two lights; one high in the sky, the other lower; it appeared as though they were shooting red and white laser beams at each other."

A spokesman for the MOD was sceptical of the report and suggested that they had seen a helicopter.

(Sources: Personal interview/UFO Mystery of strange lights in the sky – *Kent Evening News*, 20.10.87 'Was it a close encounter for a family?')

22nd October 1987 – RAF Harrier jet crashes into ocean

At 4.59pm, pilot Humphrey Taylor Scott took off from BAE, Dunsfold, Surrey, in a British RAF Harrier Jet BAE GR5 (ZD325) on what is believed to have been a pre delivery

Haunted Skies Volume Ten

flight. At 5.05pm, all radio contact was lost while the plane was over Wiltshire. (The last radio message had been a routine one to Boscombe Down Airbase.)

An examination of this unusual incident revealed that other aircraft were alerted following loss of radio contact. A C-5 Galaxy American military transport aircraft reported a visual on the Harrier 90 miles to the west of the south-west tip of Ireland, and managed to video film the Harrier, which was seen to have no cockpit canopy or pilot! The American plane followed the Harrier for 410 miles before it went down into the ocean.

The following day, gamekeeper – Mr Ken Pitman – discovered the body of the pilot lying in a field near the

village of Winterbourne Stoke, near Stonehenge, overlooking a field where some crop circles had formed on the 22nd August 1987. His secondary parachute was found nearby, and a dinghy was found in the corner of the same field in which crop circles had previously appeared. Colin Andrews heard of the incident and set out to have a look, because the location was already familiar to him, and after arriving at Winterbourne Stoke made his way to the field.

> "A battery of floodlights cut into the darkened countryside and surrounded a spot in the field, opposite to the site of our set of mystery circles. A large gathering of military personnel could be seen moving around inside the illuminated area; a parachute lay nearby. In the darkness I could just make out two army vehicles, parked in the corner. Whoever was in the vehicle was guarding an inflatable dinghy."

Contacting the MOD

Colin decided to contact the MOD, hoping to learn more about the highly unusual circumstances surrounding the death of the pilot concerned. On 7th November 1988 he telephoned 'Boscombe Down Airfield, who advised him the enquiry was being dealt with at Prospect House, London, by Squadron Leader Graham Davis. When Colin telephoned the number given, he was told by Squadron Leader Pike that Squadron Leader Davis was still out on Salisbury Plain, carrying out an investigation, and that the enquiry should be continued with Squadron Leader Davis. Colin decided to tell Squadron Leader Pike about the newly found circles, which had been found near the village of Winterbourne Stoke. He was very interested in what Colin had to say and asked him questions like:

> "How do you think these circles are formed and what kind of energy is involved?"

Haunted Skies Volume Ten

Colin:

> *"I told him I believed the phenomenon was very rare indeed, although worldwide, and that this part of southern England was experiencing a far higher frequency of reports than any other part of the world. I concluded the conversation by adding that the field in which the four circles were recently formed lies beneath the area in space where it seems this pilot was taken out of his £13.5 million pounds worth of Jet Fighter. Later the same day, I received a telephone call telling me that my information had been passed onto Squadron Leader Davis and the 'Boss', whoever that is.*
>
> *After hearing nothing else, I continued my own enquiries into the matter and obtained some information to the effect that the Harrier Jet was seen to change its course by a few degrees right over the field which had the circles, and that the pilot inexplicably left his aircraft at about that point of the flight. He was not ejected by the ejector seat fitted into the aircraft. An inflatable dinghy left the aircraft with him, as did his main parachute. This was found in shreds north of Stonehenge."*

Tony Dodd, Colin Andrews with Robert Dean. Right: Crop formation at Westbury

The inquest

This was held on Monday, 28th March 1988. The MOD stated that without being able to examine the ejector seat, which was in the aircraft at the bottom of the sea, they were unable to positively identify the cause of the tragedy. However, the most plausible reason was the *"inadvertent firing of a manual separation device, designed for use after the ejector seat had left the aircraft. This firing may have been caused by a lead lamp having fallen from its clip and become lodged under the manual override operating rod on the right of the seat, which linked the handle to the cartridge firing unit"* i.e., the pilot was inadvertently removed from the cockpit by the seat separation drogue gun, leaving the Harrier to fly unmanned, with the broken canopy attached. Without having seen the film taken by the C5 Galaxy, can we take it that the broken canopy, or remains of it, was still attached?

Colin took the opportunity to speak to Squadron Leader Davis, that evening, and was surprised to hear him admit:

> *"We do not know what caused this, quite honestly. We do not think the mystery circles which I have also seen, and this, are related on this occasion."*

He admitted the circle formations were puzzling phenomenon and asked that he be kept updated, should any further information come to light.

The layman may well consider (and we fall into that bracket) a number of pertinent questions as to how this happened, in view of not being able to obtain sight of any of the official Board of Enquiry/Inquest documents.

We have tried to form our own answers, hopefully based on common sense and research rather than considering any 'external cause', which we believe highly unlikely on this occasion, as although we have a number of reports of UFOs reported around that month, we have nothing to substantiate any association between these objects and those sightings.

Question 1 – *Why did the pilot decide to leave the aircraft, because the canopy was blown?*

Answer: He may not have had any choice; in normal circumstances the ejector seat handle, situated between the legs of the pilot, is pulled upwards to operate. The charge shatters the cockpit canopy. An ejection gun fires the seat up the guide rails to clear the aircraft. Then the rocket pack fires the seat upwards. These fire for one fifth of a second and push the seat 330ft away from the aircraft. This is followed by an explosive charge, which opens a small parachute and slows down the seat and opens the main parachute. When the main parachute opens, the pilot then floats to safety. However, in this instance, it is possible the parachute deployer rocket pack malfunctioned and the drogue chute pulled the pilot out through the remains of the cockpit, no doubt causing serious injury to the upper torso and shredding the parachute (which was recovered from near Stonehenge, in shreds). **Our conclusion:** More than likely.

It would be of interest to ascertain whether any testing was conducted on the parachute to determine how this damage had been caused – presumably, in contact with the jagged canopy? **Our conclusion:** Not known.

Question 2 – *What were the injuries to the pilot?*

Answer: A post mortem must have taken place to determine the presence of any alcohol or drugs in the body as a matter of course with accidents like this, not forgetting glass/plastic fragments in the clothing worn. **Our conclusion:** Not known.

Question 3 – *Why take the dinghy out with him?*

Answer: Again, we presume it is deflated in the aircraft and then inflated in flight. The dinghy would have been ejected as a matter of course, as it is connected to the ejector seat system and automatically inflates on ejection from the aircraft. Our conclusion: Quite possibly.

The tragic death of the pilot under what *initially appears* to be highly unusual circumstances provides many questions with no answers, other than speculative ones.

The only routine radio transmission took place six minutes after take-off with no hint of any problems or defects, which suggests that there were none.

The reader should bear in mind that although ejection seat technology appears simplistic to members of the public, and that safety systems in operation aboard aircraft are foolproof, of course in real life they are not. A look at over 500 ejections reveals that a surprising number of these were fatal, and that amongst the rest some of the pilots received a variety of medical injuries which were not life threatening but considered serious injuries. This puts things into a different perspective!

We emailed the MOD in 2013, asking if these documents can be viewed by the public, but remain pessimistic of the outcome.

Clearly we were unable to take this matter any further, and express our heartfelt condolences to any of the family concerned.

---

*Boscombe Down is owned by the MOD and operated by DERA (Defence Evaluation and Research Agency). Boscombe Down has hosted an International Air Tattoo in 1990, and an Air Tournament International in 1992, but that was before DERA took over the Base. It is notable that although Boscombe Down is an ideal venue for the Royal International Air Tattoo in 2000, while RAF Fairford is having its runways upgraded, it has been announced that it definitely will not be taking place there, by a DERA spokesman.

23rd October 1987 – Two bright 'lights' over Essex

At 3.10am, two police officers on night patrol in the Ford End area of Chelmsford saw two bright *'lights'* in the sky, heading in a south-west direction. They watched them for about five minutes, until out of sight.

(Source: Declassified MOD Report)

28th October 1987 – Strange lights over A635, West Yorkshire

At 9.10pm on the above date, a motorist and his wife were driving over the Trans-Pennine road, heading towards Holmfirth, from Greenfield when they noticed a bright white *'light'*, with a small red light underneath it, stationary in the sky. The man continued on his journey for about five minutes, before deciding to stop when he realised the *'lights'* were now overhead.

> *"Looking upwards we saw a circle of white, red/orange lights in the sky. After about five minutes the lights moved slowly away, southwards, over the moors; we estimated the lights had been about a 100ft in diameter and 800ft in height."*

Enquiries made by Andy Roberts with Holmfirth Police proved unsuccessful, although in a letter sent to Andy by Chief Inspector Brian Smith, on 21st December, the officer suggested a helicopter was the most likely culprit. (The lack of any rotor blade noise appears to rule this out.) At 10.30pm, the same evening, ambulance workers Clive Pearson and Brenda Coyne, from Aldridge Ambulance Station, were on duty when they noticed a large bright light hovering silently in the sky. Ambulance driver, Brenda, said:

> *"We watched it for about five minutes. It wasn't very high and hovering over the trees at the back, and then it shot away to our right. We telephoned Birmingham Airport and asked them to check their radar. They told us about two aircraft which we could see over the sky."*

(Source: Personal interview/*Walsall Observer*, 6.11.1987 – 'Light in Sky was UFO – drivers')

October 1987 – UFO with green lights over viaduct

Stephen Kenny of Penplas, Swansea, was on his way to work, one early, bitterly cold morning, in October 1987, and was about to cross over the viaduct, when he saw:

> *"... a dark shadow over the bridge. I first thought to myself, that's a strange place to put a sign. As I came closer, now about 100ft away from it, I heard a dull sound and realised that it was emanating from this mass, which was slowly changing shape, with two green lights revolving around it. I carried on walking, and when I got to the other side of the bridge I saw it rise vertically into the sky and disappear from sight."*

(Source: Personal interview)

CHAPTER 3

NOVEMBER TO DECEMBER 1987

NOVEMBER 1987

1987 – Bigfoot sighting, West Midlands

IN 2006, we met up with Gary Higginson, a Post Office employee from the 'Black Country' and an avid collector of books on the UFO subject – an interest sparked off by a very strange experience, which happened in 1987, while he was working on the *Sandwell Valley Archaeological project. (At the time he was living in Wednesbury and often used to run to work, a distance of four-and-a-half miles, arriving there at 7.30am. On this particular day, he decided to make the run a little longer by making his way along the road that runs adjacent to the M5 Motorway, close to a boating lake known locally as †Swan Pool.

"I just happened to look to my right across the fields and saw, with shock, what looked like a 'Bigfoot' shambling across the field. I stopped and ran away, not knowing what to do, and then rationally thought to myself 'What on earth am I doing?' It must have been some sort of hallucination, so I gingerly made my way back to where I had seen the 'creature' and cautiously looked around. There was nothing to be seen. On reflection I knew this was no hallucination, purely because I had seen it so clearly. It was approximately 6ft 6ins tall, with 2-3ins of dark brown hair covering its body (longer on the head), and seemed to be heading for Swan Pool. I saw it for 2-3secs, and admit to being frightened. My legs turned to jelly."

Having met Gary personally, and discussed his sighting of this strange creature, referred to him as a '*Bigfoot*' (which conjures up a mental image popular to American folklore, rather than the fields of England), we saw no reason to question his account as being genuine. This was not the first or last time we were to hear of strange shuffling hairy entities, or humanoids, seen by members of the public (and Military), going back to the 1940s.

Werewolves seen!

On 26th April 2007, the *Stafford Post* told their readers of *'a rash of sightings'* of a *'werewolf'-type* creature, seen prowling in and around the outskirts of Stafford, which were brought to the attention of the West Midlands Ghost Club. They confirmed of having been contacted by a number of shocked residents, who claimed to have seen a *'hairy wolf-type creature'* walking on its hind legs around the German War Cemetery, just off Camp Road, in between Stafford and Cannock. Several of them alleged the creature sprang up on its hind legs and ran into the nearby bushes when it was spotted. Research into the local area revealed a number of other similar sightings of mysterious figures and *'beasts'* on Cannock Chase – a Staffordshire beauty spot, which lies 15 miles (approx.) away from Sandwell Valley. The reports included the sighting of a *'tall female, pale grey in colour, apparently naked but with no visible breasts or genitalia, with large hypnotic eyes'* that totally transfixed the woman motorist, who found herself in dread and unable to move a muscle after being caught in the headlights of a car, while driving past Springslade Lodge at 11.30pm.

Nick Duffy, West Midlands Ghost Club:

> "With regard to the Chase area in general, there has been a considerable wealth of peculiar encounters with numerous potentially paranormal creatures. Recently, sightings of what resembled 'werewolves' have been brought to my attention – a subject that has received quite a bit of coverage by the local Press and the internet. Over recent decades, the area has given birth to a considerable number of sightings, involving numerous mysterious entities. Such experiences not only feature the more traditional tales of ghosts and alien big cats, but also perplexing accounts of hairy humanoids and, more recently, 'werewolf' type creatures."

7th November 1987 – UFO over Essex

At 11pm, Telecom engineer Michael Alan Rogers (44) of Goodmayes, Essex, and his wife, Dorothy, and friend Lesley Blair, were driving back to London from Portsmouth, along the A3, near Cherry Tree Road, close to Milford, Surrey, when he saw a strange *'red light'* in the sky through the windscreen.

> "It seemed to be travelling in a straight line and as it didn't look like an aircraft, we stopped to have a closer look. I pulled the car over into a lay-by next to the White Lion Public House, and wound the window down. I remembered I had a camera in my glovebox and took two photographs, although I had difficulty in framing the light in the viewfinder as it was small."

According to his wife, and friend Lesley, they both claimed that the *'light'* had moved across the sky in a zigzag action, before disappearing behind trees. Mr Rogers wrote to Jenny Randles about what had taken place and then sent the negatives to her for examination. The result of that examination is unknown.

(Source: Ron West)

---

*The valley is actually a valley of the River Tame and takes its name from the Holy Well, or Sandwell, which is near its centre, with evidence of human activity in the valley going back to the Stone Age, between six and eight thousand years ago. There has been continuous human habitation around the Sandwell area from the 12th century until the early 20th century).

†Swan Pool, originally known as Wasson Pool, forms part of the Sandwell Valley Nature Reserve. The pool originally the sump pool for the now defunct Colliery has been landscaped, but the actual water is still there. There are reports of wavy white shapes seen floating about in the dark, over the pool, which were reported as ghostly activity and was the subject of some investigation by the now defunct *Smethwick Telephone* newspaper.

Haunted Skies Volume Ten

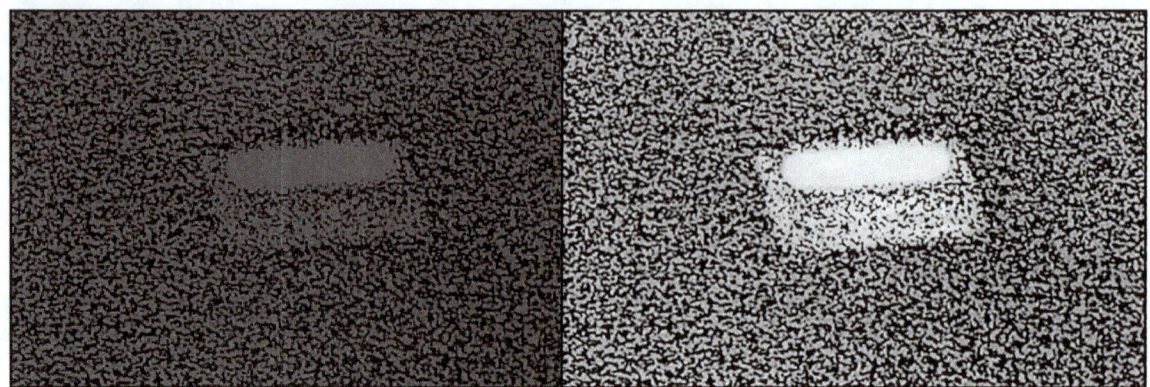

Left: Enlargement of one of two images that Mike Rogers managed to snap on the A3 near to Milford, Surrey, November 1987.
Right: A Photoshop enhancement of the same shot.

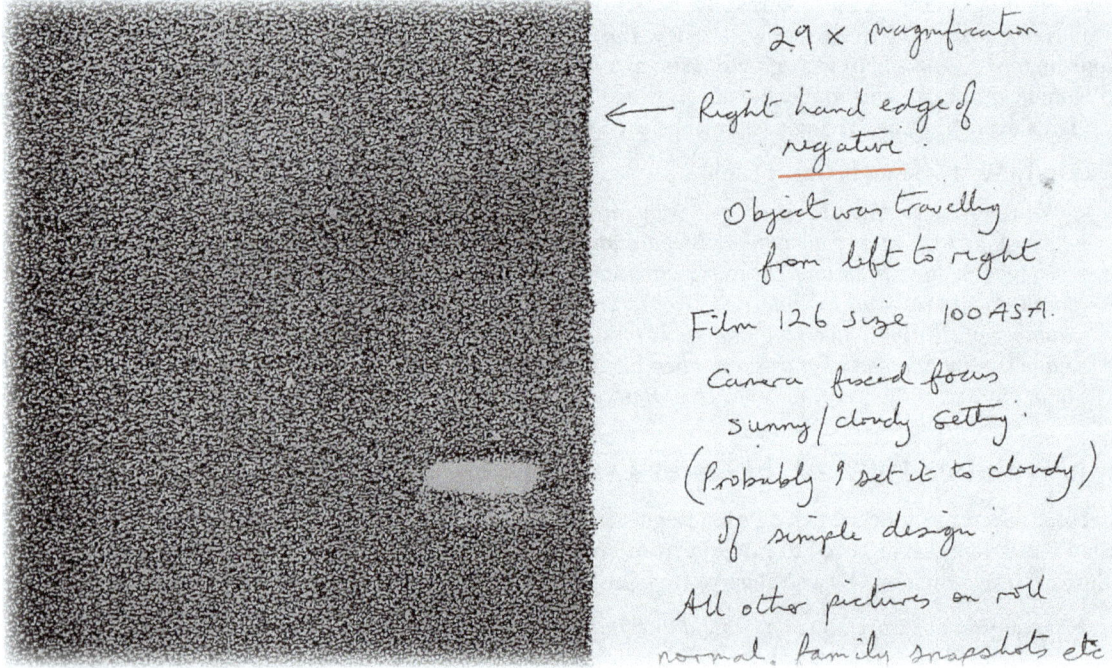

12th November 1987 – UFO crash landing – Nottinghamshire

Something strange happened on the night of 12th November 1987, just south of Mansfield, in Nottinghamshire. It was reported in the local papers as a *'freak storm'*, or more accurately, a *'freak thunderbolt'* that caused considerable damage to a number of properties in the Kirkby area, including one house that was almost destroyed. However, it seems that this was no ordinary thunderbolt, as Mike West (who dealt with many of the insurance claims) can verify.

> *"It just doesn't make any sense"*, he told a group of local residents.

> *"Every claim that I've dealt with in the past 26 years has been logical and reasonable, but this defies reason. It did not even travel in a straight line (as you would expect if it was a thunderbolt, following the line of least resistance).*

It zigzagged across the sky, before diving down over the hills. It is as if the whole area was blanketed with electromagnetic radiation."

The effects were felt over a large area. Many people in Mansfield were awoken, at 1.30am, by a sound *'like an explosion'*. Somewhat ironically, many of those still awake were watching an old war movie, *The Battle of Britain,* on TV. Coincidently, the film had just reached the point where German bombers were dropping their payload onto a British aerodrome!

As the explosion resounded, lights came on all by themselves; others that had been switched on exploded, while TV aerials were split in two.

Local insurance companies were inundated with claims for video players and TVs damaged by the so-called *'thunderbolt'*. In one street alone, 40 claims were made. A TV and video repairman, who was working at home late that evening, reported that all of a sudden the lights started to dim and light bulbs started to pop in the house. To add to this, the electrical 'trip switch' blew, and the following day, he was flooded with calls from people whose equipment had been damaged by the *'thunderbolt'*. There were also some claims that this event could have been the result of ball lightning. However, as Mike West discovered, this could not fully explain the events of that night.

He said:

> "I spoke to one old lady, who was petrified. She saw it flying straight towards her house. It looped and double-looped, and was doing some other manoeuvres in the sky. Another man saw it from a distance, and described the sky as 'suddenly becoming bright red'."

The amount of energy required to create an explosion that was heard and felt over an area of 7-8 miles radius (some people reported being practically thrown out of bed) would be far more than conventional physics attributes to ball lightning. As Mike West stated, he has dealt with numerous insurance claims that have come about as a result of ball lightning and thunderbolt damage. He has never witnessed a case such as this one.

Andrew Emerson and Dominic Beglin

To judge by the body of evidence, there has to be another explanation. On some streets, windows imploded and exploded in alternate houses! The headlines in the local newspaper reported that lightning had struck a house, causing severe damage, and demolished the gable end. However, the media reports disguised what UFO researchers Andrew Emerson and Dominic Beglin believe to be the truth behind one of Great Britain's most spectacular cover-ups.

ARE YOU A WINNER? FIND THE BALL: PAGE 39

Freak storm... or UFO crash and cover-up?

CLAIMS that a UFO crashed in north Notts ten years ago will be made at a public meeting in the city this weekend.

On November 12, 1987, homes in Kirkby-in-Ashfield were damaged, and a block of flats almost cut in half, by what official reports said was a freak thunderstorm.

Witnesses spoke of a ball of fire speeding across the sky.

Dominic Beglin, a member of the British UFO Research Association, who will speak at a meeting tomorrow, believes a UFO crashed that night and what followed was a top secret cover-up.

He said: "A possible crash site has since been found in the Warren, just north of Hucknall. Apparently after the incident the area was closed off by the military."

The *Post* has spoken to a Kirkby businessman involved in the drama.

He asked not to be identified, but said he had seen three balls of light travelling very fast towards him before the whole house shook.

He had run outside and then: "The sky seemed to explode. It looked as if the sky was full of red dust."

He says following the incident he was visited by officials wanting to know what he had seen.

But an MoD spokesman told the *Post*: "We have no record of any UFO or aircraft crash anywhere in the UK on November 12, 1987. And we have no evidence to substantiate the existence of UFOs."

The meeting will be held at Old Basford Community Centre, Davids Lane at 4pm. Admission is £1.50.

THE NOTTINGHAM TOPPER
14 MAY 1997

TAKING FLIGHT: UFO investigators claim this is the site where a mystery craft landed 10 years ago — but say the incident has been covered up by the authorities who blame freak weather for damaging nearby homes

PICTURE BY WILL PICKERING

'UFO crash site found in Notts'

REPORT by JOHN HOWORTH

RESEARCHERS say they've uncovered new evidence to back claims that a UFO crashed in Notts 10 years ago.

A thunderball was blamed for tearing through 13 homes at Kirkby-in-Ashfield — blowing out windows and bringing down chimney stacks on November 12, 1987.

But East Midlands UFO Research Association says that theory doesn't add up.

Director Anthony James said: "An insurance expert said at the time that it defied reason.

"Folk say they were stopped in their car by a police roadblock near Annesley and told they couldn't go any further as a helicopter had come down in some woods.

"Other witnesses came forward with snippets of information. British UFORA investigator Dominic Beglin believes the object was trying to avoid built-up areas and veered south heading towards Hucknall Airfield.

"The UFO didn't make it that far and a possible crash site has since been found in the countryside north of Hucknall.

"Witnesses at the time said they saw a ball of light travel across the sky in zig-zag fashion — not in a straight line which would support the thunderbolt theory.

Anthony added 'a top secret cover-up' was later launched — and the incident hushed up.

Mr Beglin is guest speaker at the EMUFORA's meeting at Basford Community Hall on May 18 (4pm).

He will be releasing details about about the incident. Admission to the event is £1.

Haunted Skies Volume Ten

Ivan Braddow

In 2013 we emailed the *Nottingham Post* with regard to these matters, and received a telephone call from Mr Ivan Braddow (55) of Kirkby-in-Ashfield, who told us:

> "It was around 1am. I was in bed. The bottom of my bed is close to the window which overlooks the property concerned – a block of flats, about 50ft away, at the bottom of our garden. I was awoken by a strange sound, like a pulsating 'whoosh, whoosh' noise, but very fast – like something spinning. Then there was a blinding white flash, and a huge bang. My first thoughts were that a nuclear weapon had exploded over the locality. This was followed by what appeared to be a gas explosion, which blew all the windows out. Some people suggest that the block of flats was the target. I looked out of the window and everywhere was in darkness – all the street lights were out. I shouted out to my mother, 'for God's sake don't go out, you don't know what the hell that was'. I got dressed and went to have a look. By this time there were three or four fireman looking into a big hole where the chimney had been on the block of flats. It had literally lifted the whole of the roof off the block of flats, and there were tiles all over the place. (There was substantial damage caused to the flats and it was thought they might have to be demolished, but the building was later repaired.) I had a walk around and was absolutely astonished with the amount of damage caused on the Coxmoor estate, which lay behind the block of flats; every single house had window damage. In addition to this I also learnt that a lot of electrical equipment – TV's and Videos – had been damaged. Also, the telephone system was knocked out. About half a mile away is the Morton Hill area where I believe extensive damage was also reported after it was alleged something came down there. I also heard that the Military attended and that trees were burnt down on the one side, although I didn't see any evidence of this myself."

Dominic Beglin & Andrew Emerson

Dominic:

> "Residents reported seeing an object, travelling very slowly in a zigzag manner, over Mansfield in Nottinghamshire. It was said to be making a strange whining noise, as though it was in some sort of trouble. Shortly after, two more objects were observed coming from the direction of Blidworth, near Sherwood Forest. This was confirmed by some of the insurance claims, which report objects coming from three different directions and colliding in mid-air, just south of Mansfield. The 'UFOs' were seen heading towards Kirkby-in-Ashfield, when one of them seemed to encounter some kind of difficulty. According to reports, the UFO lost power and came down in a large wood, near Blidworth. The downed craft appeared to 'bounce' on impact, releasing a shock wave that left a tremendous amount of damage in its wake. One report even said that, of the three 'UFOs', one resembled some kind of craft in difficulty, while the other two 'could have been missiles'."

Many householders reported structural damage to their homes. Power lines also came down and, as a result, a number of electrical engineers were sent into the area. We have since discovered that a number of the *'property damage'* insurance claims, though investigated, were not met. The reason given was that there was no *'weather'* that night – no cloud, no wind, no rain, and no thunderbolts. Other witnesses told us that they remember the night being still and cloudless.

Independent investigations found that eyewitnesses observed a number of *'balls of white light'* converge on the UFO as it came down [missiles?]. The unidentified craft then disappeared into the wood, *'exploding'* on impact, and seemingly *'bouncing'* to a second site, where the wreckage finally came to rest. Locals say the *'craft'* came down near *Annesley Hall*, at a place known as *The Warren.

---

*The Warren – a large rock, situated amongst the outcrops in the Robin Hood Hills at Annesley, known as *Robin Hood's Seat*.

Top of clearing

Bottom of clearing

Left: Damaged trees at the site. Right: Burnt tree and soil damage at the first impact site.

According to Dominic, investigations were hampered because *Annesley Hall* lies on a private estate.

---

*Annesley Hall.is a Grade II listed building and reputed to be one of the most haunted houses in England. Now, sadly, in need of restoration, Annesley Hall was the home of Byron's boyhood sweetheart – Mary Chaworth. Mary did not return his love and married John Musters – the squire of Colwick Hall – before Byron went to Cambridge.

Unfortunately the hall suffered a fire in 1997, which caused damage to the structure and it has not been lived in since. It is now privately owned, is in very poor condition and is no longer open to the public. English Heritage have listed the building on the 'Buildings at Risk Register' as high vulnerability and deteriorating.

Haunted Skies Volume Ten

Annesley Hall

The local Fire Chief was... "Quite surprised to find that the trees facing the fire did not have a mark on them, yet the backs of the trees were smouldering".

Military helicopters arrive at scene

At 2.15am, shortly after the UFO crash, seven military helicopters came on the scene. A number of eyewitnesses then watched a *'troop-carrying helicopter'* [probably a Chinook] surrounded by Gazelles and Lynx's, flying at low speed and scanning the area with powerful searchlights. These were spotted flying over Normanton, Sutton-in-Ashfield, and Kirkby-in-Ashfield. Soon after this, the police cordoned off the first site (where the craft had first impacted), erecting roadblocks that remained in place for a number of days. The trees at this site are still badly burnt, and a large number of them have been earmarked for removal. The Army remained at the second site (the wreckage site) for three to four days. Where the UFO had first *'bounced'*, an intense fire now ensued and the local Fire Brigade were called in. Many trees were burnt down, while others turned to carbon.

Haunted Skies Volume Ten

Andrew Emerson spoke to the Firechief, who told him he was *"quite surprised to find that the trees facing the fire did not have a mark on them, yet the backs of the trees were smouldering"*. This was indeed odd, and perhaps implies some kind of microwave activity. There were even pine cones that were burnt from the inside out! When Andrew asked one of the forestry workers about the crash site fire (without introducing himself as a UFO investigator) the forester's reply was astonishing, to say the least. Without prompting, he said: *"This isn't to do with UFOs, is it?!"*

In 2013 we emailed the Nottinghamshire Fire Service, asking if we could be allowed access to any of their investigations held into these matters. We were told that they were unable to assist as, in line with their procedures, all documentary evidence had been destroyed. This was very odd, as we would have thought an important matter such as this would have been used for training purposes, rather than being obliterated from history... but there may be nothing sinister about this... What a golden opportunity lost from history, until now!

Crash site examined

Andrew also investigated the crash site with a number of his science colleagues, who contended that cursory examination suggested microwaves may have been the cause for such intense burning. They further calculated that from the damage left in the wood, the object would have had a diameter of about 60ft (this was confirmed by one eyewitness, who saw the UFO come down). They also noticed a curious bend in many of the trees left standing – the trees seem to have been bent from the base up to a height of 6ft and beyond. A rational explanation for this phenomenon has yet to be offered. At the first site, topsoil and earth was removed down to a level of about 9ins.

This was replaced with clay and covered with new topsoil – new pines and silver birch were planted. *(Who did this? Why?)*

The day after the incident, heavy military lorries came to the second site – according to Andrew:

> "... probably to clear up the wreckage. Armed guards were posted to prevent access to this area and, at the same time, government officials and spotter planes came on the scene. The man who owned the house, which had been virtually demolished, found a covering of 'metallic dust' on the trees in his garden. The dust remained for up to three weeks. Two days after announcing his find, two government officials from the MoD [Department of Scientific Intelligence] turned up. They took samples of the substance and also threatened this gentleman, telling him to keep quiet about what he knew. This chap has since suffered further threats from an unknown source, mainly by telephone."

Warned by the police to stay away

Clearly angry about the whole affair, the man attempted to drive to the site. After parking his car in a nearby lay-by, he was approached by four police patrol cars and arrested by an officer. He was then taken to the police station and advised, in no uncertain terms, to keep away from the area and warned not to talk to anyone about what had happened. If he did not *'do as he was told'*, he was informed that he would be arrested for *'making obscene phone calls'*. Andrew says that a number of eyewitnesses suffered similar threats, and claims ample evidence to establish that something extremely sensitive occurred on the night in question. He suspects some covert branch of the military was involved in what could be the biggest UFO cover-up this country has ever known.

E.M.U.F.O.R.A.
East Midlands U.F.O. Research Association

ANTHONY JAMES
8 ROOSA CLOSE
HEMPSHILL VALE
BULWELL
NOTTINGHAM
NG6 7BL
0115 9275623

The East Midlands UFO Research Association will be having a guest speaker at their next meeting. Mr Dominic Beglin will be showing slides and talking about an alleged UFO crash right here in Nottinghamshire.

The alleged crash took place on November 12th 1987 whilst most people were in bed. The silence of the night was shattered in the early hours when a 'thunderball' tore through homes in Kirkby-in-Ashfield. Freak weather was blamed at the time, but since the event, witnesses have come forward and insinuated that something 'highly sensitive' and inexplicable happened on that night. Windows were blown out in thirteen homes and chimney stacks fell through roofs causing severe damage. Ashfield District Council officer John Wood at the time stated: "God only knows how no one was killed, it was just like the Blitz".

Initial finding though do support the fact that some thing highly sensitive did occur. Claims that the thunderbolt theory just don't stand up are backed by an insurance expert who said that of the explanation (quote) "It just doesn't make any sense". He stated at the time "every claim that I've dealt with in the last 26 years has been logical and reasonable...but this defies reason.

Witnesses at the time said that the ball of light didn't even travel in a straight line. It zig-zagged across the sky and witnesses saw it dive down over distant hills.

Since then, UFO investigators have re-opened the case, and after several appeals for new information new witnesses have come forward with vital pieces of the puzzle. Some people were stopped in their car by a police road block near Annesley and told that they couldn't go any further as a helicopter had come down in some nearby woods. Other witnesses also came forward with other snippets of information and according to Investigator Dominic Beglin, the object was trying to avoid the built-up areas and veered South heading towards Hucknall Airfield. The UFO didn't make it that far and a possible crash site has since been found in the countryside just North of Hucknall.

There is talk that a top secret cover-up and clear-up operation was launched straight away and everything has been hush-hush ever since. Witnesses are now coming out of the woodwork one by one due to the upsurge of UFO literature that is now available and the sudden rise in UFO related

Haunted Skies Volume Ten

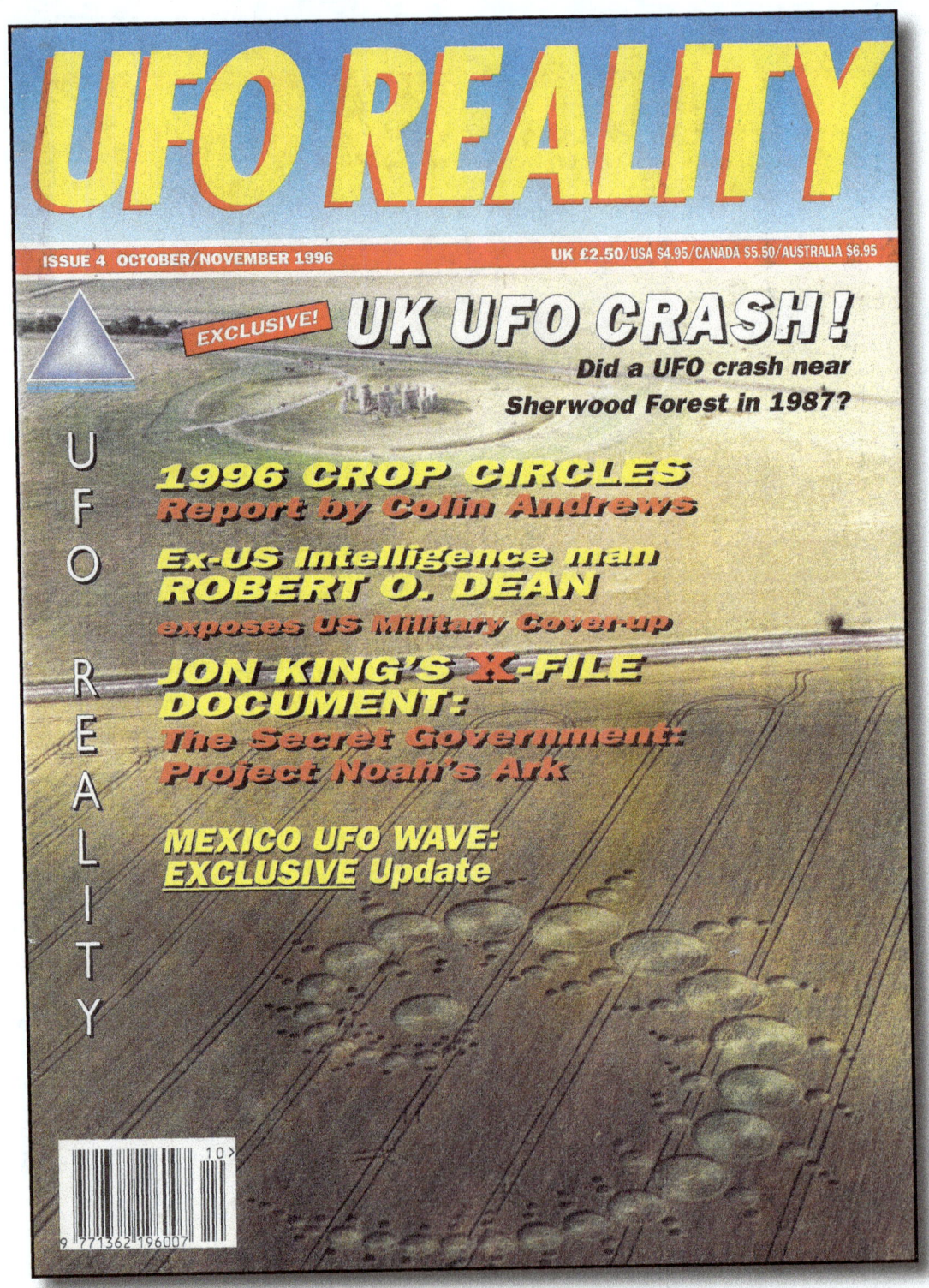

Just before impact

Andrew:

> "We believe something of a very sensitive nature occurred here. One witness – a former military man and level-headed person – lives very close to where the alleged crash occurred."

He told Andrew and Dominic:

> "Just minutes before the 'impact', my doorbell started to ring all by itself; immediately after this, six light bulbs fused simultaneously in the house. Suddenly, I heard this incredible explosion. My immediate reaction was to race upstairs and make sure my family were ok. I've never heard anything like it. I honestly expected to open my front door and find corpses in the street. I have never believed in UFOs and can't say whether the object which crashed was any 'alien' craft, and feel there is no rational explanation for what took place."

During their investigation into the matter the two men contacted a number of authorities which included the RAF and Broadcasting Companies but not surprisingly, received little assistance from those concerned.

Jon King, former editor of "*UFO Reality*":

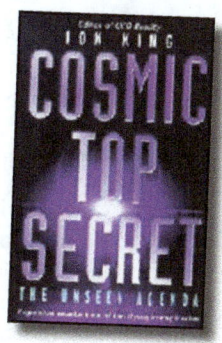

> "Andrew further told me that a number of other eyewitnesses had suffered similar threats (certainly I can confirm an irrational reluctance on the part of many witnesses to come forward with information regarding this case.) Like others who have investigated the incident Andrew now suspects that some invisible arm of the government/military was responsible for what he considers to be the biggest UFO cover-up this country has ever known. Evidence to this effect can certainly be seen at the crash site today. Over the decade since this incident occurred, topsoil and earth has been removed from the crash site down to a level of about nine inches; it has been replaced with clay and covered with fresh topsoil in which new pines and silver birch have been planted. Restoration of the site is now virtually complete. Which leaves one to ponder the fact that, whoever was responsible for the site's restoration, and whatever their reasons, it is certainly clear that somebody wanted the truth regarding this incident covered up."

Jon has also covered this incident in his book *Cosmic Top Secret*, ABE Books.

Haunted Skies Volume Ten

12th November 1987 – UFO over Staffordshire

At 4.15pm, Valerie Smith was walking back to her car at Brindley Visitors' Centre, after walking her dogs with her mother, when a brilliant *'light'* appeared in the sky towards the direction of Rugeley, which stopped briefly and then continued on its journey past the GPO Tower, before being lost from view.

> *"My mother said she could see blue and green lights around its sides. I was so excited when I reached home that I telephoned RAF Stafford to report the incident."*

(Source: Mark Hayward/Irene Bott/Graham Allen, Staffordshire UFO Group)

16th November 1987 – UFO over Blackpool

At 3am a musician was walking home, when he sighted a pulsating yellow light in the sky approaching his position. As it moved closer, the object began to descend in stages of starting and stopping.

> *"The amber light was surrounded by a shell. It began to spin at high speed, emitting red, blue, green, and white lights, before stopping still. It then headed away towards the south direction."*

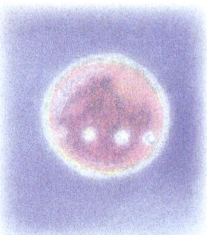

The man concerned, who asked that his personal details be kept confidential, admitted he had never been as frightened in his life.

At 6.05am, three men were travelling home from a night shift, and near Netherton, close to Meltham, West Yorkshire. It was a cool, dry, morning with little wind and scattered cloud. They noticed *'two white spotlights'*, which they first took to be a stationary car over the top of the Emley Moor TV transmitter mast. The objects then disappeared from sight.

Following an appeal in the *Huddersfield Evening Newspaper* for further witnesses, several people came forward – one of whom was Gary Howarth of Meltham Village. He was walking home, at 6.05am, when he saw two bright *'lights'* over the Emley Moor mast. He watched them for a short while, and then carried on his journey home. At this point he says the *'lights'* began to move towards his position, and alerted his wife to come and have a look.

At 3pm on Monday, 14th June 2004, Mark Windle, from Moldgreen, Huddersfield, saw what appeared to be five objects, flying in perfect formation over the Emley Moor mast. He took a photo and said:

> *"It looked to me as if they were objects that were burning up in the atmosphere. There was another plane in the sky and it looked different."*

Another onlooker said that as soon as she saw the lights she went to get her camera, but the objects were travelling fast and by the time she returned they had disappeared.

> *"We usually have planes flying past, but not in such a regular formation – it was very strange."*

Officials at the Ministry of Defence, in London, told the *Yorkshire Post* that the UFOs were probably aircraft, taking part in the NATO Air Defence Exercise, code-named *'Clean Hunter'*, which began on that Monday. Oddly, we were unable to track down a copy of the photograph on the internet or trace Mark, despite leaving messages on Facebook in 2013.

They were not the only ones. In 1979, a couple living nearby saw what they described at 10.30pm.

> *"My wife and I have seen two 'flying saucers'; the first was in 1979, at 10:30pm, at a distance of about 100 yards, at roof level, seen coming down to land, moving slowly and in a sideways motion. We had a 15 second sighting of it; it was silent and had red, orange and yellow lights, blinking on and off, around the circumference.*

I estimate it to have been about 30ft in diameter. In March 1998, at 10pm, we had another sighting on the moors when I noticed a strange ambient light as I looked out of the car window, as I drove along. I initially thought someone was having an outdoor party (it was almost 10pm). As I drove along the road, I could see what it was – a 'flying saucer', at ground level, about to take-off. As I watched it lifted into the sky, rotating like a giant Ferris wheel. 90 seconds later, it was high in the sky. My wife saw it, too, as did some clients of mine, who were in the area at 8pm, so it had been there for two hours.

This sighting – within 300 yards from the TV transmitter station, the tallest building in the area, manned 24 hours a day – should have merited some publicity. Yet not a word appeared on the local TV News. Ironically a few months afterwards the local TV News publicised a different 'flying saucer' story which they could explain – it was a mobile camera, belonging to the BBC, flying above a football ground."

Authors: That's how it always works. We have come across so many instances of where specifically the *BBC* and other branches of the media have nurtured and perpetuated stories relating to *'little green men and the alien hordes'*.

A typical example was a few years ago, after declassified documents were released by the MOD about a wave of UFO sightings around the UK, involving mysterious cross-shaped objects seen. There was little mention about this, but much discussion about the now infamous story relating to a number of hoaxed 'flying saucers' found by the public all over the country. These were constructed by students and filled with manure!

(Sources: Hazel Shanley, Blackpool UFO Society/*West Evening Gazette*, 10.12.1987 – 'UFO struck him dumb'/Andy Roberts/*Colne Valley Chronicle*, 4.12.1987 – 'More UFO sightings are reported'/Brian Vike, Director, HBCC UFO Research)

19th November 1987 – UFO over Emley Moor TV mast, Yorkshire

While making another journey home, off nights, at the same time, the men were surprised to see what appeared to be identical phenomena over Emley Moor TV mast. According to one of the men, he had this to say:

"The lights started moving slowly and followed us at a distance. When we reached the village of Netherton, we stopped and got out of the car. The object was now above the village, apparently a couple of hundred feet high in the sky. They were very bright, and on the undersides were smaller lights. A couple of minutes later it made off at great speed, silently heading in the opposite direction to when we had first seen it."

(Source: Andy Roberts)

Later the same day, two or three 'V'-shaped craft were seen flying silently in a tight formation through the sky over Penn, one of which was showing a bright light. Local resident, Pat Cropper, said:

"They looked like two boomerangs, hovering behind each other. They weren't aircraft."

Another witness was Marian Watson:

"We thought it must be a secret MOD plane; one flew really low. There was no noise. They were triangular-shaped; one was shining bright light to the ground. We thought something really weird was happening."

Haunted Skies Volume Ten

Danny Wardrobe – a representative of Halfpenny Green Airport, Bobbington – dismissed the claims as rubbish, explaining away the sighting as being aircraft on a training exercise.

(Source: *The Express & Star*, 23.11.1987 – 'UFO sightings dismissed as reports flood in')

27th November 1987 – Saucer-shaped UFO seen, Cambridgeshire

At 7am, Cambridgeshire man – Leslie Woodbridge – was driving along Main Street, when he saw:

> "... what I took to be an aircraft, but as it approached closer I saw it was saucer-shaped and glowing with bright white light. After about 30secs, it suddenly accelerated out of sight."

(Source: Brenda Slattery, Personal interview/*Cambridge News*, 30.11.1987 – 'Mystery of UFO seen cruising across the Fens)

Eric probes UFO sightings

The Cheshire UFO Studies Centre in Crewe is investigating the sighting of a "bright orange ball of light" at Nantwich.

The centre is based at the home of its chairman, Mr Eric Morris, of 117 Earle Street, who is also the North Midlands regional investigations co-ordinator for the British UFO Research Association.

"There have been a spate of sightings throughout the country in the past four months. We thought we had escaped this, but some people I know saw something in Nantwich on October 6 which we cannot seem to explain," said Mr Morris, a nurse at Nantwich's Barony Hospital.

He said it happened at about 6.30pm. Two nurses at the Barony Hospital were looking out of the window when they saw a bright orange ball of light hovering above some trees along Middlewich Road.

"They opened the window to get a better look. They said it was only a short distance away — less than a quarter of a mile — and was a ten foot globular shape.

Went

"We have tried to find an explanation and would like to hear from anyone else who saw anything unidentifiable that night," said Mr Morris. "Apparently this shape just went as if it had been switched off."

The centre is anxious to hear from anyone who sees a U.F.O. in Cheshire or the neighbouring counties. And they would like sightings reported to them as soon as possible, as they are then easier to investigate.

Explained

"We are in the business of explaining sightings. We like to keep up to date with current aircraft and what Manchester Airport and the RAF are doing, so in many cases we can give rational explanations. We have had many sightings in Crewe, and many have been explained.

"About 95 per cent of sightings are in fact explained. The rest we do not know. I don't believe in flying saucers and little green men, but am interested in the scientific aspect. I have been investigating U.F.O.s for over ten years, and my interest increases by the day."

'What they say they've seen is incredible'

Housewife spots UFO over York

AN UNIDENTIFIED flying object "the size and shape of a pumpkin" has been spotted over York.

Housewife Elizabeth Rogers of Hammerton Close, Chapelfields, York, says she was quietly watching TV with her son David, aged 8, when she noticed the night sky was getting lighter around 5.30pm yesterday.

"It just seemed to appear from the south west like a white light getting brighter. Then an orange thing in the sky appeared. It was about the size and shape of a pumpkin. It just shot across the sky and vanished," she said.

Hours later young David was still so frightened by the experience he would not go to sleep.

"I wasn't frightened, just shocked," said Mrs Rogers.

"It was close but I couldn't hear or smell anything. I opened the window to get a better look. It was definitely not a reflection.

Mrs Rogers said that two friends in her house at the time also saw the object.

DECEMBER 1987

Creature photographed at Ilkley Moor

At 7.10am on 1st December 1987, 'Philip Spencer' (a pseudonym) was walking across Ilkley Moor, Yorkshire, during falling rain – to meet his father-in-law (who lived in East Morton) – when he took one photograph of a humanoid entity, apparently walking across the moors in front of him, before *'he'* ran away. This was followed by the appearance of a silver saucer-shaped object, with a *'cube'* on top, seen to fly into the sky seconds later.

Philip then continued on his journey to Menston – the nearest village – feeling shaken, after deciding not to visit his father-in-law. During his walk to Menston (which took about 30 minutes) he was surprised to discover his compass now pointed south, instead of north, and secondly, he was surprised to find the town bustling with shoppers. He glanced up at the church clock and saw it was 10am, whereas, by his reckoning, it should have been around 8.15am.

'Spencer' was confused now. Had he really seen what appeared to be an alien, walking across the moor – had he actually taken a photograph? Would the processed photo show what he thought he saw?

He decided to catch the bus to Keighley – the nearest town with an instant film development and printing store.

Some two hours later, he had his picture of the *'creature'*, and then knew that he had not been hallucinating. It looked to be about 4ft tall, and had a blue-green tint to its skin. 'Spencer' knew he had something of importance, or at least he thought he did.

Philip later claimed two hours of 'missing time' and that his compass also went haywire. Examination of the negative by wildlife photography expert, Peter Sutherst, from *Kodak* Laboratories, in Hemel Hempstead, revealed the 'image' was no animal and the negative apparently genuine, rather than interfered with.

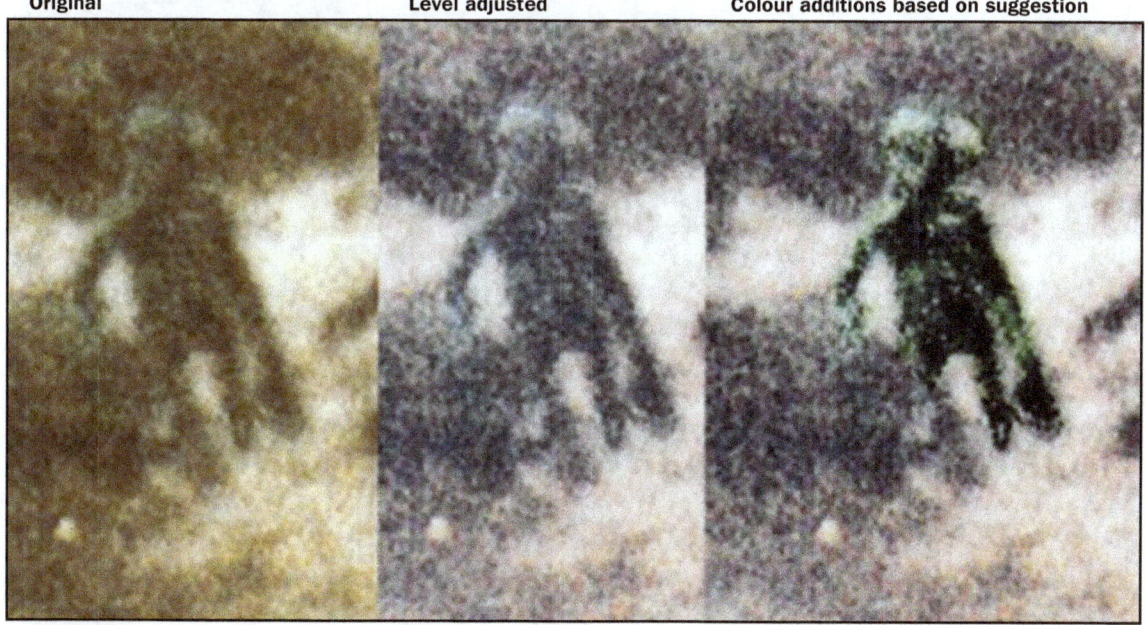

Haunted Skies Volume Ten

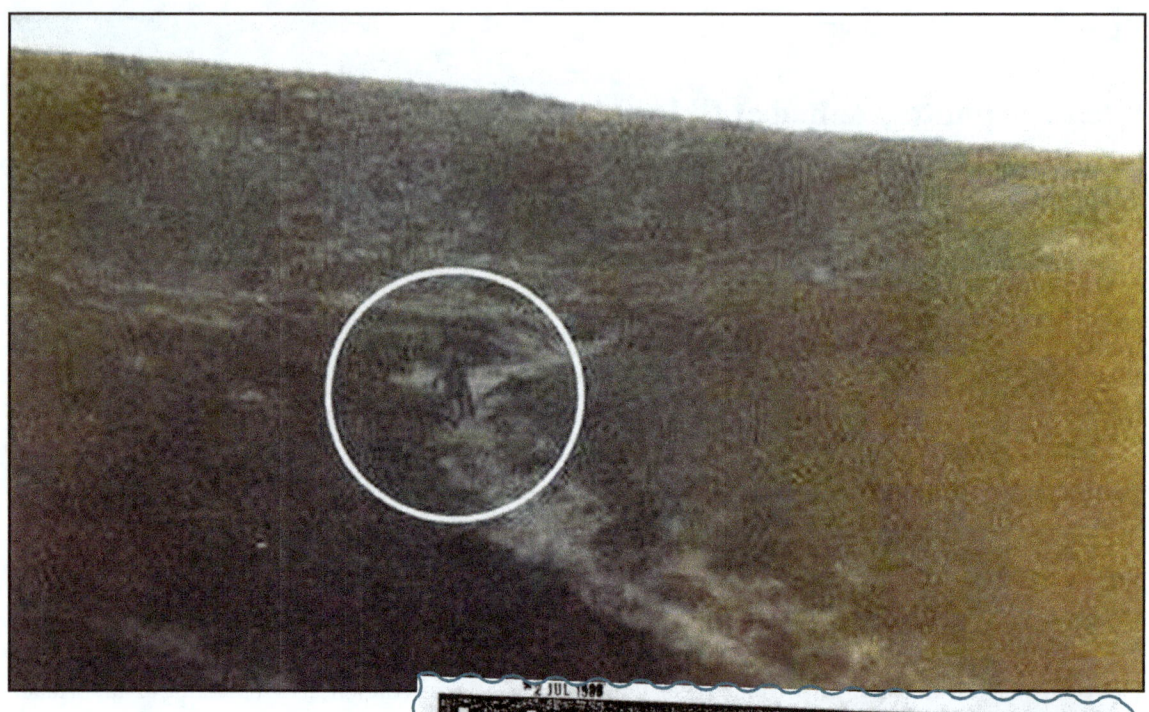

After initially contacting Jenny Randles, Jenny studied the rest of the photographs taken, using a *Prinz Mastermatic* 35mm camera, loaded with 400 ASA film but saw no other photographs of the *'Alien,'* as might be expected if a model had been used. She then arranged for the man to meet with Peter Hough, who later interviewed the man (given the pseudonym Philip Spencer) and saw no reason to question his integrity. 'Philip' told Peter he wasn't interested in making any financial gain either on the photograph or through publicity.

A visit by two men

About six weeks into the investigation, 'Spencer' received an unexpected visit from two men, who presented themselves as Royal Air Force Intelligence Officers,

who showed him their identity cards and introduced themselves as Mr Jefferson and Mr Davis. They asked 'Spencer' for the photograph he had taken on Ilkley Moor. Unfortunately for them, 'Spencer' had given the print to Peter Hough.

Clearly, without being able to trace the witness, it is impossible to form any judgement achieved through direct evidence such as personal interviews and rapport. Fortunately, Peter Hough had. In addition, this was not the only occasion we had seen similarly described photographs of what are perceived to be aliens by the human observer.

Bizarrely, in one newspaper article, following publicity about the incident, a man admitted he was the culprit that had been photographed – not any alien! Incredibly, on another site seen on the Internet (2013), it was claimed that the *'alien'* seen on the moor involved Police Officer Alan Godfrey – now that's getting it very wrong!

The strangers then left. What puzzled 'Spencer' was how these strangers could have known of the photograph's existence. Only his wife, Jenny Randles, Peter Hough, Arthur Tomlinson, and another researcher working with Hough, had any knowledge they existed. Peter Hough contacted RAF Intelligence, to confirm the visitors' identities. He was told that no such men existed and nobody from their office had visited 'Spencer'.

Regression

'Spencer' had begun to have strange dreams of starry skies, and remained still puzzled by the missing time he experienced, so it was decided to use regressive hypnosis on 'Spencer' to unlock his subconscious memories of what had taken place on that fateful morning.

The session was conducted by Dr. Jim Singleton, at Arthur Tomlinson's home, on 6th March 1988. Also present were Peter Hough, and Mathew Hill – a journalist friend of Hough, who was to operate the three tape recorders. As 'Philip Spencer' regained his missing memories, he described being taken aboard a craft that he had seen lifting up from Ilkley Moor, and then subjected to a medical examination by those onboard before being released. 'Spencer' could now remember that it was **after his release from the UFO** that he took the picture, which may clear up some ambiguities felt over the taking of the photograph and weather conditions at the time – if the memories obtained during regression were correct, which on face value appears to be so.

The memories

Jim:
>"I want you to cast your mind back to the 1st December last year, when you set off across the moor. I want you to clear your mind back to that and I want you to re-experience that. I want you to tell me what you experienced."

'Spencer':
>"I'm walking along the moor, oh! It's quite windy. There are a lot of clouds. I was walking up towards some trees. I see this little something – can't tell, but he's green; it's moving up towards me. Oh! I'm stuck. I can't move and the creature is still coming towards me. I'm stuck and everything's gone fuzzy. I'm floating along in the air. I want to get down!"

(He later told us he was levitated 2ft off the ground and the creature was in front of him – like a child, pulling a balloon on a string).

>"I still can't get down and I don't like it. I'm going round this corner and this green thing is in front of me. Oh God! I want to get down!"

Haunted Skies Volume Ten

(. . . long pause) (. . . breathing faster)

"There's a big silver saucer thing . . . there's a door in it . . . and I don't want to go in there."

(. . . worried sound in his voice) (. . . sigh)

"Everything gone black now" (. . . pause).

(It was later established that the photo had been taken **after** the *'abduction'* and the creature was waving goodbye.)

Jim:

"You say everything's gone black?"

'Spencer':

"Mmm! I can't see anything . . . like I'm asleep . . . can't hear anything (short pause). There's a bright light now. Can't see where it's coming from. I'm in a funny sort of room. I can hear this voice saying 'don't be afraid'.

I don't feel afraid anymore. I can still see this green thing but I'm not afraid anymore of it. I'm being put on a table. I can move now if I want to, but I don't feel frightened any more and there's a beam – like a pole; it's above me, it's moving up toward me. It's got a light in it – like a fluorescent tube. It's coming up from my feet. I can hear that voice again saying 'we don't mean to harm you, and don't be afraid'. Makes me feel warm as it moves up me; it's coming up over my stomach, towards my head. Close my eyes. I don't want to look at it in case it hurts my eyes. It's gone! (. . . pause) There is something – my nose feels funny (shows movement of nose) – that's gone as well. I'm standing up now. I don't know how I got stood up. I can see a door. There is one of these green creatures, motioning for me to come with him. Don't really want to go with him. I'd rather stay here. I don't feel afraid in here" (pause).

Jim:

"Can you tell me what's happening now?"

'Spencer':

"I'm walking towards a door. There is still a bright light; there is light all around. Want to know where it's coming from; it's just bright all around. Walking down a corridor; here is a window. Oh, God! (. . . sounds shocked) is that real? (. . . deep sigh) (. . . pause) (. . . sounds afraid) Don't want to be up here, want to be down there. I can hear that voice again, saying 'you've got nothing to fear'. It's pretty though – didn't realise it looked so pretty.

(He told of looking through the window, above the Earth as seen from high in space, just like the Apollo astronauts saw.)

I've gone past the window . . . now I'm walking down a corridor" (. . . long pause).

Jim:

"What's happening now?"

'Spencer':

"Come to the end of the corridor. There's a hole opened in it, so I can walk through. I'm in a big room – a big, round room. I'm on a raised platform against the wall. My camera and compass are trying to get away from me... going towards the ball. It's difficult to pull them back down again, and this ball's moved round, with strange . . . it's got some blocks on it. He says we can't stay in here too long. He wants us to go out again. The hole's closed in the wall. It's gone strange. He says I've got nothing to fear, but I'd still like to go home (. . . pause). It's got such big hands."

Jim:

"What's happening now?"

'Spencer':

"Going down a corridor again; it's very bright still. I wish I knew where the light was coming from . . . and there is another door. Going through a door; it's an empty room. Two of those green creatures have come with me. There's a picture. It's starting to move on the wall. Wonder how they get the pictures?"

Jim:

"Can you tell me what's happening at this point?"

'Spencer':

"I'm looking at the pictures on the wall" (long pause).

Jim:

"Pictures on the wall?"

'Spencer':

"Mmm . . . Creatures seem concerned at the damage that it's doing. Picture changing now; there's another picture, another film. He's asking me a question. He says 'do you understand?' I said 'yes'. It's time to go. Everything's gone black. I'm walking up the moor again; I'm walking near some trees. Some movement – I can see something – a green creature. I've shouted to it. It's turned round. I don't know what it is. I'll photograph it. It's turned around now. It's moving, quick – want to know what it is. I'm running after it. It's gone round a corner. I can't see it now. There's . . . There is a saucer (laughingly), big silver saucer! It's disappeared. I'm walking on down . . . gone past the trees."

Jim:

"What's happening now?"

'Spencer':

"I'm going home. It's ten o'clock on the town hall clock. Can't really understand – it was only eight o'clock."

Jim:

"You mentioned some green creatures; would you try to describe them to me?"

'Spencer':

"It's quite small; he's got big pointed ears. It's got big eyes; they're quite dark. He hasn't got a nose; he's only got a little mouth . . . and his hands are enormous, and his arms are long. He's got funny feet."

Jim:

"Funny feet?"

'Spencer':

"They're like a 'V' shape – like two big toes; must be difficult to walk like that. He shuffles rather than walks. I don't feel afraid of him, although he looks odd."

Jim:

"You mentioned big hands? Can you say anymore about the hands?"

'Spencer':

"It's got three big fingers – like sausages . . . big sausages. They're just very big . . . bigger than my hands."

Jim:

"About how tall would you say these creatures are?"

'Spencer':

"It's about four foot – comes to the lump on my stomach. He's about as high as – just a bit bigger than my stomach is."

Peter Hough

Arthur Tomlinson

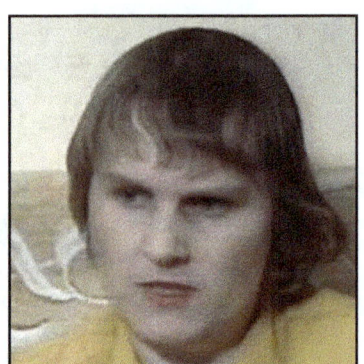
Jenny Randles

Jim:
"Okay. Now I wonder if I can ask you another question. You mentioned a film?"

'Spencer':
"There were two films."

Jim:
"Two films?"

'Spencer':
"One was lots of scenes of destruction – like on the news; can see lots of waste going into the river, and people, like Ethiopians, who are starving. It's not very good; it's not very nice."

Jim:
"Want to say anything more about that film?"

'Spencer':
"It's much of the same thing, only different."

Jim:
"What about the other film then? Do you want to tell me about it?"

'Spencer':
"I'm not supposed to."

Jim:
"I'll leave that up to you entirely. Do you want to say anything about that?"

'Spencer':
"I'm not supposed to tell anyone about the other film; it's not for them to know."

Jim:
"Is there anything more?"

'Spencer':
"No."

The account given by 'Mr Spencer' appears to be genuine, rather than fabrication. We are at a great disadvantage, as we never met him but Jenny Randles and Peter Hough did. Peter has no reason to disbelieve 'Spencer's' version of the events, and there has never been any admission of deception by the now retired Police Officer (if in fact he stayed on to complete his 30 years). He claimed, at the time, that after four years of being a Metropolitan policeman in London, he had left his job and moved with his wife and baby, to the West Yorkshire area of Ilkley Moor, to be closer to her family. The details disclosed during regression are similar to what many other UFO witnesses have reported – which appears to enhance the credibility of 'Mr Spencer' – rather than negating it. One may speculate that if, in fact, he was the subject of medical examination by the occupants of the craft, then there is far more to this incident, which we shall never know about.

(Sources: *The Complete Book of UFOs*, by Jenny Randles (1993), *UFOs and How to See Them*, by Jenny Randles (1993), *The Green Alien of Ilkley Moor* – Article in *FATE Magazine*, by Peter Hough, issue of March, 1999. *The Truth About Alien Abductions*, by Peter Hough and Dr. Moyshe Kalman (Blandford publishing, USA)

3rd December 1987 – Large bangs heard over Sussex

Riddle of huge UFO

A UFO the "size of a football pitch" was baffling police yesterday.

Dozens of people reported seeing it over Nottingham late on Wednesday night.

"They said it moved slowly, flashed lights and gave off a deep hum," said a police spokesman.

No aircraft were in the area at the time.

Bumps in the night

SOMETHING went bang last Thursday night – but nobody knows what it was.

A series of loud bangs were heard all over Sussex in the early hours of the morning.

Mrs Winifred Harris, who lives near the East Preston fire station in North Lane, heard the noises at 3.40 a.m.

"I heard three bangs, one after the other. I didn't know what it was," she said.

She woke her husband, Mr Cyril Harris, and they tried to find out the cause of the sudden noise.

They thought it came from the fire station, but nothing was happening there and the retired couple were baffled.

The cause of the strange bangs has not been discovered, but several theories have been put out.

A plane could be blamed except there weren't any around and the Ministry of Defence have said it wasn't one of theirs.

Notts UFOs: Aliens or a big secret?

– 9 DEC 1987

NOTTINGHAM EVENING [POST]

FLYING objects seen over Nottingham last week remain unidentified.

Dozens of phone calls began to flood into the Evening Post offices last Thursday morning and have continued.

Callers reported a strange series of lights in the sky last Wednesday night. So what were they?

Reports also went to the police, to East Midlands International Airport and to local radio stations.

These were not people seeking publicity for their claims — they were just baffled by what they had seen and wanted answers.

With very few exceptions, they were ordinary people who had seen something in the sky they had not seen before — and that concerned them.

They were people used to seeing and hearing aircraft at night, yet these lights immediately drew their attention.

All said they had never reported a UFO before.

Remarkable similarities

Their descriptions had remarkable similarities, as did the time of the sightings, but were not close enough to suggest a conspiracy.

From the reports, it appears that two very large objects displaying strange light configurations and emitting a constant low hum flew very slowly and low from Newark over Nottingham to the Derbyshire border and then back east over the south of the city.

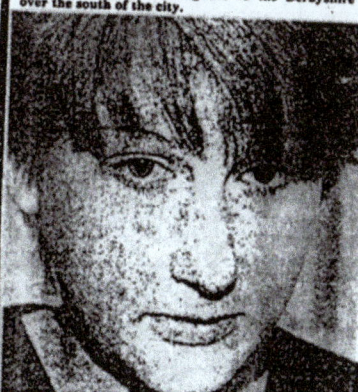
● Alison Evans — "There were rows of red lights"

Housewife Mrs Alison Evans, 26, of Henson Lane, Radcliffe-on-Trent, had friends visiting her at the time.

With Tollerton airport nearby, she is used to aircraft of all shapes and sizes.

"My friend was leaving to go. I went outside as she was getting into her car and I saw the lights coming over," she said.

"We followed the lights coming over, walking round the side of the house.

"There were two rows of lights and red lights behind. It must have been quite low and was making a low humming noise."

They went back to the front and the friend, Mrs Lindy West, was about to leave.

"We saw exactly the same thing coming over

Haunted Skies Volume Ten

4th December 1987 – Strange noises heard

At 2am, Colchester resident, Mr Owen Morgan – a drummer by profession – was walking his dog home to Edinburgh Gardens, after finishing work, when he heard:

> "... a high-pitched whirring sound on my right-hand side. The noise then went across the road in front of me and up to Portland Close, and then stopped. I admit I was scared. I didn't see anything. The noise frequency was every four seconds and the whole thing was over in seconds."

(Source: Ron West, *Colchester Evening Gazette*, 8.12.1987 – 'UFO whirring scares Owen')

8th December 1987 – Strange lights seen over Keighley

At 8pm, Winterburn Street resident Mr Azhar Ali, and his neighbours, watched a circle of reddish-brown light above the town. It was taller than a chimney and surrounded by a layer of shining light, accompanied by a small light that kept moving backwards and forwards as it hovered over the Airedale Shopping Centre.
(Source: Philip Mantle)

9th December 1987 – UFOs over Nottingham & Hull

On the 10th December 1987, Humberside based Radio Station – *Radio Viking* – told its listeners, in their news update, of having been contacted by Mrs Pauline Pindar of Sproatley. She reported seeing three UFOs in the sky on the evening of the 9th December 1987

At 4pm, the same day, *BBC Radio Humberside* also broadcast a story of a UFO sighting – this time involving Mr Philip Readymartcher. Independent UFO Network researcher – Gary Antony – learned of the broadcast and contacted *BBC Radio Humberside*, and asked them if they would repeat the broadcast – which they did – during each news bulletin. (**Authors:** One cannot imagine that a situation like this would happen in this day and age!) Philip Mantle contacted *Radio Lincoln* and appeared live on air, appealing for any witnesses to contact the UFO hotline number. Subsequently, 50 people contacted Phil and Gary about having seen strange objects in the sky. At 5pm, Mary Acey – a florist from Keyingham Holderness, accompanied by two friends – Mrs M. Hook and Mrs H. Stephenson – sighted some lights in the southern part of the sky at 45° elevation, travelling in a west to east direction in the sky, near the *River Humber*. Within 2-3 minutes, the lights were out of sight.

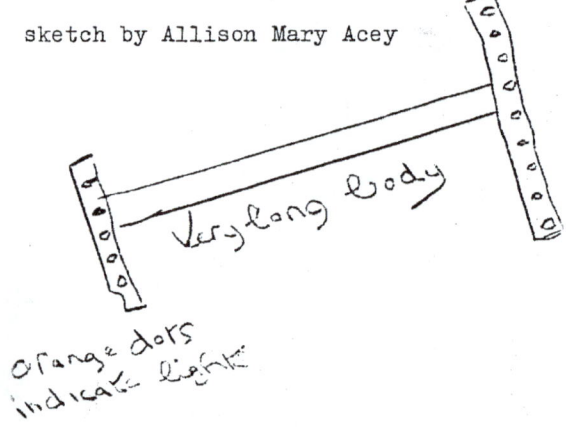

sketch by Allison Mary Acey

At 5pm, farmer John Taylor, from Fitling, East Holderness, North Humberside, was chopping wood around tea-time, when he heard a loud humming or roaring noise, which seemed close.

> "I came out of the outer house to have a look, and saw this bloody big thing come over full of lights. It was bloody enormous – full of red and white lights. It flew over the top of the house, about 500ft in the air. The lights spread out over my five acre paddock and formed an off-triangle shape, which I estimated was moving at about 250mph."

He later reported it to the police, who said they were unable to offer any explanation.

Haunted Skies Volume Ten

At 5pm, a *'huge rectangular mass of light'*, described as being 80 yards long by 30 yards wide, was sighted flying through the sky over Bramcote, Nottingham, at an estimated speed of 50mph, and a height of 500ft. This was reported by dozens of residents from the Newark, Carlton, Chilwell, Strelley, and Codnor areas of Nottingham.

Others told of seeing two very large objects, displaying strange configurations of lights, emitting a low hum, moving slowly through the sky.

Richard Breedon from Derby Road, Beeston, told of sighting:

> "... a huge object (twice as big as a football pitch) making a very loud humming noise; it had half a dozen red lights on the one side, on the other was a large bright white light. There were two red lights trailing behind it in the air."

Another witness was Mrs Allison Evans:

> "My friend was leaving, so I went outside. As she was getting into the car, I saw these lights moving low across the sky. We followed the lights, which consisted of two rows of red and white lights, by walking around to the other side of the house. Whatever it was seemed to be making a humming noise. They left a brown vapour trail in the air – still visible some time afterwards."

At 5.15pm, Hull housewife – Christine Ann Juncar – was looking out over Danson Lane Recreation Ground, towards the east, when she saw four or five sets of red and white lights heading across the sky in a north to south direction, at 45° elevation, until they disappeared from sight a few minutes later.

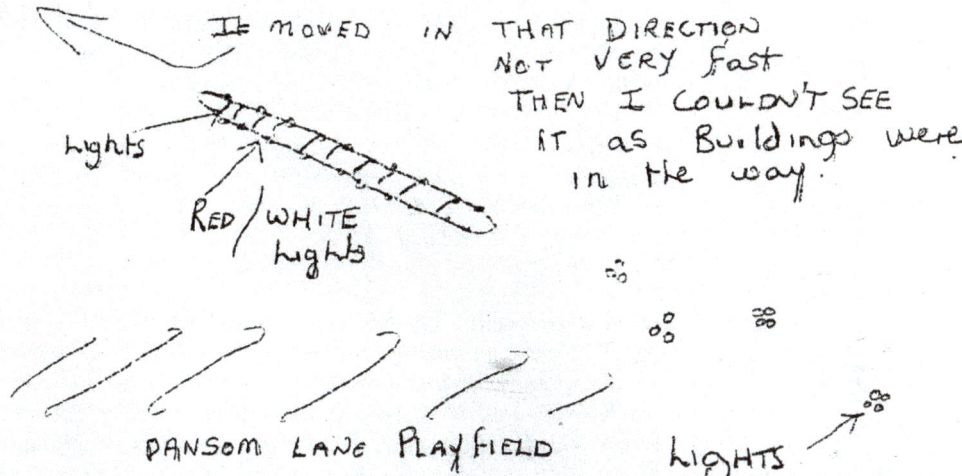

At 5.30pm, Pauline Pindar and her three children were outside, talking to a neighbour, when the children told their mother about some *'lights'* in the sky. In an interview conducted with Philip and Gary, she said:

> "It was a very bright yellow-white in colour and heading in a south to north direction. We watched them go across and dashed to the front of the house where we saw them go out of sight over Burton Constable, towards Coniston Way. The second one seemed to go up on top of the third one very closely. They resembled airships."

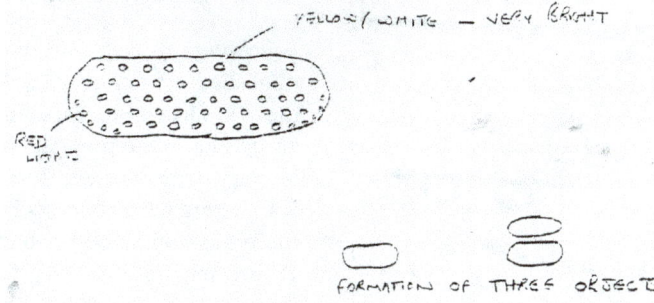

Haunted Skies Volume Ten

At 6pm, James Ellis was out walking his dog at Sigglesthorne, Holderness, four miles south-west of Hornsea, when he sighted two red lights trailing smaller lights in the east, travelling across the sky, heading northwards above cloud cover and very high.

At 6.45pm, Walter Myers was walking along Waterloo Street, Hull, on his way to a regular snooker game, when he saw

> "... an object made up of three triangular-shapes, translucent amber in colour, moving over the city, heading west to east."

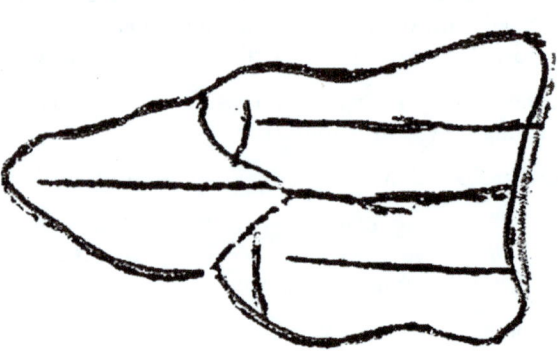

Busty Taylor and Colin Andrews

At 8.45pm, renown researcher of the Crop Circle phenomena Busty Taylor, was driving westwards on the A303, towards Thruxton, Hampshire, when ....

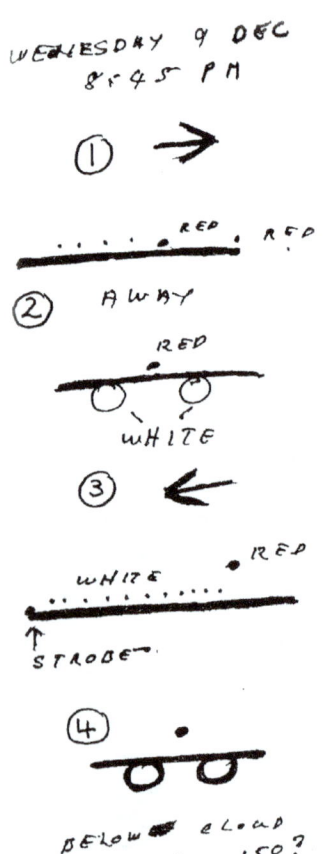

"I noticed two red lights in the sky towards the south, approaching my position, and first thought they were RAF planes from Middle Wallop. As they crossed my route I saw it was not two aircraft but one long object, with a red light on the front and another red light on the back, behind which came a row of lights – like portholes. I accelerated in order to try to get underneath it, watching it all the time. It crossed the road at least two miles or more ahead of me, some 30° off the horizon. I decided to pull-up the car on top of the bridge at Thruxton beside the White Horse Inn.

I turned my engine off and listened, but couldn't hear anything at all. The object was now moving away from me, so I was looking at the rear end of it. It had two large lights, with a red one above moving below cloud cover, at an estimated speed of 160mph. When over the Ludgershall area, the object executed a left hand turn, enabling me to see a white strobing light in front, followed by a line of white lights or windows, showing one red light above the rear. It then headed away towards the direction of west, somewhere in the vicinity of Tidworth, before being lost from view.

Following on from this, on the 11th December 1987, the *Hull Daily Mail* published a story entitled, **'Mystery Sky Sight Remains A Mystery'**. On the 30th December, (not unsurprisingly) the same newspaper published an update to the previous story, entitled: **'Aircraft Theory In Hull Big Bang Mystery'**, which misled the reader into associating airborne phenomena with a loud bang that was heard in Hull and the surrounding areas, when there was no link between the '*bang*' and the original UFO sighting of the 1st December 1987.

Haunted Skies Volume Ten

Left: Colin Andrews with Busty Taylor and right, Busty in his light aircraft

A Ministry Of Defence spokesman said:

> "90 per cent of UFO sightings turn out to be satellite debris, balloons, unusual cloud formations, or aircraft."

We learnt that an RAF/NATO refuelling exercise had taken place that evening, involving F111 and USAF KC135 aircraft. While there are some that may believe this was the explanation, the evidence of the eyewitnesses proves contrary.

(Source: *Nottingham Evening Post*, 9.12.1987 – 'Nott's. UFOs: Aliens or a big secret? /*Hull Daily Mail*, 10.12.1987 – 'Mystery sky sight remains a mystery')

18th December 1987 – 'Flying Saucer' seen at Barnsley, South Yorkshire

At 7.40am, a married couple, returning home from holiday, were being driven back to Mexborough. As they neared Barnsley, on the A628, close to Silkstone Colliery, they saw an extremely bright object, low in the sky, about 4-600ft off the ground. They first took it to be the floodlights of the nearby colliery, as it was still dark. As they approached closer, they saw it was:

> "... saucer in shape, with a brilliant orange coloured dome; beneath the dome were a row of brightly-lit square windows. Under the top section was a diamond-shaped arrangement of flashing lights. It just hung in the air and was completely silent."

(Source: Philip Mantle)

29th December 1987 – Bell-shaped UFO over Rotherham

At 10.15pm, Mary 'N' and her husband, from Wingfield, Yorkshire, were looking out of the rear bedroom window, when they noticed:

> "... a bell or helmet-shaped object moving over the rooftops, heading in the direction of Wentworth; it was very large and black. We saw it had square like windows, three at the top, three in the middle, and four at the bottom. It had a point at the front. My husband ran to the telephone and called the police and RAF Finningly."

From: C.R. Neville, Secretariat (Air Staff)2a

MINISTRY OF DEFENCE Room 8245
Main Building Whitehall London SW1A 2HB

Telephone 01-218 (Direct Dialling)
01-218 9000 (Switchboard)

Philip Mantle Esq
106 Lady Ann Road
Soothill
Batley
West Yorkshire
WF17 0PY

Our reference D/Sec(AS)12/3

Date 14 January 1988

Dear Mr Mantle,

Thank you for your letter of 19 December 1987 which asked if we possessed any information relating to sightings seen in the Humberside area on 9 December 1987. I have now spoken to the Royal Air Force and can confirm that your suspicions about the sightings being a refuelling exercise were correct. On that particular evening, it is highly likely that the objects seen by your witnesses were USAF KC135 and F111 aircraft which were exercising over the North Sea, passing over Humberside at about 5.00pm.

I am also now able to answer your earlier letter of 26 November which asked if we had received any reports which related to sightings seen in the East Midlands on 14 and 21 October 1986; and Todmorden and Halifax, West Yorkshire on 28 November, 1980. I have looked through our records files and I regret that I have been unable to trace any reports which correspond to the details you gave.

As you already know, we do try to see if we possess any report relating to sightings seen by the public but I would like to stress that we do not have the resources to offer correspondents a general answering service on the UFO subject. As such I would ask that if possible you restrict any future requests to sightings seen recently, ie. within the last year.

I hope that this is helpful.

Yours Sincerely,

> From Squadron Leader D L Webley RAF
>
> **Royal Air Force Binbrook**
> Lincoln LN3 6HF
> Telephone Binbrook (STD 047283) (GPTN 8713) 511 Ext 300
>
> Mr P Mantle
> 106 Lady Ann Road
> Soothill
> BATLEY
> West Yorkshire
> WF17 0PY
>
> Your reference
> Our reference BIN/101/,1/1/AIR
> Date 18 December 1987
>
> Dear Mr Mantle
>
> ALLEGED UFO SIGHTINGS - 9 DECEMBER 1987
>
> 1. Thank you for your enquiry about alleged UFO sightings at around 1730 hrs on 9 Dec. We also received some 4 or 5 telephone enquiries at that time; no enquiry telephone numbers were recorded though one call was understood to be from the postmaster at Great Limber near Grimsby.
>
> 2. We made appropriate enquiries at the time and were eventually satisfied that the reports concerned 2 USAF KC 135 tanker aircraft each with up to 7 F111 aircraft in trail; these aircraft from Mildenhall were operating with Midland Radar in the area at the times of the reports.
>
> 3. I hope this information is of use to you.
>
> Yours Sincerely
> D L Webley

Mr and Mrs Wentworth were out walking in the Wingfield area of Rotherham, South Yorkshire, when they saw:

> "... a strange bell-shaped object, flying through the sky over nearby rooftops; the object emitted an intense white glow and showed red, blue, and orange light. It also had a revolving central section."

(Source: Yorkshire UFO Society [YUFOS], Graham and Mark Birdsall/Ron West)

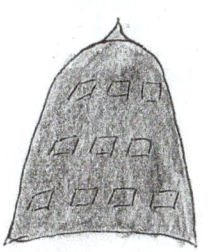

31st December 1987 – Triangular UFO over South Yorkshire

Former security officer Derrick Anders from Goldthorpe, South Yorkshire, told of what he saw, at 7am:

> "I had just taken the dog outside into the garden, when these 'lights' caught my eye passing silently across the sky. They were triangular in shape and consisted of eight orange and one white light. I watched them stop overhead, as if somehow looking for something, then head out towards the south-west direction, where they stopped for a short time before disappearing, but reappearing in the south-east. It's still vivid in my mind."

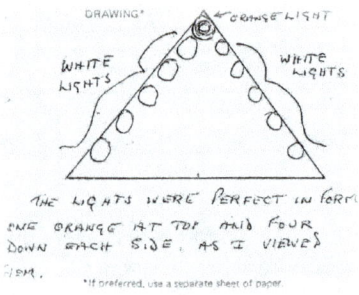

Mr Anders contacted the local newspaper, who published his report. Over thirty people telephoned him about having seen a similar object.

(Source: *South Yorkshire Times,* **15.1.1988/Interview by David Clarke, UFOIN)**

In *Flying Saucer Review,* Volume 35, No. 2, June Quarter, 1990, Gordon Creighton commented on the ever growing reports of Triangular UFOs, seen over the Plymouth and Devonshire areas. These were later explained away on the front pages of the *Daily Telegraph* (18.7.1989) as being sightings of the Stealth Bomber!

1988

MARGARET Thatcher becomes the longest serving British Prime Minister this century, in power for eight years. Actor Rowan Atkinson launches the new *Comic Relief* charity. Labour Party leader Neil Kinnock calls for a further £1.3 billion to be made available for the *National Health Service*. Football hooliganism sees 41 suspected hooligans arrested at the *FA Cup* third round tie between *Arsenal* and *Millwall*, at Highbury. Unemployment figures released at the end of 1987, showing the 18th successive monthly fall. Just over 2,600,000 people are now jobless in the United Kingdom. The 'Birmingham Six' lose an appeal against their convictions. Margaret Thatcher announces a £3 billion regeneration scheme to improve a series of inner city areas by the year 2000. It is revealed that the average price of a house in Britain reached £60,000 at the end of last year, compared to £47,000 in December 1986. IRA campaign continues with bombing and attacks.

The Prince of Wales narrowly avoids death in an avalanche, while on a skiing holiday in Switzerland. US President Ronald Reagan makes a visit to Britain. 80,000 people attend a concert at *Wembley Stadium* in honour of Nelson Mandela, the South African anti-apartheid campaigner, who turned 70 on that day and had been in prison since 1964. Five British soldiers are killed by the IRA in Lisburn. Piper Alpha oil rig disaster in the *North Sea* explodes and results in the death of 167 workers. Pan Am Flight 103 explodes over the Scottish town of Lockerbie, Dumfries and Galloway, killing a total of 270 people – 11 on the ground and all 259 who were on board. Our condolences go out to the people that were murdered and to the loved ones that remain, whose lives will never be the same. We will always honour the innocent victims of murder in this book, no matter what the chosen subject.

CHAPTER 4

JANUARY TO MARCH 1988

JANUARY 1988

2nd January 1988 – UFO over Thames

JANUARY was to be a busy month for the Yorkshire based UFO Society ran by Mark and Graham Birdsall, to whom we had the pleasure of talking many times over the years, but never actually met! On this evening, a UFO was sighted hovering over the *Thames Estuary* by local resident – Mrs Jean Williams.

> "I thought I was seeing things, when I saw this pink shape whizzing round and round – like a child's spinning top. I called my son, Shaun. He watched it through binoculars; it resembled a jellyfish in appearance. At one stage, a red dot whizzed past the main object."

Shaun:

> "It was rotating and kept changing shape each time. I could see circular objects with lines leading away from them. We were shaking. The whole thing was very eerie."

Was there any connection with a report of a mysterious explosion, which shook the windows of a Billericay house, the same evening, followed by an eerie white glow seen on the skyline, hovering over Basildon, near the A127?

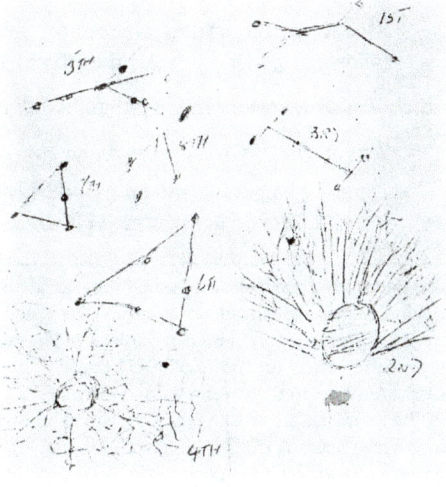

At 7.30pm, two people living in a village near Worksop later contacted Graham and Mark, after sighting two unusual flying triangular objects moving around in the sky for several minutes.

At 7.50pm, Leeds resident – Ray Barron – was about to go into his house, when he saw something very unusual in the night sky.

> "It was plate-shaped, orange and yellow in colour, and was spinning or rolling as it moved across the sky. It appeared to descend a fraction, at which point I noticed some kind of smoke, or vapour, being emitted

Haunted Skies Volume Ten

> *from the rear of the object. The light was brilliant and quite large, about half the size of a full moon. It then just vanished, but to my surprise I could still see the spiralling smoke continuing on its journey."*

He was not the only one to report having seen strange aerial activity that evening. At about the same time, Jane Marsden and Vivienne O'Donnell, from Dewsbury, were sat in a parked car, talking, when they noticed a large *'ball of light'* pass through the night sky. Their first reaction was to wonder if this was an aircraft in trouble. Further scrutiny revealed a *"brightly lit orange and yellow object, with a pale blue flame behind, and a red tail."*

At about 9pm, Mr Edward Johnson, living north-west of Leeds, sighted a large orange and yellow coloured *'ball of light'* streaming grey smoke behind as it headed across the sky, apparently following the contours of a nearby valley. After the object was lost from view, the vapour trail that it left remained in the sky for some time afterwards.

At about 9.30pm, Basildon resident Mr J Colby (43) – a head teacher by profession – was sat reading, when an explosion or shock wave rocked the house in Bell Hill Close.

> *"My mother came in straightaway, soon joined by my son, Mark, who had seen a flash – then heard the sound of an explosion. We looked out of the first floor window and saw a large illuminated patch of ground (approximately the size of two football fields) with light shooting up from it."*

Mrs Mary Alice Redmond (71):

> *"It was evening and dark. I was in the kitchen at the back of the house, when I heard an explosion and the double-glazed windows vibrated and the house shook. It reminded me of the blast effects of bombs, dropped in the war at Bromley, Kent, where I lived at the time. I rushed outside but saw no sign of any damage. I looked south over Basildon, and saw a large area lit-up, south of the A127, which faded from view about 30 minutes later."*

(Source: Ron West/*Southend Evening Echo*, 7.1.1988 – 'Flying Saucer in explosion riddle'/Personal interview)

Spinning UFO over London

At 10pm, Zena Sfeir from the *The Little Boltons, Kensington, London (then aged 16) was looking up at the night sky through her telescope.

> *"When I first saw the UFO, it resembled the stereotyped grey 'Flying Saucer', with pink blobs, hemispherical in shape, attached to a circle in its underside. As it spun around, it changed colour to electric blue.*
>
> *A police officer arrived. He couldn't believe his eyes and radioed in, asking for other officers to attend. Before long, there were eight officers watching the object . . .*

which was now resembling a jellyfish *'ball of light'*, during the early hours of 3rd January 1988.

> *This is what I wrote in my diary, covering those events for the 2nd January 1988 –*
>
> *10pm – I go outside my house and I begin to look at the moon through my telescope, but my position is not comfortable so I stop. I choose to look at something else that I have noticed through the naked*

*The Boltons is a street located in the Brompton district of the Royal Borough of Kensington and Chelsea, London, England (postcode SW10). The street is divided into two crescents to the west and east, with large expensive houses and communal gardens in the centre. Both ends of the street are manned by armed Diplomatic Protection Group officers because it houses several embassies, including those of Israel and Russia. As prices in the street soared in the past decade, the makers of *Monopoly* chose it as the top square on the board ahead of Mayfair. The second most expensive street is The Boltons, Kensington, where the average house is £13.3million, with Frognal Way, Camden, third at £10.6million. In fact, the top ten expensive streets are all in London.

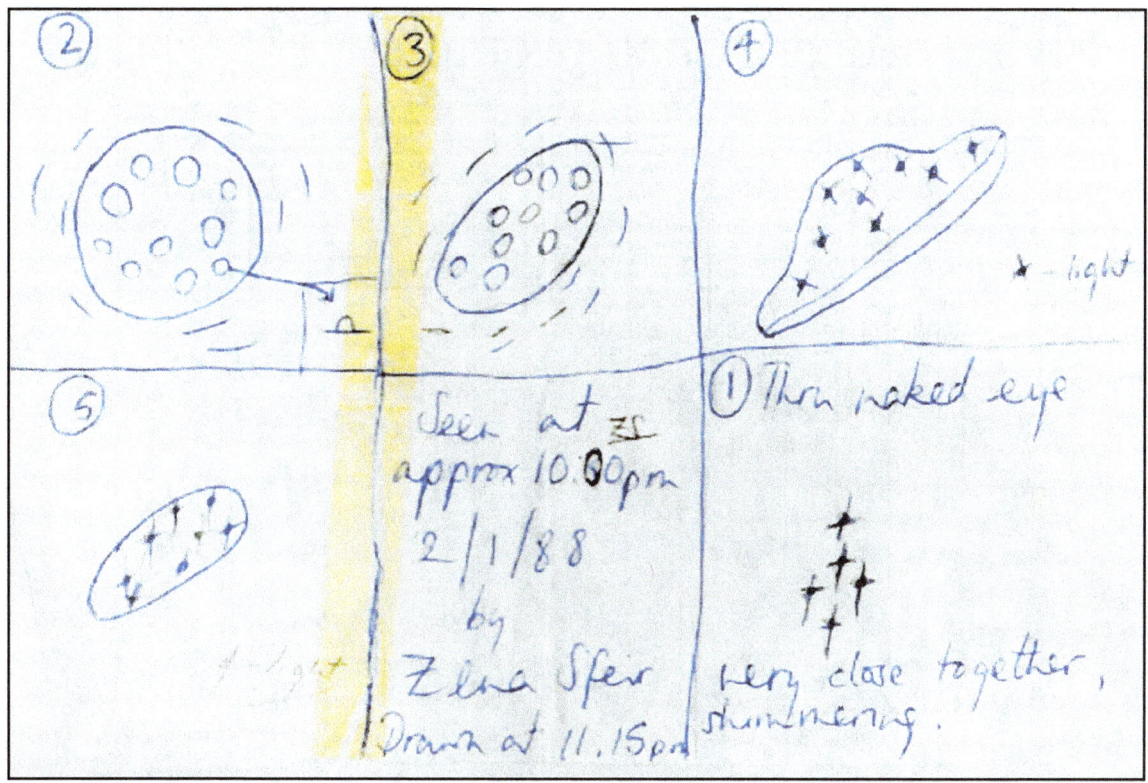

eye. Straight ahead of me, looking down (south-east) the street (The Little Boltons, London SW10) quite low in the sky, is a cluster of four bright lights. 10.30pm – I point my telescope at this and am shocked by what I see in clear focus. The object is round, grey/green in colour and has pink hemispheres attached. It is clear that I am looking at the underside; the object slowly rotates to reveal itself to be saucer-shaped. The saucer shape is defined by small white lights. It strongly resembles the stereotypical 'flying saucer' of cartoons and illustrations. Clouds soon obscure my view and I return indoors to tell my incredulous family – each of whom is in bed.

11.30pm – Still taken aback by what I had seen. I look outside to see if it is still visible to the naked eye. I see that it is now smaller and has moved from its original south-east position to a southern position. I bring out my telescope again and decide to call the police at my local Kensington Station. By the time the first policeman arrives, it looks, to the naked eye, like a bright star but for a neon-like glow which distinguishes it from other surrounding stars. Through the telescope, it looks more like a pulsating jellyfish – a ball of pink and blue light. The policeman is dumbfounded by what he sees and radios in another policeman. All in all, that night, eight policemen come to have a look through the telescope. They are all amazed by the unexplained object they see. We watch it for over an hour.

3rd January, the next day – Two officers, unsolicited and very kindly, came to my house to tell me that they had recorded the event in their log and that if anyone 'thought I was mad', they should come to the station and see the log.

4th January – A crime reporter from the 'Mirror' picks up the story at the police station and runs an article which is picked up by the media."

Flying saucer squad prompts UFO dispute

By Peter Dunn

A FLYING SAUCER has been witnessed by eight policemen over London, opening up old wounds between the promoters and debunkers of unidentified flying objects.

The UFO was seen in the early hours of Sunday morning by Zena Sfeir, 16, a Rugby School pupil who was raking the sky with her telescope looking for the full moon. Miss Sfeir, who lives in Kensington, London, said yesterday that the flat, saucer-shaped UFO, grey-green with pink blobs, looked like a "swimming jellyfish". When it spun round, it changed to electric blue.

After an hour's tracking the Sfeir household telephoned the local police. "One policeman came round, saw it and called in a few more," Miss Sfeir said. "They called in two more and they called in two more. In the end eight policemen were witnesses. The moment they saw it they were complete believers."

News of the sighting put the Aetherius Society on full alert at its headquarters, a converted shop in Fulham Road, London. The society, which is passionate about flying saucers, regards the Kensington spaceship as further vindication of its beliefs and a well-earned rebuff for mockers like the astronomer, Patrick Moore.

"We're just literally on the phone to the police about it now," Dr Richard Laurence, the society's secretary, said. "There's a lot of police interest in flying saucers because they're always on duty looking at the sky. They get a lot of sightings and often feel frustrated because I think they're up against some sort of policy of no comment.

"For instance, my colleague's been shifted from department to department for 40 minutes and ended up at the same place three times. That's always a sign there's a bit of a panic on.

"Patrick Moore says it's just Jupiter. I know him of old. I've been on TV with him. As I said to him then, I wouldn't talk about astronomy because I don't know enough about it and he doesn't know anything about flying saucers and should keep quiet about them. Patrick Moore is one of those people who've set out to debunk the subject. Another one is the science correspondent of The Daily Telegraph whose name eludes me at the moment. None of them knows anything about it. They're all prejudiced. We don't think it's strange or eccentric to believe in flying saucers. On the contrary, we think it's eccentric to disbelieve."

Independant Newspaper 6th January 1988

DAILY MIRROR, Tuesday, January 5, 1988   PAGE 3

'ELLO UFO! COPS SPY A JELLY IN THE SKY

By SYLVIA JONES

A LAUGHING policeman's smirk turned to wide-eyed wonder when he answered a midnight call from a schoolgirl astronomer.

He found himself gazing at a saucer-shaped UFO, dazzling in colour and slowly changing shape "like a swimming jellyfish," as it moved across the sky. The astonished officer radioed in and TWO colleagues in Kensington, West London, arrived.

They took one look, radioed in and another FIVE coppets turned up.

The eight spent 40 minutes tracking the UFO through binoculars and a telescope which Zena Sfeir, 16, had mounted on her doorstep.

EXCLUSIVE

Blobs

Zena said: "They were all prepared to treat it as a joke... but you should have seen their faces when they all saw it. They were astounded.

"It was shimmering and first looked grey-green with pink blobs.

"When it turned round completely it seemed an electric blue colour with flashing lights. It was the most incredible sight I have ever seen."

Astronomer Patrick Moore reckons the Saturday night sighting was probably the planet Jupiter.

But the goggle-eyed policemen beg to differ.

And the object has been officially reported as a UFO at Kensington station, where a spokesman said: "The officers saw it long enough to be completely convinced."

'Ello, 'ello.. that's a UFO

by Peter Wilson

A UFO has been spotted in the night skies over London... and that's official, according to Scotland Yard today.

A total of eight startled police officers watched the grey-green, pink and electric blue object as it spun, banked and hovered above Kensington.

A Yard spokesman said: "Police officers saw an unidentified object after a call from a members of the public. We are unable to say what it was."

The bizarre incident, which has been reported as a UFO in the station log at Kensington, took place shortly after midnight on Saturday

Alerted

Zena Sfeir, 16, had mounted a telescope on the doorstep of the family home in The Little Boltons after spotting a light in the sky.

She called in the local law to verify her sighting. The first sceptical P-c to arrive was astounded to see a saucer-shaped object, dazzling in colour.

He asked for assistance and a further two officers arrived. They in turn called back to the station and five more came along.

They spent thirty minutes watching the UFO through the telescope and a pair of binoculars.

LONDON STANDARD JAN. 5, 1988

Scotland Yard Police

A Scotland Yard spokesman confirmed the sighting:

> 'Police officers saw an unidentified object, after a call from a member of the public. We are unable to say what it was'.

This was an incident which was to attract much media attention. Unfortunately, and albeit naively, little did Zena know her courage in reporting the matter was to bring ridicule upon her. Astronomer Patrick Moore suggested they had seen the planet Jupiter – an explanation firmly rejected by the officers and Zena.

Derek Jameson and John Stalker

Chief Constable John Stalker

Zena was invited onto Derek Jameson's show – then being hosted by former head of Manchester Police, ex Chief Constable John Stalker – who dealt with her in what appears to be a condescending and sceptical manner, making the usual quips that one would expect from a man in the public eye and authority, who would have no comprehension or knowledge of the subject. The *British Astronomical Association* suggested Venus – very bright at that time – could have been responsible! Mike Wootten, of BUFORA, established that what they had seen was Jupiter!

Over 25 years later, Zena still rejects this explanation for what she and the officers saw (and so do we, based on *all of* the evidence).

There have been other occasions when police officers have seen strange things in the sky. On the evening of 10th March 1999, officers watched four diamond-shaped *'lights'* move silently over Stamford Bridge, in south-west London, hovering over Chelsea Football Club's stadium, for about 15 seconds. The officer said the *'lights'* were *"not like anything seen before and moved across the sky fairly quickly, changing shape slowly"*.

The *'lights'* reportedly moving from east to west, were also seen by another officer from Chesham, Buckinghamshire. Although it was a clear night, he was unable to state the size of the object.

(Source: Personal interview/*Independent* Newspaper, 6.1.1988 -'Flying Squad prompts UFO dispute'/ *London Evening Standard*, 5.1.1988 – 'Ello ello, that's a UFO'/*The Daily Mirror*, 5.1.1988 – 'Ello UFO! Cops Spy a Jelly in the Sky'/BBC 6 o'clock news/Ministry of Defence declassified files)

3rd January 1988 – UFO seen over Essex

At 5pm, York woman Annette McDonaldson and her young daughter – Clare – set off home, after having been to see some friends in Grimsby. As they neared the outskirts of the city, Annette noticed some bright lights in the rear view mirror and decided to slow down, in order to let the vehicle overtake. After the vehicle (presumed to be a lorry) failed to overtake, Annette asked her daughter to have a look – which she did – then exclaimed in astonishment that the *'lights'* were actually above the ground. Suddenly, they loomed closer and then inexplicably vanished from view.

Within seconds they reappeared, now over the top of the car. Annette, panicking, increased the speed of the car to well past the regulation speed limit of 70mph; incredibly, the *'lights'* were then seen ahead of the car, just above the road.

The phenomena kept pace with the car, for a couple of miles, before shooting straight up into the sky and finally disappearing for good.

Haunted Skies Volume Ten

At about 6pm, MOD employee Reginald Rawlings (63), from Foulness Island, was driving home from work.

As he went over the Havengore Bridge, Essex, he noticed a very bright light in the sky.

> *"At first I thought it was a bright star, although it was still light. I continued on my journey for about three miles. When I reached Church End village, I was shocked to see a large black mass, showing a huge green light at either side, hovering at about 3,500ft. It then moved silently away towards the north-west direction; it was something very strange."*

Ron West wrote to the MOD, hoping to interview him at work, and was told it would not be possible.

In 2013 we spoke to his daughter – Doreen Tilbrook – about the matter. She remembers her father talking about the incident, but was not inclined to treat it with any seriousness at the time.

Havengore Bridge, Essex

At 9.30pm, Leeds housewife – Pauline Russell – was out walking near her home, when she sighted an *"egg-shaped object, moving slowly across the sky"*. Suddenly, an aircraft was seen approaching the object from the opposite direction. The UFO moved in a zigzag motion across the sky, and passed very close to the right-hand side of the aircraft. (**Source: Yorkshire UFO Society, Graham Birdsall/Ron West & Brenda Butler**)

4th January 1988 – Heavy UFO activity over Yorkshire

This was the Yorkshire UFO Society's busiest days of the year for reports of UFO activity. It began at 5.25pm, when a married couple saw a massive white sphere moving just above cloud cover, over Harewood, near Harrogate.

Glowing white object

At 7pm, a glowing white object, showing several dark points or patches on its body, was seen over Leeds, at an estimated height of 1,000ft, moving slowly southwards. Twenty minutes later a cluster of red and yellow coloured lights were seen at a height of 500-1000ft, over Mosborough, Sheffield, by a local man. He telephoned the UFO hotline number and Allan Petre made his way out to the scene and confirmed the sighting.

Glowing orange object

At 7.30pm, ex RAF Officer Mr J.S. Rhodes was outside his house, when he saw a glowing orange object in the sky over Scholes, West Yorkshire.

> "I could see five darkened portholes running along the side of its body. Nearby were two aircraft, possibly military. I could hear their engines, but not the object. Within seconds, it moved away and out off sight."

Fifteen minutes later, three brilliantly lit spheres were seen over the centre of Derby by two women, on their way home from work.

Large circular object

At 7.46pm, two men in a parked vehicle at Chellaston, Derby centre, saw what they described as:

> "... a large circular object, resembling a piece of glass sewn together by threads."

'Globes of light' seen

At 8pm Mr Bill Moran from Kimberworth, Rotherham, sighted a *'bright ball'* of yellow and orange light, heading slowly, low in the sky, towards the north-west direction.

Two minutes later, a bright *'ball of light'* was seen over Roundhay, Leeds. This was followed by what appeared to be three aircraft. We believe it is possible they were no such thing and more likely to be UFOs.

Object resembling V1 Flying Bomb

At 8.15pm, a man from York saw what looked like an old V1 Flying Bomb, heading across the sky at low altitude, trailing sparks, debris, and flame. At the same time, a large luminous green *'ball of light'* was seen moving slowly through the sky over Kirkhamgate, near Wakefield, by a family who said they had seen some kind of vapour being left behind the object as it went away, apparently following the course of the M1 Motorway. Was this the same UFO seen over York, at about the same time, described as a brilliant yellow-orange sphere?

Lemon-shaped UFO

Two minutes later, at 8.17pm, Mr Lee was driving along the dual carriageway of the A38, near Shelton Lock, Derbyshire, when he saw:

> "... a large lemon-shaped object heading across the sky, westwards. It was white in colour and was surrounded by a blue or green glowing halo of light. At one point it was that low, I thought it was going to crash into the ground."

Object resembling V1 Flying Bomb

At 8.45pm, an object resembling a V1 Rocket was seen moving through the air, emitting sparks and debris, over Blubberhouses, North Yorkshire, by two men hiking over the top of the moor.

'Globes of light' seen

Five minutes later, two extremely large glowing white spheres moving side by side (identical to what was sighted by the co-author, John Hanson, in June 1996) were seen over Collingham, West Yorkshire, by two men travelling in a car. At one point, the two objects descended quite close to their vehicle before moving away and out of sight.

'Green beam of light'

Unusually (if one can designate such a category in this plethora of unusual sightings) a thin green *'laser beam of light'* was seen to shoot across the sky from one horizon to the other, by ex-RAF serviceman – Mr Jones of Guisley, West Yorkshire. The reader will hear more about these mysterious phenomena later in this same year. Was this the same *'beam'*, described as a thin pencil-shaped object, over Selby, North Yorkshire, at 8.50pm?

Mysterious UFO

At 9.10pm, Gordon Blake – an ex-RAF serviceman from Leeds – was outdoors, at the time, when he saw a large glowing *'light'* in the sky. As it approached closer, he was surprised to see . . .

> "something truly gigantic and about 400ft in diameter. It was showing several layers, with twelve lights flashing in and around the formation."

Object resembling 'Flying Bomb'

Still in the same locality, Mrs Robson and her friend were close to their home in Morley, Leeds, when they sighted a rocket-shaped object, *"resembling a flying bomb"*, moving across the sky at high speed, trailing blue and red flames from its rear. Although this couldn't have been the answer, the next photo showing a real flying bomb taken during World War 2, is a frightening reminder of what people had to endure during the Blitz. Chillingly one wonders about the likely victims of this terrible weapon of modern warfare as it struck home.

Three points of light

Fifteen minutes later, a large white *'light'*, with several smaller lights inside, was seen in the sky close to the A1, near Wetherby, West Yorkshire.

At 9.16pm, one minute later following the previous report, a glowing orange coloured object was seen at high altitude, practically stationary above the town. Shortly afterwards it moved slowly towards their position, enabling them to see three separate points of orange and yellow coloured lights, inset into the main body of whatever it was.

UFO display over Dewsbury, West Yorkshire

Finally, at 11.30pm, an elderly couple from Dewsbury, West Yorkshire, was in the process of retiring for the night. While in the process of closing the bedroom curtains, they saw a brightly lit object,

> *"like a dinner plate, moving backwards and forwards across the sky, making a swishing noise."*

The couple watched what they referred to as the best aerial display since Guy Fawkes Night, until whatever it was inexplicably vanished from sight.

Triangular UFO over Southampton

Also seen during this period of time (the exact date is unknown – just early January 1988) a triangular-shaped object was seen over Milbrook, Southampton. A few days later, Geoff McWilliams, Mathew Cadden and Simon Cade, were sat on a bench at Riverside Park, when a strange *'ball of light'* shot across the nearby football pitch.

Geoff:

> *"It was the size of a football, hovering about 30ft off the ground and performing triangular motions. It suddenly shot towards us and we ran away."*

(Source: Bob Price)

5th January 1988 – UFO seen over Barnsley, South Yorkshire

A coal miner from Stairfoot, Barnsley, was motorcycling home, after night duty at Redbrook Colliery. As he drove along Huddersfield Road, which leads into Barnsley town centre, he saw some unusual *'bright lights'* above the trees and decided to pull-in to take a closer look.

> *"I watched them for a few minutes, and then a red light appeared under the lights, which began to move towards me at an angle. As it approached my position, as God is my judge, I saw what looked like 8-10 windows all in a line, and what appeared to be an object which looked solid. It then tilted slightly, enabling me to see the shape of the red light and three small lights flashing. I sat on my bike watching, for a couple of minutes, and then it came to a stop. By now I was scared, so put my bike into gear ready to go. I glanced across again and saw it tilt the same way I was going. Its lights went off and it disappeared from sight."*

In an interview later conducted at the scene by Philip Mantle and Andy Roberts, the witness (who asked that his personal details be confidential) said:

> *"The object was cross-shaped; two red lights were positioned on the end of each 'wing' and the underside was metallic grey or silver and covered in indentations, resembling boxes or machinery – like the spaceships used in* Star Wars.*"*

Philip:

> *"He also remarked on an eerie silence while the object was nearby, and that no cars or people were seen during the incident."*

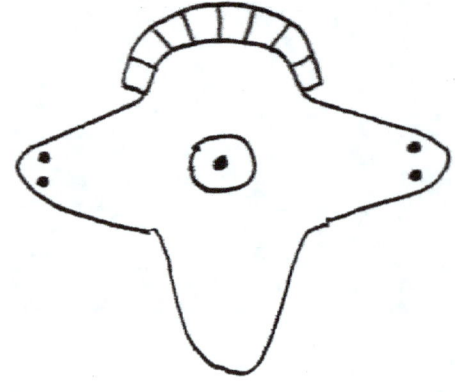

At 5pm, Shaun Roy Williams (19) of Canvey Island, sighted a strange object in the sky and called out his mother to have a look. (**Source: Philip Mantle, Andy Roberts**)

6th January 1988 – UFO, York

At 10.30am, an odd cross-shaped object, black in colour, was sighted moving across the sky over Yorkshire.

Later that evening, a number of people contacted the Yorkshire UFO Society, reporting having sighted 'cross-shaped objects' flying through the sky over the Rotherham area.

At 5.30pm, following a number of UFO reports centered over the York area, Mrs Elizabeth Rogers of Chapelfields, York, was watching TV with her son, when they noticed the sky was becoming appreciably lighter, followed by the appearance of a white object – the shape and size of a pumpkin in the sky – totally unlike any aircraft ever seen before. In addition to this was a report of three orange 'balls of light', seen at 7.45pm, heading southwards over Yorkshire.

At 8.20pm, a UFO was seen over the Eastwood estate, described as a large 'flying cross', approximately 60ft in diameter.

It is said that twelve photographs were taken of yellow-orange coloured light – still present in the sky after the 'cross' had disappeared over the horizon.

According to Mick Hanson, of the *Yorkshire UFO Society*, it was disclosed that a UFO was chased by a RAF jet during the evening of this day, although we have no further details at the present time but will endeavor to find out more information.

At 8.55pm, Rosetta Webley from St. Albans, Hertfordshire, was lying down on the couch at her St. Albans home, when she experienced a strange feeling. She looked through the window of the dining room and saw a huge round object, showing red, yellow, and white lights. She got up, opened the window and peered out, seeing:

> "... a completely circular spinning object, with a dark dome on top. Around the lower part were many square lit windows of red, white and yellow – in that sequence. Beneath each square there was another light – all very bright and dazzling. It reminded me of a fireworks display. The entire object was rotating slowly and seemed inclined or tilting, first one way and then the other. As it rotated, the coloured lights all appeared to blend into each other. It looked like a child's spinning top. Whilst this was going on, I was aware of a great silence. I couldn't hear anything. I gathered that my husband, Gary, was calling me. After a few minutes, I became aware of my surroundings and called him. He came over and looked out. By this time the object had began to recede into the distance. He then ran into the garden with my daughter, Cheryl (15), by which time it was moving northwards towards Harpenden."

In a letter later sent to Gordon Creighton – the Editor of *Flying Saucer Review* – about the incident. Rosetta (previously a sceptic of such matters) told him she had developed precognitions of future events, and an increase in psychic awareness.

During the same evening, Andrew Findlay of Yaverland Drive, Bagshot, was cleaning out his rabbit hutch. He happened to look upwards into the sky, when, through a gap in the clouds, out flew:

> "... a bright white flying saucer-shaped thing, with green lights in the middle of it. It hovered for about 7-8 seconds, completely silently, before disappearing through another gap in the cloud. As it went, I could see this glow coming from its underneath".

(Source: Gordon Creighton/*Watford and West Hertfordshire Review*, 14.1.88/Susan Stevenage/*Farnborough Mail*, 12.1.1988 – 'Three claim UFO sightings in night sky'/The *Star*, 7.1.1988 – 'UFOs on the prowl in York'/*FSR*, Volume 39, No. 2, Summer 1994)

7th January 1988 – UFO over Chesterfield

At about 8pm, Stephanie Thorneycroft was at her home address in Old Road, Brampton, Chesterfield, when she noticed a large disc-shaped object in the sky, accompanied by three smaller ones, hovering low down over some trees. She shouted her husband, Geoffrey – a retired college lecturer – who came to the window to have a look, and then alerted neighbours David Wheatcroft and his family, along with another householder, who watched the objects until they dropped down behind the trees.

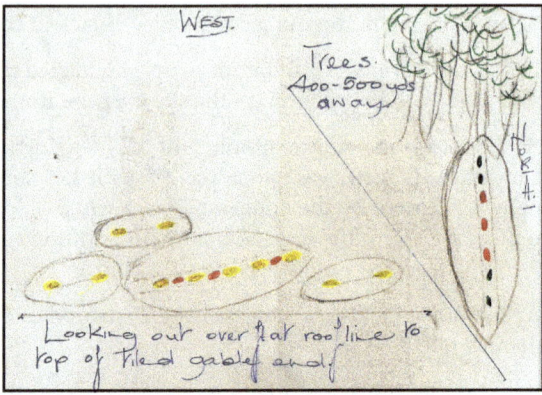

Mr Thorneycroft contacted the police at Chesterfield, to report the matter.

We spoke to Stephanie, in 2006, about the incident. Sadly, Geoffrey had passed away some years ago, but she was more than willing to send us an illustration of what had been seen.

In February 1988 the couple appeared live on ITV's – *The Time, The Place* – to tell of what they had witnessed. Although there were once again attempts made to explain away what the couple had seen as being celestial bodies, we discovered that Leeds salesman – Chris Triggs – was driving along the A38, between Burton-on-Trent and Derby, when he saw:

> "...a circular white, blue and green, sparkling light in the sky – the size of a plate – moving at about 100mph in an east to west direction."

Coincidently, Elsa Lee – a member of YUFOS – was on the way to see Mr and Mrs Thorneycroft, to collect some sighting reports, several days later, when she saw *"three strange objects in the sky"*.

(Source: *The Chesterfield & Dronfield Gazette*, 14.1.1988 – 'UFO spotted over Brampton'/*Derby Evening Telegraph*, 'County UFO alert'/Personal interview/Wikipedia 2014)

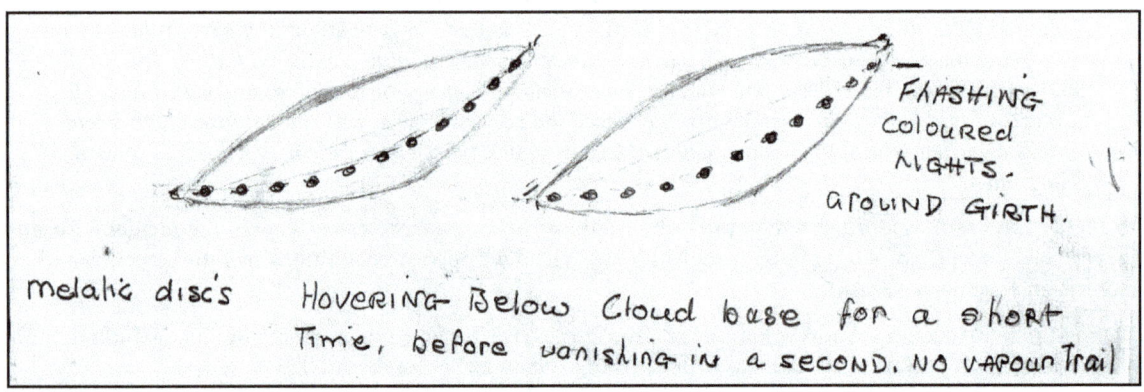

The Time, The Place was a British audience participation talk show that was produced by a number of different ITV companies, and broadcast live on ITV from 1987-1998. *TTTP* was presented by Mike Scott from 1987–1993 and by John Stapleton from 1991-1998. Henry Kelly also presented the programme for a period before Stapleton took over full time. The program was developed as ITV's competition to the BBC's *Kilroy* morning discussion show, which premiered in 1986. It differed from *Kilroy* in that *Kilroy* delved into more political and current event related issues, while *TTTP* focused on human interest topics. The programme toured the country and came from the various ITV regional studios, including Aberdeen after the Piper Alpha. Towards the end of its run, the programme came from London at least three days a week to save money. It was axed on 20th March 1998, to make way for the less topical, more issue-led programme *Vanessa*, which mainly dealt with personal matters.

11th January 1988 – UFO seen over Farnborough

At 6.30am, Farnborough man – Fred Clark – was driving to work along the A31, towards Alton, accompanied by his stepson – Darryl Robson – when they noticed a bright *'light'* in the sky, with a smaller one below it. On reaching Bentley, Fred stopped to visit a shop and was amazed to see:

> "... a massive object, moving slowly towards Farnham, shaped like a 50pence piece. It had a light at opposite ends and was making a droning noise."

At 10.30am, a retired professor of organic chemistry (65) and his wife (67) were travelling towards Skipton, by car, and were about one mile from the Grassington side of the *Craven Heifer* Public House, when they saw what they described as a flat hovercraft, or disc-shaped object, descending from a height of some 2-300ft in the air. They first took it to be a weather balloon, falling to earth in a south-west to north-east direction.

> "The object seemed to have a flange or rim, which undulated as it came down. It had appeared in front of us very suddenly, as though it made a very rapid descent. It then changed direction to move parallel with the ground. The front edge of the object appeared to be moving towards us initially, as it passed in front of our car. It had sharpened edges and was silvery pink in colour. It then veered to the left of the car as if to land, but then disappeared from view."

The sighting was reported to Tony Dodd – Head of UFO investigations for the South Yorkshire UFO Society – who retired from the police, in 1988, as a sergeant. Tony made a visit to the locality known as *Crookrise Plantation*, but found nothing untoward. Over the course of the years, I (John) was involved in other investigations handed down to me by him, after joining Quest in the later years. Sadly, Tony passed away some years ago. According to Yorkshire UFO Society investigator – Mick Hanson, RAF Jet Fighters were seen chasing UFOs over the Rotherham area during this time, although we do not know the dates of when this actually took place.

(Source: *Camberley News* [Surrey] 29.1.1988 – 'UFO claim by father and his stepson'/Tony Dodd)

16th January 1988 – Mysterious 'red light' over Sheffield solved?

Police Inspector David Tingle and Sergeant Chris Thompson, from Woodseats Police Station, Sheffield, were driving along the road near *Fanny's* nightclub, at 12.45am, when they saw a bright 'red light' in the sky – apparently hanging over the Greenhill, area. The officers thought it might have been a flare, discharged by a local Territorial Army unit. Enquiries made with them revealed no knowledge. According to UFO researcher

---

Baffled by red sky at night

POLICE are baffled by a mysterious red light which hung over Sheffield late at night.

Inspector David Tingle and Sergeant Chris Thompson, from Woodseats, watched the light for more than half a minute as they drove back from the Derbyshire peaks shortly after midnight.

Police switchboards received calls from across the city about it.

Inspector Tingle said: "We were driving along the road near Fanny's nightclub at Owler Bar when we saw a bright red light in the sky. It seemed to be hanging over the Greenhill, Low Edges area but it was difficult to make out its size.

"At first we thought it was just a flare, perhaps from a local Territorial Army unit, but when we checked they had no knowledge of the light.

"When we got back to the station we found there had been a lot of calls from members of the public but, as yet, we are unable to explain what it was," said Insp Tingle.

Sheffield Star 23.1.1988

David Clarke, following enquiries made by him, he received a letter from the Chief Superintendent of South Yorkshire Police, who told him it had been a flare which was seen to land on a local golf course.
(Source: *Sheffield Star*, 23.1.1988)

19th January 1988 – UFOs captured on cine film over Wentworth

The *Rotherham Advertiser,* South Yorkshire (22.1.1988), told of being contacted by two people, who claimed they had captured two brightly lit doughnut-shaped objects on cine-film, seen flying across the sky over the Wentworth area.

22nd January 1988 – Triangular UFO over North Yorkshire

At 9pm, Mr and Mrs Alan Davidson were driving northwards and near Kettlewell, North Yorkshire, when they saw a large triangular-shaped object directly in front of their car, moving from left to right. In the few seconds they had before the object was lost from view, they saw it had a bank of lights on its base with several others in the centre, which were flashing on and off – its length estimated to be 60ft. The couple, who were shaken by the strange encounter, pulled up, hoping to see the craft again – but nothing remained of any interest.
(Source: YUFOS)

23rd January 1988 – UFO seen over Derbyshire

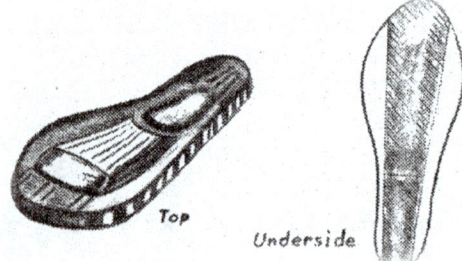

Mr Ivan Spenceley from Chesterfield, Derbyshire, was out exercising his dog, at 12.45am, when the animal became agitated. Glancing upwards he saw what looked like a window in a large object, about 250ft away from where he was stood, which was:

> " . . . *dark black in colour, like the sole of a shoe in shape. It was lit up inside with tinted windows, and a series of blue and red lights. It then shot off upwards into the sky.*"

He contacted Graham and Mark Birdsall about the matter, and was later selected by *Central TV* to appear on their programme – *The Time, The Place* – which he did later in the year, we believe. (**Source:** YUFOS)

27th January 1988 – UFO reported over Pyle, South Wales

Western Mail, Cardiff — 28 JAN 1988

Dawn UFO spotter no hoaxer — police

POLICE ARE taking seriously reports that a giant UFO paid a flying visit to South Wales yesterday.

The sighting was made by a resident of Pyle during an early-morning walk along a lane near Meadow Street in North Cornelly.

A statement from South Wales police said, "His attention was drawn to a large object in the sky roughly over the area of South Cornelly."

Coloured

"He described the object as being the size of three maisonettes with three rows of different coloured lights.

"The object moved off, but he could not state in which direction."

Officers have interviewed the man, who does not want to be named, and are satisfied he is no hoaxer.

Essex Chronicle, Chelmsford — 29 JAN 1988

Mystery light: more sightings

HAVE you seen any UFOs over Chelmsford recently?

A Witham man recently spotted a mystery object shooting across the sky above the town — and several other people have since come forward to confirm that they saw a UFO at about the same time.

Mr Rodney Cullum, of Chalks Road, Witham, saw the object while driving with his wife on the A12 at Hatfield Peverel, about 5pm on Sunday (January 17).

"We were travelling towards Chelmsford and we suddenly saw a small speck travelling at a terrific speed across the sky. As it passed it started to glow and then suddenly it lit up and disappeared. It left a vapour trail for several minutes.

"I am not a crank but my wife and I definitely saw something. I suppose it could have been a satellite or something from an aircraft — but I'm not sure. I really don't know what it was.

"Since the incident I have received calls from several people in the area who saw the same thing."

CONFIRM

Mr Alan Pope, of Boreham, this week called Chelmsford Police to confirm that he saw a mystery object flying over the Chelmsford area about 3.45pm on the afternoon of January 17.

Mr Pope said the object was visible long enough for him to fetch a pair of binoculars and call his wife.

The object was cylindrical with a bright metal finish and no wings. It was emitting a red or orange trail behind.

A police spokesman this week said that all reported sightings will be added to their files.

29th January 1988 – 'Flying Saucers' over Oldham

At 2am, Mrs Lynda Alker was at her home in Eustace Street, Chadderton, Oldham, when she sighted a bright flashing light in the sky.

> "At first I thought it was a helicopter, because it wasn't moving – then I saw two lights on either side, with a bright flashing light in its centre. I watched it from a landing window for about 30 seconds, before it dropped vertically behind some trees and vanished."

In a conversation held with her, many years after the event, Lynda told us:

> "I remember it coming down through the air at a slant. I still can't find an explanation for what it

was I saw. When I contacted the newspaper, I was ridiculed by so many people. I got sick of people referring to 'little green men' and 'Martians'. The whole thing made me ill. I wish I had never bothered to report it now."

As dawn broke, *'a large jet black saucer-shaped object, with a silver centre'* was seen passing over the Marjorie Lees Health Centre, Oldham, by local woman – Jose Ludlam. Enquiries with the police revealed they had received no other reports. (**Source:** *Oldham Evening Chronicle,* 29.1.1988 – 'José's close encounter')

31st January 1988 – UFO over Manchester

At 6.20am a bright stationary object was seen in the sky over Manchester, by a police officer. The result of any investigation is not known, although brief details are shown on the PRUFOS website, run by retired police officer Gary Heseltine. We are unsure if there is any connection with a report made during the early hours of 2nd February 1988, when a glowing, spinning, *'craft'* was seen by patrolling Cheshire police officers – Ian Walmsley and Chris Evans. After reporting the incident, the officers were told by air traffic controllers, at Manchester Airport, that they had seen a British Airways jet arriving from New York! – An explanation which was rejected by them.

(**Source:** *Doncaster Star,* 6.2.1988 – 'Police saw UFO hover overhead'/*Daily Express,* 2.2.1988 – 'U Foolish Officers Rocket for two PCs with stars in their eyes')

FEBRUARY 1988

2nd February 1988 – Flurry of UFO sightings over South Yorkshire

A number of people contacted the authorities, after sighting something strange in the sky during the evening.

At 7.15pm, David Jones – a miner – of Sunnyside, Rotherham, was on his way home from work on what was a cold night, with rain coming down, when he sighted a number of red lights through his car window, which were stationary in the sky to his right. He last saw whatever it was moving towards the Parkgate, Wentworth direction.

Also at 7.15pm, Miss Smith – an ex-CID Officer, living in a bungalow on the hillside above Deepcar – was watching TV, when she noticed an object in the sky towards the west, in the direction of *Underbank Reservoir*, near Midhopestones, which she described as being:

> "... a very large elliptical object, covered in between 20-30 sharply defined brilliant white lights".

Miss Smith kept the object under observation for 25 minutes, by which time she had called a neighbour to witness the phenomena. The two women watched the object, apparently manoeuvring over the Moors beyond Midhope. It then turned left, twice, and right once, where it continued to hover for a short while, before disappearing from view.

Another witness was businessman Jim Lovett, who had stopped his car in Wentworth village, when he sighted a similar object to that seen by David Jones.

Police officers on patrol sight UFO

Police Constable 3249 Susan Jackson (29) decided to go out on mobile patrol, after a number of people telephoned to report having seen a UFO cross the City. According to contemporary newspaper accounts, within a few minutes the officer saw a bright red 'V'-shaped UFO hovering above the car, making a whirring sound. A few hundred yards away, PC 1979 John Boam was outside Ecclesfield Police Station, when he also saw the UFO covered in rows of flashing red lights pass through the sky, heading off towards the Grenoside area, before being lost from view.

Bolton Evening News — 1 FEB 1988

New UFO sighting

A BOLTON civil servant is the latest witness to an unidentified flying object over the moors north of the town.

Julie Nuttall, of Rosedale Avenue, Sharples, got a clear view of an object floating above Winter Hill.

It is one of many UFO sightings in the area this year.

Julie said: "I was travelling home from a friend's house along Old Kiln Lane. I saw something in my windscreen and I thought it was just a reflection.

"I got out of the car and got a clear view of this object.

"It was shaped like a flattened rugby ball lying flat on its side. It was circled with white lights which seemed to be revolving."

● Letters — Page 6

DAILY MIRROR, Monday, February 8, 1988 — PAGE 3

MAY THE FORCE BE WITH YOU

Cops see mystery UFO over the nick

'ELLO 'ELLO — the old hands at the cop shop swapped knowing grins when a policewoman breathlessly radioed in to report: "I can see a UFO."

But then they heard a strange droning noise pass over the station.

WPC Sue Jackson was sent to investigate when the nick was flooded with phone calls reporting a bizarre craft floating in the sky over Ecclesfield, near Sheffield, Yorks.

As Sue, 29, drove along in her Panda she suddenly spotted a V-shaped machine hovering just yards away.

A row of flashing red lights along its side lit up the entire area.

Blank

Thirty seconds later the mystery craft flew off — and then, as stunned Sue radioed the station, officers there heard a whirring overhead.

A check with RAF Finningley near Doncaster revealed that nothing had appeared on their radar.

A police spokesman yesterday said: "It was snowy and dark — but we did hear SOMETHING pass over the nick."

Unidentified flying oranges...

A FLEET of giant ORANGES has been sighted flying over the Midlands.

Witnesses claim the oversize Outspans give off an orange glow that has left some people with sunburn.

A woman from Beeston, Nottingham, said the oranges were about the size of a house. They hovered just above the ground and gave off a humming noise.

The UFO Investigation Society said: "We have had dozens of reports about these oranges."

Mystery of UF... Oranges!

A FLEET OF giant flying oranges is being probed by UFO experts.

They're the size of a house and leave people who spot them with a dose of sunburn.

They glow bright orange and have been sighted throughout the Midlands in recent weeks, according to Dennis Harriman, co-ordinator for the UFO Investigation Society.

Checks

He has received reports of the strange shapes being seen as far afield as Nottingham and Lichfield, Staffs.

People have claimed the giant jaffa lookalikes hover just above the ground.

And a 35-year-old woman from Beeston, Notts, reported: "I was totally amazed. My husband didn't believe me, but I'm not given to hallucinations."

Checks with the RAF and the Ministry of Defence have failed to link the weird sightings with aircraft.

Mr. Harriman said: "I am not saying they are from another planet but you cannot rule out the possibility."

Haunted Skies Volume Ten

Local UFO Researcher – Michael Hanson – confirmed he had received three other calls of a UFO seen over Kimberley Park, and above Shardlows Steel Works, at Blackburn Meadows. The matter was brought to the attention of David Clarke, who made arrangements to speak to the two officers at Ecclesfield Police Station on the 12th February 1988, when the truth of what had been seen was established.

Susan Jackson:

> "It was Tuesday, 2nd February, and I was driving down Primrose Drive at about 7.45pm, when I heard some interference on my radio. I was going to turn into Floodgate Road, but I changed my mind and carried straight on and came to the junction with Primrose Drive. I saw something in the sky. I thought it was an aeroplane but there were too many lights for it to be. It had bright red lights – really big. It must have been high up because I couldn't actually see the shape of it, but I saw the red lights – bright red lights in rows. It was like an arrowhead coming towards me. It had bright red lights on the side and then on the inside like two rows of five. It made a loud humming noise and went straight over my head – that was it."

*David Clarke asked Susan a number of other questions in his very professional and thorough manner, eliciting answers relating to the sighting, in which she told him she had radioed in to Force Control about the sighting and that the barmaid at the *Black Bull* had also seen it.

Dr. David Clarke displaying his book published by The National Archives

*David Clarke, now Dr. David Clarke, is currently a senior lecturer in journalism at Sheffield Hallam University. In 2009 he wrote a book entitled *The UFO Files: The Inside Story of Real-Life Sightings* – an official history of British UFO reports published by The National Archives in 2009.

Haunted Skies Volume Ten

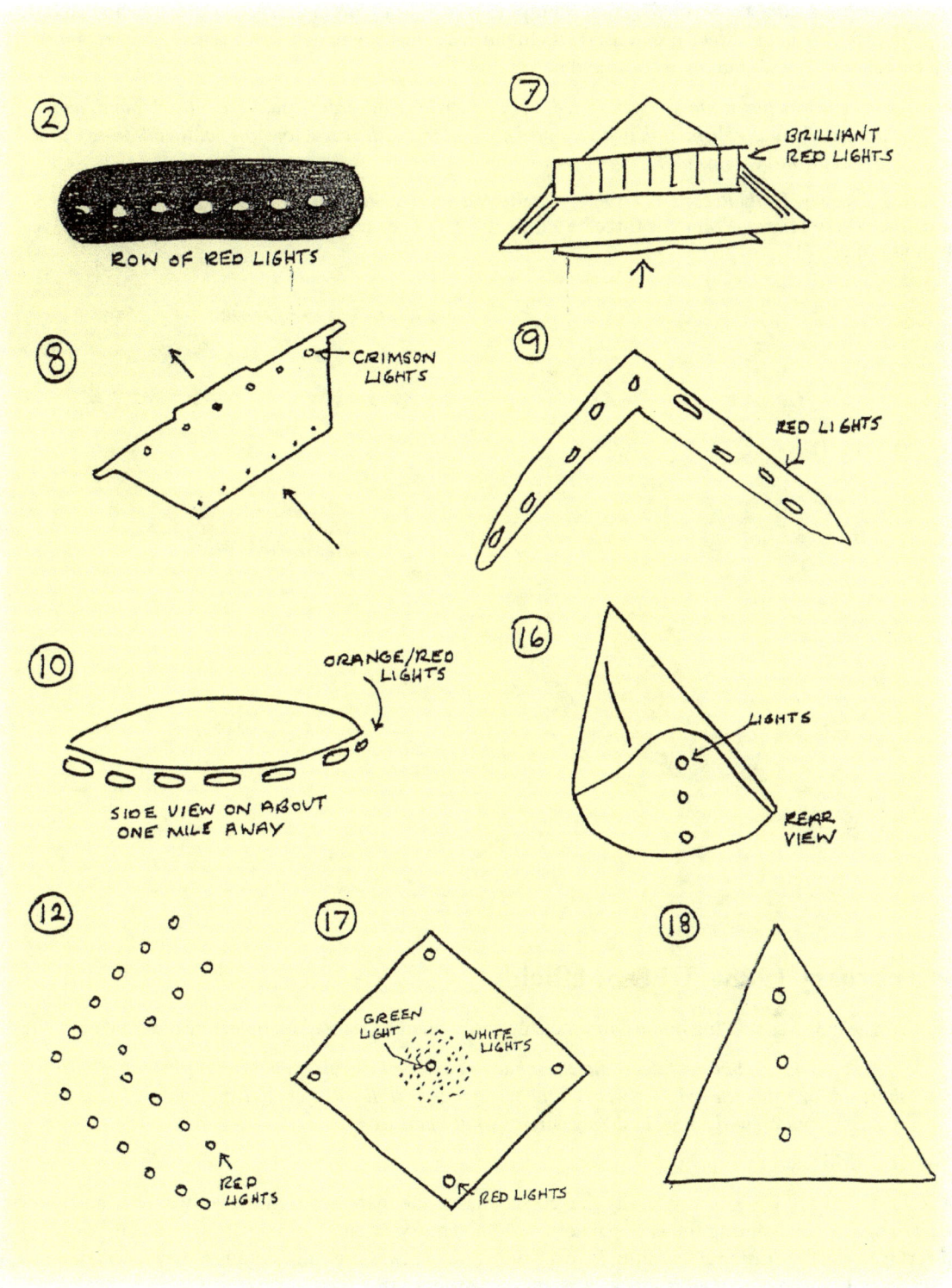

Haunted Skies Volume Ten

At 11.10pm, tobacconist shop owner Glen Kamiya (32) of South Woodham Ferrers, Essex (who had only just taken over the business a week previously) was in the back garden when he saw a saucer-shaped object in the sky. He called out to his family to come and have a look.

> "At first it was just a mass of yellow light, but as we looked harder, could see a black band, above which was an orange light. It then accelerated away at fantastic speed, towards Southend-on-sea, and that was the last we saw of it."

(Sources: *Glasgow Daily Record*, 8.2.1988 – 'Crafty'/*Doncaster Star* - 'Yorkshire Police saw UFO hover overhead'/*Daily Mirror* – 'May the force be with you – Cops see mystery UFO over the Nick'/Ron West/ Brenda Butler)

3rd February 1988 – UFO Sheffield

Scott Worne (13) was walking home from the chip shop, when he sighted an object he described as being:

> "... like a triangle but not fully complete; it had red and white lights on it. White lights ran along the short side of it and the red ones were on the triangular part. It was a cool, clear, night with scattered cloud. When I arrived home, I told my parents what I had seen."

(Source: David Clarke)

Was this the sort of UFO he saw, taking into consideration the increased sightings of what became known as the Triangular UFO, during the later part of the 20th century, often described as large, silent, black objects, hovering or slowly cruising at low altitudes over cities and highways, usually at night? They are often described as having pulsing coloured lights that appear at each corner of the triangle.

4th February 1988 – UFO over Hertford

At 4.30am, Sheffield taxi driver Alan Butterworth (33) had just dropped off a fare at Wincobank, when he happened to look over the valley where Tinsley, Meadowhall, and Blackburn Meadows, are situated, and saw:

> "... a bright object, which I am sure wasn't a plane or helicopter. It had a reddish outline, and every ten to fifteen seconds a bright light shone down from it and then went out. The object was cigar-shaped and headed away in a south-westerly direction, before disappearing from view behind houses."

At 10.30pm, three pupils from Sale School, Hertford – Hayley Farthing (14), Lisa Childs (15) and Martin Purdom (14) – were being driven in a car belonging to Adrian Tummon (17) – a former pupil at the school at Goldings, near Hertford. They saw a massive object, estimated to be 200ft long and covered with lights, hovering just above the ground, half a mile away from them, before disappearing a few minutes later behind a mound. Needless to say, after reporting the matter, the youths were subjected to the usual quips about *'little green men'* from their friends at school.

(Source: *Hertfordshire Mercury*, 5.2.1988 – 'Schoolchildren see UFO – claim')

5th February 1988 – UFO over South Wales

Mr J.W. Hewer of Park Place, Risca, Gwent, wrote to Ecclesfield Police to report what he had observed, after reading in the *Daily Mirror* about the UFO seen by two police officers.

> "I was in my garden on Friday, 5th February, at 5.10pm, when I heard a roaring noise – like a low flying aircraft – and looked upwards to see a 'V'-shaped craft, streaking across the sky, at high altitude. It had flashing lights along one side. My wife and neighbours, who had been alerted by the noise, rushed outside but didn't see it pass by."

Haunted Skies Volume Ten

David Clarke, who investigated this incident and spoke to the witness, believes that he may have seen a military aircraft of some sort, on exercise from one of the RAF Bases in the South Wales area.

The Mansfield UFO Society told of a sighting brought to their attention from a local man, who was walking along Westbourne Road, at Sutton, when he saw two objects meet in the sky, at 8.15pm.

> "Instead of passing each other, the first one swung around the stationary one, for one complete turn, before joining it. It then increased in brightness and shot off at incredible speed, northwards."

(Source: *Mansfield Advertiser*, 18.2.1988 – 'UFO is sighted')

6th February 1988 – Police sight UFO, Telford

At 6.45pm, following a call from a member of the public to the Police, five police officers from Telford, Shropshire, sighted a UFO over the City Centre, which they described as showing green, yellow, and blue lights, before it was soon lost from view.

8th February 1988 – Fireball over Hampshire

At 2.30pm, gardner Raymond Brown was in Barker Park, Kimberworth, about to take a tea break with a colleague, when he saw:

> "... a bright orange cigar-shaped UFO near to ground level, right in front of us, stationary and silent. Ten seconds later, it appeared to turn on its side and vanish from sight."

During the evening Ann Hollis and her 17-year-old daughter, from Shawfield Road, Ash, Hampshire, witnessed a huge pink fireball passing across the sky, with smoke coming from its rear, described as looking like a distorted bright pink moon in size.

Ann Hollis:

> "It came across the front of the house and was stationary for a moment – I know it sounds ridiculous, but almost as if it was looking at us. After that, it moved up across the sky, dropped down again, and disappeared behind some houses."

At 8.20pm, Ian Smith – a member of the South Yorkshire UFO Society – was in Fenton Road, Kimberworth, when he saw:

> "... a cigar-shaped object in the sky that seemed to switch on like a light; it headed northwards, for about half a mile, and then 'switched off'."

Ten minutes later, Kimberworth resident – Ian Petres – sighted:

> "... an object in the sky, shaped like an ice-cream cone, showing a pale orange light at the back, with a flashing white light at the front."

Mick Hanson of the South Yorkshire UFO Society

Mick Hanson – the Rotherham based chairman of the South Yorkshire UFO Society – disclosed that since 26th December 1987, they had received 85 reported sightings – 30 of them over South Yorkshire. In another published article by the *Rotherham Record* on the 18th February, Mick Hanson told of further UFO sightings from around this locality, which included a sighting of a red object, shaped like a diamond, seen rising in the sky over Greasebrough and Upper Haugh areas, by South Yorkshire UFO Society members – Paul Garner and Ian Smith – before descending again. (**Source:** *Midweek News*, 9.2.1988 – '**Mother and Daughter spot UFO**')

Haunted Skies Volume Ten

UFO's – FACT OR FICTION?

Recent sightings at Kimberworth fuel speculation

Special report by Phil Coleman

The Rotherham based chairman of the South Yorkshire UFO Society has reported recent spates of UFO sightings over the Rotherham area.

The latest sightings over the Kimberworth area on Monday night, said UFO Society's Area Co-ordinator Mick Hanson.

Mick, of Goldsmith Drive, East Herringthorpe, told the Record this week: "We've just received reports of two sightings over Fenton Road, Kimberworth."

"The first, at 8.20 p.m., was seen by our member Ian Smith."

Ian, 41, of the Lanes, East Deane, described seeing "a cigar shaped object above Fenton Road."

Said Mick: "Ian said that he saw the object 'switch on like a light'. It travelled northwards for about half a mile and then just switched off again."

The second sighting — only ten minutes later, and again over Fenton Road — was made by a Mr. Ian Petres, of Claremont Street, Kimberworth.

His sighting, said Mick, was of an object "shaped like an ice cream cone, with a pale orange light at the back and a flashing white light at the front."

Mick said: "These are just two of many recent sightings in this area. Since December 26th, we've received 85 reported sightings — 30 of them over south Yorkshire."

He added: "The interesting thing is that these reports are being confirmed — with times — by different people in different places — and they all seem to be credible witnesses."

Mick cited the recent sightings over Ecclesfield, Sheffield, reported by a police woman and a policeman, and corroborated by other independent witnesses.

So, might there be some down to earth explanation?

"It seems highly unlikely," said Mick. "The Kimberworth sightings were made by men who know what to look for — and they definitely wouldn't be fooled by a cloud formation or a plane seen under unusual circumstances."

He added: "There was also a third witness, who doesn't wish to be named. He says he's seen similar sightings over the last five or so years."

Mick added that society members have also collected photographic evidence of recent sightings which is now being analysed at the UFO Society's Leeds Headquarters.

Asked whether the large number of UFO sightings worried him, Martin replied: "No, I'm just frustrated. Every time I go UFO spotting, they all seem to disappear."

Record readers photograph of alleged sighting of UFO over Kimberworth approximately ten years ago.

ROTHERHAM RECORD, FEBRUARY 11, 1988

9th February 1988 – Mysterious 'fog' kills dog in Shropshire

At 6am, Sheffield post office worker – Susan Jackson – was on her way to work, when she sighted:

> "... two lights, side by side in the sky. I tried to identify the source, as they weren't street lights, because they were the wrong colour and also too high in the sky on what was an extremely dark morning."

When Susan came out of work an hour later, for a break, there was no sign of them.

What lay behind a chilling incident that allegedly took place at 8am, involving a report from a man and woman from Oswestry, Shropshire, who were out exercising their dog? They came across a 45ft diameter yellow glowing cloud of something resembling fog, seen straddling a hedgerow, accompanied by a noise like rushing air, tingling sensation, and sulphurous smell. According to the unnamed couple, the dog ran into the *'fog'* and disappeared for a short time, before being found unconscious, wet and hot; its eyes were red and it died a few weeks later. (**Source: Jenny Randles,** *Time Storms*)

10th February 1988 – UFOs over South Yorkshire

Unemployed miner, Stephen Millard of Carleton Green (to the north-east of Barnsley, South Yorkshire) told of seeing:

> "... an object in the sky at 6.50pm. I first thought it was a communications satellite, but then realised it was too low for that.
>
> It couldn't have been an aircraft, as they have forward movement. I watched it for a few minutes and noticed that it was tilting – the full cross visible. When it tilted towards me, I could see a small dome on top. The round portholes were of less density and flickered. It was three times the size of a Jumbo Jet and about 600ft in altitude. It was aluminium in colour and had brightness like an electric welding arc."

'Hovercraft' shaped UFO

At 7pm, Harold Swift of Findon Street, Hillsborough, Sheffield, was with his wife, Janet, and 9-year-old daughter, and were driving up the hill on Chapeltown Road, towards *Asda*.

> "Just as we passed Ecclesfield Road School, we saw a number of red and green lights to out left, over rooftops. We were only moving at 30mph, so were able to see them clearly. The lights made us think of a hovercraft shape. As we drove down the hill, we lost sight of them."

Old-fashioned steam iron

Fifteen minutes later, Susan Killick of Parsons Cross, and her friend – Miss M. Wright – were on their way to a dog show and driving along Wordsworth Avenue, at the time.

> "As we were approaching the garage I looked up into the sky and saw several red lights in a line, and brought my friend's attention to it. We tried to follow, but lost sight of the objects as they headed away towards the direction of Ecclesfield."

Susan telephoned the police at Ecclesfield, and told them what had been seen. In a further interview she described the objects as:

> "... arrow-shaped lines of red lights – a bit like an old-fashioned steam iron. They also made a soft whirring, purring, sound."

Diamond-shaped UFO

At 7.20pm, Mr and Mrs Upton were about to put their car into its garage at Rotherham Road, Monk Bretton, Barnsley, when they saw:

> "... a large 'diamond'-shaped object pass over the roof of the garage, at low altitude. It was brilliantly-lit with banks of red, green, and white lights; it also had a dark central section inside. As it passed overhead, we heard a low humming noise."

Another witness was a woman resident of Wombwell, who was walking down Albany Road, on what was a very black night, with bright stars. She was nearly at her gate when she heard a droning noise, which increased in sound. Her first thoughts were that it was an aircraft, about to crash. She looked up into the sky and saw a large black mass, underneath which were a number of bright red and silver lights.

> "Although I didn't feel at all frightened, I must admit the hairs stood up on the back of my neck. I thought, for a few moments, that if anything happened to me, there was no-one to see where I've gone. I wondered if I watched it disappear over the main road, I might see the shape of it. It started to climb very steadily, heading towards the direction of Hoyland, and I could only see the lights. I went into my house and my husband said to me 'You look as if you've seen a ghost'."

Diamond or pyramid-shaped UFO

Just before 7.30pm, Mr Hoyle of Wombwell was sat in his parked car in the town centre, when he saw an object appear over the rooftops, at a height of approximately 200ft, moving slowly in a south-east direction, towards Hoyland. He described the object as:

> "... diamond, or pyramid-shaped, with apparently five sides to its 'body', surrounded by a mass of different coloured lights, but primarily white, green, and pink-red. I watched the object, which was moving very slowly, for less than a minute, and heard a whirring noise when it was closest from me (100ft away)".

Mr Hoyle described the object as a fantastic sight and unlike any aircraft he had ever seen. He also reported that, at the time of the sighting, another group of people beside a car had also seen it.

Triangular-shaped object over Yorkshire

At 7.30pm, a housewife from Birdwell, and her 24 year-old daughter, were on their way home, driving along the one-way system in Hoyland, after having left an aerobics class in the town centre. As they proceeded up the road towards Birdwell/Sheffield Road, they were astonished to see, directly in front of them, hanging in the sky, a strange object just behind *Oliver's Public House*. The object was described as very big, black, and triangular in shape – like a set square, pointing downwards – with a number of red and green lights inside it. The couple watched, transfixed, soon to be joined by another car, which pulled up behind them – the occupants also apparently having seen it as well.

Due to the daughter not being in possession of her glasses and unable to focus clearly on the unidentified object, the couple made their way home, collected the spectacles, and returned back to the original scene – this time driving down Milton Lane, towards Elsecar. The UFO had moved around three-quarters of a mile, in a south-east direction, and was now hovering directly above an electricity pylon, in the direction of Wentworth.

The object was huge in size, well over 200ft in length, and very low in altitude – approximately 200-300ft. It had bright green lights around its perimeter and a mass of randomly distributed red lights inside it, which were pulsating on and off. The object behind the light resembled a black metallic set square, which had changed position; the second time it was observed over the pylons in the fields behind the houses. The UFO was then seen to move away along the length of the electricity pylons, erratically through the air in a straight line, stopping and starting before disappearing from sight at around 7.45pm.

Following their return home, at 9.15pm, the couple looked through the front window of their house and saw the UFO once again, but this time high in the sky and travelling rapidly towards the West direction – its many coloured lights pulsating in the night sky.

At approximately 10.15pm, a woman resident of Dronfield was travelling towards Sheffield, having been to a dance at Holmfirth Community Hall with three friends. While driving along the A629 road, not far from Penistone, they saw some very bright *'spotlights'* in the sky and decided to stop the car, in order to obtain a closer look.

> *"The object came nearer and we realised it wasn't either an aeroplane or helicopter, as it kept stopping and starting – apart from that we couldn't hear any noise, such as rotor blades. It was in sight for approximately five minutes and appeared to be about 600ft off the ground, moving erratically in a North direction. It was diamond-shaped, dull metallic in colour, and very bulky in depth, with a row of brilliantly-lit cabin windows along the front section, which had three very bright 'spotlights'. The rear section was indistinct, though it appeared to be much bigger than a double-decker bus and was completely silent."*

Independent UFO Network researcher – Andy Walmsley – made enquiries into these matters, and found Venus and Jupiter were prominent in the south-western night sky at the place and time in question. Andy also considered auto kinesis, due to cloud movement of some kind, of lighted kite or balloon, but accepted it was impossible to confirm that this was, indeed, the explanation.

11th February 1988 – UFO over Lancashire

At Dodworth, near Barnsley, a miner (who asked that his name be kept confidential) was walking towards the family home, at 6.35am, when he saw a bright *'light'* in the distance.

> *"I thought it was unusual because it was larger and brighter than any star that I had seen. I stood and looked at it for a while and then fetched my wife. By this time the 'light' was almost above our heads, enabling us to see underneath it.*
>
> *We watched it move slowly away for a few minutes, heading in an East to North direction, gaining altitude as it did so."*

At 11.30pm, a ball-shaped object was visible in the eastern part of the sky over Carlton, near Barnsley, for over half an hour, until it disappeared from sight.

11th February 1988 – Triangular UFO over Beira

On the same date we learnt of an incident reported to Cynthia Hind, concerning a UFO sighted by the Chief Pilot of *Mozambique Airlines – Captain Simplicio Pinto – who was on a flight from Quelimane to the capital of Maputo Mozambique in a Boeing 737. The report makes very interesting reading, as it involves the sighting of three separate objects forming a triangle in the sky.

As there was no fuel at Quelimane he made a short stop at Beira, where he landed at 6.10pm. At the end of the runway there is a designated turnaround area, at which point he glanced up into the sky and saw a strange object described as:

> " . . . looking like a wing parachute or 'flying mattress', and appeared in layers. The object had a fluorescent light, like those mercury lamps which give off an intense white light. It seemed to be stationary, or moving extremely slow, and was nothing like I hade ever seen before".

After the passengers had disembarked, Chief Steward Isabel Lobo opened the door of the plane to allow one hundred and fourteen travellers to come aboard. As she did so, some of the people came running up onto the flight deck to ask her if she had seen the strange object in the sky.

Captain Pinto asked his co-pilot, Jamal, to make some enquiries with the Control Tower, to see if they had sent up a weather balloon. When Jamal spoke to the control tower, they told him it had appeared at 3pm about 125kilometres from Beira and that Air Force Radars had picked it up, but they had no idea what it was.

About half an hour later, Captain Pinto radioed the control tower asking for permission to take-off. At this point the object was still in the sky. The control tower asked him if he was willing to do so while the object was still there. Captain Pinto advised them he was going to take-off and he did, heading southwards towards Maputo.

*Linhas Aéreas de Moçambique Ltd., operating as LAM Mozambique Airlines (Portuguese: *LAM Linhas Aéreas de Moçambique*), is the flag carrier of Mozambique. The airline was established by the Portuguese colonial government of Mozambique, in August 1936, as a charter carrier named *Direcção de Exploração de Transportes Aéreos*, and was renamed in 1980 following reorganisation. LAM Mozambique Airlines is based in Maputo, and operates scheduled services in southern Africa and Europe. The company is a member of the International Air Transport Association, and the African Airlines Association since 1976. LAM Mozambique Airlines is on the list of airlines banned in the EU, as of April 2011

Captain Pinto:

> "As soon as we were up, I could see the object from much closer. I had no further doubts. It was not a plane; it was not a weather balloon. I continued to head southwards, by which time it was getting darker on land although much lighter in the air. The sun was on my right, allowing me to see this 'thing'; it was simply enormous. It seemed to be stationary south of Beira, but did not seem to be as high up as I had originally calculated. I climbed above 11,000ft but had to veer right a bit, as the lights were so intense they blinded me – there were three, like searchlights, placed in a triangle."

Captain Pinto then switched on the landing lights of the aircraft and switched them off, twice, seeking to establish any response from the object. The object then began to climb vertically – its lights dimming as it headed away from the observers.

> "I tried to locate the object on the radar, but no image showed. By this time we were flying at 24,000ft and 'it' seemed stationary above the mouth of the Save River, near Mambone, Mozambique. I continued to climb but it appeared very far away, even when we reached our cruising speed at 30,000ft."

Following enquiries made by Captain Pinto, he ascertained that two days before his sighting, an object with similar characteristics was seen over Medellin Airport, Colombia, South America, and that a UFO was seen over Madrid, a couple of days later.

Twinned with the UK

As part of the United Nations Africa Liberation Day, the city of Bristol, UK, signed a friendship agreement with Beira, in Mozambique, on 11 December 1990, to promote lasting peace and development, and enhance understanding between the two cities. During the past 20 years, Bristol and Beira have established a strong link through education programmes, cultural events and development work facilitated through the Bristol Link with Beira (BLB). The Link works closely with Bristol and Beira City Councils to organise projects and activities, promoting understanding of Beira in Bristol and contributing to the development of Beira. The link also involves exchange visits, joint educational work, cultural events, financial appeals and donation of equipment. BLB is a member of BITA and works closely with the Mozambique High Commission, in London, and the British High Commission in Maputo.

(Sources: Cynthia Hind, *AFRINEWS*, No. 3, May 1990/*The UFO Report*, Timothy Good, Avon Books, 1991)

12th February 1988 – UFO over Sheffield

Schoolgirl Joanne Shepherd, from Fox Hill, was sat watching the TV, when she was startled to see five bright *'lights'* in the sky.

> "I jumped up and went to the window, where I saw this large round egg shape, with red and blue lights on it, for about ten seconds. It then began to move away over our roof, and disappeared. I told my mum when she got in, and she said it sounded like a UFO."

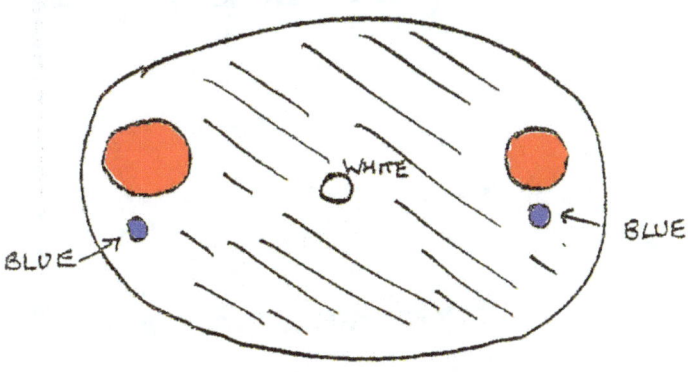

The next day's newspaper carried a story about a UFO seen over Ecclesfield. The witness on this occasion was Denise Watson of Shiregreen, near Ecclesfield. She told of being at home with her husband, when a friend of hers – Mrs Carol Cragg, who lives opposite – told her about something strange in the sky.

> "We saw some pale amber lights, with a pale pink and blue tint in places. The lights were not in the same place on the object and seemed to be in a circular motion

Haunted Skies Volume Ten

around it. At the same time an aircraft was flying overhead, but you could tell what we were seeing was no aircraft. The object seemed to hover in one place, for several minutes, until the aircraft passed it – then it moved northwards, towards Rotherham, when it disappeared at 8.10pm into clouds. I then reported it to Ecclesfield Police."

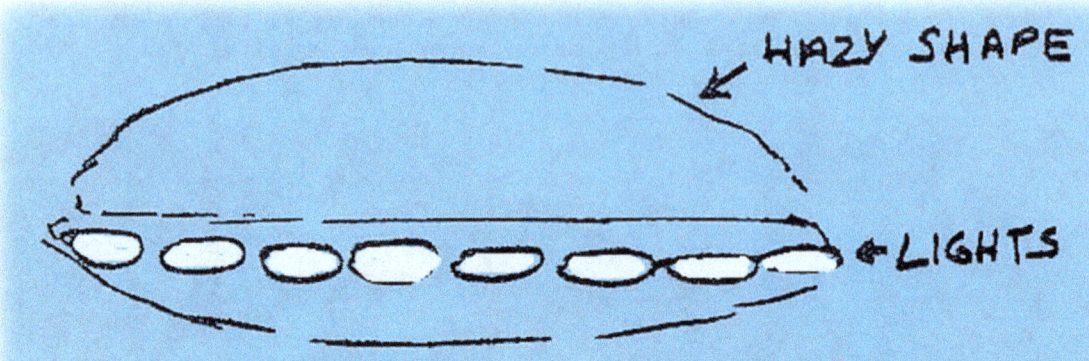

14th February 1988 – UFO over Essex

At 6.40pm, Mr R. Clarke was observing the night sky, when he saw:

> "...a light – the size of a star – appear in the west and slowly move eastwards. It then grew larger and changed into a cigar-shaped object, roughly about a quarter of the size of a full moon, before changing back in size to that of a star and disappeared from view."

(Source: Ron West)

16th February 1988 – Police sight UFO over West Midlands

At 9pm, West Midlands Police Sergeant Steve Godwin was on patrol in Delves Road, driving towards Caldmore, Walsall, accompanied by his Inspector – Roger Clarke. Steve told us:

"We noticed this massive object in the sky; it was bigger than anything I had ever seen in the sky before, and covered in flashing lights. As it was heading along the main flight path into Birmingham

Airport. I radioed the sighting into the Police Force Control Room, and later discovered two other police officers, who had been on foot patrol in Rose Hill, Willenhall, had seen what they described as an oblong object, showing red and green flashing lights, rotating around a fixed light source – presumably the same UFO we saw."

A spokesman for RAF Strike Command, at High Wycombe, commented on the officers' sighting, saying:

"We have yet to establish that there are such things as 'flying saucers', with 'little green men' inside".

Between 6.30pm and 7.30pm, antiques dealer Mr Swinnels from Mexborough, near Doncaster, and his son-in-law, watched a brilliant *'ball'* of orange light hovering over Marr Woods, in the direction of Barnburgh Church. After a short time it decreased in size, before fading from sight.

At 9.17pm, Police Sergeant Stuart Griffiths, and his colleague – PC Michael Powell – were on patrol in the Rosehill area of Willenhall, Staffordshire, when they saw:

" . . . a spinning object in the night sky; it had red and green flashing lights all around its circumference."

It appears that the same object *was* also seen by a Redditch, Worcestershire, housewife – Mrs Margaret Brannan – who watched what resembled *"a floating city in the sky, showing tiny windows"* pass over the Hewell Recreation Club, Tardebigge, on the same evening.

During the same month there was a spate of UFO activity around the Chase and Burntwood areas of the West Midlands, important enough to catch the attention of the Press.

(Sources: Sky Scan, Worcester/*Redditch Weekly Mail*, 26.2.1988 – 'It came from Outer Space'/Personal interviews)

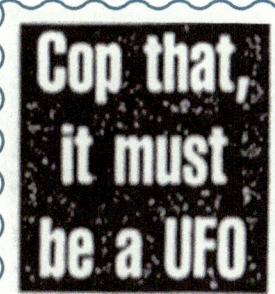

John Hurley

UFOs OVER CHASE: RAF CALLED IN

by **LYNETTE LLOYD**

It was this week confirmed that RAF Strike Command - the nerve centre of the RAF - is 'extremely interested' in a huge number of unexplained UFO sightings over the Chase area.

In the last month there have been no less than 38 unexplained sightings - 26 of them over Rugeley, and others over Burntwood, Boney Hay, Lichfield, Brownhills, Willenhall and Walsall.

The normal monthly average is four. Of these two may well be explained away.

The figures were confirmed by John Hurley of the Unidentified Flying Objects Studies and Investigations, who is in the process of submitting a report to Strike Command.

"Something very strange is going on," said John. "These people are quite definitely seeing something extraordinary."

"They are the unexplained sightings which can't be pinned down to being aircraft or air balloons or constellations in the sky.

"In just two hours over Rugeley we had 16 sightings. One of them was from a very frightened 12 year old girl who was with two friends when they saw a huge oval shaped craft hovering at around 600 feet. The bottom of the craft was covered in green, blue and white lights and had a small blue light which moved in and out of the object. It made no noise as it hovered, only when it moved off at a fast pace" said John.

"Whatever she was, it terrified her and she's been too frightened to leave her home since," said John.

"We had similar sightings from four police officers - two in Walsall and two in Willenhall

Many of the people who've spotted the craft give descriptions that are amazingly similar.

Most of the sightings occur at night, after 10.30pm.

A Lichfield man spotted a 'cigar-shaped' object hovering over a Lichfield church one morning recently, just before 8am.

Mr Edwards, of Friday Acre, said: "It was huge and had a mushroom shaped top which came doen to a long cigar shape underneath.

The latest incident came on Saturday when two men spotted a 'cigar-shaped' object near Rugeley Road in the Hazel Slade area

The two men, Robert Brough and Andrew Onions, say the object rise from behind trees

18th February 1988 – UFO seen over Sheffield

Another witness to something very odd, that evening, was Elise Oxley, who was then studying for a Degree at Sheffield University. She was interviewed by David Clarke and had this to say:

> "I was driving home from college, at about 6.30pm, when an object appeared in my windscreen. It seemed very low. It carried on heading in a westerly direction for about ten seconds, then turned 90° to fly south over Sheffield, before disappearing into cloud cover. After about 20 seconds, I stopped the car to have a better look. When I arrived home in Binstead Gardens, Wadsley Bridge, a minute later, I spoke to my husband, who told me he had also heard it and seen it disappear into clouds (my car radio had been on during the sighting, so I never heard any noise). About ten minutes later, we heard a noise and looked out of the back door and saw the object flying directly over our house. It appeared to be either very low or, if as high as previously seen, very big. It then tilted almost 90°, with the underside facing due west. We then lost sight of it 30 seconds later."

At 6.30pm, Caroline Glossop (45) – a graphic designer from Stannington, near Sheffield – was just driving through the village, when she also saw a strange object through her car windscreen.

> "It was massive in proportion to the car and was moving very slow and appeared low. It moved to my right. There were lights all around the outside of it, which gave an impression of a spinning motion. I wasn't frightened but elated. I drove home, parked the car, and rushed to the back of the house, where I was in time to see it fade away."

At 9.20pm an object, showing red and green lights, making a humming noise, was seen heading across the sky in a north to south direction over Sheffield. This was reported to the MOD. Mysterious flashing lights, travelling at high speed across the sky, were seen over Amptill and Stewartby, Bedfordshire, during this evening.

19th February 1988 – UFO display over Sheffield

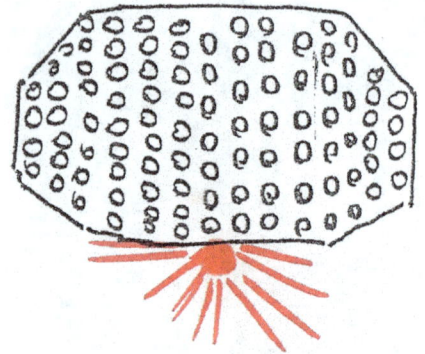

At 6.10am, Mr R. Helliwell of Greenoside, Sheffield, sighted a number of flickering bright lights in the sky, in the middle of which was a red light that gave out a beam. He called his wife, who then joined him to watch them, one of which occasionally shot away. They kept the lights under observation for 10-15mins, before losing sight of them. He later reported it to the *Sheffield Star*.

At 6.25am, a glass worker from Swinton, near Mexborough, was on the way home off nights, when he saw what appeared to be the same phenomena. Initially, he saw a bright light in the sky and mistook it for a star but then realised it wasn't moving.

"At the end of the road I stood and watched, as it came nearer and brighter. I watched it as it moved overhead, at a height of about 50ft, taking five or six minutes. It then headed away towards the direction of Swinton. The lights were in rows, like banks of flying floodlights – it was that low. I could have thrown a stone at it."

February 1988 – Blazing orange lights seen over Farnborough

In the same month, Farnborough taxi driver – Gerry Hurn – had just picked up Danielle from her boyfriend's house in Keith Lucas Road, when they saw:

". . . three bright blazing orange lights in the sky – like a helicopter formation – just hovering. All of a sudden, they veered away and vanished."

The couple drove around the Royal Aircraft Establishment and Southwood Golf Course, in an unsuccessful attempt to discover where the lights had gone, and later reported the incident to Omar Fowler, who said the description given was consistent with other reports of UFO activity in the area.

Mid-February 1988 – UFO photographed over Middleborough

The *Evening Gazette* (22.2.1988) told of a UFO sighted by amateur photographer Andrew Fornaby, and his friend – Mark Savage.

MY SPACE INVADERS!

Weird visitor in the night sky...

By MALCOLM PICKERING

AMATEUR photographer Andrew Farnaby believes he has captured real-life space invaders on film. 2374.

The 20-year-old community programme database worker was with four pals when, he claims, they saw a strange bright object in the night sky above Coulby Newham.

Andrew, of Forber Road, Linthorpe, Middlesbrough, dashed into his home to get his camera and tripod before the "visitors" and their "UFO" disappeared.

"I set it up on a long time exposure and the picture shows it quite clearly. It is like a bright tadpole with two tails."

One of his mates who also saw the "UFO" was Mark Savage, 18, of Rochester Road, who said: "It was really weird.

"There was no way it could have been a plane or a helicopter.

"It stayed too still. It was there for about 25 minutes, then it just went whoosh and vanished."

Said Andrew: "We did not tell anyone expect our parents what we had seen, because we were sure no-one would believe us.

"But when the film came back, there it was. It wasn't a star. The stars show up on the photo in a completely different way."

Cleveland Police say they had no other reports of UFO sightings on the night in question, last Wednesday.

● UFO spotters Andrey Farnaby, left, and Mark Savage with the photograph they claim is of a "flying saucer" — shown below in an enlargement.

Mysterious lights spark UFO alert

MYSTERIOUS flashing objects, travelling silently at a high speed, have been sighted in the skies over Ampthill.

Witness Patrick Lyall said he saw 20 or 30 lights grouped over Ampthill and Stewartby, coloured orange, red and white and moving erratically.

And he has dismissed suggestions that they could simply be aircraft or stars.

"Two of them went right over my head," said Patrick, of Cornwell Road, Bedford. "I could see seven or eight different lights on them and the strange thing was that they made no noise whatsoever.

"There's no way I could have mistaken them for anything but UFOs."

Speed

The 21-year-old decorator first noticed the objects as he and his friend, Robert Finch, drove from Bedford to Ampthill.

"We watched them for about half an hour. Sometimes two would join into one and they would move off at high speed. We weren't frightened. It was fascinating."

Needless to say, nobody believed him when he arrived home.

The incident happened last Thursday night and although no sightings were reported to the police, a spokesman at Cranfield aerodrome air traffic control confirmed that there had been queries about similar sightings on the same night.

Nearby RAF Chicksands confirmed that they had no suspicious radar signals on that night.

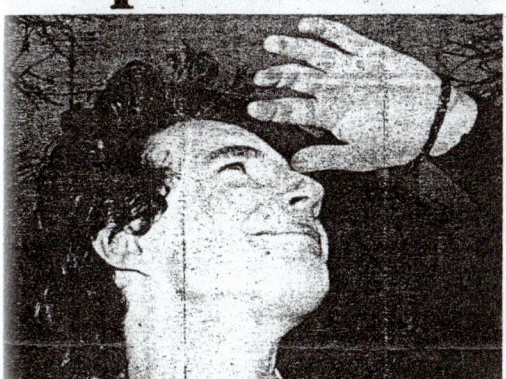

● Watcher of the skies: Patrick Lyall.

22nd February 1988 – Bright blue light over Bournemouth

At 7.35pm, teenagers – Michelle Dodd, Robert Cook, Dean Hyde, Peter Roberts and Gary Day – contacted the *Bournemouth Advertiser*, after sighting brilliant blue lights that lit up the sky for about 15 seconds.

26th February 1988 – UFO over Bury

At 7.30pm, a small white *'light'*, with a *'tail'*, was seen to pass under a light aircraft flying over Tile Hall, Wickhambrook, by the Reverend Dr. Scrivener, who was so intrigued he contacted RAF Honington, Wattisham, Mildenhall and Lakenheath, but they were unable to explain what it was that he had seen. After the sighting was published by the *Bury Free Press,* Sharon Alcock later contacted the newspaper to tell them she had also seen the object, which *"wriggled off into the distance."*

Timothy Good

Also on this date was a lecture given by Tim Good, at Croydon and District Writers Circle, held at the United Reformed Church in Addiscombe Grove, East Croydon. Tim showed copies of Top Secret documents, passed between the American CIA and the President's Office, along with sworn statements of encounters with UFOs by astronauts and pilots.

(Sources: *Bury Free Press,* 4.3.1988 – 'Priest puzzled by UFO, 11.3.1988/*Beckenham & Penge Advertiser,* Kent, 22.2.1988 – 'UFO expert drops in')

28th February 1988 – UFO over Rotherham

At 7.20pm, Robert Hodgson was walking up Central Drive, Rotherham. It was a beautiful clear evening, with a moonlit sky showing plenty of stars, when he saw what he took to be the fuselage of an aircraft in the sky.

> *"About a quarter of the object – the rear end – came away, with sparks coming from it. I thought it might have been a bomb that exploded. All of sudden, it vanished."*

According to David Clarke, enquiries made revealed that a Mrs Dimbleby of Ravenfield, Rotherham, had seen what she described as *"a big shooting star"* moving over the sky, at about the same time (give or take a few minutes), the back end of which appeared to fall away and disintegrate in flight. It appears the parties involved may have seen a fireball, rather than a UFO, on this occasion.

29th February 1988 – UFO over Lichfield

Mr George Edwards contacted the *Lichfield Mercury,* reporting that he had sighted a long, silvery cigar-shaped object, hovering over the Cherry Orchard area, at 8am. The newspaper published his story on the 11th March 1988 – 'Sightings endorses reports of UFOs'. It also included an account from another man, who told of having seen a similar object in the sky over Eastern Avenue.

MARCH 1988

1st March 1988 – UFO over Wales and Essex

At 9.30pm, Sally Aspden of Conwy, Gwynedd, was out walking near her home, with two members of her family, when they saw a *'bright light'* in the western sky, low over the mountains.

> *"Due to low cloud, no other stars were seen. After about five minutes it began to rise towards us – slow to begin with, then increasing gradually, curving round as it did so, flying towards the south. As it turned, the white light at the front was no longer visible; instead we saw two red lights, forming a line perpendicular to its flight. Two more red lights appeared in front of these, as if the front of the 'craft' were rising in comparison to the rear. Their brightness seemed to be increasing and decreasing*

regularly at intervals of about half a second. It made a noise like an old-fashioned airplane – a steady low pitched droning, as it rose towards us, and fading as it turned away – before disappearing beyond the mountain, south of the village. The next evening, 2nd March 1988, we saw the object again; that was the last time we ever saw it."

(Source: *FSR,* Volume 33, No. 3, 1988)

At 9.40pm, Malcolm Burnage (41) of Kendall Road, Colchester, Essex, was walking home, when his attention was caught by a vapour trail in the sky.

"I discounted an aeroplane, because the vapour trail was red. I then wondered if it was a meteor but realised it was cigar-shaped, with pinpricks of lights along its side. It halted in mid-air, before flashing across the sky at a terrific speed."

(Source: Ron West/Brenda Butler)

2nd March 1988 – UFO over Bath

At 6.35am, night nurse Elda Coretti was finishing her shift at Bath's Royal United Hospital, when she saw *"a yellow-orange glowing object – as big as a double-decker bus – rushing across the sky, which changed from circular to cigar in shape, before vanishing over the horizon"*, leaving her shocked. After ringing the police, the matter was brought to the attention of Squadron Leader Ernie Dunsford, from RAF Lyneham, who was quoted as saying:

"I don't think this lady should be knocked. We certainly had no planes in the air. I've got to keep an open mind on this."

(Source: *Daily Star,* 2.3.1988 – 'My UFO encounter – by shocked Nurse')

MY UFO ENCOUNTER – BY SHOCKED NURSE

NIGHT nurse Elda Coretti sparked a military alert yesterday after seeing a UFO.

The glowing object—as big as a double-decker bus—soared across the sky before turning from circular to cigar shape.

Then it vanished over the horizon leaving Elda, 50, stunned and shocked.

Police and defence officials immediately launched a probe into the sighting, which happened at 6.35 a.m. as Elda was finishing her shift at Bath's Royal United Hospital.

STAR REPORTER

She said: "I watched it from the window as long as I could. It was 'yellow-orange.

"I ran in and told my colleagues, then rang the police."

Elda added: "I hadn't been drinking or dabbling in the medicine cupboard —I know what I saw."

At nearby RAF Lyneham, Squadron Leader Ernie Dunsford said: "I don't think this lady should be knocked.

"We certainly had no planes up in the air. I've got to keep an open mind on this."

● A new organisation called Skyscan has been set up in Worcester to probe the recent flood of UFO sightings all over Britain.

THE STAR, Wednesday, March 2, 1988

3rd March 1988 – UFO over South Yorkshire

At 9.20pm, a group of four students were driving from Manchester to Sheffield, travelling on the A628 Woodhead Road, which runs over the Moors, when they noticed an unusual plane in the sky. This was no aircraft bound for Manchester Airport but a triangular-shaped object, showing six or seven bright red lights, flying point first over Howden Moors, towards the direction of Emley Moor TV mast. The object was in sight for about 5mins, at an estimated height of 3,000ft, before being lost from view. Another witness to what undoubtedly appears to have been the same UFO was lorry driver Barry Bellamy, from York, who was travelling along the A1 in Sheffield.

4th March 1988 – UFOs tracked on radar

SURREY MIRROR
Reigate and Redhill edition

No. 5814   THURSDAY, MARCH 10, 1988   Editorial: Phone Reigate 223411 Price 20p

UFO SIGHTING CONFIRMED BY GATWICK RADAR

MYSTERY IN THE SKY

Surrey Mirror, Redhill. 10 MAR 1988

By Christine Milne

A STRANGE UFO hung ominously over the Reigate area for four hours on Friday evening.

Two very bright white lights shone out from the unknown object which a Reigate man estimated to be nearly 200 feet across.

After hovering almost stationery over the Buckland area, the craft slowly moved away to the north west.

The UFO could also be seen by people in Redhill and Dorking, and New Scotland Yard had had reports of sightings from as far away as Watford and Wimbledon.

And Gatwick Airport radar controllers said something showed on their radar screens which they could not account for.

"It was so strange said Mr Joe Clarke, aged 35, from West Street, Reigate. "It was an ominous presence because it was something that should not have been there."

The night-time drama began at 6 pm when Mr Clarke's wife and daughter told him they could see two parallel bright lights approaching in the sky from the west.

He didn't take much notice but when he went into the garden an hour later the lights were still there, hanging somewhere over Buckland.

He telephoned a relative in Dorking who could also see the lights, and his father and sister in Redhill spotted them too.

From the distance between the lights and by taking bearings from various objects in the landscape, Mr Clarke reckoned the UFO was between 100 to 200 feet wide, and about 2,000 feet up in the sky.

At 8.20 pm Mr Clarke, a caretaker at East Surrey College's School of Art, rang Reigate police station to report the sighting.

Three police officers turned up and asked: "Where are the little green men then?"

"But their attitude changed when I took them into the garden and showed them the lights," said Mr Clarke.

Checks by police with Heathrow Airport revealed that people in Watford and Wimbledon had reported the UFO sighting to New Scotland Yard.

They also contacted Gatwick and were told: "Yes, there's something strange on the screen we can't account for."

Mr Clarke and his family watched the object for another hour and a half before it started to move slowly away into the wind over Box Hill.

Mr Clarke points to the spot where he saw the UFO.

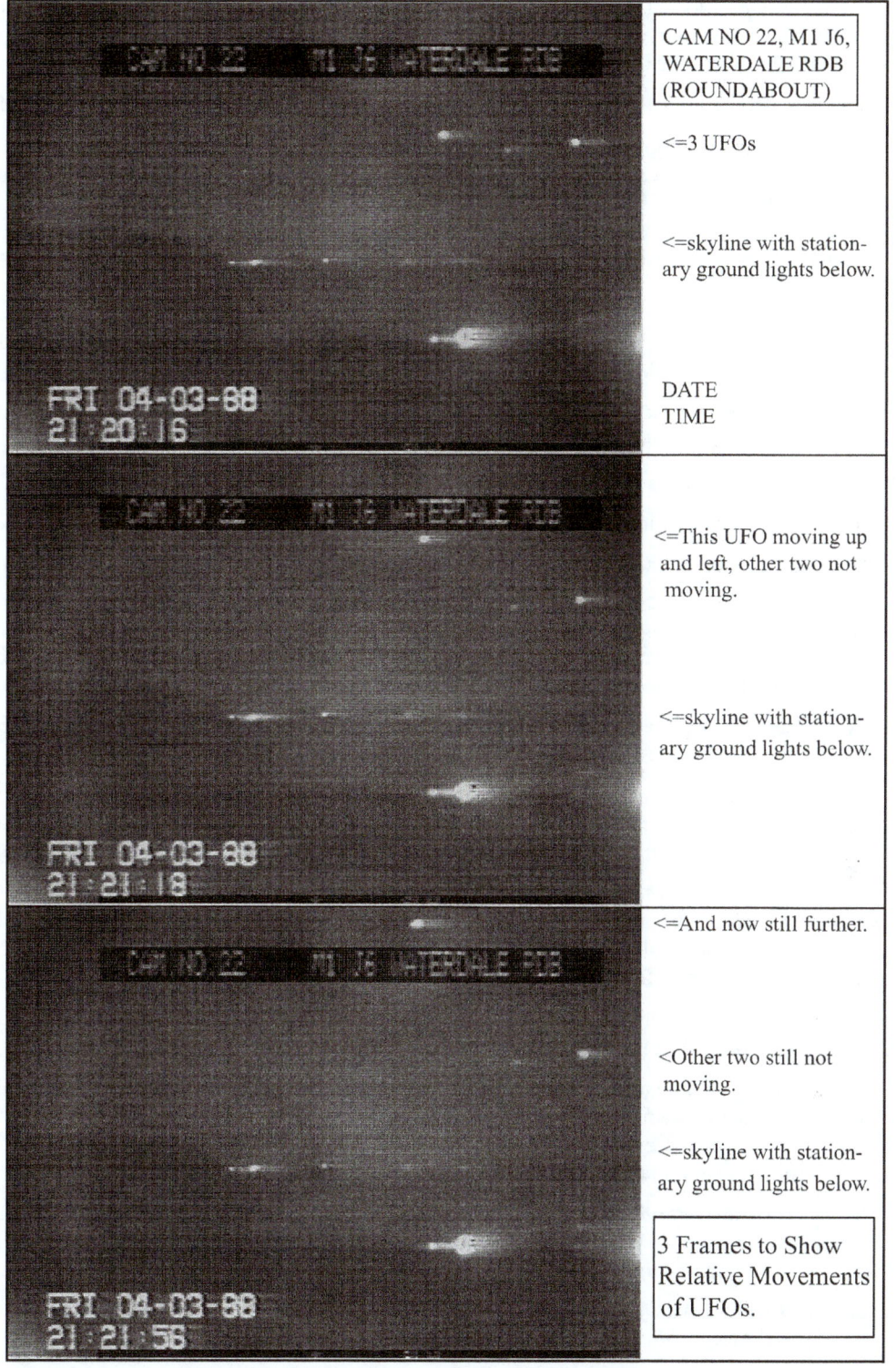

At 6pm, Reigate resident – Joe Clarke – was approached by his wife and daughter, who told him about two strange *'lights'* they had seen in the sky, approaching their position. Initially he didn't take much attention, but when he went into the garden he was surprised to see:

> "... two lights, hovering in the sky, 100-200ft apart, about 2,000ft high, over the direction of Buckland".

His curiosity aroused, Joe telephoned a relative in Dorking and father and sister at Redhill, who confirmed that they had the two *'lights'* under observation. He then telephoned the police, who sent three officers. When they arrived, they jokingly asked him *"where the little green men were?"* ... an attitude which soon changed when they saw the lights for themselves, before they eventually moved away towards Box Hill. The officers contacted Gatwick Airport and asked them to check the radar, and were told:

> "Yes, we have something strange on the radar screen. We can't account for it."

Between 9pm-9.40pm, the same evening, several bright *'lights'* were seen in the sky and captured on the M25 Motorway observation video. Chief Inspector Chris Partridge, of the Hertfordshire Police, said:

> "The lights were filmed by a police car in the area. Despite every effort to find out what they are, nobody has been able to come up with an explanation. The tapes will stay in police records."

He contacted Air Traffic Control. They told him:

> "We are unable to establish what they are. Two lights were moving – the other two were stationary."

Gordon Creighton, Editor of *FSR*, was able to obtain a copy of this film. He discovered, from careful examination, that:

> "There were at least three large white spheres present simultaneously, either totally stationary or moving about – sometimes very slowly; other times, very quickly – over the Rickmansworth area. The video also shows a total of six large white spheres, captured on the police video camera."

One of the witnesses was Daphne Knapp, of Rickmansworth, who told Gordon Creighton and his colleague – Brian Drummond:

> "I happened to look out of the front door of the house and see a shining green object, moving towards me in front of the houses, just above the level of the bungalows. It was flat bottomed, showing two red lights at the rear – not flashing like aircraft lights would do. It made this humming noise as it moved along."

Another witness was Mrs G. Dawn (aged 46) of Grimwade Street, Ipswich, in Suffolk. She was outside, looking up at the night sky, at 9pm, when she saw a pearl-shaped object moving through the sky, accompanied by some other smaller luminous objects. (**Source: Ron West, Brenda Butler**)

In May 1991, Gordon wrote to the editor of the *Watford Observer*, giving the facts of what had taken place, after having examined the police video. He was totally ignored by them!

Gordon was also to hear of a huge object reported in the sky over the airport, south of Gatwick, which was there for some hours, before being seen to move away towards the direction of Watford. Further enquiries made with the principal of the East Surrey College at Redhill, to trace and interview Mr Joe Clarke, were unsuccessful. Gordon was told that they had nobody of that name having worked for them.

On 23rd March 1988, the *Watford Observer* published this comment, under the heading of 'UFO down to Venus': *'Experts have scotched fears about a round white light spotted above Rickmansworth. Passers-by thought the light was a UFO but experts say there is no cause for alarm; the light was simply a planet, probably Venus'.*

(**Sources:** *Surrey Mirror* [Reigate and Redhill edition] 10.3.1988 – 'UFO sighting confirmed by Gatwick Radar – mystery in the sky'/*FSR*, Volume 42, No. 3, August 1997)

6th March 1988 – UFO over Godmanchester

Bridge Place

Pauline Emerson (then aged 14) was attending to her horse 'Charlie' at the family home in Bridge Place, Godmanchester, Huntingdonshire, located off the A14, north-west of Cambridge, at 7.30pm when she heard a faint noise, which she took to be an aircraft approaching.

> "I glanced casually upwards and saw this awful thing. It was like a black dense square, with a 'bump' in its middle, covered in perforations, with what looked like antennas sticking out of each corner, and was about one and a half metres wide and twenty metres long. As it passed overhead, it made a disgusting noise, leaving a horrible smell in the air. I was very frightened and ran into the house screaming for my mother and father, who hadn't seen the UFO but told me they had heard a loud vibrating sound, followed by the air being sucked out of the room and then an awful smell."

Enquiries made by Ron West – an Investigator for the East Anglia UFO & Paranormal Research Association – with RAF Alconbury, Connington, Wyton and little Storton, revealed no aircraft had been flying over Godmanchester at the time given.

During an interview with Pauline, Ron West discovered that her eyesight had been affected by the incident; she complained of blurred vision and was later treated for enlarged pupils. Weather conditions for that day were fine, with high cloud. The object was first seen over the top of nearby council offices, heading in an east to west direction. It was observed disappearing behind a nearby road bridge.

Ron West contacted RAF Alconbury (about three miles away from the

Pauline Emerson

incident) about this matter, and was informed that no aircraft from the Base were flying. The pony was left in a very agitated state.

Ron:

> "Could it have been hydrogen sulphide, often associated with the smell – sometimes noted with UFOs?"

Tea-hee... how the teabag UFO might look

Teabag UFO zaps Pauline

SCHOOLGIRL Pauline Emerson was stirred up yesterday—after a close encounter with a teabag-shaped UFO.

Pauline, 14, was feeding animals in her garden when the smelly spaceship—black with little perforations—zoomed within five yards of her.

Now she is off school and taking tranquillisers to get over the shock.

Yesterday she said: "It was like a teabag. It was so black it shone out. The smell was really disgusting.

"Charlie, my horse, was trembling and my radio went off."

Her mum Barbara was inside their home near Godmanchester, Cambs, at the time and remembers it shaking and the sensation of oxygen being sucked from it.

An education welfare officer who interviewed Pauline afterwards said: "She is a truthful kid, she wouldn't make this up."

Earlier this week a school dinner lady reported UFOs shaped like oranges flying over Beeston, Notts.

We contacted Pauline – now married and living in the Lincoln area – who told us she still suffers from eyesight problems following the appearance of the UFO, and that despite many visits to the opticians, the situation remains unchanged. Oddly, her eyesight appears to improve with age rather than deteriorate.

(Source: As above/Personal interview)

For her courage in reporting the matter to the Press, she was ridiculed by many – especially after the banner grabbing headlines 'Smelly Spaceship', showing an alien piloting a teabag. According to Ron West, who took charge of the investigation, together with Brenda Butler, the matter was later discussed with the School Education Officer, who spoke highly of Pauline's character and said she was well regarded at school, but felt he had no other course of action than to move her to another school, because of the unwarranted attention she was now receiving.

We were told that, as a result of a newspaper appeal, at least two other people came forward to say they had seen a similar *'craft'* moving across the Cambridgeshire sky, but not on the same day when Pauline saw it.

UFO SIGHTING ACCOUNT FORM

SECTION A

Please write an account of your sighting, make a drawing of what you saw and then answer the questions in section B overleaf as fully as possible. Write in BLOCK CAPITALS using a ball point pen.

On Wednesday the 2nd of March at 4 o'clock I went outside to clean out my animals. At 7 o'clock I was mucking out my horses stable and he was out in the field. At 7.30 I was packing away my tools which I had been using and whent to pick up my radio which I had stood near the wall. As I went to do this I heard a faint noise I didn't take any notice at first as I thought it would be an areoplane but then I looked again. I could see a real black square in the sky blacker than black could ever be. It was making a terrible noise and there was a disgusting smell so horrible it is impossible for me to describe. It was about 1 and a ½ metres long and 20 mm

Please continue on a separate sheet if necessary.

DRAWING*

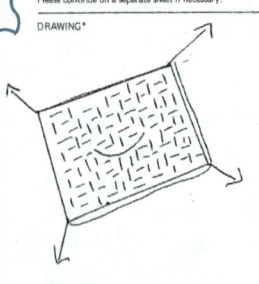

Your full name (Mr/Mrs/Miss/Ms) PAULINE EMERSON Age 14
Address 27 BRIDGE PLACE
GODMANCHESTER, CAMBRIDGESHIRE
Telephone No. 411838 (STD 0480)
Occupation during last two years: Schoolgirl
Any professional, technical or academic qualifications or special interests

Do you object to the publication of your name?
*Yes/No. *Delete as applicable.
Today's Date 9-5-88. Signature P. Emerson

*If preferred, use a separate sheet of paper.

Haunted Skies Volume Ten

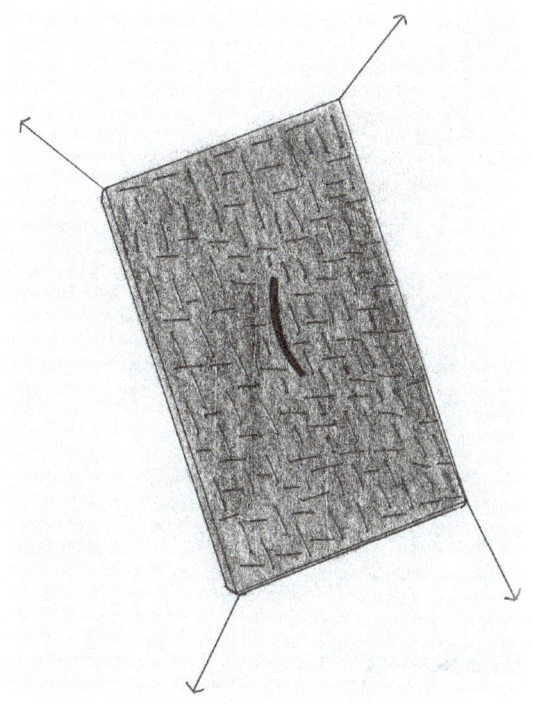

7th March 1988 – Bright red 'ball of light' seen, Walsall

Francois Butler (10) of Sutton Road, Walsall, was looking southwards, when he saw a bright red *'ball of light'* stationary in the sky for about five minutes, before it disappeared from view. Suggestions for what he saw included Jupiter and Venus as being responsible. He wasn't the only one to see this phenomenon. (**Source: John Hurley**)

President George Bush & UFOs

On 7th March 1988, during a Presidents Rally in Rogers, Arkansas, Vice President George Bush was about to go into a building to meet with reporters, when Charles Huffer – a UFO researcher – approached him. (This was in the days before 911). Mr Huffer asked George Bush:

> "Will you tell the people the truth about UFOs?"
>
> "Yes"...

replied George Bush ... then realising what he had just said, Bush added:

> "If we can find it, what it is. We are really interested".

Huffer replied:

> "You'll have it, you'll have it. It's in there." (I meant it would be in his briefing when he became president). Declassify it and tell us, ok?"

George Bush:

> "OK, alright, yes."

George Bush then entered the building, where he met with the local Arkansas Press. Huffer remained outside, waiting for Bush to come back out. When he did emerge from the building, Huffer, with his tape-recorder running, told George Bush, *"Going to hold you to that promise."*

Haunted Skies Volume Ten

"Alright, OK", said Huffer, *"You're going to get it."* (I meant the UFO information)

"Why don't you send me some information about it?" asked Bush.

"No", said Huffer, *"You're a CIA man. You know all that stuff."*

"I know some", replied Bush. *"I know a fair amount."*

10th March 1988 – UFO over Ossett

At 8.45pm on the 10th March 1988, UFO investigators on the A61 highway, North of Sheffield, England, saw a large pulsating orange ovoid UFO fly by at 400ft altitude.

At 10.55pm, Dianne Wild (28) was closing the kitchen curtains, when she noticed a brilliant yellow light approaching from the south direction, accompanied by a distinct humming noise. She looked out to see an object in the sky heading towards her position.

> *"It was shaped like a cross and about the size of a football field. I could see a red flashing light towards its rear and yellow lights along its side. Underneath was grey, with black stripes, as it passed overhead slightly to the left of our house. I have never seen anything as big or as clear in the sky before."*

(Source: Mark Birdsall, YUFOS/Timothy Good, *The UFO Report 1990*, p25)

18th March 1988 – spate of sightings over Staffordshire

During the middle period of this month, many people contacted the newspaper and police, telling of having seen two *'bright lights'* in the sky. They included housewife Veronica Yates of Drayton Street, Walsall. She was hanging washing on the line when:

> *"... 'light' appeared above me. It had a dome on top and two searchlights on the front. I was rooted to the spot. I turned around. When I looked back, it had gone."*

Other sightings of similar objects occurred all over the Dorking area during this period, many of which were explained away as being Venus and Jupiter, in conjunction with each other, reflecting the sun. According to the various astronomical institutions, the two planets were highly visible (weather permitting) between 6pm and 10pm. We accept that this may well have been the explanation for some of the sightings but not all.

(Sources: *Dorking and Leatherhead Advertiser* [Surrey], 17.3.1988 – 'Venus is to blame for distraction'/ *Walsall Observer*, 18.3.1988 – 'A UFO invasion by Jupiter')

20th March 1988 – Orange 'globe' over Essex

At 5.45pm, housewife Jane Hancock (48) of Radwinter Road, Ashdon, Saffron Waldon, Essex, happened to look out of the window, when she was amazed to see:

> *"... a large red-orange 'ball of light' moving through the sky, in an east to west direction; it then slowed down before increasing its speed, and was soon lost from view."*

(Source: Ron West, Brenda Butler)

SIZE OF TEA PLATE

26th March 1988 – Rotherham UFO Conference

Rotherham assembly rooms were the venue for the annual Yorkshire UFO Society UFO Conference, entitled: *UFOs Above Top Secret*. The speakers included Timothy Good.

(Sources: *Doncaster Star*, 25.3.1988/ *Yorkshire Post*, 21.3.1988 – 'UFOs in the frame'/*Rotherham and South Yorkshire Advertiser*, 18.3.1988 – 'UFO spotters flock to town')

Also on this date was a talk given by Andy Roberts, at Sheffield, held at the Library Theatre, entitled *Spook Lights of the Pennine Moors*.

26/27th March 1988 – UFO over Luton

Irene Armstrong of Manton Drive, Luton, Bedfordshire, contacted the *Luton News* after sighting something strange in the sky, two nights running.

> "I first saw it Saturday night, between 8.30pm and 10.30pm. It looked as if it was over Dunstable area. On Sunday night, 27th March, it was there again, so I had a look through binoculars and saw a long shape – like a disjointed arrow, with orange lights on it. It resembled a cluster of diamonds."

(Source: *Luton News*, 31.3.1988 – 'Strange sight in the sky')

Close encounter of the wierd kind

A DRIVER has had a close encounter of a strange kind on a dark country lane near South Harting.

Mr. Dennis Hoare, of Barncroft Way, Leigh Park, Havant, was driving his Ford Granada on the B2146 near the National Trust house Uppark when the car began to behave strangely.

"It was dark, all of a sudden the radio started buzzing and the next thing I knew the headlights were going dim then I saw my ammeter was at full discharge," he said.

"Then I looked to my left where there is a dell and the land sweeps up. I could see what looked like arc lamps on top."

NORMAL

As he drove on the radio and ammeter returned to normal as he went on to South Harting.

But on the way home later the same evening the radio began to buzz again as he reached the road near Uppark.

"I just kept my toe down – I didn't want to stop in the middle of nowhere. When you are right out in a dark place like that you imagine all sorts of things," he said, adding that the car had worked perfectly well both before and since that evening.

UNUSUAL

"I just wonder if anyone else has had something like this happen to them."

A spokesman for the nearby Bordon garrison said it would be very unusual for the army to be doing any exercises in this area because it was not MoD land.

"I would very much doubt if it was any of our exercises," said Col. David Bagnall-Oakley. He added that it was not likely either to be the RAF flying helicopters in this particular area.

Petersfield Post. 9 March 1988.

30th March 1988 – Close encounter, Birmingham

At 5.30am, Carol Thomas (45) and her daughter Helen (25) were walking to work in the Castle Vale area of Birmingham – a regular journey that normally lasted 15 minutes – when they both heard a distant humming noise, which seemed odd as most factories in the area were closed. Carol:

> "Suddenly we were both startled to see a light shining down on us from above – like a bright torch. We stopped and became frightened, as the light grew larger and larger until it was directly above our heads. I remember holding my daughter's hand and then starting to feel dizzy. The next thing I remember was walking along the alley with my daughter, but something was wrong. We were both in a daze and walking erratically, because we were so dizzy. My daughter was wearing a leather coat, which was wet – yet it hadn't been raining. We felt very strange and, when we reached the mill, the security guard commented that we were very late for work. We don't remember much about that day at all, but since then we have been very nervous when we walk to work."

Haunted Skies Volume Ten

HYPNOTIC CLUE TO SPACE KIDNAPPERS

UFO watcher Tony Dodd claims spacemen kidnap Britons from their beds and beam them up to their flying saucers.

Once on board the spacecraft the humans are medically examined by the aliens.

Ex-cop Tony says the aliens blank out the memories of the people they have examined before setting them free.

But details of the encounters can still be unlocked under hypnosis.

People who experience the sensation of having lost part of their day may have been abducted by aliens, says Tony.

He claims a 41-year-old housewife from Colne, Lancs, was snatched from bed while her husband slept next to her.

Under hypnosis she recalled a three-hour ordeal at the hands of three silver-suited spacemen who examined her on an operating table in their craft.

Two friends from Keighley, Yorks, also experienced a 45-minute memory loss during a car journey together across local moors.

Ordeal

Under hypnosis they remembered being beamed up to an alien craft.

A 32-year-old Halifax woman is claimed to have been beamed up to a spacecraft in a ball of brilliant light. The terror of her ordeal was later unlocked by hypnosis.

On some occasions the examination of humans are carried out by robots under the aliens' command, say the UFO experts.

THE FORCE... ex-copper Tony

John Hurley

The matter was initially brought to the attention of John Hurley – then Secretary of the Birmingham Group – UFOSIS, who spoke to the women and then contacted UFO Investigator Tony Dodd – a retired Police Sergeant from West Yorkshire.

Tony Dodd

During interviews held with the two women, they complained of having suffered *reddening and blistering of the skin on their faces and arms – like sunburn – nosebleeds, and a discharge from their navels.* Helen also found a patch of hair missing from the nape of her neck.

Hypnosis conducted by professional hypnotist Joyce Dinsdale

On 12th March 1994, following a session of hypnosis, arranged by Tony, both women described being subjected to *"an examination by 'little men',"* described as having *"tiny ears, big black eyes, with three long fingers"*, while lying naked on some sort of examination table, with what looked like netting over their legs.

Carol told of *"some sort of operation conducted, involving the application of a tube that was pushed into her stomach"*, used to extract what she presumes to have been human eggs. She also mentions about *'their'* interest in her hair and a pulling sensation (which may be consistent with the later discovery of a patch of hair missing?) Some time later, she was allowed off the table and shown a large screen on which was seen a succession of symbols, including triangles, squares and wavy lines, followed by film footage showing wars and explosions – a familiar theme of so many other accounts brought to our attention, over the years.

Carol mentioned having seen other *'beings'* in the room,

> "one of whom was tall, with long blonde hair and blue eyes, and wearing a silver suit, with a blue badge containing a circle, triangle, and two wavy lines".

The next thing she remembered was putting on her clothes, feeling dizzy and disorientated, and being back in the alley with Helen, who was asking her why her leather coat was wet.

Helen told more or less the same story, although she described her captors as having *"two fingers"*. One of them pushed a thin rod, with a *'silver ball'* on the end, into her nose. When the rod was withdrawn, the *'silver ball'* was missing.

> "A piece of wire was inserted into my ear, followed by a glass tube being placed into my navel fluid and then drained [as in her mother's case]. A large 'D'-shaped glass cup was placed onto my head. A small circular object was placed onto my hair at the bottom of my neck, pulling my hair – which I didn't like. I remember seeing some sort of 'screen', with symbols, followed by a 'wafer' being placed into my mouth, which I spat out. I was then taken back into the room, where I saw my mother stood next to a tall blonde, beautiful woman, who was wearing a silver badge [as previously described by her mother] and was given back my clothes. The next thing I was aware of was being back in the alley."

We hoped to find out more about this interesting matter, but there is very little information about it other than on Roy Lake's website. Details of the incident and subsequent allegation of abduction were published in an edition of *UFO* magazine during in September/October 1994. It would have been of great interest to have spoken to them with regard to their experience as an update but this has proved unsuccessful so far. We were also unsuccessful in tracing any knowledge of the hypnotherapist Joyce Dinsdale, which seemed strange, but these events were, after all, a quarter of a Century ago now!

(Source: As above/Tony Dodd/Quest *Alien Investigator*/*UFO Magazine* September/October 1994)

According to John Hurley, of UFOSIS, there was an upsurge of UFO sightings for the end of February/March 1988, over the Cannock Chase area, and included 38 separate reports from places such as Rugeley, Burntwood, Boney Hay, Lichfield, Brownhills, Willenhall and Walsall.

> "In just two hours, over Rugeley, we had 16 sightings. One of them was from a very frightened 12-year-old girl, who was with friends, when they saw a huge oval object hovering in the sky, about 600ft off the ground. It was covered in green, blue, and white lights, and had a small blue light moving in and out of it. The girl doesn't want to leave her house – that's the effect it had on her."

Carol Thomas (right) and daughter Helen

CHAPTER 5

APRIL TO MAY 1988

APRIL 1988

7th April 1988 - 'Ball of Fire' over Essex

AT 1.30am, William Johnson (aged 62) of Tanys Dell, Harlow, Essex, had occasion to go to the bathroom. As he entered the room, he saw that it was illuminated by flickering orange flames from outside.

"I drew the curtains and saw a red pulsating fire or light in the air, to the right-hand side of the frosted window."

By the time he made his way to an open window, there was nothing to be seen. When he told his family what he had observed, they laughed at him. (According to other sources, similar objects were seen that evening over the Midlands.)

Another witness was Betty Fudge, who lived a short distance along the same street. She was getting ready for bed, at 1.30am, when the room was lit up with red light,

"... bright enough to read by. I went to the window, thinking one of the houses nearby was on fire. I threw back the curtains and saw this 'ball of fire', stationary in the sky; it looked to be about 2ft in diameter. I stood there staring at it, not knowing what to do, as it began to move slowly towards the direction of The Stow."

Brenda Mumford, living halfway down the same road, was awoken by a swishing noise and orange lights streaming through the venetian blinds.

"I rushed over, thinking someone's house was on fire, and looked out, seeing a football sized orange object, about level with our rooftop. I was so pleased to find out that other people had seen the object. I thought I was going mad."

(Source: Ron West/Brenda Butler/East Anglian UFO & Paranormal Research Association/ *Harlow & Epping Newspaper*, 5.5.1988 - 'Gee whiz, more flying oranges!')

Haunted Skies Volume Ten

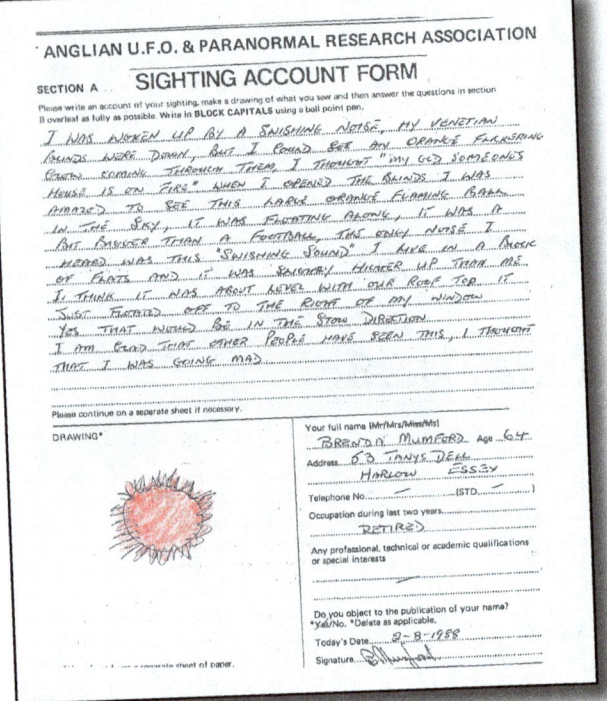

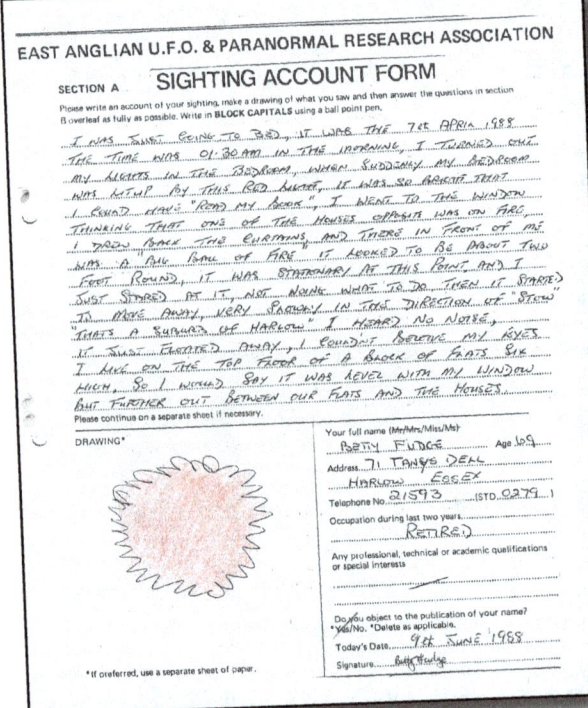

10th April 1988 – 'Red Light' over Oxfordshire

At 11pm, Oxford resident – David White – was driving home from Blewbury, Oxfordshire, when he noticed a *'red light'* in the sky, apparently following his car, travelling several hundred feet above him. When he stopped the car and wound down the window, the light halted. Puzzled, he continued on his journey.

"I drove towards Wantage; it moved with me again. I kept flashing my lights; I stopped, it stopped – now stationary in the sky above me, and occasionally zigzagging. As I drove through Faringdon, I saw it – then a few miles down the road it vanished."

(Source: Personal interview/*Oxford Star*, 14.4.1988 – 'David's close encounter – mystery red glow follows his car')

As dawn rose at 5am, Eddie and Molly Owers of Royston, Hertfordshire, were astonished to see *"a huge glowing yellow 'casserole' shape"* hovering over the Buntingford area, before disappearing from view, several minutes later. When Eddie contacted the police, he was told others had also reported seeing a UFO the same morning.

(Source: *Unknown newspaper,* 15.4.1988 – 'Couple in UFO mystery')

Eddie and Molly Owers

'Rings' found in road surface, Derbyshire

Could there have been any connection with *'two 12ft in diameter round 'rings', discovered in the tarmac road surface'* at Farley, near Matlock, Derbyshire, which we believe were seen by Police Sergeant Sidney Earnshaw, in early to mid-April 1988, who wrote to us with details of this and other incidents?

(Sources: Personal interview/*Chesterfield and Dronfield Gazette*, 14.4.1988 – 'UFO Alert'/*Nottingham Evening Post*, 11.4.88 – 'Ring Road for UFOs?')

Mid-April 1988 – Cigar-shaped UFO over Henfield

A strange cigar-shaped object, with blue shafts of light coming out of it, was seen over the house of actress Selena Gilbert and her husband, Terry. The couple from Horn Lane, Henfield, and two friends, reported the matter to Steyning Police. They sent two officers – Police Constable John Hughes and Peter Smith. The officers reported back to the Royal Greenwich Observatory who explained away that what they had seen was Venus. The police suggested an over vivid imagination! Even worse, an officer said:

"I have never come across a sighting that hasn't been explained."

(Source: *Chesterfield and Dronfield Gazette*, 14.4.1988 – 'UFO? No it's Venus Love')

Allegation of Abduction

In addition to this was a bizarre story published in the media about Cheshire woman Jackie Smith, as below, who went missing after she reported having been abducted by aliens. (*Sun*, London 11.4.1988 'Riddle of lost girl in UFO kidnap'/*Daily Star*, 11.4.1988 – 'Jackie may be on run from aliens') *Sun*, London, 12th April 1988, 'Missing girl is back')

Nottingham Evening Post 11 APR 1988

Ring road for UFOs?

STRANGE markings on a country road which puzzled police have led to a flying saucer alert.

Two rings, 12ft in diameter, have been found in the road surface at Farley near Matlock in Derbyshire.

Police are baffled but a spokesman for local UFOn spotters said: "They could be linked with a UFO landing.

"Over the past few months we have had many sitings reported in Derbyshire."

Today, London 11 APR 1988

ALIENS WOMAN MISSING

A FRIGHTENED secretary has vanished a day after claiming she had an encounter with aliens.

Jackie Smith, 39, disappeared leaving her first month's wages from a new job untouched and furniture at a new house unpacked.

She was reported missing at the weekend two weeks after she vanished, by a distant aunt, her only relative.

Her boss Andy Egan has hired a UFO investigator to find her.

Jackie, of Warrington, Cheshire, had arrived at work in a panic after her alleged encounter, he said yesterday.

She said green men got into her car which was whisked into the air. The next she remembered was waking up and finding blue dots on her ankles.

Andy, 25, said: "It may sound like a joke but it most certainly isn't. She turned up at the office in a hell of a panic."

UFO expert Jenny Randles said: "People have been known to experience the same sort of encounter as Jackie.

"The blue dots are a classic sign of alien presence. Jackie may now be hiding somewhere terrified that they will come back and get her."

Haunted Skies Volume Ten

What lay behind this chilling allegation? Was there a happy ending, despite Jackie eventually returning home?

13th April 1988 – 'Flying Oranges' over the UK

During the same month, a number of bright glowing orange spheres were sighted crossing the Midland Counties of Nottingham and Staffordshire, described by people as resembling *'Giant Jaffa lookalikes, hovering above the ground'*. At 1.40am, birdwatcher Ronald Clarke was out on Wallasey Marshes, one mile south of the *River Crouch*, near Bambers Timber Wharf. He noticed a round bright orange *'light'* in the clear sky, moving slowly in a north-east to south-west direction, at a height of 5,000-10,000ft. He kept it under observation for 15 minutes, until out of sight.

Frank Large (74) of Minerva Way, Cambridge, was walking home from bingo, at 9.15pm, when he sighted an unusual object in the sky. He made his way home and alerted his wife. The couple went outside and watched the object, described as showing three *'prongs'*, until 10.15pm, when it moved away. The illustration appears similar to others sighted around this period.

(Source: Ron West)

GEE WHIZ: FLYING ORANGES

UNIDENTIFIED flying objects whizzing over the skies of Harlow caused a stir on Thursday.

The bright orange balls were first spotted by an STC accountant, Bill Johnson, when he paid a visit to the bathroom at 1.30am.

"I saw something through the frosted glass window and at first thought there was a car on fire in the street outside," said Bill, who lives in Tanys Dell.

"The curtains seemed to be ablaze with fire and flames appeared to be flickering up the window."

Bill, a grandfather, said: "When I told the family, they said dad's losing his marbles."

But Bill's discovery was substantiated when he read a report in a national paper about flying oranges seen in the sky over the Midlands that night.

Two of his neighbours also saw something strange,

"I don't think there are any little Martians sitting up there, but there are some things we can't explain," he told the Star.

A spokesman from the Ministry of Defence commented:"Our sole interest in UFOs is if they have a military connotation. You do see some peculiar things in the sky."

HARLOW STAR -Essex-

Daily Mirror, London
13 APR 1988

Unidentified Flying Oranges..

A FLEET of giant ORANGES has been sighted flying over the Midlands.

Witnesses claim the oversize Outspans give off an orange glow that has left some people with sunburn.

A woman from Beeston, Nottingham, said the oranges were about the size of a house. They hovered just above the ground and gave off a humming noise.

The UFO Investigation Society said: "We have had dozens of reports about these oranges."

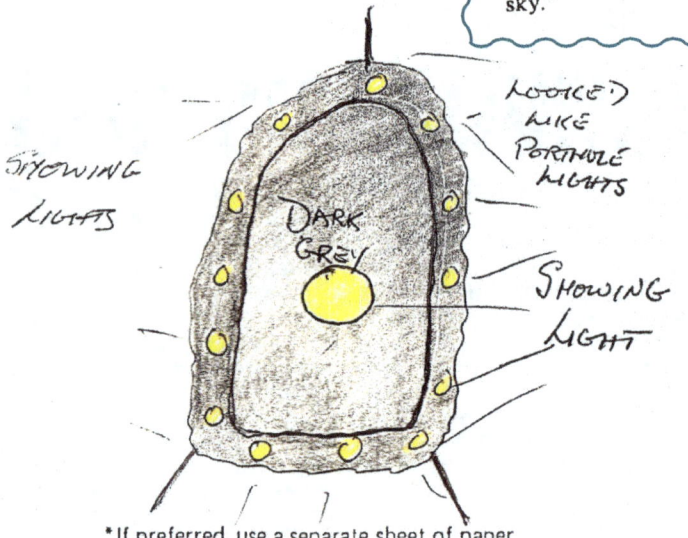

*If preferred, use a separate sheet of paper

Haunted Skies Volume Ten

At 10.10pm, Mr Joseph Herring, from Southend, was watching *Hill Street Blues* on TV, when his neighbour – Mrs Teesdale (who was fetching the washing off the line) – shouted out to him:

"There's something strange in the sky".

Joseph went outside and saw:

" . . . a very large circular object, showing a semi-triangular shape inside, hovering in the sky; I watched it for a short time, and then went back in to continue watching my programme. When I came out, at 10.58pm, it had gone."

(Source: Ron West/Brenda Butler/*Daily Star*, 13.4.1988 – 'Mystery of the UF . . . Oranges'/Dennis Harriman, UFO Investigation Society)

13th April 1988 – UFO over Essex

At 9pm, John Steven Cook (37) of Fairleigh Drive, Leigh-on-Sea, Essex, was pointing out some stars to his daughter, when he noticed a small object in the night sky that kept flashing red and green. Further scrutiny revealed three lights, set in a triangular formation, which was completely still in the sky. John called his wife, Linda, to come and have a look. She confirmed seeing the same object. An hour later, the object/three lights disappeared from view.

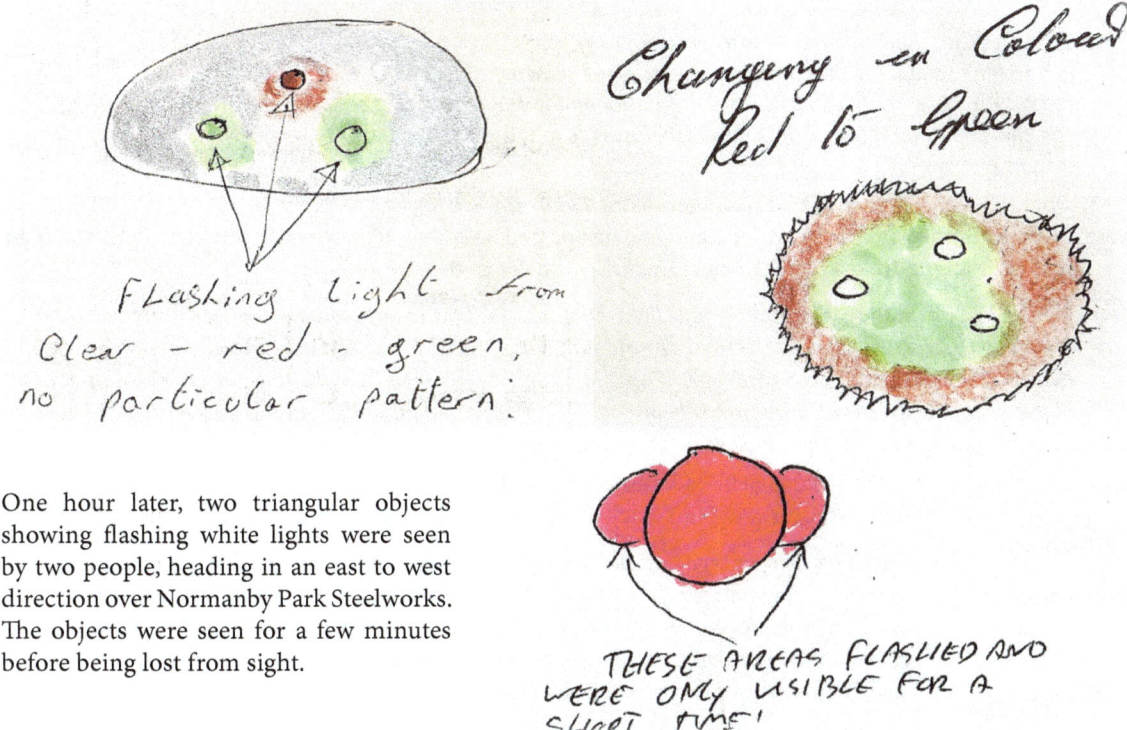

One hour later, two triangular objects showing flashing white lights were seen by two people, heading in an east to west direction over Normanby Park Steelworks. The objects were seen for a few minutes before being lost from sight.

Haunted Skies Volume Ten

14th April 1988 – Orange UFOs over Southend

At 8.15pm, Mr H. Bentley of Thorpe Bay, Southend, was cycling along the road, when he saw a bright object in the sky, which was:

> "... all lit up, with a slight orange tinge to it – bright enough to light up the sky towards the south. I carried on to the top of the road, where I managed to obtain a better look at the object. All of a sudden it vanished. I made my way to a friend's house and sketched what I had seen."

In due course a letter was sent to the *British Astronomical Association,* asking them whether it could have been a fireball, although Mr Bentley believed this not to be likely.

Jean Armstrong and her husband, Leslie, were driving along Maplin Way, towards the seafront, at 8.15pm, when they noticed an object:

> "... as big as dinner plate in the sky, glowing orange and red, slightly elongated in shape, before it eventually disappeared over Westcliff."

At 8.15pm, Donald Everett was being driven along the seafront by his wife, when she brought his attention to an object in the sky.

> "I looked up and saw a mushroom-shaped object – apparently made up of numerous globules of glowing red and orange lights – that seemed to be following the coastline, heading towards the Old Leigh, losing height as it went."

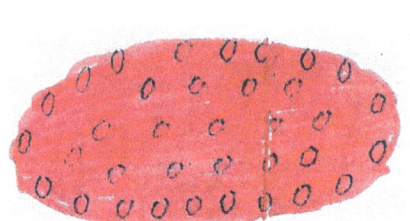

At 8.20pm, Norman and Sharon Firminger, from Leigh-on-Sea, were travelling home with their two sons, and had just passed Southend Pier, when one of their sons – Stephen – brought their attention to a strange object that he could see in the sky. Sharon:

> "We looked up and saw this pink/mauve light, circular in shape, travelling inland towards the Royals Shopping Precinct. It followed the road around and disappeared from view behind trees on the top of the cliffs." UFO Investigator, Ron West: "Over thirty-one people sighted a glowing red/orange/mauve object as it flew over from the south side of Southend Pier, came inland for approximately 6-700yds, before turning or swerving to the left in a westerly direction, towards Leigh-on-Sea."

Between 8.15pm and 8.20pm, Janet Self – a housewife from Somerset Avenue, Southend-on-Sea – was sat in her living room, watching TV, when she noticed a bright *'light'* in the sky. She had this to say:

> "A very bright orange and red 'ball of light' caught my attention, hovering between two bungalows opposite. All of a sudden a smaller piece appeared to fall away from it, straight down – then the larger 'ball' went straight and disappeared from view." Another witness – Tina Anderson – described seeing: "... two orange-red 'balls of light' in the sky, which gradually fell downwards over the tree line".

Haunted Skies Volume Ten

Between 8.15pm-8.30pm, James Lee was sat in his house in Lancaster Gardens, looking out of the window overlooking south, over the Pier, when he saw:

> "... a fairly large rotating spherical object, with very bright lights, heading south; it then disappeared from view over the rooftops of nearby houses."

At 10.10pm, the same evening, Mrs M. Bowen (72) was walking along Hardwick Close, Rayleigh, in Essex. She had this to say:

> "I noticed lights coming towards me in the sky. I stopped and watched a square-shaped object, with lights on it, pass overhead, heading towards London."

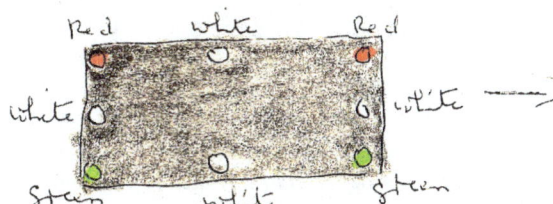

We presume that Mrs Bowen may have passed away, as she would be aged 97 if alive. We are sure she would have been pleased that her sighting and illustration is now available for people to see.

A number of bright glowing orange spheres were also sighted throughout the Midlands, during April 1988, according to Dennis Harriman of the UFO Investigation Society, who told of being contacted by people from Nottingham, Lichfield and Staffordshire, some of whom described seeing what looked like *'giant oranges, hovering above the ground'*.

(Source: Ron West)

20th April 1988 – UFO over Benfleet

At 7pm, Brian Heale was stood in his kitchen at Benfleet, Essex, when he noticed a bright orange *'light'* hovering in the sky. He watched it for a minute or so, before it vanished from view.

At 8.30pm, on the same evening, a young couple was walking along Warren Lane, Staincross, north-west of Barnsley, near the village of Woolley, when they noticed a man sat in a car, with what looked like an aerial on a post. The man seemed to be intently looking at the sky. About 15-30 minutes later, a triangular object flew overhead really slow, and then shot off over fields and disappeared from sight.

A few seconds afterwards three or four cars, with *'great big lights'*, appeared on the lane and appeared to be chasing the object. Andy Roberts later interviewed the witness from whom he obtained further information to the effect that the object was displaying ten lights on it, and about the size of an aircraft, making a hissing noise. Andy made some enquiries and was told one possible explanation could have been a model aircraft. A possible contender for this may have been one that was manufactured by *Dragon Models* of Wrexham, Wales, taking into consideration an article that appeared in the 11th August edition of *Executive Post*, during which Mr Ray Jones – the founder and director of the company – spoke of a reproduced B52 Bomber, over 25ft in length, for use in a TV production. He also disclosed the construction of specially adapted models for use by the police, civil authorities, local councils, and that the MOD was currently involved in business with *Dragon Models*. Presumably these would have been for pilotless surveillance craft, to be used in military operations, which is of no consequence to us. We appreciated that it was unlikely *Dragon* would be able to remember specifically whether one of their craft had been flown on that evening, but felt it was worth asking them if they had produced any remote craft of a triangular design to be used at night.

In October 2013 we emailed them about this, wondering if, at the end of the day, the couple had seen a remote controlled model aircraft, hoping to obtain further information but never received any reply despite having written to them also about this matter.

> **That UFO again!**
>
> MRS. L. SAGE, Everill Gate Lane, Broomhill:
>
> PLEASE tell the Darfield lady and the Barugh lady that my daughter and myself saw the U.F.O. on Wednesday, April 20, around 9.45 p.m.
>
> We were walking from Wombwell down into the village of Broomhill where we live, and half-way down the lane, my daughter saw this thing in the sky, with red lights and big white lights, some flashing on and off.
>
> It turned all its lights out as it got nearer us, then came hovering round us and put two big white spot lights on us for a few seconds.
>
> We were both a bit scared when it did this, and I said: "Come on, let's go home."
>
> As we started to walk again, it put red, green and white lights on, and went towards Wombwell way. When we got home I told my son about this. He thought we were mad, so I didn't tell anyone else till I saw it in the paper.
>
> But I know it was really a U.F.O. and won't ever forget that night I can tell you. I don't wish to remain anonymous!

At 9.45pm Linda Sage of Broomhill, near Barnsley, was walking from Wombwell down to Broomhill, when her daughter said to her:

"Look at that funny thing in the sky, Mummy!"

As Linda approached closer, she saw an object showing red, green and white, flashing lights on the body.

"As it reached our position it hovered and descended lower. It then turned all its lights out and put two large white spotlights on us. By this time my daughter had become frightened, and we decided to make our way homewards. As we did so, the big lights went out and the small ones came on again. When we arrived home, I told my son about what had taken place. He asked me if I had gone mad."

At 10pm a UFO was reported over Darfield, Barnsley, by an anonymous woman, who wrote to the *Barnsley Chronicle*. They published her sighting on the 6th May, which also included other reports for that evening.

At 10.30pm, Harry Reynolds – an apprentice turner of Curdsworth, Barnsley – had just finished work at *Redfearn Glass*, Monk Bretton, near Barnsley, and was walking to the car park situated in Banton Road, with two other colleagues – the last few in a line of six or seven other men – when they saw something in the sky.

"I first thought it was an airplane and that it was too low for some reason I can't explain. We stopped walking and stared in astonishment, because it wasn't moving; it had green red and white lights, flashing alternately – then two large searchlights came on, shining almost straight down. It was very hard to discern any shape. I could not see a solid body, but I had an impression it was oblong – narrower at one end than the other. There were lots of lights running the length of it. One of my friends said, 'It looks like a row of arcades'. It was totally silent and then started to move in a series of thrusting movements – almost like a dragonfly – before disappearing from view towards the south-west direction."

20th April 1988 – UFO Display over Barnsley

At 8.45pm, Mrs Jessop, of Dodworth, was with her son when they saw an object in the south-west direction of the sky. She immediately told her husband, Eric, and the family watched the object they described as being about the size of a tennis ball in the sky.

"We saw it move across the sky, where it was joined by two other UFOs forming a 45° angle. They circled around the perimeter in an anticlockwise direction – showing red, green, orange, pink, blue, violet and yellow, lights but mostly blue. These lights resembled the motion made by caterpillar tracks on a bulldozer. The outer surface of the objects looked like a grey white skin, with 'veins' on it. After moving from an elevation of 45° to 15°, they vanished from view."

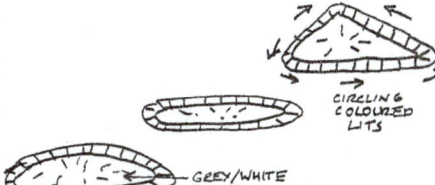

23 APR 1988

Alert over new 'veg' from outer space

TERROR OF THE UFO CARROTS

STAR REPORTER

FRIGHTENED people ran for cover from giant flying carrots, only a few miles from where oranges as big as houses were spotted whizzing across the sky.

Two carrot-shaped objects the size of hot air balloons but a lot faster were seen over Kirk Hallam, Derbyshire.

The unidentified flying oranges were reported by terrified witnesses in Beeston, Notts, last week.

A Kirk Hallam pensioner who spotted one of the carrots said: "I saw it drop below the back of the house towards a pond."

The pensioner, who refused to be named, added: "It looked like a stumpy carrot with smoke coming out of the end."

Flames

"I went to look at it. It was glowing, but there was no noise. It was eerie — I was too frightened to go down to the pond to see what happened.

"My dog was whining and seemed nervous, too."

Another witness, Ann Mart, 43, of Worksworth Road, said: "It was too bright for a star and too stationary for a plane. It was massive and it was glowing.

"So many people have seen this carrot that it can't be my imagination.

"You don't like to say anything because people think you are a raving nutter."

Her husband Trevor, 53, said: "This thing was 400ft. in the air and glowing. It hovered for ages then zoomed off at incredible speed."

The UFO Investigation Society's international co-ordinator Dennis Harriman, said: "The latest objects were round at the top and tempered like carrots with flames spouting out.

"Several people saw them loop the loop then one zoomed off to nearby Belper while another apparently crashed into a pond.

"People who went to find it saw something move then ran off in terror. The next day there was no trace of anything there."

64TS/PQ
From: C R Neville, Sec (AS)2a, Room 8245
MINISTRY OF DEFENCE
Main Building Whitehall London SW1A 2HB
Telephone 01-218 (Direct Dialling)
01-218 9000 (Switchboard)

P Mantle Esq
106 Lady Ann Road
Soothill
Batley
West Yorkshire
WF17 0PY

Your reference

Our reference
D/Sec(AS)12/3

Date
8 July 1988

Dear Mr Mantle

Thank you for your letter of 15 May 1988 asking for information that we might have received on any Unidentified Flying Object (UFO) sightings in the South Yorkshire area on and around 20 April 1988.

I have looked through our files and am sorry to say that we did not receive any reports which relate to the details supplied in your letter.

I can also confirm that we are not aware of any flying operations in the area concerned, although I cannot discount the possibility that there might have been the odd individual training sortie here and there.

I hope that this is of help.

Yours sincerely,

26th April 1988 – 'V'-shaped UFO over Dodworth

A 'V' or triangular-shaped object was sighted moving across the sky, heading from the Penistone area in the north-west, towards the Worsbrough area, two miles south of Barnsley in the south-west. According to the witness:

"My first thoughts were that it was an RAF heavy bomber

Haunted Skies Volume Ten

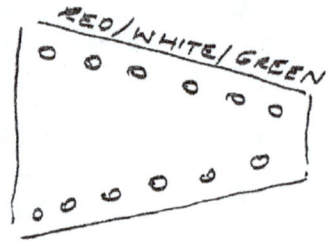

on night training, as I have seen others at rooftop level, but it wasn't like an aircraft – there were no sign of any wings. The red, white, and green lights, positioned below, were like fairground lights, rather than navigation lights. They were fixed and in a 'V' formation. I saw it for about 30secs as it passed between cloud formations, at approximately 250-500ft altitude."

A married woman from Hoyland, Barnsley, was with her two children and about to collect her husband from work, when they saw a large white 'light', surrounded by red and green flashing lights, hovering over fields outside their house. Extremely curious, the woman and the children got into the family car and drove to the Grenoside Road, then onto Hoyland Common, and through Pilley Close, to what is named locally as 'Witches Wood' (part of Tankersley Park) when they realised the object appeared to be following them. The woman stopped the vehicle and got out, as the object silently passed overhead, close to the traffic island, heading towards Stocksbridge and Penistone area.

The family then continued on their journey to Sheffield, where they picked-up the husband, who thought they were pulling his leg!

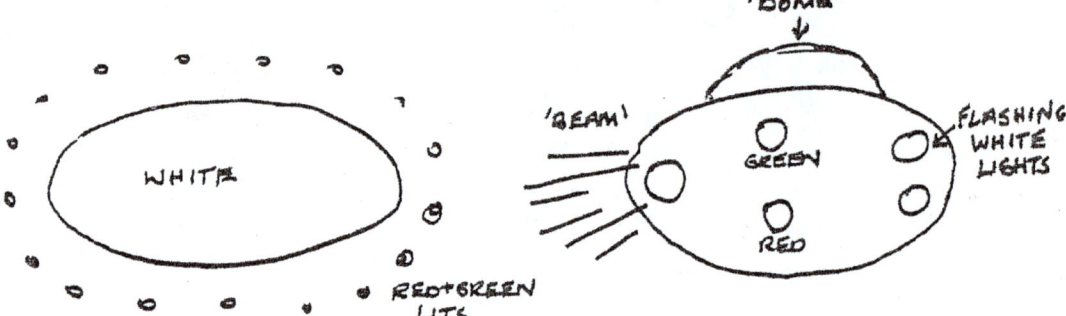

UFO Hoyland sighting

AN Elsecar man was amazed last week to see a UFO hovering over Hoyland and Elsecar for about 40 minutes.

As he drove home from his work in Ecclesfield at 10 p.m., the man stopped the car twice so he could study the silent object more carefully.

"It was really very strange," he said. "Although it was dark I could see it was a vague box-shape and there were big green, white and red lights on it which stayed lit up all the time. It was huge and it was absolutely still, and what really surprised me was that it didn't make a sound.

"I thought it must be some sort of aircraft, but it was so still and quiet it couldn't possibly have been."

The 38-year-old man drove home, keeping his eye on the object, but lost sight of it when he put his put in the drive.

"The next-door neighbour was just about to take the dog out for a walk, so I told her about it and we went down the road to see if it was still there, but there was no sign of it," he said.

He went in the house, told his 37-year-old wife what he had seen, and kept looking out of the window to see if he could catch sight of it again.

"I couldn't believe it when I saw it there again, so I called my wife to have a look," he said.

She looked out of the window and saw the object just as her husband had described, then watched it move slowly across the sky and disappear.

"We even opened the window to see if we could hear a noise, but it didn't make a sound," she said. "I couldn't believe how big it was. Then it suddenly disappeared.

"Neither of us have ever experienced anything like it before, and I don't particularly want to e er again — although we weren't frightened, just inquisitive really."

The couple wanted to remain anonymous for fear they would be laughed at. "I don't want people to think we are crackpots," said the man.

"I know it sounds stupid but I know what I saw and I'm glad my wife witnessed it too. It's just a pity that we didn't have a film for our camera. If we had managed to take a picture of it people would have had to believe us!"

BARNSLEY CHRONICLE, APRIL 29, 1988

UFO sighting sparks off probe

BARNSLEY CHRONICLE, MAY 6, 1988

THE sighting of a UFO over Hoyland and Elsecar a fortnight ago is being investigated by a nation-wide team of UFO spotters.

The object was spotted by an Elsecar man as he drove home from his work in Ecclesfield at 10 p.m. The man stopped the car twice so he could study the object more closely.

When he arrived home, he told his wife, who looked out of the window and saw the box-shaped object with flashing green, white and red lights.

David Clarke, a student at Sheffield University, who is a member of the group of UFO spotters, said that it appeared to be similar to an object seen at Hoyland, Elsecar, Wombwell and Penistone on Wednesday, February 10.

On that evening a 200 ft. long diamond-shaped object with flashing lights was seen hovering 150 ft. above Wombwell town centre by two or three people and later witnesses reported that it followed the power lines between Hoyland and Elsecar.

At 10.30 p.m. a motorist on Penistone by-pass saw a similar object moving towards Manchester.

Mr. Clarke said all the incidents were being investigated, and he is now looking for more witnesses. His phone number: Sheffield 694537.

Footnote: Photographs of a UFO (left), seen flying over Sheffield Road, Barnsley, which appeared in the Chronicle last year, are now being studied by space experts at Nassau.

(See letters, page 4).

We also saw the UFO

"DARFIELD LADY":
PLEASE tell the Elsecar man and his wife that I don't think they are crackpots — I saw the U.F.O. too!

I was walking down the street in Darfield at 10 o'clock on Wednesday, 20th April, with a friend. I looked up and said jokingly, "Hey look — a U.F.O.!" My friend looked up and said, "What is it?"

In the sky was this silent object. It was very still and didn't make any sound whatsoever. It was quite large and had white, red and green lights on.

We looked up and watched it for two or three minutes. Then my friend said, "Come on let's go — they might come down and get us!" We laughed and walked away.

I would be interested to know whether anyone else in the area saw anything. Also whether anyone could offer any rational explanation for what it could be.

The absence of any sound and complete lack of movement rules out most types of aircraft. Are the Ministry of Defence using any that we don't know about?

"BARUGH LADY":
I ALSO saw the U.F.O. seen by your reader. Although you do not state the actual date of his sighting, I saw it on Wednesday, 20th April at around 10 o'clock to the rear of Keresforth Hall.

It was dark at the time and although it could have been some distance away it still looked quite large and had two white lights (one on each end) and a third white light which was flashing on and off.

It was definitely hovering and completely silent. As I drove off, it moved silently away from me.

It would be interesting to know if your reader saw it on the same night. I also wish to remain anonymous.

East Anglian Psychical Research Group

Haunting at '*Bellinas Chocolate Shop*', Bury St Edmunds

Emphasizing that, on occasion, Brenda Butler and Ron West also dealt with reports of paranormal activity (despite the massive 'wave' of UFO sightings from around the Essex area in this year) was a matter investigated by member Eric Quigley, from Bury St, Edmunds. This involved reports of a ghostly monk seen at *Bellinas Belgian Chocolate Shop*, 3 Buttermarket, *Bury St Edmunds. (According to the *Internet 2013* – 38 Buttermarket, currently a bookshop, was the source of similar reports.) Although most of the current buildings are less than 200 years old, the cellars and foundations are as much as 500. Under all of these shops runs a network of passages cut into the soft chalk. Many of these have never been fully explored and are usually bricked-up when discovered.

Ghostly monks seen

It is rumoured that the monks dug these passages to carry out clandestine liaisons. On the 24th September 1975, Sandra Overden was opening up her shop – *Annabells Togs*, at number 47 Abbeygate Street – when she saw the figure of a monk, in a brown habit, cross the shop near the checkout and pass through the wall. The Hadleigh-based East Anglian Psychical Research Group sent Mr Malcolm Ramplin to investigate. On the 24th October they held a psychic 'sit in' but failed to make any contact, although mysterious footsteps were heard. During the same week, at 21 Churchgate Street, a 40ft well was found in the shop cellar, after someone nearly fell down it. There was also a report of a ghostly figure seen at this location. The manifestation was believed to have arisen after workmen found a trapdoor in the well, leading to a tunnel complex. The property next to *Bellinas* – *Milletts* at No. 2 the Buttermarket – also has a well in its downstairs shop, which was level with Bellinas stockroom where ghostly sightings took place. Eric managed to interview the girl concerned, but forgot to make a note of her name.

> "I went down to use the toilet on the morning of the 28th April 1988. As I reached the bottom of the stairs, I saw a shadow go into the store, at the far end of the room, and felt cold. I rushed back upstairs and spoke to my friend, Pat, who said she had also seen the same thing herself that week. Pat said that she had also heard banging noises."

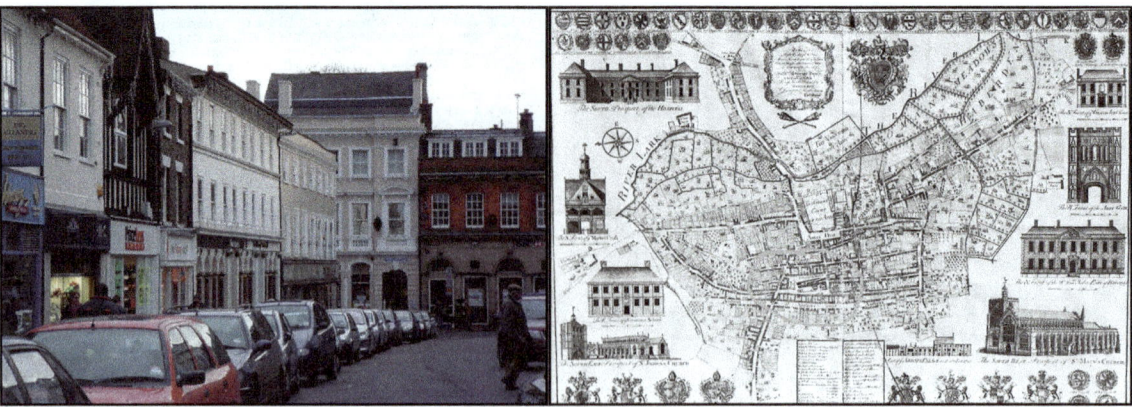

*Bury St Edmunds is a market town in the county of Suffolk, England, and formerly the county town of West Suffolk. It is the main town in the borough of St. Edmundsbury and known for the ruined abbey near the town centre. The town, originally called Beodericsworth, is known for brewing and malting (with the large *Greene King* brewery) and for a British Sugar processing factory. Many large and small businesses are located in Bury, which traditionally has given Bury an affluent economy with low unemployment, with the town being the main cultural and retail centre for West Suffolk. Tourism is also a major part of the economy, plus local government.

MAY 1988

7th May 1988 – Saucer-shaped UFO over Suffolk

At 10.15pm, Peter Fleming from Haverhill, Suffolk, was out exercising the family dog, 'Smudge', accompanied by his girlfriend – Julie Rondeau.

As the couple strolled along Clarendon Road, towards the direction of Puddlebrook, picking out the constellations in the night sky, they noticed a bright pinprick of light towards the south-east horizon, and presumed it to be the headlights of a car, or the glow of a bonfire.

> "We kept our eye on it as we walked along, noticing that it was heading towards the direction of Ladygate Woods. To our surprise it stopped in mid-air, and hovered over the woods, about a mile away from us. All of a sudden, a beam of light came on illuminating the woods below it, allowing us to see that it was saucer-shaped with what appeared to be windows set into its side. A short time later, the beam was extinguished and the 'saucer' began to move right to left, in a zigzag manner across the sky, and then returned to its original position again, where the beam came on once more. We stood watching it for about 20 minutes, until it moved once more, but this time it headed towards where we were standing and passed overhead, enabling us to see what looked like a tennis ball, squashed in the middle, with a sort of square box underneath, displaying red and green lights. As it headed eastwards I could just about make out its outline, when what sounded like engines started up. After arriving home we were astonished to discover that we had been out for some hours, rather than what appeared to be a much shorter time-span."

During the same evening Barnsley man David Grimme told of being chased by a UFO while on the way home.

Haunted Skies Volume Ten

UFO SIGHTING ACCOUNT FORM

SECTION A

Please write an account of your sighting, make a drawing of what you saw and then answer the questions in section B overleaf as fully as possible. Write in BLOCK CAPITALS using a ball point pen.

The field is situated at the back of Greenacres way, to get to it we passed through a mass of houses just off the Clements Estate. We didn't notice anything at first, until Pete pointed out something glowing to the right of Ladygate Woods. It could have been a fire or torch, but we realised it wasn't when it moved to left and up in the sky, hovering just above the woods, and there was no sound. At this point, sometimes it moved quickly and then very slowly or stayed still and seemed to light up the whole top of the trees. We both seemed transfixed on this object as we couldn't really believe what we were seeing. We stood there for about 25 minutes. The shape only appeared

DRAWING*

Your full name (Mr/Mrs/Miss/Ms) Julie Rondeau Age 17
Address 9 Argyl Court
Clements Estate, Haverhill
Telephone No. 704112 (STD. 0440)
Occupation during last two years: Student / Trainee Secretary
Any professional, technical or academic qualifications or special interests
O'level, 5 CSE's, 2 City Guilds

Do you object to the publication of your name?
*Yes/No. *Delete as applicable.
Today's Date 5/6/88
Signature Julie Rondeau

Chased by UFO

TERRIFIED steelworker David Grimme told last night how he was chased by a massive shoebox-shaped UFO.

The spooky space craft chilled him to the bone as he drove home from work late at night.

"Although it was pitch dark, I could see it was like a vague, black shoebox — with dazzling lights," he said.

The UFO suddenly disappeared when Dave, 38, arrived home in Barnsley.

SUNDAY SPORT MAY 8. 1988

12th May 1988 – UFO over Chester

At 4pm, a woman employee of Chester Zoo was stood in her house, when she heard a strange whirring noise. She looked out of the window and saw:

> "... a greyish red coloured object rising in the air, 7-8ft above the hedge, which continued to ascend until just a tiny spot in the sky."

(Source: MOD Declassified records, 2010)

14th May 1988 – UFO over Germany

Mr Kenneth Jackson (60) of Sherringham, Norfolk, with a diploma in psychology and plastic technologist by occupation, was working in West Germany at the time. At noon on the above date he was out cycling just outside the village of *Achstetten, when he sighted something highly usual, approximately two miles away. Upon his return to the UK, Mr Jackson wrote to Arnold West of BUFORA. Here is his letter:

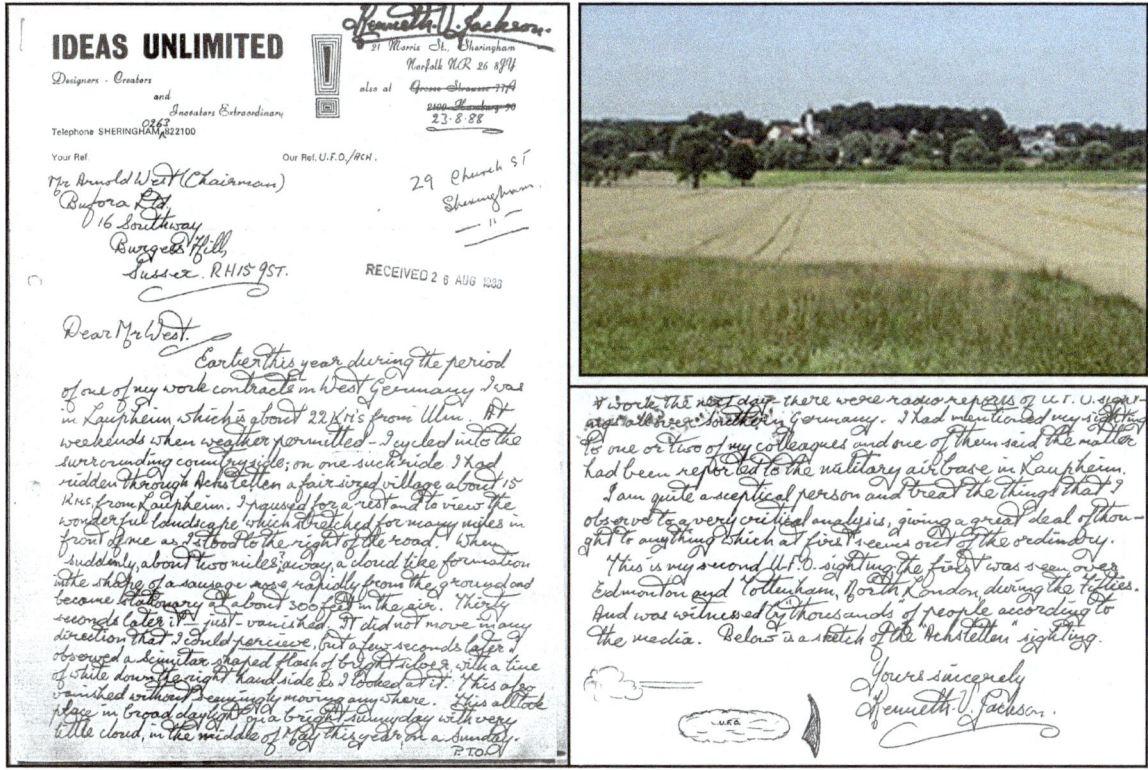

*Achstetten is the northernmost municipality in the district of Biberach, in the region of Upper Swabia in Baden-Württemberg, Germany. As of 30 September 2008, it has a population of 4.141. The villages of Oberholzheim, Bronnen and Stetten were incorporated into the municipality of Achstetten between 1972 and 1975. The strung-out village is situated west of the federal road Bundesstraße 30. The river Rot runs through it. Achstetten lies approximately 4 km north of the city of Laupheim and approximately 18 km south of the city of Ulm. The name *Achstetten* is derived from the Old High German words *aha* meaning water, and *stet*, meaning place; the name meaning thus *place close to water* Close to the road to Ersingen, tumuli from the Hallstatt period have been discovered. This indicates that the area has been settled for at least 2,500 years. Celtic tribes are associated with Hallstatt culture. During the Roman period, Achstetten was also a place of settlement, indicated by the remains of Roman villa. The outlines of this structure are visible on aerial photographs.

:TURN FORM TO:–	LOCATION
	EVAL'N
	UFO CLASS: CE1
	CLOSED

UFO SIGHTING ACCOUNT FORM

SECTION A

Please write an account of your sighting, make a drawing of what you saw and then answer the questions in section B overleaf as fully as possible. Write in **BLOCK CAPITALS** using a ball point pen.

Earlier this year during the period of one of my work contracts in West Germany I was in Laupheim which is about 22 Kms from Ulm. At weekends when weather permitted I cycled into the surrounding countryside; on one such ride I had ridden through Achstetten a fair sized village some 15 Kms from Laupheim. I paused for a rest and to view the wonderful landscape which stretched for many miles in front of me as I stood to the right of the road. When suddenly, about two miles? away, a cloud like formation in the shape of a sausage rose rapidly from the ground and became stationary at about 300 feet in the air. Thirty seconds later it – just vanished. It did not move in any direction that I could perceive, but a few seconds later I observed a Scimitar shaped flash of bright silver with a line of white down the right hand side as I looked at it. This also vanished without seemingly moving anywhere. This all took place in broad daylight on a bright sunny day with very little cloud, in the middle of May on a Sunday.

Please continue on a separate sheet if necessary.

DRAWING*

*If preferred, use a separate sheet of paper.

Your full name (Mr/~~Mrs/Miss/Ms~~) KENNETH V JACKSON Age 60

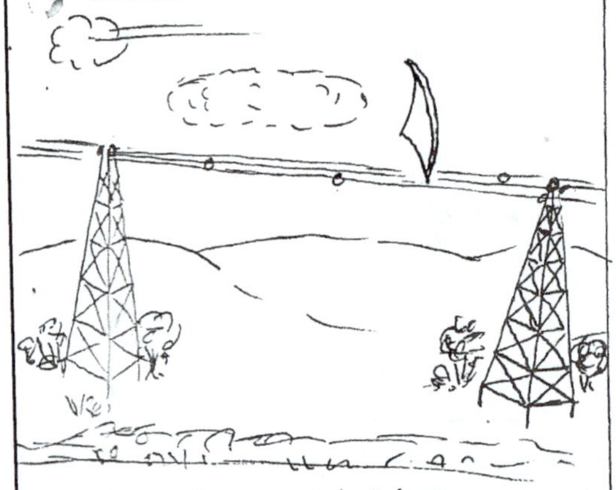

Address 21 MORRIS STREET

SHERINGHAM NORFOLK NR26 8JY

Telephone No 822100 (STD 0263)

Occupation during last two years REINFORCED PLASTICS TECHNOLOGIST (PATTERN MAKER)

Any professional, technical or academic qualifications or special interests

PHSYCOLOGY (DIPLOMA)

Do you object to the publication of your name? *~~Yes~~/No. *Delete as applicable.

Today's Date 11-10-88

Signature Kenneth V Jackson

Published by the British UFO Research Association (BUFORA LTD.) for the use of investigators throughout Great Britain. Further copies may be obtained from BUFORA Research Headquarters.; Newchapel Observatory; Newchapel, Stoke-on-Trent, Staffs:, England

Form R1

BUFORA LTD 16 SOUTHWAY BURGESS HILL SUSSEX RH15 9ST

Haunted Skies Volume Ten

An example of two 'flying triangles'. This photo was taken by Dawn Holloway at Barmouth, North Wales in the summer of 1991. At the time of the photograph Dawn does not remember seeing an object in the sky.

16th May 1988 – 'Flying Triangles' over Cannock

During this evening Steven Delaney from Gnosall, Staffordshire, was driving back from Reading, in Berkshire, along the A5108 Staffordshire road, near Haughton, when he noticed two triangular objects in the sky,

> "... hovering at an estimated height of some 30ft above trees, approximately three quarters of a mile away, which appeared solid, with a single red light on the jet-black underneath, resembling what I took to be a type of military aircraft I had never seen before – totally silent. I watched as they flew away, before being lost from view behind a bank of trees towards the eastern side of Haughton. The closest thing I could compare them to was the Stealth Bomber, so my impression was of something possibly man-made rather than alien."

Graham Allen

At around 9.55pm the same evening, Rugeley man – Graham Allen – was enjoying a family barbecue, on what was an exceptionally warm evening, when his brother brought his attention to two *'lights'*, travelling one behind the other horizontally across the sky, over the Cannock Chase area.

> "One by one we all joined in to watch the two lights, which performed a number of strange movements as the headed across the sky, towards Stafford, before suddenly executing a U-turn and approaching our position. As they moved nearer, I asked my mother to fetch a camera; unfortunately, there was no film in it. All we could do was watch as the two (now triangular-shaped) objects passed overhead – like two Christmas trees all lit up – with a bright light in each corner and several underneath, bluish white in appearance. I could not see any navigation lights as you would expect if they had been aircraft – apart from that, they were totally silent."

Graham and his family were not the only ones to see the UFOs as they passed over Cannock Chase that evening. Many people around the Rugeley and Cannock areas contacted the authorities, reporting having seen similar objects flying through the air.

One of them was ex-RAF Eileen Ballard, from Uttoxeter – now a civilian worker, employed by the Staffordshire Police – who was accompanied by five other people in Fernwood Road, when one of the party shouted out, *"What's that?"*, pointing upwards.

> *"I looked up and saw two perfect circles of bright yellow light, heading across the sky at a height of about 1,000ft, reminding me of two car headlights. They flew slowly and silently overhead. It was an amazing sight. Nobody seemed frightened. I kept thinking I should go and get the camera but knew that, by the time I had put some film in it, the lights would have gone. As it turned out, I would have had plenty of time and still regret not having fetched the camera. Eventually, the lights slowly changed into an oval shape, turning as they did so, allowing us to see they had mass but only obvious from the underside, showing panels of multicoloured lights – quite dull in comparison when first seen."*

Eileen firmly rejected a later suggestion put forward, explaining the incident away as RAF *VC10* Airliners, adapted as fuel transporters, based at Brize Norton Airbase, Oxfordshire; whilst BUFORA suggested that the mystery objects were, in fact, top secret radar proof *F19 Stealth Fighters*, from RAF Alconbury, or a remote controlled reconnaissance vehicle – used in battle zones, such as Northern Island and Israel.

Eileen:

> *"I knew from my days in the RAF that what I had witnessed was not an aircraft; I contacted RAF Shawbury and was put through to the control tower. I described what I had seen and was told that no night flying of military aircraft had been logged for the time given. As a result of having contacted the local newspaper and been given some publicity, I received a telephone call from an ex- RAF Squadron Leader, or Wing Commander, who told me that while returning home after having picked up his grandchildren from RAF Stafford Air Training Cadets, he sighted some very bright circular lights in the sky – almost level with the top of Weston Bank along Weston Road – and decided to stop the car to have a closer look. He told me that the objects were like nothing he had ever seen before. Many people*

have suggested that what I saw was the Stealth Bomber, but if it was Stealth why would anyone spend billions to develop a new strike bomber, invisible to radar, and then light it up like a Christmas tree?"

Elaine Willacy from Littleworth, Staffordshire, was stood outside, talking to her next door neighbour, when they saw a triangular object passing overhead.

> "It was huge. The size and shape was so different from any aircraft I had ever seen before. We watched it for 10-15 minutes as it almost turned a full circle, before moving back the way it had come. It was like the sketch in the paper (provided by Mrs Ballard) – a bright array of orange red and blue lights."

A conflicting opinion was obtained from John Teasdale, who was driving near Cannock Chase on the way back from Burton-on-Trent, Staffordshire. Looking towards Cannock Chase, he noticed a collection of lights, which he was unable to identify. Curious, he pulled up on the outskirts of Rugeley and got out, watching the lights for 15mins, which were:

> " . . . heading slightly south of east/north-west, that appeared to turn, when they reached NW of Cannock Chase, but came back – now moving overhead. I looked through a pair of binoculars and saw what appeared to be the engines of a VC10; the lights were on the wings. This solved the mystery for me."

Other witnesses to the event were Joan and Michael Acocks of Hillcote Hollow, Stafford, who was walking home at 9.50pm, when they saw two triangular shapes,

> " . . . hovering above some trees, all lit up, but didn't look solid objects. We stood looking. All of a sudden, it just disappeared. We waited and it reappeared in the same place, hovered, then finally it disappeared. We continued on walking."

Graham Allen – then head of the Staffordshire based UFO Group – subsequently produced a DVD of the incident, which outlines much of the information above and includes an interview and dedication to the late Graham Birdsall, who died two years later (7.5.54 to 19.9.2000).

MP Bill Cash

The sightings were brought to the attention of Stafford MP Bill Cash, who wrote to Roger Freeman at the MOD asking him to make some enquiries, and let him know his views, adding:

> "Several independent individuals in the constituency, who can be regarded as reliable witnesses, saw these things and caused a great deal of concern. I don't know what they were".

When the question was raised in the House of Commons, Mr Freeman advised Mr Cash:

> "It was busy air traffic going into Birmingham Airport"

– a ludicrous explanation, according to Bill Cash.

MP Bill Cash

Graham Allen

We wrote a number of emails to MP Bill Cash, hoping that he may have been prepared to let us have his opinion regarding this matter, and his subsequent interest, but never received an answer. A letter was then sent 'Recorded Delivery' to him at his parliamentary address, in January 2010; this was also treated in the same manner. Oddly, in conversation with Graham Allen,

> **AFTER MP's PLEA, MORE TELL OF UFO MYSTERY**
>
> **'I stood under it for 15 minutes'**
>
> *By Barry Heafield*
>
> A REQUEST by Stafford MP Bill Cash for more details on last month's UFOs has brought further reports from witnesses.
>
> Last week, Mr Cash said he would be putting the strange sightings to Defence Minister Roger Freeman for official investigation.
>
> But this week, The Newsletter received several new reports. The most startling was from Joan and Michael Acocks, of Hilcote Hollow, Stafford.
>
> Mrs Acocks said she and her husband actually saw the object appear and disappear in exactly the same position several times.
>
> "We were just on the way back from a stroll on the Monday night and we saw two triangular shapes hovering above some trees. They were lit up, but somehow they didn't seem solid objects.
>
> "I stood there looking and all of a sudden it just disappeared. I stood there for a while and then it appeared again exactly as before in the same place, hovering for a few seconds before it disappeared again and we walked on."
>
> Mrs Acocks said she and her husband, who is an accountant, saw the UFO at the same time as previous reports, 9.50pm on Monday, May 16.
>
> "What struck me more than anything was that it was absolutely silent," added Mrs Acocks.
>
> Another witness, Elaine Willacy, of Harrowby Street, Littleworth, said she had a look at the object through binoculars with two neighbours.
>
> "It came across the sky, looking just like the sketch in the paper," said Mrs Willacy, "then it seemed to turn quickly and as it came over, it was just an array of bright lights, orange, red and blue.
>
> "We had a look through binoculars but we couldn't see any markings or anything to identify it. The amazing thing about it was that it was so quiet, there was no sound at all.
>
> "It was going very slowly and seemed in no rush to go anywhere. It felt as though someone was looking down on us and taking pictures."
>
> David Myatt from Marston House Farm, Church Eaton phoned in and said he'd seen exactly the same things seven years ago.
>
> "There were reports about it at the time," said Mr Myatt, "I saw it just outside Brocton on my way to Stafford. I looked up and saw it and stopped and it was right over head, about 50 feet from end to end, completely motionless and completely silent.
>
> "There were a lot of lights around it. I got out of the car and stood for about 15 minutes, hoping it was going to land, but it just drifted off.
>
> "It definitely wasn't a plane, there was no sound at all."
>
> But the British UFO Research Association still maintain the mystery objects are the American top secret radar proof F-19 Stealth fighter.
>
> Director of investigations at BUFORA, Jenny Randals, said: "It's often very difficult to make factual observations at night. If it has a lot of lights and suddenly they're put out, it's easy for the observer to assume it's disappeared.
>
> "Hovering can be an illusion because it's difficult to judge distance and the complete silence can be caused if the engines are highly tuned and the wind's blowing away from you.
>
> "I'm as certain as I can be that there's a conventional explanation to this one, probably the F-19 or remotely controlled reconnaissance aircraft known as RPVs which are all sorts of shapes and sizes and are also an open secret. They can hover and they're fairly quiet and they're used a lot in Northern Ireland."
>
> Mr Cash reiterated his request for all information on the subject from witnesses to be sent directly to him so that it could be put to the minister.

in February 2010, we learn that his attempts to elicit some response from the same MP had also been doomed to failure – which seems rather discourteous, taking into consideration that a self-addressed envelope was enclosed. Graham remains sceptical (as we also do) of the explanation offered that what was seen were *VC10s*. If this was the case, why weren't they heard passing overhead? They were low enough. The illustrations provided indicate the strongest of likelihoods that this was yet another example of what was to become labelled as the Triangular UFO. As Graham Birdsall said, both on CD and in conversations with us, over the years, these are not anything new, irrespective of the hype!

(Sources: Graham Allen, Staffordshire UFO Group – *Stafford Newsletter,* 24.6.1988 – 'UFO witness Plea'/ 27.5.88 – 'Strange lights riddle still hover over the town', *Stafford Newsletter,* 1.7.88 – 'After MPs plea, more tell of UFO Mystery'/*Cannock Chase Post,* Wolverhampton, 11.10.2001 – 'Visitors light up a spring night')

MOD release Documents

In 2008 The Ministry of Defence made available its findings about the May 1988 *Staffordshire UFO sightings* to the National Archives. They explained away the reports of the two triangular objects seen in the skies above Uttoxeter on Monday, May 16, 1988, as two aircraft on a refuelling exercise.

The MOD report accepted that several other people in Uttoxeter had also seen the dazzling display, but were too afraid to come forward and that strange clusters of orange and red lights seen around the same time of the evening were reported in Wolverhampton and Penkridge, where they *"flitted about the sky, disappearing and then reappearing"*.

In July 2012, the MOD released further sighting reports – part of 25 files released from the 1980s to the current day (2012). They included a reference to this date (16.5.1988). Quote:

A set of triangular-shaped objects were seen moving across the sky over Staffordshire, including Uttoxeter.

One eyewitness stated:

"It was around 9.45pm, and I was in the garden and saw two lights in the shape of a cross. They hovered for a while, before zooming off towards Uttoxeter."

Another eyewitness added:

"I saw bright lights coming towards my direction. As they flew overhead, I started to make out two perfect triangles, with flashing lights. I cannot begin to explain what it was, but I know of no plane that can manoeuvre like this object did."

In response to the sightings, a letter sent from the Ministry of Defence (MOD) stated:

"We can confirm that we received a number of reports from members of the public. The MOD receives and co-ordinates information about UFOs usually in the form of brief reports of the sightings. Our sole concern is then to establish whether or not the sightings present a threat to the security and defence of the UK. Unless we judge that they do, and this is not normally the case, we do not usually attempt any further investigation. I am advised by staff that the reported phenomenon is quite likely to be connected with civil air traffic going into Birmingham Airport, which was exceptionally busy at the time. Our experience is certainly that most sightings can be adequately explained in term of natural occurrences, such as aircraft observed at unusual angles, satellite debris, meteorological balloons, to mention just a few."

Authors: It is patently obvious, in our opinion, that the explanation given by the MOD does not fit, and is extremely unlikely to be the explanation for what was seen during that time and on many other occasions when Triangular UFOs and displays of UFO light phenomena have been brought to our notice.

18th May 1988 – Strange lights over Cambridgeshire

At 10pm, Deborah Cowe of Longstanton, Cambridgeshire, was at her home address, when she saw two lights, about 30yds apart, hovering in the sky.

"They grew brighter and zoomed backwards, dimming as they did so – then they spun around in a full circle, and seemed to split into two directions, one of them showing a red flashing light. Within a few minutes, they had gone."

At 3am, a white *'light'*, accompanied by four yellow *'lights'* was seen stationary in the sky above Pentland ski slopes, over the Pentland Hills, by a police officer. Previous to this, two people had contacted the police reporting having sighted three objects in the sky.

(Source: *The Doncaster Star*, 6.2.1988/Brenda Butler/Ron West)

21st May 1988 – UFO seen, burn marks found

BUFORA researcher Eric Morris, from Crew, employed as a nurse at the Barony Hospital in Nantwich, whom we never met but spoke to on a few occasions over the years, until his death in 2008, told of a sighting which took place at Audlem, in Cheshire, involving a UFO landing. This was reported by a man from Hankelow, and a group of four people in a car that stopped to take a closer look, after sighting a bright red object which dropped out of the sky and landed in a nearby field. The object remained on the ground, before taking off a few minutes later. Eric:

"I investigated this case and found the grass was burnt over a 40ft diameter. I also found two dead cats and a dead badger in the vicinity."

The samples and photographs taken were passed on to Dr. Henry Adjakdel – an Armenian physicist – who, it is said, specialised in close encounter cases. Eric also confirmed that the MOD had contacted him about this matter. In February 1989, Eric and his wife, Cornelia, were interviewed by the *Stoke-on-Trent Evening Sentinel*.

(Sources: *Crewe Chronicle*, 5.10.1988 – 'UFO expert called in'/*Crew Chronicle*, 8.2.1989 – 'Study made of samples from UFO'/*Stoke-on-Trent Evening Sentinel*, 9.2.1989. 'UFO buff's down-to-earth view of spacemen')

CHAPTER 6

JUNE TO AUGUST 1988

JUNE 1988

June 1988 – Eagle-shaped UFO over Lancashire

MRS Edna Tudge of Hillside Avenue, Blackrod, Bolton, Lancashire, contacted the *Bolton Evening News* after seeing an object in the shape of an eagle hovering in the sky, which occasionally turned round, before it headed off towards Horwich Moor. Efforts to capture it on photograph, by using her son and daughter's camera, proved fruitless. Incredibly, Mrs Tudge maintained she had been seeing the object on and off over a period of a few weeks.

(Source: Steve Balon, UFO Investigator/*Bolton Evening News*, 6.6.1988 – 'Grandmother's UFO mystery')

18th June 1988 – £1 admission, UFO Conference, Blackpool

The Blackpool and Fylde UFO Society held a UFO conference at the Friends Meeting House, Raikes Parade, Blackpool.

Guest speaker was Timothy Good. Admission was £1 for adults and 75pence for children and OAPs.

Haunted Skies Volume Ten

20th June 1988 – UFO over the sea

At 4.30pm, Terrence Taylor (50) was out on the seafront with his wife, at Clacton-on-Sea, when they noticed a black, square-shaped object, on the horizon out to sea.

> "It was very low and seemed to be skimming the sea, heading westwards at about 50mph. We reported it to the coastguard and police."

26th June 1988 – Triangular UFO seen over the coast of Essex

28th June 1988 – UFO over Dorset

At 1.30am, Mr and Mrs Strickland of Chine Hill, Puddeltown – a small village 5miles east of Dorchester – were disturbed and went to the window to look out.

> "We saw a circular object hovering over the adjacent field, near power lines. It was larger than the full moon. Suddenly it shot upwards, and then moved left, near houses, making a whining or humming noise. A light shone out of it and it disappeared from view."

30th June 1988 – Special Constable alleges abduction

On this date the *Yorkshire Evening Post* newspaper published details of an allegation of alien abduction by a Special Police Constable, which took place in Roundhay Park, Leeds, and was the subject of investigation by the British UFO Research, Association.

JULY 1988

10th July 1988 – UFO over Essex

At 9.45pm, Anthony Wallace (20) from Rosemary Avenue, Braintree, in Essex, was walking his dog. He said:

"Suddenly, a huge dish-shaped object appeared in the sky about 50ft above me. I stood there in amazement as it silently headed towards the Colchester area, gaining height."

13th July 1988 – UFO over Wiltshire

During this evening, Miss Mary Freeman from Marlborough, Wiltshire, was driving home in her Renault 5, from Winterbourne Monkton, one mile north of the Avebury stone circle. As she drove through Avebury on the A361, at 11.13pm, with about 70% cloud cover, she saw, through the driver's window, a large golden disc-shaped object within the cloud, out of which projected a bright white parallel beam of light, at an angle of about 65°, shining across the sky towards *Silbury Hill, one and a half miles to the south.

"I was amazed but not frightened; it was ethereal. Suddenly about half a dozen articles, which were in a recessed pocket along the dashboard, rose up and flew backwards, landing in my lap and onto the passenger seat next to me. It was as if a surge of energy had passed through the car."

*Silbury Hill is the tallest prehistoric man-made mound in Europe and one of the tallest in the world. It is estimated by archaeologists to have been built about 4,750 years ago. The mound is located in Wiltshire, England, and it overlooks West Kennett Long Barrow, a Neolithic tomb. Both archaeological sites are a little less than a mile south of one of the largest monolithic standing stone rings in the world, built around 2,600 BC. Silbury Hill, when seen for the first time, is breathtaking and still remains so irrespective of how many times you visit the area. There is a timeless quality about the landscape which enthuses one with a magical quality found nowhere else, even at Stonehenge. During the mid-1990s we were to spend much time down there, conducting our own research into all manner of strange phenomenon brought to our attention, which will be covered in later volumes.

Haunted Skies Volume Ten

On 15th July, unusual marks were photographed in the field adjacent to Silbury Hill and subsequently photographed by Colin Andrews and Pat Delgado. This photograph appeared in *Circular Evidence*, (Bloomsbury Publishing, 1989) written by Andrew and Pat, both known to us and well respected on the international stage for their efforts to preserve a unique and very important part of our social history. Colin Andrews has provided much assistance to the authors of the *Haunted Skies* series of books. He has always been there for us and we are proud of our friendship with him. His work has attracted the interest of Royalty and people such as David Mitchell MP as the following letters show . . . As a token of our appreciation, we would like to publish a photo of his beloved dog 'Angie' – now passed away.

From: David Mitchell, M.P.

HOUSE OF COMMONS
LONDON SW1A 0AA

9 September 1989

Colin Andrews Esq MASEE AILE

Andover
Hants

Dear Mr Andrews

I was glad of the opportunity of meeting you and going through matters again. I agree that the matter of the circles is something which the Government should assist in investigating and I shall make represntations to the Minister concerned. In addition I look forward to receiving photographs which are most effective in demonstrating firstly that it is not crop lodging because the crop is all neatly turned and laid and secondly that the circle is too scientifically a circle and not generally an area of the falling down of crop. Also the extraordinary photograph that shows satellite circles would be most effective in demonstrating the points you are making.

As soon as I have these photographs I will write to the appropriate Minister. If it is possible it would be helpful if I could have three sets of each photograph so that I can approach more than one Minister.

Yours sincerely

(Dictated by Sir David
but signed in his absence)

Haunted Skies Volume Ten

From: Brigadier Clive Robertson

BUCKINGHAM PALACE

31st October, 1989

The Duke of Edinburgh has asked me to write to thank you for your letter of 23rd October which His Royal Highness was most interested to read. Prince Philip would certainly like you to update him with significant developments on the Circles Phenomenon. Thank you again.

Yours sincerely,
Clive Robertson

Colin Andrews, Esq.,

BUCKINGHAM PALACE

10th May, 1990.

Dear Mr Andrews,

Thank you for your letter of 2nd May, which has been shown to The Queen. Her Majesty has taken an interest in the mysterious crop circles for some time, and was consequently sad to hear that your results of years of research into the question are at risk through lack of funds.

Haunted Skies Volume Ten

  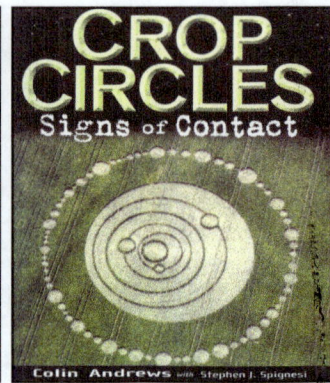 

Army helicopter lands

During numerous visits made there, many years ago, we also saw some very odd things in and around this ancient part of the country. This photo, taken by Colin, shows an Army helicopter landing close to Silbury Hill. A soldier was seen to jump out and apparently recover a video tape from a hedgerow below the hill.

Colin:

> "You can just make out people stood on top of Silbury Hill (illegally) who witnessed this. I happened to see the helicopter activity and took this photo. The next photograph was taken by me personally, from West Kennett Long Barrow, facing south-east, during the summer of 2003. I was visiting with my friend, Dr. Melih Arici, and both of us took random photos of the wonderful countryside in that area. When the large Hercules military aircraft appeared, I snapped two more photos. Neither of us saw this peculiar object to the left of the Hercules at the time, but back home in the US, about two weeks later, when looking through all of the photos, there it was. The second photo of the aircraft did not have the object in it."

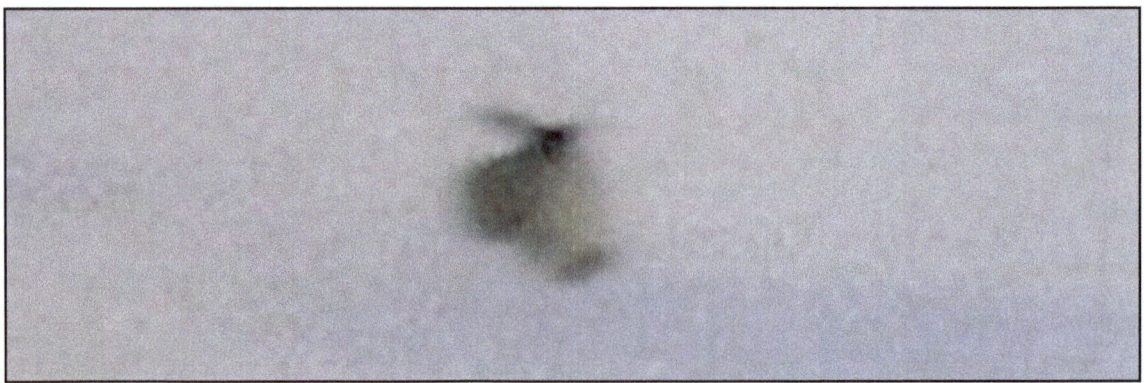

Haunted Skies Volume Ten

Another photograph shown was taken between 2-3pm on a Saturday afternoon in August 2010, by a person who wishes to remain anonymous. The camera is facing south over West Kennett Long Barrow. The classic UFO shape appeared over the Barrow and in the same region of sky as my own, seven years earlier. This unexplained object was not seen at the time the photo was taken, but seen when viewing later – again just like my own, between 2-3pm on a Saturday afternoon in August 2010. I would like to add that when the picture was taken, I was taking a picture of the Long Barrow and the UFO was only discovered when I got home and transferred the picture to my PC. It is a genuine picture and best seen zoomed in. It does look like the UFO is coming down from the right."

Photographs 1 and 2 taken near West Kennett Long Barrow, next to Silbury Hill, on 4th August 2009, by Audrey Davies and Stephen Morris.

Crop Circles – according to *Wikipedia*, 2013

According to *Wikipedia*: 'A crop circle is a sizable pattern created by the flattening of a crop such as wheat, barley, rye, maize, or rapeseed. Crop circles are also referred to as crop formations because they are not always circular in shape. The documented cases have substantially increased from the 1970s to current times. In 1991, two hoaxers claimed authorship of many circles throughout England. Twenty-six countries reported approximately 10,000 crop circles in the last third of the 20th century; 90% of those were located in Southern England. Circles in the United Kingdom are not spread randomly across the landscape, but they appear near roads, areas of medium to dense population, and cultural heritage monuments, such as Stonehenge or Avebury, and always in areas of easy access. Archeological remains can cause crop marks in the fields in the shapes of circles and squares, but they do not appear overnight, and they are always in the same places every year. The scientific consensus is that most or all crop circles are man-made, with a few possible exceptions due to meteorological or other natural phenomena.'

Colin Andrews: Now the reality!

On the 24th April 2013 Colin Andrews had occasion to write the following article, as found on his website, relating to the corruption of facts and history by *Wikipedia*, which is a serious issue …

> "Unlike Wikileaks who uncovered truths and could still have long-term positive influence on our future, its near name-sake, Wikipedia will not, the way it's going. The idea started off as a great one but its accuracy depended upon integrity in our adding or subtracting information. For those

in our ranks who have an axe to grind though, the exact opposite is what they have in mind; they it seems, will destroy this concept. I published some concerns on Jan 5, 2010. My own place in crop circle history is a good example of what is happening. My own input is well known by those who have followed my work, since I created the term 'Crop Circle' in the early 1980s, but those who are seemingly determined to re-write the subject inaccurately have changed all that. I have informed the moderator of the page but each time anything related to my involvement is entered, it's removed, leaving a great deal of the research I've done unaccredited, which is a large amount. As of the time I wrote my 2010 article, all the references to me have been deleted which leaves most of my 30 years work on the subject unaccredited by the Wikipedia site.

You would never know that I remain the longest living researcher of the subject along with my friend Busty Taylor. We took part in all the first series of TV documentaries and most of those that followed, did most of the ground work researching with Pat Delgado and Dr. Terence Meaden. I wrote the first book on the subject with Pat in 1989, 'Circular Evidence', featured in the first DVD and videos ever made on the subject and travelled the planet investigating and presenting as well as writing reports for my Prime Minister and Head of State, etc (BIO). It's a whole different story according to Wikipedia and that for all other subjects and the education of our children, this behaviour is of great concern."

UFOs – according to *Wikipedia*, 2013

'An unidentified flying object, or UFO, in its most general definition, is any apparent anomaly in the sky (or near or on the ground, but observed hovering, landing, or departing into the sky) that is not readily identifiable as any known object or phenomenon by visual observation and/or use of associated instrumentation such as radar. These anomalies were referred to popularly as "flying saucers" or "flying discs" during the late 1940s and early 1950s. The term "UFO" (or "UFOB") was officially created in 1953 by the United States Air Force (USAF) to replace the more popular terms because of the variety of shapes described other than "discs" or "saucers." It was stated that a "UFOB" was "any airborne object which by performance, aerodynamic characteristics, or unusual features, does not conform to any presently known aircraft or missile type, or which cannot be positively identified as a familiar object." As originally defined, the term was restricted to that fraction of cases which remained unidentified after investigation, with USAF interest being for potential national security reasons and/or "technical aspects." (See Air Force Regulation 200-2).

The term UFO became more widespread during the 1950s, at first in professional literature, but later in popular use. UFOs garnered considerable interest during the Cold War, an era associated with a heightened concern for national security. Various studies have concluded that the phenomenon does not represent a threat to national security nor does it contain anything worthy of scientific pursuit (e.g., 1953 CIA Robertson Panel, USAF Project Blue Book, Condon Committee). Culturally, the phenomenon has often been associated with extraterrestrial life or government-related conspiracy theories, and has become a popular theme in fiction.

Studies have established that the majority of UFO observations are misidentified conventional objects or natural phenomena—most commonly aircraft, balloons, noctilucent clouds, nacreous clouds, or astronomical objects such as meteors or bright planets with a small percentage even being hoaxes. Between 5% and 20% of reported sightings are not explained, and therefore can be classified as unidentified in the strictest sense.

While proponents of the extraterrestrial hypothesis (ETH) suggest that these unexplained reports are of alien spacecraft, the null hypothesis cannot be excluded that these reports are simply other more prosaic phenomena that cannot be identified due to lack of complete information or due to the necessary subjectivity of the reports. While UFOs have been the subject of extensive investigation by various governments and although a few scientists have supported the extraterrestrial hypothesis, almost no scientific papers about UFOs have

Haunted Skies: Now for reality!

We agree wholeheartedly with the comments made by Colin Andrews. Surely by now, it is patently obvious that during a period in the last 60 years of UFO history on this planet, involving many periods of intense UFO activity, the real facts surrounding what had taken place is still continuing to be kept from us. Despite our best efforts, we have been unable to attract any interest from the Media with regard to our continuing long-term commitment to preserving the social history of what UFOs have represented. Through publication of **nine** intense *Haunted Skies* Volumes, covering the years 1940-1988, we believe we have overwhelmingly shown, from the evidence presented, that while it may have nothing to do with an extraterrestrial presence on Earth, it is clearly *worthy of investigation*.

July 1988 – Woolaston, Gloucestershire

In the same month, Tom Gwinnett – a farmer from Woolaston, near the Forest of Dean – was driving past a wheat field, one July evening in 1988, when his car's electrics suddenly failed. He was trying to rectify the problem, without success, when he became aware of a strange whirring noise.

> "I looked into the adjacent field, and saw a dull red 'ball', the size of a football. It was not a solid sphere; rather, it appeared to consist of a cluster of red sparks, and the sparks seem to be coming from the tops of the wheat."

Spellbound, Gwinett watched the mysterious *'ball'* for a minute or two, the mechanical sound continuing throughout. The object then suddenly disappeared and all was quiet. At the precise moment, the electrical fault on his car righted itself, his headlights came back on and he was able to continue his journey. He did not inspect the field that evening, but the following morning he discovered a six-metre crop circle in the spot where he had seen the mysterious *'ball'* of red sparks.

16th July 1988 – Cigar-shaped object over Buckinghamshire

Gerald Twaites, his wife, Sue, and son, Danny, were driving along the A5 at Little Brickhill, Milton Keynes, Buckinghamshire, during the evening, when they sighted a blazing cigar-shaped object hovering over the road, estimated to be about five miles away. Gerry managed to take some film of the object with a video camera he had taken with him to an earlier wedding, and later reported it to Arnold West, of BUFORA, and the police.

According to an MOD spokesperson, who was consulted, he said:

> "I've seen flying oranges until they turned out to be balloons; it depends on the time of the day, the position of the person, the weather. We follow some of the reports up, but we've never yet been able to prove the existence of 'little green men'." ...

A typical response from somebody whose knowledge of the UFO subject was clearly limited.

(Source: Personal interview/*Citizen*, 21.7.1988 – 'Mystery objects spark a probe')

Another motorist to see something unusual that evening was Malcolm Naylor (26). He was driving home from Colchester, at midnight, near to Lawford, when:

> "... a very large triangular object, showing no lights, swooped very low over the car, about 150ft high. It had a wingspan of 4-500ft and had three pointed ends at the rear, with what looked like rods sticking out. Another car heading towards me swerved, but managed to avoid a collision. I was shaking like a leaf and felt sick. I had to stop the car to recover."

18th July 1988 – UFO sighted by Ron West

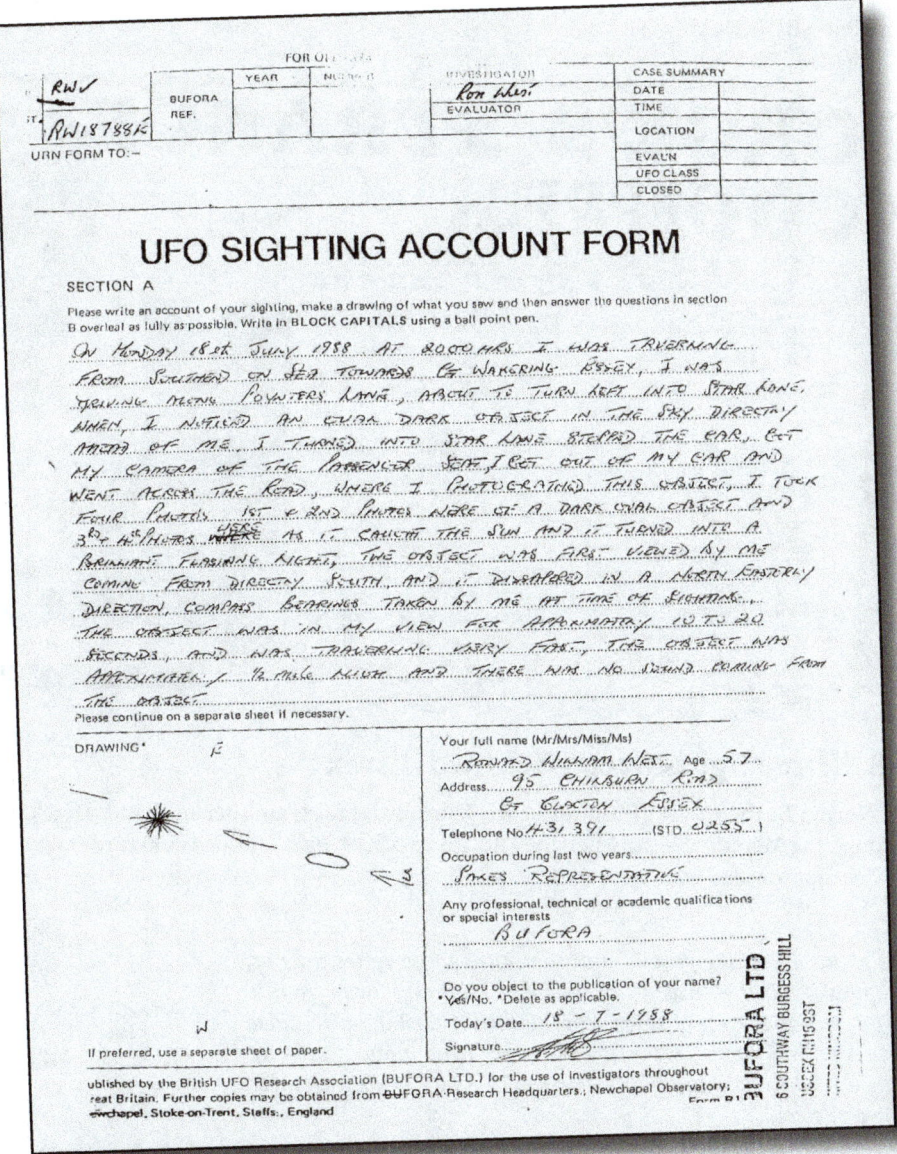

20th July 1988 – UFO over flight path, Essex

At 10pm, Sarah (aged 32) from Prospect Lane, Woodford Green, Essex, was in the kitchen, making a cup of tea, when she noticed a brilliant light in the sky.

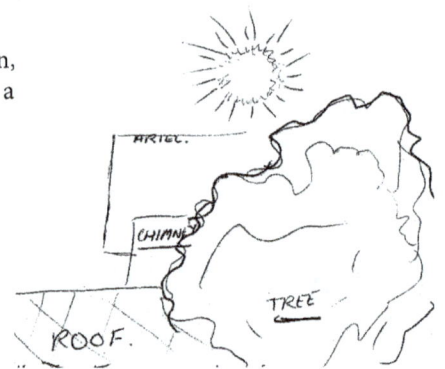

> "We are on a major flight path, so I am fully conversant with air traffic. This thing was totally silent and stationary in the sky and pulsating slightly. A few seconds later it dimmed and then flared up with light, illuminating the whole area, before vanishing completely."

(Source: Tony Pace, BUFORA)

July 1988 - Three lights over Wickford, Essex

At 10.30pm, Norma Burnett (44) of Mount Close, Wickford, Essex, and her husband, Derek, were walking their dog through the Memorial Park, when they noticed a bright *'light'*, about 4-500 yards away, which moved to the left as they approached it.

Norma:

> "It was about 4ft off the ground and continued to move towards us; when approximately 200yds away, we turned left and away from it. The 'light' was made up of three separate lights, forming a lopsided triangle. A few minutes later we saw an orange light, motionless in the sky – then a white light moved upwards to it. As it did so, it changed to orange in colour."

(Source: Brenda Butler/Ron West, East Anglian UFO & Paranormal Research Association)

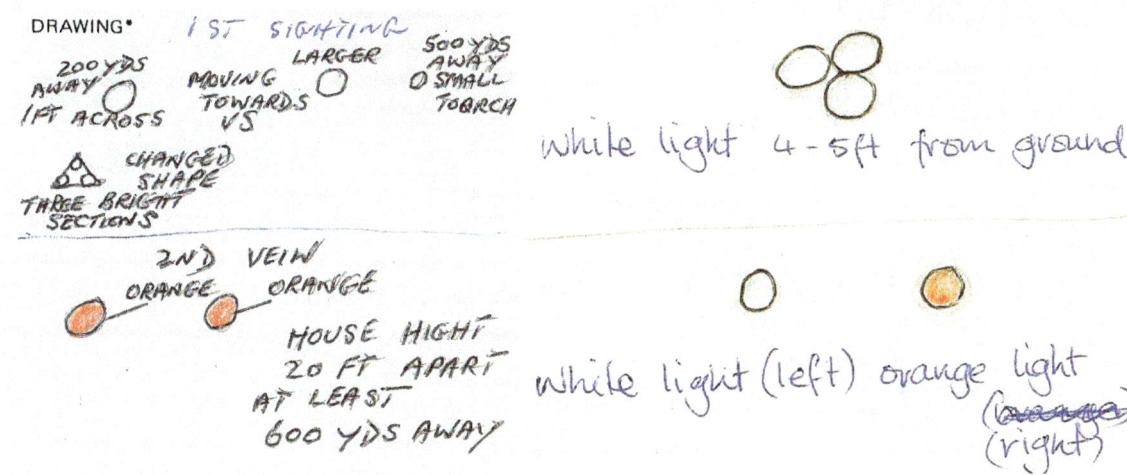

25th July 1988 – UFO over Warwick

At 10.30pm, a mysterious neon-lit round object, with flashing red and blue lights, was seen stationary in the sky over Warwick, by two girls returning home to Stratford-upon-Avon, before suddenly dropping down, reversing, moving to the left, and disappearing from view.

(Source: *Leamington Spa Morning News*, 29.7.1988 – 'Mystery or imagination?')

They were not the only ones to sight strange phenomena. A taxi driver and two passengers were driving in the early hours of that morning when they reported having been chased by a saucer-shaped object, close to the *Marsden Inn* at Whitburn.

Haunted Skies Volume Ten

26th July 1988 – UFO over Essex

At 6.51pm, Margaret Rose Preston from Gascoyne Road, Colchester, in Essex, was out driving with her husband, when he drew her attention to an object in the sky.

> *"It was elliptical in shape and not moving. We watched it for a few minutes before it moved away."*

27th July 1988 – 'Plank' UFO over Harlow

At 9pm, John McDonald (34) of Harlow, Essex, was in his back garden, watering the plants in his greenhouse.

> *"I happened to look up into the darkening sky and saw a long, thin, horizontal 'plank' of orange light. It was fading in and out, glowing and pulsating. I watched it for 30 minutes, until my wife called me in for my bath."*

29th July 1988 – UFO over St. Osyth

At 10.15pm, Hospital porter Neil Jones (19) was outside, when he sighted a pulsating triangular object in the sky, about half a mile away; he was not the only one. At least 40 people gathered around to witness the *'craft'*.

(Source: Brenda Butler/Ron West, East Anglian UFO & Paranormal Research Association)

July 1988 – UFO over Sunderland

In the same month, an object described as *"some kind of machine, with grey metal on top, 80ft long, with red lights on top and bottom, with a string of white lights along its rim"*, was seen at 3am, over the 'Marsden Inn', at Whitburn, Sunderland, by a woman taxi driver and her male passenger, who reported the matter to the police, after being followed by the *'saucer'* along the coast road, before it disappeared over the local golf course. A police spokesman said:

> *"We get quite a few reports of UFO sightings, but this is the most dramatic I have ever come across. This woman and man are not crackpots, and did not know each other before the incident, so there is nothing to indicate they would have made the story up. The whole thing is a mystery."*

Haunted Skies Volume Ten

AUGUST 1988

3rd August 1988 – Crop marks found in field at Beckhampton, Wiltshire

9th August 1988 – Glowing UFO over Saffron Walden, Essex

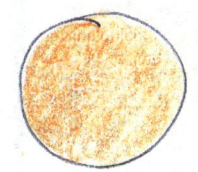

At 10pm, housewife Jane Hancock (48) was in her garden, when she was shocked to see another appearance of a mysterious red globe, the size of a tea plate in the sky, moving in a westerly direction.

"Suddenly it stopped for a good ten minutes, before vanishing from view."

12th August 1988 – Diamond-shaped UFO

At 12.30am, Stephen Ely – an accountant by occupation – was with two friends in the garden, studying the night sky, hoping for a glimpse of meteorites. Their patience was rewarded when, after about an hour, 15-20 meteors were seen flashing across the sky.

"All of a sudden a diamond-shaped object appeared in the sky, right of the North direction. It was clearly defined externally, but the interior was misty – a blue-grey in colour – and swirling about inside. I found it impossible to calculate the size of the object compared with its height above the ground, but it was about a foot in size in the sky. We saw it head east to west and then disappear out of view."

(Source: Brenda Butler/Ron West, East Anglian UFO & Paranormal Research Association)

14th August 1988 – UFOs over Mansfield, Nottinghamshire

UFO investigator Mr William Blythe from Padley Hill, Mansfield, who was responsible for assisting the authors some years ago with local sightings reports, was in the backyard, at 11pm,

"...when I saw a brilliant object, travelling just above rooftops of a nearby house, and called my wife. We dashed into the street to get a better look and saw, with surprise, that the lights had dimmed and we were looking at a large white craft, with a row of orange portholes along its side. We continued watching until it disappeared behind the skyline."

According to William, another sighting took place over Forest Town, Nottinghamshire, that evening, involving a report of a large shape, covered in many small lights, with a red light at the rear. Mr Blythe contacted the *Mansfield Observer*, who published his story on 22nd September 1988.

16th August 1988 – UFOs over Essex

At 2.30am, Private security officers David Smith (28) and Alan Todd (52) were on patrol, driving down Thorney Bay Road, Canvey Island. They saw three lights – white, blue and red – hovering about 150ft above a nearby field adjacent to a holiday camp. The men stopped the car to take a closer look.

Haunted Skies Volume Ten

EAST ANGLIAN U.F.O. & PARANORMAL RESEARCH ASSOCIATION

SECTION A — SIGHTING ACCOUNT FORM

Please write an account of your sighting, make a drawing of what you saw and then answer the questions in section B overleaf as fully as possible. Write in BLOCK CAPITALS using a ball point pen.

1/9/58

Approx 6 weeks' on night Patrol myself and another Person Return to Base, approx 2-30 in the early hrs of the morning, I saw 3 lights white, blue, and red, in that order, approx 150-200 ft in the air approx 400 yrds distance, we stop the motor and watched the light for a few seconds, later it turned slowly in a Hovering Position and took off a great speed, towards South and in a Zig Zag way, a great Speed, as close as we were, to these lights, a no time deal of or any sound of Engine, or sound of any Propellers. These light were so bright that it shrouded the object that was carrying these light.

DRAWING: BLUE RED WHITE — LARGE BRIGHT LIGHTS — APROX 15 ft 20 ft — 400 ft

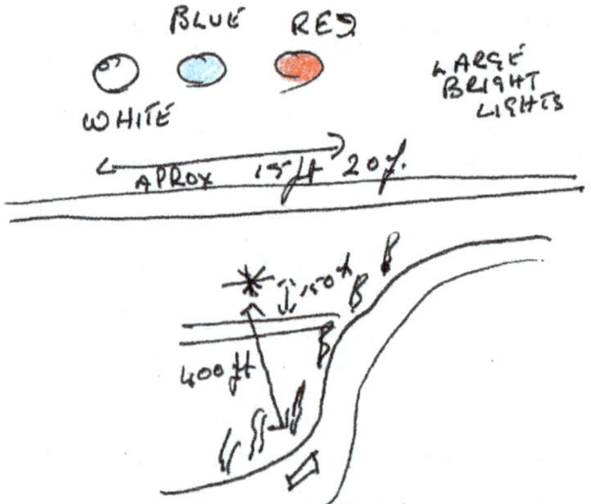

Your full name: T.O.D.D. CALLAM   Age: 52
Address: 12 LEIGH RD, CANVEY ISLAND
Telephone No: 685169 (STD. 0268)
Occupation during last two years: SIGNWRITER

Today's Date: 29/9/58

David:

"There was no engine noise. We watched them for about 30 seconds; suddenly they banked away at a speed faster than anything I have ever seen before, and headed towards the direction of Shoeburyness."

(Source: Brenda Butler/Ron West, East Anglian UFO & Paranormal Research Association)

21st August 1988 – UFO over Hawarth

On or about the 21st August 1988, Keighley pensioner – Mrs Margaret Snowdon – was talking to her neighbour – Edith Spencer – in her 9th floor flat at Parkwood Rise, when their conversation was interrupted by a buzzing noise. Looking out of the window the women saw:

> "... a weird oval-shaped object, black on top with a silver rim around its centre, flying towards Keighley from the direction of Hawarth."

The incident was later explained away by local UFO Researcher, David Barclay, as likely to have been pressure in the rocks (just before a rainfall) creating the effect of an Earthlight.

(Source: *Bradford Telegraph & Argus*, West Yorkshire, 20.8.1988 – 'Afternoon cuppa disturbed by a UFO', 21.8.88 – 'Oval flying saucer shocks Margaret – Rain Theory over that silver UFO')

27th August 1988 – UFO seen over Essex

At 9.10pm, amateur astronomer Mr Colin Pell (64) of Cambridge Road, Southend-on-Sea, was outside, adjusting the finder on his Tasco 11T Newtonian telescope, using the pole star as a guide, when:

> "... an object passed across my line of sight, heading south-west to north-east. I managed to keep it in track for some 10° – I then looked with eyesight and was able to pick it up and follow to ground level. This was not any earthbound satellite (of which I have seen many) as it didn't roll and usually disappear after 10-15°. What made this one different was that its brightness stayed with it all the time of observation."

UFO seen – Angel hair found?

Could there have been a connection with what took place at Thorpe Bay, Essex, during the same evening, involving Mrs T Sullivan (62)? She was in bed at Wansfell Gardens, when she was shocked to see what looked like a *"train, or railway carriage,"* moving across the sky. Enquiries made by Ron West revealed that others living in the same locality had sighted a *'black object'* hovering in the sky, at around the same time.

The next morning, when she got up, she was surprised to see a large amount of grey, hard pointed, debris scattered over the local golf course. She told Ron that she had collected some for analysis, but it disappeared before this could be done. Was this Angel hair – a sticky, fibrous substance, reported in connection with UFO sightings, described as being like a cobweb, or a jelly? It is named for its similarity to fine hair, or spider webs, and in some cases, the substance has been found to be the web threads of migrating spiders. Reports of Angel hair say that it disintegrates or evaporates within a short time of forming.

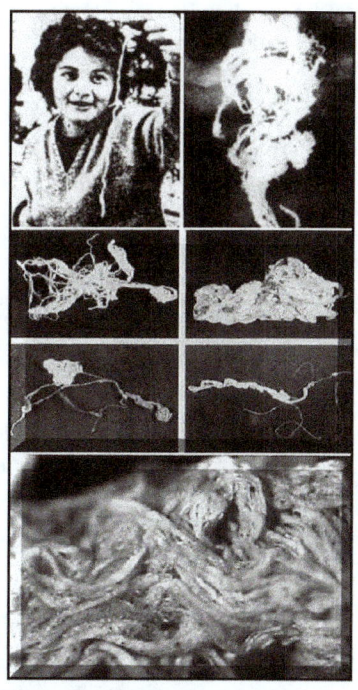

(Source: Ron West, Brenda Butler, East Anglian UFO & Paranormal Research Association)

Starjelly

Late August 1988 – Triangular UFO over Essex

At 9.30pm, Valerie Knight of Boundary Road, Leigh-on-Sea, was sat in her lounge when she noticed some bright blue, yellow and white, lights in the sky. As they weren't flashing, as one might have expected from an aircraft (bearing in mind the close proximity of nearby Southend Airport) she ran into the back garden, accompanied by her son. They were stunned to see a silvery, triangular object, moving towards the direction of Hockley. A minute later it was out of sight.

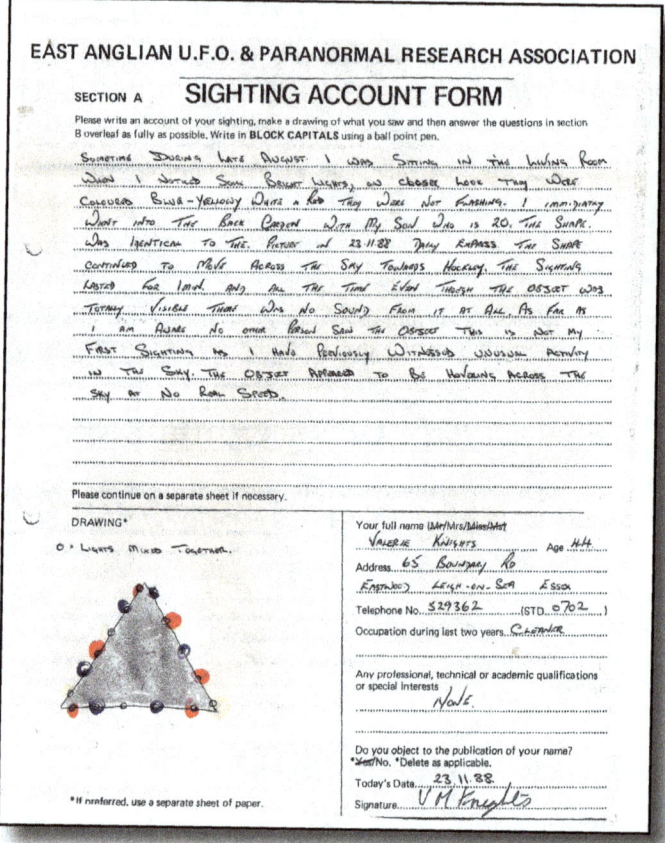

Late August 1988 – Three UFOs over Essex

Also in this month was a sighting of what should now be all too familiar to the reader, involving the appearance of three separate *globes of light*. On this occasion they were seen by Shirley Muir of Galleywood, Chelmsford, Essex. She was settling back to bed after having attended to her small boy, who woke up at 1.20am.

> "I was getting back into bed, when I noticed some bright lights through a gap in the bedroom curtains. I first thought it might be something to do with the Marconi Research Station, as we can see the mast from our house. I looked out and saw three lights, forming a triangle, low down in the sky towards the Danbury direction. I watched them for about 25mins but then began to feel a little frightened, so I closed the curtains and went back to bed. The next morning, I looked out and realised the object had been nowhere near the mast."

28th August 1988 – Triangular UFO seen over Essex

At 8pm, Mr William Evans (76) of Fobbing, Essex, was with his wife when they saw a number of coloured lights moving across the sky.

> "All were in the shape of triangles. We watched them for over an hour. When aircraft flew overhead, the lights from the objects would extinguish but come on again as soon as the aircraft were out of sight."

At 10pm, Carlton McVey (51), of Westcliff-on-Sea, was out in his garden when he noticed a triangle of three lights, heading northwards at speed.

> "They then turned upon themselves and returned along the path previously taken. Cloud height was 40,000ft and they were judged to be considerably higher."

(Source: Ron West/Brenda Butler, East Anglian UFO & Paranormal Research Association)

CHAPTER 7

SEPTEMBER TO OCTOBER 1988

SEPTEMBER 1988

Electrical discharge over Sandling Road, Kent – Autumn 1988

DURING the same month, housewife and freelance writer – Mrs Monika Newman (75) of Moray Lodge, Sandling Road, Saltwood, Kent, was awoken at 1am by what sounded like an explosion. As a result of what she saw, she later wrote to Ron West.

> K/89/226
> Moray Lodge
> Sandling Road
> Saltwood, Nr. Hythe
> Kent CT21 4QN
> Phone: 0303-66676
>
> June 4th 1989
>
> Dear Mr Robson,
>
> I saw your letter in the Adscene paper yesterday, about UFOs. I must say that I cannot really believe in these, but I did have an extraordinary thing happen just outside our house last autumn, and on reading your letter I have come to the conclusion that what I saw must have been on the same night in November that something odd happened around Castle Road here in Saltwood. I did not make a note of the date, but the time was just after 1 am. I was asleep and awakened by a bang (not a very big one). This was followed immediately by a curious noise as if some highly combustible fluid had suddenly caught fire and I could see a red flash through the curtains. My first thought was that there must have been a car accident just outside the entrance to our house. I pulled back the curtains and all I could see was a mass flames, not red now but more coloured in blue and white, rising from the ground and moving along the telephone wire from the road towards the house. I particularly remember seeing the white painted woodwork on the gables of the house lit up as the flames rose upwards. Then suddenly it was all over. There was no sound at all. I went out early in the morning to see if there was any sign of burning where all this had happened, but I could find no trace of any kind of damage. I have thought a lot about this and the only thing I can suggest is that it was some kind of electrical discharge. Many years ago, on a day of thunder storms, my father, who was driving a horse and cart, was followed by a glowing ball which floated along about a foot above the ground but finally changed direction and disappeared. I also had a friend who was sitting in a room with a door open on one side and a window on the other. Suddenly one of these globes of electricity floated in through the window, crossed the room and went out through the door without causing any noise or damage. Both these incidents happened in Finland. Could you tell me who it was that reported the blue-white light around Castle Road. I would be interested to speak to the person who reported this.
>
> When I told my family of what I had seen during the night, they would not believe it and insisted that I must have been dreaming, but I am quite certain that I was fully awake. A dream fades very quickly from memory, but I can remember exactly what it all looked like and the sound of the explosion also.
>
> Yours sincerely,
> Monica Newman
>
> K/89/226

Haunted Skies Volume Ten

1st September 1988 – Triangular 'Lights' over Essex

At 2pm, Fred Tidey (57) of Tankerton, Kent – a foundry foreman by occupation – was working in his rear garden when he saw:

> "... a 'traffic light' amber coloured object, shaped like a peanut, heading through the sky. I called my wife, Marjorie (59). She told me it was an airplane. I fetched some binoculars and looked through to see a 'delta wing' object showing striped vertical lines of red and yellow, over its outer surface. It then suddenly changed shape from triangular to 'knife edge'. I watched it heading northwards."

2nd September 1988 - 'Lights' over Essex

At 2.30am, Jacky – a resident of Bournemouth Park Road, Southend, in Essex – was having trouble sleeping, when all of a sudden the night sky was flooded with a brilliant light that illuminated the bedroom. Wondering what on earth was going on, she rushed to the window and looked out, seeing:

> "... a number of bright longish oval 'lights', split by smaller green lights forming a semicircle in the sky, hovering silently over the tops of nearby houses".

Frightened, she went back to bed and hid under the covers.

(Source: Ron West/Brenda Butler, East Anglian UFO & Paranormal Research Association)

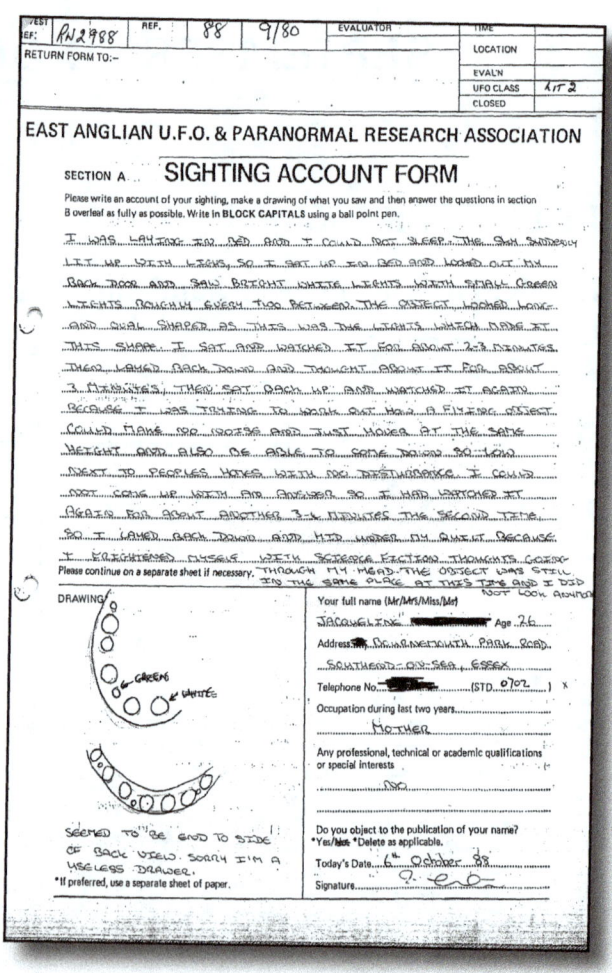

3rd September 1988 – Unidentified pulsating 'mist' seen in Suffolk

At 11am, Norman Ernest Trent from Eye, Suffolk – known to Brenda Butler and extremely interested in both UFO and paranormal subjects, who had the misfortune to have met David Daniels, the alleged reptilian (See Volume 9 of *Haunted Skies*) – was at his home address, accompanied by Miss W.I. Trent, when he noticed:

'On the chilly autumn evening of 16th November 1963, 17 year-old John Flaxton, 18 year-old Mervyn Hutchinson, and two other youths, were walking home from a party on Sandling Road, in the county of Kent, when they saw a silent, glowing, orb-like object, described as being just a few metres in diameter, hovering above a field. It was then seen to make its way behind trees and settle into the shadow infested foliage of the woods at Sandling Park. Moments later a shambling, quasi-humanoid, figure emerged from the woods and waddled towards them. The *'beast'*, looking like a headless bat, was approximately 5ft tall, with large webbed feet, and wings protruding from its back. Needless to say, the youths made their escape. (See Volume 2 of *Haunted Skies* for full 'write-up').

"... a semi-luminous shape of grey pulsating 'mist', floating in the north-west corner of his garden, over where garden rubbish is normally burnt. (There had not been a fire there for a few days.) It was about 3ft in diameter but wasn't truly circular. The edges were ragged and hazy. Three minutes later (timed by my watch) it began to grow brighter – as if illuminated internally. At 11.04am it moved along the boundary hedge, before suddenly disappearing from view."

(Source: Ron West/Brenda Butler, East Anglian UFO & Paranormal Research Association)

4th September 1988 – 'Box' UFO over Essex

At 10.15pm, Marian Bowers (72) of Hardwick Close, Rayleigh, Essex, was in the road when she noticed an object moving through the sky, which she described as:

"... lit-up like a Christmas tree, heading northwards. It had these white, red, blue and green lights, flashing as it did so. It was more box shape than aircraft".

(Source: Ron West/Brenda Butler, East Anglian UFO & Paranormal Research Association)

7th September 1988 – Formation of UFOs over Essex

At 12.30am, John Pizzey (28) of South Stifford, Grays, was out 'sky watching', when he saw, through binoculars, some fast moving objects high up in the sky.

"There were four of them, flying in tight lines; they moved into a 'V' shape and then into a 'ball', before moving back into tight lines."

8th September 1988 – UFO over Wickford, Essex

At 9.20pm, Chris Johnson (43) was out walking the dog at Canvey Island, when he sighted two strange lights moving through the sky, heading westwards. Chris later contacted Ron West to tell him about what he had seen.

At 10.30pm, Miss Y. Burnett from Mount Close, Wickford, Essex, was sat in the bedroom, talking to her boyfriend, when he noticed a strange red 'light' in the sky.

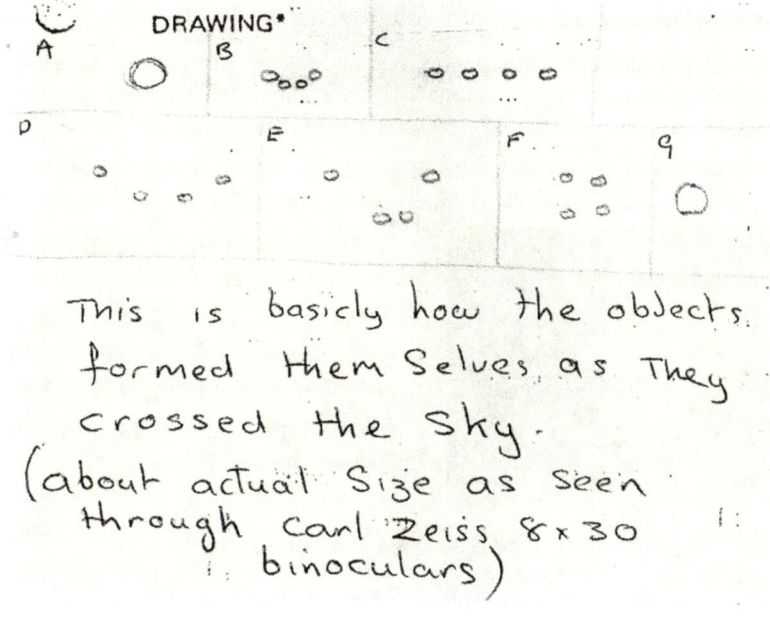

"I looked out and saw, just above some trees, two red lights; they were much lower than aircraft. All of a sudden, they shot away at speed and were gone."

Haunted Skies Volume Ten

9th September 1988 – Triangular & Rectangular UFOs seen over Essex

At 6.45pm, painter and decorator Steve Smith (32) was driving from Billericay, towards Mount Cressing, when he noticed a disc-shaped object motionless in the sky, before vanishing from sight seconds later.

At 9pm, Sylvia Murray (46) was walking home from visiting a friend, and near her home in Langdon, when she noticed a collection of lights, stationary in the sky.

"They were red, orange and white, forming a triangular shape. I stood and watched it for 10-15 minutes. I began to feel frightened and ran inside."

Geoffrey Welling (40) was driving home from having been to see his mother in Ilford, Essex. About half a mile from the *Fortune of War Public House* roundabout, eastbound along the A127, he noticed a brightly-lit object, showing a cluster of various coloured lights in the sky to his right. He thought no more of it, until he read about UFOs being sighted on that evening.

At 10.15pm, Mr Elliot 'S' (18) from Laindon, Essex, was walking through the shopping centre on his way home.

He noticed a large black diamond-shaped object, motionless in the sky, with two *'balls of light'* in the centre, about 200ft up in the air. He watched it for ten minutes, after which time it began to go *'fuzzy'* before completely vanishing from view. A number of black rectangular shapes, showing blue and white lights, were seen in the sky over Pitsea, for a few minutes, before fading away.

At 10.30pm, another witness was engineer Peter Aldridge of Clayburn Circle, Basildon, who saw a single orange *'light'*, accompanied by a humming noise, while out walking with his dog.

"After a few minutes it seemed to split into two and come together again, and then shoot off like the dot when you turn the TV off."

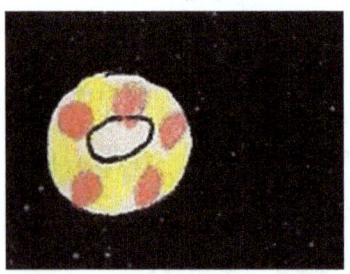

At 11.10pm, Sheila Johnson (22) from Basildon sighted a *'ring of lights'* in the sky over the *Barge Public House*.

"They were very low and travelling slowly, from east to west. The lights in front were red and yellow, mixed in with orange lights. I heard no noise during the ten minutes I watched it."

She was not the only one. Mr J. Petty saw what appeared to be the same lights over the sea off Southend.

10th September 1988 – UFO over the sea

At 2.15am, Barry Smith – a fisherman from Barling Magna, Essex – was heading out towards the North Sea, along the *River Crouch*, when he noticed a bright object in the sky.

"At first I thought it was a flare, but flares don't hover or stay for long. I watched it for a good five minutes, noticing that its reflection was caught in the sea below it. As I was passing the Buxey Buoy

out from Clacton-on-Sea, I saw it again – small, to begin with, but then increasing in size. I called the first mate – Mr Stow – to come up on deck and have a look.

We watched it for a further ten minutes and checked the onboard Radar, which hadn't picked it up. It then disappeared."

At 10.15pm, Mr Peter Mason (41) was driving his bus along High Street, Basildon, Essex, when he saw:

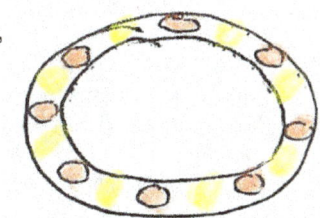

"... a ring of white and orange coloured lights, high up in the sky. I stopped the bus and shouted to the conductor to come and have a look. He suggested it was an aircraft. I told him that it couldn't be, as this thing was the shape of a doughnut and was covered in lights."

(Source: Ron West and Brenda Butler)

11th September 1988 – UFOs and Crop Circle, Suffolk

At 1am, Dave 'W' – then a serving member of the Armed Forces, from Billericay, Essex – was on his way home, with eight other servicemen, after a night out.

"We were surprised to see, in the sky over South Green, three stationary objects showing orange lights. The far right one was spinning around very fast . We watched them for about a minute, until they suddenly went out and disappeared from view."

At 9.30pm, Mr Horace Grimwood Carter (76) and his wife Patricia (57) from Grays, Essex, sighted what they thought was a bright star in the sky, until they realised it was moving. As it passed overhead, Mr Carter managed to look at it through binoculars, when he saw a delta winged-shaped object with bright lights attached to it.

```
0375 380961                                    33, Palmers Ave.,
                        CASE 88/9/93             Grays,
                                                   Essex, RM17 5TX.

The Editor,                                    17th. Sept 1988.
Thurrock Gazette,
Orsett Road,
Grays.

Dear Sir,
        Last Sunday 11th. Sept. at about 9.30p.m. my wife was at our front door.
She called me to come and look at what she at first thought to be a very bright Star
but realised that it was moving.
        We observed this, it was travelling comparitively slowly for an aircraft
in a North North Westerly direction at approximately 320° and passed immediately
over our heads.  Unlike a normal Aircraft it was brilliantly lit with bright WHITE
lights and appeared to me to be of a Delta Wing shape but we could not hear any
engine noise.
        It must have been seen by many people. I am not suggesting that it was
an Unidentified Flying Object but it was unusual and I rather expected some
mention of it in the Media but the only report that I saw or heard was a rather
scathing/jocular reference by Derek Jamiesin in his programe on Monday morning.
        I wonder, can you give an explanation of its origin, wither it was bound
and what type of Aircraft it was.

                                Yours faithfully,

                                    H.G. Carter.
```

Haunted Skies Volume Ten

Also at 9.30pm, schoolboy Peter Topham (aged 11) from Tutt Hill, Fornham All Saints, near Bury St. Edmunds, Suffolk (close to the junction with the B1106 and B1112) was getting ready for bed, when he saw, through the open bedroom window, a bright object in the sky.

On 23rd September 1988, in an interview conducted by Derek Newman and Ron West, from the East Anglian UFO & Paranormal Research Association, Peter told them:

> *"I went upstairs to get ready for bed, and looked out of the bedroom window, when I saw a bright light come out of the sky from nowhere – like a bullet. I went down to tell my sisters, who came upstairs. We could see other lights on it. I tried to stay awake all night, but I fell asleep. We had heard no noise and the colours of the lights were four purple lights and three different colours on it, and they changed colours – blue, changing red. There was no noise – just these 'sparks' of light going across the field."*

Rebecca (15):

> *"After following my brother upstairs, I looked out of the window. The first thing I noticed was four purple lights. After a while, maybe ten minutes, a large rectangular-shaped light came on very brightly. While this was happening, I saw small darting lights across the field (these were white). The following Monday we went up to the area where we had seen it land; there was a large round circle of flattened sugar beet. On the Wednesday we took my Dad to the area. He pointed out that the sugar beet and soil in the circle was dry, while the field was wet from rain. I didn't hear any noise."*

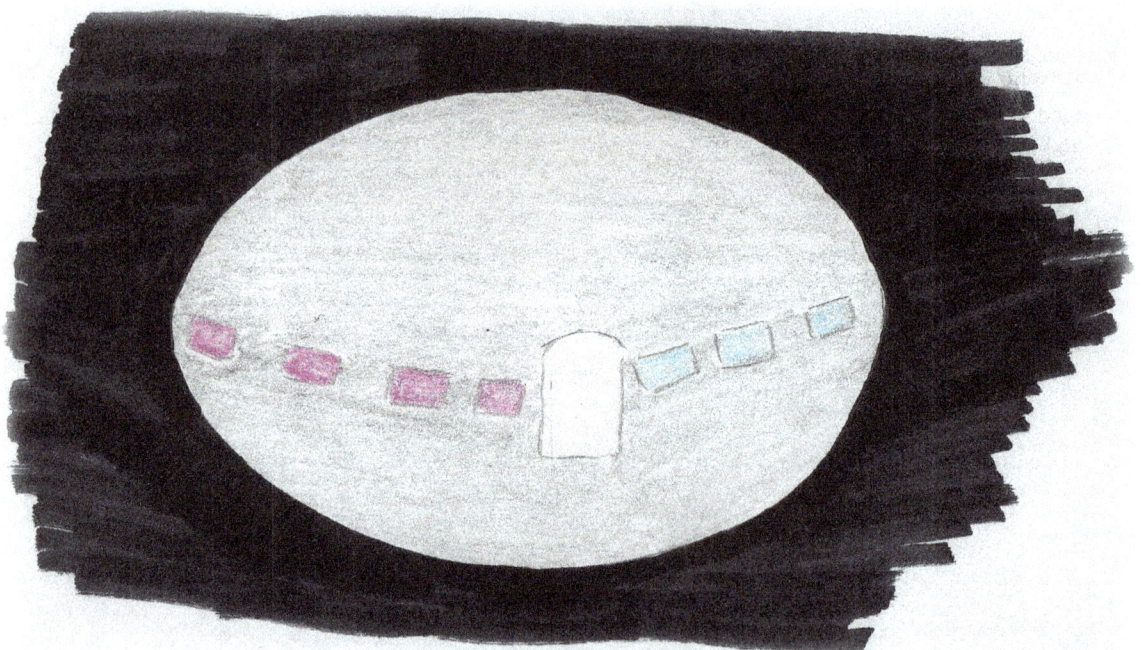

Josephine (10):

> *"At 9.30pm Peter came rushing down to tell us to come up, so we went up and saw a big light in the middle and other lights either side, over the field, and then they started flashing different colours – a few minutes later, the light in the middle went even brighter, then I decided to go to bed. There was a big light in the middle, and white lights on the left, with green, red, blue and orange, ones on the other side."*

Del and Ron made their way to the scene of the incident, where they examined the circle of flattened beet. Del:

> "The ground was bone dry; the remainder of the field was moist – the sugar beet within this circle was flattened compared to the rest of the field. The beet inside the circle was showing signs of decay, with yellowing leaves, in contrast to the outside, which was still thriving with dark green leaves. We found no indentations within the circle or outside. We measured the flattened area and found it to be 30metres, but it was not a perfect circle."

Fears grow crafts buzz

By ANDY RUSSELL

IT was 9.30 p.m. when schoolboy Peter Topham felt compelled to look out of his bedroom window, over the fenlands near his East Anglia home.

But what he saw had him staring wide-eyed in disbelief.

There, at the end of the field, was a weird craft with flashing red, green and purple lights.

"It was a flying saucer," says Peter. "It also flashed a large white light, like a camera, which seemed to cover the entire field."

He is one of the many terrified people who have seen—but haven't been able to explain—mysterious lights in the sky over East Anglia.

The following day Peter, of Fornham All Saints, near Bury St. Edmunds, stepped out into the field to see if there was any trace of the strange craft.

In the middle of the large crop of beet, there was 100ft-wide circle which had been flattened.

The story reached Del Newman, a UFO expert in Ipswich and two weeks after the sighting he interviewed Peter and inspected the field.

"Even after that amount of time, the circle was still distinguishable from the rest of the field," says Del who helps run the East Anglia UFO and Paranormal Research Society.

Disturbing

Peter's conviction that a UFO visited the fens of East Anglia is backed by dozens of unexplained and disturbing sightings.

"The United States air force bases at Mildenhall and Woodbridge and the nuclear power station at Sizewell would be areas of interest to visitors from space," says Del Newman.

Among the frightening close encounters was that of former teacher Janet Richards.

She was driving along the A12 at Blyburgh in Suffolk one evening with daughter Cathy, 23.

"We were chatting away about this and that when I noticed a sort of ball of white light in the sky," says Janet, 52.

"We got out of the car and there was a humming sound and the light came towards us and passed overhead."

Saucer

Nurse and qualified pilot Melanie Hartley of Bury St Edmunds had a similar experience when she was driving home near the village of Fornham All Saints.

"It was about 11 p.m. and I noticed a very bright light reflecting on our car bonnet from above. Both my daughters were in the back and they saw an object to the left and above the car," says Melanie, 41.

She described the saucer-shaped object as being about the length of three double-decker buses.

Artist James Aish saw a similar object while he was looking out of his bedroom window at home in Tydd St Giles, near Wisbech in Cambrid-

Haunted Skies Volume Ten

– 7 OCT 1988 Bury Free Press

Experts support UFO claim

Report by Andy Cooper

EXPERTS are giving their backing to a young boy's claim that he saw an unidentified flying object land in a field at the rear of his home.

Two ufologists have visited ten-year-old Peter Topham at his Fornham All Saints home and have confirmed they believe his story of seeing a strange craft.

Radiation

They carried out radiation tests on the site of scorched sugar beet where Peter says the UFO landed and took photographs and notes at the scene.

And this week they said the results of their findings backed up Peter's claim and they asked for other witnesses to come forward.

Mr Ron West, founder member of the East Anglian UFO Research Association, said: "We have been to investigate the incident in Fornham All Saints on the night of September 11 and we believe Peter's story."

Mr West, who was one of the ufologists to visit the field at the rear of Peter's home at Tut Hill, said the description sounded like a flying saucer.

Saucer-like

"Certainly from the configuration of the lights which were described to us by Peter, I can only presume we are talking about a saucer-like craft," he added.

The strange tale of the mysterious craft was told by Peter in the Free Press on September 30. He says he saw an object with bright flashing lights hovering at the end of a field near his home.

As a result of some considerable newspaper publicity given to the incident, along with an appeal from Del and Ron, seeking any other witnesses, a Mrs Susan Slinger of the White House, Bury Road, Fornham All Saints, claimed that she and her husband, Cecil, had seen: *"a cigar-shaped object, hovering in the night sky at around the same period"*.

Other witnesses to something strange observed in the sky over Bury St. Edmunds, during this month, were Reuben Eaves and his sister, Esther. They were cycling home, close to Prigg Walk in Bury Road, at 4pm, when they saw:

"... a long shape, to begin with, then it formed the shape of an umbrella and seemed to be moving like it was opening and closing; it was a frightening experience."

At 10.15pm, Paul Sullivan was sat in his car with his girlfriend, in Basildon Car Park, when they saw a large, round object, displaying red and blue lights around it, moving across the sky.

"It was very high up and was silent. We could see what looked like a dome in the middle. It then shot over the nearby Police Station, being watched by two Police Officers outside, and headed towards the west. Five minutes later, it was out of sight."

(Source: *Bury Free Press*, 28.10.1988 – 'Yes we also saw UFO'/East Anglian UFO & Paranormal Research Association)

12th September 1988 – 'Black Triangle' seen over Essex

At 9.30pm, Jean Temple (61) of Wickford, Essex, was out walking her dog, when she sighted two bright lights in the sky.

"They were dancing around all over the place. Sometimes they would separate but then rejoin; other times they zigzagged across the sky, before making a sharp square movement as they did so. About five minutes later, they all shot off towards the east and disappeared from view."

At 11.30pm, Steven Warner from Pitsea, Essex, was looking out over the *River Thames*, when he noticed *"a large black triangular object, flashing with lights"* hovering silently over the river. Was there any connection with what Brenda Butler later reported having seen at the same time, from her office window, at the Leiston Care Home where she worked?

Brenda:

"I saw what looked like a torch light going past, a bright light moving slowly across the sky, towards the Sizewell direction."

(Source: Brenda Butler & Ron West)

13th September 1988 – UFO Display over Essex and Cheshire

Clare Howard (59) was living in Long Meadow Drive, Wickford, in Essex. At 3am, while returning from the bathroom, she noticed a bright *'light'* in the sky over the cemetery, which faces the front of the house. She thought it might have been a flare, until it moved away towards the west. At about the same time, a number of young people were walking along the beach at Thorpeness, Suffolk, when they sighted a number of yellow lights *'dancing'* in the sky and behaving erratically. The light display continued until 3am, and then disappeared from sight.

At 8.45pm, Ronald Goodge (35) was driving home along the A127, towards Southend, with his girlfriend – Kym Lillian Bansiak. As they approached the Research Centre turn-off, near Laindon, Ronald instinctively ducked in his seat as a large black object, showing pulsating lights in the middle, moved across the front of the car from left to right.

At 10pm, another display of UFO activity took place near Basildon, involving about eight 'lights' seen darting about all over the sky, by Mr Jeffrey Palmer (44) – then driving home towards Basildon.

At 10.45pm, Geraldine Stacey (64) of Wickford, Essex, was calling her cats inside.

"I was frightened to see a massive triangular object in the sky. It seemed to float along and was about 500ft off the ground. I couldn't sleep much that night, wondering what it was."

Triangular UFO seen

She wasn't the only one. Nurse Sylvia Belton (34), also of Wickford, had this to say:

"I was walking my dog 'Sheba' when she suddenly became very frightened and began to strain at the lead, trying to go back home. I thought there might have been a dog about and looked around. Then, out of the corner of my eye, I caught a sudden movement and, looking upwards, I saw a black-grey triangular-shaped object in the sky. I estimated it was 800ft long. It covered the roadway I was walking on, side to side. There was a row of green lights on the back, with two or three white lights on the front. In the middle of the object was what looked like a round ring; it was some 150ft above me and moving slowly. I watched, frightened, as it headed away over the rooftops and was then lost from view."

Was this the same UFO seen 15 minutes later by Terrence Elliston (59) of Moreland Road, Wickford?

Haunted Skies Volume Ten

"I had just parked my car in the driveway, when I looked up and saw two triangular-shaped craft I estimated to be 500ft long, moving slowly through the sky at a height of about 300ft. At the back of the objects was a row of nine green lights; at the front, two white lights."

Another witness was Mr & Mrs Jackson, who reported seeing this object between 10.30pm and 11pm.

They later received a visit by Ron West, who interviewed them about what they had seen.

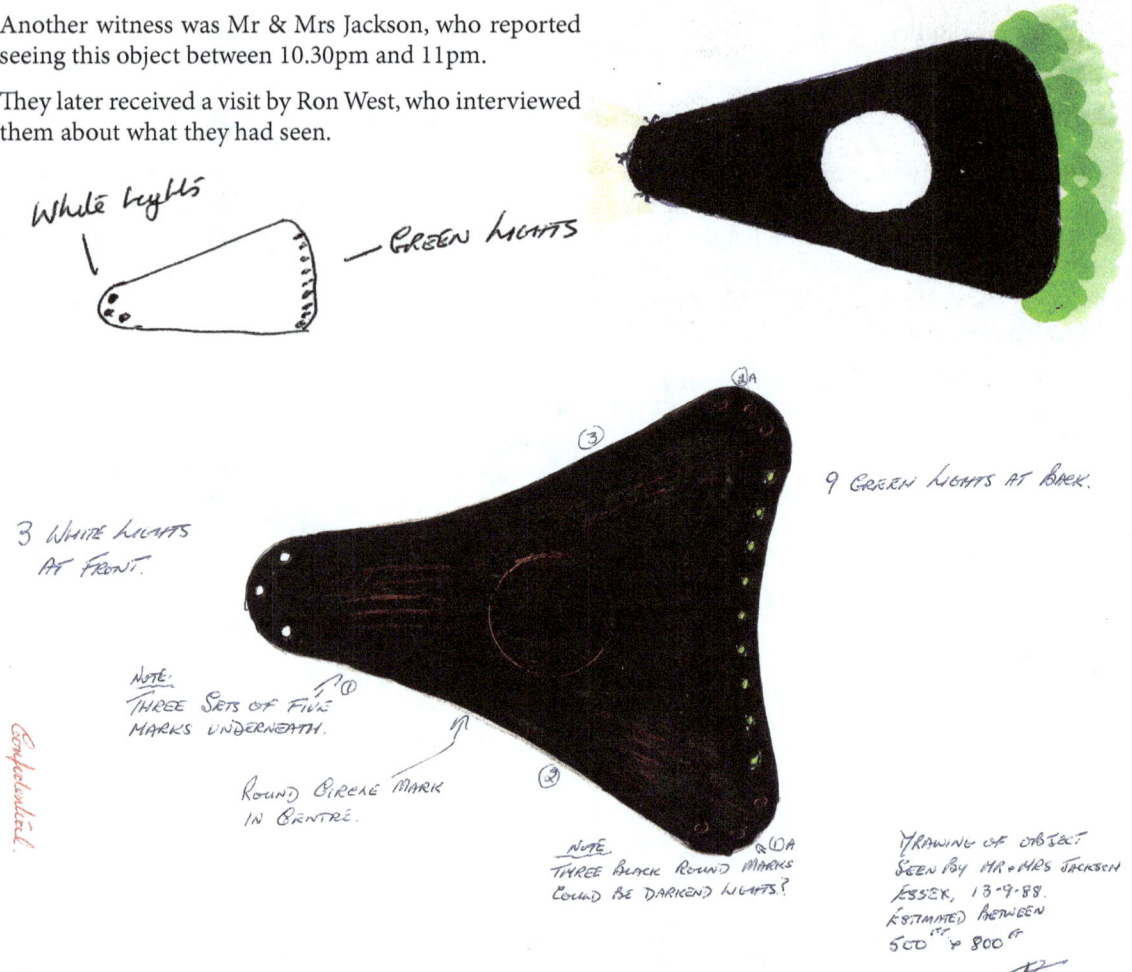

Also at about 10.45pm, Mary and Peter 'J' (59) of Walnut Drive, Wickford, Essex, were walking the family dog, when Peter pointed out a black shape in the sky and asked his wife what it was. Mary (who asked that her details be kept confidential) said:

"I looked up and saw this black shape in the sky; it was huge – bigger than any aeroplane I had ever seen before. It had some green lights on the back and white lights on the front. It was completely silent. Suddenly, it shot off at great speed.

It was going so fast, you couldn't see it go. It seemed to fill the whole sky when hovering. We reported it to the Police, but they told us that they had not received any other reports. We also checked with Southend Airport; they said nothing had been picked up on radar."

In addition, during the same evening, we were to learn of a spate of UFOs sighted around the Nantwich, Crewe, Winsford, and Northwich areas of Cheshire. Eric Morris, Regional coordinator for BUFORA, said:

> *"Two men reported having seen two bright lights, with flashing red lights at the rear, hovering in the sky. Some time later, they saw the same object fly over a red 'ball'. The red 'ball' appeared to chase the first UFO for some seconds, before being lost from view."*

(Source: Ron West and Brenda Butler)

Authors: It should not now come of any surprise to learn that in addition to this display of UFO activity, examples of which we have given countless times in *Haunted Skies*, there is the appearance of what many describe as structured objects. For those that may suggest Triangular UFOs are no more than examples of covert Top Secret technology, how do they explain the association between these and the UFO *'displays'* which appear in the sky?

We believe, from the evidence presented so far, that we are dealing with a phenomenon that has the propensity to create or manufacture, through an applied energy, something clearly not constructed by human hands.

September 1988 – UFO over Southampton

The Evening Post (17.9.1988) published a sighting from their own reporter – Tim Boone – who was on the beach at Southampton, with a group of friends, one Saturday evening, when a brightly-lit object was seen heading through the sky – too fast to be a shooting star or satellite.

Tim:

> *"It disappeared over treetops, only to remerge seconds later, and flew gracefully back in the direction which it had come from, slowing down. It stopped and hovered above the City and stayed there all night. The truly remarkable thing was that it would occasionally disappear and then light up again, shining brightly in a cloudless sky. A passenger plane, easily identified by its warning lights, later flew on what we believed to be a collision course with the bright light. As the plane drew close, the light disappeared. When the plane passed, it lit up again. Two hours later the object was still shining on and off in the sky when we saw another plane, heading in the same direction as the first, behind which could be seen a second smaller 'light' apparently tracking the aircraft for a few minutes, before it disappeared from view."*

It appears that Tim and his friends were not the only ones to witness something unusual that evening. We discovered that at least four people reported having seen *'formations of red, yellow, orange and white lights, and triangular shapes, moving quickly across the sky'*.

(Source: *Weekend Evening Post*, 17.9.1988 – 'Did I really see a UFO? Mystery flying object baffles journalist, Tim')

18th September 1988 – UFO seen over Yeovil

At 10.30pm, Marion and Stan Sampson from Tytherleigh, near Axminster, contacted their local newspaper, after sighting:

> *"... a circular object, as big as six full moons, with about a dozen lights inside, flying at a height of 3,000ft and heading in the direction of Chard."*

(Source: *Pullman's Weekly News*, 26.9.1988 – 'Strange sight in the sky'/*Chard & Illminster News*, Somerset, 21.9.1988 – 'Was mystery object a UFO?')

Haunted Skies Volume Ten

Was mystery object a UFO?

AN unusual object was sighted on Sunday night in the sky above in Tytherleigh.

Mrs Marion Sampson, of Culverfield, Tytherleigh, near Chard, was looking out of her bedroom window at about 10.30pm and saw a large circle of white lights.

"It came over from the Axminster area, passing over our house, and going towards Chard. There were about ten to a dozen white lights each as big as grapefruits forming a large circle. It was very low and no noise came from the object. I called my husband Stanley to come over and look and we watched it for about five minutes. I got him out of bed because I knew he wouldn't have believed me in the morning."

A spokesman from Yeovilton could give no answer for this mysterious object.

The last time The News was notified of an unidentified flying object was in 1979 when two young schoolboys reported a sighting at Halcombe, Chard.

20th September 1988 – UFO over Basildon

At 10.30pm, Engineer Peter Aldridge (41) of Clayburn Circle, Basildon, was about to walk his dogs, when he noticed a stationary orange glowing *'light'* in the sky, making a constant humming noise.

> "I stood there for a couple of minutes and called my wife, Siobhan, to come out and have a look. About a minute later, it split into two and headed away across the sky. To our great surprise, it reformed into one object and moved out of sight."

(Source: Ron West & Brenda Butler)

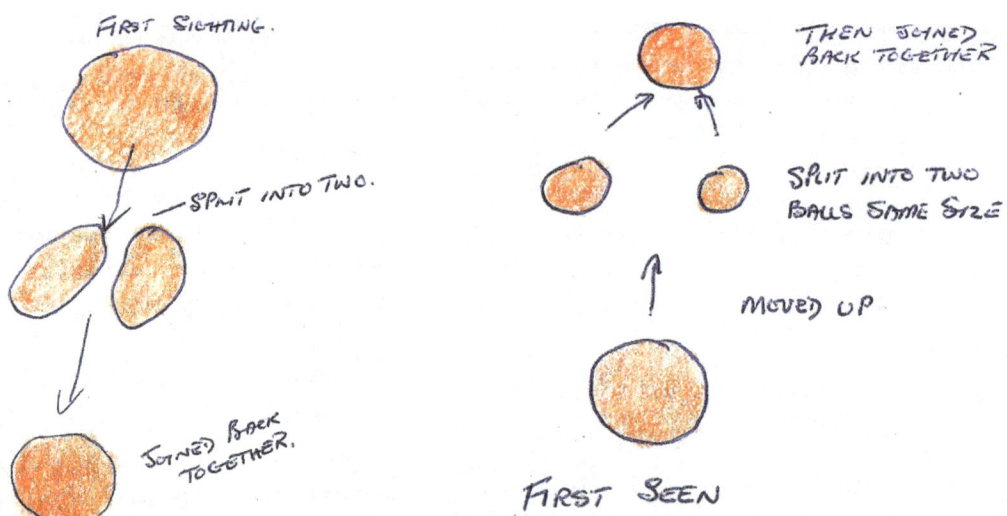

23rd September 1988 – UFO Display over Essex – 95 witnesses!

At 8.15pm, Steven Leonard Mounter (28) of Rochford, Essex, was attending a caravan rally at Burnham-on-Crouch, Essex, and sat outside his caravan, when he noticed some lights appear in the sky that he first took to be an aircraft.

> "I called my wife and we watched the three red lights above a large white one for a good five minutes, until it began to move away from us."

At 8.25pm, Ron West – Head of the East Anglian UFO & Paranormal Research Association – received a telephone call from a Mr Haron about some strange lights seen in the sky over Leigh-on-Sea, and decided to go and have a look himself.

EAST ANGLIAN U.F.O. & PARANORMAL RESEARCH ASSOCIATION

SECTION A — SIGHTING ACCOUNT FORM

Please write an account of your sighting, make a drawing of what you saw and then answer the questions in section B overleaf as fully as possible. Write in **BLOCK CAPITALS** using a ball point pen.

On the 23rd September 1988 at 8.25pm a Mr Haron telephoned me to say he was watching lights in the sky at Leigh on Sea Essex and could I see them. I looked out of the door window and directly south east of me I could see three white shining lights (these were not stars) they were hovering. Then I noticed a ring of lights yellow, orange, red and white directly in front of me, the whole ring of lights were the size of a golf ball. These suddenly blinked out and I was left with the three lights still hovering. Then the far right one moved in a triangular movement and then back to original position then all of them disappeared. At 8.58 1 red light appeared moving east to west. Then two white shining lights appeared one to the west other to east. The red light was now moving towards me growing bigger. It got to the size of a pea then turned east, then it stopped and hovered. Hovered for six minutes then moved to the east again and disappeared behind a large tree. I didn't see the red light again. In the meantime another white light had appeared and was hovering. P.T.O.

Please continue on a separate sheet if necessary.

DRAWING* 1st Sighting 8.35 — Disappeared 8.40

2nd Sighting 1st then grew to

TREE

If preferred, use a separate sheet of paper.

This one went straight over my house. No noise.

Your full name (Mr/Mrs/Miss/Ms): Ronald West Age: 57
Address: 95 Edilburn Rd, Gt Clacton, Essex
Telephone No. 431391 (STD 0255)
Occupation during last two years: Sales Rep
Any professional, technical or academic qualifications or special interests: —

Do you object to the publication of your name?
*Yes/No. *Delete as applicable.

Today's Date: 23-9-88
Signature: [signed]

Haunted Skies Volume Ten

At 8.30pm, resident John Alfred Sutherby was at his home address in Rayleigh, Essex, when he saw a number of strange *'lights'* flying all over the sky, and alerted his wife – Grace.

> "I went and told my neighbour and telephoned Southend Airport, after seeing two of them hovering over that location, but they were unable to help. I then telephoned the police and asked them if they had received any reports of at least nine UFOs being seen in the sky over Rayleigh. They also replied in the negative, so I told them to get one of their officers to go out and have a look. As the objects passed overhead they formed a triangle of lights, reminding me of a hang-glider with lights. During the time they were in the sky, I could also see a vapour trail in the shape of a 'V'."

At 8.30pm, Gillian Cadman (30) of Suffolk Way, Canvey Island, was walking home along Link Road, when she noticed four white, green, red and yellow, individual lights in the sky. Gillian watched them for about an hour, before continuing on her journey.

At 8.30pm, Lisa Gunn (15) of Roundtree Field, Basildon, was called outside by her sister, Karen, who told her of some strange lights in the sky.

> "I ran outside and saw six or seven sets of red, white, yellow and blue lights, travelling in a scattered formation high up in the sky. They then came together into a single group and headed away towards the direction of London."

At 8.30pm, Peter Webb (58) of Thundersley, Essex, also saw them go over.

"I saw nine flashing lights, forming a triangle, in the sky. I watched them until 9pm, until they disappeared from view."

At 8.30pm, Rita Clarke (53) from Canvey Island, Essex, sighted five or six sets of lights in the sky and the arrival of one set from the direction of the North Star. Twenty minutes later, they were gone from view.

At 8.30pm, Mr John Willett (61) of Canvey Island was out in his back garden.

"I was bringing in the washing, when I noticed all these coloured lights in the sky; I counted ten of them. They were completely silent. It was a wonderful sight."

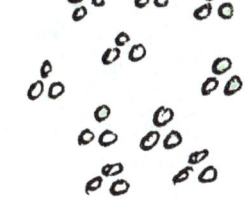

At 8.30pm, Mrs Chafer, from Benfleet, was stood at the front door of her house, when she saw two bright lights in the sky and thought they were aircraft, stacking.

"I then saw a third light moving about in the air, but not going anywhere. I went inside but came out ten minutes later – they were still there."

At 8.30pm, Westcliff-on-sea resident – Mrs S. Mapleton – saw what she thought was a plane approaching through the sky en route to Southend Airport – then realised this was not the case.

"The three lights formed an upside-down triangle and were silent. As they moved overhead, they projected powerful beams of light through the air. 10 or 15 minutes later, they were still in the sky. I thought no more of it, until I read the Evening Echo.*"*

At 8.30pm, Raymond Abraham (46) was driving to Basildon with his son, on a clear starlight night, showing a full moon with what appeared to be a huge vapour trail across the sky . . .

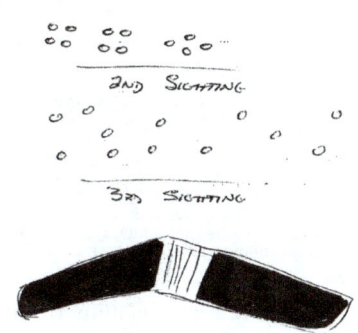

"We saw two sets of square lights, showing red and yellow lights, and a diamond shape of lights. Suddenly one of the lights broke away and dropped downwards, enabling us to see a delta wing-shaped object. I didn't believe in UFOs before – now I do."

At 8.30pm, Valerie Cowell (44) was on her way back from Bolton, Lancashire, and approaching Heathrow Airport, when:

"I saw three bright silver lights in a triangle in the sky. I thought they were something to do with the landing strip, but realised they were too high up."

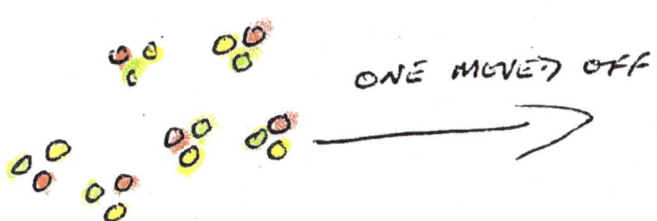

At 8.40pm, Ann Caliendo (37) – also from Canvey Island – was with her son and about to leave the family home, when he pointed out what they first thought were a number of helicopters, performing stunts in the sky.

"I looked up and saw five or six triangular-shaped lights, hovering in the sky towards the west. One of them moved away into another direction."

At 8.45pm, civil servant Margaret Hollinger (34), of Shoeburyness, sighted them in the sky

"... just sat there in sets of three, forming a triangle."

At 8.45pm, Toby Heath (54), of Leigh-on-Sea, saw seven triangular objects in the sky, moving in circles over the Southend, Rochford, Rayleigh, and Leigh-on-Sea areas.

> "They had two bright lights at the front, like headlights, with a slight beam. I could see red and yellow lights at the back and along the sides. They just kept circling in the sky. A strange thing happened; two of the lights seemed to merge together – then separated. I watched them for a good hour before they went eastwards, out over the sea, and were then lost from view."

(Handwritten note: TWO WHITE / YELLOW / FOUR RED / SEVEN OF THEM)

UFO sightings are soaring

THE NUMBER of UFO sightings in South East Essex is soaring, say experts.

And 19 families in the last year claim to have made contact with a creature from out of space — some 'losing' up to three hours of their lives after their close encounters.

Sheridan Lane, of the East Anglian UFO and Paranormal Association, said 1,400 sky searchers contacted them between July 1988 and July this year.

She said: "The number of sightings has dramatically increased. There seems to be more and more visitations by unidentified objects.

"Nineteen people have told us that they have made contact with an alien. In most cases individuals have been driving along when their car has suddenly stalled.

"In most cases their memories have been vague as to what has actually happened but the amount of time they have lost has varied between 20 minutes and three hours."

In the last fortnight dozens of people have contacted the society's hotline to report sightings.

On September 29, two pensioners on their way home from bingo in Southend report seeing a huge object, much bigger than an aeroplane. It was diamond shaped with a brilliant white light shining through two windows.

Earlier that night a man in Stanford-le-Hope said he saw a triangular object above his house.

On the same night a Basildon couple watched an object with red, green and white lights hovering above the Basildon telephone exchange.

On October 1, a widower in Tilbury was woken from his sleep at 12.15am by a bright white light which lit up his whole bedroom and garden.

On October 2, a husband, wife and daughter walking their dog along Underhill Road, South Benfleet, spotted a triangular shaped object. It was very large with red, green, blue and white lights. It sped away after they had watched it for 20 minutes.

And on October 4, a couple in Canvey saw a huge saucer shaped like a skate fish at 9.30pm.

Ms Sheridan said: "We are still investigating all these cases but so far we have uncovered no explanations. We believe each call to be genuine."

At 8.50pm, Margaret Collins, from Westcliff, Essex, was driving along the M25 Motorway, accompanied by her son, Gavin, when they noticed:

> "... a number of bright objects darting across the sky, zooming up and down; they could not have been aircraft, because they would have crashed. A much larger 'light' appeared, shaped like a Mercedes car sign, and dropped down over some trees. I was lucky not to have crashed the car; the lights were darting about everywhere on what was a busy motorway."

At 8.55pm, Shirley Baker (43) was driving along the A13, heading towards the Dartford Tunnel, with her friend, when she noticed two sets of lights in the sky towards the Croydon area. This was followed by the appearance of a cluster of four or five sets of other luminous objects seen above them, which appeared to be following them. When they came out of the other side of the tunnel, the lights had gone. After visiting a 'cash and carry' warehouse, they were astonished to see a total of eleven triangular objects in the sky over the Basildon area. During their journey back, they formed an impression of once again being followed by the lights, which were last seen heading towards the Southend-on-Sea direction.

Also at 8.55pm, Sara Drolin (11) from Blyth Avenue, Shoeburyness, was playing in the back garden with her friend, Betty Henderson, when they saw:

"... a large flashing light, heading across the sky. As it passed over, we saw about four red lights zigzagging behind it."

At 9pm, Philip Reeve and his wife, of Kingsmere, Thunderley, Essex, sighted two large white 'lights' in the sky over their house; one was towards the north-east, the other north-west. Through a telescope Philip was able to see:

"... a large object in the sky, covered in smaller yellow and green lights which occasionally pulsed".

He managed to take a short piece of video film showing the objects, which were kept under observation for a period of two-and-a-half hours, between 9pm-11.30pm.

We spoke to Mrs Reeve about the incident, in 2005. She had no idea where the film had gone and told us that her husband had passed away, some years previously, but believes there was probably a natural explanation for what was seen, such as fireworks or stars.

At 9.15pm, Mr H. Phillimore was walking along Prince Avenue, Southend, towards the town (opposite the airport) when he happened to look up and see an off-white object heading across the sky, in a south-easterly direction, before being lost from view as it moved into or behind clouds.

A few minutes later, Paul O'Brien (15) of Canvey Island, was out sunbathing in a field near his home, with his friend – Jason Peterson (15) – when they saw two small 'lights', high in the sky, forming a square shape.

Paul:

"It appeared to be hovering – then it zigzagged across the sky and disappeared from sight."

At 9.30pm, Jean Woof of Winter Gardens, Canvey Island, sighted something very strange in the night sky.

The reader should bear in mind that Ron, Brenda, and Derek Newman, received more than 250 calls from the public, reporting the sightings of *'black diamond, and triangular-shaped orange lights, darting about erratically in the night sky, accompanied by a humming noise'*, over Southend, Canvey, Billericay and Wickford, during a two week period covering the end of September to the beginning of October 1988. Over 32 separate UFO reports from the Basildon area alone were received.

We could have filled out another half a dozen pages on what appears to have been the largest display of UFO behaviour we had come across, over the years.

(Source: Ron West/Brenda Butler)

24th September 1988 – UFO Display over Suffolk

A man from Basildon was disturbed by a noise at 2.30am. When he went to the window to look out, he was astonished to see a triangular object in the sky.

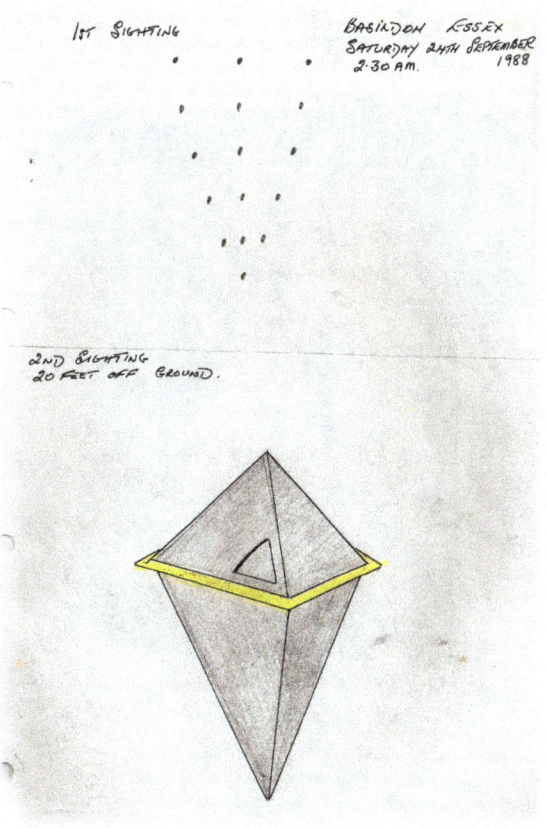

Haunted Skies Volume Ten

I saw a object in the Sky and I thought at that very instance that in my opine it was in some difficult, as I was worried I thought it was trying to make a landing, as it seemed completly out of shape to any other aircraft but as I continue my watching, it seemed to straighten itself out of its difficulties and to my suprise I saw very clear Brilliant Reds Inderwal and White Seperate Bulbs like what you would see in a amusement Arcade. But my hearing is very good and I cannot say that I heard any aircraft I normaly hear various planes. I just saying a prayed that who ever the were that they would have a safe journey

Please continue on a separate sheet if necessary.

DRAWING

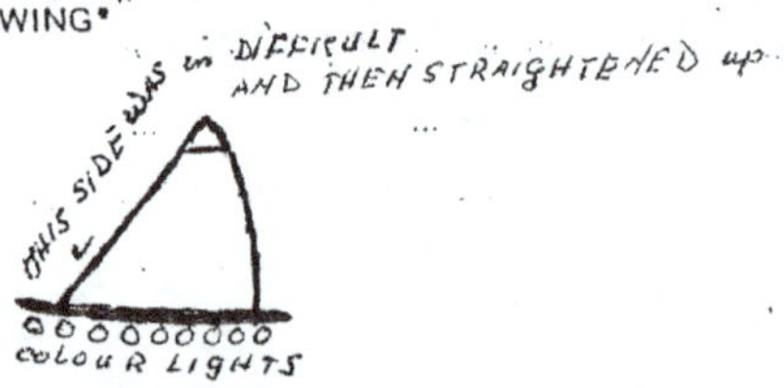

THIS SIDE WAS IN DIFFICULT AND THEN STRAIGHTENED UP

COLOUR LIGHTS

Your full name (Mr/Mrs/Miss/Ms) JEAN WOOF Age 68
Address PEZZO 39 RUSKOI ROAD WINTER GDS. CANDEY ISLAND ESSEX
Telephone No 683860 (STD)
Occupation during last two years RETIRED HOUSEWIFE

Any professional, technical or academic qualifications or special interests
AUX NURSE HELPING + VISITING THE HOUSE BOUND

Do you object to the publication of your name?
*Yes/No. *Delete as applicable. Because I LIVE ALONE WIDOW.
Today's Date 20/10/1988
Signature J Woof

RAYLEIGH, ESSEX
FRIDAY 23RD SEPTEMBER 1988
8 PM THROUGH 9.30 PM
4 WITNESSES THIS SIGHTING
95 WITNESSES OVERALL.

At 8pm, Eric William Bailey (46) was driving from Bury St. Edmunds to Brandon, in Suffolk. When about two miles from Brandon, he noticed a cluster of red, green and pale yellow lights, in a formation, which was narrow at the front and wide at the back, moving slowly across the sky before being lost from view.

(Source: Derek Newman)

25th September 1988 – UFO over Lowestoft

At 2.30am, Alan Symonds (42) and his wife, from Clayburn Circle, Basildon, returned from a holiday to Portugal.

After going to bed, Alan awoke at 8.30am and told his wife about a weird dream he had experienced, involving the sighting of a UFO. She laughed at him.

Alan:

> "All I know I was in bed – then I was in my garden, looking up into the sky. I saw 16 silver objects in a formation of three fives and one main object. They were shaped like a diamond, with a rim around the middle.
>
> It was a clear night and a full moon. I just put it down to a dream, until I read the Evening Echo, which brought the dream back to me."

Authors: Was it a dream? We shall never know, but wonder how many other Essex people had similar dreams that night on what was probably the busiest night of UFO activity for many years.

Coincidently, Carole O'Brien (35) of Maurice Road, Canvey Island, contacted Ron West and Brenda Butler, telling them of a strange dream she had during the same night.

> "I seemed to be on some sort of train and being taken away by aliens. I wasn't frightened. In the dream they appeared friendly. A door opened in the compartment and a man floated in. He was wearing a grey or silvery suit, and hat. I can't remember his facial features."

At 6.45pm, Sara Mills (31) of Basildon, Essex, was at her home address when her daughter Natasha (6) and her friend, came rushing downstairs in a very frightened state, telling her that they had just seen a black object with red, yellow, and white lights on it, heading towards the bedroom in which they had been playing. According to the daughter, it then went out of the window and over nearby rooftops.

At 8.15pm, Heidi Brooks and Emma Scrivens (12) from Lowestoft, had just left their local youth club and were crossing a field, when they became aware of a buzzing noise.

In a tape-recorded interview, later conducted by UFO enthusiast David Spoor, Heidi had this to say:

> "Emma and me carried on until we got to the middle of the field – then I noticed this circle of light going around us like a lighthouse, but it never touched the ground at knee height. We looked up and saw it gradually getting closer. Emma was so scared she froze with fear; I grabbed hold of her and made her run away. When we got to the top of the field, we looked back and saw the UFO starting to come towards us again, so we ran home."

At midnight, Marie Lloyd (19) from Chichester, Southend, sighted a large red light, with a *'tail'*, pass over the sky – which frightened her so much that she ran inside. How would she have reacted if she had known that she was one of countless scores of people that had reported seeing highly unusual objects in the night sky that night?

(Source: David Spoor/Personal interview/Ron West, Brenda Butler)

26th September 1988 – Triangular formation of UFOs seen

Just after midnight, into the early hours of the above date, schoolboy Simon Karim (15) was in his bedroom in Kelverdon Close, Billericay, Essex, looking out of the window. He was surprised to see:

> "... three triangular objects – each one consisting of six red, white, and yellow lights forming an even larger triangle crossing the sky. The back one was spinning around like a top. I watched them as they headed towards the direction of Canvey Island, before losing sight of them".

27th September 1988 – Oblong UFO over Essex

At 1am, Miss A. Fisher was looking out through a window over the river, towards the south-west, when she saw:

> "... a large oblong object, showing two yellow lights in the sky, with two lines running down the left-hand side – two on the right and two on the underneath".

Further enquiries revealed the sighting took place over a Shell refinery chimney (which burns off waste gas) a few miles away.

At 3.45am on this date, a mysterious blue light was seen stationary in the sky over Ipswich, close to Norwich Road Railway Bridge. Three people separately contacted Brenda Butler, telling her of having seen this. The light given off was strong enough to illuminate buildings in its path. In addition to this, five other reports of a similar nature were reported to Ron West.

At 8.45pm, three strange *'lights'* – red, white and blue – were seen hovering in the sky over the Essex area, by a family returning home. A plane passed overhead on its way into London Airport. As it did so, the red and blue *'lights'* left and followed the course taken by the aircraft. The family went back inside and heard a heavy loud noise, like a dynamo, but was unable to locate the cause.

28th September 1988 – 'Flying Saucers' over Essex

Mr Bill Mathews (58) of Benfleet, Essex, was up at 3am, after suffering stomach-ache. He happened to glance through the kitchen window, and saw:

> "... a round object to my right, and a saucer-shaped object, with coloured lights around it, to my left, approximately 300yds away, hovering over the direction of Hadleigh. Within seconds they had gone."

29th September 1988 – Formation of Lights over Essex

At 7pm, Dennis Goodfellow (46) – a surveyor by profession – was driving along the A13, heading towards Southend-on-Sea, on a straight stretch of road between the Five Bells roundabout and the Pitsea Flyover, when he noticed four *'lights'* in the sky, which consisted of two on the left and two on the right, placed horizontally.

> "They were the size of the North Star and low down, towards the East. Suddenly they shot upwards, at fantastic speed, and faded from view."

At 8.45pm, Shoeburyness schoolboys – Mark Tame (14) and Toby Longbottom – sighted two bright orange lights over the *Thames Estuary*.

> "They looked like two ice-cream cones and would move towards the sea and then fly back again to where we first saw them, before repeating the cycle again."

A few minutes later, the objects vanished from view.

(Source: Ron West/Brenda Butler)

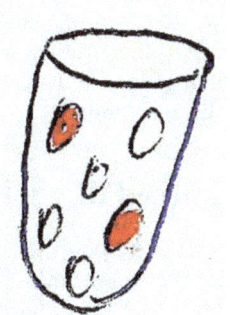

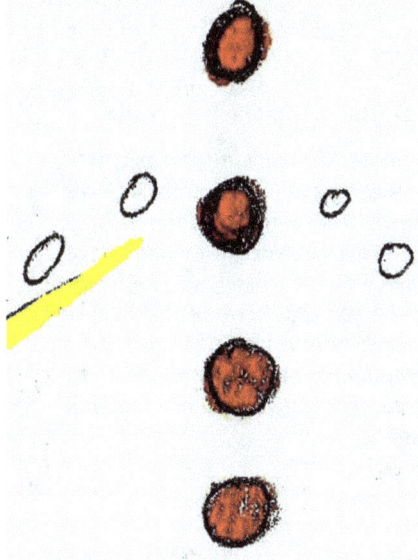

30th September 1988 – Formation of lights over Essex

At 9.30pm, Mark Johnson – a student from Westcliff-on-Sea – was in his back garden, when he happened to look up and see a formation of lights passing overhead, forming what looked like an arrow image in the sky, with its beam projecting sideways.

Many miles away, in Suffolk, Brenda Butler was sat on the cliff tops at Sizewell beach, at 10.30pm, when she saw some unusual lights out to sea, followed by a bright light that shot through the air overhead.

At 7.15pm, Bill Goulding and his wife, Mabel, were driving on the Bacup road, out of Burnley, when they saw four bright white lights in the sky ahead of them.

> "We stopped the car and watched in complete silence, for about five minutes. They then moved away, banked a little, and disappeared. We tried to look at them through binoculars, but couldn't see much as they were so dazzling."

Later that evening, people living in the Tilehurst and Caversham area of Berkshire contacted the authorities, after sighting bright lights speeding across the sky. They included Kevin and Donna Wallace, who were driving home from Bradfield to Laytom Rise, when:

> "We noticed this large bright object lighting up the sky. We first thought it was a plane, but it stayed in the same position. When we got home we saw up to eight objects in the sky, moving backwards and forwards at great speed. There seemed to be one main light, which the others were coming back to; some of them were red, green, and blue. They were in the sky for several hours and were not fireworks."

(Source: *Burnley Express*, 4.10.1988 – 'Actor Bill sees strange lights'/*Reading Evening Post*, 1.11.1988 – 'Was it a bird, was it a plane – or UFO?')

September 1988 – 'Flying Saucer' examined by MOD!

During a 'wave' of sightings of mysterious orange *'globes of light'* seen dashing across the sky over the Essex area during this period, invariably many explanations were offered as to their cause.

In 1988 a man from Southend, Essex, contacted a local newspaper, expressing a wish to be put in touch with members of the East Anglian UFO & Paranormal Research Association. This man was later the subject of a tape-recorded interview conducted by members Sheridan Lane, Ron West, and two others. Unfortunately, we do not have a taped copy of this interview – only a typed resumé. We believe this bizarre story to be total fabrication, but felt it was worth bringing to the reader's attention to illustrate the lengths that some people will go to. Admittedly it is a scenario which may well have taken place previously, for all we know, but not on this occasion.

Forced down by the US Military?

This man, who was given the pseudonym Paul Cain, claimed in 1984 that a *'flying saucer'* was *'forced down'* by the American military authorities in Arizona, and that a decision was made to tow the *'flying saucer'* to 'Foulness Island, Shoeburyness, near Southend, by using a *'Battle cruiser'* [it could not be flown out] in order that an examination could be made of the object, as previous attempts to open it had proven unsuccessful. Paul stated that he served in the Armed Forces and had seen service in Africa during the Mau Mau uprising. He also disclosed he was an advisor to Tom Adams' Government in the West Indies, and in more recent times, a member of an elite group of sixteen personnel employed by the MOD. This is what he had to say:

> *"In September 1988 I was asked by certain parties whether I was interested in looking at a 'machine' they had acquired. I was picked up by a civilian driver and on arrival at the site [Foulness Island] was stripped and X-rayed. I was then taken along with about a dozen others in a vehicle to a large, slightly curved 'hoarding', 10-15ft high and about a mile long, three miles away. This area was surrounded by trees. About 3-400yds away I saw other smaller 'hoardings'. When I saw the 'machine' I had been called in to investigate, I asked a group of other men there 'what the hell is it?' Two of them spoke English; another man spoke in Russian. I learnt, later, that he was a psychic and specially flown to the UK as part of a desperate attempt to gain access to the interior of the 'flying saucer'. [Paul refers to a four years examination of the object, which indicates 1984 when it was first recovered] I was told that if we didn't manage to open the object, it would be encased in concrete.*

Measuring the 'Flying Saucer'

The 'flying saucer' was neither hot nor cold to the touch; when paced it had a circumference of 1.538 paces. Its height was 4 feet and three and a quarter inches. It weighed an estimated 3,000 tonnes. The shape was flat, thin and round. It shimmered like water when seen from a distance, but the real colour was light silver-grey. Its texture was smooth, but microscopic inspection showed it was made from millions of minute coloured particles which looked round until you touched the outer surface, that was eggshell thick. I asked if it could be made from organic material and was told it may actually be a vegetable substance. Five months after working on the project, electromagnetic resonances successfully caused a flap on the underside to open; this was the result of work carried out by an unnamed science professor from Edinburgh University. If you were to get a piece of plasticine and pull

it out, you would not see any joins – that is how the door and flaps are attached. There are two elastic type contraptions which drop away and then swing down."

Entry gained

According to Paul, during the opening of the flap, around 200 people were present; initial investigation of the dark interior was conducted by torchlight. The men entered an oval-shaped tube, where they discovered numerous round *'balls'* but didn't pick them up.

Paul:
> "The Russian physic, 'Melk', then entered the 'vehicle' after everyone else had left. When he came out he was in possession of one of the 'balls', which were orange and coloured the same as the craft. He said, 'I can bend it; I can feel it bending – it's moving, it's bending with me'. These 'balls' absorb and give out a multitude of shades of light reflection. Incredibly, they only weigh about a quarter of an ounce. Efforts to break one have not been successful, despite being subjected to a pressure of 100 tonnes".

Paul's narrative of the event mentions that eleven flaps on the top of the vehicle were finally opened, too small to enter; they measure 14 inches across. They are later determined to be inspection hatches. Probes with cameras and tubes were inserted and they discovered each inspection hatch goes into a tube. The tubes run into each other via linked flaps. The hatches slant diagonally about 30-40°. Apart from the thousands of peculiar *'balls'*, nothing has ever been found inside the *'flying saucer'*. There are no instrument panels, flashing lights, seats, or storage compartments. Only two areas remain not investigated and are completely sealed. These are attached in a half circle, running from the centre of the craft. Sonic soundings have established them to be hollow.

Haunted Skies Volume Ten

Paul:

> "In one of the tubes is a tank, inside which can be seen little black hairs. It probably contains a liquid, but the device is totally sealed. It is believed to be the brainchild of the craft, storing information. They believe the 'saucer' sucks in light while flying, which then spins around a tube. What has been learnt so far covers a short period. The opening of the machine and everything else has all happened in a matter of months. More people will come on the scene; people like me will be a thing of the past. New people, new ideas, new technology, machinery and testing methods, will emerge. They may even cut out a piece from these similar machines. It may be developed for our own use. Many countries are involved in this project – Britain, USA, Russia, France, Germany, India and Israel. International finance is involved but, until now, the only people to have known anything about this originally highly secret project have worked on a need to know basis."

Paul was asked why he was willing to speak out now, and replied:

> "I'm concerned about the loss of around 200 of the odd little coloured 'balls'. These and many others became activated by our investigations. Some flew out of the ship and were lost. Local coastal areas have received reports of sightings of these 'balls'; people have seen them in their gardens. Anyone finding them shouldn't touch the objects, but must contact the local police or official source."

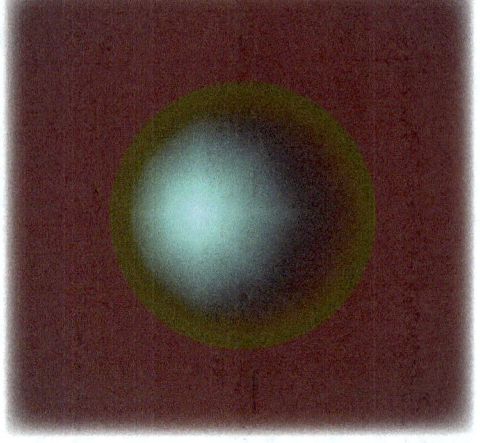

Paul mentioned to a superior that he was thinking of writing a book about the project, and was told:

> "Do so. No one will believe you."

On the 29th May 1988, Paul told the UFO group that he had received a telephone call, telling him the *'saucer'* had been removed to Australia. We felt unwilling to take any of this information as valid. The United States has far more resources to commit into carrying out specialist work of this nature and would no doubt rely on the expertise of personnel from Area 51 and Wright Patterson Base, rather than shipping anything of such importance to the UK.

What was the purpose behind this man contacting the UFO group in the first place? Was it a flight of fanciful imagination, concocted by someone who had his own agenda for wishing to disseminate a story like this, or was it disinformation? We shall never know! We would like to add that we infer no criticism of the people concerned in this investigation. Without their efforts to preserve what is, after all, a huge slice of important Essex based UFO history, we would be the worse off.

Late September 1988 – UFO over West Midlands

Michael Lander from Sutton Coldfield, West Midlands, contacted us with regard to what he and his wife saw, one early evening in late September 1988, while driving home along the A453, at Bassetts Pole, towards Mile Oak (the scene of a number of other UFO reports over the years).

---

*Foulness Island is Essex's best kept secret; a 6,000-acre nature magnet of scrub and marshland, which is only a short range rocket launch from the hustle and bustle of Southend. The island's Ministry of Defence owners do not welcome casual visitors. For nearly a century, the MOD has used Foulness as a testing centre for military weapons, propelling all manner of deadly devices into the Maplin Sands. It includes grenades, explosive shells and guided missile systems, all of which have their destructive capabilities assessed here by specialists ahead of rubber stamping and delivery to global war zones. Apparently Atomic weapons were also on the agenda in the Fifties.

"My wife drew my attention to a large elliptical glow in the sky, moving from left to right. I tried to keep my eyes on it, estimating it to be travelling only a few hundred feet off the ground, heading towards the A5, but soon lost sight of it. The next morning I was flabbergasted to hear, while listening to the local radio station, that a number of people in the Yardley area, south of Birmingham, had reported seeing an identical object later that same evening."

OCTOBER 1988

1st October 1988 – UFO over Essex

At 7.20pm, Basildon man John Maddex (43) was outside his house, when he noticed a yellow object moving up and down in the sky.

2nd October 1988 – UFO over Essex

At 7.30pm, a triangle of green, red, and white lights was seen heading across the sky over Basildon, by Mrs D. Hope (59), her son, and next door neighbour. Ten minutes later, they were gone from view.

3rd October 1988 – UFO over Peterborough

At 6.30pm, Paul Crow and Brian Twyman were out fishing at the City's Stanground backwater. As dusk began to fall, they were shocked to see a circle of red and orange lights appear behind them, moving from side to side.

According to the two men, the phenomena went on for four hours before they managed to run away.

(Source: *Peterborough Evening Telegraph*, 10.10.1988 – 'Anglers in UFO sighting drama')

4th October 1988 – UFO Display over Army Barracks, Colchester

Mrs M. Stephens – then the wife of a serving soldier, living in married accommodation at Colchester Army Barracks – contacted Ron West (after finding his name in the telephone book) to report that she and a number of army personnel had seen a silent display of lights in the sky over the Barracks, at 8.30pm. This incident was not released to the Press and kept under wraps for nearly 25 years.

"There were beautiful lights, all colours – red, blue, yellow and green – moving in a circle. Then a big shape appeared, like a dome, with all these lights around it. The army later told us that it had been helicopters, on exercise."

5th October 1988 – UFOs over Westcliff-on-sea

At 9.45pm, Eva Deleur (72) of Prittlewell Chase, Westcliff-on-sea, was sat in the kitchen, having a cigarette.

"I noticed a blue and yellow light in the sky through the window. I thought I was seeing things and carried on smoking, then the lights appeared again – strong enough to illuminate the rooms inside the house. I decided to take the dog for a walk and reached about 100yds up the road and looked back at my house, when I was astonished to see that only my house was lit-up by a pale blue light; other houses were in darkness. This lasted for a couple of minutes. I returned home. As I did so, the house was lit-up again. Puzzled, I looked up and saw a weird shape in the sky, surrounded by a blue haze. I went to bed and, although the bedroom was still lit, fell asleep."

7th October 1988 – UFOs over Derbyshire

At 7.25pm, UFO Investigators – Mr D. Walters and Mr L. Trueman – were travelling along the Derby to Kirkby-in-Ashfield road, heading in the direction of Mansfield, in order to interview a witness at Ilkeston.

After making a right-hand turn onto the road leading to Junction 27 on the M1 Motorway, close to the roundabout with Underwood and Eastwood, a glowing object was seen moving slowly, low down in the sky.

Mr Trueman commented that it was a strange looking aircraft, so Mr D. Walters opened the passenger side window and saw, through binoculars:

> "... nothing like I had ever encountered before. It appeared as two 'V' formations of light, one above the other, a short distance apart, and was composed of numerous small lights. The 'V's pointed downwards, with white lights forming the left-hand of the 'V', whilst the right-hand side was made up of red lights. We could hear a faint sound of engines above the sound of traffic passing us; most of the time we were on the road.
>
> We saw the object – now 45° high in the sky – slowly travel from right to left, approximately over the Derby direction, towards Mansfield, and as it passed away from us the 'V' configuration changed, until it appeared as two clusters of lights, separated horizontally by a space. By now it was some distance away, showing as a cluster of mixed red and white lights, with a small flashing light on the top of each cluster of light – out of sight by 7.30pm."

(Source: Peter Tate, Bristol)

8th October 1988 – Rectangular UFO over Sunderland

At 5.15am, Mrs A Rawlings from Redfern House, Sunderland, was looking out of her bedroom window, when she saw what appeared to be a rectangular object, displaying flashing white lights at the centre and left-hand section, with a red semicircular shape underneath it. All of sudden, it rose upwards and disappeared from view.

(Source: *Sunderland Echo*, 15.10.1988 – 'Strange light')

At 7.20pm, Carol Howe (34) of Buxhall, Stowmarket, Suffolk, was out in the garden, fetching the washing in, when she saw a big black circle moving slowly across the sky, which disappeared into cloud cover 30 seconds later.

At 7.25pm, Frank Wells (69) – the father of Carol – was out walking near the playing field, when he also saw what appears to have been the same object, although he describes it as resembling a car headlight – gone in 30 seconds.

9th October 1988 – 'Beam of light' seen

At 7.15pm, Mrs Phyllis Greenman (51) of Wethersfield Way, Wickford, Essex, was outside her house, saying goodbye to Mr and Mrs D. Smith, when the sky was lit-up in one particular direction, as if a searchlight beam of intense light had been switched on. According to Phyllis, the beam originated specifically from some sort of *'craft'* in the sky, although she was unable to make out any detail.

At 11.55pm, Ron West was driving home on the A120 bypass, around Colchester, when he noticed something unusual, as a result of which he found himself later writing his own UFO report for his own organisation!

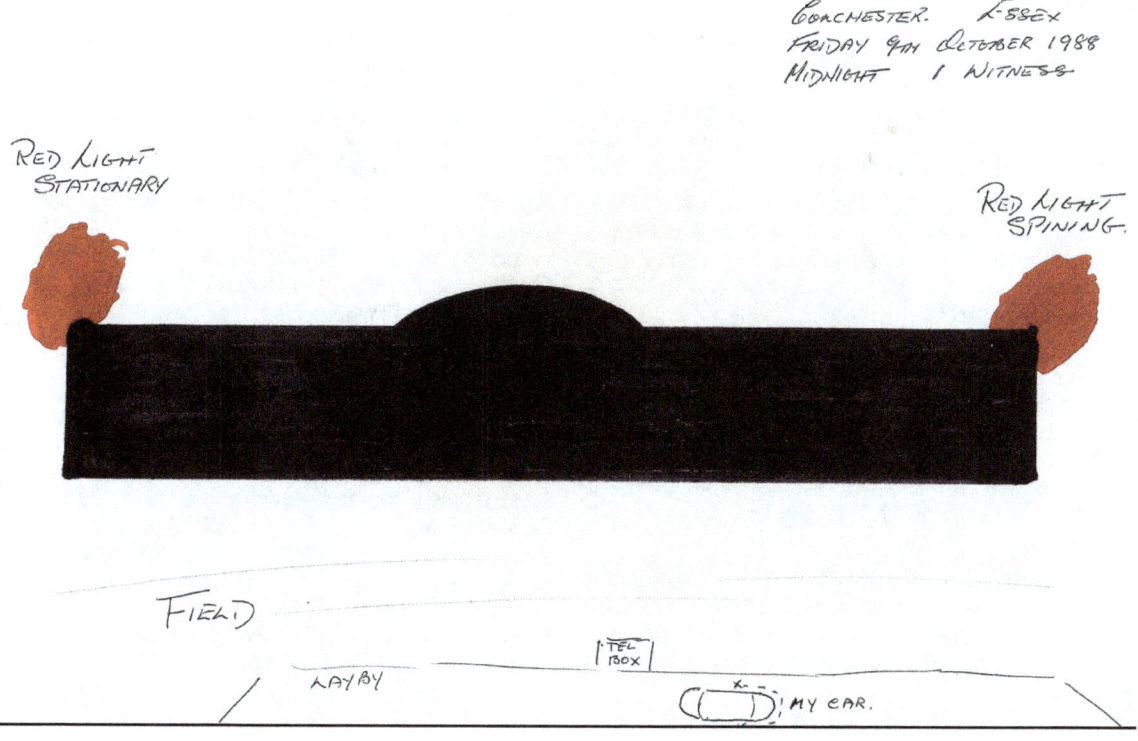

13th October 1988 – 'Necklace' UFO over Essex

At 11pm, Mrs Maureen Newberry (58) of Castleford Gardens, Westcliff-on-Sea, was getting ready for bed.

As she drew the curtains, she was stunned to see a huge circle of lights hovering in the sky.

> "It resembled a necklace of brilliant lights and was brown in colour, with a brilliant white light on the right-hand side. Behind it were some faint red lights. I watched it until 11.30pm, and then went to bed."

(Source: Ron West/Brenda Butler)

14th October 1988 – Crescent-shaped UFO over Basildon

At 9.30pm, David Harrington (43) of Meadowland Road, Wickford, Essex, was returning home from a night out with his wife – Helen, two sons – Mark and Paul – and daughter, Jean. Near Basildon, Mark pointed out an object in the sky to his father.

Haunted Skies Volume Ten

Sunday People, London — 9 OCT 1988
MEN ON MARS

ALL the recent hoo-hah in America about a strange "face" on the surface of Mars being created by intelligent life forms, comes as no surprise to Britain's UFO experts.

They've always believed that there's life on Mars — and on Venus, Pluto, Neptune and Saturn too.

The fuss in America has been caused by scientists who have been studying in minute detail the photos sent back from Mars by the spacecraft Viking in 1976.

They have identified a mile wide "face" on the surface complete with hair, eye socket, pupils and eyeball — all in the perfect proportions of a human face.

They also say there seems to be a weird "city" of pyramid structures on the surface.

Esteemed boffin Dr Mark Carlotto of Boston's Analytic Science Corporation says that these two features show intelligent design and cannot be a trick of nature.

And he's backed by other scientists who are calling for another expedition to Mars as soon as possible.

"It's a great step forward that scientists are now considering the real possibility of life on Mars," said Christine Aubry, who co-ordinates the hot line of UFO sightings in Britain from the society's London office.

Should you spot a visiting martian, or any other UFO, the society would like you to ring their hot line on 01 731 1094, 10am - 10pm seven days a week.

"It was orange-yellow in colour, surrounded by a reddish glow, and was heading towards the centre of Basildon; due to traffic, we were unable to stop and lost sight of it within seconds. It was not the moon, as this was visible in another part of the sky."

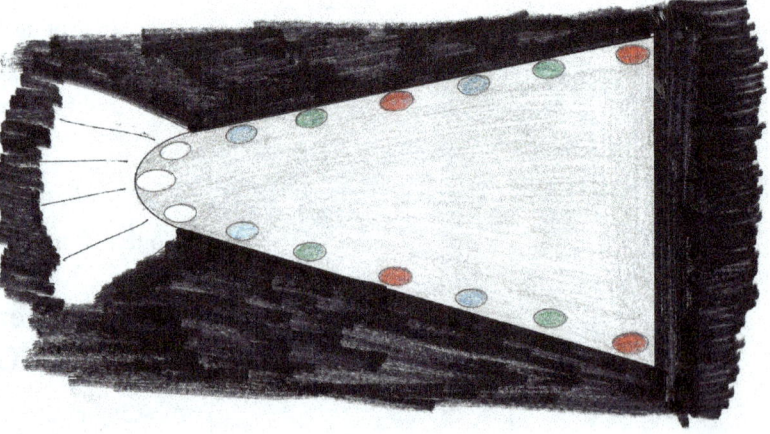

Langdon Hills, Basildon. Wednesday 18th October 1988 8.30 p.m. 2 witnesses.

At 10.35pm, Patricia Brooks (32), from Clacton-on-Sea, had just let the dog out into the garden, when she was amazed to see an elongated (elliptical) bright green light – the size of a rugby ball – shoot across the sky and climb upwards at terrific speed, before being lost in cloud five seconds later.

19th October 1988 – Strange lights, Southend-on-Sea

At 3am, Sue Chelu of Lancaster Gardens, Southend-on-Sea, close to the seafront – who has no problems sleeping through the night – was awoken by a bright white/blue light that lasted for about ten seconds,

"... like someone shining several lights through the window".

20th October 1988 – Orange and blue lights seen

In the early hours, Mrs P. Hewitt of Lydden, Dover, Kent, was awoken by what she took to be electric blue lightning, constantly flashing, for over half an hour. When she looked out of the window all she could see was a blue *'light'*, covered in thick mist that shrouded the landscape.

21st October 1988 – UFOs seen over Essex

At 8pm, Mr Keith Rodgers of Cheapside, East Rayleigh, was taking his dog for a walk in the local Swyne School playing fields, accompanied by his son, and daughter – Michelle (6).

"Something in the sky caught my attention; I looked upwards and saw five objects moving across the sky in a spinning action, showing a red light on the one side. I told my daughter to fetch my wife – Julie (28) and son – Daniel (9). After they arrived, we watched the object for some 15 minutes. At this point I decided to continue exercising the dog and carried on keeping my eye on them for another 40 minutes, during which time my parents – Donald (65) and Ruby (62) – turned up to watch."

At 8.10pm, Audrey Bushton (39) was sat in her car, parked on her mother's driveway at Wickford, Essex, saying her goodbyes. A light appeared in the sky and disappeared behind nearby trees. Audrey says that the object had a round *'head'*, tapering to a *'tail'*, and was luminous green in colour. It had an orange-red glow to the top and bottom edge. Within seconds it was gone from view.

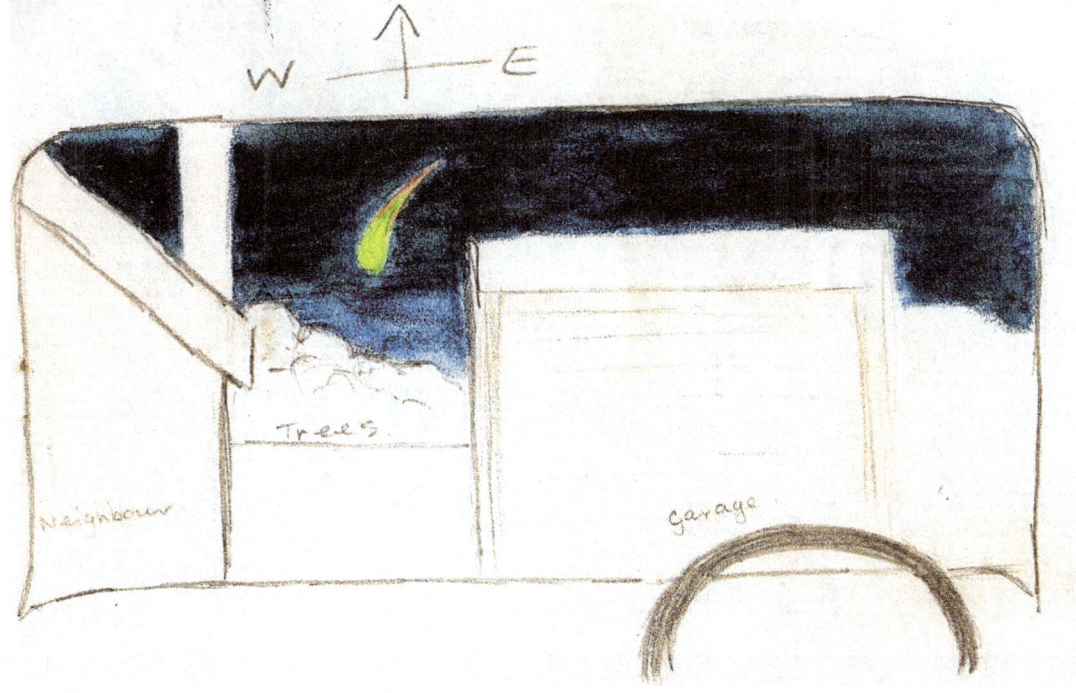

Haunted Skies Volume Ten

OUR SECRET ARMY AGAINST THE ALIENS

Whitehall denies that DI55 exists to watch UFOs

DEEP down the dark corridors of Whitehall lies an office which officially does not exist. Behind its closed doors, faceless men and women gather intelligence on a subject which also officially does not exist.

The department is known as Defence Intelligence 55 and its task is to investigate the possible threat to Britain from alien forces who regularly cross our skies in UFOs.

At DI55, nationwide reports from the armed services, police and the public are meticulously logged and carefully studied in preparation for the day when a UFO lands on Earth.

For the Ministry of Defence, in line with over half Britain's population, secretly accepts that there are probably other more advanced life forms in the universe which sooner or later will make contact.

The MOD will neither confirm, nor deny, the existence of the secret department. A spokesman said: "We do not discuss the work of intelligence departments at all."

But engineer Michael Hanson has no reservations. As southern co-ordinator of the Yorkshire UFO Society he recalls how he telephoned the MOD with a routine sighting inquiry.

As usual he was put through to the RAF's Air Staff Two department which checks out sightings against aircraft operating in the area. But apparently by accident Michael was then passed on to another department — DI55.

Said Michael: "Air Staff Two said they had no information on the UFO. I think they thought I was something to do with the Ministry because they said they would transfer me to DI55.

"Someone answered the phone but as I explained who I was I was returned to the switchboard and after a long wait was told no one was available.

"The strange thing is when I rang back later and asked for DI55 I was told it did not exist. When I said I had already talked to them the operator said I shouldn't have been put through."

A colleague of Michael's, Mark Birdsall, who is the Yorkshire UFO Society's chief investigator, then tried the same telephone procedure but was met with a brick wall.

Mark said: "I have had my suspicions for a number of years that such a department exists. The British public deserves to know that there is a covert intelligence department which deals with UFO reports for what can only be one reason — in case of visitors from other planets."

Mark says 1988 is becoming the Year of the UFO with increased numbers of sightings throughout Britain.

He believes the MOD has recorded the sudden increase but adds: "We used to get a great deal of co-operation but now they have clamped down completely.

"I have watched military aircraft turn and follow UFOs but when I've asked the Ministry about such an incident it usually denies that there were even any aircraft in the area at the time.

"We are currently in the biggest wave of UFO sightings in the last six years and we feel something is going to happen soon because everyone is becoming very uneasy about it all.

"We have noticed the pattern of flights has changed with the craft hugging the terrain, possibly to avoid detection. But we have no idea what they represent or what their purpose is here on Earth.

"The craft have remarkable agility. Some appear to be almost remotely controlled while others seem to be piloted."

Serious UFO followers like Mark admit that at least 90 per cent of so-called UFO sightings have perfectly normal explanations. And they have no time for people who claim to have been beamed up into alien spaceships.

Such abduction stories began in 1957 when a Brazilian farmworker claimed four men seized him and took him on to their craft where he was forced to make love to a white woman with oriental eyes and red hair. Since then many people claim to have been space-napped with their minds and bodies probed by aliens.

But Mark and his colleagues say such ludicrous stories simply give the whole subject of UFOs a bad name when there is a small, but significant, proportion of sightings which even officialdom admits cannot be explained.

An RAF spokesman said: "We have one secretary who as part of her normal duties deals with UFOs. She passes on reports to Air Staff Two. Checks are made to see if we have any aircraft in the area at the time.

"We do not inform people of our findings because of a lack of facilities and personnel. But we do not deny there are peculiar things in the sky which we cannot explain. My personal view is that we would be very silly not to concede that there could be life elsewhere where technology could be light years ahead of us.

"Years ago as an RAF navigator 24 of us in 12 jets in formation over Cyprus saw a silver ball which we could not explain. It held station alongside us at about 400mph and then shot away at about 1500mph. We all put in UFO reports to our base.

"Today if a spaceship lands on Earth I can assure you we will be very interested but I can also assure you there is no cover-up."

But Dr Richard Lawrence, director of the largest international UFO society with branches in every continent, is adamant: "There is a cover-up." As European Secretary of the Aetherius Society Dr Lawrence lectures throughout the world on unexplained phenomena. And he has a deep suspicion of the British Ministry of Defence.

He says: "The Ministry says it does not release details because of a lack of finance and personnel, and they tell us thousands of files were destroyed because of a shortage of space. They were files which would now be available under the Public Records Act. Now we are waiting for 1992 when more files become available unless of course the MOD comes up with another excuse for destroying them.

"I know the Ministry is deliberately hiding things. People, particularly journalists, are amazed by the brick wall they are met with.

"But the public today are not so easily satisfied or fooled. After all far more people have seen flying saucers than have seen an African tribesmen and they know the tribesmen exist, so why not UFOs?"

One of Britain's leading authors on UFOs, Timothy Good, says he has proof of the existence of department DI55 through a copy of an MOD document distribution list which has come into his hands.

He says: "It is nonsense to say UFO reports are just handled by a secretary. I know they are dealt with by Defence Intelligence, or to be more precise, by the RAF Provost and Counter Intelligence Branch.

"Top secret investigations into a possible UFO threat to Britain have been carried out since the late 1950s. It is the most sensitive intelligence matter of all time.

"There are many at the Ministry who can honestly say they know of no such investigations. But the details are only given to a few on a need-to-know basis with an appropriate security clearance level."

And Arnold West, chairman of the British UFO Research Association, says: "The Government knows of many more cases than we do. We receive a polite but guarded response to our inquiries, usually from a junior information officer. But certainly Whitehall has far more information than ever sees the light of day."

Throughout the world UFOs have now been sighted by millions of people and yet scientific research into the subject is almost nil.

A recent American Gallup poll found that one in 11 adults had seen a UFO and half the people polled believed in them.

Britain is an even stronger nation of UFO believers. A poll of 2,000 people in 11 cities revealed one in six had seen a UFO and 60 per cent believed in them.

LAURIE MANSBRIDGE

Haunted Skies Volume Ten

MYSTERY: 1988 is proving to be a record year for reports of strange glowing objects in the sky. RIGHT: Top UFO investigator Mark Birdsall

SPACESHIP TAILS CAB

THESE are just a few of the UFO sightings reported from various parts of Britain since the start of the year:

- A taxi driver in South Shields, Tyneside, described an 80ft saucer covered in bright lights which first hovered and then followed his cab. The driver said: "At one stage it was just 30ft above us. It was made of grey metal. But the weirdest thing was it made no noise. I got out of the car with my passenger to have a closer look and then it backed off and disappeared."

- At Barnsley, Yorkshire, a 38-year-old man saw "a huge, box-shaped object with green, white and red lights. It didn't make a sound. It followed me home and I called the wife who also saw it."

- Youth club warden John Rees was walking his dog at Aberdare, Glamorgan, when he saw a cylindrical luminous object with two downward parallel beams moving spirally without any noise. "I watched it for about 45 minutes and have never seen anything like it in my life. I had never believed in UFOs before."

- Frank Barnes, delivering morning newspapers at Winchester, Hants, said: "Two yellow saucers, each about the size of a house, flew over me at about 30mph. There was a hissing sound."

- Oxford art studio boss David White was followed for 40 minutes by a red glowing object as he drove home. "When I stopped it stopped" he said. "I thought I was going crazy. There was no real shape to it, just a red glow with a white centre and no noise."

- Husband and wife Eddie and Molly Owers were baffled by a dawn sighting of a glowing yellow shape hovering above them at Stevenage, Herts. Said Eddie: "We watched it for several minutes. It was a huge casserole-shaped object."

- Pensioner George Moore was going to bed at his home in Rotherham, Yorks, when his terrier Harry "went beserk, whimpering and leaping around in terror". George thought he had burglars but when he looked out of the window he saw a "luminous cone-shaped object" which he watched for five minutes.

Haunted Skies Volume Ten

23rd October 1988 – UFO over Kent

At Biddenden, Kent, a strange object was seen passing over Woodlands Caravan Park, at an estimated height of 500ft, by teenagers – Joanna Dickinson and Julie Jessop – described as oval, with four lights, displaying a bright red light in the middle, emitting a deep hum, before shooting vertically into the late evening sky and disappearing from sight.

The girls later contacted the *Kent & Sussex Courier* (4.11.1988) complaining that the object had *'knocked out the telephone line'*.

24th October 1988 – UFOs over Northamptonshire

Terri Oakensen (then aged 10) – granddaughter of Elise Oakensen, whose spectacular UFO sighting can be found in Volume 7 of *Haunted Skies* (November 1978) – was walking home towards Weedon, when she noticed an eye-shaped object with red, green and blue, coloured lights around it.

> "On the top was a light, which flashed blue and red. When all the lights went off a black thing came out of the bottom, and when it moved away the whole thing went white. There was no noise."

According to Elsie, with whom we had the pleasure of meeting and talking to, many times over the years – then the Daventry representative for the British UFO Research Association – she mentioned:

> "Other people had also reported seeing UFOs that evening. At 6.05pm, there were three separate sightings of a group of six objects. At 6.25pm, there were another three sightings of a group of three UFOs."

(Sources: *Daventry Weekly Express*, 24.11.1988 – 'Schoolgirl sees alien craft buzz house'/ Personal interviews)

25th October 1988 – Diamond-shaped UFO over Lowestoft

At 4.30pm, Beverley Denise Roberts (32) was walking along Queen Anne's Drive, Westcliff-on-Sea, with her two sons, when her eldest shouted out:

> "Look Mum, there's a 'flying saucer'."

Beverley:

> "I looked out and saw a 'flying saucer', hovering in the sky above some bungalows opposite. It was grayish-white in colour, had twinkling blue lights and brilliant orange windows – then it changed into a glowing tube and disappeared from sight."

At 8.40pm, a diamond-shaped object was seen passing over Mutford, near Lowestoft, by Lowestoft Chemist – James Edington – who said:

> "I have never seen anything like it before. I was standing with an elderly neighbour of mine. We both saw it, and noticed a flashing light at each point of the diamond. It was silent – all we could hear was the swishing of air as it passed over."

Enquiries with the nearby airfield revealed that the only aircraft up at the time was a Sikorksy helicopter, which landed at 8.50pm.

During the same evening, members of the Sawyer family from Great Wakering, Southend-on-Sea, sighted:

> "... a large light in the sky, accompanied by two or three smaller ones around it, and were being approached by two aircraft, which kept moving towards them but appeared to be 'pushed away'".

The sighting, which also included reports of triangular and circular lights over Essex, at 9.00pm the same evening, was later explained away by the British Astronomical Association as being the planet Venus!

(Sources: *Lowestoft Journal & Mercury*, Suffolk, 28.10.88 – 'Mystery of the silent UFO'/East Anglian UFO & Paranormal Research Association)

SECTION A — SIGHTING ACCOUNT FORM

Please write an account of your sighting, make a drawing of what you saw and then answer the questions in section B overleaf as fully as possible. Write in BLOCK CAPITALS using a ball point pen.

My wife, two sons and daughter, and I, were returning from a meal out in Basildon. The time was 9.30 p.m. by my car clock. One of my sons Mark pointed out to me this crescent shaped object in the sky it was an orange/yellow colour with a reddish glow surrounding it. It seemed to be moving towards the centre of Basildon. We were unable to stop due to the traffic, and we lost sight of it within four or five seconds. THERE WERE NO LIGHTS TO BE SEEN AND WE COULD SEE THE MOON.

It was published in the Evening Echo two days later, that it had been seen in Basildon.

Please continue on a separate sheet if necessary.

DRAWING* — ORANGE/YELLOW, RED GLOW.

Your full name (Mr/Mrs/Miss/Ms): DAVID HARRINGTON Age 43
Address: 15, MEADOWLAND ROAD, WICKFORD, ESSEX
Telephone No. — (STD. —)
Occupation during last two years: SHELL OIL DEPOT
Any professional, technical or academic qualifications or special interests: ....

Do you object to the publication of your name? *Yes/No. *Delete as applicable.
Today's Date: 22-10-88
Signature: D. Harrington

*If preferred, use a separate sheet of paper.

26th October 1988 – UFO seen over Leigh-on-Sea, Essex

At 3am, Denis Colin Nicoll (59) – a senior lecturer living in Southchurch Boulevard, Southend-on-Sea – was awoken by a brilliant *'light'*. Thinking lightning had struck the house, he rushed to the window – but there was nothing to be seen. According to Colin, the next morning, *Radio London* explained it away as being a meteorite.

At 2.30pm, ex-pilot Mr Lindsay Guy Fraser (35) living in Holland Road, Westcliff-on-Sea, Essex, was with Lee Stannard (19) and Kevin Barton (23) when they saw a dazzling *'ball of light'* appear in the sky *'as big as the Sun'*. Five minutes later, it suddenly disappeared from view.

At 4.30pm, Dora McQuillan (72) living on the top floor of an eleven storey block of flats at St. Clements Court, Leigh-on-Sea, was sat talking to her sister (78), while looking out of the window, facing south-east, on what was a cloudless day.

Dora:

> "We often see many aircraft heading in and out of Southend Airport from this window. Suddenly I saw what I took to be an aircraft, behaving in a most odd manner; it was moving backwards and forwards all the time. I shouted to my sister to come and have a look. She has exceptionally good long-range vision and was fascinated to see whatever it was performing these movements in the air, some way off."

(Source: Brenda Butler/Ron West)

At 6.30pm, Kellie Drane (19) – from Wakering, Essex – was walking home from work when she sighted a glowing *'light'* in the sky, about two or three miles away. The *'light'* was then seen to travel around in a semicircle and fade away.

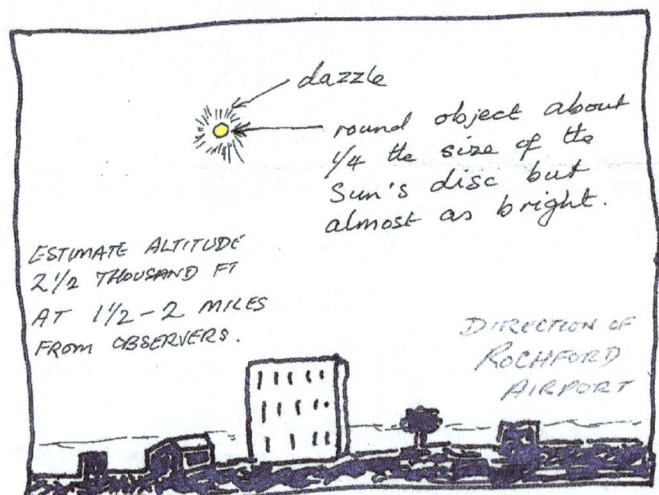

At 8pm, Kerry Hawes (11) of Canvey Island saw something strange. Other witnesses were Barbara and Bernard Boniface (62) and their son Brian (26) of Poplar Road, Rayleigh, Essex. The couple contacted Ron West, the following day, to report what they and their neighbours – John and Grace Sutherby – had not only seen but videoed. Unfortunately the whereabouts of the tape remains currently unknown.

	REF.	YEAR	NUMBER	INVESTIGATOR Ron West	CASE SUMMARY	
RW261088		88	10/58	EVALUATOR	DATE	
RN FORM TO:-					TIME	
					LOCATION	
					EVAL'N	
					UFO CLASS	
					CLOSED	

EAST ANGLIAN U.F.O. & PARANORMAL RESEARCH ASSOCIATION

SECTION A — SIGHTING ACCOUNT FORM

Please write an account of your sighting, make a drawing of what you saw and then answer the questions in section B overleaf as fully as possible. Write in BLOCK CAPITALS using a ball point pen.

THESE OBJECTS WERE AS REPORTED TO YOU ON 23RD SEPT 88 REGARDING NUMBERS — AREA OF OPERATION — SHAPE — TIME AND PATTERN OF FLYING.

ONCE AGAIN APPROX 8-10 OBJECTS WERE OBSERVED OVER THE TILBURY AREA FLYING IN A LARGE CIRCULAR AREA AS BEFORE. LIGHTS WERE NOT FLASHING AND NO NOISE WAS HEARD. ONE WAS SITED OVER SOUTHEND AIRPORT WHICH WAS VISIBLE AT 8 O'CLOCK TO THE MOON. THIS OBJECT WAS RECORDED ON VIDEO WHICH YOU NOW HAVE. IT REMAINED FOR APPROX 15 MINS BEFORE LEAVING TO REJOIN OTHERS OVER TILBURY AREA. AND WITH THIS OBJECT NO NOISE OR FLASHING LIGHTS WERE OBSERVED. IT WAS CLEARLY SEEN AS TRIANGULAR IN SHAPE WITH TWO BRIGHT WHITE LIGHTS IN FRONT WITH ONE RED LIGHT AT THE REAR. TOTAL PERIOD OF OBSERVATION 1¼ HRS FROM 2000 HRS — 2115 HRS.

Please continue on a separate sheet if necessary.

DRAWING

OBJECT WAS TRIANGULAR IN SHAPE WITH TWO WHITE LIGHTS IN THE FRONT AND ONE RED AT REAR WITH NO ENGINE SOUND.

Your full name (Mr/Mrs/Miss/Ms) BERNARD BONIFACE Age 62
Address 8 POPLAR ROAD
RAYLEIGH ESSEX SS6 8SL
Telephone No. 770084 (STD. 0268)
Occupation during last two years RETIRED (CIVIL SERVANT)

Any professional, technical or academic qualifications or special interests NONE

Do you object to the publication of your name? Yes/No. *Delete as applicable.
Today's Date 8-11-88
Signature B.Boniface

Haunted Skies Volume Ten

27th October 1988 – Blue flashes of light over Essex

Amateur astronomer Cecil Bailey (62) of Haverhill, Suffolk, awoke at 3.15am to make a cup of tea for his disabled wife. While waiting for the kettle to boil, he went out into the backyard and looked up into the clear night sky, apart from wispy cloud and a moon on the wane.

> "A green-blue light appeared in the sky and obscured the light given off by the moon, for a few seconds. I then saw a vapour trail heading south-east, with a dark object in front of it."

Mr Bailey expressed an opinion to UFO investigators – Julie Rondeau and Peter Fleming – who came to see him, that what had been observed wasn't a meteor, as it was going too slow and left no trail or sparks.

A12 Chelmsford Bypass, Essex

Felixstowe British Rail worker Eric Wallis was on shunting duty, at 3.45am, with colleague Michael Scarfe, when the immediate area around the Container terminal became illuminated by a bright blue light. This was followed by the appearance of a brightly-lit object seen heading across the sky, showing silver-blue flames.

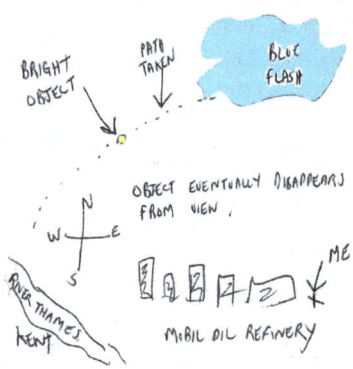

At 3.20am, David Osborne (53) and his wife, Thelma, were travelling along the A12 Chelmsford Bypass, when the whole of the sky lit-up for a few seconds. The couple's first thought was that Bradwell Power Station had blown up. However, after seeing an aircraft en route to Stansted Airport, they wondered if the landing lights had been switched on and off.

At Wivenhoe, bird life on the River Colne became agitated, following the brilliant blue flash, and took a few minutes to settle down again. John Whitehead was on night shift at the Mobil oil refinery at Coryton, Stanford-le-Hope. At 3.30am, while sweeping up on Unit 18, a bright blue flash in the sky caught his attention.

> "Out of this 'flash' appeared a bright object, moving very fast, resembling a 'rocket' firework. The object headed away in a south direction, towards Kent. I first thought it was a meteor or shooting star, until I read in the Evening Echo about other sightings."

Maldon, Essex

At 3.40am, housewife Barbara Melville of Maldon Close, Maldon, Essex, was in the process of getting back into bed, after attending to her baby, when a blue light lit-up the house.

> "As it died down, I saw a silver half-moon shaped object hovering in the sky. Ten seconds later it shot away at speed, heading silently North towards Clacton."

Another witness was Jane Banks (79) of School Road, Wickham Bishops, Malden, Essex, who thought it was lightning, but on looking out saw that the sky was clear.

Essex area

At 3.40am, milkman Kevin Cook was getting ready to start work and went outside to bring the dog in, when there was a huge flash of blue light, which lasted for a few seconds.

"My dog came running into the house and went straight into his basket, clearly frightened."

Other people who reported it were Jane Banks (79), Harry Edmund (55), Mr C. Moss (56), Gina Rose (53), Doris Watson (67), Sandra Janet Marlow 43), Caroline Ann Spooner (17) and Mrs P. Noakes (54).

Ashford, Kent

At 3.45am, Police Constable Norman Sells and Robin Buxton were on duty at Gascoignes Corner, High Halden, Ashford, Kent, when the whole of the night sky became as bright as daylight, lasting for 3-4 seconds. When the officers radioed in the incident, they found the phenomenon had been seen by residents of Deal, Sheerness, and Sittingbourne. This appears to have been a fireball 'bolide' breaking-up in the atmosphere, especially as there was a report of a blue *'ball of light'* seen to descend through the sky over Biddenden, by Stephen Button, who was driving along the road at the time.

Also at 3.45am, Mr Basil John Watson (60) – then a security guard – was driving home along Valley Road, Clacton-on-Sea, after finishing work at Point Clear Holiday Park when:

"... a huge flash of blue and white light lit-up the sky – strong enough to blot out the stars. I stopped the car and spoke to the driver of another vehicle, which had pulled up in front of him. The 'flash' went back on itself to a spot in the sky, behind which was a long white vapour trail."

Ipswich, Suffolk

At the same time, Brian Williams of Brookfield Road, Ipswich, was outside having a breath of air, after watching the late night film.

"I saw this shaft of blue light in the sky, moving over the direction of Norwich Railway Bridge. It appeared to cover a distance of several hundred yards and was visible for about 5mins. It reminded me of a torch being switched on and off."

Another witness to this phenomenon was Mr Graham Abbott of Carlsford Court, Ipswich.

"I was about to put the light on, when the room was lit-up with what appeared to be lightning. I went to the window and looked out to see a large round circle – bigger than the moon in the sky; it had what appeared to be a vapour trail behind it. Within 2-3 seconds it vanished from view."

High Wycombe, Buckinghamshire

HGV driver Mr Nelson Bibby (48) was driving along the M40, at High Wycombe, when the sky was lit-up for two seconds by a huge flash of blue light.

Chelmsford, Essex

Mrs Winifred Friedlein (67) of White House Farm, North Fambridge, Chelmsford, Essex, got up to turn-off the water heater.

As she was about to settle down for the night, a huge flash lit-up the house for about 20 seconds.

> "At the same time I heard this humming noise, which I thought was an airplane, and went to bed. The next morning, my husband told me that there had been other reports about this on Essex Radio"

At 3.50am, John Herbert Hill from Chelmsford, Essex, was awoken by a blinding flash of light.

Mr Hill told Ron West in an interview, later, that:

> "The other 'light' was seen to climb rapidly through the sky, heading southwards at an angle of 45°, before disappearing into cloud. The main object I saw was flying about as fast as a USAF Flying Fortress, as seen in the Second World War, but had no apparent wings."

Hockley, Essex

Other witnesses to this phenomena included Ross Davis (11) from Hockley, Essex. According to Ross's mother, the mysterious *'light'* – likened to that of a searchlight rather than the sky being flooded with lights, as one might expect from a fireball – was the subject of discussion by BBC *Radio Essex and Radio Medway*. It was said that an astronomer by the name of Mr Rolphindy, of Hawkwell, explained away the light phenomena as being a meteor shower! The matter was also the subject of conversation by teachers and pupils at the Greenwood School, in Hockley, the next day.

Some miles away in Ipswich, Suffolk, Vivien Humphrey (49), of Warrington Road, was also awoken by a bright blue flash of light.

Westcliff-on-Sea

At 4.45pm, Jeanne 'H' (37), of Queen Anne Drive, was on her way to the local shop before it closed, accompanied her by her six year-old son and his friends.

> "I noticed the sky in the south was an unusual deep blue colour – almost mauve. I wondered if it was connected with the Power Station chimneys on the River Thames, as they are always giving off chemicals. It was a cloudy day, with orange clouds as the sun began to set. My son screamed out that he could see a 'flying saucer'. I told him not to be silly, as I do not believe that such things exist, and looked up. I was shocked to see a 'flying saucer'-shaped object in the sky over the Foulness area of the North Sea. It was something that defied explanation and was not to be confused with aircraft, airships, moon or stars. My son told me it plunged down from the sky, although I didn't see this happen. One of his friends said he could see it giving off little flashes of light as it left, but I didn't see that as well."

Rayleigh, Essex

At 5pm, Elizabeth Seymour (82) from 50 Deepdean Road, Rayleigh, Essex, was waiting for a bus outside the community hall at Havengore, Pitsea, with other members of the old-age pensioners club, when she noticed:

> "... three lights in the sky, situated like a triangle, underneath which were four small dull lights. I also saw a number of aircraft flying about."

According to Mr Bainbridge who interviewed her, following contact with her daughter, Pauline, none of the others would allow him to interview them. Elizabeth would be long gone now, but her story lives on and will not be forgotten.

At 5.45pm, Sarah Burton (11) was looking out of her bedroom window in Rayleigh, Essex, when she saw a huge black object, showing a red light and ring of lights underneath, cross the sky and fly over the house, before disappearing from view.

Hadleigh, Essex

At 7.15pm, Kamlesh Trivedi (30) was on his way to Southend from London, driving along the A127 on what was a clear night, with a full moon, accompanied by passenger Mr M. Ali (34). As he passed Hadleigh, he saw a bright object, stationary in the sky over a field close to Hadleigh Castle.

> "It was made up of five bright objects, forming a rectangle in shape. I took them to be aircraft, until I looked again and saw they were still in the same position and showing bright blue and white lights. The objects were there for at least 45 minutes and kept circling in the sky. They reminded me of Chinese lanterns and were silent."

Kamlesh stopped the car. As he drew nearer the object, it suddenly dived into the ground and was gone from sight.

At 7.30pm, Pamela Osborne (35) of Cambridge Road, Canvey Island, was inside her house, when she was summoned by the next door neighbour to come out and have a look at something strange in the sky.

> "I went upstairs and opened the bedroom window and leaned out alongside my next door neighbour, who was doing the same. We saw nine separate lights in the sky, which flew in either a south or north direction before returning back to the original location, which was occupied by one single light that stayed there throughout the two hours time we watched them. We knew they couldn't have been aircraft or helicopters, as they often flew next to each other while in flight."

Wakering, Essex

At 7.45pm, Peter Sayer (33) of Beach Court, Wakering, Essex, and his wife, Susan – an enrolled nurse – were approached by their daughter, who told him about a bright *'star'* which had appeared in the sky.

Peter:

> "I went to have a look and saw a bright light in the western sky. There were about six smaller lights moving backwards and forwards from it. This went on for two hours. I contacted the airport at Southend, and was told no aircraft were in the sky over our location. I took some photos."

[The whereabouts of these photos is unknown, although according to UFO investigator – Mr Martin Bainbridge – they were *'poor photos, but showed a 'V'-shaped formation of lights'*]. The object was also seen by neighbours Kelly and Joy Booth of 2, Beach Court, and Sylvia Karer and Shaun Davies of 1, Beach Court.

Stanford-le-Hope

At 8pm, the UFOs were now being observed over Stanford-le-Hope, according to Mr R.J. Ward (34) and his wife, who thought initially, like so many others that evening, that they were aircraft – until the sky became flooded with the lights.

> "They would appear from all directions and hover, before flying away into the sky. Sometimes two or

three would converge on each other and hover in the same place, before moving away. There were at least 50 of them – sharply defined, white in colour, and totally silent. We watched them for an hour before they disappeared from view."

Kent

At 8.30pm, Mrs J. Knowles (61) of Riverside Close, *Kingsnorth, Ashford, Kent, was at home when her husband shouted out to her that he was watching an object moving over nearby houses. His wife ran outside and was astonished to see a silver saucer-shaped object, approximately 10ft in diameter, moving low down in the sky towards them. The object then halted and began to hover over a nearby paddock, at a height estimated to be between 10-15metres off the ground. A light then came on, which moved like a searchlight over various parts of the paddock. About twenty minutes later the light withdrew into the object, which was swinging backwards and forwards in a curious pendulum movement, before shooting up into the sky vertically, and was lost from sight.

(Source: John T. Robson)

Stanford-le-Hope

At 9.10pm, Terrence Ernest Harding (40) – a telecom engineer by employment – was walking across the car park, with companion John Chesney, when a huge flash of light lit-up the sky. Both men ducked, wondering what was happening. They looked up and were surprised to see a light blue tubular-shaped object, motionless in the sky. A second later, it inexplicably vanished from sight.

(Source: Mr T. Robson, UFO Investigator /Martin Bainbridge, Ron West/Brenda Butler/ *Kent & Sussex Courier,* 4.11.1988 – 'Village beat Lit up')

Pitsea, Essex

Towards the end of another spectacular day's sighting of strange phenomena, Sonia George (28) of Kenneth Road, Pitsea, was in the process of putting out empty milk bottles on the doorstep, at 11pm, when a brilliant white light – *'long in shape'* – appeared in the sky, followed by a loud booming noise. She went to close the door and the light reappeared.

> "I went outside and saw a shadow in the clouds; I ran inside and alerted the lodger and my husband as to what was happening. They just laughed at me, so I ran back outside and along the pathway leading to Pitsea Centre and looked up. The object was enormous, silvery bronze in colour, showing squares on its side and making a humming noise. It then moved into thick cloud. I was jumping up and down with excitement – then it was gone."

---

*A Roman settlement was discovered at the crossing of two important Roman roads on Westhawk Farm. The centre of the settlement has been preserved unexcavated as an open space, but before building began on the rest of the site, part of a Roman road was uncovered. There was evidence to show that there had been timber buildings at the side of the road, some of which were associated with ironworking. A shrine or temple was also found with a water-hole which contained 74, mostly 2nd-century coins probably left as offerings. Over 250 coins and many other artefacts were discovered on the site, together with a Roman cemetery and an Iron Age burial. A site at Park Farm, which is crossed by one of the Roman roads, also yielded Roman pottery fragments, some of which were associated with the regional distribution of salt, probably made on Romney Marsh. The RAF and USAAF occupied RAF Kingsnorth, an airfield close to the village, during World War II.

Haunted Skies Volume Ten

Southend Evening Echo, Essex — 28 OCT 1988

UFO: One of the first flying saucer sightings was made over Iran by a 16-year-old student

UFOs: An Essex landing imminent

By FRED HAMMERTON

A UFO may soon land in South East Essex.

That's the prediction of one of the county's most experienced researchers.

His claim follows what has been the most amazing few weeks for spacecraft spotters and comes in the wake of a barrage of new sightings of a mysterious blazing light early yesterday off Southend.

In September, according to Ron West of the East Anglian UFO Research Association, there were 270 reported sightings in the Basildon and Southend areas. These figures were way up on previous months.

What does it mean? Ron, 57, said: "I know you will think I am crank but I believe we are going to get a landing. They will not harm us."

What will these inter-galactic travellers look like?

Ron, a former infantryman who works for an oil company, believes they could be similar to a 10ft tall blond male.

This is the rundown for daily sightings in the Basildon and Southend areas in September: Mondays 15, Tuesdays 10, Wednesdays 48, Thursdays 13, Fridays 54, Saturdays 35 and Sundays 25.

The Friday figures are bumped up by the coloured lights spotted over Southend on September 23.

The British Unidentified Flying Object Research Association, of which Ron is an Essex accredited investigator, had 25 calls about these mysterious sightings.

Window

He received a call from a Southend man and was able to watch them for an hour from where he lives in Clacton.

Ron said: "I have been interested in UFOs for 20 years but these are the first I have seen.

"The official line was that the lights were stacking aircraft but you don't see stacking aircraft moving around like this and you don't get blue lights on aircraft."

Ron, who said he was very excited by his first sight of UFOs, believes Southend along the Thames is a window in the sky through which spacecraft enter the earth's atmosphere.

Ufologists believe there are specific windows on earth through which space craft enter. Two are the North and South Poles. Apart from the Southend window the next is at Lowestoft in Suffolk.

The lights over Southend were seen in the Basildon area and surrounding districts. They were triangular in red, green, yellow, white and blue.

The only reported abduction in Essex was on October 27, 1974.

John and Sue Day from Aveley were driving home after seeing relatives. It was 10.20 pm and their three children were asleep in the back of the car. They saw a blue light in the sky and rounding a bend went through some green mist. As they did this their radio sparked.

Dreams

They then drove out of the mist but were amazed to discover it was then 1 pm.

For the next three years they had psychic experiences including objects moving around and seeing lights in the sky.

They also had recurring dreams of being in a room with small ugly creatures.

The family approached UFO Research and hypnosis was carried out. Their story was that they were drawn out of their car and had hazy memories of entering a UFO where they saw tall, human-like figures in silver suits with helmets.

Smaller creatures carried out medical examinations on them.

Mr West says 90 per cent of reported UFO sightings are fakes but this still leaves 10 per cent unexplained.

He and colleagues in UFO research advise anyone who sees a UFO not to approach it and never touch it.

They say: "Try not to interfere with the activities of a UFO occupant. It may be hostile or indifferent to your fragility.

"If it shows signs of wishing to communicate comply as best you can. Try not to allow your natural panic from allowing you to do so."

Radiation

The researchers also say you should consult your doctor following the incident to ensure you are not suffering from the effects of radiation.

They add: "As soon as you can, write down everything you can remember about the experience and make as many drawings as possible.

"You should repeat this about four days later without looking at the previous drawings then make a comparison to see how far you are out between first and second drawings."

The East Anglia UFO hotline is 0728 830757.

'You will think I'm a crank but we're going to get a landing'

READY: Ron West keeps an eagle eye on developments

ALIEN: This is an impression of how Ron West expects the aliens to appear, up to 10 feet tall with blond hair

Experts ready to meet aliens from space

A Skywatch with Ron West

Haunted Skies Volume Ten

28th October – 1988 UFOs over Essex

Billericay, Essex

At 2.30am, Mrs Eileen Storer (70) of Crays View, Billericay, Essex, was unable to sleep, so her husband went down to make some tea.

> "I looked out and saw a large silver 'ball' reminding me of a ballroom dancing globe, apparently bouncing in the air over the nearby treetops. Within seconds it was out of view."

Leigh-on-Sea

At 3am, Mr J. Jackson of Manchester Drive, Leigh-on-Sea, was in bed when he heard a humming noise – like a spinning top. On looking through the window he saw a cigar-shaped object, horizontal in the sky, which had a red light on one end and a blue one on the other. As he watched the object, it changed into a 'Y'-shape (lying down) and then a half-moon shape, before disappearing from view.

Southend-on-Sea

At 4am, baker Roger 'D' (43), from Southend-on-Sea, was walking to work along Maple Avenue.

> "I heard a soft 'swishing noise' coming from over my head. I looked up and saw a disc-shaped object, about 2-300ft in the air, passing overhead. It was dark in colour and was showing red and white lights around its outer rim. I estimated it to be 6ft across. I watched it head away until out of sight, 10 seconds later."

Wickford, Essex

At 7.45pm, Diana Fitt (65) of Wickford, Essex, sighted a brilliant white object – *'much larger than a tennis ball'* – moving across the sky on what was a very clear, cold night.

Rochford, Essex

The activity continued with a report from Anna Argent (51) of Rochford Garden Way, Rochford, Essex, who was outside her house, at 9.30pm, talking to a neighbour.

> "We noticed a sharply defined, silent, jet black, triangular-shaped object in the sky; it had red, green and yellow lights on it, and was moving slowly – as if looking for something. It headed away towards Leigh-on-Sea."

(Source: Brenda Butler/Ron West)

29th October 1988 – Square-shaped UFO seen, Westcliff-on-Sea, Essex

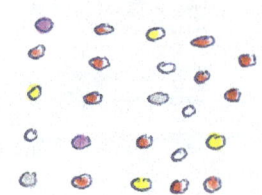

At 12.45am, Lesley Jones (aged 31) was walking home from a night out with his two friends, when they saw a number of bright lights of various colours, forming

a square or block in the sky, which stopped briefly overhead before travelling eastwards, towards the direction of Shoeburyness. The duration of observation was five minutes.

At 00.45, 01.44, 02.20, and 03.30hrs, people living in the Thundersly area of Essex reported seeing a bright flash of light that lit-up the sky for a split second. Was this space debris, meteors entering the earth's atmosphere, or the prelude to a UFO sighting?

Wickford, Essex

Other witnesses to UFO activity that early morning were Emma Fairbairn (17). She and her two unnamed friends were standing in the Memorial Park, at 1.00am, when they noticed a blue light shining through the branches of nearby trees. They wondered if it was an aircraft in trouble, because the lights were just over the tops of the trees.

> "Gradually the lights moved over; at one stage we thought they were going to crash into the football fields. They then moved away, at which point I saw what looked like two propellers above the five lights."

At 2am, Mr G. Suckling (67) of May Avenue, Canvey Island, had retired to bed. Before going up he opened the back door which faces south and immediately noticed a bright object in the sky that appeared to change shape.

> "Suddenly from the object's bottom right-hand side appeared what looked like a shooting star. This veered off to the right – like a comet. The object then changed colour from green to red, but still remained stationary in the sky. I presumed that I was watching a star, burning up, and observed it for about 30mins before going to bed."

Southend-on-Sea

At 4.25pm, a taxi driver noticed a large blue light, stationary in the sky. He stopped the car and got out.

> "It was like a round blue football; it looked like the moon but wasn't. A few minutes later it suddenly shot off across the sky, towards the East."

At 11.30pm, Rayleigh, Essex, resident – Roy Watson (63) – was in the process of leaving the *White Horse Public House*, accompanied by his wife and daughter, and walking to the pub car park. A bright moving *'light'* caught his attention in the clear night sky.

> "I expected it to burn out. I then saw that it was actually a strip of four or five lights. Somebody behind me shouted out 'It's a UFO'. I watched the yellow-grey strip of lights, which were at an angle in the sky and had pointed ends, head away into the distance."

At 11.15pm, Gina Cook (28) of Kenneth Road, Thundersley, Essex, saw a vivid flash in the sky, which caught her attention. She decided to continue her observations of the night sky and was rewarded, over the next few hours, with other examples of strange activity – which she carefully made a note of.

(Source: Brenda Butler/Ron West)

30th October 1988 – UFO Display, Berkshire

Bright *'lights'* were seen speeding across the sky over Tilehurst, Caversham and Reading, during the night of 30th October 1988. The witnesses included Kevin and Donna Wallace, who were driving home from Bradfield to Laytom Rise, Tilehurst, Reading, when they noticed a large bright object in the sky.

Donna:

> *"We first thought it was a plane, but it stayed at the same position. When we arrived home, we counted up to eight objects in the sky – all moving backwards and forwards at a great speed. There seemed to be one main light which the others were coming back to; some of them were red, green, and blue. They were not fireworks, as they stayed in the sky for several hours."*

Between 7pm and 9pm that evening, Clark Roberts (16) from Rutland Avenue, Southend-on-Sea, was alerted by the sound of dogs, barking, and went out to have a look at what was causing the commotion. He was shocked to see a number of *'lights'* moving across the sky and alerted his neighbours; who came out to watch.

A spokesman for the MOD confirmed that they had received some reports from the public and would be investigating whether the craft had illegally entered British airspace!

(Source: *Reading Evening Post,* 1.11.1988 – 'Was it a bird? Was it a plane – or UFO? /Personal interview)

31st October 1988 – Pear-shaped UFO seen over Essex

Canvey Island

At 1.30am, Gillian Cadman, of Kings Holiday Park, was in her bedroom, after having visited the bathroom.

She decided to have a look outside, to view the weather conditions, and was stunned to see what she described as:

> *". . . a mauve coloured object, shaped like a cone with the top cut off, with a white underneath, heading across the sky at high altitude."*

She watched it for a few minutes, during which time she alerted her mother, who later confirmed the sighting to Ron West, of the East Anglian UFO & Paranormal Research Association.

Basildon, Essex

At 6.20pm on the same day, June Grace Habberley (43) of Basildon, Essex, noticed a strange *'star'* in the sky. She went into the garden and called her daughter, Carla (19) to come and have a look.

> *"It was pulsating red, blue and white, lights. I looked at it through binoculars; it looked like a bunch of Christmas tree lights – apparently stationary in the sky. It then began to slowly move away, heading in a north-west direction. Above it was a red dot, zigzagging over the top and sides of the other lights. The red dot of light stayed for about five minutes, before disappearing from view."*

Carla:

> *"I thought it was a star, to begin with, then realised it was pear-shaped, with lights rotating around it."*

Another witness was Mr A. Bolton – the lodger of Mrs Habberley. He was just on his way out, when she asked him to look up into the sky. When he did so, he saw three (red, green and white) flashing lights *"moving at an extraordinarily low speed through the sky"*.

EAST ANGLIAN U.F.O. & PARANORMAL RESEARCH ASSOCIATION

SECTION A — SIGHTING ACCOUNT FORM

Please write an account of your sighting, make a drawing of what you saw and then answer the questions in section B overleaf as fully as possible. Write in BLOCK CAPITALS using a ball point pen.

On 31st October, at roughly 6.20 pm, I noticed what appeared to be a very large star in the sky. I called my friend to come outside, into the garden, and asked him what it might be. He said it was not a star and it was pulsating red, blue and white light. I looked at the object and could also see the colours. We watched for about 5 mins and then I got some binoculars out and continued viewing. It first appeared stationary but was moving at a pace of roughly 4 mile an hour, or slower, it appeared to be heading in a North Westerly route. I continued watching for about 45 mins and noticed a red dot moving over the top of object and zig-zagging at the side (continued)

Please continue on a separate sheet if necessary.

DRAWING

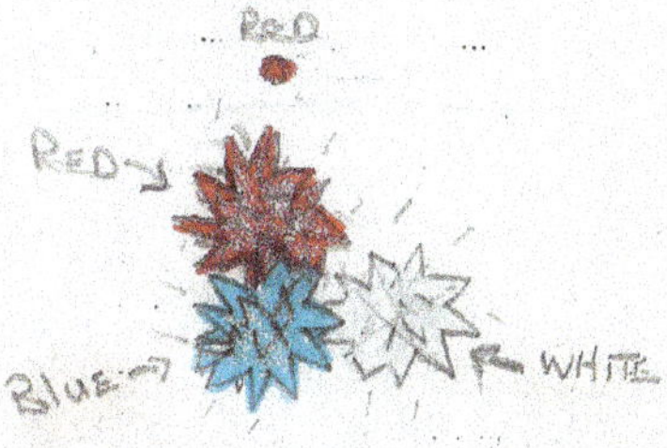

RED
RED →
BLUE → ← WHITE

I CAN NOT DRAW AT ALL, BUT WOULD SAY THE OBJECTS LOOKED LIKE A BUNCH OF CHRISTMAS TREE LIGHTS.

If preferred, use a separate sheet of paper.

Your full name (Mr/Mrs/Miss/Ms) JUNE GRACE HABBERLEY Age 43

Address 121 DANACRE LINDON BASILDON ESSEX

Telephone No BAS 419618 (STD)

Occupation during last two years MOTHER AND LANDLADY

Any professional, technical or academic qualifications or special interests INTERESTED IN THE LATE MR GEORGE ADAMSKI & HIS BOOKS

Do you object to the publication of your name? ~~Yes~~/NO *Delete as applicable.

Today's Date 13 NOV 1988

Signature J G Habberley

Peterborough

At 7pm, housewife Lucy Kennedy, from Arundel Road, was with her husband, David, looking out of the window at an early bonfire party, when she noticed a smoke ring about 50ft across, hovering in the air

> "... like a giant Polo mint. Suddenly, it rose upwards into the clouds and was gone."

At 7.10pm, Mr Mason (32) – a bookkeeper – of Church Road, Basildon, sighted what he referred to as:

> "... a strange atmospheric phenomenon, rather than any UFO incursion; it was an intense band of luminous light, stationed in the sky above the local town centre, stretching from south-west to north-west. It resembled a searchlight beam, yet didn't emanate from anything. The W/NW section of the band was dimmer, but curiously the band of light was vanishing and reappearing in a rapid 'on and off' cycle. By 7.30pm, it had faded away."

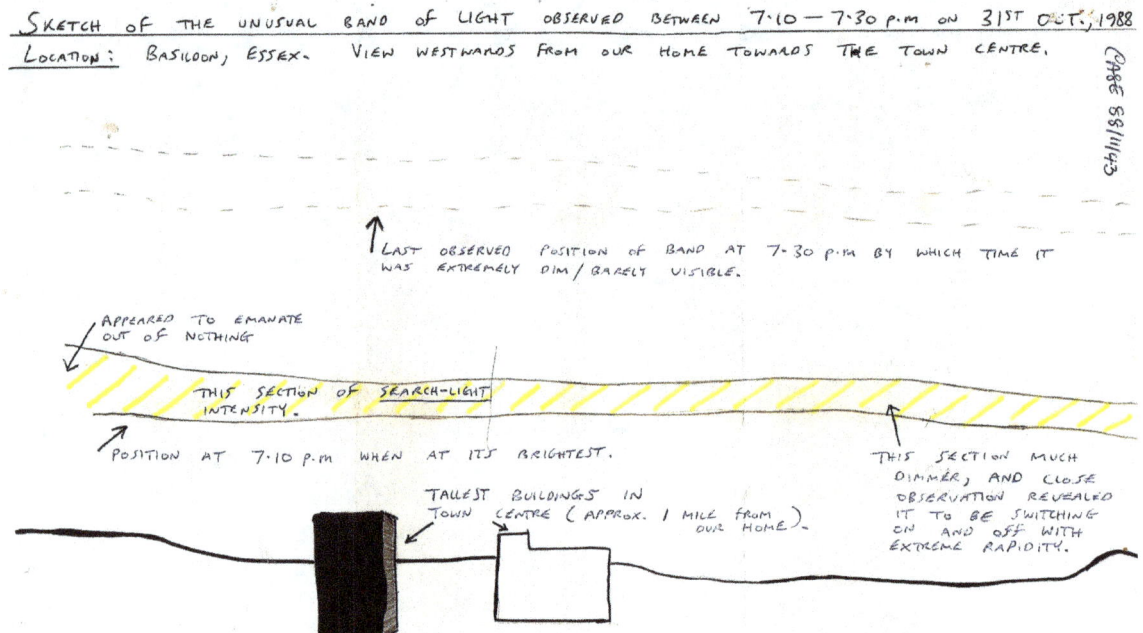

Canvey Island

At 8pm the same evening, Leon Hawes (aged 14 at the time) had just come out of his house in North Avenue, and was talking to his friend, Sean Harding, when they saw three *'lights'* (one red, the other two forming a triangular shape) moving in a south-east direction through the sky.

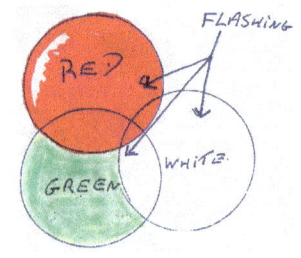

Westcliff-on-Sea

Another witness to what appears to have been the same UFO, at the same time, was Sarah Clarke (11) of Prince Avenue.

She, her sister, and two sons, saw a circle of flashing lights in the sky, close to the local airport, accompanied by a humming noise that she took to be an aircraft, until the lights stopped flashing. Sarah was astounded to see a silver object, made up of triangular '*cuts*'. Twenty minutes later, the object shot straight upwards and was gone from sight.

(Source: Brenda Butler/Ron West/*Peterborough Evening Telegraph*, 2.11.1988 - 'UFO like a Polo mint')

EAST ANGLIAN U.F.O. & PARANORMAL RESEARCH ASSOCIATION

SECTION A — SIGHTING ACCOUNT FORM

Please write an account of your sighting, make a drawing of what you saw and then answer the questions in section B overleaf as fully as possible. Write in **BLOCK CAPITALS** using a ball point pen.

> First of all I saw all different sorts of lights flashing in circle form at first I thought it was an aeroplane but when it stopped it just floated for about 20 minutes then after that it zoomed off upwards very fast I waited incase it came back but it didnt so I went to my sisters. and also it had triangular cuts around the Bottom And the had the lights in between.
>
> Sorry I forgot to write in block capitals I hope you can read it.

Your full name: Sarah Louise (Miss) CLARK
Age: 16
Address: 570 Prince Avenue Westcliff on Sea
Telephone No. .... (STD. ....)
Occupation during last two years: ....

Any professional, technical or academic qualifications or special interests:
Special interests are Animals and to Look after them and to Join Stop the fox Hunting

Do you object to the publication of your name? Yes/*No. *Delete as applicable.

Today's Date: 5/11/88
Signature: S L Clark

*If preferred, use a separate sheet of paper.

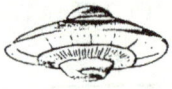 **East Anglian UFO & Paranormal Research**

WHO ARE THEY ?

WHERE DO THEY COME FROM ?

WHY ARE THEY HERE ?

AND WHAT DO THEY WANT FROM US ?

THE U.F.O. PHENOMENON

THESE ARE ONLY SOME OF THE QUESTIONS ASKED WHEN PEOPLE HAVE SEEN SOMETHING IN THE SKY IN DAY TIME OR AT NIGHT,TO WHICH THEY CANNO'T EXPLAIN.IF YOU THINK THAT YOU MAY HAVE SEEN SOMETHING OR HAD AN EXPERIENCE OF THIS NATURE THAN PLEASE CONTACT US AND LET US DEAL WITH IT,OUR HOT-LINE NUMBER IS----- 0268-286079,OR IF YOU WOULD LIKE TO BECOME AN ACTIVE MEMBER THE NUMBER IS JUST THE SAME,WE WILL BE ONLY TO PLEASED TO RECIEVE YOUR CALLS AND YOU WILL BE ADVISED ON WHAT TO DO.IF YOU WISH TO BECOME A MEMBER YOU WILL BE ADVISED ON HOW TO ENROLL WITH US.

AS WE HAVE ALL READ IN THE DAILY PAPERS ABOUT THESE PHENOMENAS WE ARE LOOKING FOR PEOPLE TO BECOME MEMBERS AND HELP WITH OUR INVESTIGATION WORK, THIS IS APP'LICABLE TO BOTH MALE/FEMALES OVER THE AGE OF 18YRS OF AGE AND OWN TRANSPORT WOULD BE A BENEFIT AS WELL FOR THE INVESTIGATION WORK INVOLVED.

SO PICK UP YOUR PHONE AND CONTACT US NOW ON THE NUMBER GIVEN.

RING US NOW

CHAPTER 8

NOVEMBER TO DECEMBER 1988

NOVEMBER 1988

1st November 1988 – UFO over Essex

AT 9.20pm, checkout supervisor Mrs Tomlinson of Tilbury, Essex, was travelling along the A13, heading towards the Tilbury turn-off, accompanied by her sister-in-law – Mrs Shovler. As they passed Orsett Hospital, they saw an object in the sky.

> *"It was round and had what looked like car headlights on the bottom, with red light in the middle. We stopped the car to take a closer look. It was stationary in the sky, but after a couple of minutes moved alongside of us, enabling us to see other lights underneath. Strangely, this was the second time in a week I had seen something like this along the same stretch of road."*

At 9.30pm, an oblong object showing blue and red lights, with a *'blob'* on top, about 30-40ft in length, was seen motionless in the sky over Hockley, Essex, by ex-pilot Mr C. Ebbs (49), who estimated it was at a height of about 2,000ft and was no firework. Five minutes later, it vanished from view.

(Source: Martin Bainbridge)

At 9.30pm, Ian Davidson (42) of Canvey Island,

Giant blond men visit
Get ready for UFO landing

by SR Reporter

A UFO MAY soon land in South East Essex.
That's the prediction of one of the county's most experienced researchers.
His claim follows what has been the most amazing few weeks for spacecraft spotters and comes in the wake a barrage of new sightings of a mysterious blazing light last week off Southend.
In September, according to Ron West of the East Anglian UFO Research Association, there were 270 reported sightings in the Basildon and Southend areas.
These figures were way up on previous months.
What does it mean?
Ron, 57, said: "I know you will think I am crank but I believe we are going to get a landing. They will not harm us."
What will these intergalactic travellers look like?
Ron, a former infantry-man who works for an oil company, believes they could be similar to a three-metre tall blond male.

Sightings

This is the rundown for daily sightings in the Basildon and Southend areas in September: Mondays 15, Tuesdays 10, Wednesdays 48, Thursdays 13, Fridays 54, Saturdays 36 and Sundays 25.
The Friday figures are bumped up by the coloured lights spotted over Southend on September 23.
The British Unidentified Flying Object Research Association, of which Ron is an Essex accredited investigator, had 25 calls about these mysterious sightings.
He received a call from a Southend man and was able to watch them for an hour from where he lives in Clacton.
Ron said: "I have been interested in UFOs for 20 years but these are the first I have seen.
"The official line was that the lights were stacking aircraft but you don't see stacking aircraft moving around like this and you don't get blue lights on aircraft."
Ron, who said he was very excited by his first sight of UFOs, believes Southend along the Thames is a window in the sky through which spacecraft enter the earth's atmosphere.
UFologists believe there are specific windows on earth through which space craft enter.
Two are the North and South Poles. Apart from the Southend window the next is at Lowestoft in Suffolk.
The lights over Southend were seen in the Basildon area and surrounding districts.
They were triangular in red, green, yellow, white and blue.
The only reported abduction in Essex was on October 27, 1974.
John and Sue Day from Aveley were driving home after seeing relatives. It was 10.20 pm and their three children were asleep in the back of the car.
They saw a blue light in the sky and rounding a bend went through some green mist. As they did this their radio sparked.
They then drove out of the mist but were amazed to discover it was then 1pm.
For the next three years they had psychic experiences including objects moving around and seeing lights in the sky.
They also had recurring dreams of being in a room with small ugly creatures.

Family

The family approached UFO Research and hypnosis was carried out.
Their story was that they were drawn out of their car and had hazy memories of entering a UFO where they saw tall human-like figures in silver suits with helmets.
Smaller creatures carried out medical examinations on them.
Mr West says 90 per cent of reported UFO sightings are fakes but this still leaves 10 per cent.
The East Anglia UFO hotline is 0726 830757.

Southend Standard
Essex 4.11.1988

Essex, was outside when he saw a thick blue beam of light emanating from the direction of the MOD establishment, at Shoeburyness. He reported it to Ron West and believes it was a laser light being tested at the Base.

2nd November 1988 – Triangular UFO over East Sussex

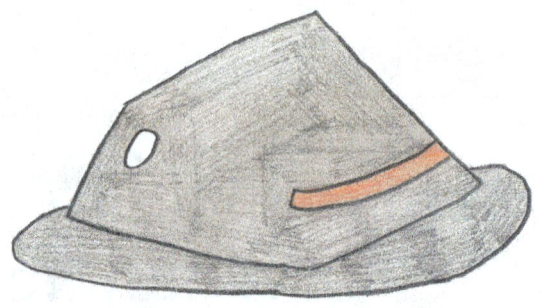

Another example of what was to become known as a 'Triangular UFO', which was to plague Europe in the late 1980s, took place on 2nd November 1988, involving 14-year-old schoolboy Kevin Laker from Derwent Avenue, Rayleigh, South-East Essex, who described seeing:

> "...a triangle with an extra side, which met at a point, with a white light and a long red light. It didn't make any noise and went off towards the Canvey direction.

Later the same evening, baffling *'bright lights'*, described as long with green and red flashing lights, were seen hovering over the Tilehurst area of Reading. One of the witnesses was Simon Baker (15), who said:

> *"I was really frightened. This long thing, showing green and red flashing lights, was hovering over the sky."*

At 9pm, Mr L Johnson (61) of Creek Cottages, Old Hall Lane, Walton-on-the-Naze, was out exercising his dog at the back of his property, situated at the bottom of a 400ft hill.

> *"Suddenly a strong wide beam of light projected down from the top of the hill. Wondering what had caused it, I went up to the top of the hill. When I reached the summit I switched on my torch, which throws a beam a light a mile long into the sky, but saw no sign of the strange light, which was much more powerful and stronger than my torchlight.*
>
> *I even went back the next day, and checked the ground, but found nothing of any interest."*

(Sources: *Reading Evening Post*, 3.11.1988 – 'Children see UFO'/*Southend Evening Echo*, Essex, 4.11.1988 – 'New UFO sighting is a puzzler')

3rd November 1988 – UFO Display over Essex

At 6.15pm, Steven Smith (14) of Wickford, Essex, went out to feed the cats, when he noticed an orange object in the sky and shouted his mother, who came running outside. His mother, Jenny (39), told him it must have been a star – until it suddenly increased in size. It then moved to the left, then back to its original position. An aircraft appeared, at which point the object took up a position behind the plane – both *'craft'* being lost from view, due to trees restricting their observations. The plane was seen shortly afterwards, but nothing more of the object.

At 6.40pm, State Registered Nurse – Isabelle 'Q' of Park Drive, Southend, was at her home address, when she saw something unusual and called her father to come and have a look. It began with a pair of red and blue lights that were seen stationary in the clear sky, rotating around a common centre, about the height of an aircraft. After about a minute the lights accelerated away, at tremendous velocity, towards the North. By this time she had called her father, who had made a written log of what he and his daughter had seen.

Haunted Skies Volume Ten

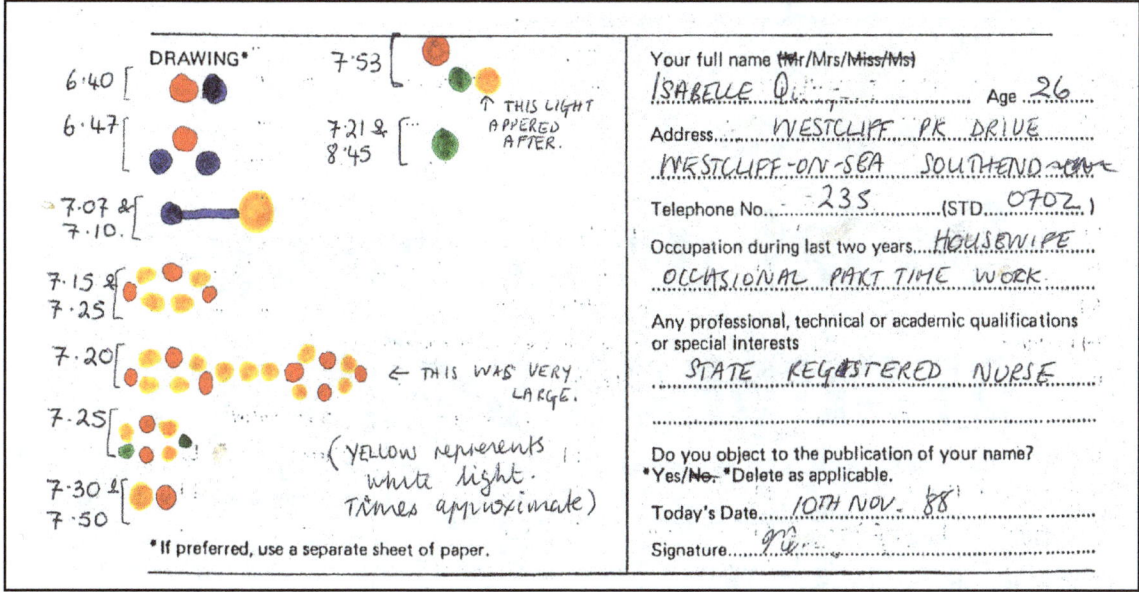

Log...

At 6.47pm, a triangular pattern of coloured lights, consisting of a red light at the apex and a blue light occupying the other two corners appeared. This also accelerates upwards and out of sight.

At 7.04pm, a bright white flash of light was seen moving horizontally towards the coast, heading southwards. This appeared to have a tail and was believed to have been a meteor.

At 7.05pm, Hazel Morag Reid (13), of Westcliffe-on-Sea, was delivering newspapers, accompanied by her brothers – Graham and Michael – when they saw a spinning object, moving at a fantastic speed across the sky, before disappearing into clouds.

> "It was shimmering and changed colour from white to orange-red, and then orange-brown, before we lost sight of it."

At 7.07pm, a bright light, trailing a slender blue trail, close to a second smaller light, was seen moving in a northwards direction but at a much lower altitude. A few minutes later, a second object was seen moving at the same altitude and velocity. As this disappeared another one reappeared, showing a blue light at the top of the cluster. [Authors: most likely the one and same object] A bright red light was then seen, moving across the sky. This was seen to change into a *'disc'* of light, showing alternating white and red lights.

At 7.20pm, two *'discs'* were seen in the sky but at a much lower altitude. This was followed by a large green light, heading northwards. This UFO activity continued up to 8.45pm and included sightings of further green, red, and yellow, lights in the sky.

At 8.30pm, Mr William Figg (33) of Westcliff-on-Sea went outside to put the rubbish out, when he saw a blue light in the sky, very high up over the *River Thames*.

> "It stayed still for about 5-10mins, then moved sideways and dropped down behind a cloud. That was the last time I saw it."

(Source: Geraldine Dillon/Ron West, East Anglian UFO & Paranormal Research Association)

BURY FREE PRESS — 4 NOV 1988

No let up in number of strange sightings

TWO more UFO spotters have contacted the Free Press after recent stories in the paper from people who claimed they saw strange objects in the sky.

And one is backing up the tale of a strange umbrella-shaped craft seen over Bury St Edmunds by a brother and sister who recounted their experience in last week's Free Press.

Mrs Ann Self and her eight-year-old daughter Carla also saw the craft as it passed over the town near to their home in Eastgate Street.

Mrs Self said: "Carla just said 'What's that in the sky' and we looked up and there was this strange black thing hovering a long distance away.

"It's hard to say exactly what it was. I wouldn't like to say whether it was a UFO but it didn't look like a plane either. It wasn't really moving very fast — it was just hanging in the air," she added.

Mrs Self saw the object on the same night as Rueben and Esther Eaves claimed they had spotted an umbrella-shaped craft near their home in Prigg Walk, Bury.

The second spotting took palce at Red Lodge in the early hours of last Thursday morning when Jerri Upshaw was returning home with her boyfriend.

As they neared the porch of her home in Gorse Close, she says she saw a green light shining from behind them.

"At first I thought my boyfriend was shining a flash light to show the way but when he looked back as well we saw this orangey-red glow go across the sky.

"It was very frightening and my stomach started to turn. I was so amazed at what I saw that I ran in to wake up my mum and tell her about it," she added.

A spate of UFO sightings have been reported recently in the Free Press, following an article in September when a Fornham All Saints boy reported seeing one in a field at the rear of his home.

We cannot be sure of the exact date, but according to the *Yorkshire Advertiser* (4.11.1988) a housewife at Wingfield, Rotherham, reported having seen *"a cylindrical object, showing white lights underneath, and orange lights moving around the top"*, while returning from the local fish and chip shop, at 6pm.

5th November 1988 – UFO over Essex

At 3.45am, Mr Kamlesh J Trivedi (30) of London Road, Southend-on-Sea, Essex, was driving along the A13 Road, near Hadleigh, Essex, heading homewards, when he was shocked to see a highly unusual object low down in the sky.

At 8.30pm, Norah Murdoch was out walking her dogs near the steps leading onto the sea front at Leigh-on-Sea, when a firework exploding in the sky caught her attention.

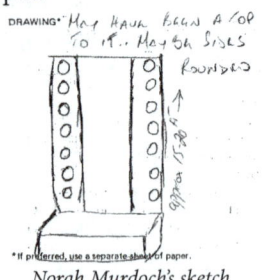

Norah Murdoch's sketch

EAST ANGLIAN U.F.O. & PARANORMAL RESEARCH ASSOCIATION

SECTION A — SIGHTING ACCOUNT FORM

Please write an account of your sighting, make a drawing of what you saw and then answer the questions in section B overleaf as fully as possible. Write in BLOCK CAPITALS using a ball point pen.

I WAS TRAVELLING ON A13 LONDON ROAD, HADLEIGH ESSEX AT ABOUT 3-45 AM IN DIRECTION OF SOUTHEND. ON MY RIGHT OVER A FIELD THERE IA IT WAS; A THREE DIMENSIONAL OBJECT EITHER A RETANGULAR OR A WITH COLOURED LIGHTS COVERING IT. (COLOURS RED, BLUE, WHITE). WITH A DIAMOND SHAPE TOP. FLYING VERTICALLY. AS MY CAR APPROACHED THIS OBJECT IT DIVED OUT OF MY VIEW. ITS SIZE WAS ABOUT A LARGE CAR; VOLVO OR MERCEDES. IT APPEARED TO BE ABOUT 150-200 FEET AWAY. IT DISAPPEARED WHAT I SEED OR BEEN THE HORIZON. I WAITED FOR A WHILE BUT IT DID NOT REAPPEAR.

DRAWING: LIGHTS, DARK OBJECT, SOUTHEND ↑, FIELD, SEA, MY CAR

Your full name: KAMLESH T TRIVEDI Age 30
Address: 166 LONDON ROAD, SOUTHEND-ON-SEA ESSEX
Telephone No. 333557 (STD. 0282)
Occupation during last two years: BUSINESS PROPRIETOR
Any professional, technical or academic qualifications or special interests: READING
Do you object to the publication of your name? Yes/No.
Today's Date: 9/3/89
Signature: Trivedi

Clear Sky	☑	Cold	☑	None	☑	Dry	☑	Stars	☑
Scattered cloud	☐	Cool	☐	Breeze	☐	Fog or mist	☐	Moon	☐
Much cloud	☐	Warm	☐	Moderate	☐	Rain	☐	Planet	☐
Overcast	☐	Hot	☐	Strong	☐	Snow	☐	Sun	☐

"I looked around and was shocked to see an object stationary in the sky over Billet Lane. I crossed over a nearby bridge to get a closer look, but by then it had gone."

At 9.45pm, Bernard Bowden (42) from Springfield Drive, Westcliff-on-Sea, was in his back garden when he saw a bright light shoot across the sky, heading in a north to south direction. He was adamant that this was no firework because it was so huge. He was interviewed about the matter some 12 months later by Ron West and Geraldine Dillon, who found him to be still very excited about what he had seen.

Haunted Skies Volume Ten

6th November 1988 – UFO over Essex

At 6.15pm, Julie Denham (24) of Thundersley, Essex, was in her back garden, accompanied by her husband, Kevin, brothers Jason and Darren Reeve, and their parents Philip and Daphne. They saw a circular pulsating orange and red object in the sky.

"It was dimming and glowing and moving up and down, side to side, as it headed across the sky."

In the same month, Douglas Harrison (70) of Harvest Road, Canvey Island, Essex, was outside his house, at 8pm, when he saw:

"... something I had never seen in all the years of my life – two rows of lights, with a larger light on top, heading across the sky towards Southend-on-Sea direction."

At 8.30pm, Mr Scott Ryden (22) of the *Jog Inn*, Halstead, Essex, was out walking with his friend – Jason Thompson – over the Borley area.

"Suddenly three yellow, white and blue, lights appeared over nearby treetops, forming a triangle pattern, before slowly descending into a nearby wood. We became frightened and ran back to the roadway, then made our way home to tell the family what we had seen."

7th November 1988 – UFO over Essex

At 4.20pm, Dennis Hursthouse and his wife, from Colchester, Essex, were about to leave the house when they saw a white object in the sky heading towards their position, about a mile away. The couple watched the white globe of light for about five minutes, before they lost sight of it.

At 6.15pm, Steven Mark Smith of Wickford, Essex, went outside to feed the cats, and saw an orange *'star'* moving about in the sky and called his mother, Jenny, to come out and have a look. The orange light dropped downwards, and then closed up behind an aircraft which was flying over at the time. When the aircraft reappeared after moving behind trees, the light was gone.

8th November 1988 – UFO over Essex

At 8.15am, John Bannon (40) – manager of a gent's outfitters – was travelling to work on the Southend to London train.

"We had just passed Leigh-on-Sea Station, when I noticed two almost circular objects joined together in the sky, hovering over *Hadleigh Castle. As the train proceeded towards Benfleet Station, they or it accelerated into the sky and disappeared from sight."

*Hadleigh Castle in the English county of Essex overlooks the Thames estuary from a ridge to the south of the town of Hadleigh. Built after 1215 during the reign of Henry III by Hubert de Burgh, the castle was surrounded by parkland and had an important economic, as well as defensive role. Hadleigh was significantly expanded by Edward III, who turned it into a grander property, designed to defend against potential French attack as well as provide the king with a convenient private residence close to London. Built on geologically unstable hill made of London clay, the castle has often been subject to subsidence; this, combined with the sale of its stonework in the 16th century has led to it now being ruined. The castle is now preserved by English Heritage as a Grade I listed building and scheduled monument. **(Source: Wikipedia 2013)**

9th November 1988 – 'Blue light' over Westcliff, Essex

At approximately 9.30pm, Robert Rossi (20) of Prince Avenue, Westcliffe, accompanied by his friend, Paul Thwaites, was driving down Annerley Road, Southend, when he saw:

> "... a blue flash of light come from the doors of the Church, opposite. A few seconds later this was repeated, and the car's electrics failed. The next day, the car was taken to a local garage. An inspection revealed no sign of what had caused the malfunction."

At 11.30pm, Mathew Charles Single (16) of Cedar Drive – then a schoolboy at Park School, Raleigh – was walking across his back garden, heading towards his house.

> "A thin 'blue light', about 12ft long, showing a touch of red and yellow, suddenly shot up into the sky at an angle from a point between the back door and kitchen window, about 2ft from the house. It was moving that fast, the eye could hardly register. I examined the area, but saw nothing which would explain where that beam of light (resembling a laser light) had come from."

(Source: Ron West)

Did you see the bl-UFO?

Southend Evening Echo, Essex – 10 NOV 1988

UFO 2374 investigators want to speak to more witnesses who might have seen a mysterious blue light over South East Essex.

They already have an astonishing sighting by an engineer who was woken by a blue light that bathed his bedroom.

He thought it was a car's headlamps but looked out to see a craft about 1,000 to 2,000ft up coming towards his house.

The craft was round at the front and square at the back. He said a smaller craft detached itself from the parent and went off in a different direction.

A similar object was seen at Canvey.

If anyone else saw the light they are asked to contact the UFO hotline on 0728 830757.

13th November 1988 – UFO over Rainham, Essex

At 7am, Maureen Howell (46) – a dressmaker by trade – was on her way to work in her car. While stopped at traffic lights on the A13, near to Rainham Police Station, she saw a golden *'ball'* in the sky,

> "... like a goldfish bowl; it stayed there for quite a while on what was a sunny morning. Suddenly it disappeared, leaving a white 'ball' underneath, which moved away across the sky and out of sight."

At 7.30pm, Fred Tidey (57) of Newton Road, Tankerton, Kent, was walking his dog on the seafront at Maplin Sands, when he sighted a white and red *'light'*, static in the sky, at an elevation of 40°, which he then brought to the attention of local woman – Mrs Spratt.

14th November 1988 – UFO over Leigh-on-Sea, Essex

At 1.10am, Mrs P. Selman, from New Court, was looking out her window, when she saw a bright blue object hovering in the sky over the *Thames Estuary*. She watched it for about 15 minutes, before it began to drift away and then decided to go back to bed. **(Source: Geraldine and Deanne Dillon)**

EAST ANGLIAN U.F.O. & PARANORMAL RESEARCH ASSOCIATION

SECTION A — SIGHTING ACCOUNT FORM

Please write an account of your sighting, make a drawing of what you saw and then answer the questions in section B overleaf as fully as possible. Write in **BLOCK CAPITALS** using a ball point pen.

I WALK MY DOG ON TANKERTON SEA FRONT MOST SUNDAY MORNINGS.
DATE OF SIGHTING IS I HOPE A GOOD APPROXIMATION.
TWO LADIES I SPOKE TO 10-20 MIN. AFTER I HAD SEEN LIGHTS WOULD NO DOUBT BE WITNESSES., BUT LADY FROM TUNISIA WILL BE VERY HARD TO CONTACT. SHE WOULD BE THE PERSON TO GIVE CORRECT DATE OF SIGHTING AS SHE TOLD ME SHE HAD FLOWN BACK TO LONDON FROM TUNISIA RECENTLY.
THE LOCAL LADY MRS SPRATT DOES REMEMBER ME SPEAKING TO HER ABOUT SEEING LIGHTS OUT TO SEA.
SHE ALSO SPOKE TO LADY FROM LONDON AND TUNISIA.

DRAWING* — ESSEX, MAPLIN SANDS, NORTH SEA, O WHITE LIGHT, ● RED LIGHT, SOUTHEND PIER, R. THAMES, ISLAND OF SHEPPEY, FAVERSHAM CREEK, WHITSTABLE, TANKERTON, "I STAND HERE", KENT

Your full name (Mr/~~Mrs/Miss/Ms~~) MR FRED TIDEY Age 57
Address 27 NEWTON ROAD TANKERTON, CT5 2YD
Telephone No.................(STD.........)
Occupation during last two years... FOUNDRY FOREMAN
Any professional, technical or academic qualifications or special interests
Do you object to the publication of your name? ~~Yes~~/No. *Delete as applicable.
Today's Date 31/5/89
Signature F. Tidey

*If preferred, use a separate sheet of paper.

Scattered cloud ☐	Cool ☐	Breeze ☑	Fog or mist ☐	Moon ☐
Much cloud ☐	Warm ☐	Moderate ☐	Rain ☐	Planet ☐
Overcast ☐	Hot ☐	Strong ☐	Snow ☐	Sun ☐

At 4.30pm, Essex couple Michael Foreman (38) – a carpet fitter by trade – accompanied by his wife, Jackie, were visiting their parents in Nottinghamshire. They were travelling from Shirebrook to Warsop Vale, in an Austin Metro, when they saw several amber lights in the sky over Shirebrook Colliery. A couple of minutes later the lights vanished from view.

Haunted Skies Volume Ten

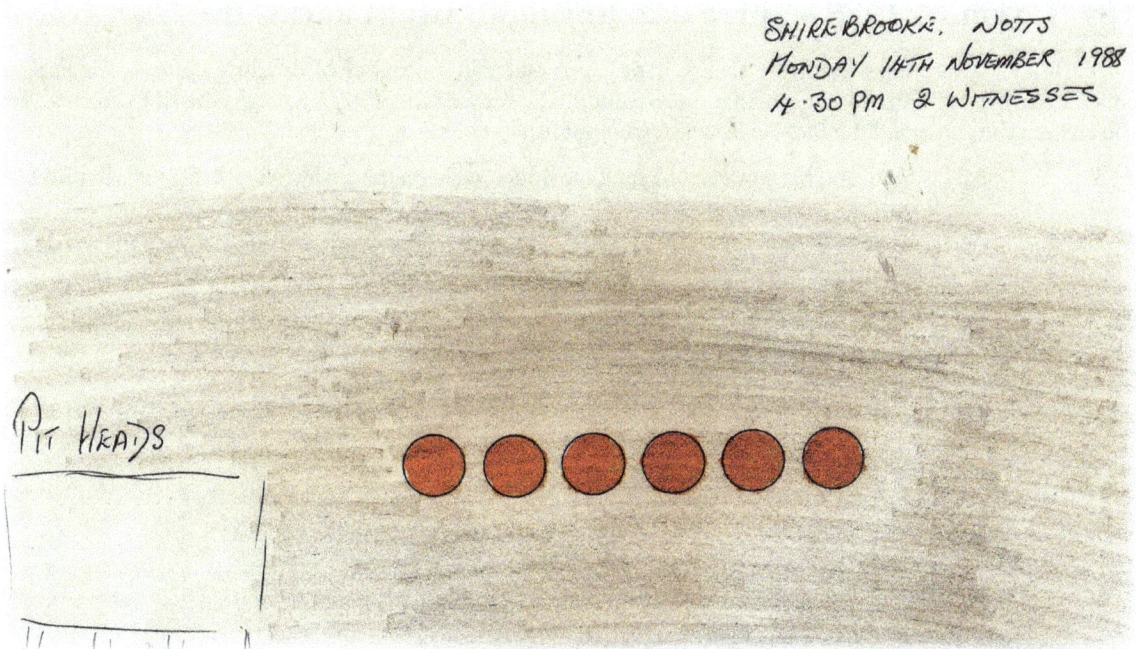

16th November 1988 – UFO over Hullbridge, Essex

At 9.30pm, Mrs J. Seymour and her two young daughters, of Lower Road, Hullbridge, Essex, were looking out into the night sky, when two strange lights appeared in the sky and began to dart around.

> "They then stopped in mid-flight, for a couple of minutes, before shooting straight towards us – almost brushing the chimney as they did so. The brightness of the lights was amazing; our garden was flooded with blue light. The lights headed away towards the North, before being lost from view."

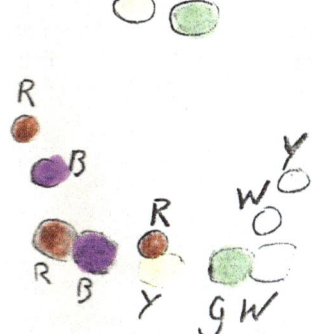

17th November 1988 – UFO over West Yorkshire

As seen by Gary Howarth and Tony Armitage:

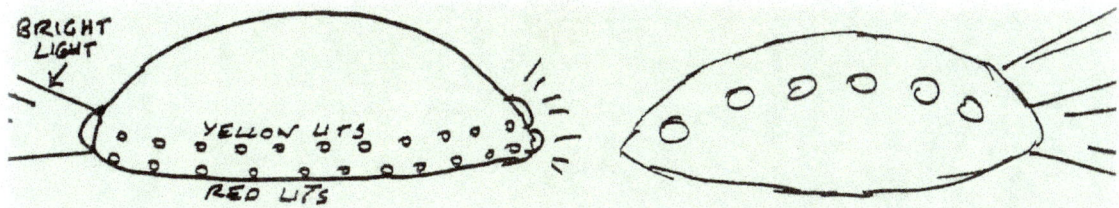

Drawings of objects sighted by Gary Howarth (left) and Tony Armitage (right) on 17-11-88, Melthan, West Yorkshire.

18th November 1988 – Three dazzling lights over Lancashire

Eileen Riley of Carholme Avenue, Burnley, Lancashire, watched a number of dazzling lights – one large, a smaller one behind, with an even smaller one behind that – moving in formation across the sky. Curious as to the answer, she contacted the *Burnley Express*, who published her story.

At 5.20pm, Ronald Murrill and his workmate, Frank Devinuae, were on their way to work. This is what Ronald wrote about the incident.

> On the morning of the 18th November 1988 myself and a workmate a Mr. Frank Devinuae were going to work from Basildon to Southend on the A127. We observed a bright light which caught our attention. This light fascinated both of us with its zig-zaging across us and stopping above us when we stoped at traffic lights near Rayleigh when we moved so did it. Another fascinating point was the speed it could excellerate and slow down. This observation went on all the way down the 127 from the Rayleigh weir, to Priory Park Southend.

At 5pm, Derek Drury (62) of Holland-on-Sea, Essex, was stood on his driveway, with his wife and granddaughter, when they noticed two stationary orange *'lights'* in the sky out to sea, at an angle of some 45°. Ten minutes later, they vanished from sight. (**Source: Brenda Butler**)

Holland on Sea Essex
Friday 18th November 1988
5pm 3 witnesses.

Like car head lights but with no beam stationary.

19th November 1988 – UFO over Wickford

At 7.15pm a bright white light was seen rushing across the sky in a west to east direction, by Cabinet Maker Mr Robert Young.

20th November 1988 – Flashes of light over Canvey Island

At 10.30pm, mysterious flashes of light that were seen to strike the ground took place over Canvey Island, according to Mr Flowers, who was out walking near the sea wall (close to Maurice Road) with his son, Barry, and Anita Flowers. This was followed by the appearance of an unidentified flying object, described as triangular in shape, and an elliptical-shaped object, showing lights all around it. **(Source: Ron West and Brenda Butler)**

21st November 1988 – UFO over Halesowen & green 'ball of light', Essex

Mrs Betty Griffin from Drews Holloway, Haleswowen, was driving along Two Gates, at lunchtime on 21st November 1988, with her husband, when they saw two disc-shaped objects hovering in the sky above the town.

> *"They looked to be a few thousand feet up in the sky. We could see what looked like a pearl necklace around each of them. Their 'bodies' looked like aluminum and we had a clear view."*

(Source: Personal interview)

At 5.15pm Carol Price, from Clacton-on-Sea, was in the kitchen of her house, when she saw a pure white *'light'* streak horizontally across the sky – gone in a few seconds. At the same time Brian Hopgood (56) from Lake Avenue, was in the back garden, collecting the washing from the line, when he saw:

> *"... a large bright green, ball-shaped object, shoot diagonally downwards, as though it was going to hit the ground, but then it did a 'U' turn and shot straight up into the clouds and vanished from sight. I admit to being frightened by the incident."*

Mr Hopgood contacted the police and coastguard, but they declined to comment.

Robert William Moss (45) was driving home along London Road, Little Clacton, at 6.15pm, when he observed:

> *"... a bright green 'light' moving across the sky. Suddenly, it seemed to dip and start to descend, before I lost sight of it due to some trees obscuring my vision. I expected to hear an explosion, but after nothing happened pulled up. To my astonishment, the green light reappeared, now going upwards into the sky, where I lost sight of it – the whole episode over in seconds."*

At 9.45pm Mrs Francis Bragg (53) was driving home along the A12 near Colchester when she saw a green oval shaped object flying across the sky from east to west through her rear mirror.

22nd November 1988 – Orange 'ball' over Little Clacton, Essex

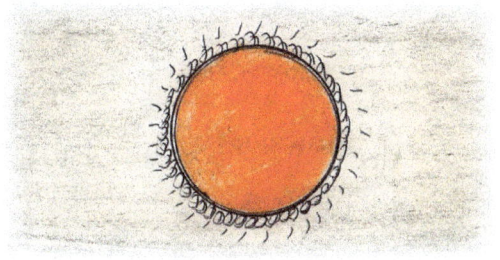

At 5.25am Mrs Linda Marsh (79) of Edward Close was having problems sleeping, due to arthritis, and was sat up at the time of the sighting ...

3rd December 1988 – Whirling noise heard

Mrs O'Brien from Maurice Road, Canvey Island, was jolted from sleep, at 2.45am, by a whirling sound from above her, which went on for 10-15 minutes before fading away. Mrs O'Brien reported the incident to UFO researcher Ron West, and told him of a strange dream she experienced about four weeks previously. In that dream she had been walking down Canvey Island High Street, talking to a stranger, when he began to metamorphose into something resembling an insect, with lots of legs.

5th December 1988 – UFO over Essex

At 5.15pm on 5th December 1988, Mr Eric Prior (47) was putting the shopping into the car at Gateways Supermarket, Clacton-on-Sea, when a large *'ball'* of white light was seen moving southwards, slowly across the sky.

Seconds later, it was out of view.

6th December 1988 – UFO over Essex

At 6.30pm, Mr David Harrington (43) was travelling home along the A13, heading towards Basildon, accompanied by his work mate, Ken Sharpe, when they sighted a bright orange *'ball of light'* moving parallel with their car, at a height of about 2,000ft. They stopped the car and wound down the windows, but could not hear anything; ten seconds later, it had gone out of sight.

11th December 1988 – UFO over Martlesham, Ipswich

At 5.15pm, Derek Newman – who was a member of the East Anglian UFO & Paranormal Research Association, run by his friends Brenda Butler and Ron West – had just let the dog out, when he saw a large *'light'* in the sky, travelling at high speed, under light cloud cover. To the left of it was what looked like lightning; two seconds later it disappeared from view.

12th December 1988 – UFO over Ilford, Essex

This was a second sighting for Anita and Barry Flowers of Seaview Road, Canvey Island, who were out walking near the seawall, at 1.40am, when they saw a number of *'lights'* in the sky – some of them moving, others stationary – accompanied by a whirring noise.

At 8.10am on 12th December 1988, a crowded passenger train crashed into the rear of another train that had stopped at a signal, at Clapham Junction Railway Station, London. An empty train, travelling in the other direction, crashed into the debris. Thirty-five people died and five hundred were injured. The collision was caused by a signal failure, due to a wiring fault. British Rail was fined £250,000 for violations of health and safety law in connection with the accident.

Pupils and teachers from the adjacent Emanuel School were first on the scene of the disaster. They were later commended for their service by Prime Minister, Margaret Thatcher.

Five minutes after the crash, Mrs Pullman (42) of Chase Lane, Barkingside, Ilford, Essex, was looking out of her living room window when she saw a silver-grey object in the sky, moving out from behind trees.

> "I first thought it was a child's balloon but then I saw two more similar objects behind the first one, to my left-hand side. They didn't blow away from each other as one might have expected in the wind, but stayed together at the same distance from each other. I kept them under observation for several minutes, until they were lost in the eastern direction over distant rooftops."

13th December 1988 – UFO over Rainham, Essex

Mrs Howell (46) of Durrants Close – a dressmaker by profession – and her daughter, Natalie (15), had just alighted from the bus in Briscoe Road, at 5.50pm, when:

> "... something dropped out of the sky in front of us. It was very large and about the size of a house, covered in mist, showing quite a few lights on it. It then shot upwards into the sky, and headed towards the base of the full moon – now just rising above the horizon. Then it completed half a circle of the moon and began to descend again. It was about three times the size of an aircraft."

Mid-December 1988 – 'Flying railway carriage'

During mid-December 1988, two UFOs were sighted over Boney Hay, Burntwood, Staffordshire – matters that were brought to the attention of Inspector Robert Langley of Chasetown Police, who confirmed they had been contacted by people in Longfellow Road, and that Air Traffic Control had been notified.

Haunted Skies Volume Ten

Councillor Paul Atkins

Former Councillor Paul Atkins was one of the witnesses, who described the frightening sight of what looked like "… *two railway carriageways, joined together, covered with about 15 flashing lights, making a whining sound*", while walking back from the local corner shop.

We contacted Paul in 2007. He told us that it was still something he could never forget and that, following the incident, he was interviewed by two police officers, who had also seen the UFO. Mrs Brenda Bardell was the other witness. She said:

> "It was massive – nothing like a plane, more like a really long strip, tubular in shape, showing lots of lights."

(Source: UFOSIS, Birmingham/*Chase Post*, 17.12.1988 – 'Puzzle of Boney Hay UFO probe')

About a week before Christmas 1988, playgroup leader Mrs Bridie Humphreys (45) of The Gore, Basildon, was saying goodbye to her next door neighbour and children, who had been visiting, at 10.30pm.

> "I was talking about how cold it was when we noticed a white sausage-shaped object, showing bright lights underneath and making a humming noise, moving across the sky. We watched it for about ten minutes and then went inside."

20th December 1988 – UFO over Essex & Staffordshire

At 10.15pm, Frinton-on-Sea residents – Mr & Mrs J Camp (60) – were watching TV. During the adverts, they looked out of the window at Frinton Lodge when they were stunned to see a saucer-shaped object in the western part of the sky, over the sea.

Mrs Camp:

> "We watched it for about ten minutes and then it headed away, towards Clacton-on-Sea."

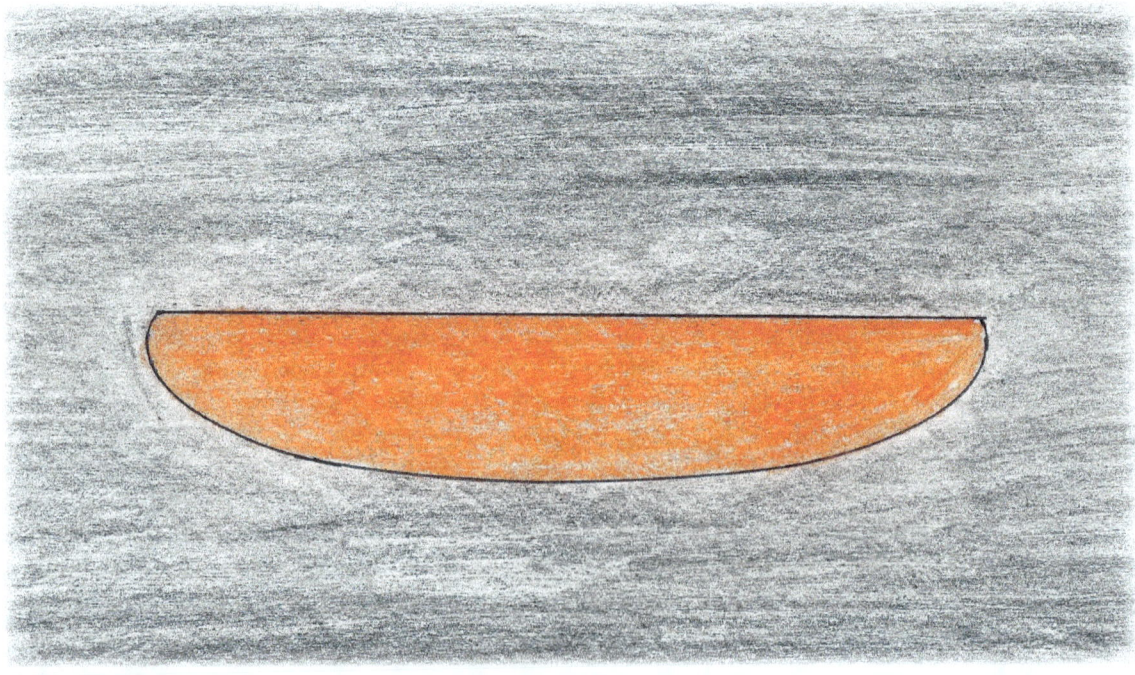

At 11.45pm, pensioner Mrs Helena Steers from Prospect Drive, Shirebrook, Nottinghamshire, was at home when her husband called her. Helena went outside and saw a bright yellow object, stationary in the sky, with what looked like prongs sticking out of it – *'similar to a mine'*. She took four photographs of the UFO, using a Kodak camera, equipped with a 110 film.

Mr W. Grant from Ashfield UFO Research & Investigation Group of Associates (AURIGA) developed the negatives, but found nothing of value – not unexpected, owing to the distance and night-time when the photos were taken. Ken Rogers, Chairman of the Unexplained Society in London, asked for any readers to contact him – should they have seen a mysterious light crossing the sky on the 20th of December 1988,

> *"Evidence suggests that we may be in for another prolonged spate of UFO activity in the New Year. Sightings come in cycles. Our research shows that the star of Bethlehem was probably nothing more than such a classic UFO sighting."*

21st December 1988 – Mystery 'lights' seen over Essex

John Paul Dearman (22) from Springwater Road, Eastwood, Leigh-on-Sea, was working outside, at 5pm, with Albert Outten (52), when they saw a bright *'light'* appear in the sky, surrounded by another fifteen similar *'lights'* forming an elliptical object. The *'lights'*, about the size of a dinner plate in the sky, were then seen to move away before being lost from view.

December 1988 – Orange 'lights' over Colchester

In the same week, two UFOs were seen hovering over a field next to the A128, at Colchester, by local Chadwell St. Mary haulage contractor – Martin Bennett, and his friend Terrence Fagan – who were driving along Tilbury Road, at 11.40pm, in mid-December 1988, when:

> *"... we saw a scattering of bright orange lights, hovering over a field opposite a farmhouse, about a quarter of a mile from the railway bridge, and slowed down to obtain a closer look. By this time, other drivers had also slowed down. Suddenly the lights, which had increased in size and brightness, moved away towards the direction of Horndon-on-the-Hill. We tried to follow them, but couldn't keep up."*

(Source: East Anglian UFO & Paranormal Research Association/*Yellow Advertiser*, 23.12.1988 – 'Strange lights were UFOs say men who followed them')

22nd December 1988 – UFO seen over Kent

Norah Greenfield of Sandown Road, Deal, in Kent, awoke at 3.30am, needing to visit the bathroom.

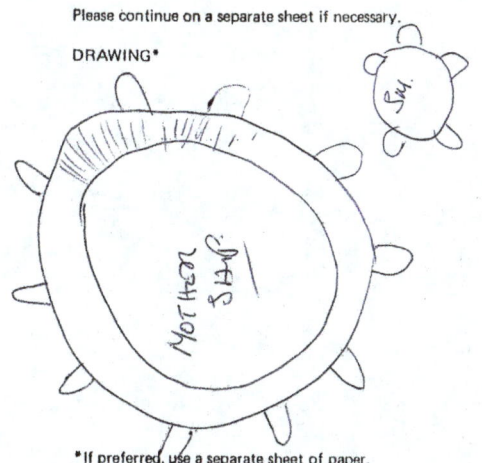

> *"As I was on my way back to bed, I heard a buzzing noise and looked out of the window to see a fairly large object, with lights all around it, moving slowly across the sky. Following the object was a smaller one. They both headed away towards the Channel – that was the last I saw of them."*

PART 2
1943 TO 1954

DINOSAURS first appeared during the Triassic period, 231.4 million years ago, and were the dominant terrestrial vertebrates for 135 million years, from the beginning of the Jurassic (about 201 million years ago) until the end of the Cretaceous (66 million years ago), when the Cretaceous-Palaeocene extinction event led to the extinction of most dinosaur groups at the close of the Mesozoic era. We all know that dinosaurs are ancient residents of this planet, but to be reminded that they were the dominant species for 135million years sends a chill through the body, knowing that we could not possibly imagine, in our wildest dreams, where the next few hundred years will take the human race, never mind millennia. We believe that the normally invisible UFOs and their occupants who have plagued us during our lifetimes were there then, and are as ancient as the planet itself.

Another beautiful hand drawn painting from artist Robert Townshend depicts that scenario (opposite).

We had hoped to include details of British 1989 UFO activity in this volume of *Haunted Skies* but, due to the enormous numbers of sightings catalogued covering this period in time, realised that we were unlikely to have the space – so Volume 11 will begin from 1989, cover 1990 at least, and hopefully, include the next part of the historical 'catch up' from 1963 onwards.

Mysterious flying objects encountered by pilots during the Second World War

In the Second World War, during missions over Germany and Japan, both allied and Axis aircraft pilots described sighting mysterious aerial phenomena in the skies over the European and Pacific theatres of operations. We have documented some of these in Volume 1 of *Haunted Skies*.

Though the term foo fighter was initially used to describe a type of UFO reported and named by the US 415th Night Fighter Squadron, it became a common form of reference to reports of anomalous phenomena during that period, which included reports of triangular or Christmas tree-shaped objects, sometimes apparently pacing the aircraft. Other ex-RAF aircrew we spoke to reported firing their weapons at the objects, believing they represented examples of German technology.

Green fireballs

Who could not be fascinated by reports of mysterious green fireballs over Los Alamos, Las Vegas and the West Texas Triangle, which began on the 5th December 1948? These were not meteorites falling to earth and were judged sufficiently important to be classified top secret by the American USAF, under the heading Project Sign. (Project Grudge was succeeded by Project Sign in February 1949, and was then followed by Project Blue Book. The project formally ended in December 1949, but continued in a minimal capacity until late 1951).

Ghost rockets

One wonders if there is a connection between these green fireballs and reports of flying objects, labelled as 'ghost rockets', seen on the 26th February 1946, by Finnish observers. About 2,000 sightings of these 'rockets' were logged between May and December 1946, with peaks on the 9th and 11th August 1946. Two hundred sightings were verified with radar returns, and it is alleged the authorities recovered physical fragments attributed to the landing of these objects. It was suggested they originated from the former German rocket facility at Peenemunde, and were long-range tests by the Russians of captured German V-1 or V-2 missiles, or maybe an early form of cruise missile, because of the ways they were sometimes seen to manoeuvre. This prompted the Swedish Army to issue a directive stating that newspapers were not to report the exact location of 'ghost rocket' sightings, or any information regarding the direction or speed of the object. This information, they reasoned, was vital for evaluation purposes to the nation or nations performing the tests.

UFO's can harm your health!

The effects of UFO exposure to human beings, interference to electrical installations, and complaints from motorists worldwide, of their vehicles being rendered inoperative following UFO activity, have, we believe, been well documented.

We could no longer ignore the fact that on occasion, albeit inadvertently rather than any deliberate action, common sense dictated the effects of the field of energy which surround UFOs has caused aircraft compass, radio, and other sensitive electronic instruments to malfunction, sometimes with disastrous consequences. Whilst we can neither prove nor disprove such actions were responsible for the loss of aircraft and life, it is clear from the very circumstances of some of these harrowing tragedies that they may well be attributed to UFO activity, and our hearts and condolences go out to those who perished.

WORLDWIDE EVENTS

Finally we wanted to recognise the commitment made to UFO research by those from America, Australia, New Zealand and Tasmania, which allow us and the readers the opportunity to learn of some fascinating investigations, many of which we had not heard about before. We would like to say a special thank you to researchers Bill Chalker, George Simpson, Keith Basterfield, John Auchetti, Diane Harrison & Robert Frola, Co-Directors of AUFORN, Paul Jackson, Keith Roberts, of the Tasmanian UFO Investigation Centre, for their assistance, Mary Rodwell, and many others. We would also like to pay our respects to those that have now passed away. They include Judy Magee, Paul Norman, and Bruce Leonard Cathie – former Airline Captain, from New Zealand – whom we spoke to on occasion, many years ago.

Paul Norman and Judy Magee

Bruce Leonard Cathie

Bruce produced a number of books on the UFO subject, over the years, including Harmonic 33, Harmonic 288, and Harmonic 695. Bruce, who believed that UFOs used the Earth's magnetic power grid as a source of energy for their visits to this planet, was born in 1930 and lived at Takapuna, Auckland, New Zealand. He passed away on the 2nd June 2013.

UFO and Paranormal Research Society of Australia

Thanks to the UFO and Paranormal Research Society of Australia, run by Dominic McNamara and Larraine Cilia, now personal friends, we were able to obtain an insight into some of the cases investigated by them, which included filmed re-enactments of those UFO/Paranormal encounters using 'period' motor vehicles and settings, giving an authentic feel to what had transpired many years ago. This illustrates a dedication not normally found in UFO groups, and they should be applauded for their part in preserving the history of Australian UFO sightings for future generations.

Larraine is President of the UFO-PRSA, which was established in 2000, and is a senior researcher for RACE (Research of Australian Close Encounters) having been a member of the society since its founding in the year 2000. Larraine is also the New South Wales Director with AUFORN (Australian UFO Research Network). Originally from the UK, Larraine has had many experiences involving the paranormal and UFOs. This prompted her to join the group to study and investigate the phenomenon.

During her research into reported UFO phenomena, Larraine developed an interest in counselling and taking reports from people who were perplexed by their sightings and close encounters with other worldly craft

Haunted Skies Volume Ten

and beings. Larraine is co-ordinator and spokesperson for Project Bluewater, gathering reports from NSW coastal areas for a database, and has presented evidence at numerous conferences. Larraine is also a member of the Paranormal Investigators team that appeared in Paranormal Investigators, The Challenge Series Two, aired on TVS1 Sydney, C31 Melbourne, QTV Brisbane and C31 Adelaide, in 2009, and currently screening on Community TV Perth.

This group holds public meetings once a month at the Campbelltown Arts Centre (Corner of Queen Street and Camden Road, opposite Quandong Information Centre, starting from 7pm and concluding at 10pm.

Disclosure Australia

Originally from Adelaide, South Australia, Dominic is a former chairperson of the AURA group (Australian UFO Research Association). Whilst in Adelaide, Dominic and Keith Basterfield began 'Disclosure Australia'. In this was the steady and patient discovery and public availability of government documents held, which covered the UFO topic but were not part of the public domain. This project took nearly four years and around $4,000 of private funds to exhaust, to the point where the group could officially close off the project such as it was, and leaves open only that interest which keeps the maintenance of such a catalogue up to date. Currently, there are around 1,500 case reports on the catalogue.

Dominic relocated to Sydney in 2006. He now holds the position of Secretary and has recently taken on the role of Webmaster. He is the technical inquisitor of events and excursions covered by the UFO-PRSA group. As such, he is involved in attempts to procure equipment other than 'off the shelf' and is busily developing the next family of night vision. Dominic is interested in hearing about any kind of bizarre circumstance, inexplicable events, psychic ability or UFO sightings, as he believes that many such stories and the information contained within them, is important enough to record but is often simply lost through the lack of a structured recording system. He believes that all events of a nature which defies logical explanation, or are significantly inexplicable by ordinary means, deserve better than to be lost forever.

In addition to this, in 2013, we renewed out contact with Jack Morgan and his spectacular photographs, taken over the Queensland sky in the late 1990s, which will be shown in due course.

Although primarily we were only interested in the events that had occurred in Great Britain during the middle to the end of the 20th Century, we realised that there was little difference, if any, between what had been sighted in the UK and reports of UFO displays, close encounters, and motorists being pursued by strange glowing

Larraine Cilia

Robert Frola

Dominic McNamara

'balls of light' along the towns and highways of Australia; wherever possible we will contrast (within reason) details of British sightings against their Australian counterparts, as common sense dictates that there may be a connection. We have also included many interesting but brief references found in Mr Ron West's archives, painstakingly catalogued by him, relating to worldwide reports of UFO activity, which the reader may feel warrants further investigation by themselves. Unfortunately, the source of the majority of this material is not known – a matter for which we apologise, but no doubt checks made with local libraries will yield further information about these incidents.

Eerie sightings, involving the passage through the sky of mysterious 'lights' and the occasional, disturbing close encounter between people on the ground and UFOs, are nothing new to the UK – nor are they to the Australian subcontinent, the United States, and other parts of the world. In addition to these incidents, we were intrigued to read about the mysterious losses of vessels in the Bass Strait, and saddened to learn of the tragic loss of young pilot – Frederick Valentich – following his close encounter with a UFO in 1979.

In the now declassified file, released by the Australian Authorities, we learnt about what friends, family and colleagues of Frederick had to say about him, following an investigation made into the matter – and could not help but feel moved by what we read.

Some people believe that many of the reported incidents, involving contact between human beings and UFOs (and their occasional alien occupants), are as a result of an undetermined agenda being carried out, while others believe it is random. Although, by now, we know a great deal about their behaviour and effects on the luckless few who have the misfortune to encounter them, we are still unable to identity the purpose (if, in fact, there is any) of these spasmodic continuing appearances, which undoubtedly have influenced the decisions of our race on this planet, going back many thousands of years.

Greg Bishop with John Keel

In his book, 'UFOs – Operation Trojan Horse' (published in 1973), author John Alva Keel tells us in the foreword of this book:

> "My files include thousands of letters, affidavits and other materials encompassing many unpublished cases, which correlated with and confirmed the events and conclusions discussed in this book. Numerous other researchers around the world have confirmed my findings through events in their own areas. The real problems hidden behind the UFO Phenomenon are staggering and so complex that they will seem almost incomprehensible at first. The popular beliefs and speculations are largely founded upon biased reporting, gross misrepresentations, and the inability to see beyond the limits of any one of many frames of reference. Cunning techniques of deception and psychological warfare have been employed by the UFO source to keep us confused and sceptical. Man's tendency to create a deep and inflexible belief on the basis of little or no evidence has been exploited. Those beliefs have created tunnel vision and blinded many to the real nature of the phenomenon."

Haunted Skies Volume Ten

Nuremberg 1561 – What may have been an early example of a UFO display took place over the city, as painted by Derek Samson, a West Midlands UFO researcher and member of NICAP, UK, who spent many years researching the UFO subject.

NUREMBERG PHENOMENA.

A recording in Nuremberg tells us that on the 4th April 1561, large numbers of flying objects were seen flying near the Sun at Sunrise, they were described as blood red and bluish black globes, some of the globes were flying side by side with blood coloured crosses. Two large tubes were seen to contain smaller discs or globes, their was also a great black object shaped like a spear, it looked as if the objects were fighting each other, after an hour they fell to the ground were they let off a lot of steam.

In 1880, long before the expression 'flying saucer' or UFO came into use, there were reports of strange aerial phenomena seen.

On 22nd March, an enormous number of luminous bodies were seen rising up from the horizon, heading eastwards, over Germany. In May, Mr J.W. Robertson was a passenger aboard the British India Company Paddle Steamer, *Patna*, heading up through the Persian Gulf, at 11.30pm.

> "There suddenly appeared on each side of the ship an enormous luminous wheel whirling around, the spokes of which seemed to brush the ship along. The spokes were 200-300 yards long and resembled the birch rods of the dames' schools. Each wheel contained about sixteen spokes and, although 500 or 600 yards in diameter, they could be seen all the way round. The phosphorescent gleam seemed to glide flat along the surface of the sea, no lights being visible in the air above the water. The appearance of the spokes could be almost exactly represented by standing in a boat and flashing a bull's-eye lantern horizontally along the surface of the water round and round."

The wheels followed the ship for about twenty minutes and were also witnessed by Captain Avern and third officer – Mr Manning. (**Source:** *Knowledge*, 28.12.1883)

On 28th July, an object was reported in the sky over St. Louis and Louisville, USA, between 6pm and 7pm, described as, *"moving in various directions – ascending, descending – seemingly under control"*. Later, an object with what looked like a ball at each end – sometimes seen in circular form; others oval – headed northwards across the sky.

(**Source:** *Louisville Courier-Journal*, 29.7.1880)

On 30th July a large, circular, luminous vessel, followed by two smaller ones, was seen moving over a ravine at St. Petersburg, Russia.

On 20th August, a white/gold cigar-shaped object, with pointed ends, was observed by Mr M. Treul of the French Academy. A smaller object is seen to leave the parent *'craft'*, creating a trail of sparks in its wake.

Australia: 1881 – 11th June – At 4am, an illuminated object was seen in the sky over Melbourne and Victoria.

Australia: 1893 – Report from central New South Wales of landed silver object by local farmer, who described encountering a *'man in strange clothing'*, who shone what looked like a torch at him, which threw the witness to the ground. When he recovered consciousness the object had gone. The unnamed man suffered a cut to his hand and was paralysed in that limb for life.

Australia: 1925 – Near Moora, two men came across an object which was resting in a paddock; it was described as resembling *'two saucers, edge to edge'*, which rested on four legs and had oval windows; around the outside was some type of heat haze. The object then took off. It was said that after the object had gone, the earth was found to have been scuffed up.

Australia: 1927 – At Ferndale, in New South Wales, a large disc-shaped object was seen on the ground, with some sort of dome on top, illuminating the valley with brilliant light. The next day, a 10 metre diameter of scorched grass was discovered.

Australia: March 1933 – At Nambour, Queensland, a young boy observed an object on the ground, a few feet away. A white *'mist'* then appeared between the boy and the object, causing a tight feeling in the head. Later that night, the youth found large white blisters on both hands. These burst, releasing a clear watery fluid, following which he felt much better.

Haunted Skies Volume Ten

1936/37: UFO display

In late spring, Richard Keller (13) was out with his family on a Sunday afternoon drive, at Narragansett, Rhode Island – a town in Washington County, Rhode Island, United States. They stopped the car at North Avenue to pick up some toffee apples from a nearby stall, and continued on their journey. Richard happened to be looking through the back window, where he saw:

> "... 10 or 12 objects, cavorting about in the sky and doing acrobatics, for approximately 10 minutes, when suddenly they converged, as if on signal, to a point under the clouds, stacking one above the other and climbing vertically up into the cloud bank, before disappearing from sight."

This was one of the earliest 'displays of UFO behaviour' we had come across; bearing in mind we had covered many identical incidents involving the movement of these objects, over more recent years. The purpose behind these displays is not known, although on occasion, they can herald the arrival of a larger object, often described as apparently solid or mechanical in structure. Perhaps the 'display' in some way generates the arrival of the 'main event'. Who really knows the answers? (**Source:** *The Hynek UFO Report*, **Dr. J. Allen Hynek**)

1942 – UFO over Bass Strait

According to British UFO investigator Harold T. Wilkins – also author of *Flying Saucers On The Attack* – he was contacted by a Major in the RAAF, who was stationed at the Secret Weapons Establishment, Woomera –who told him:

> "We had orders, not long after the Japanese attack on Darwin, to patrol the Bass Strait, where fisherman had reported seeing mysterious lights in the sea. At 5.50pm we were flying some miles east of the Tasman Peninsula, when suddenly out of a cloud bank appeared a singular airfoil of glistening bronze colour, about 150ft long and 50ft in diameter. It had a sort of a beak on its prow and the surface seemed burled or rippled or fluted. On its upper surface was a dome or cupola from which I seemed to see reflective flashes as the sun struck something which might or might not have been a helmet worn by something inside? The other end of the airfoil thinned out into a sort of fin. Every now and then there came from its keel greenish blue flashes. It turned at a small angle to us and I was amazed to see, framed in a white circle on the front of the dome, an image of a large grinning Cheshire cat. The dam thing flew parallel to us for some minutes and then abruptly flew away; as it did so it showed four things, like fins, on its belly side. It went off at a pace, turned, and dived straight down into the Pacific and went under, throwing up a regular whirlpool of wave, as if it had been a submarine. No, the Japanese had nothing like that in their amphibian line like that mysterious bird. What do you think that was?"

Authors: to those that would perhaps dismiss this out of hand, they should think again. This was not the only time we had been told of something similar, as the reader will find out in due course.

1944 – 'Dark shadow' seen over Bass Strait

Mr T.R.H. Royal was piloting a Beaufort Bomber over Bass Strait, when a dark 'shadow' appeared alongside and kept pace for eighteen to twenty minutes. The object seemed to have a flickering light, and belched flames from its rear end. It maintained a distance of thirty to fifty metres from the aircraft before accelerating away. During the event, all radio and direction finding equipment was said to have malfunctioned. (**Source:** *The Australian Saucer Record*, 1957/Project 1947, Keith Basterfield/WWW, 2014)

Haunted Skies Volume Ten

USA: 1945 Summer – US Pilot Ensign Roland D. Powell, based at the US Naval Station Pascoe, Washington, was one of five F6F Hellcat pilots scrambled to intercept a UFO described as being the *"size of three aircraft carriers side by side"* seen hovering at high altitude above the top secret plutonium production facility for the world's first nuclear bombs, at Hanford.

1947

Australia: 1947 – A woman driving through Maffra, Victoria, reported having almost collided with a dazzling gold coloured *'ball'* seen hovering in front of her on the road, followed by a wind that buffeted at the point of impact. The object then appeared to roll over the side of the embankment and disappear behind tall maize; the wind then ceased.

USA: 14th June 1947 – At 2.15pm, pilot Richard Rankin, and a young boy companion, sighted ten *'almost round'* or *'flying flapjack'*-shaped objects in formation moving across the sky, at an estimated height of 9,000ft and between 300-400mph, heading northwards on a straight course through the sky. Seven of the UFOs were then seen to return on a reverse 'S' course later. (**Source: McDonald List; FUFOR, Ted Bloecher, 1967**)

14th June 1947 – Field of debris found in New Mexico – was it a crashed UFO?

On the 14th of June 1947, William Brazel – foreman for a ranch in Roswell, New Mexico – was with his son Vernon (8) checking livestock, some seven to eight miles from the ranch house of JB Foster, when he came across a large area of wreckage made up of rubber strips, tinfoil, tough paper and sticks.

On July 4th, he and his wife, accompanied by their two children, Vernon and Betty, went back to the scene and collected some of the material. Brazel took some of the pieces to show Floyd and Loretta Proctor at their ranch nearby. They suggested it could have been wreckage from an alien spacecraft, or a government project, and that he should report it to the local County Sheriff. Brazel then collected a sample of the debris and showed it to George Wilcox, of the Chaves County, New Mexico's Sheriff Office, where, after discussion, Wilcox fetched Major Jesse Marcel from the Roswell Army Air Field (RAAF) to examine the debris.

Haunted Skies Volume Ten

The 'road to nowhere' near to Roswell. A photograph taken at the Brazel Ranch and the Proctor Ranch sign

Harassed Rancher who Located 'Saucer' Sorry He Told About It

W. W. Brazel, 48, Lincoln county rancher living 30 miles south east of Corona, today told his story of finding what the army at first described as a flying disk, but the publicity which attended his find caused him to add that if he ever found anything else short of a bomb he sure wasn't going to say anything about it.

Brazel was brought here late yesterday by W. E. Whitmore, of radio station KGFL, had his picture taken and gave an interview to the Record and Jason Kellahin, sent here from the Albuquerque bureau of the Associated Press to cover the story. The picture he posed for was sent out over AP telephoto wire sending machine specially set up in the Record office by R. D. Adair, AP wire chief sent here from Albuquerque for the sole purpose of getting out his picture and that of sheriff George Wilcox, to whom Brazel originally gave the information of his find.

Brazel related that on June 14 he and an 8-year old son, Vernon, were about 7 or 8 miles from the ranch house of the J. B. Foster ranch, which he operates, when they came upon a large area of bright wreckage made up on rubber strips, tinfoil, a rather tough paper and sticks.

At the time Brazel was in a hurry to get his round made and he did not pay much attention to it. But he did remark about what he had seen and on July 4 he, his wife, Vernon and a daughter Betty, age 14, went back to the spot and gathered up quite a bit of the debris.

The next day he first heard about the flying disks, and he wondered if what he had found might be the remnants of one of these.

Monday he came to town to sell some wool and while here he went to see sheriff George Wilcox and "whispered kinda confidential like" that he might have found a flying disk.

Wilcox got in touch with the Roswell Army Air Field and Maj. Jesse A. Marcel and a man in plain clothes accompanied him home, where they picked up the rest of the pieces of the "disk" and went to his home to try to reconstruct it.

According to Brazel they simply could not reconstruct it at all. They tried to make a kite out of it, but could not do that and could not find any way to put it back together so that it would fit.

Then Major Marcel brought it to Roswell and that was the last he heard of it until the story broke that he had found a flying disk.

Brazel said that he did not see it fall from the sky and did not see it before it was torn up, so he did not know the size or shape it might have been, but he thought it might have been about as large as a table top. The balloon which held it up, if that was how it worked, must have been about 12 feet long, he felt, measuring the distance by the size of the room in which he sat. The rubber was smoky gray in color and scattered over an area about 200 yards in diameter.

When the debris was gathered up the tinfoil, paper, tape, and sticks made a bundle about three feet long and 7 or 8 inches thick, while the rubber made a bundle about 18 or 20 inches long and about 8 inches thick. In all, he estimated, the entire lot would have weighed maybe five pounds.

There was no sign of any metal in the area which might have been used for an engine and no sign of any propellers of any kind, although at least one paper fin had been glued onto some of the tinfoil.

There were no words to be found anywhere on the instrument, although there were letters on some of the parts. Considerable scotch tape and some tape with flowers printed upon it had been used in the construction.

No strings or wire were to be found but there were some eyelets in the paper to indicate that some sort of attachment may have been used.

Brazel said that he had previously found two weather observation balloons on the ranch, but that what he found this time did not in any way resemble either of these.

"I am sure what I found was not any weather observation balloon," he said. "But if I find anything else, besides a bomb they are going to have a hard time getting me to say anything about it."

On the 8th July 1947, the Roswell Army Air Field (RAAF) public information officer – Walter Haut – issued a Press release, stating that personnel from the field's 509th Operations Group had recovered a 'flying disk', which had crashed on a ranch near Roswell. Later that day, the press reported that Roger Ramey – Commanding General of the Eighth Air Force – had stated that a weather balloon was recovered. A Press conference was held featuring debris (foil, rubber and wood) said to be from the crashed object, which seemed to confirm its description as a weather balloon. Subsequently, the incident faded from the attention of UFO researchers for over 30 years. In 1978, physicist Stanton T. Friedman interviewed Major Jesse Marcel, who was

involved with the original recovery of the debris in 1947. Marcel expressed his belief that the military covered up the recovery of an alien spacecraft.

In February 1980, the *National Enquirer* ran its own interview with Marcel, garnering national and worldwide attention for the Roswell incident. Additional witnesses added significant new details, including claims of a large-scale operation dedicated to recovering alien craft and aliens themselves, at as many as 11 crash sites, and alleged witness intimidation.

Project Mogul or dummies was the answer!

In 1989, former mortician – Glenn Dennis – claimed alien autopsies were carried out at the Roswell Base, after being asked to provide a number of child-sized coffins by them. In response to the allegations made by Mr. Dennis and other witnesses, the United States Air Force carried out an internal investigation. The result was summarised in two reports. The first, released in 1995, concluded the recovered material in 1947 was likely to have been debris from *Project Mogul.* Their second report, released in 1997, suggested recovered *'alien bodies'* were likely to be a combination of either innocently transformed memories of military accidents, innocently transformed memories of the recovery of anthropomorphic dummies in military programs like *Operation High Dive,* conducted in the 1950s, or hoaxes perpetrated by various witnesses and UFO proponents. The psychological effects of time compression and confusion about when events occurred explained

Haunted Skies Volume Ten

Project Mogul. A series of rubber weather balloons and tinfoil radar 'kites', strung together in a row for carrying listening devices into the sky.

New Mexico Magazine, January 1948

"One of the experiments there [Alamogordo] is probably responsible for newspaper stories last summer about flying discs and flying saucers, for at Alamogordo the Watson Laboratories of the Air Materiel Command are experimenting with long range radar detection, using balloon piloted observation radar targets. Under certain conditions these targets could well be identified as flying saucers, the balloons appearing as saucers and the tin-foil covered targets as the wings of the flying discs."

the discrepancy with the years in question. These reports were dismissed by UFO proponents as being either disinformation or simply implausible.

Project Mogul – In 1994-1995, in response to an official inquiry by New Mexico Congressman Steven Schiff, the Air Force published a report that suggested that Mogul Flight 4, launched from Alamogordo on 4th June 1947, crashed near or on the J.B. Foster Ranch at Roswell, New Mexico, and formed the source of the debris that sparked the Roswell UFO Incident (as seen by 'Mac' Brazel on the 14th). Examination of the Mogul flight summary table shows cancelled and missing Flights 2, 3, & 4, with flight 5 from 5th June 1947 being the first documented New Mexico Mogul flight. Whether it was, 4 or 5 seems irrelevant to what was claimed to have happened, as these took place before the 14th June 1947. The balloon consisted of 23 x 15ft diameter meteorological balloons, stretching 650ft into the air.

It carried three radar reflectors, manufactured by a New York Novelty Company using reinforcing tape used to hold it together, showing a flower like lavender design on it, which has been suggested was the hieroglyphics found on some of the material recovered by Mac Brazel. Also on board were large metal foil kites, called Rawin targets, low frequency acoustic microphones and metal boxes packed with batteries for the acoustic devices, sonobuoys attached to three and four inch diameter aluminium rings, tubes holding ballast and altitude switches.

The grim reality

In 2007, following the death of Walter Haut, a sworn affidavit was opened in which he stated the weather balloon claim was a cover story, and that the real object had been recovered by the military and stored in Hangar 84. He described seeing not only the craft but alien bodies, after being taken there by Colonel Blanchard.

> "It was a metallic egg-shaped object, around 12-15ft in length and 6ft wide. I did not see any windows, wings, tail, landing gear, or other features. I saw two bodies on the floor, partially covered by a tarpaulin, about 4ft tall, with disproportionately large heads. I am convinced that what I personally observed was some kind of craft and its crew from outer space."

The affidavit also talks about a high-level meeting he attended with Base Commander Colonel William Blanchard, and the Commander of the Eighth Army Air Force – General Roger Ramey. Haut states that at this meeting, pieces of wreckage were handed around for participants to touch, with nobody able to identify the material. He says the Press release was issued because locals were already aware of the crash site, but in fact there had been a second crash site, where more debris from the craft had fallen. The plan was that an announcement acknowledging the first site, which had been discovered by a rancher, would divert attention from the second and more important location. Haut also spoke about a clean-up operation, where for months afterwards military personnel scoured both crash sites searching for all remaining pieces of debris, removing them and erasing all signs that anything unusual had occurred.

If aliens crashed at New Mexico in 1947, which appears to have been the case, then something of monumental importance took place that would have had ramifications for the human race on this planet. An acceptance would have been its proudest defining moment. However, shamefully, we decided to camouflage those events in subterfuge, disinformation, and probably downright lies, in an effort to conceal the real truth from the public. Is it not an irony that our probes sent out into the far reaches of space contain the warmest of greetings, and the open hand of friendship, when, in truth, we regard the aliens and their craft as being representative of a hostile race, whose presence on this planet is a hostile act rather the opposite? Logically, although we cannot prove alien beings were recovered, there is ample evidence to justify the strongest of likelihoods just from the nature of the massive wealth of evidence presented that an alien device did crash-land in 1947, and that alien bodies were recovered.

Colonel Blanchard went on leave on the 8th July 1947, at the time Major Marcel was flying the crashed debris to Carswell. Reporters who tried to get in touch with the Colonel were told he was on leave and unavailable for interview. According to *The Roswell Incident* written by Charles Berlitz and William Moore, in the late 1970s, we learn that Stanton Friedman (who offered to assist us with a foreword for one of the *Haunted Skies* books) interviewed General Blanchard's widow, who told him *"the wreckage he sent to Carswell did not belong to any balloon and was nothing made by us. At first he thought it might be Russian, because of the strange symbols on it; later he realised it wasn't Russian either."*

Whether this incident has anything to do with thousands of UFO sightings worldwide, involving all manner or strange craft (and their occupants) seen since, can of course, only be conjecture! However, we would not be surprised if it was! One of these days the world will wake up to the reality that we truly are not on our own. Until then, the UFO subject will be ignored and continue to be the butt of jokes and ridicule.

Coincidentally, we spoke to Jesse Marcel Junior on a number of occasions before his death on the 24th of August 2013 and felt privileged when he agreed to write the foreword for a future volume of *Haunted Skies*. Sadly, that did not happen. We would like to pay our respects to Jesse, who was well regarded and very much liked by those that had the privilege to talk to him over the years.

Haunted Skies Volume Ten

The full facts surrounding the whole, fascinating and disturbing incident, are far too much to incorporate in this volume, but veteran UFO researcher, author of several books on the UFO subject, and current editor of the on-line *UFO Today* magazine – Philip Mantle – was lucky enough to visit the locality some years ago, and kindly sent his photographs, which set the scene for what is undoubtedly still the most talked about UFO incident – now over 60 years later.

USA: 24th June 1947 – Kenneth Arnold UFO sighting – what happened to the missing film?

An appropriate time to show what Kenneth Arnold saw, while over the Cascade Mountains, Mount Rainier, Washington, as painted by Derek Samson (opposite).

Interestingly, Kenneth was to illustrate something of a quite different shape in the books that he wrote with Ray Palmer. This was not his last sighting. He went on to observe several more, including the incident in July 1947, when he filmed an object while in flight, which he stated could not be seen without the aid of a jeweller's glass. We tried unsuccessfully to track down this film, and wrote to his daughter on more than one occasion, over the years, but never received any answer.

In 1962, Kenneth Arnold said:

> "After 14 years of extensive research, it is my conclusion that the so-called UFOs that have been in our atmosphere are not spaceships from another planet at all, but are groups and masses of living organisms that are much a part of our atmosphere and space as the life we find in the depth of our oceans. The only major difference in the space and atmospheric organisms are that they have the natural ability to change their densities at will."

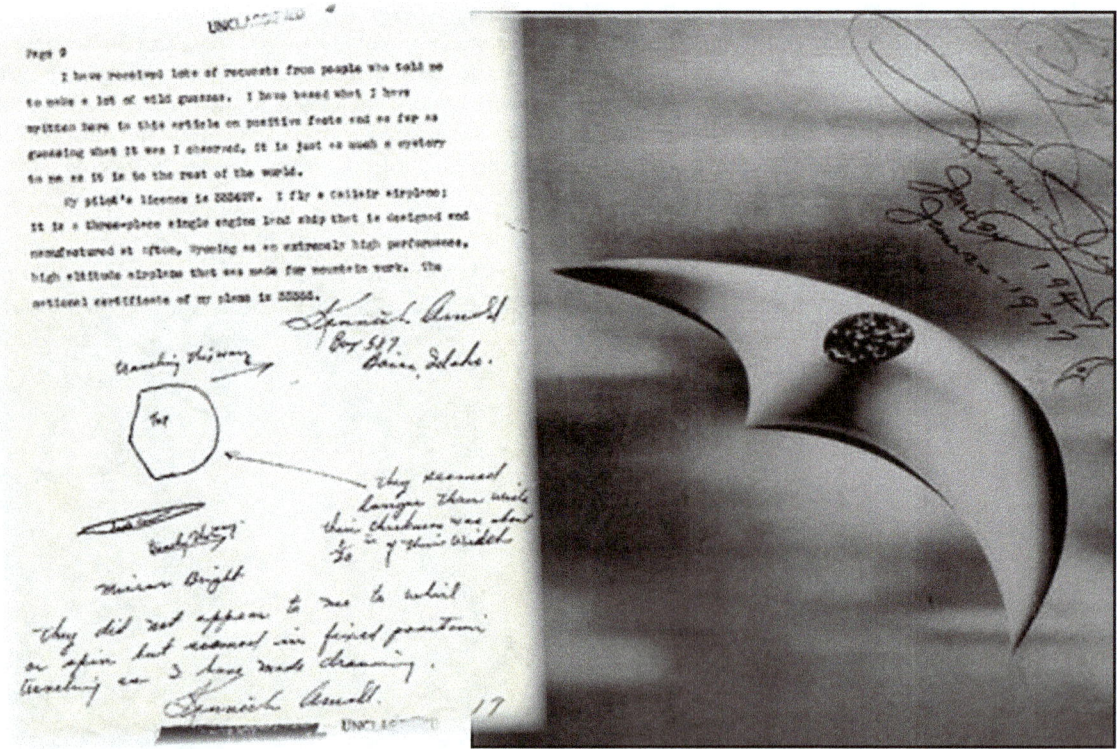

THE KENNETH ARNOLD STORY.

On Tuesday 24th June 1947, a businessman Kenneth Arnold, aged 32, was flying his own plane over Mount Rainier at a height of 10,000 feet, suddenly a flash caught Arnolds eye, flying over the mountain peaks, and shineing in the sun were nine unusual objects, Arnold described them as "shaped like frying pans" "or a saucer shape", the name Flying Saucer soon caught on, and before long the newspaper reporters and the public were refering to unusual flying objects as "Saucers" as these were unidentified, they became known as U.F.O.s. "Unidentified Flying Objects".

USA: 25th June 1947 – A saucer-shaped object was reported moving southwards over Silver City, New Mexico, by local dentist Dr. R.F. Sensenbaugher.

USA: 26th June 1947 – Dr. Leon Oetinger of Lexington, Kentucky, was with three others when they sighted a large silver ball-shaped object, travelling at high speed near the end of the Grand Canyon. The men rejected any suggestion that it was either a balloon of dirigible.

USA: 27th June 1947 – At 9.50am a white disc *'glowing like an electric light bulb'* passed over Pope, New Mexico, according to local resident – Mr W.C. Dobbs. Minutes later, a similar object was sighted travelling south-west over the White Sands Missile Range by Captain E Detchmendy. The incident was reported to Colonel Turner, who, fearing hysteria, explained it away as being a daytime meteorite.

At 10am, Mrs David Appelzoller of San Miguel, New Mexico, sighted a similar object heading south-west. On the same day, John Petsche – an electrician at Phelps-Dodge Corporation – sighted a disc-shaped object overhead, which apparently came to earth at around 10.30am, near Tintown, in the vicinity of Bisbee in south-eastern Arizona, near the Mexico border.

USA: 28th June 1947 – Captain F. Dvyn was flying over the vicinity of Alamogordo, New Mexico, when he saw: "...a 'ball of fire', with a fiery blue trail behind it. It passed underneath the aircraft and appeared to disintegrate."

Did a UFO crash-land?

USA: 29th June 1947 – Army Air Force pilots conducted a search for an object, reported to have fallen near Cliff, New Mexico, but found nothing although a curious odour was noted. On the same day, a team of rocket scientists, headed by Dr. C.J. Zohn, were on duty at White Sands Proving Grounds, when a silver coloured 'disc' was seen to carry out a series of manoeuvres over the secret rocket range.

Later, Major George B. Wilcox of Warren, Arizona, sighted a series of eight or nine perfectly spaced *'discs'*, at three second intervals, heading through the sky, eastwards, at high speed, showing a wobbling motion in flight.

He estimated them to be at a height of about 1,000ft. (**Sources: 25th-29th June, FOIA/***The Roswell Incident***, Charles Berlitz and William Moore**)

USA: July 1947 – prolific period of UFO activity

We were shocked to find just how many UFO sightings took place in this month. A look at the NICAP website, in 2014, contains the following information, which we believe is of great interest, taking into consideration the ramifications of what took place at Roswell. If nothing else, it shows just how prolific the activity was for this month. While it would be so easy to become blasé, due to the enormous numbers of sightings, we must not forget that each of these reports generated tremendous excitement to those involved, as it surely would if you or I glanced through the window and saw something so extraordinary it would change our perspective on everyday life

1st July 1947 – Mr and Mrs Frank Munn sighted a large object, moving eastwards over Phoenix, at 9am.

On the same day, a bluish disc-shaped object was sighted heading across the north-western sky of Albuquerque, by Mr Max Hood.

2nd July 1947 – At 9.50pm, a fireball was seen passing over Roswell, by Dan Wilmot, his wife, and son – Paul, before disappearing over Six Mile Mountain.

> "It was shaped like two inverted saucers, mouth to mouth, and glowing inside, and out of sight in 40-50 seconds."

Mrs Wilmot told of hearing a slight swishing noise, as the object passed by. (**Source:** *Roswell Daily Record*, 8.7.1947)

Charles Berlitz and William Moore believe the UFO which fell to earth on the 2nd July 1947, was the same object seen by Mr and Mrs Wilmot, and that north of Roswell, the object was struck by lightning during an intense electrical storm, following which it shed a large amount of wreckage before crashing into the area west of Socorro, known as the Plains of San Agustin which was later found by 'Mac' Brazel. It appears that this may not be the case as Mac Brazel says he found the wreckage on the 14th of June but we may be wrong.

3rd July 1947 – UFO sightings flood in

At 12.45pm, on this date motor mechanics Chief Robert L. Jackson and Chief William Baker from San Diego, California, sighted three aluminium saucer-shaped objects twice the size of navy aircraft, moving at a speed of about 400mph over the ocean, west of San Diego.

Formation of coloured lights seen

At 2.30pm, South Brooksville-Harborside, Maine, astronomer John F. Cole was disturbed by a roaring noise overhead. Looking upwards he saw approximately ten light coloured objects, between 50-100ft wide, towards the North, at about 50° elevation, in a formation initially about 1.5° wide, with two dark forms to their left or two objects which had darker projections, somewhat like wings, moving like a swarm of bees to the north-west, between 600-1,200 mph through a 30° arc. 10-15 seconds later, they were out of sight.

Alien craft with occupants found near Magdalena?

In addition to these spectacular sightings was a report from Socorro civilian engineer – Mr Grady Landon 'Barney' Barnett (1892-1969) – who talked of seeing a craft and the dead bodies of the alien flight crew, to his friends Alice Knight, Vern Maltais, Harold Baca, and J.F. 'Fleck' Danley. According to those parties, Barnett was described as being a reliable man who was not given to practical jokes, nor one who told tall tales.

Barnett told of driving through the desert on the 3rd July 1947, near Magdalena, when a flash of light caught his attention. He turned toward it and came upon a crashed disc-shaped object. Vern said that Barnett told him the craft was metallic, dull gray, and *"pretty good sized"*. According to Maltais, Barnett thought it had burst open as it slammed into a low ridge line. There was almost no wreckage scattered around the damaged ship. Barnett also said that he saw the flight crew. The beings were *"small, with pear-shaped heads, skinny arms and legs, and no hair. They seemed to be all males. All wore metallic-like, form-fitting grey/silver 'flight suits', without buttons or zippers."*

While on the site, Barnett was joined by a handful of archaeologists, who claimed they were part of an archaeological research team from the University of Pennsylvania. Barney says that at this stage he and they were stood around, looking at the dead bodies on the ground and ones still inside the machine, which was not at all that big and apparently made of what looked like dirty stainless steel, which had been split open by the explosion or impact. Before they could do much more, the military arrived, and warned them that what they had seen was classified top secret, and then escorted them from the site.

For those that may be inclined to dismiss the story as an example of vivid imagination, we doubt that this was the case.

Grady was a veteran of World War 1 and saw service as a 2nd Lieutenant with the 313th Engineers and past Commander of the America Legion Post at Mosquero, New Mexico, prior to working as an engineer for the US Soil Conservation Service for 20 years, until his retirement in 1957.

The activity continued at 4.50pm with a sighting of an object, described as resembling *'a giant pocket watch'*, seen 1,000ft above the main runway of Santa Rosa Naval auxiliary station. It was seen to move north to the end of the runway, before banking and turning eastwards. Exciting as these sightings were, now 66 years ago, what can we make of an enthralling incident that occurred at St. Maries, Idaho, on the same day, involving Mrs Walter Johnson of Dishman, Idaho, and nine other witnesses, who observed eight objects that landed on a mountainside at Butlers Bay, Idaho. According to Mrs Johnson, the *'saucers'* came into view at an extreme speed, travelling south to north, and suddenly slowed before fluttering downwards, like leaves to the ground.

This matter was reported to intelligence officers from the Spokane Army Air Base, following which an intensive air search was carried out by two missions of the National Guard's 116th Fighter Group. Local sheriff's deputies also made a ground search, but no trace of the objects was found.

Within 24 hours, reports of UFO sightings flooded in from hundreds of bewildered citizens, who contacted newspapers and police stations all over the country, and adjacent areas as well, from Southern California to New Brunswick, and from Louisiana to North Dakota. People everywhere experienced the beginning of one of the most massive 'waves' of UFO sightings on record. **(Source: San Diego, CA Union, 4th July 1947, Bloecher Case 194/Berliner; Dr. James McDonald, 1968; FOIA; Ted Bloecher, 1967/Jan Aldrich, Loren Gross, Santa Rosa Press-Democrat)**

4th July 1947 – At 11am, C.J. Bogne of Tigard, Oregon, and other witnesses in a car near Redmond, sighted four flying *'discs'* moving at high speed past Mount Jefferson, on a straight course. **(Source: McDonald List; FOIA; Ruppelt, p20; Bloecher, 1967/*The Roswell Incident*, Charles Berlitz and William Moore)**

'Flying Discs' seen

At 1.05pm, a multi witness sighting took place over Portland, Milwaukee, Oregon, and Vancouver, Washington, involving the following:

Radio newsman Frank Cooley of Station KOIN, employees in the Portland Oregon Journal Building, Clark County Sheriff's Deputy, Fred Krives, Deputy Clarence McKay, Sgt. John Sullivan, Portland Police Officer Kenneth A. McDowell, Harbor Patrol Captain K.A. Prahn, Harbor Patrolmen A.T. Austad and K.C. Hoff, Portland Police Officers Earl J. Patterson, Walter A. Lissy and Robert Ellis, Oregon Highway Patrol Sgt. Claude Cross, and many others over a wide area, sighted five large *'flying discs'* moving at high speed – two of them flying southwards, the other three eastwards. The objects were seen to be making an oscillating or wobbling motion, sudden 90° turns, or zigzagging.

Radio reports alerted other officers who saw the objects – aluminium or chromium in colour, disc or hubcap, or pie-pan or half-moon shape – flashing in the sun; no vapour trail, no noise (except possible humming), some at 10,000-40,000ft, others at about 1,000ft. McDowell noticed pigeons reacted. Sullivan, McKay and Krives noted a low humming sound and reported 20-30 objects. Frank Cooley reported seeing 12 *'flying discs'* moving through the sky at a height of about 20,000ft. Further sightings took place at 2pm, 4.30pm, and 5pm.

Airline pilots sight UFOs

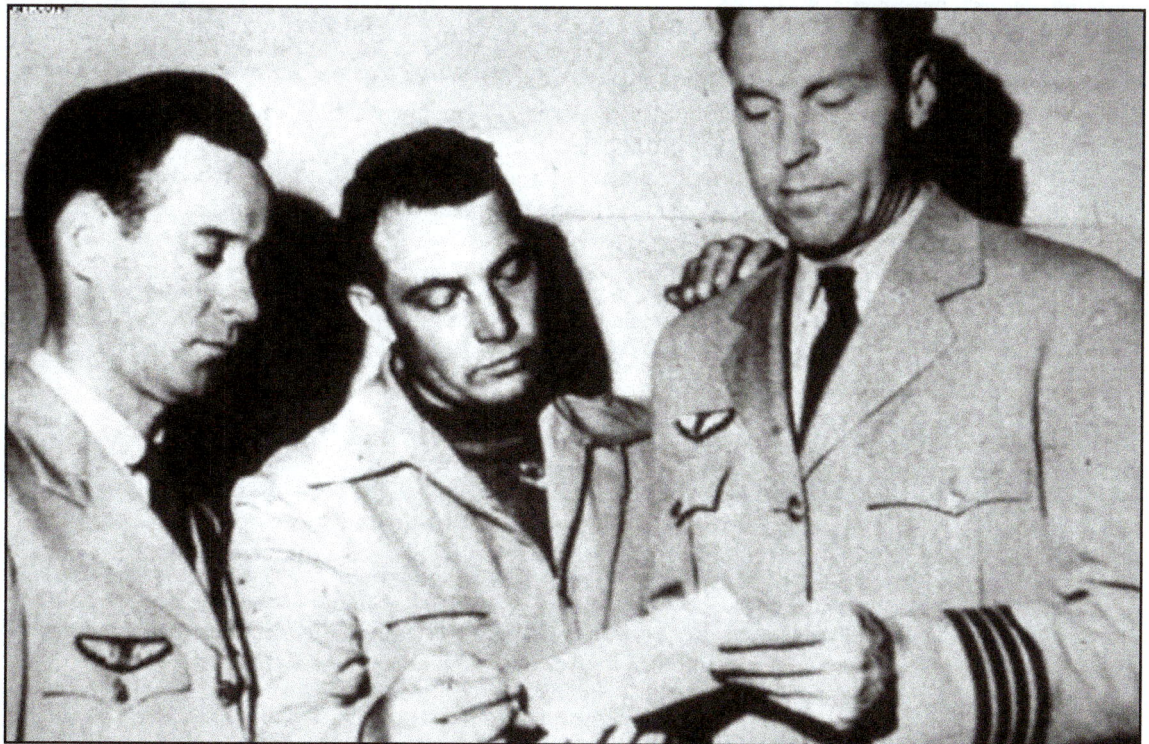

Co-pilot Ralph Stevens, Kenneth Arnold, and Capt. Emil. J. Smith

On the evening of the 4th July at Boise, Idaho, United Airlines Captain Emil Smith was walking up the ramp to board his plane, flight 105, for a trip to Seattle, when someone mentioned the massive *'wave'* of *'flying saucers'* seen taking place all day over the north-west. Captain Smith joked: *"I'll believe in those discs when I see them."*

The airliner lifted off at 9:04pm, and turned towards Seattle. As Captain Smith remembers it, the control tower at Boise bid him farewell by *"... joshingly warning us to be on the lookout for 'flying saucers'."*

Shortly after take-off, five *'disc'*-like objects, one larger than the rest, approached Captain Smith's DC-3 head-on. Stunned, Captain Smith and his co-pilot – Ralph Stevens – watched as the objects quickly reversed direction and took up a course that paralleled their own. For 45 miles Captain Smith was able to keep the objects in sight. Co-pilot Stevens thought the objects were aircraft at first, and flashed the airliner's landing lights. The objects reacted by changing formation from a very tight cluster to a more open one. The cluster of *'discs'* then began to open and close repeatedly, before settling down into a loose formation. After vanishing from sight another group of four came into view, which soon merged and vanished into the north-west. The airliner's stewardess – Miss Marty Morrow – verified the sightings. (**Source: J. Allen Hynek, *The UFO Report*, p1002, Dr James McDonald, 1968, FOIA/Ted Bloecher, 1967**)

At 9am on 5th July 1947, at Albuquerque, New Mexico, five *'discs'* were seen to fly eastwards over the City; one of which then circled back, to the original point of observation. In the afternoon, five witnesses saw a sphere manoeuvre in and out of clouds. (**Source: Jan Aldrich, Project 1947: A Preliminary Report on the 1947 UFO Sighting Wave;** *Albuquerque Journal*, **6th July 1947**)

At 12.40pm on the same day, at Seattle, Washington, Sergeant Raynar Cain, USMC, reported seeing two

Haunted Skies Volume Ten

football-shaped, *'disc'*-like objects, one of which was seen to bank slightly, at a height of about 8,000ft, before shooting upwards, heading north. The second one followed a short time later, both of them *'wobbling'* in flight as they headed north, climbing, before being lost from sight. **(Source: Ted Bloecher)**

On the night of 4th July 1947, radar indicated that the object had gone down about 30-40 miles north-west of Roswell. William Woody, who lived east of Roswell, said he remembered being outside with his father on the night of 4th July 1947, when he saw a brilliant object plunge to the ground. The debris site was closed for several days, while the wreckage was cleared, and Schmitt and Randle say that when Woody and his father tried to locate the area of the crash Woody said they were stopped by military personnel, who ordered them out of the area.

We learn that on the 5th July, tinfoil and paper wreckage of a RAWIN target device was discovered on the ground by Sherman Campbell – a local farmer. On the 8th of the same month, a similar device was found by David C. Heffner. In both instances the wreckage was handed back to the authorities.

Sightings of 'flying discs' continue to be reported

During the following day (6th July 1947) at Buckley, Colorado, LeRoy Krieger – Aerologist, Second Class – and James Cavalieri – hospital apprentice – reported sighting a bright, round, silvery object, shooting up and down noiselessly in the sky, for several minutes, before leaving at high speed. **(Source: Ted Bloecher)**

They were not the only ones. At Travis Air Force Base, California, Captain and Mrs James H. Burniston saw a highly reflective, round, flat object, having no wings or tail, the size of a C-54 transport plane (118ft) roll from side-to-side, three times, in the sky and then fly away fast from north-west to the south-west direction at 10,000ft. **(Source: Ted Bloecher, 1967)**

At 1.45pm, Major A.B. Browning and his crew were flying a B-25 eastwards to Kansas City, when they saw a silvery circular object, 30-50ft in diameter, pacing the aircraft at a little lower altitude. This was then seen to shoot off at high speed, heading eastwards at 11,000ft, and 210mph. **(Source: Project 1947, FOIA, Ted Bloecher, 1967)**

7th July 1947 – Heavy UFO activity reported on this day

On the morning of 7th July 1947, a bright silver object was seen in the sky, seven miles north of Shreveport, Louisiana, by a pilot. Other sightings for this day included a silver balloon-like object, with what looked like a silver disc attached to it (no cables seen) observed over Hickam Field Air Force Base, Hawaii.

At Muroc Army Air Field, California, test pilot Major Jowell C. Wise was powering up an XP-84 Jet on the runway, at 10.10am, when he saw other people gazing up into the sky. He looked up and saw, in the northwards direction, a yellowish-white sphere, about 5-10ft in diameter, oscillating in a *'forward whirling'* motion, without losing altitude, at about 10,000-12,000ft altitude, moving west to east, at about 200-225mph. **(Source: FOIA)**

Around noon, at Willow Springs, Illinois, Robert Meegan and his 14-year-old son, John, heard a buzzing noise overhead, while working in the fields on their farm, near the *Des Plains River*, not far from the Argonne National Laboratories. Looking up they saw thirteen round objects all going east, single file, in a straight line. They described the objects as: *"... round, with flat bottoms, about as big as a house, and bluish-grey in colour; which flew on a straight and level course toward the east."*

Between 1pm and 2pm, at Lakeland, Florida, five round shiny objects were seen in the north-east direction, climbing at 7,500ft, accompanied by a shrill noise. **(Source: Mary Castner/CUFOS)**

UFO drops into sea!

At 3.10pm, two people out surf fishing at Fort Bragg, California, sighted a flat, glistening object – the size of a lorry tyre – approach them from the ocean, at high speed. This was seen to drop rapidly and hit the water approximately a quarter of a mile offshore, with an enormous splash. Just before it hit the water, they heard a humming sound. The object floated for a few minutes and then appeared to sink. **(Source: Carl W Feindt)**

Between 10.30pm and 11pm, Lt. Colonel Cobb from Arlington, Virginia, saw a *'blob'* – the size of a small airplane – reflecting white light, flying at less than 500ft above ground, heading south-east, at about 1,350mph. **(Source: FOIA)**

On the same day a grey elliptical object, about 30ft in diameter with visible *'canopy'*, was seen heading across the sky at an estimated speed of about 500mph, over Phoenix, Arizona. A photograph was taken of the UFO by the witness – William Rhodes. Unfortunately, while it looks very genuine, there has been considerable controversy about its authenticity. **(Source: Project Sign)**

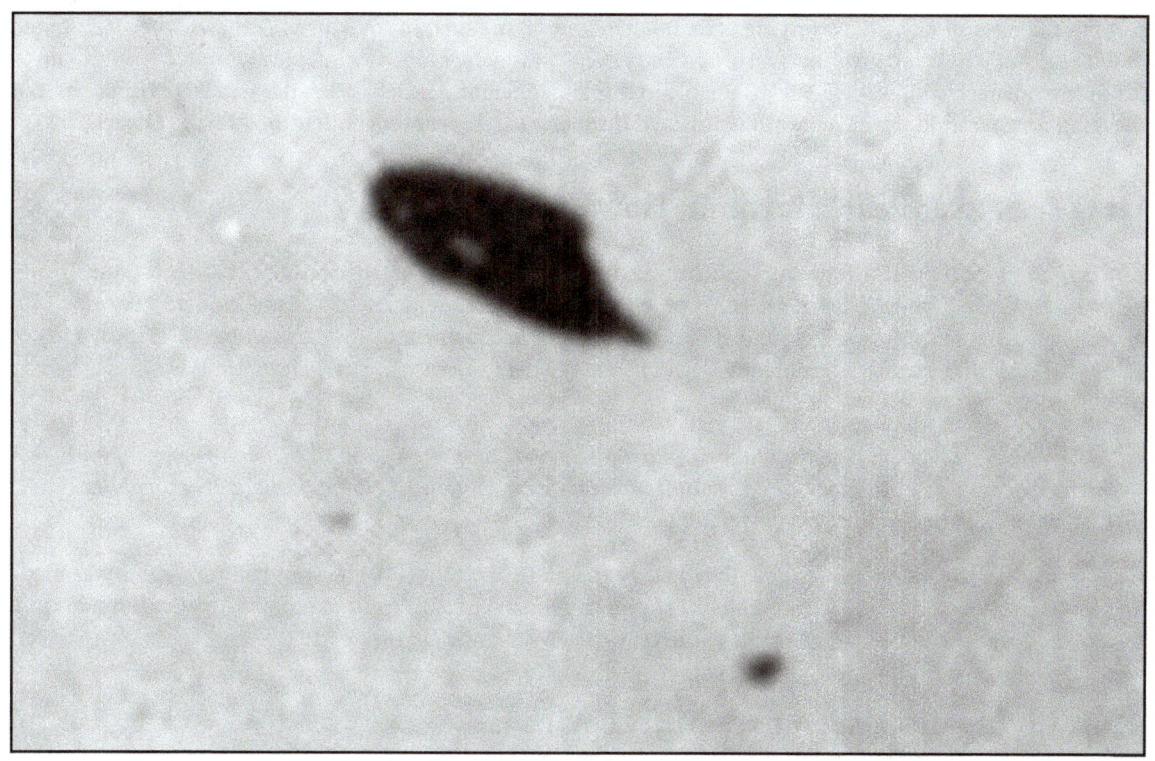

UFO photographed by William Rhodes over Phoenix, Arizona

At 9.45am on the 8th July, another sighting was reported from Muroc Army Air Field, California. This involved 1st Lt. Joseph C. McHenry, T/Sgt. Joseph Ruvolo, S/Sgt. Gerald E. Nauman, and Miss Jannette Marie Scott, who sighted two *'saucer'* or *'disc'*-shaped objects, silver and apparently metallic, flying in a wide circular pattern, at a height of approximately 7,500-8,000ft and travelling at 350-400mph, heading 320° north-west toward the Mojave. Before the first two objects had disappeared, a third similar *'disc'* or spherical silver object reflecting sunlight was seen, with additional five witnesses to the north, flying tight circles at about 7,000-8,000ft, beyond what was felt as the capability of current aircraft. No sound or trails were noted. Surprisingly, this was not the last time UFOs were seen on that day. At 11.50am, experimental test pilot Capt. John Paul Strapp, Mr Lenz from Wright Field, and two others in an observation truck, at Area 3, near Rogers Dry Lake, for a P-82 ejection seat test, saw a round, silver or aluminium-white object. At first this was thought to be a parachute, about 25ft wide, falling from a height below the 20,000ft of the test aircraft at 3x the rate for an ejection seat test, drifting horizontally toward Mt. Wilson (to the south) at less than 50-80mph. When close to the horizon, the object appeared to have an oval outline with two thick fins, or knobs, on the upper surface that seemed to rotate or oscillate (no propellers), slowly disappearing below the mountain tops in the distance after 90 seconds.

At 12 noon, Muroc (now Edwards Air Force Base) Commanding Officer Colonel Signa A. Gilkey, and engineer Major Richard R. Shoop and wife, each saw from a different location five to eight miles away to the (believed north) apparently the same falling object, described as resembling thin metallic aluminium and the size of a pursuit aircraft [50ft?], reflecting sunlight and oscillating. It was observed to descend to ground level, then rise again and move slowly off in the distance for a total of eight minutes. No sound or trail was reported. **(Source: FOIA; Vallée Jacques, *Magonia* 60)**

At 4pm the pilot of an F-51 was flying at 20,000ft, about 40 miles south of Muroc Airbase, when he sighted *"a flat object of a light reflecting nature; it had no vertical fin or wings"* above him. He attempted to climb up to it, but was unsuccessful, as the F-51 was unable to reach that height. All airbases in the area were contacted, but they had no aircraft in the area. **(Source: Edward Ruppelt, *The Report on Unidentified Flying Objects*, p22)**

UFO seen over Pearl Harbour, Hawaii

At 5:30pm, more than 100 Navy men, including Yeoman 2nd Class – Ted Purdue (21) of McClain, Texas, Yeoman 1st Class – Douglas Kacherle (22) of New Bedford, Mass., Seaman 1st Class – Donald Ferguson (19) of Indiana, Yeoman – Morris Kzamme (13) of LaCrosse, Wisconsin, and Seaman – Albert Delancey (19) of Salem, West Virginia, watched an oblong object in the sky over the base at Pearl Harbour. It was described by most witnesses as:

> *". . . silvery coloured, like aluminium, with no wings or tail, sort of round or oblong-shaped, and moving both slow and fast, very high, and moving westward toward Honolulu in alternating bursts of speed, and in a slow, zigzagging flight path."*

Navy officials at the base reported that they had begun an investigation. A check of balloon flights was made and it was learned that at 4.35pm, a weather balloon had been sent aloft from Honolulu Airport, but had risen quickly and was carried off to the south. **(Source: Case 769, *The UFO Wave of 1947*)**

More 'flying discs' seen over Muroc Airbase

At 9.30am on the 9th July 1947, a 1st Lieutenant, stationed at Muroc Airbase, was about to enter his office, when he happened to glance up into the sky, after hearing the noise of an aircraft moving over. He was astonished to see two silver, spherical or *'disc'*-shaped objects, heading north-west across the sky, at a height of about 8,000ft and speed estimated to be 300mph.

The officer brought this to the attention of two others and then ran into the dispensary to alert the staff there, and point out the objects to them. When he looked back into the sky he saw another object, at great height, moving around in circles. He was adamant that these could not be explained away as being weather balloons or aircraft, due to the tight circles the objects were making. **(Source: Project Sign)**

Black 'disc' seen over Idaho

At 12.17pm on this date, *Idaho Statesman* aviation editor and former (AAF) B-29 pilot – Dave Johnson – was flying in an Idaho Air National Guard AT-6, between Meridian and Boise, Idaho, when he saw a black *'disc'*, standing out against the clouds, make a half-roll, then a stair-step climb. The object was the size of a 25-cent coin [at arm's length?] (**Source: Berliner, Sparks, Wilson**)

9th July 1947 – Grand Falls, Newfoundland, Canada

At 11.30pm, Eric Kearsay – a Newfoundland Constable – arrived home. He was asked by his wife if he had seen *'flying saucers'*. Just minutes earlier, his wife and his mother-in-law, and Mr John Jackman, saw four round objects, flying in an easterly direction. Mr Jackman said that the objects were flying side by side, at a terrific rate of speed. As Eric Kearsay looked skyward, he, his wife and Mr Jackman, saw a round object – like a huge jellyfish, with a phosphorous glow – flash across the sky in a rocking motion. The direction of this object was not stated. (**Source: Dan Wilson**)

Between 3pm and 5pm, Mr A.R. Leidy, Mr J.N. Mehrman, and Mr J.E. Woodruff, employed as ground crewmen with Pan American Airways, briefly saw a translucent *'disc'* or silvery wheel-shaped object – the size of a C-54 transport aircraft – flying very fast, at about 10,000ft, leaving a dark bluish-black trail. It was then lost from sight as it entered cloud cover. (**Source: Berliner; FOIA**)

10th/11th July 1947

At 4.47pm, Dr. Lincoln La Paz was driving West on Highway 60, near Fort Sumner, New Mexico, with his wife and two teenage daughters, when they saw a sharply outlined, white, ellipsoidal, seemingly luminous, 200ft object, wobbling in the distance to the west, about 25 miles away.

It is alleged that this incident was reported in a *LIFE* magazine article on UFOs, in 1952, though Mr La Paz was not identified at the time.

> *"All four of us almost simultaneously became aware of a curious bright object, almost motionless, among the clouds.*
>
> *As seen projected against these dark clouds, the object gave the strongest impression of self-luminosity. It showed a sharp and firm regular outline, namely one of a smooth elliptical character much harder and sharper than the edges of the cloudlets... The hue of the luminous object was somewhat less white than the light of Jupiter in a dark sky, not aluminium or silver-coloured...The object clearly exhibited a sort of wobbling motion...This wobbling motion served to set off the object as a rigid, if not solid body. After remaining stationary for about 30 seconds, it then suddenly rose. This remarkably sudden ascent thoroughly convinced me that we were dealing with an absolutely novel airborne device."*

Whether this sighting had anything to do with a report of six *'flying discs'* seen by the pilot and crew of a plane over Morristown, New Jersey, on the same day, can only be speculation.

The following day (11th July 1947) Auxiliary Air Force Colonel Perry, stationed at Elmendorf Air Base, Anchorage, Alaska, was with a colleague, at 6.30pm, when they sighted a round 3ft aluminium coloured object, heading southwards at great speed. (**Source: FOIA; *FUFOR Index***)

12th July 1947 – At 6.35pm, Seaman John C. Kennedy and Seaman Ben Bobberly, stationed at Sand Point Naval Air Station, Washington, sighted a silvery, perfectly round and silent disc-like object flying eastwards, toward Kirkland, over Lake Washington. (**Source: Jan Aldrich, Bloecher Case**)

Haunted Skies Volume Ten

24th July 1947 – During the morning Joseph Muka, Seaman 2nd class, and John Francis Nihen, of Squantum Naval Air Station, Massachusetts, were carrying out a routine weather check on the Operations Building, when they saw a highly polished *'silver ball'* hurtle though the air, between 8,000-10,000ft, at a speed of 300mph, and rising towards the north-west direction.

Four days later, at 8.34pm on the 28th, the crew of a Seattle-bound United Airlines Mainliner DC-3 over Boise, Idaho, reported sighting a disc-like object in the sky, at a height of 9,000ft, at the same time as a twin-engine airliner was seen flying at 7,500ft. The C.A.A said that no other planes were in the area identified by the pilot as where he saw the *'disc'*. (**Source: News clipping, Dan Wilson**)

At 12 noon on July the 29th, three men sighted a 3ft shimmering object which was rising, descending, hovering and fluttering, while moving through the sky at tremendous speed, over Canyon Ferry, Montana, at a height of about 3000ft. (**Source: McDonald List;** *FUFOR Index*)

29th July 1947 – At 2.50pm Hamilton Field, California assistant Base Operations Officer – Captain William H. Ryherd, and B-29 pilot – 1st Lt. Ward Stewart, sighted two round, shiny, white objects, estimated to be 15-25ft in diameter, flying three to four times the apparent speed of a P-80, at a height of 6,000-10,000ft, heading south or south-east, at 120°. One object flew straight and level; the other weaved from side-to-side, like an escort fighter. (**Source: Berliner; FOIA;** *FUFOR Index*)

Capt. Edward J Ruppelt:

> *"By the end of July (1947) the UFO security lid was down tight. The few members of the Press who did inquire about what the Air Force was doing got the same treatment that you would get today if you inquired about the number of thermonuclear weapons stock-piled in the U.S. atomic arsenal . . . (At ATIC there was) confusion almost to the point of panic."*

(**Source:** *Report On Unidentified Flying Objects*, p.39)

USA: Twin Fall County, 13th August 1947

At 9.30am on this day, County Commissioner Hawkins – a former County Sheriff from Filer – was at Salmon Dam, 20 miles west of Twin Falls, when he heard the sound like a motor and looked upwards in time to see two circular objects, travelling at great speed and higher than normal aircraft height, across the sky.

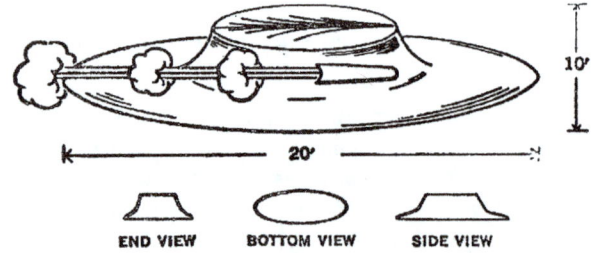

At 1pm, Mr A.C. Urie – then in charge of the Auger Falls trout farm, six miles west of Blue Lake Ranch – had walked down to Snake River Canyon to see if his two sons – Keith (8) and Billy (10) – were alright, as they were crossing the river by boat.

> *"I had a side view at a distance of about 300ft, almost level with the 'thing'. My sons, who were below me, also saw the object. It was all one colour, sort of light sky blue, with a red tubular fiery glow at the side or the top. It rode up and down over the hills and hollows, at a speed indicating some type of control faster than the reflexes of man. In my opinion it appeared guided by instruments and must be powered by atomic energy, as it made little noise – just a swish as it passed by. It was about 20ft long by 10ft high and 10ft wide, forming an oblong shape.*
>
> *It might be described as looking like an inverted pie plate or broad brimmed straw hat that had been compressed from two sides."*

Kirtland AFB Tech-Area-1

During the latter part of this year, Colonel William P. Hayes – Infantry Component Affairs Officer, from Kirtland Air Force Base – was driving his car at 10pm, along Highway 60 near Vaughn, New Mexico, when he noticed an object, 4-500ft in the sky, which was descending slowly in a vertical movement.

> *"It was slightly larger than a basketball, bright white in colour – like a miniature sun; on reaching a point about 200ft above the ground it appeared to explode, although no noise was heard. I stopped my car and got out to take a closer look. By this time it was 40-60 yards away and completely silent. At this time the fragments assumed a fiery red colour and dropped downwards – like numerous sparks, which extinguished before they struck the ground."*

In an interview conducted on the 9th December 1948, the officer told investigators that he had seen the same phenomena on the 3rd or 4th of November 1948, and the 23rd November, in the same location.

Mr K.D. Flock – forest supervisor of Santa Fe Forest, Federal Court House, Santa Fe, Mexico – was contacted by Madeleine Merchant, who told him she was out prospecting with her husband, in New Mexico, and that during a five week period, she and her husband had witnessed various objects crossing the sky, which she described as being cigar-shaped, with glowing tips.

Declassified 'Project Sign' documents relating to reports of UFO activity received revealed it was policy to carry out (sometimes with the assistance of the FBI and local police) into the personal backgrounds of many witnesses. This often included speaking to friends, relatives and employees, in order to evaluate the character of the witness involved.

On this one occasion it was said that Madeleine had an extensive file on her, which related to many incidents of UFO activity witnessed by her over a two-year period. As she was also known to correspond with Communist Front organisations, she was considered dangerous! **(Source: National Archives)**

Birth of 'Project Sign' Restricted!

By the end of 1947 a secret memo on 'flying discs' began to circulate amongst senior military leaders at the Pentagon. Major General Craig, Deputy Chief of Staff to the Commanding General Air Material Command at Wright Patterson, Ohio, dated 30th December 1947, declared:

> "It is Air Force policy not to ignore reports of sightings and phenomena in the atmosphere but to recognise that part of its mission is to collect, collate, evaluate and act on information on this nature. It is desired that the Air Force Air Material Command set up a project whose purpose is to collect, collate and distribute to interested government agencies and contractors all information concerning sightings and phenomena in the atmosphere which can be construed to be of concern to the national security. The Project is assigned 2A with a security classification of 'restricted' and code name Sign. Where data of a classification higher than restricted is handled by the project, such data should be classified accordingly. Signed by, Command Chief of Staff".

7th January 1948: Godman Field sight UFO

At 1.20pm, the tower crew at Godman Field, Kentucky, sighted a disc-shaped object, which they kept under observation for several minutes, and then asked the commander – Colonel Guy Hix – to come and have a look. He described it as being:

> "... very white; looks like an umbrella. I just don't know what it is. Through binoculars it appears to have a red border at the bottom, at times, and a red border at the top at times."

Authors: Was the object rotating in flight?

About five minutes later (1.25pm), four 51P Mustangs happened to be en route from Mariette, Georgia, to Standiford Field, Louisville, Kentucky. As they appeared in the sky, the Commanding Officer contacted the flight leader NG3869 Captain Thomas Mantell and asked him to take a look at the object, as they were unable to identify it. One fighter plane piloted by Henricks NG336 turns away and landed at 3.1pm.

The other three piloted by Pilot Clements NG800, Pilot Hammond NG737 turn south. Mantell moves forward of the two wingmen and, after confirming he has sighted it, radios back, saying: *"...object travelling at half my speed and directly ahead of me and above. I'm closing in to take a good look at it.* [He is asked for a description] *It's above me; it looks metallic and it's tremendous in size. It's above me and I'm gaining on it; I'm going to 20,000ft."*

At 2pm on this date, Kentucky State Police contacted Fort Knox reporting an unusual aircraft or object flying through the sky. It was circular in appearance and approximately 250-300ft in diameter, moving briskly westwards. At approximately 3.15pm, Godman Tower loses sight of the UFO and Mantell's aircraft. Five minutes later, a telephone call is received to inform them that the plane has been located; it has crashed. The Captain's decapitated body is found nearby; it is alleged his watch has stopped at 3.10pm.

We presume that his watch either stopped due to the impact sustained, following collision with the ground, or that it stopped in flight. If this was the second case, should we consider that the watch may have been rendered inoperative, due to the field of electrical energy which surrounded the UFO? However, according to Godman Tower, the engine of the plane was still being heard at 3.15pm, although not seen by ground observers, due to its height, or was there another explanation? [The object was kept under observations until 4pm].

It is claimed an Officer Walker arrived at the crash scene and found that the pilot's body had been removed from the aircraft while other accounts say he was thrown out by the impact.

We were confused by the actual time relating to when the aircraft was found; some accounts give a much later time of 4.45pm. We were puzzled as to why the alleged comment made by Captain Mantell *"it looks metallic and it's tremendous in size"* was not made public until 1985, following declassification of a Top Secret Air Force Naval Intelligence letter, dated 1948. Although according to *The Riddle Of The Flying Saucers*, written by Gerald Heard, and published in 1950, it contained this information which suggests authenticity.

This may suggests that it was probably common knowledge at the time. Another rumour which has proliferated through time was that Captain Mantell told of experiencing unusual heat as he neared the object. According to Frank Edwards, who wrote *Flying Saucers – Serious Business* (1966), he tells of a conversation held with an unnamed radar operator, who was present at the time that this was said. If it was mentioned, it was not officially recorded.

Captain Thomas Mantell

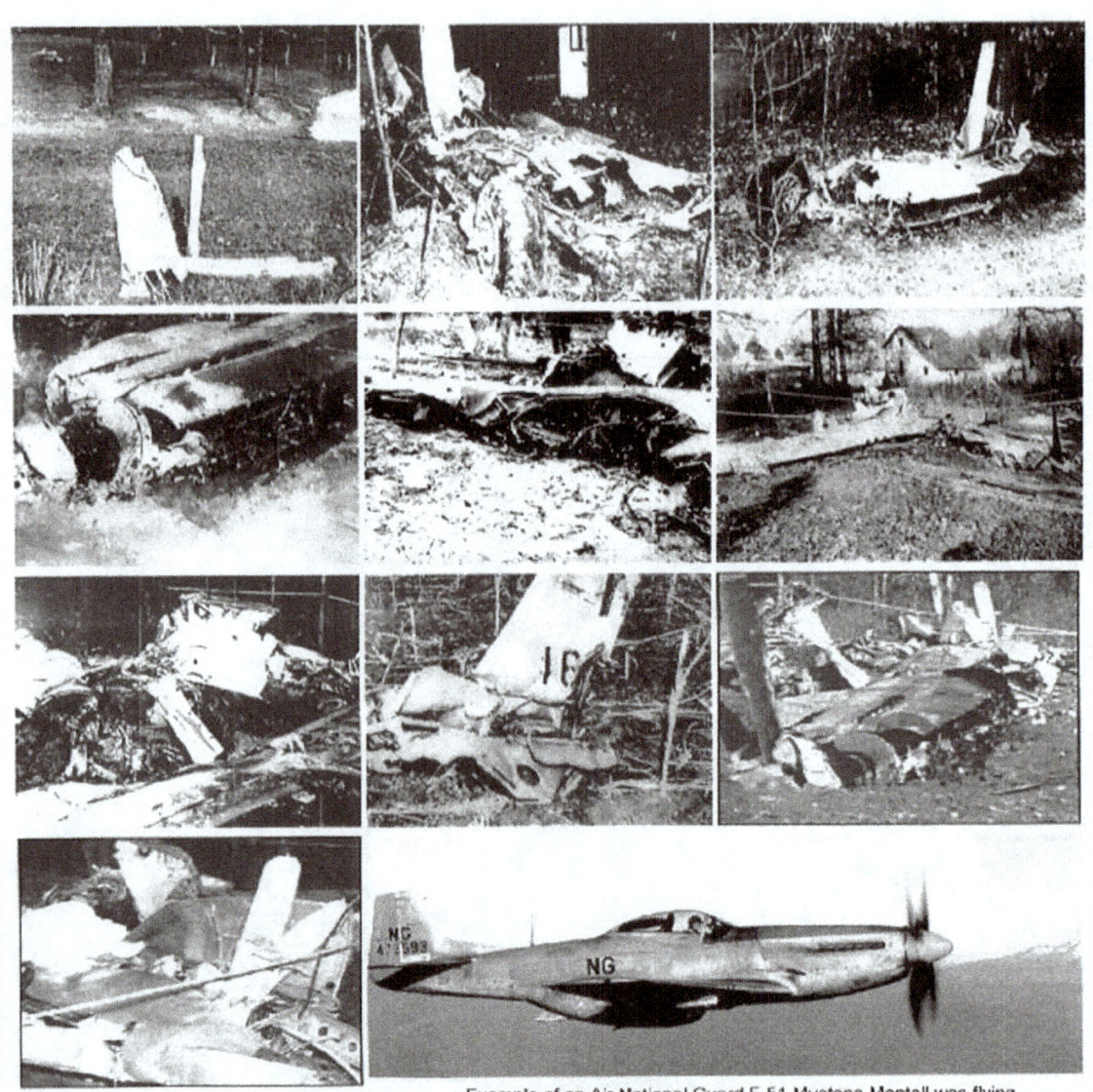

Example of an Air National Guard F-51 Mustang Mantell was flying

Oxygen starvation, Venus, or weather balloon?

The tragedy was later initially explained away by the authorities, following an investigation, as due to oxygen starvation and that the aircraft being trimmed continued to climb until increasing altitude caused a sufficient loss of power for it to level out. It then turned to the left, due to torque, and as the wing dropped so did the nose, until the aircraft was in a tight diving spiral. The uncontrolled decent, resulting in excessive speed, caused

CAPT:THOMAS MANTELL,AND THE FORT KNOX SAUCER,1948.

On the 7th January 1948,Capt.Mantell in Command of a scout fleet of three P.5I planes,was flying over Godman Airfield when the tower operator radioed Mantell for assistance,he was requested that if he had enough fuel would he investigate an object that they had failed to identify. Capt.Mantell climed to about I5,00 feet,he radioed to the tower that the object was in sight ahead and above him,he described it as huge and round,about 500 feet across from around the saucers rim Mantell could see blasts of red flame.His last message to the tower was "am going to 22,00 feet, for a closer look"he did not call again, the wreckage of his plane was found one hour later,Capt.Mantell was dead,his death is still a mystery today.

The wreckage of Captain Mantell's P-51 Mustang. Picture retouched to remove scratches.

the aircraft to disintegrate. It was suggested that the officer never regained consciousness. The canopy lock was still in place, discounting any attempt to abandon the plane. Another suggestion was that the object being chased was Venus! – Extremely unlikely, as it was 33° above the horizon.

It was then suggested the object was, in fact, a 'skyhook' weather balloon! Checks made with the Meteorological Office and Naval Centre for the Study of Cosmic Rays, at Minneapolis, revealed neither of them had released any balloons on that day.

We know that following the impact made with the ground, the left wing and tail of the Mustang came off. There was no fire, no sign of blood in the cockpit, no scratches on the aircraft's body to indicate forward movement. Part of the skull and scalp were found, as shown on page 46 of *Project Blue Book*, edited by Brad Steiger.

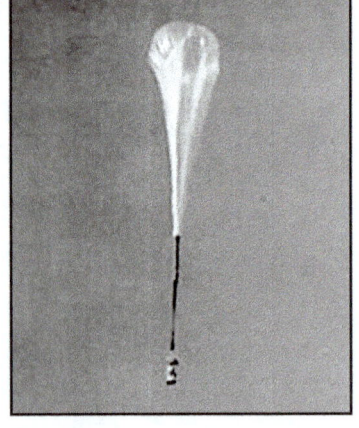

The propeller blades showed no scratch marks to show it had been rotating at the time of impact. There was no swathe or furrows left in the ground, as one may have expected if the pilot was attempting to land the plane. It was as if the plane had 'belly flopped' onto the ground. There have been suggestions made that the plane ran out of fuel, but Captain Mantell told the tower before attempting to intercept the object that he had plenty of 'gas'. Exactly how much 'gas' is, of course, open to speculation.

According to *Project Blue Book*, the aircraft exploded in the air and wreckage was scattered over an area of about half a mile; the tail section, one wing and the propeller, were not located. It is said that the canopy was still in the locked position; fragments of the canopy were found, nearby. What caused the safety belt, which was still around the pilot, to be shredded?

Shortly afterwards an object was not only seen in the sky again over Godman, but tracked moving at 250mph in a WSW direction. A *'great ball of light'* was also reported over St. Louis Tower. Clearly this matter is far from as simple as one may be inclined to believe. We know, from calculations made, that this could not have been Venus, a mock sun, weather balloon, or the result of an attack by Martians, as suggested in some newspapers! It is clear that this is an excellent example of when you have eliminated the impossible, whatever remains, however improbable, must be

Flying Disc Brings Death To Pursuing Guard Pilot

Sky Phenomenon Observed At Ohio Air Base

WILMINGTON, O., Jan. 8.—(*P*)—A phenomenon of the skies, a flaming red cone trailing a gaseous green mist, appeared near the Clinton County Army air base last night, and today continued to provide a mystery for the thousands of people who saw it.

The Army air base late today issued a formal statement on the matter, but, a spokesman said, officials there still had no idea what it was or what it might mean.

"The sky phenomenon, described by observers at the Clinton county air base as having the appearance of

Astronomers Declare Object Apparently Balloon

LOUISVILLE, Ky., Jan. 8—(*P*)—Several areas of Kentucky and adjoining states were excited today over reports of "flying saucers" which led to the death of one National Guard flier and fruitless chases by several other pilots.

The National Guard headquarters at Louisville said Capt. Thomas F. Mantell, Jr., 25, was killed late Wednesday while chasing what was reported as a "flying saucer" near Franklin, Ky.

Two other members of the Kentucky National Guard, also assigned to a flying investigation of re-

the truth. Eyewitness testimony from various people on the ground corroborates the fact that this object was travelling at 500mph, leaving a long flame in its track. It was last seen between 5pm and 5.20pm over Lockbourne, Ohio, now silver-grey to amber in colour, before disappearing over the horizon. On the next day a large metallic object was seen over Circleville, Ohio, displaying an orange light near the ground.

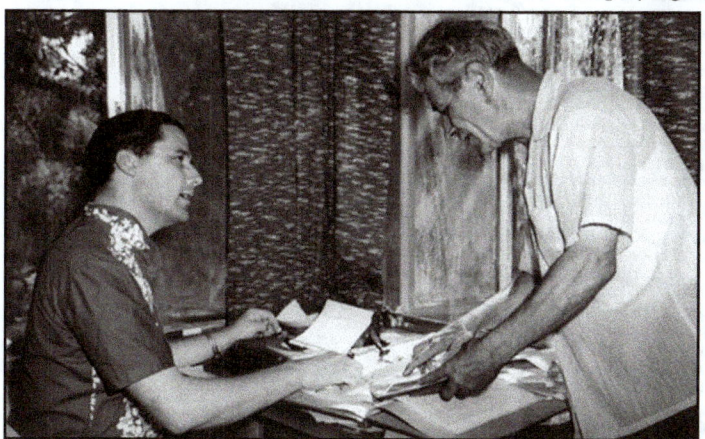

Desmond Leslie, seen here in 1954 with George Adamski at Palomar Terraces, USA

Ex-RAF Spitfire Pilot – Desmond Arthur Peter Leslie (his father was a first cousin of Winston Churchill) – wrote about this matter, which was published in *Flying Saucer Review*, Volume 1, No. 5, November/December 1955. Desmond tells of meeting an engineer from Godman Field, who witnessed the event during a trip to the States. The man told Desmond that the object . . .

> ". . . came across the county slowly, at a speed estimated to be 110miles per hour, at a height of 5-7000ft, and was 250-350ft in size. It passed

over Benning Field, which notified Godman Field that a UFO was approaching their position. It is then said that although three F51 Mustang Fighters were available, only one was fuelled and ready to scramble. It was a huge dull silver, circular, disc and flew along at an angle with a heavy list, so that the upper structure was plainly visible. The structure was a huge flattened dome and everyone on the field had a perfect view of it; it was breathtaking. This was no weather balloon or atmospheric effect. The wreckage of the plane was spread over an area of six square miles, according to the witness, who claimed it did not fall in pieces but came down like confetti. We watched the flight leader – Captain Mantell – try to intercept it. In addition to what was reported, he also described it as having a ring of portholes surrounding the rim, but this was deleted from the voice transmission."

*This is incorrect. One landed, leaving the other three to investigate.

http://www.bluebookarchive.org/page.aspx?PageCode=MAXW-PBB3-719

THIS PAGE IS UNCLASSIFIED

CONFIDENTIAL A/hag
315TH AF BASE UNIT
GODMAN FIELD, FORT KNOX, KENTUCKY

9 January 1948

At approximately 1420, 7 Jan 48, I accompanied Lt. Col. E.G. Wood to the Godman Field Control Tower to observe "an object hanging high in the sky south of Godman".

Shortly after reaching the tower, Col. Guy F. Hix, Commanding Officer, was summoned; it was at that time that I first sighted the bright silver object.

Approximately five minutes after Col. Hix came into the tower, a flight of four P-51's flew over Godman. An officer in the tower requested that the Tower Operator call this flight and ask the Flight Leader to investigate this object if he had sufficient fuel. The Flight Leader (Capt. Thomas F. Mantell) answered that he would, and requested a bearing to this object. At that time one member of the flight informed the leader that it was time for him to land and broke off from the formation. This A/C was heard requesting landing instructions from his home field, Standiford, in Louisville.

In the meantime the remaining three P-51's were climbing on the course given to them by Godman Tower towards this object that still appeared stationary. The Tower then advised the Flight Leader to correct his course 5 degrees to the lft; the Flight Leader acknowledged this correction and also reported his position at 7,500 feet and climbing. Immediately following the Flight Leader's transmission, another member of the Flight asked "where in the hell are we going?" In a few minutes the Flight Leader called out an object "twelve o'clock high". Asked to describe this object, he said that it was bright and that it was climbing away from him. When asked about its speed, the Flight Leader stated it was going about half his speed, approximately 180 M.P.H.

Those of us in the Tower lost sight of the flight, but could still see this object. Shortly after the last transmission, the Flight Leader said he was at 15,000 ft, and still climbing after "it", but that he judged its speed to be the same as his. At that time a member of the flight called to the leader and requested that he "level off", but we heard no reply from the leader. That was the last message received from any member of the flight by Godman Tower.

DOWNGRADED AT 3 YEAR INTERVALS.
DECLASSIFIED AFTER 12 YEARS.
DOD DIR 5200.10

"CERTIFIED A TRUE COPY"

/s/ James F. Duesler, Jr.
JAMES F. DUESLER, JR.
Captain, USAF

JAMES F. DUESLER, JR.
CAPTAIN, USAF

CONFIDENTIAL

UNCLASSIFIED

Desmond:

> "I have flown Spitfire Mk V1s during the war and knew of pilots crashing as result of oxygen failure. When this happened, the out of control plane dives earthwards and buries itself into the ground, but it comes down in one piece. Lack of oxygen cannot and never will disintegrate a plane in the air, but this did. Every fragment was painstakingly gathered up and made to disappear."

During further conversation with the engineer, Desmond asked him if Captain Mantell had taken any aggressive action. According to him, during the last exchange between Mantell and the control tower, the pilot had told of becoming fed up with the way that the thing kept accelerating out of reach as he was going to open fire. He was going to open fire if he could not get any closer.

In late 1951, Captain Edward J. Ruppelt became the director of Project Grudge until it became Project Blue Book, in March 1952; he remained with Blue Book until late 1953. He decided to re-examine the file on the Mantell case and found the microfilm housing the original document was degraded, as if somebody had spilled something onto it. Many of the sections were so badly faded that they were illegible. Worse, practically none of the original military persons were available to re-interview.

Captain Edward J. Ruppelt

Cigar-shaped UFO seen by pilots – 24th July 1948

USA: 24th July 1948 – Pilots Clarence S. Chiles and John B. Whitted were 20 miles south-west of Montgomery, USA, when an unidentified flying object, showing two rows of windows, leaving a 50ft trail of orange-red flame, shot past the aircraft.

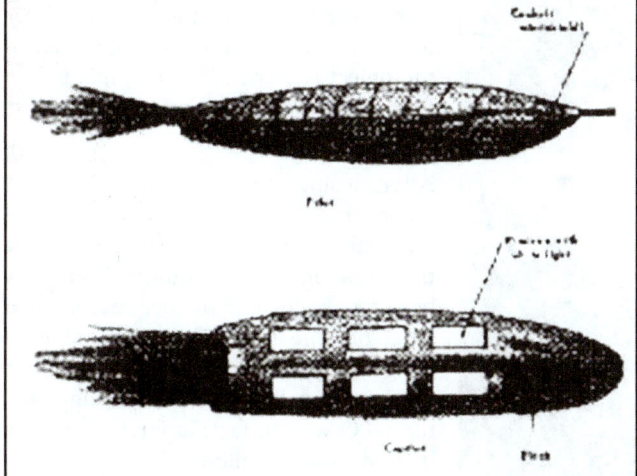

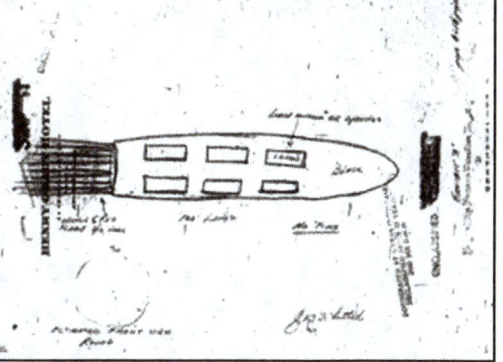

Haunted Skies Volume Ten

USA: Richmond, California, 23rd September 1948 – Retired butcher – Sylvester Bentham (70) – was visiting Castro's Ranch and engaged in conversation with Colonel Horace Eakins, when the Officer brought his attention to something in the sky.

> "I looked up and saw a rectangular object; it was sharply outlined, buff or grey in colour, showing several darker vertical lines, like ribs. It looked like a flying vegetable crate."

(Source: National Archives)

USA: Louisiana, 5th September 1948 – Dairy farmer – Elma McDaniels (58) of Tangipahoa – was disturbed by a noise she described as resembling a steaming train, flying through the sky between 3pm and 3.30pm. She told investigators that she had heard the sound before at 3pm on the 5th September 1948. Enquiries made with her neighbours revealed she was known for having a vivid imagination and had spoken of paranormal activities which occurred around the area. History may well record that there was far more substance to her allegations than many believed and that she wasn't delusional! **(Source: Chief of Staff, Wright Patterson Air Force Base/National Archives)**

USA: Southern Colorado, 12th September 1948 – Green fireball seen moving through the sky, by Mr Harold Wright.

USA: 1st October 1948 – Pilot George Gorman (25) of the North Dakota National Guard was on landing approach to Fargo, USA, flying a P51 Mustang, at around 8.30pm. Due to the clear conditions, he decided to carry out some night-time flying at 9pm. While in the air he noticed an object to the west, which was showing a blinking light. After ascertaining that no other aircraft were in the vicinity, other than a Piper Cub (piloted by Dr. A.D. Cannon, accompanied by Einar Nelson, who also confirmed a visual on this object), George told Air Traffic controllers – L.D. Jensen and Manuel E. Johnson – that he was going to pursue the object to determine its identity, but soon realised the object was moving faster than his top speed. He then made a right turn and approached the object (described as a '*simple ball of light, eight inches in diameter*') head-on, at 5,000ft.

After losing sight of it, the object reappeared again. Interestingly he noted that when '*it*' increased its speed, the blinking (or pulsating) effect grew brighter. Following further attempts in what became referred to as a dogfight he gave up the chase and landed. An investigation into the matter suggested the UFO was, in fact, Jupiter! . . . then a lighted weather balloon!

USA: Indiana, 13th October 1948 – At 11.40am on this day, secretary Florence Brooke and Cyril Thompson – Chief Clerk engineer of the Studebaker Corporation – sighted a spinning, flashing, flat silver object, moving through the sky at terrific speed, over the City of South Bend, at a height estimated to be 1,500ft. The couple said the object, which had no visible fins or protrusions on its body, was in view for about ten seconds.

(Source: Wright Patterson Air Force Base, declassified file)

USA: Sterling, Utah, 16th October 1948 – Frederick Nash of Salt Lake City was out hunting with a number of colleagues, eight miles east of Sterling, at 11.45am. At the time of the sighting the group were on a ridge 9,000ft above sea level, when only Fredrick saw:

> "... an object resembling a flat football, about 9ins long by 6ins wide and 3ins thick, pass at a height of some 500ft above me. There were no visible signs of an exhaust, but from the rear an opening was seen in the centre. It was silver and black, showing a silver stripe down the centre from front to rear. It was moving at a speed of about 300mph."

(Source: Project Sign Office of Special Investigations/National Archives)

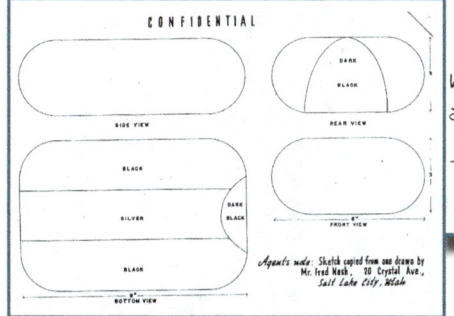

Formation of unidentified flying objects seen over the Washington area

USA: Washington, 30th October 1948 – Major Homer William Morris of the 318th Fighter Interceptor Squadron, McChord Air Force Base, Washington, was interviewed on the 7th December 1948, by OSI Agent Donald C. Hildreth. The typed statement taken from the officer with regard to a UFO, as seen by his radar observer – Lt. Robert Kunzman – follows the declaration:

> "I make the following statement after having heard the 24th Article of War, which was explained to me by Donald C. Hildreth, whom I know to be a Special Agent Officer of Special Investigations. No force, threats, or promises, have been used to induce me to make this statement and I realise that anything I say may be used for or against me in a court of law."

The officer described a flight, while 10-20 miles off the coast of Washington and 15 miles north of Grays Harbour, in an F-82-F, involving checking out their instruments, during the early afternoon, when Lt. Kunzman told him he had seen a fast moving object in the air, while descending over the ocean at a height between 500-1000ft. By the time the Major looked, it had gone.

Lt. Kunzman:

> "At about 2.30pm, I saw a small compact group of objects, which seemed to string out in line formation at my 11 o'clock position. The first colour I noticed was rather yellow. As they came to a 1 o'clock position, they appeared white and egg-shaped. I thought they were seagulls – 10-20 of them – until they came round to my 3 o'clock position in the same formation, before turning back to the '2.30' position, parallel with our course, and faded – much as exhaust fume from an airplane would."

The officer said the time of observation was about 20 seconds, and that they had been on a westerly course initially, before changing to a north direction. Major Morris stated that the only reason he allowed this report to go through was because Ground Control Station said they had picked up a target, but later denied this to him. We could not help but wonder if there was any connection with what Kenneth Arnold had seen, the previous year?

USA: Fargo, 24th November 1948 – Mr Lloyd Sanders – manager of Swift and Co., North Fargo – was driving towards the town with his wife, Jean, at 5.45pm, when they saw an object suddenly appear in the sky, travelling at terrific speed, about 1,000ft high. As the couple reached the outskirts of Moorhead, the object made a sharp right-hand turn and headed northwards. Seconds later, as if a light was switched off, the object vanished from view. (The authors believe its luminosity may have been extinguished, leaving the impression that it had vanished from view, when, in fact, it was still there) **(Source: Special Inquiry Report on Information on Flying Discs, Wright Patterson Air Force Base/National Archives)**

USA: Waco, Texas, 23rd September 1948 – Mr Ruble Angier was stood outside Santa Fe Radio Station, at 9.40am, watching a plane descending towards Los Alamos Airport, when he noticed an object in the sky, at a height he estimated to be 30,000ft, and size of 150ft in diameter.

> "It was a perfect white object, circular in appearance, the side visible to me as flat as a coin would appear when seen from a distance. There were no projections, air trails or exhaust, of any kind. I called Mr Fairchild's attention to it and we watched it for about eight minutes. After duration of 20 minutes, I left and returned to Waco."

(Source: reported to Captain E. McCall, Intelligence Department, USAF/National Archives)

USA: New Orleans, 1st October 1948 – Bank Manager Bernard Williams was out squirrel hunting, at 5.40am, near a clearing which runs from Highway North to the swamps, when he saw:

> ". . . an object, which looked like an ice-cream cone, heading from west to east. The larger end in the front looked white hot, like mantles in a gasoline lantern; towards the rear if became gradually darker red. The object was silent and appeared to be about three quarters of a mile away from me, at an elevation of about 2500ft. I estimated it was travelling at 300mph."

USA: Indiana 13th October 1948 – Florence Brooke sighted something strange in the sky over Indiana

USA: San Francisco, 29th November 1948 – A UFO was seen by local resident Mr Robert Thatcher, heading in an east to north-west direction, at 9.15pm on that date, before being lost from view as it entered a fog bank. **(Source: Project Sign/Wright Patterson AFB, National Archives)**

In compliance with request contained in "Elements of Essential Information, Project, Sign", Miss FLORENCE BROOKE, on 1 December 1948 executed and signed the following statement.

THE STUDEBAKER CORPORATION
South Bend 27, Indiana

December 1, 1948

At approximately 11:45 AM on October 13, 1948, while looking out through our office window facing North, I noticed a very dark colored plane flying directly North, but it was so far away I could not determine what type plane it was other than the fact that I felt it was not a transport plane inasmuch as we see transports very frequently, they are sliver in color and travel East and West, or Southeast and Northwest while within our scope of vision from this location.

While I watched the above described plane fade from view, another object caught my attention. At first I thought this object was a piece of paper being blown along by the wind, however on closer observation, I noted that it was much higher than would be possible to see a piece of paper floating. Also the object was traveling at what seemed to be a very high rate of speed, although it was impossible for me to determine the altitude at which it was moving. The object was sliver in color and seemed to be turning or spinning so that the sun reflected on it. As it was traveling very rapidly and at what seemed a very high altitude, it was not possible to determine its shape, although I am certain it was not an airplane. It did not appear to be a smooth surfaced object because of the flashing of the sunrays against it. The object was traveling a direct course from Northwest to Southeast and was within my scope of vision for perhaps 15 to 20 seconds.

s/ Florence Brooke
t/ Florence Brooke,
Secy. to S. W. Sparrow,
V.P. in Chg. of Engrg.

USA: Kirtland Air Force Base, 6th December 1948 – At 9.30pm, the pilot of a C-47, flying from Lowry Air Force Base to Williams Air Force Base, 10 miles east of Albuquerque, reported seeing a green flare rise up from the ground, at an altitude of 500ft, on the slopes of the Sandia Mountains, at 9.27pm.

Haunted Skies Volume Ten

Sandia Mountains

At 11pm on the same date, Captain Van Lloyd – pilot of a Pioneer air flight – contacted Kirtland to tell them he had seen a pale green light, west of Las Vegas, at 9.35pm.

> *"It appeared to be coming straight towards my airplane and I attempted to jerk the aircraft from its course to avoid the light."*

He first thought this was a *'shooting star'*, but then realised it was too near the ground and wondered if it had been a flare fired from a pistol.

USA: Sandia Base, 6th December 1948 – At the top secret Sandia Base – then the principal nuclear weapons installation of the United States Department of Defense, situated on the south-eastern edge of Albuquerque, New Mexico – Joseph H. Tolouse, AEC Security representative, observed a greenish flare in the sky, almost directly over the base, while driving west near the base …

> *"The flare was about one third of the size of the moon and a slight arch ensued, falling from east to west; a few seconds later it vanished from sight."*

For 25 years, the top secret Sandia Base and its subsidiary installation, Manzano Base, carried on the atomic weapons research, development, design, testing, and training, commenced by the Manhattan Project during World War Two. Fabrication, assembly and storage, of nuclear weapons were also done at Sandia Base. The base played a key role in the United States nuclear deterrence capability during the Cold War. In 1971, it was merged into Kirtland Air Force Base.

USA: Near Las Vegas, 8th December 1948 – OSI Special Agents Stahl and Neef – trained Pilots with the USAF – (presumably the one and same Captain Neef that attended the secret conference on the 16th February 1949) took off from Kirtland Air Force Base in a T-7 Aircraft, at 5.45pm. At 6.33pm, while flying at 11,500ft 20 miles east of Las Vegas, at 160mph, on what was a clear evening with good visibility, Special Agent Neef (who was co-pilot) first saw the phenomenon, followed by Mr Stahl. This was the sighting of a green flare, at an estimated altitude of 2,000ft higher than the aircraft. Although the object was similar in appearance to a burning green flare of common use in the Air Force, this was larger than a normal flare and lasted a couple of seconds, before it appeared to burn out. The following day, Special Agent Stahl flew back out to the locality and conducted a search of the terrain over a number of hours, but saw nothing untoward. (**Source: National Archives**)

Dr. La Paz's second sighting was of a green fireball, soon after he began his investigations into the phenomenon for the Air Force, in December 1948. The sighting was on the 12th December and the phenomenon was also seen over Los Alamos, enabling Mr La Paz to perform triangulation. This showed that the object's path was directly over the very sensitive Los Alamos.

USA: Pennsylvania, 17th December 1948 – At 1.30am, Charles Werner was working as yardmaster in the railway yard, north of Ambridge, when he saw a formation of spherical objects at a 45° angle above the northern horizon, heading southwards.

> "The top object appeared to dive beneath the formation and make a sharp 90° turn to the right, before disappearing from view westwards. They were visible for 30 seconds and appeared to be rotating around their axis."

Mr Peter Hildebrand, who was also working at the same location, was interviewed. He confirmed the sighting and said they resembled solid white wheels, turning around their hubs. Both men said they had not seen any wings, fins, propellers, or openings. (**Source: National Archives**)

USA: Boise Idaho, 18th December 1948 – Mr Maynard Rogers was employed at Boise Municipal Airport as a meteorological aide. While driving to work from his home a few miles away, at about 7.20am, he sighted what looked like '*a big ball of fire*' in the sky, about 15 miles away from him, described as being a brilliant fire orange in colour, before it grew in brilliance to '*white hot*'.

> "It was the same size of the moon; it left a trail of deep grey smoke. The width of this was about four times the size of the object itself [This trail took four hours to dissipate]. It was in sight for four minutes, and was located at 43° 24 minutes north, 116° 06 minutes west. The object was heading in a straight line north-east and at a height of about 8,000ft. I believed the object to be a meteor."

(Source: *Idahoe Statesman,* 18.12.1948)

USA: Point Eagle, Utah, 29th December 1948

At 8.53pm, Mr G.S. Skipper was driving over *State Route 4, 390 miles north of Bandelier National Monument cut off, when he saw what he thought was a meteorite, moving from left to right through the sky.

> "It was the size of a tennis ball and glaring white in colour, similar to white hot steel in a furnace. It had a small conical-shaped tail, which appeared to be greenish in colour, seeming of a gaseous nature. It appeared to be travelling on a controlled course and was visible for a second or two, before disappearing from view behind trees. As I made a sharp right-hand turn on the road, I saw it again for about a second, when I saw a small light to the right of the object which appeared to be travelling with it. This light was similar to a running light on an aircraft, and was reddish in colour. The object and light was then lost from view."

UFO seen to separate in flight

Captain Shea and Inspector William D. Wilson were on patrol along 405 Interstate Highway, Southern California, at 8.54pm the same evening, when they saw:

> ". . . an object making a path through the sky, in a west to east direction – possibly southerly. It was travelling in an almost flat trajectory and its decline formed an angle with the horizon of approximately 20°. It then disappeared behind the mountain directly to the north-east of Point Eagle; total time of visibly one and a half seconds. It was an intense blue-white light, about the size of basketball. As the object traversed the sky, there was a faint trail behind it. Two objects, the size of a baseball, separated from the main body. These objects were of the same colour and intensity of the main body and trailed behind it directly in its path at even intervals of distance, equal to approximately three times the diameter of the main body. The size of the main body was one quarter the size of the moon."

(Source: National Archives)

---

*State Route 4 (SR 4) is a state highway in the US State of California, routed from Interstate 80 in the San Francisco Bay area to State Route 89 in the Sierra Nevada.

USA: Los Alamos. At 8.10pm, on the 30th December 1948, a series of strange sounds was heard by AESS Inspectors Hodges, Krug, and Pierce, employed at Station 340. The matter was reported to Dr. Lincoln La Paz, who asked USAF Major C. Philips to investigate the incident.

According to Hodges and Krug they both heard what they thought was a truck, labouring up the highway, close to their station. When they went outside, the road was empty. Repetitions of this seven seconds duration of sound were measured on a stopwatch and found to occur at eight-and-a-half seconds duration. Ten minutes later, at 8.20pm, the same noise was heard. Once again, the men went out to have a look but saw nothing. At 8.50pm, following the previous departure of Mr Krug, another strange noise was heard but this was determined to be emanating from the sky, as opposed to the road. It appears that this was followed by what was referred to as a *'bogey alarm'* at 8.50pm, i.e. possible aircraft approaching. At Station 390, it was ascertained from conversation with an Inspector Herbert Myers and William Putman that while they had not heard of the three strange noises reported from Station 340, they did hear what sounded like the rumbling of heavy wagons on the highway, just after 9pm. This lasted 45 seconds. At Station 350, statements were taken from Inspector Harry S. Wellborn and Arnold F. Ross. They confirmed having heard a noise in the sky at 8.10pm, which they thought was the engine of a 140HP Cub aircraft. As a result of an apparent aircraft overflying a prohibited *'no fly zone'* location, a complete blackout of the installation was ordered. Despite this, no lights were seen on that aircraft. At 8.50pm, the sound was heard again. This initiated a *'bogey warning'* being transmitted to all stations.

Los Alamos founded during World War II as a secret, centralized facility to coordinate the scientific research of the Manhattan Project, the Allied project to develop the first nuclear weapons. The location was a total secret. Its only mailing address was post office box number 1663, in Santa Fe, New Mexico.

1949

USA: Mississippi, 1st January 1949 – Airport Manager Thomas Rush and his wife, accompanied by pilot Mr T.A. Doolittle (and his wife) were flying from Gulfport to North Jackson Air Park in a Stinson aircraft, at 1,700ft, at 125mph. Two miles east of Jackson, half a mile north of Highway 80E, close to the *Pearl River* swamp and the Knox Glass bottling company, at approximately 5pm, they sighted an object which was 500ft in front of them. Observation of this object, which lasted 10secs, revealed it to be . . .

> *". . . dark blue or black, 60-70-ft in length, 8-10ft in diameter, and of solid construction. The front end tapered to 3ft at the rear. It resembled a large sleeve target, the front opening much larger than the opening of a 60ft sleeve target. It was flying horizontally towards the south-west, at about 200mph; then it turned, picking up tremendous speed, making a slow fluttering action as it departed. I did not see any exhaust effect on clouds, lights, supports or propulsion. Although I didn't hear it, my wife and Mrs Doolittle heard what they describe as a roaring noise as it left the vicinity."*

Mr Jackson then reported the incident to the Commanding Officer at Jackson Air Force Base, and was subsequently interviewed by a representative from Wright Patterson Air Force Base. Copies of the 'Project Sign' report were forwarded as a matter of course to 5th OSI District and Wright Patterson Air Force Base by Major Edward Ford.

USA: Albuquerque, New Mexico, 6th January 1949 – Private First Class, Meredith J. Everett, of the Service Company, 8450th MP Group, Sandia Base (nuclear weapons installation, located on the south-eastern edge of Albuquerque, New Mexico) was on security patrol, guarding a C-97 Aircraft, when he saw a *'bright light'* travelling across the sky, heading south-east to north-west.

> *"It was diamond-shaped, about 2ft long, and much brighter in the centre than the sides. It was flying at an estimated height of 1,500-2,000ft in the air."*

Other members of the same security patrol – Sgt. Richard Welesgoe and Corporal Wilson – on duty close by, did not see the object. **(Source: National Archives)**

USA: Kentucky, 16th January 1949 – At 4.30pm, Mr Paul Brannon of Paris, Kentucky, was driving towards Paris, accompanied by his wife, Irene, and their niece, Elizabeth Fritz, when they sighted a walnut-shaped object emerging from behind cloud, which vanished from view a minute later, leaving a *'tube'* of vapour that was photographed by Irene. Another witness was Harold White, of the same City. He noticed a streak of vapour which was climbing up in the sky for about three minutes. In addition to this, Mr David Isgrig contacted the authorities after seeing a vapour trail building up in the sky, which did not have any source. The matter was reported to Special Agent Arthur Littleton, Wright Patterson Air Force Base, Dayton, Ohio, via telephone call from Captain B. Sneider, Technical Intelligence Division, to Major Farrell, and filed at OSI. **(Source: National Archives)**

USA: 30th January 1949 – Large fall of green fireballs reported over northern New Mexico

USA: Oklahoma, 31st January 1949 – Between 1.15am and 2am, an unidentified flying, lit object, showing a bluish-green pulsating light – about the size of a car wheel – was seen in the vicinity of Orlando Air Force Base and Winter Park, Florida, by five USAF policemen and three police officers. The object was seen heading silently in a south-westerly direction, at an angle of between 20° and 45° above the horizon.

About 1.30am, police patrolman Paul Early of the Winter Park Police, Florida, was out checking property on Fairbanks Avenue, when he saw a blue-green round object approaching skywards, which he first thought was an airplane crashing. Another officer – John W. Huggins – described seeing the same UFO, also while on duty at that time. During the late evening of the same day, a number of people contacted the local radio station in the Oklahoma area, after sighting *'fireballs'* moving across the sky.

It was also established that an object, showing a green exhaust flame, was seen flying over Tampa Municipal Airport, at 1.10am on the 31st January 1949. One of the observers – Patrick B. Lawless employed as a CAA Communicator at Orlando Municipal Airport – went outside, after the object had gone, and became aware of a peculiar odour similar to that of burning garbage.

USA: Los Alamos, New Mexico, 3rd March 1949 – Sergeant D. Rickard, from station 101, Atomic Energy Security (AESS) was facing eastwards and talking to Lt. Buckley, at 1.59am, when a bright green light fell almost straight downwards in the sky, north-east of Station 101.

Other sightings of green objects seen crossing the sky took place on the 8th March 1949, at 6.35pm, by Inspector Patterson, Section 3 of the Protective Force HQ, who was at station 103, Bayo Canyon, when he was startled to see what he took to be an aircraft on fire.

> *"It had a silver or aluminium body inside a flame or glow, resembling the fuselage of a wartime German plane. From behind the wing to just in front of the tail assembly, flames were visible. It appeared to be about half a mile away and its outline – very distinctive."*

At 6.36pm, from station 106, Inspector Leonard Lang sighted what appears to have been the same object just above the horizon, moving South to North, at an estimated speed of 800mph, roughly parallel to the mountains. 13th March 1949 – Private First Class – Robert Espina of the Military Police Battalion, at Sandia Base – was on sentry duty, when he saw a bluish or greenish *'ball of light'* leaving a similar coloured trail, 20° above the horizon, at 9.53pm. A few seconds later it was out of view.

On the 31st March Charles Sradomski, Charles Boles and Pete Hildebrand – employees of the Spang Chalfont Company, situated at Ambridge, Pennsylvania – sighted 20 *'flying saucers'*, golden in colour, moving silently across the sky, northwards. Over the next 20 minutess, two further formations were seen; the first contained 12 objects, the third about eight. (**Source:** *Ambridge Newspaper*, 31st March/National Archives)

USA: 5th April 1949, Salt Lake City – Hundreds of people contacted the authorities, after seeing *'balls of fire'* rushing through the sky over the city. This was accompanied by the sounds of jarring mid-air explosions; the first at 10.30am.

At 9.45am an object, resembling a tracer bullet or tunnel shape, was sighted in the south-west part of the sky by Fred Sears, who owned a flower shop in Logan, Utah. The object then disappeared in a bright orange flash, at a height of about 11,000ft, followed by an explosion, but left a bluish white vapour trail that lasted 15 minutes.

At 10am police patrolman – L.N. Jeppeson, of the Utah State Highway Patrol – also sighted the phenomena, which he described as being two trails of blue-white vapour, one above the other in the sky, at a height he thought was about 11,000-12,000ft. About a minute later he heard and felt a strong explosion, but took it to be blasting in the local area.

A second mid-air explosion was heard at 11.15am. Witness to this phenomena stretched along a 10 mile wide by 100 mile long area, from Salt Lake City in the north, through Ogden, to Logan and the Idaho line. A *'ball'* of red glowing fire was seen high in the sky by Ted Martin – chief controller at Salt Lake Airport – at an estimated height of 20,000ft.

At 1.45pm, Cliff Nielson – a news correspondent with the *Salt Lake City* – reported having sighted six UFOs speeding across the sky, heading north-west.

Triangular UFO seen

At 12.50pm, Frank Petersen was part of a crew clearing branches back from power lines, north-west of Logan, when he saw a triangular-shaped object high in the sky, descending rapidly with the base (seen as 3ft in length, total length 6ft) changing colour as it did so from blue, to purple, orange, yellow, and finally bright green, before disappearing. The angle of descent was 45°. Many people heard an explosion and ran outside in time to see a puff of smoke, or vapour, high in the sky. These incidents were brought to the attention of FBI Agent – Leo J. Nulty – by the police. He then informed Captain Pelham – Burnett District Commander of the 16th District OSI.

USA: 6th April 1949, Denver – At 8pm, a round object was seen heading across the sky over the US weather bureau at Stapleton Airfield, by a number of people, who estimated it to be 15,000 to 25,000ft high. A check with the radar system, then in use, revealed nothing untoward had been tracked, although there appears to be a suggestion that this might have been a weather balloon.

USA: 18th May 1949, New Orleans – A housewife was outside, watering her lawn, when she noticed a silver disc-shaped object, approximately the size of a small aircraft, travelling in an east to north-west direction on the outskirts of the City, in the vicinity of Lake Pontchartrain, two miles away, at an angle of 45° off the horizon.

USA: 21st May 21st 1949 – An F-82 Fighter aircraft was dispatched from Moses Lake Air Force Base, near Hanford, Washington, to intercept a *'flying disc'* that was observed hovering in restricted airspace over Hanford Atomic Power Plant by employees, at an altitude of 17-20,000ft, which was plotted on radar. Before the aircraft could take-off, the object shot off in a southerly direction at a speed greater than the jet fighter.

Conference at Los Alamos – On the 16th February 1949, a top secret conference was held to consider the recent *'wave'* of green fireballs sighted during the 5th December 1949.

Haunted Skies Volume Ten

Page 18

Dr. LaPaz: May I make the observation that if you look in the chapter by........ you'll find that in Alaska where this observation was reported, there are very few times at this season of the year when you can't see an aurora.

Dr. Teller: I have the feeling that it is....either a discovery in physical psychology or.....

Dr. LaPaz: I thought that psychological element would come in here!

Dr. Teller: Here is a slightly irrelevant question - you brought in the flying discs. What is the connection?

Dr. LaPaz: I didn't bring in the flying discs.

Mr. Newburger: I brought in the matter of the flying discs because the Air Force, as I understand, now have classed the flying discs and these fireballs into one category.

Captain Neef: ...The only indication we have is a letter from MAC in Washington Saturday where they indicated the old project Sign is now project Grudge, which includes the phenomena observed in New Mexico. They knew of this meeting and were going to send a representative.

Dr. LaPaz: I just asked Mr. Hoyt a moment ago how he would compare the brillance of this object with that of an aircraft flare. He said they were of comparable magnitude. I think that was definitely ruled out...

Dr. Teller: I understood that a reasonable explanation of the flying discs - and I suppose that it is generally known - is that they are meteorological balloons.... I understand that in quite a number of cases there have been very close directions established....I must say that from what you have said it certainly sounds like everything else but meteors. The thing that impresses me is your evidence of the horizontal flight. Meteors do not usually come in like that...

(mumbled talk between Drs. Bradbury and Teller)

Captain Neef:.....Change of direction such that we haven't been able to follow it up yet. One of our men was returning Sunday night when our tower operator saw this object to the Southwest from Kirtland Field and.....Arizona reported it was Southeast from them. From the Kirtland tower it was a bronze color. The time checks, but from....Arizona it was green until it turned straight down and veered going.....

Dr. LaPaz: Dr. Teller, may I mention this one other instance that shows maybe why I have more concern than is merited by the evidence I am able to present. I deal with Vic Regener and I know that the physicist doesn't like to work with anything that can't be photographed. I share that view but a meteorist is not available sometimes to photograph shooting stars, even the conventional type. During the war I was acting as Director of the Ohio Section of the American Meteor Society and all at once we began to get reports of large numbers of stationary fireballs; not moving. The burst

Conference on AERIAL PHENOMENA

Page 20

Dr. LaPaz: It should be possible ...The conventional meteor cannot be photographed at the present time. The so-called meteorschmitts that Harvard College is now having produced at very great expense, they expect to go down to the 4th and possibly fainter. With one of those, a bright green fireball might be photographed, but they are not available...

Mr. Newburger: Does anybody know if there were any experiments carried out in Europe, prior to the war when our last best information came from over there, along this line?

Dr. LaPaz: Not to my knowledge. I raised that question with Dr. Kaplan and he gave me some rather surprising information. Dr. Kaplan had attended the IAU meetings in Syria ? and the Russians had a large representation there. Sufficiently large, as a matter of fact, to beat down the proposal that the IAU appoint an international committee to investigate the so-called.... meteorite crater produced in the fall of 1947, February 12. On the contrary, at the Oswald, I think it was, conference of the International Geophysical Union, none of the Russian geophysicists were present. Kaplan's interpretation was that they feel so far ahead of us that they didn't think they could learn anything, and they were taking the precaution that no leak occurred.

Mr. Newburger: Were the Germans experimenting in any phase that was possibly connected with it?

Dr. LaPaz: Well, they had the so-called stations in space ...might have some attachment to it.

Comdr. Mandelkorn: You don't have any record of experiments.

Dr. LaPaz: No, no knowledge of experiments. I have the belief that no country in the world has there been meteoritics developed as it has in Russia in recent years. Recently, the Academy of Science of the USRR has been issuing a so-called meteoritic, an extradorinary publication - very little work of the caliber being done by the Russians has been conducted in the United States. Apparently, there it has big support; here, it is an individual matter. Until we had some military interest in meteoritics, we were never able to found even an institute in meteoritics in the United States. The one in New Mexico is an outgrowth of application of meteoritics to determine, say, ballistic coefficien for shells of unconventional design like the proximity fuze shell with the radi in its nose, and that sort of thing. That's where we got a start. Apparently, the Russians got that earlier and have full-fledged state support.

Dr. Holloway: How much interest would the military have if they found out these things were landing all over the country, Canada, Hawaii, etc.?... Have you contacted people in the East?

Dr. LaPaz: Olivia, C.C. Olivia, President of the AMERICAN Meteor Society, King, Leonard, Pruitt, Kaplan, etc. Most of them have been observing; Kaplan, I imagine, has not, because he is now preoccupied with laboratory

Attending this were Mr N.E. Bradbury, Mr Marshall Holloway, Mr Fred Reines, Mr John Manley, Mr Edward Teller, Mr Elmo Morgan, Mr Sidney Neuberger (security). The 4th Army were represented by Major William A. Godsoe, 4th Army Intelligence Liaison Officer, and Major Wynn. USAF Captain Neef, 17th District OSI. Dr. Lincoln LaPaz, Director of the Institute of Meteorites, and associated with the Operations and Analysis Division, USA, employed on secret or top secret USAF contracts, from the University of New Mexico, was also invited.

Others included Captain Groseclose, Technical Intelligence Adviser, Lt. Smith, of the same department, and Sandia Base Commander, Richard Mandlekorn. [This matter was documented in a 25 page (approx) file, declassified some years ago. It makes fascinating reading but we have decided not to duplicate the whole content, which includes considerable geometric technical information about the velocities and trajectories of meteorites, but to pinpoint the gist of that meeting].

Captain Neef opened the meeting and told the audience that the investigation into the matter was a classified military secret under the name Project Grudge and that since 5th December 1948, there had been more than ten incidents of green fireballs brought to the attention of the authorities, and some 20 more presenting minor deviations which should be considered as connected with the phenomena, separate from a number of normal shooting stars and meteors seen.

He also mentioned there was no direct association that could be made between the green fireball incidents and *'flying discs'*. Whatever these things were, they were judged important enough to raise concern and arrange a high-powered conference to discuss the matter. Statistics were then given by Dr. La Paz, who pointed out that the phenomena could not be explained away as normal meteorite falls, as he had himself witnessed one of the objects at the 'Starvation Peak' on the 5th December 1948. Dr .La Paz (page 8) refers to the 'Town meteorite' that fell on 18th February 1948, which appears to have attracted some speculation it was a Russian bomb, although this was quashed when meteorites were recovered from the scene. He then refers to the daylight occurrence of bright white objects seen in Memphis, Tennessee, during May 1948 (page 11).

Dr. La Paz was asked what he believes these *'things'* are. He said:

> "The only explanation is the one I gave in the beginning and had my ears promptly boxed for. I think these are defensive manoeuvres of some higher US Command and they are practising in the neighbour of the regions that are going to defend, so naturally your localization of light near the atomic bomb installations, but boy, am I scolded for that.
>
> Even Dr. Kaplan [physicist] of the FAD tells me no, no, the FAD would all know about it and they don't have any facts."

Mr Teller then discussed the velocity and mass of these objects as they passed through the sky and expressed an opinion they were not physical objects, as no shock waves or loud noises had been heard as one would have expected with the fall of a rocket or missile.

One of the strangest comments made by Dr. LaPaz is shown (opposite), as well as a reference to the flying discs!

Development of the Atomic Bomb

The Los Alamos area, sprawled over several north central New Mexico mesas in a region known as the Pajarito Plateau, is historically characterized by remoteness. Many undisturbed prehistoric Pueblo Indian ruins still dot the region. After the arrival of Europeans in the mid 1700s, the Plateau slumbered for some 150 years as a secluded grazing and timbering area. The few homesteads and ranches that arrived in the late 1800s and early 1900s were mostly seasonal. In 1917, an elite preparatory school for boys took over the year-around.

Haunted Skies Volume Ten

Los Los Alamos Ranch School occupied a large, central portion of the Plateau and was operated until 1943, when outside events forced it, along with a number of homesteads, to vacate the premises. The Manhattan Project dramatically transformed the Los Alamos area into a bustling scientific and military complex with several outreach sites, much of it fenced and all of it guarded by U.S. Army patrols on horseback or in jeeps. Staffed by many of the world's top scientists, the Los Alamos weapons laboratory designed, built, and tested at White Sands, New Mexico, the world's first atomic bomb. (**Source: Los Alamos County WWW 2014**)

USA: New Mexico, 8th March 1949 – At 6.35pm, a luminous green object was seen in the sky towards the south-east direction, from Kirtland Air Force Base tower – also reported from Los Alamos as greenish white, with a white flaming tail, moving in a floating or 'lazy' manner through the sky from cloud layer ... gone in a few seconds.

1950

USA: 31st March 1950 – Airline Pilots Adams and Anderson were flying a DC-3, 130 miles from Memphis to Little Rock, when a huge glowing saucer-shaped object was seen.

> *"It had a central cupola, showing bright blue and white flashing lights, with what looked like eight to ten portholes or vents on the body."*

USA: 27th April 1950 – Pilot Captain Adickes was en route to Chicago, at 200mph, when he saw an object resembling:

> *"... a giant red wheel – like stainless steel – flying on edge, like a tyre through the sky. It dropped downwards over South Bend and that was the last I saw of it."*

Great Britain: 14th August 1950 – A spectacular sighting took place at RAF Farnborough, according to Stanley Hubbard then a Flt. Lt. Test Pilot with the RAF.

> *"It was a warm day and unusually quiet for a base that normally resonated with the sound of general noise and aircraft engines. As I trudged across the runway, heading towards the Mess where I was billeted, I became aware of a strange sound coming from somewhere behind me. I stopped and turned around, curious as to the source of this noise, and was very much taken aback to see an object, looking like a 'flying sports discus', rocking from side-to-side in a regular rhythm of movement, (approximately 20-25 degrees either side), heading across the sky at about a thousand feet off the ground. I watched as it moved over, noting that the exterior of the craft appeared to be light grey in colour – a bit like mother-of-pearl – blurred, rather than sharply defined. As it passed overhead, it allowed me to determine it was obviously reflecting light because, as it rocked, it reminded me of a pan lid, rotating segments of light. Around the edges were what looked like tiny crackling, sparkling lights, accompanied by a powerful smell of ozone. The next thing I was aware of was the arrival of the female dispatcher from the radio shack nearby. She was hysterical. She screamed out my name and said, 'Did you see that horrible thing go over?' I walked over to the Wing Commander's, office, and explained what l had seen. He made a telephone call to the Air Ministry, who interviewed me, a few hours later, following which I was advised not to make any enquiries about the incident, or discuss it with anybody else."*

Great Britain: 5th September 1950 – Incredibly, Stan Hubbard was to find himself once again sighting something unusual over Farnborough. On this occasion he was outside with a group of men, watching the sky near the Flying Control building, waiting for the return of a Hawker P108 out on test flight, when he noticed an object to the south.

Flt. Lt. Stanley Hubbard, Test Pilot with the RAF.

A Bristol Brabazon photographed at Farnbrough air show in the 1950s

"I grabbed hold of the nearest person, my civilian boss – Jack Spencer, and asked him what he thought the object was. When he saw it he shouted 'Oh, my God' and called for someone to fetch a camera. Nobody moved. He told someone to fetch a pair of binoculars and 'Taffy' Evans came up with a pair – by which time a number of people were gathered watching the performance of this unidentified object as it took off from what appeared to be an unstable hovering position to incredible speeds across the sky, in great angular steps of movement, ranging between 180-330°."

Once again, after bringing the incident to the attention of the Wing Commander, Stan was interviewed by a group of men from the Scientific Intelligence Department.

"They were very, very, specific that I was not to discuss the matter with anybody, because it was highly classified."

Over fifty years later, a search of declassified documents at the Public Records Office found the report into the incidents, submitted by Scientific Intelligence. A copy was obtained and shown to Mr Hubbard, who was shocked to discover that both incidents had been explained away as either hallucinations, or misidentifications.

1951

Australia: 7th January 1951 – At 6am a steel blue coloured object, as big as a full moon and completely silent, was seen to rise up through the sky into clouds over Bowral, New South Wales.

Australia: 26th October 1951 – Train crew sight UFO

At 4am the driver of a transcontinental trail on the east-west railway line sighted an object, which illuminated the countryside like the full moon.

"It came close to the train, appeared to land in the desert and then took off again, before disappearing from view."

(Source: MUFOB, Volume 6, No. 2/*Uknown Melbourne newspaper*/*Flying Saucers On The Attack*, Harold T. Wilkins)

Was there any connection with an earlier report, made in September 1951, when it was claimed a group of Unmatjera aborigines sighted a shiny circular object land near a similar craft, about 40ft in diameter? They alleged that several minutes later a dwarf dressed in a shiny suit, with a round shiny head, emerged and entered the other. Both then took off, making a buzzing noise.

(Source: Frank Edwards, *Flying Saucers Serious Business*)

1952

Australia: 3rd May 1952 – A gleaming silver disc, with a dome, was seen flying through the sky over Melbourne, Victoria, leaving a blue-white vapour trail. Also on this date was a report of a wingless cigar-shaped object with blazing lights, seen over Sydney, and a report by an airline pilot, and many others, of a wingless cigar-shaped object, about the size of an airliner, showing a pair of blazing lights at the end, seen rushing across the sky at 6am. Others described it as resembling a submarine lit-up like an ocean-going liner.

A 16-page file, which includes a clipping from the *Daily Telegraph*, dated 6th May 1952, described three servicemen's reports of a *'flying saucer'* seen over Sydney on the 3rd May 1952. Their reports were given to Dr. J.H. Piddington – Principal research officer of the radio physics Division of the CSIRO – rather than to the

RAAF. Later documents on the file indicate that the object, a *'ball of light'*, seen at about 6.10am, was a meteor-like object, which appeared in the south-eastern sky and travelled due east, as seen from Sydney.

The object was also seen from widely separated places such as Sydney, Canberra, Wollongong and Melbourne. A detailed report was prepared by Flt. Lt. W.J. Sadler and Squadron Leader M.C. Murray. This 6-page document gathered observations, and analysed them. Their conclusion was that ...

> *"The light was probably caused by a meteor or similar body".*

(Source: Michael Hervey, *UFOs over the Southern Hemisphere*/Keith Basterfield, WWW, 2014)

An explanation which of course might have satisfied many at the time but with the advantage of hindsight, and the opportunity of being able to examine the accumulated weight of evidence relating to reported UFO activity, not only in the UK but in the Southern Hemisphere, it is clear this is not the case!

Australia: 6th May 1952 – At 6am, a large cigar-shaped object, some 30 meters in length and five or six meters wide, showing a bright red nose and portholes along the sides, was seen approximately 400ft away in New South Wales, by tractor driver – Mr Geppart. It then shot away at speed. (**Source:** *UFOs over the Southern Hemisphere*, **Michael Hervey)**

Australia: 11th May 1952 – A silvery *'ball'*, surrounded by a halo, was seen in the sky over Parramatta, New South Wales; suddenly it vanished from view. The local meteorological officer was unable to offer any explanation.

USA: Clarksburg, West Virginia, 21st May 1952 – UFO landing?

Harold T. Wilkins wrote of the following account that was passed on to him by Gray Barker – editor of the *Saucerian Bulletin* – from teenager Rose Murphy. It appears genuine. Unfortunately, we are unable to re-investigate matters like this (and so many others), as we are now talking about a period of 60 years ago.

On this evening, Rose and her friends – Hank and Ellen – were out horse riding, along a narrow path between a dry creek bed and a dense wood, when Hank's horse reared up and began acting in a skittish manner.

> *"My horse then reared up and pawed the air. I looked and saw a huge light blue saucer-shaped object descending less than 200ft from the ground. The horses seemed frozen in their tracks. The thing landed and hit a tree with a resounding crash, illuminating the surrounding countryside with an eerie blue light. The noise seemed to break the spell over us and I heard Ellen, who was behind me, turn her horse. I didn't wait. We rode back home, not even stopping to open Lingenfelters gate, but jumping over it."*

Next day, they went back on foot to the area and found many trees down – some broken in half, neatly. In the sand was found an enormous brown indentation in the creek bed. There was no circus or carnival in the area. The location was more than 10 miles from Peoria Airport.

Somewhat as a footnote to this peculiar incident was a second letter, sent on 10th August 1954, by Miss Murphy, who had this to say:

> *"I am real scared. I can't help thinking that what since happened came from the 'saucer'. My mare's last year's filly – three months old – has died. We thought, at first, that she had lockjaw. She seemed to respond to treatment – then on July 1st she just literally dropped dead. I didn't think anything of it at the time, but today I had a letter from Frank; both Lous and Coaly's foals were born dead. The foals were not deformed. They looked perfectly healthy, average size, weight, etc. Here is what scared me: Lady has been bred eight times this year. When she came on heat again yesterday, I took her over to the veterinary. They gave her smear and other tests, which proved that my mare, Lady, is now sterile.*

Haunted Skies Volume Ten

> *The vets can find no reason for it. A seven year mare, perfectly healthy, just goes sterile! You will probably think 'I'm off my rocker' for supposing that the 'saucer' had anything to do with this. Well, if you do, I won't go mad.*
>
> *Sincerely,*
> *Rose Murphy."*

Australia: 7th June 1952 – At 7.30am, three RAAF employees, en route to their base in New South Wales, sighted a cigar-shaped UFO, showing several *'portholes'* visible along one side, spilling out orange light and a *'tail'* that had what were described as several raised flukes. Its *'nose'* was sharply pointed with a fore cabin, emitting an almost dazzling light and flying at a height of 2-3,000ft. (**Source: Michael Hervey, *UFOs over the Southern Hemisphere*)**

On the same day, (7th June 1952) at 1pm, two witnesses reported a *'flying saucer'* appearing above Meknes, Morocco. One of them said he saw a bright *'light'* in the sky, moving at lightning speed, and contrasted its speed to some T-33 planes, flying near the Meknes Base, which seemed very slow by comparison. Was there a connection with a sighting made by the crew of a B52 Bomber, at 11.18am, who were over Albuquerque, New Mexico, at 11,500ft, when they sighted a rectangular aluminium object, about 6ft x 4ft in size, flying 250-300ft below them? (**Source: (USA) Francis Ridge, NICAP**)

Australia: 22nd July 1952 – At 8pm, Albert Thomas – a Sydney railway security guard – was leaving his house, when he saw an object looking like a hot coal, with smoke around it, passing through the sky.

> *"It was travelling at about 400mph. My arms started to tingle, like an electric shock. It then changed to what looked like a hurricane lamp, which someone had thrown into the air. My revolver under my belt was vibrating."*

(Source: 1952, Sighting Archive http://www.auforn.com/1952.htm)

(OPEN ABOVE CLIPPING)

New Zealand – Summer 1952 – UFO sighted over airfield

Another witness to strange phenomena was Bruce Cathie – a Fokker Friendship Captain of New Zealand's National Airways Corporation – whom we spoke to, some years ago. He launched his own investigation, after witnessing something unusual in the summer of 1952.

Bruce:

"I was driving a friend to the local *aero club at Mangere, Auckland, when she pointed up into the sky and asked me, 'what is that object?' I looked and saw a glaring light, hanging motionless in the sky over Manukau Harbour. I told her it was Venus, although I knew from its altitude this could not be the case.

When we arrived at the club, I went in and asked five members to come outside and see it, which they did.

There were gasps of surprise and disbelief. We rushed down to the main gate of the airfield and scrutinised the object, no more than 2,000ft high in the sky. We saw a smaller red light several hundred feet to one side and on the same level as the larger white object. This action went on for ten minutes – then both lights began a slow descent before moving horizontally southwards, perhaps a quarter of a mile. Five minutes later the red light disappeared and the white light increased in brilliance, before shooting upwards into the clear sky – then gone from view."

Later that evening, Bruce rang the duty officer at Whenuapai Air Force Control Tower and explained what he and the others had seen. The officer confirmed he had received other reports before ours, and was unable to offer any explanation. Bruce, who had

Air Force Studying New 'Saucer' Report

TRIBUNE, Scranton, PA - July 17, 1952

WASHINGTON (AP) — The Air Force followed a familiar routine today—sending through channels its latest flying saucer report.

Two airline pilots, First Officers W. B. Nash and W. H. Fortenberry, reported in Miami eight objects 100 feet in diameter glowing like red hot coals and traveling 1,000 miles an hour passed directly beneath their plane over Chesapeake Bay on Tuesday night.

The Air Force said it has made a preliminary report to the Air Force's technical intelligence center at Dayton, Ohio, and that a complete written report is expected to follow.

Until this report is made, the Air Force added, no evaluation can be made of this reported sighting.

Capt. E. J. Ruppelt of the air technical intelligence center at Wright-Patterson Air Force Base near Dayton, said today 60 reports of flying saucers from throughout the nation have been channeled to the base.

Roy T. Ellis of Dayton reported seeing an object almost like an ice cream cone with an elliptical dark object in the center where the ice cream would rest in the cone.

Ellis, an amateur astronomer, said he was looking for comets Sunday night when he saw the object. He said it moved "very deliberately."

Col. Richard H. Magee, Dayton Civil Defense director, said "There is something flying around our skies and I wish I knew what it was."

Asked if flying saucers could be the reason for the "skywatch operation," Colonel Magee said no specific reason had been given, "but that could be the answer."

---

*Mangere Aerodrome was the original home of the Auckland Aero Club. It is now the site of Auckland Airport.

previously felt that reports of UFOs could be explained away as hallucinations or misidentified aircraft, like so many others [including the authors of this book], decided to find out for himself what lay behind reports of UFO sightings. Little did he know that this was to be the first of five UFO sightings!

USA: UFO crash-lands at Flatwoods, West Virginia – 12th September 1952

At 7.15pm, two brothers – Edward (13) and Fred May (12) – and their friend – Tommy Hyde (10) – reported having seen a bright object cross the sky, which then appeared to come to rest on land belonging to local farmer G. Bailey Fisher. The boys then made their way to the home of Mrs Kathleen May, where they reported seeing a UFO crash-land in the hills. From there Mrs May, accompanied by three boys – local children Neil Nunley (14), Ronnie Shaver (10), and 17-year-old West Virginia National Guardsman Eugene 'Gene' Lemon – travelled to the Fisher farm in an effort to locate whatever it was that the boys had seen. Lemon's dog ran ahead, out of sight, and suddenly began barking; moments later it ran back to the group with its tail between its legs. After travelling about a quarter of a mile (400m), the group reached the top of a hill, where they reportedly saw a large pulsating *'ball of fire'*, about 50ft (15m) to their right. They also detected a pungent *'mist'* that made their eyes and noses burn.

Creature seen

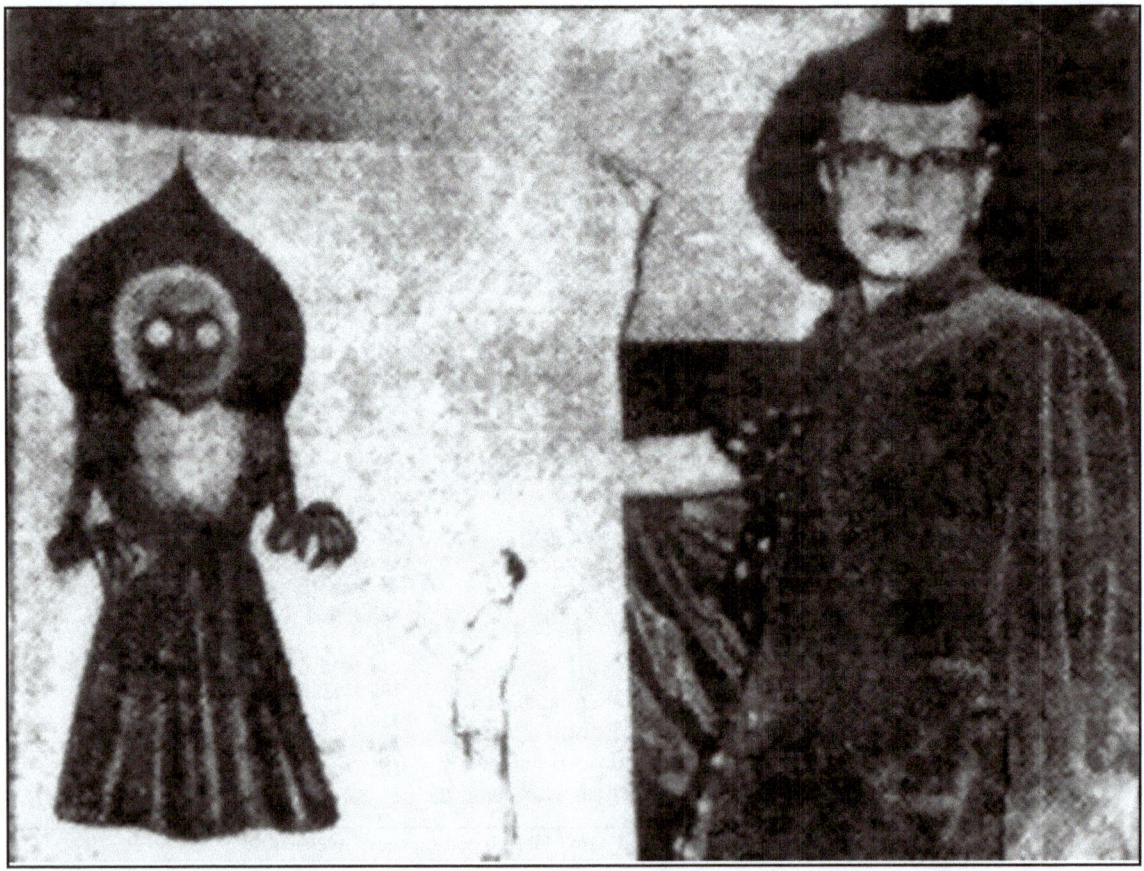

Braxton Co. Residents Faint, Become Ill After Run-In With Weird 10-Foot Monster

Seven Braxton County residents Saturday reporting being a 10-foot Frankenstein-like monster in the hills above Flatwood.

They said they saw the monster Friday night when they climbed a wooded hill to investigate reports that a flying saucer had landed.

Mrs. Kathlyn May, Flatwood, said she and six boys, including a 17-year-old member of the National Guard, started to search for a bright object which her two small sons said they had seen come down.

However, State Police laughed the reports off as hysteria. They said the so-called monster had grown from seven to 17 feet in 24 hours.

The National Guard member, Gene Lemon, was leading the group when he said he saw what appeared to be a pair of bright eyes in a tree. At first he thought it was an opossum or a raccoon but when he shone his flashlight on it, he said, he saw a 10-foot monster with a blood-red face and a green body that seemed to glow.

Mrs. May said Lemon let out a terrified scream and fell over backwards. She said the monster started toward them with a bounding motion.

All of the party agreed that there was an overpowering smell that burned the nostrils and made them sick. Several of the party fainted and vomited for several hours after returning to town.

A. Lee Stewart, co-publisher of the Braxton County Democrat, said he and several men armed with shotguns returned with Lemon about a half-hour to an hour later and reported a sickening odor still present. He said there were also slight heat waves in the air.

"Those people were the most scared people I've ever seen," Stewart said. "People don't make up that kind of story that quickly."

Both Mrs. May and Lemon described the thing as having the shape of a man, blood-red face, bright green body, protruding eyes and hand extended forward and appeared to give off an eerie light. They said it had a black shield affair in the shape of an ace of spades behind it and wore what looked like a pleated metallic shirt.

"It looked worse than Frankenstein," Mrs. May said.

Lemon then noticed two small lights to the left of the object, underneath a nearby oak tree, and directed his flashlight towards them, revealing a *'creature'* described as, at least 10 feet tall showing a red face which appeared to glow from within, and a green body. It had bulging, non-human eyes. Behind was what looked like a large heart shaped cowling. The *'creature's'* body was described as being man-shaped and clad in a dark pleated skirt; later described as being green. Some accounts record it had no visible arms, while others describe it as having short, stubby arms; ending in long, claw-like fingers, which protruded from the front of its body.

It was reported to have emitted a shrill, hissing noise, before gliding towards them, changing direction and then heading off towards the red light. At this point the group fled in panic. Mrs Eugene Lemon reported that, at the approximate time of the crash, her house had been violently shaken and her radio had cut out for 45 minutes.

Upon returning home, Mrs May contacted local Sheriff – Robert Carr – and Mr A. Lee Stewart – co-owner of the *Braxton Democrat*, a local newspaper. Stewart conducted a number of interviews and returned to the site with Lemon later that night, where he reported that *"there was a sickening, burnt, metallic odour still prevailing"*. Sheriff Carr and his deputy – Burnell Long – searched the area separately, but reported finding no trace of the encounter. Enquiries made into the event by William and Donna Smith, from Civilian Saucer Investigation revealed another report by a mother and her 21-year-old daughter, who claimed to have encountered a creature with the same appearance and odour, a week prior to the 12th September incident; the encounter reportedly affected the daughter so badly that she was confined to Clarksburg Hospital for three weeks. Another sighting came from a director of the local Board of Education, who claimed to have seen a *'flying saucer'* taking off at 6.30am on 13th September.

After-effects of encounter

After encountering the *'creature'*, several members of the 12th September group reported being overcome with similar symptoms that persisted for some time, which they attributed to having been exposed to the 'mist' emitted by the creature. The symptoms included irritation of the nose and swelling of the throat. Lemon

Haunted Skies Volume Ten

suffered from vomiting and convulsions throughout the night, and had difficulties with his throat for several weeks afterwards. Over the years this incident has been explained away as being a meteor, a pulsating red light of an aircraft, and the creature or alien as being an owl! **(Source: William and Donna Smith, Civilian Saucer Investigation)**

Great Britain: 17th September 1952 – 'Flying Saucer' seen by RAF Pilots over RAF Topcliffe (See Volume 1, *Haunted Skies*)

Australia: 8th October 1952 – Woomera radar operator – Mr Turner – was tracking an aircraft on the radar scope, at 1.45pm, on what was a fine day, with high cloud at 25,000ft, and a North wind moving at 25-30mph, when he acquired a target similar to that of a large aircraft. From 2.05pm and 2.29pm, the invisible target, was plotted moving at heights of between 1,500ft and 5,600ft, was tracked to within a mile of the base. *"At times, during the movement of the target, smaller targets seemed to detach themselves from the larger one and drift away."* The official explanation was a possible neutron cloud. **(Source: National Archives of Australia, File D174)**

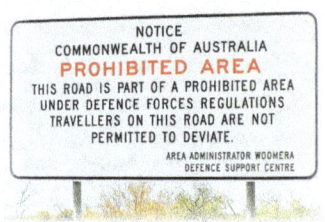

Australia: 12th October 1952 – A red and blue illuminated object, letting out a terrible whistling noise, was seen over Melbourne on this date, by Mr J. McKay and J. Robinson.

Australia: 18th October 1952 – Adelaide journalist – Keith Hooper – was on his way home, at 9.45pm, when he saw:

> *". . . a greenish-white iridescent, cigar-shaped, object about the size of a Boeing 707, about ten miles away moving from left to right across my front, heading in a south-east to north-west direction."*

Keith stood still and watched the object which climbed steeply upwards and vanished from sight at incredible speed.

Great Britain: 21st October 1952 – RAF Pilots scrambled at RAF Little Rissington and sight three UFOs. (See Volume 1, *Haunted Skies*)

New Zealand: 6th December 1952 – At 9.45pm a green ovoid object, making a faint hissing noise, was seen in the sky moving south-east, over Palmerston North, and was joined by two other objects – one green, the other blue. During the same evening people living in Christchurch, Kyeburn, Invercargill, and Waipahi, sighted a *'blue disc'*, making a hissing noise, at a speed estimated to be 600mph. Another report told of a bright green luminous sphere, showing a brand of brighter dots, moving southwards over Plimmerton, making a faint hissing noise. [Ron West tells of a sighting in Invercargill, in 1910, when a major, vicar and police officer, sighted a cigar-shaped object hovering in the sky, 100ft off the ground. A *'man'* was alleged to have shouted in an unknown language at the party below].

New Zealand: 16th December 1952 – A luminous blue object, with a light spot in the centre, was seen moving erratically across the sky, at 8pm, over Gisbourne.

1953

New Zealand: 1st January 1953 – At 7pm a bright circular object was seen over Napier, which faded to a reddish glow before disappearing.

Great Britain, January 1953 – UFO over RAF Marham

Mrs M.L. Martin, wife of a RAF serviceman stationed at RAF Marham, Norfolk, was looking out of the window, at 3pm, when she saw what she took to be a jet aircraft crossing the clear blue sky, at high altitude. To her horror, both *'wings'* left the fuselage but instead of crashing to earth, they rushed across the sky, one behind the other, before coming to a halt, glinting as they caught the sun before suddenly rising upwards and disappearing out of sight.

"When I later discussed what I had seen with my husband, he told me all personnel at the airbase had been warned not to breathe a word about a UFO which had, apparently, been seen by other airmen."

(Source: *Warnings from Flying Friends*, Arthur Shuttlewood)

Australia: 3rd January 1953 – A bright yellow object, with a luminous halo that kept disappearing and reappearing, was seen in the sky over Geelong, Victoria, at 10pm.

New Zealand: 6th January 1953 – At 9.28pm, over Paporoa, a bright orange light was seen near the horizon, heading south-east to north-west. One minute later, an object – slightly smaller than a full moon – was seen over Whangarei.

Another report at 9.30pm, made from a boat on the river Ngunguru, told of an object showing what appeared to be an illuminated porthole, and from its *'tail'* emitting a rocket-like flame, which was seen to accelerate to a higher altitude and then make a 'U'-turn, before disappearing from view. Also at this time

Whangarei, New Zealand

was a report from Henderson Valley, Auckland, of the sighting of a luminous cigar-shaped object, showing an orange flame at the rear; at 10.10pm two *'discs'* – a blue one, with a green one above – were seen in the sky over Karori.

New Zealand: 8th January 1953 – At 10.20pm a triangular reddish glow was seen over Mosgiel, which was seen to fade and then reappear performing a rising and falling motion. This was accompanied by a small white light; ten minutes later, it was gone from view. [**Authors**: the presence of a smaller light is a familiar background to reported UFO sightings, and may well form part of the larger object.]

New Zealand: 9th January 1953 – At 9pm a dull *'disc'* of light yellow-orange in colour, almost circular, with a slight flattening over a third of its circumference, was seen in the sky over Christchurch.

At 9.27pm an object was sighted from an aircraft, described as a brilliant orange light, with a red tail, moving in a west to east direction.

New Zealand: 14th January 1953 – A blue light, showing a gold red rim, was sighted heading south-west, over Otago, at an estimated speed of 500mph.

New Zealand: 18th January 1953 – At 10.20pm a bright yellow object, resembling a *'stingray'*, was seen over Sockburn.

Australia: 21st January 1953 – Two men in a truck at Graceville sighted a bright light, accompanied by a smaller blue/red one. As they approached the object, it shot into the sky and circled before landing again. It appears the men decided not to get involved any further and drove away from the scene.

(Source: *UFOs over the Southern Hemisphere*, Michael Verney)

Australia: 22nd February 1953 – A retired Australian Air Force officer, and his wife, were sat outside on their verandah, at about noon, when they were astonished to see the appearance of two rotating *'discs'* in the sky, a short distance apart. The objects then dropped downwards, before ascending and vanishing from view. The man ran into the house for his binoculars, and was in time to see the objects almost meet up with each other once again, before moving out of sight.

New Zealand: 16th April 1953 – A strange thread-like substance was reported seen falling from the sky, over Ongaonga, near Hastings. Was this 'Angel hair' or cobwebs? ('Ongaonga' is a Maori word meaning distaste, dislike or repulsive and may refer to Ongaonga (town), a township in New Zealand.)

Australia: 17th May 1953 – Captain B.L. Jones, who was piloting a DC-3, reported having sighted a brightly

Haunted Skies Volume Ten

illuminated glass domed object, beaming a light down onto the aerodrome below. The UFO then moved around the aircraft and crossed its path, before moving away and out of sight.

Australia: 18th May 1953 – An object, the size of a pinhead to the naked eye, was seen in the sky over Rockhampton Airport, Queensland. Through binoculars, a silver crescent-shaped object was seen to change course several times.

Great Britain: 21st April 1953 – At 7.45pm, a brightly-lit object was seen hovering motionless in the sky, over Norwich, by spectators at a football match, before being lost from view, at 8.15pm. It is likely this was the same UFO sighted by a member of the Royal Observer Corps at 8.15pm, north of Lowestoft. Through the lens of a telescope, he saw *'what looked like a plastic lighter refuel capsule, with a sharp pointed end'*, move towards the south-west before turning north-east and disappearing from view, 30 minutes later. (**Source:** *Evening News, Norwich, 25.4.53*)

Australia: 23rd May 1953 – A long silver rocket like object, about 100ft in length, was seen in the sky over the Surrey Hills, moving at an estimated speed of 500mph.

New Zealand: 27th May 1953 – At 4am an unusual light was seen moving northwards, over Otumoetai, at an estimated height of 30,000ft.

New Zealand: 29th May 1953 – an unusual light seen over Tauranga, at an estimated height of 10,000ft. A similar object, blue in colour, was seen over Palmerstone North during the same night. Other reports included the sighting of a fiery object that shot across the sky over Waikato.

New Zealand: 2nd June 1953 – At 6.30pm, a 70ft long object, 3ft in depth, was seen over Hastings, at a height of some 8,000ft. Also on the same date, but many thousands of miles away in Great Britain, Dawn Gould – who had served in the Women's Land Army during the Second World War, and with the Civil Defence – described what she saw at midday on 2nd June 1953:

> "I was living at Melplash Court, Bridport, Dorset, and pegging the washing on the line, when I happened to look upwards and see five saucer-shaped objects, like white circles, high up in the blue sky, 'line abreast,' – just hovering there. Before I could shout out or fetch someone, they changed to line astern and moved forwards and upwards, until out of sight. I've never forgotten what I saw."

(Source: Personal interview, 2006)

Australia: 21st June 1953 – UFO sighted over Dunoon

Mr Sidney Callow and his wife, from Dunoon, were outside on the 21st June 1953, when they noticed:

> "... an object the size of a football, appear from out of the clouds. [Cloud ceiling 5-6,000ft] It was spinning in a clockwise direction and stood on edge before going straight upwards into the sky, leaving a black trail behind it."

(Source: *Glasgow Herald/Glasgow Evening Times*)

Australia: 28th July 1953 – 'Flying Saucer' at Stowport

At 5pm, a Stowport mother – Mrs J.B. Hulton – whose husband was Burnie, Manager at Trans-Australian Airways, reported that after being called outside by her 13-year-old son, Anthony, she and her three young children sighted a dark grey object moving inland from the Bass Strait area, apparently diving downwards, from high altitude, at great speed.

"It was spinning slowly and when it reached a height of 800ft it opened out like a big parachute; it was some distance away and seemed to float among the trees, drifting westwards over Round Hill. At times, when partly obscured by hills, it looked like a half moon. It eventually resumed its top shape and disappeared from sight. It was unlike any aeroplane I had ever seen and left me with a queer feeling."

The Mercury newspaper, Hobart, Tasmania (29.7.54), which published the sighting, told of an incident that had taken place two months previously, when John Howarth of Sulphur Creek, had been awoken, just before dawn, by a luminous spinning object seen hovering outside his window, moving back and forth in the sky, about the size of an aeroplane.

Australia: 9th October 1953 – A resident of Caulfield Victoria, Melbourne, came across a long silken thread, hanging down from a telegraph pole at 3.50pm. When touched, it dissolved. Was it a long cobweb or Angel hair? Analysis conducted on these threads, which had a tendency to disintegrate on handling, revealed they consisted of nylon like amorphous mass with traces of Mg, Ca, and Si. The material some which was stored in air tight containers was found to have shrunk from a metre to 2.5centimeters without leaving a residue.

Great Britain: 9th October 1953 – A saucer-shaped object was seen stationary in the sky, over the English Channel, by the crew of a BEA Airliner en route from London to Paris. The incident which was later brought to the attention of the media, involved Captain Peter Fletcher and his first officer – Mr R.L. Lemon. In an interview held with a reporter from the *Sunday Dispatch* newspaper, Captain Fletcher said:

"Our Elizabethan flight left London Airport at 9am. There was a certain amount of low cloud and fog but when we climbed, we found ourselves in an absolutely clear atmosphere with a clear blue sky. It was one of those rare days when you could see an aircraft 50-60 miles away. It was so clear that when we were over the English Channel, we could see aircraft over the Airport at Orly, 100 miles

away. I reported our position to Control when we were over Seaford, Sussex, on a course of 150°, who informed me of a Constellation aircraft overtaking on our left. I watched as it reached its cruising altitude of some 13,500ft, immediately ahead of me and above. At this stage the relative position of my aircraft to the Constellation and the sun was such that the sun's light was reflected to me from the top surface of the aircraft's wing, making the lit surface very easy to see, while a darker shadow etched in the lower part. It was then that I noticed the 'flying saucer'. It was apparently another aircraft above the Constellation and a little away to the left and it seemed to have similar sun reflections. When the Constellation was getting on for 30 miles ahead of us, the irregularities of fuselage, engines and tail, could still be distinguished breaking up the reflecting surface of the top wing. But it was quite different with 'our flying saucers', which had the appearance of two shallow saucers, with their rims together. 1. Its relative position remained unchanged for the whole of the 30 minutes we kept it under observation. It appeared to be still. 2. The intensity of reflected light from the top surface remained absolutely steady until the last ten minutes of observation, when it gradually dwindled away at a speed consistent with the changing position of the sun 3. The top reflecting surface was smooth and unbroken. It was more highly polished than is normally the case with an aircraft's skin. We had no doubt whatsoever that the object was solid, having a shape approximately that of an aircraft, and constructed of a metal similar to that used for aircraft construction – only more highly polished. In 18 years of flying, I have never seen anything like it before. If it had been visible for a few seconds, or even a few minutes, I would have dismissed it as a trick of the light."

(Source: *Sunday Dispatch*, 18.10.53)

Australia: 28th November 1953 – At Lismore, New South Wales, four people were outside, at 11.42pm, when they saw an illuminated circular object in the sky, which gave off an ivory glow. It was judged to be 30ft in diameter and was last seen heading southwards. **(Source: Michael Hervey, *UFOs over the Southern Hemisphere*)**

Great Britain: 1st December 1953 – Owen Moor from Beccles, Norfolk, was cycling home at 5.30pm when he noticed an object, moving across the night sky at fantastic speed, heading towards the Midlands.

"It was like a shooting star but flying level in the sky. As it passed my position, I detected a peculiar humming noise. The first person I met was a railwayman. I asked him if he believed in 'flying saucers'. He answered 'yes', you saw the thing go over?' I saw it discharging a blue/green light and turn towards Norwich, climbing at great height."

(Source: Ivan W. Bunn)

They were not the only ones to sight something unusual in our sky. Strange silver *'balls of flame'* were seen shooting across the sky at 6pm over Nottingham and Leicestershire.

Great Britain: 2nd December 1953 – People living in the Birmingham area sighted fiery streaks of light crossing the sky. One witness described seeing what looked like *'a large sheet of flame flying towards the northeast, before breaking up into smaller pieces, at a height of 2-3,000 ft.'* Apparently, some charred fragments were seen to fall through the sky over Sutton Coldfield to the north of Birmingham, accompanied by a peculiar chugging sound likened to a World War Two aircraft.

Even stranger was a report from Exmouth, Devon, of what *'looked like a dagger, seen travelling handle first across the sky, forming a letter Z'*. Was the continuing public interest into reports of *'flying saucers'*, now seen all over the world, one of the reasons why RAF Fighter Command issued a restricted directive on 16th December 1953? The directive was ordering that *'sightings of aerial phenomena were to be immediately reported, in writing, to the Deputy Director of Intelligence, at the Air Ministry, together with a request for UFO reports to be made to them from the public.'*

Haunted Skies **Volume Ten**

The Topcliffe Saucer

Australia: 6th December 1953 – *'Flying saucers'* were reported on this date. No other information.

Australia: 12th December 1953 – Five people at Black Rock, Victoria, sighted what looked like a large electric *'globe'*, tapering to a point, heading northwards, at 6.40pm.

According to Wikipedia, 2014, during the period between February and December 1953, there were eight separate incidents involving collisions between RAF aircraft, but no mention of the above incident at all. Likewise, there was no mention in Wikipedia's list of accidents and incidents, involving military aircraft, of the tragedy which befell Captain Mantell on the 1st January 1948, or of an incident involving eight jet fighters which crashed over Dayton, Ohio, when three pilots were killed. There was also no reference to the RAF Topcliffe incident on 15th November 1953, when a number of aircrew sighted *'flying saucers'*, or Flight Lt. James Salandin's encounter with a UFO over England, in 1954. The list would, no doubt, go on. Whilst we have nothing but praise for Wikipedia for preserving the history of world events, it appears that reports involving involvement with UFO activity and aircraft are being deliberately omitted, not for any sinister reasons but probably because of fear of attracting ridicule.

Great Britain: 16th December 1953 – It was reported that four Meteor Jets flew into thick fog over Waterbeach, Cambridgeshire, after taking off. Within minutes, all of the jets crashed without collision. Two pilots baled out; one was hurt, three of the jets came down in Cambridgeshire, and the other in Suffolk. The official explanation was that "They ran out of fuel" – which seems very odd, but this was not an isolated incident. [We cannot find any trace of this report on the internet 2014]

Great Britain: 23rd December 1953 - A huge explosion was heard at 3.38pm all over South and West London. Police were unable to offer any explanation.

1954

Australia: 1st January 1954 – Off duty pilot sights UFO

On New Year's Day, 1954, at 10.15am, *Captain Douglas Barker – a commercial pilot, with more than 14,000 flying hours and 17 years experience – was sat on the edge of the dining table in his home at East Kew, Melbourne, when:

> "I noticed a clear, plastic-like, outsize 'mushroom' shaped object oscillating rapidly in and out of the thick cloud, which was at 1,800 to 2,000ft, flying over the Templestowe Brickworks. The object was flying well below the safety level in that area, travelling faster than any jet I have ever seen, and roughly four times the size of a DC4 seen side-on. It appeared to have something trailing beneath it, like a thick stalk. When I reported it to Flight Control, they said I should take more water with it and told me a Convair was in the air in that position at 10.15am; my 'flying mushroom' was nothing like a Convair in appearance. I have been flying since 1937 for ANA, and served for three years with the RAAF, so there is no question of confusion."

Douglas speculated whether the *'stalk'* could have been a small observation car.

> "I am not interested in impressing anyone, neither had I been celebrating the New Year. I was in bed at 11pm."

---

*Captain Barker was badly injured on the 19th March 1943, when while piloting a Douglas Airliner, 'Warana'; he was forced to land in a paddock, two miles from Melbourne Airport. Although both wings and engines on the plane were torn off during landing, twelve passengers survived unhurt but Captain Barker suffered a fractured skull, thigh, and rib injuries. (**Source:** *Northern Star*, Lismore, NSW – 'Crew hurt in Air Liner Crash', 20.3.1943)

Following further humour being directed towards him, followed by a suggestion that he might have seen a flock of birds flying through the air, Captain Barker reiterated what he had seen.

> "Its main body was elliptical, with a long shaft, about the same length as its body, hanging below it. At the end of this thin, slightly curved, shaft was a sort of control tower. It would fly for a short time into the clouds, then sink down to the clear sky. Its colour seemed to be changing from clear plastic to sky blue. I couldn't possibly confuse this with any plane. It was four times as big and travelling 10 times as fast as a DC3."

Appeal made by Air Traffic Control Civic Aviation Department

Separate from the ridicule that was being aimed at him, Mr Seymour – then Superintendent of Air Traffic Control of the Civil Aviation department – told a different story:

> "We do not regard this business as a joke; people are definitely seeing objects which have not been explained."

Was this the same object seen on the same day by racing spectators at Hanging Rock, Victoria, described as a round silvery 'disc', seen motionless in the sky for about two minutes, before it turned on edge and vanished from view?

Haunted Skies Volume Ten

Mrs Jerrams of Camberwell Road, Camberwell:

> "I saw a perfectly round silver 'disc' in the sky and pointed it out to my two sisters-in-law. It was visible for about one minute; it was stationary and made no noise and could see it clearly through the trees. It turned on its side and disappeared."

Other sightings for this day included observers at Box Hill and Melbourne, who told of sighting a box-shaped object, rotating in the sky, at 2.30pm.

Mr A. Heinrichs, of Victoria, was with his wife when they saw what looked like a large box, or balloon, hanging in the sky.

> "Something dived on it at terrific speed, at a 45° angle. The second object looked like a 'ball' of vapour, with a jet trail behind it. A few seconds later they vanished from view, behind some houses."

(Source: *Melbourne Sun*, 4.1.1954)

At 3.17pm a clear plastic looking object, resembling a dish, was seen rushing across the sky over Hampton Beach, Victoria.

At 8.45pm a huge silver object was seen in the sky from other locations around Victoria, trailing a streamer of vivid red and blue flame, before vanishing from sight.

Mr Seymour made an appeal through the Press for people to contact him about other sightings. In just one week they received 50 reports, describing *'discs'*, *'saucers'*, and rocket-shaped objects, seen by the public. They were also contacted by Mr J.U.W. Boyle – Vice President of the Victorian branch of the British Astronomical Association – who told them of other sightings brought to his attention. One high ranking RAAF (unnamed) officer admitted the service had been investigating such reports since 1947. (**Source: Melbourne's *The Argus*, on 2nd January 1954**) broke the story with the slightly mocking headline: **'Airman sights a 'mushroom' in the clouds. Flying mushrooms are with us!'**/*The Sydney Morning Herald*, 2.1.1954 – 'Pilot reports strange object in air'/*Star*, 30.1.1954 – 'Flying Saucers no joke to Australians'/*Melbourne Herald*, 6.1.1954)

During this year of prolific activity, it appears that there were four categories of unidentified objects brought to the attention of the Australian UFO investigators. They included rotating *'discs'*, often seen in pairs, showing a rotary motion, with small ball-like wheels inset, cigar-shaped glowing objects sighted during night-time, lights seen to flash, hover, and inexplicably vanish from view, moving across the sky at speed, during night and day.

Australia: 3rd January 1954 – Melbourne resident John Boyle – Vice President of the Victorian Branch of the British Astronomical Association, from Carlisle, St. Kilda, who had previously retained an open mind on the UFO subject – told of what he saw, at 11am, on this date.

> "I was taking my son, Ian (4), to the beach when we saw this object in view for 15-20 seconds. I first thought it was a piece of paper being blown along by the wind, but it was a calm day with little wind. As it rocked from side to side, it flashed in the sunlight like a piece of aluminum; each time it flashed, a purplish halo appeared around it. I am certain it did not give any light of its own and there were no vapour trails or jets. Ian described it as a silver butterfly. It was impossible to estimate its height, but I was able to calculate its speed to be five degrees per second. This means that if the objects were flying at, say, 30,000ft, its speed would be 1,800mph and about 60ft wide. I cannot find an explanation for what we saw."

(Source: *Melbourne Sun*, 12.1.1954)

Australia: 6th January 1954 – Australian National Airways pilot – Captain Ivan Wooley – was mowing his grass at West Footscray, Victoria, when he noticed a number of:

"... queer things, like brown scraps of thin metal, floating down from the sky. When they reached an estimated height of 200ft, the 'scraps' shot upwards at tremendous speed."

At 11am, Bryan Francis Ryan (17) of Virginia Street, Springvale, was driving along Dandedong Road, near Oakleigh, when he saw:

"... a silver disc-shaped object, showing what looked like glass observation cockpits on its top and bottom, about twice the size of an aircraft and travelling between 7-800mph."

At 2.15pm, Mrs W. Elliot of Flemington, North West Melbourne, and her husband, watched,

"... two small bright lights circling our district for five minutes, before they flew towards North Melbourne and then back again."

(Source: *Melbourne Age*, 7.1.1954)

Ken Gilbert was out working, with several colleagues, at the North Melbourne railway yard, at 2.15pm, when:

"We saw a rotating 'disc', high in the sky overhead. It gave out white flashes at two second intervals. We watched it for about ten minutes – then it began to climb upwards, before disappearing from sight."

At 7.30pm, Mr A.J. Parr of Blackwood Street, Carnegie, Melbourne, was walking along the road, on the way to the picture house, when:

"... a man drew my attention to a disc-shaped object, heading silently in a south to north direction, at terrific speed; it wasn't a plane. Several seconds later, it was gone."

(Source: *The Victorian UFO Report*, 1954/*Melbourne Argus*, 7.1.1954)

Australia: 7th January 1954 – At 3.30am, Mr D.R. McDonald was out in a motor boat on Gippsland Lakes, Victoria, on the way to start fishing with two companions, when he noticed a brightly-lit object in the sky which he took to be a star.

"Then it began to approach out position, flying at about a 1000ft or so, about the same speed as a Vampire Jet Fighter. Well you know what a bright new ball-bearing looks like, if you cut one in half this is exactly what it looked like. It had a flat round bottom, with a hemispherical top, which seemed to reduce down to the tail at the stern. It had no wings and flew past us and then turned due east, flying directly into the wind."

Mr. McDonald was unable to confirm the object was silent or not, due to the sound of the boat engine. (Source: *Melbourne Herald*, 7.1.1954)

At 4.20pm, Mr X. Karamastos and A. Pantazis of the Victorian Fish Café, in Grey Street, sighted a strange object moving through the sky over the roof of the Frost Engineering Works. The men described it as being:

"... a silver object, circular in shape, with a parachute like adjunct – [something attached to another in a dependent or subordinate position] – it remained stationary for about 20 seconds and then sped away, at terrific speed, before disappearing from view."

Later that evening, Miss I. Lutze from Ballarat, Victoria, reported being 'dive-bombed' by a group of silver-white objects, while out driving. (**Source:** *Hamilton Spectator*, 12.1.1954)

Awoken by loud humming noise

After retiring to bed at 10pm, a woman resident of Bonbeach, Victoria, was awoken by a loud humming noise. Her first thoughts were that it was a malfunction with the fuse box, or electricity cables outside. She awoke her husband, and they went outside to investigate further. On seeing nothing, they went back to bed. The humming noise persisted. On two further occasions, clearly perplexed about the source of this unusual sound, she went outside to have a look – but still saw nothing. While returning to bed she glanced through the window and saw a shining gold coloured object, with hazy edges, circling in the sky – almost the size of the moon. She rushed outside and saw it move across the sky for a few seconds before is vanished over the horizon, brightly illuminated by moonlight. The woman waited for a few minutes, and was rewarded by the appearance of a cigar-shaped object, which shot up into the sky from the same location where the first object was last seen.

> "It did three or four loops, with a slight pause between each other. Each time it did this, it left a puff of white smoke. It then disappeared. As it did so the noise ceased abruptly."

(Source: *Melbourne Herald*, 31.7.1954/*The Victorian UFO Report*, 1954)

Australia: 8th January 1954 – Former RAAF employee – Mr A. Brown from Hamilton, Victoria – went outside to water his tomatoes.

> "As I turned around I saw a bright object in the sky, moving steadily from the north-west direction and then over towards Coleraine. It was high in the sky and seemed very distant. After about three to four minutes, it gradually grew smaller until disappearing from sight in the distance, towards Mt. Gambier. It was bright orange in colour – like two saucers, the upper one placed upside-down against the lower one – it left a vapour trail which fanned out a little towards the rear. I got my field glasses and looked through; it showed up the same but only bigger of course. There was no alteration in its structural shape, but as it banked to turn away, a sort of spout showed at the bottom towards the rear – the same bright orange colour as the rest."

Mr Brown pointed out that it was not an aircraft of any conventional design he had ever seen before.

(Source: *Melbourne Herald*, 8.1.1954)

At 1.05pm on the same day, Mr W Allen – manager of a shoe shop in Glenferrie Road, Malvern – sighted a shining silver, circular, halo-shaped object, at an estimated height of 2,000ft, leaving a red vapour in the sky. It was last seen heading towards the bay. (Source: *Melbourne Herald*, 8.1.1954/*The Victorian UFO Report*, 1954)

Australia: 9th January 1954 – Captain W. Booth was piloting an aircraft 100 miles north-east of Adelaide, when he noticed a strange object moving erratically, after sunset. It circled slowly across the sky, moving from side to side.

Australia: 10th January 1954 – At 2.30am, four people from Adelaide sighted a white to deep orange coloured *'planet-like object'* hovering in the sky, moving sideways, vertically, and then back to sideways. A bright pinprick of light was seen to circle the larger object, twice, at immense speed.

On the same day, in fine weather, a BOAC Comet Jet airliner crashed into the sea off Elba Island. No distress call was made prior to the accident, although Italian fishermen claimed to have heard three almost simultaneous explosions above a belt of cloud, followed by a silver object being seen to flash out of the cloud and hit the water. During a medical examination of fifteen bodies of the deceased recovered, it was discovered that there was an absence of water in the lungs of those involved and that only fragments of the upper clothing were found. Mr Lennox-Boyd, the British Transport Minister, disclosed that some of the passengers sitting in the rear of the aircraft appear to have been struck from behind by some sort of explosion. Our condolences are offered to the families of those concerned who lost their lives.

Germany: 11th January 1954 – At night-time on this date three US Air Force Sabre Jets were flying, near Darmstadt, when something caused all the pilots to bale out. The whereabouts of the third pilot has never been ascertained. It is alleged a similar incident took place on 16th December 1953, over East Midlands, UK, when RAF Jets ran out of fuel. (**Source:** *Flying Saucers on the Attack*, **Harold T. Wilkins**)

We were unable to discover any information relating to the matter over Germany. The only reference we could find with regard to RAF Fighter aircraft running out of fuel was a tragic incident, which occurred on 8th February 1956, when a flight of eight RAF Hunters were redirected to another airfield, owing to adverse weather conditions. Six of the eight aircraft ran out of fuel and crashed, killing one pilot.

Other sightings for January 1954 (undated) included a UFO, described as being larger than a dinner plate in the sky, seen over Texas, New South Wales, by three men. It then raced towards the men, but promptly vanished behind a tree. Another sighting for the same month tells of an object *'like a large sheet of aluminum, rocking from side to side'*, seen high in the sky over the St. Kildar beach, near Melbourne, at 11am. Also in the same month were reports of a bright dazzling orange object, resembling a double saucer, seen in the sky over Hamilton, at 9.45pm. It left a vapour trail, which was present for 20 minutes. At Brighton Golf Links, Victoria, Mr White was on the course when he saw a number of golden *'discs'* move over in a 'V' formation, heading eastwards. At Armadale a boomerang-shaped object, trailing a ribbon of black smoke, was seen.

February 1954

Australia: 10th February 1954 – At 4am on this date four Australian aborigines awoke prospectors Mark Mitchell and his wife, at Harts Range 100 miles from Alice Springs to tell them about a strange whining noise heard in the sky. At midnight, Mr R. Cobain from Sale, Victoria, saw an object with a corrugated top, low on the horizon. It flashed crimson lights, which changed to misty-green in colour. It moved up and down a number of times, finally flashing crimson, once, before disappearing from view.

New Zealand: 15th February 1954 – Nine objects seen over Auckland, in daylight. Some reports told of twelve objects seen. Mid-March – white shining object, with black sides, seen zigzagging across the sky over Wellington.

USA: Muroc Airbase, 1954 – Did aliens meet the President of the United States?

Desmond Leslie was interviewed by writer George Hunt Williamson, for *Valor Magazine*, on 9th October 1954.

Desmond told him that discreet enquiries made during a visit to the Muroc area with an unnamed Air Force man had revealed a *'flying saucer'* was kept under guard in Hanger 27, and that President Eisenhower had visited the Base to see the craft, while at vacation in Palm Springs. It is, of course, claimed that Eisenhower had a meeting with aliens and secret talks with them on the 20th February 1954. Information to this effect was supplied to Lord Clancarty, who discussed it with Gordon Creighton. According to Lord Clancarty, he was told that *"five different types of alien craft landed at Muroc Airbase; three were of the 'flying saucer' shape and two were long cigar-shaped."*

As a result of this unprecedented visit, Eisenhower (who was on holiday at Palm Springs) hurried to the Base, where he was introduced to the aliens.

Haunted Skies Volume Ten

US President Eisenhower

It is then claimed the aliens agreed with the views expressed by the President that the world was not yet ready to become involved in being made aware of their presence on this planet, and that it would cause panic and confusion, after the *'aliens'* told him they were interested in initiating an educational programme for the people of Earth to make mankind aware of their presence, and showed how they could make themselves invisible to human eyes.

It is difficult to know what to make of this. For a start, we do not understand why different species of aliens would use different *'spaceships'* – unless they wanted to give this perceived impression. Some years ago, a British UFO researcher of note tried to convince people that the aliens update their spacecraft from simplistic *'flying saucers'* to triangular craft – which appears nonsense, in our opinion. As far as educating humans was concerned, haven't *'they'* been doing this for millennia? We feel distinctly uncomfortable about accepting this version of events as being genuine. Was it disinformation? Time will of course tell . . . more to the point, have they anything to fear from us?

Leslie also wrote the foreword for Margaret Fry's book – *Who Are They?* – published in 2004, and began: *"Did you know that the UK had its own Roswell?"* This was an incident that had been reinvestigated by us and involved the spectacular landing of a saucer-shaped object at Bexleyheath, Kent, in July 1955. (See Volume 1, *Haunted Skies*). Not many people know about this. Sadly, Desmond Leslie passed away on the 21st February, 2001.

Great Britain: 1st March 1954 – Mrs Edith Capes from Lowestoft contacted the local newspaper, *The Eastern Evening News* (2.3.54), after sighting an object looking like a child's spinning top with a light underneath it, travelling over the town at 7.30pm. Later the same evening Mr P. Goreham from Norwich reported having seen a spinning *'ball of light'* in the sky, which changed into a *'triangle'* as it headed across the sea.

On 4th March 1954, of a saucer-shaped object was seen heading south-west over Lowestoft, at 10.40pm.

New Zealand: 9th March 1954 – A round flat object was seen in the sky over Nelson Bay, at an estimated height of 30,000ft.

New Zealand: 19th March 1954 – During this day, Nelson was rocked by a series of aerial explosions, followed by flashes of lights and unidentified flying objects seen.

In February/March of the same year it is claimed, during springtime, three men captured a UFO on photographic film and cine, which paced their vehicle. A RAAF aircraft landed nearby and the pilot ordered the men to hand over the film and photos, which were never seen again. Just as strange was a report of a 40ft diameter object, emitting streams of smoke and making a terrible noise, *'like a drum laden truck on a bad road'* in the sky, over Alice Springs, on the 17th March 1954.

Australia: 2nd April 1954 – A whirring object, trailing a shower of orange sparks, was seen over Moorabin.

Australia: 28th April 1954 – UFO sighted over railway train, at Geelong

At 7.20pm, two Australian railroad men – engineer Ted Smith, and Colin Beacon (23) – had a frightening experience 45 miles from Geelong, Victoria, between Duverney and Berrybank, when a gigantic object swooped down on the train.

Ted:

> *"I nearly fell out of the cab of the engine when I saw a huge, round, dark mass plunging straight down at the train. It screamed downwards and then suddenly raced towards the sky. The adventure lasted four minutes; it was terrifying."*

I couldn't see any doors or windows in it. Trees in the background looked like matchsticks against its vast bulk. It could have been a quarter of a mile in diameter. I called my fireman, and we both saw it stand still in the air, like a huge monster hovering over us and unlike any possible aircraft. It was a beautiful clear morning and it came within 350ft from us. The way it careered around the sky, you would have thought it was driven by an amateur. After plunging about the sky, it rose higher and higher and went out of sight."

In an interview conducted later with the *Melbourne Argus*, published on the 30th April 1954, Mr Smith told them:

"It was colossal. We watched it for four minutes; it partly obscured the sun, but all the time the light was clear. I felt that the weird thing was piloted."

New Zealand: May 1954 – A brightly coloured 'light' was seen manoeuvring about in the sky, over Invercargill. In the same month it is reported that a UFO was seen to descend close to the ground, at 12.40am, over Melbourne. Apparently human figures were seen through portholes in the object.

Local UFO clubs

In the edition of *Flying Saucer News*, Summer/Autumn 1954, we learn that Mr John Stuart – previously of Hamilton Flying Saucer Investigation Society – had formed 'flying saucer' investigators, and that their theories behind the 'flying saucer' phenomena have been sent to the New Zealand Prime Minister. In addition to this, Mr Fred Stone of the Australian Flying Saucer Club had now amalgamated with the Australian Flying Saucer Bureau, whose director was a Mr E.R. Jarrold. Interestingly, Mr Jarrold disclosed that he had received a large number of *'hysterical'* letters, enquiring about a piece of a *'flying saucer'* in possession of the Bureau, but admitted the Bureau was in possession of a 30ft length of a UFO, which was one of a number that was seen over Shepparton, Victoria, on the '12th May!

(Source: *New Zealand Herald*, 25.5.1954/Mr H.H Fulton, President of New Zealand Civilian Saucer Investigation Group/*Flying Saucer News,* Summer/Autumn 1954, Page 19)

Such was the interest in UFOs during this period that on the 20th November 1953, Alec Downer – the member for the Federal Division of Angas – enquired during Question Time in the House of Representatives, about whether the RAAF was actively investigating the UFO phenomenon.

The then Minister for Air, William McMahon (later Prime Minister) replied that the *'saucers'* were a problem *"more for psychologists than for defence authorities"*. In July 1954, AFSIC released a study of 55 sightings. The *'flying saucer'* topic came under intense criticism. Public support for the continuation of investigation into the UFO phenomenon was driven by newspaper coverage of the 1954 sightings.

Alec Downer

Then Federal Minister for External Affairs and Minister in charge of the Commonwealth Scientific and Industrial Research Organisation – Richard Casey – wrote a letter to *The Advertiser* newspaper (Adelaide), which was published on 30th January 1954, and declared:

"I have lists of the dates over the last several years on which people have reported having seen 'flying saucers' in Australia and have compared them with the dates on which the Earth passes through the principal (sic) meteoric showers. There appears to be a noticeable relationship between these two sets of dates."

New Zealand: 12th May 1954 – At 4pm, Mr Ramon Estrada, of Shepparton, sighted silk-like threads floating down from the sky, together with several long strands of this material sailing northward. The average length of these strands was 30ft. At 4.30pm, there was a similar occurrence, only the number of strands was doubled. Mr Estrada gathered some of these filaments and, although they became wrinkled, they did not disintegrate. These were sent in an airtight container to the headquarters of AFSB which, in its subsequent report, said that the substance was pure white in colour, and silky in formation, though harder in texture. It was odourless, warm to the touch – like cotton – and different from cobwebs which, after a time, became sticky and grey. A microscopic examination revealed a mass formation of uniform threads of a very fine type. A comparison with the microscopic analysis of cobwebs showed that the Shepparton filaments were coarser. There was some resemblance to white raw silk, or even nylon. The *'Cosmic Silk'* was highly susceptible to the disintegrating action of the atmosphere and the sample had to be kept in a tightly-closed container. The substance did not dissolve in water. A test in a strong caustic soda solution caused the matter to disappear momentarily. It burned rapidly, leaving no smell or ash – unlike wool, cotton, silk, or cobwebs. The threads were not sticky, or oily, but dry. Like silk they stretched easily at the ends, as little hairs were detached from the spool. The most important characteristic was the length of the original strands coming down from the sky, which averaged 30ft. It appears from the size given this was the item of interest referred to by Mr Jarrold, rather than a substantial fragment of solid material. **(Source: Hervey, M. (1969),** *UFOs over the Southern Hemisphere*)

In the same month, people living in Sydney reported having sighted a peculiar object, which was revolving in the sky for about ten minutes. According to many of the witnesses, it looked solid and appered to be dented on one side

Great Britain: 14th May 1954 – At 3.45pm, USAF fighters (from 91st Fighter Squadron, RAF Bentwaters, Suffolk) piloted by Captain Kenneth Scott, Jnr., Lt. Harry Joseph Eckes and Lt. David Clarby, were scrambled by GCI Radar type 7 at Bawdy, to intercept a UFO eight miles from their position. It was travelling at 240 knots and had been sighted visually as a 30ft. in diameter, silver/grey round object, showing a thin silhouette as it turned, at a height estimated at 50-60,000ft. Unfortunately, the pilots were unable to get anywhere near the UFO. What the pilots would not have known is that, on the same day, Marine Corps pilots chased a formation of sixteen UFOs near Dallas, Texas.

(Source: NICAP *'The UFO Evidence'*, 1964/Personal interview with Jill Clarby)

Australia: 15th May 1954 – At Roma, Queensland, a bright yellow 'V'-shaped object, the size of a large car, completely soundless, showing two red lights at the rear, was seen in the sky.

Australia: 18th May 1954 – At 10.30pm a strange object was seen in the sky over Melbourne, trailing flame and smoke.

New Zealand: 24th May 1954 – Three UFOs over Eastern Taranaki

At daybreak, three (unnamed) pilots, flying over eastern Taranaki, at 135mph, sighted:

> *"... three strange orange objects, oval in shape, with reddish flames coming from them; they appeared to be hovering at about 7,000ft above us, but it was difficult to tell whether or not they were moving. We flew on and noticed a number of others, flying in a single line formation. Suddenly they all climbed rapidly upwards, at great speed, and disappeared from view."*

The pilots were later interviewed on the radio about their sighting and told of observing 15 huge *'discs'*. Details of this sighting report were sent to *Flying Saucer News*, as published by Captain E.L. Plunkett – a Bristol-based UFO researcher from 71, Chedworth Road, Horfield, Bristol 7 [whose son Dennis took over the Magazine following his death, and was a great source of assistance with some of the earlier editions of *Haunted Skies*].

Great Britain: 20th May 1954 – Nigel Frapple sights landed UFO at Wincanton, Somerset and reports it to the police. BBC interview Nigel. He is later visited by two men who allege they are from the Ministry and threaten him to keep quiet. (See Volume 1 *Haunted Skies* for full story and pictures).

Australia: 25th May 1954 – At midnight, a yellow object – described as silent and 'V'-shaped, with two red lights at the rear – was sighted in the sky over Queensland, and was reported to have followed a stretch of road for 100 miles.

Australia: 30th May 1954 – UFOs over Victoria

A saucer-shaped object was seen moving through the sky over Victoria, Australia, at 8pm. The following day it was sighted again at the same time, swooping across the sky, backing up, vanishing, then reappearing and flattening out. This was observed by a number of people and described as like a white football, leaving a trail of sparks. Another object was reported as being as big as a railroad car, *'with dark shapes inside it, like people'*.

(Source: *Melbourne Argus*, 31.5.1954/*Melbourne Sun*, 31.5.1954)

Tasmania: 31st May 1954 – Two people, living in Elizabeth Town, saw a dark object rise up from ground level and head straight up into the sky, at fantastic speed, leaving a white vapour trail behind it.

Australia: 1st June 1954 – A mushroom-shaped object with a long tail, inside which was seen an entity, along with a second UFO that was revolving next to it, were reported seen over Melbourne, at 5.45pm.

Australia: 2nd June 1954 – Sixty miles from Melbourne, a white and green coloured *'globe'*, with a yellow tail, was sighted over rooftops. Seconds later it split into two and vanished from sight.

Australia: 6th June 1954 – 'Flying Saucer' over East Malvern

At 12.25am, a group of seven people from East Malvern, Victoria, sighted an oval *'saucer'*, with what appeared to be objects inside it, flying over nearby treetops at high speed. Later that day, at 5.45pm, a very strange object – described as resembling a white balloon, flying at tremendous speed, with a long tapering tail and what looked like a mushroom or umbrella-shaped object inside – was seen over Melbourne. During the same evening, a revolving *'red light'* was seen heading across the sky, shuttling backwards and forwards as it did so. Suddenly it spun three times, as if it had been a plate, and vanished from view. At 5.30am on the 2nd June 1954, thousands of people living on the waterfront, at Sydney, awoke after hearing a mysterious explosion. Police failed to discover the cause. A local observatory found no tremors had registered on its seismographs.

Australia: 9th June 1954 – 'Flying Saucer' over Melbourne

Janette Brown (16) and Jeanette Johnston (13) both of Dandenong East – a Melbourne outer suburb – were out walking, at 6.20pm, when they heard a loud drumming noise.

Janette:

> "I left my home to meet Jeanette Johnston. I was standing outside the main gate of a partly-built factory on Prince's Highway, waiting for Jeanette, when I heard a loud drumming noise – like a motorcycle. I looked toward the factory, and hovering over the top of the end dome of the building I saw a large dark shape. I flashed my torch in its direction, and it came towards me; it had three lights, one on top and two on the ends, lit up. I thought they were rays and fell to the ground. I was terrified. It was terribly weird and fascinating. I just couldn't move or even run away, I was so scared. Then it came towards me and stopped, hovering about 20 yards away on the top of the factory gate, as if it deliberately wanted me to look at it – or it wanted to look at me. It was a cylindrical shape, about 30ft long and 15ft high, with a canopy and window on top and a window on each end. I was so close I could even see how it worked. The undercarriage consisted of three wheels, which were half turning and making a low clicking sound."

Haunted Skies Volume Ten

Just then, a car came along the road. The *'saucer'* must have heard it or seen the approaching lights, because it swung around and settled behind the caretaker's house. At this stage Jeanette arrived to meet Janette, who told her to watch the house.

Jeanette said:

> "As I watched the house, a silvery coloured cylinder rose into the air. It stayed there, hovering for about two minutes, and then swept away in a wide circle to another factory – the International Harvester factory – a few hundred yards away. It stayed on top of the factory for about one minute, where the bright lights flashed out and only the top and left lights kept shining. Suddenly, the left light spun around to the right-hand side of the *'saucer'* and it crossed the road and disappeared behind the tree."

Mrs Johnston said her daughter hoped the story would not be published, in case the object attacked them. Her daughter had asked her to move to another suburb, because she feared the *'saucer'* might try to destroy her home and family. **(Source:** *Melbourne Argus***, June 1954 –'TEENAGE GIRLS SEE SAUCER They're Sleepless now'/***Sunday Telegraph***, 13.6.1954/Australian UFO Research Network)**

UFO sightings continue . . .

Sightings of *'flying saucers'* continued to be reported over Victoria during the 5th, 6th, 9th and 10th of June 1954. An object resembling a *'railway car'*, jetting blue flames, was sighted over Botany Bay, at 5.55am on the 18th June 1954. Was there a connection with peculiar multicoloured *'lights'* seen over Sydney, the previous evening, at 7pm?

Australia: 28th June 1954 – A giant spherical object was seen spinning in the sky and moving in many directions, at 6.30pm, over Montmorency, Victoria. Was this an example of a UFO display, as reported many times over in our books?

In this month the *Melbourne Argus* offered £1,000 for the first authentic photographs of a *'flying saucer'*, as seen by Captain Howard on the 1st July 1954, over the Atlantic Ocean.

Australia: 5th July 1954 – Two cigar-shaped objects were seen in the sky over Melbourne, leaving a bright vapour trail as they moved away at an estimated height of 5,000ft.

Australia: 6th July 1954 – At Queanbeyan, New South Wales, a wingless silent object, belching green flame, apparently under controlled flight, was reported seen crossing the sky by Mr G. Burnett and Mr T. Kerr. **(Source: Michael Hervey,** *UFOs over the Southern Hemisphere***)**

New Zealand: 7th July 1954 – At 8.30pm, an object, trailing sparks, was seen over Taranga.

Great Britain: 7th July 1954 – A huge object, resembling a question mark, was seen drifting in the sky, at an estimated height of 15 miles above London, sparking off thousands of calls from the public. In one hour, the *Evening Standard* received over 2,000 calls from concerned citizens, who caused traffic jams after getting out of their cars and gazing upwards into the sky. The incident was later explained away as being a cosmic ray balloon, with a width of 600ft and depth of 200ft, released by Bristol University, at Cardington, Bedfordshire. **(Source:** *Evening Standard***, 7.7.1954)**

Great Britain: 8th July 1954 – Harold Hill, an amateur astronomer, sights 13-15 saucer-shaped objects in the sky, through a telescope, over Wigan, Lancashire. (See Volume 1, *Haunted Skies*, for full report and images).

Australia: 10th July 1954 – A dazzling object, larger than an aircraft, was seen moving through the sky, at great speed, over Pascoe Vale State School, Victoria, at 8pm, by Thomas Blake (19) and Allan Jackson (20). It passed over the roof of the school no more than 30 yards away, making a soft buzzing noise.

Australia: 11th July 1954 – A bright red *'globe'* was seen moving across the sky over Melbourne, at 8.30pm.

NUMBER SIX SUMMER/AUTUMN 1954.

FLYING SAUCER NEWS

THE JOURNAL OF THE BRITISH FLYING SAUCER BUREAU & FLYING SAUCER CLUB.

B.O.A.C. "FLYING JELLYFISH" Report

```
"CHAOS & CONFUSION" (Editorial)..3      B.F.S.B. NEWSLETTER........13
A strange sight over WIGAN...... 7      More Saucer-men Claims....18
"CRAB SHIPS" Mystery............ 8      News from Australasia.....19
Saucer over Hants & Somerset.... 9      Saucers over BERLIN.......20
SIGHTINGS, home and abroad......10      "Star Letter".............23
```

Haunted Skies **Volume Ten**

Tasmania: Summer 1954 – UFO photographed at Oyster Cove, Queensland

At 5.30am a farmer's daughter, from Oyster Cove, was helping her father to bring in the cows. They heard a low whirring noise, followed by the locality being illuminated with light. Looking upwards, towards the eastern direction, they saw a silver oval object, with a dome on top, showing red and white lights, shining a beam of light downwards. The cows became agitated; at this point her father ran into the house and took some photographs of the object, which shot off over the sea. The father processed the photographs and contacted someone in authority to report the matter. The couple received a visit from two men in dark blue serge jackets, who demanded the negatives. When they refused to acquiesce, the men became threatening but eventually left with five photographs. In 1967 the house and its contents, including the negatives, were destroyed in a bushfire. **(Source: Keith Roberts, TUFOIC)**

USA: 30th July 1954 – UFO display over New York

At 9.40pm, Robert Frenhoff – a science teacher at a Yonkers school – was outside, tending to his lawn, when he glanced upwards and saw:

"A queer thing – like a child's gyroscope or spinning top – whirling along at high altitude. It was mainly yellow, with a crimson glow at the edges, which might have been an exhaust. I shouted to my wife and the neighbours, who came out.

It moved around in a fantastic manner. One moment it would hover near the Great Bear constellation and then in a sudden rush dart away at an angel of 90°, and then stop short – as if it had hit a brick wall. There was no way of estimating its immense height in the sky. It repeated these hovering and rushing manoeuvres until close on midnight."

(Source: *Flying Saucers Uncensored,* **Harold T. Wilkins)**

New Zealand: 1st August 1954 – At 2.20pm, an oval object was seen in the sky near New Plymouth. As it flew over, it changed shape to about 8ft across.

Great Britain: 6th August 1954 – George Hortrop, who contacted us in 2003, described what he and his companion saw at 5.45pm, while sitting on the beach at the 'Knap', enjoying the afternoon, when their attention was caught by a stationary object in the sky over the Bristol Channel, towards the south-west, well out towards Rhoose Point.

"It was brilliant silver in colour and conveyed the impression of a light reflecting on chromium, or silver plate. The thing that struck us was, although there was a slight westerly wind, the object continued to remain stationary. The weather was perfect that evening, with an exceptionally blue sky, apart from one or two small patches of fractocumulus cloud. During the time we were watching the object, it altered its shape to a silvery dumb-bell before eventually disappearing from view, two hours later."

George discovered they were not the only ones to see this object. Two security guards, stationed outside the main entry gate to the BP Chemical Plant, also witnessed the incident. A few days later he learnt, through the National Press, that a number of experienced observers from RAF St. Athan and Rhoose, including a flying officer, reported having sighted an object resembling a large double convex lens, viewed in vertical profile, stationary in the sky.

George wrote an account of the incident and sent it to Lord Clancarty (formerly the Hon. William Francis Brinsley Le Poer Trench, born 18th September 1911, died 18th May 1995) – a major figure in British UFO research – who spoke on the subject in the House of Lords, and wrote many books on the UFO subject. He was editor of *Flying Saucer Review* from 1956 to 1959, and founded the worldwide organisation, *Contact*, while vice-president of BUFORA (The British UFO Research Association). He wrote back to George, informing him that the UFO sighting would be referred to during a debate on the subject in the House of Lords.

An hour and a half later, two silver circular objects were seen over Cheltenham, at 7.15pm, by a number of people. One such person was Eric Jones, who had seen them through his binoculars. He noted that one of the objects was tilted and showed a conical tower, similar to the Adamski-type *'saucer'* illustrations then in vogue at the time. The other was smaller in appearance and constantly moving up and down in the air – almost as if *'playing tag'* – at a height estimated to be 6-20,000ft. Was this the same object reported earlier by Mr Hortrop? Could it have been connected with what was sighted by Lt. O'Farrell?

(Sources: *Townsville Daily Bulletin*, 17.12.54 – 'Saucer confirmed by radar'/*Riverine Herald*, 17.12.1954 – 'Navy probe on flying saucers'/*Queensland Times*, 17.12.1954 – 'Saucers circled plane, says pilot'/*The Mercury*, Hobart, 16.12.1954 – 'Navy finds flying saucers'/*The Canberra Times*, 17.12.1954 – 'Navy to check report of saucers over Goulburn'/*Morning Bulletin*, Rockhampton, 17.12.1954 – 'Investigating saucer reports'/*Sydney Morning Herald*, 17.12.1954 – 'Saucer alert explained'/*Examiner,* Launceston, 17.12.1954 – 'Eisenhower on saucers' /*The Argus*, Melbourne, 16.12.1954 – 'Navy saw saucers'/*Sydney Morning Herald*, 16.12.1954 – 'Saucer check at Nowra'/*Goulburn Evening Post*, 16.12.1954 – 'Nowra pilot saw flying saucers here'/*Barrier Miner*, 17.12.1954 – 'Flying saucers over Goulburn'/*The Canberra Times*, 11.6 1968 – 'UFOs in the Open'/*Newcastle Morning Herald and Miners Advocate*, 17.12.1954 – 'Vague shapes under plane'/*News Adelaide*, 16.12.1954 – 'RAN Saucers a complete mystery')

Australia: 10th August 1954 – A vivid green object was seen over Canberra, moving towards the direction of Sydney, at 5.20pm, at an estimated speed of 600mph. Other sources mentioned a dark bodied object, with a green flare at one end, and the suggestion of a central green *'globe'*, which may have been spinning in flight. The RAAF and Weather Bureau were unable to offer any explanation. (**Source: Michael Hervey, *UFOs over the Southern Hemisphere*)**

New Zealand: 18th August 1954 – A bright blue-green cigar-shaped *'light'* was seen in the centre of a black storm cloud, over Whenuapai Air Force Base.

Australia: 27th August 1954 – A glowing orange object was sighted in the sky over Wonthaggi, Victoria.

Australia: 31st August 1954 – RAAF pilot sights saucer-shaped objects tracked on radar

According to Nowra Radar, two *'flying saucers'* were tracked flying together, after having been reported chasing Lt. J.A. O'Farrell – an Australian Navy Pilot. The Australian Navy Minster disclosed that the objects were seen to draw away from the plane, moving at 285mph, on the 31st August 1954, over Goulburn, New South Wales, and that the sighting was not released for three months. The pilot contacted Nowra Radar, who confirmed they had three echoes on screen. The two bright lights reformed at 'nine o'clock' and disappeared on a north-easterly heading. It was later suggested the pilot had seen meteorites! [Some sources give the date as 15th December 1954, which may have been when it was released into the media]

The full circumstances of the incident were that Lieutenant J.A. 'Shamus' O'Farrell was returning to the Royal Australian Navy Air Station of Nowra, after a night cross-country flight in a Sea Fury aircraft. After contacting Nowra, at about 7.10pm, O'Farrell saw a very bright *'light'* closing fast at a 'one o'clock' position, which crossed in front of his aircraft, taking up a position on his port beam, where it appeared to orbit. A second and similar *'light'* was then observed at 'nine o'clock'. It passed about a mile away from of the Sea Fury and then turned in the position where the first *'light'* was observed. According to O'Farrell, the apparent crossing speeds of the 'lights' were the fastest he had ever encountered. He had been flying at 220 knots. O'Farrell contacted Nowra simply to ask if there were other aircraft, as he was reluctant to explain that he was in company of UFOs. Petty Officer Keith Jessop, at Nowra, then confirmed that they had two radar *'paints'* in company with him. The radar operator – Petty Officer Keith Jessop – confirmed the presence of two objects near the Sea Fury on the G.C.I. remote display. The two *'lights'* reformed at 'nine o'clock' and then disappeared on a north-easterly heading. O'Farrell could only make out *"a vague shape, with the white light situated centrally on top"*.

When he landed, O'Farrell was thoroughly checked, to ensure that he had not been drinking. The Directorate of Naval Intelligence, at the time, wrote that O'Farrell was:

> *". . . an entirely credible witness and that he was visibly shaken by his experience, but remains adamant that he saw these objects".*

The Australian Ministry of Navy was immediately alerted and, in the same year, the Minister of Air – William McMahon – ordered an investigation on this case and other similar cases. Dr. J. Allen Hynek interviewed the pilot in 1973. In a later interview, Mr O'Farrell said:

> *"I was about to press the button and tell them at Nowra the two aircraft were departing, when they called me up and told me the two aircraft appeared to be departing at high speed, towards the north-east. Is that correct? They asked me and I replied in the affirmative. They said 'Roger', we will see if we can track them – which they did for a while, before losing them."*

The case has been researched in depth by Australian investigator – Bill Chalker (*The Oz Files – The Australian Story*) who had this to say:

> *"Upon my request made on 13th July 1982, the Director of Naval Intelligence declassified documents relating to this incident of the 31st August 1954. The file included written statements made by the pilot and the radar operator at Nowra. It also included a confidential memorandum from the DNI to DAFI."*

(Sources: James E. McDonald, Senior Physicist, Institute of Atmospheric Physics, and Professor, Department of Meteorology, The University of Arizona, Tucson, Arizona, to the House Committee on Science and Astronautics at July 29, 1968, Symposium on Unidentified Flying Objects, Rayburn Bldg., Washington, D.C., 1968, *Study of Official Australian Government Involvement in UFO Controversy, a Progress Report*, by Bill Chalker, 1982, *The Sea Fury Incident*, Bill Chalker, 1982/*Project 1947*, Ian Aldritch/*Of Planes and UFOs*, Moira McGhee, INUFO, 1988)

New Zealand: 9th September 1954 – It is claimed a photograph was taken of a disc-like object, seen hovering over Nelson.

Australia: 9th September 1954 – At Wonthaggi, Victoria, a motorist gave chase to a UFO – unusual, bearing in mind that normally it is the UFO that does the chasing, but strangeness is paramount to this phenomena!

Great Britain: 12th September 1954 – At 11am a bright silver object, shaped like a dumb-bell, was seen flying slowly through the sky over St. Helens, Lancashire, by Mrs Rimmer, *'catching the sun like a mirror'*, as it moved westwards.

Great Britain: October 1954 – Staffordshire housewife – Mrs Jessie Roestenberg (known to the authors) – was with her two children when they sighted a UFO, with occupants, over a remote farmhouse. (See Volume 1, *Haunted Skies*, for full interview and images).

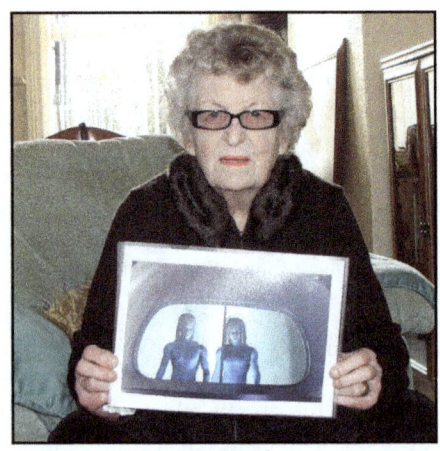

Jessie Roestenberg

Haunted Skies Volume Ten

Great Britain: Sunday 14th October 1954 – RAF pilot sights three saucer-shaped objects over Essex

RAF Auxiliary Officer, Flight Lt. James Salandin, MBE, (29) who was stationed at RAF North Weald, Essex, near Epping (then attached to 604 County of Middlesex Squadron) described the mysterious encounter he had while on an air test, climbing towards Southend, Essex, on 14th October 1954, *"...still vivid in my memory, despite it having happened over 50 years ago."*

Mr Salandin, to whom we had the pleasure of speaking many times over the years, told about his service with the Fleet Air Arm and the RAF, having logged 1,800hrs flying time on a variety of aircraft, including 300hrs in the famous Spitfire.

> *"I took off at about 4.15pm. Flying conditions were perfect. When at a height of some 16,000ft I noticed a number of contrails in the sky, approximately 30 to 40,000ft, over North Foreland. Through the middle of these trails I could see three objects, which at first I took to be aircraft, although there was no sign of any vapour trail that one would associate with the movement of an aircraft in high atmosphere. When they got within a certain distance, two of them went off to my port side; one was gold in colour, the other silver. The third object headed towards me and closed to within a few hundred yards, almost filling the middle of the aircraft windscreen before departing towards my port side. I tried to turn and follow, but it had disappeared from view. The object I saw through the front*

cockpit of my Meteor 8 Jet Aircraft was saucer-shaped, with a 'bun' on top and underneath. I didn't see any portholes, windows, or other exterior extrusions that one would associate with the passage of an aircraft through the air. There weren't even any flames coming from the objects."

In 2008, we met up with James Salandin at his home in rural North Yorkshire, and had the opportunity to personally discuss with him what he had seen.

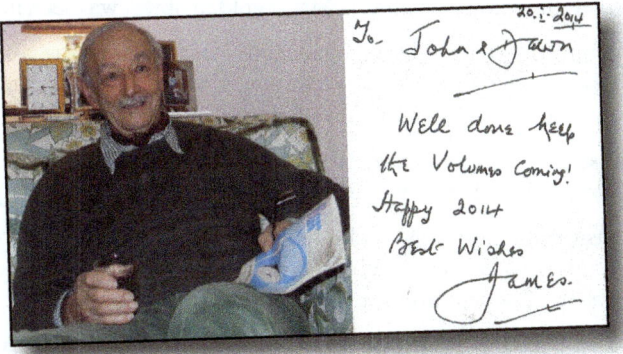

"It is now 54 years since my sighting of three UFOs in October 1954. At the time I was bound by the Official Secrets Act and if it hadn't been for leaks, nothing more would have been heard of the incident. I have always said that I know what I saw and my story has never varied over the years – the picture is still clear in my mind. However, I have not at any time given an opinion as to my thoughts on the subject but I feel that now is the moment to do so. Since my wife, Margaret, passed away nearly two years ago I've had plenty of time to reflect and would like to voice my true feelings, as most people appear to be sceptical or just not interested in UFOs. I was a volunteer in the Fleet Air Arm, from 1943 until demobilisation in 1947, my flight training being with the United States Navy, after which I served with 604 County of Middlesex Fighter Squadron 'R' Auxiliary Air Force from 1947, until we were disbanded in 1957. The last five years of my service I was 'B' Flight Commander. During this Decade, 604 were equipped with Spitfires, Vampires, and Gloster Meteors, the Squadron motto being, 'Si vis pacem para bellum', (If you want peace prepare for war!) I mention all of this because I was an experienced pilot and I have never seen, in all the years of my service, anything like I saw on that day."

(Source: *The London Daily Sketch*, 24.2.1955 – 'A flying saucer buzzed me, says Meteor Jet Pilot – It flew straight at me at staggering speed')

Ohio: 22nd October 1954 – web like material found after UFO sighting (see Volume 1, *Haunted Skies*)

Venice: 27th October 1954 – 'Angel hair' falls (See Volume 1, *Haunted Skies*)

Australia: 3rd November 1954 – UFO photographed over New South Wales

At 4pm, sheep station hand Keith Weston – son of the manager at Mena Murtie Station, Wilcannia – was near the woolshed with a groom, when they saw a silver coloured object, showing a tower on top, with two portholes on the side, approaching from the south-west, at a height of about 500ft, moving between 80-100mph. Keith fetched a camera and took three photos of the object in the sky, which was *"making a terrible sound; it looked like an inverted saucer, with an inverted teacup on top"*. They told Constable Cosatto, of Wilcannia Police, that it was over 100ft long and resembled a *'flying saucer'*. This appears to have been a genuine sighting. Unfortunately we were unable to trace a copy of the photographs and ascertain the result of any analysis carried out as to their authenticity. (Sources: *The Barrier Miner*, 5.11.1954 – 'Mother of lad at Wilcannia tells of origin'/*News of Adelaide*, 5.11.1954 – 'Men claim they saw flying saucer'/*The Barrier Miner*, Broken Hill, 9.11.1954 – 'Flying saucer negatives are wanted')

New Zealand: 5th November 1954 – An orange elliptical object, showing blue portholes, was seen over Lookout Point.

Australia: 9th December 1954 – A housewife, from Melbourne, was awoken by a powerful buzzing sound. On going to the window to look out, she saw a huge *'flying saucer'*-shaped object hovering over a nearby field.

Australia: 12th December 1954 – A golden object was seen in the sky over Bonbeach, Port Phillip Bay, Victoria.

A short time later, a second object appeared – this one was cigar-shaped, which was seen to perform a loop in the sky and then fly away, leaving puffs of black smoke. Earlier that morning, a witness living in Melbourne reported having heard a buzzing noise, followed by the appearance of an enormous saucer-shaped object.

Australia: 18th December 1954 – A pear-shaped object – like an electric *'globe'*, tapering to a point – was seen flying across the sky over Black Rock, Victoria, by seven people.

Great Britain: 18th December, 1954 – At 12.30pm, three shining circular objects, *'resembling a smaller version of the full moon'*, were sighted one after the other, moving across the sky over Otley, in Yorkshire, by Mr and Mrs H.J. Cooper. (**Source:** *UFOLOG*)

Australia: 19th December 1954 – A milkman and four security guards reported having sighted a strange object, jetting out flames like red hot lava rushing out of a cloud, streaking across the sky, showing a blue-green tail of light on its underside.

Australia: 25th December 1954 – An object, described as resembling an orange *'flying saucer'*, was seen heading silently south-east, over Victoria, by a man and his son. A short time later, a four-engine plane flew over on its way to Essendon Airport. (**Source:** *Flying Saucers Uncensored*, **Harold T. Wilkins**)

PART 3

1955 TO 1960

1955

Australia: 1st January 1955 – Mysterious clouds seen over Sydney

MR P. Griffith Taylor and his wife were on the Manby ferry, at about 9.40pm, on a cloudless day, with the moon in its first quarter low in the western sky.

"Suddenly a luminous cloud, abnormally persistent in shape and position, appeared moving slowly from our right and downwards. After it had disappeared, another one came into view. This was bell-shaped and brighter in its upper and outer parts. It also moved to the right and downwards, and then split into four egg-shaped parts, which gradually vanished. Now a smaller cloud appeared to the right and condensed into two more parts – then formed into one luminous oval shape and vanished."

(Source: *Flying Saucers Uncensored*, Harold T. Wilkins)

USA: 1st January 1955 – At 6.44am, a *'metallic disc'* was sighted at Cochise, New Mexico, described as resembling two pie tins, face-to-face. On the same date were reports from Brazil, involving a family and an employee who were out fishing, just past midnight, when they saw a 30-metre in length, disc-shaped object at an estimated altitude of 200 metres. The light from the descending object lit up the surrounding area. When about a metre off the water, a figure was seen within the light on the cupola, believed to be about 5-6ft in height. Others reports were of a UFO, which hovered in the sky over Peru, and a *'flying disc'* at Bloemfontein. **(Source: Project Blue Book)**

Great Britain: 10th January 1955 – At 4pm, Staffordshire housewife – Jessie Roestenberg – sights an orange cigar-shaped object, followed by the appearance of a RAF Jet.

Great Britain: 18th January 1955 – A disc-like object was reported over the sea at Southport, by Mr Peter Walsh, who contacted the police and coastguards. **(Source: *The Daily Express*, 19.1.1955)**

Air Marshall Lord Dowding speaks at the Flying Saucer Club, London

On the 23rd January, Air Marshall Lord Dowding told the Flying Saucer Club, in London:

> *"It's rude to fire AA guns and send fighters to shoot them down; you never know what they could do to you. I believe these objects come from planets hundreds of years ahead of us in scientific knowledge; there is no material we know that could travel 9,000 miles per hour, which was the recorded speed of one saucer, without becoming white hot."*

USA: 26th January 1955 – At 6.15pm over Lakeland, Florida, a black smoke trail/circle explosion and some objects fell. Explanation: Missile.

USA: 27th January 1955 – Object seen playing *'tag'* in the sky over Valley Centre, California. Was this an example of UFO display? Other sightings for this period included reports of fireballs and what were explained away as meteorites rushing through the sky. (**Source: Project Blue Book**)

February 1955

Great Britain: 2nd February 1955 – At 7.30am, Len Scott sights a UFO over Immingham.

New Zealand: 6th February 1955 – During this day, Greymouth was rocked by a series of aerial explosions, followed by flashes of lights and unidentified flying objects seen.

New Zealand: 7th February 1955 – Explosions heard

A mysterious explosion of terrific force shook the west coast of New Zealand, after people reported sighting a strange silver shape flash overhead. Various descriptions were given of this object, including cigar, barrel, or saucepan-shaped, throwing out a dazzling light. It was first seen 200ft above Inchbonnie (a farming community 30 miles inland) heading towards the mountains. An explosion was heard and felt over several hundred square miles, followed by a plume of smoke seen rising from the Southern Alps. This was explained away as being a meteor.

USA: 7th February 1955 – Pilot sights three white lights

It appears the same phenomenon was seen over South Florida, USA, causing pilots to swerve out of the way to avoid striking it. Pilot Captain Charles Elmore, reported seeing three bright white *'lights'* due south of the DC-6B, at 8.35pm, as they crossed Biscayne Bay at 1,200ft.

> *"The lights were 15° higher than the plane and had fuzzy edges and were round. They appeared to hover with the front two connected by a line of light between them. Suddenly they blinked out. The tower also saw them, but couldn't identify them."*

(Source: Mr H.B. Williams/*The Daily Telegraph*, 7.2.1955)

Australia: 10th February 1955 – Flashing light seen in the sky

An object, described as resembling a poached egg with a yellow core, surrounded by a white edge, making a whining noise, was seen heading out to sea over Melbourne. In the same month, the *Melbourne Times* (16th February 1955 – 'Sky Mystery') told of a sighting by Mr John Ginty and his wife, who were watching television, one evening, when they noticed a strange *'light'* in the backyard. When he went to have a look, there was nothing to be seen. A short time later, Mrs Ginty brought her husband's attention to another *'flash of light'* in the sky, just west of the new drive-in theatre on the Kissimmee Highway. Intrigued, they watched the night sky and recorded flashes bright enough to light up the whole countryside, at 10.05pm, 10.06pm, and 10.27pm. He said:

> *"It was like looking into the sun – a bright yellow circle, with a large corona around it, going darker red towards the edges. The flashes came instantly, but died more slowly."*

Nick Dean – Airport manager at Melbourne Airport – was contacted. He suggested the flashes were probably something to do with the Patrick Air Force Base, as he had seen them several times before. When Nick spoke to an official at the airbase, he was told they were flares being shot into the sky as some sort of experiment. Major S.A. Pelle was contacted. He denied any such work being carried out at the missile testing base. Curiously, when Mr Ginty telephoned the airbase, he was told it was some type of aerial photography going on at Avon Park. The truth of the matter was that the base had no idea what was causing the mystery flashes and, in fact, asked for the public's assistance.

Oddly, an Auckland groundkeeper – Mr C.M. Callander, at the Mount Roskill Bowling Club – was in the process of re-laying turf, when a bright red fireball came from behind and landed inches from his feet, followed by a loud clap of thunder. Mr Callander, who admitted to having run away, returned to the scene and found no trace of the object having landed on the green. (**Source:** *The UFO Annual*, **edited by M.K. Jessup/ Harold Fulton)**

Great Britain: 11th February 1955 – Six 'flying saucers' were seen in the sky over Chichester.

USA: 11th February 1955 – Captain King was flying between Miami and New York.

> *"Suddenly, close to the plane and under the wings, two strange reddish-green objects passed by. They were also seen by some of the passengers.*
>
> *I hadn't believed in 'flying saucers' before, but after this incident my opinion had quickly changed."*

USA: 24th February 1955 – Green fireball seen over Texas

Streaking silently through the sky, the mysterious object was observed by thousands – including three control-tower operators at Pound's Field, one of whom was Mr J. N. Aber, who said:

> *"It was about midnight; this light seemed to pop out of the sky directly over us, like a huge electric arc. It was greenish, like the tip of a welder's torch. It was a blinding light, the brightest that I ever saw. The whole room lit up for a second."*

All three operators agreed that the fireball was moving so swiftly that it crossed the horizon in little more than a second. Its fiery glow was seen as far east as Jackson, Mississippi.

March 1955

Australia: 1st March 1955 – A silver object was seen in the sky over Moola Boola Station, which reversed course from north-west to south-east in flight.

USA: 2nd March 1955 – At 3pm a hovering, rectangular-shaped, object was seen rocking in the sky over Tucson, Arizona. One hour later, at about 5pm, a car driving ten miles north of Huntley, Illinois, was followed for ten minutes by three elongated *'balloons'*. The objects were each about seven meters long and showed eight red lights.

Haunted Skies Volume Ten

Did a UFO cause the crash of aircraft on this day?

At 5.50pm on 9th March 1955, Eugene Metcalfe of Paris, Illinois, reported that he was watching a jet fighter shoot across the sky, when suddenly, a gigantic object . . .

> "shaped like a call bell, descended over it. This object literally swallowed up the fast moving jet as easy as a hawk would a chicken, and then disappeared upwards with its prey".

We were unable to confirm that any jet fighter aircraft was reported missing on that date. However, two aircraft did crash on the same day – caused, it is believed, by snow storms that struck the area, rather than any UFO interaction.

Beechcraft

One of them was a Beechcraft aircraft flying from Chicago to Arcata, California; it went down on its way from Rock Springs to Salt Lake City in rugged mountain territory. A search was conducted but called off on the 21st March. Almost two months later the plane was found by two sheep men – Bill Sorenson and Pete Mower – about 18 miles from Evanston, Wyoming. They were herding sheep into the area when they came across the wreckage, scattered over a large patch of ground covered in snow. The bodies of five persons – Robert J. Willis, 38-year-old Chicago plywood broker and owner of the plane, his 9-year-old son, Jacques, Pilot George Dott (37), Harry W. Gindelle, and a fifth body – believed to be Harry Knutson, from San Francisco, a Costa Rica lumberman were recovered – positive identification being made by Sheriff Frank L. Narramore of Uinta County, Wyoming.

B52 bomber

This was not the only air crash on that day; an Air Force B-25 also came down. The B-25 was discovered on Mt. Timpanogos four days later. The bodies of three men who died in the crash were found, two were still missing. Until the climbers reached the B-25 and sent a radioed message to planes overhead, nobody knew whether it was the Beechcraft or B-25 due to the fact that the remains were buried under 9ft of snow.

Aboard the B-25, on its flight from Great Falls, Montana, to March Air Force Base, California, were Major Daniel C. Howley (33) Springfield, Massachusetts – pilot. 2nd Lt. Howard E. St. John, Jr. (25) Mendham, New Jersey – co-pilot. Airman Second Class C Doyle Dempsey, (22) Hawkins, Texas – engineer. Donald R. Cubbage (45) of Great Falls, Montana – a civilian engineer working for the Air Force, and Maurice McNulty (30) a Wyoming man, also a civilian engineer working for the Air Force. We offer our condolences. (**Source: Project Blue Book /** ***Ogden Standard Examiner**, Utah, 5.6.1955)*

Mr Arthur Constance – a legend of the 20th Century

UK: 24th March 1955 – Was it a Meteor or UFO?

Following the sighting of a UFO over the UK by thousands of people, at 5.50pm, and attempts to intercept by the RAF (later explained away as a meteor!) Arthur Constance – Cheltenham Journalist and UFO author/researcher, who at the age of 69 (in 1960) had written nine million words, ten thousand articles, twenty-three books (including *The Inexplicable Sky* and 260 radio broadcasts) – handed over his 18,000 word report into his investigation of the events that took place on 24th March 1955, compiled from 180 different newspaper cuttings. Arthur also possessed an impressive library of over two million Press cuttings and sixteen thousand reference books devoted to strange phenomena. What happened to them? (See Volume 1 of *Haunted Skies* for further information).

April 1955

During this month in the USA, further sightings of *'green fireballs'* continued to be seen, which were once again explained away as meteors.

USA: 8th April 1955 – At 9.30am over Rockford, Illinois, USAF Pilots open fire on a big object, which explodes after ejecting a small round object. Balloon-like objects observed. Two 'balls' were observed by more than four military witnesses. Explanation: Balloon.

Australia: 22nd April 1955 – A motorist driving through Tintinarra, at 7.45am, was astonished to see, through his rear view window, a silver sphere – some 9ft in diameter – crossing the road behind him. The object then followed the vehicle for some distance, before climbing up into the sky.

May 1955

USA: 15th May 1955 – UFO photographed over New York

Warren Siegmond took this photograph from a New York rooftop on May 15th, 1955. It is one of five exposures of the 'Surprise-Visiting' UFO

Haunted Skies Volume Ten

USA: 17th May 1955 – At 8.20pm over Mojave, California, nine grapefruit size objects were seen for 10 minutes over the desert. Radio and television interference was reported – Explanation: aircraft.

New Zealand: 24th May 1955 – At 12.35am a bright fireball was seen by a number of people, heading over Achilles Point. This exploded with a brilliant blue flash just above the waterline, between this location and Rangito Island.

June 1955

New Zealand: 11th June 1955 – A cylindrical luminous object was seen in the sky over Kumara and Greymouth, accompanied by a loud roaring noise, leaving a vapour trail as it did so.

Australia: 17th June 1955 – A silver, oblong, object was seen hovering in the sky over Adelaide, before being lost from sight as it went behind clouds.

July 1955

Great Britain: 5th July 1955 – Mystery explosions rock London.

USA: 11th July 1955 – Long Beach, California. Coastguards were contacted by a motor boat owner, who told of having sighted a *'flying saucer'* over the Santa Catalina Channel.

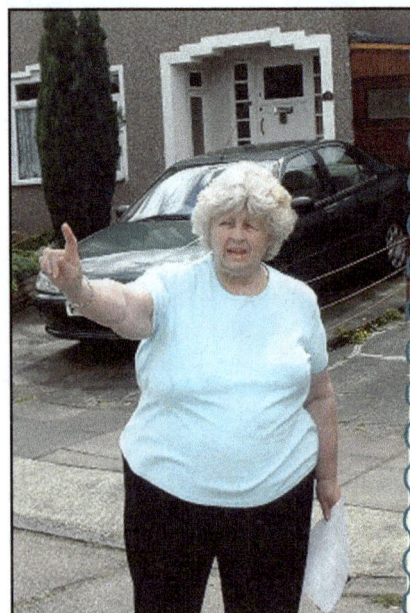

Margaret Fry

THAT BIG, BIG BANG HAS YARD BAFFLED

Air Ministry say 'Not a plane'

Evening Standard Reporter

The loud bang which woke people over a wide area of London and the Home Counties shortly before one o'clock this morning is the second mystery bang in four months.

In March police searched Hampstead Heath following reports of a bang believed to have occurred between Hampstead Heath and Parliament Hill Fields.

No explanation was found, or given, for this bang.

Is there any connection between the two incidents? No one seems to know.

Theory discounted

The Air Ministry said of today's bang that Uxbridge Report Centre had no reports of any aircraft being in the vicinity of the noise. This discounts the theory that an aircraft breaking the sound barrier could have been responsible.

The Ministry of Supply cannot help.

The possibility of an explosion at a munitions dump or factory was put forward. But the only Government explosives depot anywhere in the area is Woolwich Arsenal. Nothing has been reported from there.

Scotland Yard are still baffled. Hundreds of reports of the explosion poured into the Yard's information room. Police on foot and in cars checked and rechecked, but nothing was found.

Haunted Skies Volume Ten

Great Britain: 14th July 1955 & 17th July 1955 – Spectacular sighting of near landed UFO at Bexleyheath, in Kent, by local woman Margaret Fry, following reports of saucer-shaped objects seen in the sky by children from local school. (See Volume 1 of *Haunted Skies*, for full report).

DAILY EXPRESS

No. 17,166   SATURDAY JULY 30 1955   1 a.m. forecast: Dry; sunny intervals

WHOOSH—and the world zooms into the Jeff

FLYING SAUCERS
They will circle the earth at 18,000 miles an hour

FLYING SAUCERS have come true, and that's official. Plans to launch them were announced yesterday on behalf of President Eisenhower.

America will send up "earth satellites" 19¼ins. wide—twice the size of footballs—but weighing a hundredweight.

The metal saucers will girdle the earth in 90 minutes, from North Pole to South Pole, travelling at 18,000 miles an hour.

They will revolve round the earth at a height between 200 and 300 miles and will radio information about air density, cosmic radiation, and the weather.

The announcement of plans which will come into effect in two years was made by President Eisenhower's Press Secretary, Mr. James Haggerty, in Washington— and by a scientist in Brussels.

The saucers will be launched by rockets in America.

The results will not be secret. Forty nations, including Britain and Russia, will have listening posts.

These nations are contributing to a "Geophysical Year" from July 1957 — a period of intensive research into the earth sciences.

And the plan to launch flying saucers is America's contribution.

In the White House Mr. Haggerty said that the plan is entirely for scientific purposes, and that the cost of the project will be £3,500,000 — exclusive of the cost of the rockets.

Scientists joined Mr. Haggerty to explain the plan. They called the projected satellite "THE BIRD" and said that each would circle the earth for days or perhaps weeks.

They would then fall and disintegrate.

At the expected rate of travel the saucers could pass over London to over New York in 11 minutes, and over London to

over Brighton in 10 second The scientists at the Whit House said that observations ma by the saucers would "indic the conditions if the day com when man goes beyond the earth atmosphere in his travels."

The highest man has been far is about 18 miles up in a rock plane.

The world of Jeff Hawke, spaceships and interplaneta travel, came appreciably nea yesterday.

It would take the saucers— they could get that far—13 hou to reach the moon and th months to reach Mars.

Haunted Skies Volume Ten

USA: 1st August 1955 – In Willoughby, Ohio, a married couple and their two children were driving home when they saw a circular object descend through the sky, showing red lights, about 100ft in diameter, with a dome on top, emanating a white light. It then stopped and began to hover.

The family got out of the car and watched. Two beams of light appeared and several openings were seen. Frightened, they made their way home. (**Source:** *Flying Saucers on the Attack*, **Harold T. Wilkins**)

Great Britain: 15th August 1955 – A silver *'flying saucer'* was seen over Betley Post Office, Cheshire. (See Volume 1, of *Haunted Skies*)

August 1955

Great Britain: 16th August 1955 – Entity seen, Bradford

At 4am, Bradford lorry driver Ernest Suddards (35) was on his way home, after collecting the firm's lorry from the garage (where it was kept overnight) accompanied by his son Raymond (13). As they drove down Roundhill Street, a short distance from the family home, they saw something, or someone, approaching in the glare of the headlights.

Ernest:

> *"It looked about 4ft tall, dressed in skintight black clothes, with arms close to its sides, with feet together, and hopped, or jumped forwards, in a series of jerky movements. On its chest was a circular silver disc, with holes cut into it, below the throat. It then turned down a nearby passage. We were literally paralysed by the sight. After arriving home, we talked about it and then contacted the police, who had a look around but found nothing."*

We spoke to Ray Suddards (aged 63 in 2006) – like his father, a lorry driver by occupation.

Ray:

> *"I remember it clearly – like yesterday. It had this silver plate, with holes on its chest, hopping up Roundhill Street. After my dad reported what we had seen, he was subjected to a lot of ridicule. A few days later, he picked up a newspaper and read about a similar 'figure' being seen in Horton Lane, close to where we had seen it."*

The sighting led to much speculation. Some people believed that what the Suddards' had witnessed was the lone occupant of a downed *'flying saucer'*; others thought it might have been a ghost.

Following an appeal in the *Bradford Telegraph & Argus*, we were contacted by Detective Sergeant Paul Jackson (retired) who recalls the incident very well, because his partner at the time was Police Constable Victor Briggs – the Officer who interviewed them and made a search of the area.

> *"He (P.C. Briggs) often brought up the subject in conversation, as he believed they had genuinely sighted something highly unusual."*

Haunted Skies Volume Ten

TELEGRAPH & ARGUS, Bradford, England – May 5, 2003

RETIRED DETECTIVE GETS ON THE TRAIL OF BRADFORD UFOs

Did you see the little green man in a pointy hat?

IMAGE: Could this be the little green man seen in a Bradford street in 1954, now hunted by UFO detective John Hanson, inset

by **JANET FAULKNER**
T&A Reporter

As far as close encounters go, it seemed a strange place for aliens to land.

Not for them the White House or even Roswell, New Mexico.

But a little street off Manchester Road, a stone's throw from the city centre, became the focus, it is said, of a visitation from another world.

It was 1954, a young Queen Elizabeth reigned, and the biggest ever crowd of 102,000 watched a Challenge Cup Final replay between Halifax and Warrington at Odsal.

Just a few short months later, the aliens, perhaps intrigued by the vast crowds at Odsal, descended on the city.

It was 4am on August 16 and a 'creature' was seen creeping around Roundhill Street by a lorry driver.

And now a retired detective is on the hunt of the Close Encounter of the Holme Top kind.

John Hanson is writing a book about UFOs and other unexplained phenomena and is hunting for anyone who witnessed the little green man with a pointy hat.

The lorry driver described the creature as about four feet tall and said it was walking in a peculiar manner before it disappeared down an alleyway.

Witnesses of other "alien sightings" have reported a similar strange walk, he said.

As a CID officer, Mr Hanson was sceptical about reports of UFOs and aliens - until he heard about something he simply could not explain.

An orange ball of fire was reported in the sky above a suburb of Birmingham on January 19, 1995.

When police officers went to investigate, they saw a blue object with a bar of orange light in the centre.

Mr Hanson said: "Prior to January 19, 1995 I was a sceptic in such matters."

But he was unconvinced by the official explanation that the object was simply a shooting star.

Since then, he has spent hours of his time researching other sightings of UFOs.

"I decided to carry out my own research into the subject, working sometimes six or seven hours a day, writing up accounts given to me by people, some of whom I had to track down from the early 1950s. I'm obsessive to say the least!" he said.

He believes that many of the unexplained phenomena are connected with ancient "energy fields" which are linked to the planet itself.

"This would suggest that we are dealing with a phenomenon which is as ancient as man himself, and likely to be indigenous to the Planet rather that examples of visitations from E.T." he added.

What is clear is that 50 years of research have not found an explanation for the creature seen in Roundhill Street.

With the help of readers who remember, John Hanson hopes to get closer to the truth.

Please email Mr Hanson with any reports of UFO activity: john@recardo76.fsnet.co.uk or write to him at 1 Bunbury Gardens, Kings Norton, Birmingham B30 1BA.

SPACE: Images in the sky that John Hanson is hoping to track down and identify

USA: 21st August 1955 – Mysterious event at Kentucky – Alien or ghostly spectre?

There have been numerous books, documentaries and debates, regarding this incident, which alleges a close encounter with extraterrestrial beings on the 21st August 1955. The incident became famous and well-publicised.

It occurred at Gaither McGette's rural farmhouse, rented at the time by the Sutton family, located between the hamlet of Kelly and the small city of Hopkinsville, Christian County, Kentucky. Many people believe that it had nothing to do with any alien incursion and more in keeping with a paranormal report, involving some sort of demonic presence.

While there is no reason to suppose this was a hoax, it is worth considering whether you and I would have seen the same thing. I believe we probably would. Some claim it was investigated by the United States Air Force, which may well have been the case, bearing in mind the sketch of one of the *'creature's'* released by the American Air Force in 1969 and later redrawn by Pauline Bowen.

The seven people present in the farmhouse claimed that they were terrorised by an unknown number of *'creatures'* – often referred to as the 'Hopkinsville Goblins'. The residents of the farmhouse described them as:

> *". . . around three feet tall, with upright pointed ears, thin limbs, long arms, and claw-like hands or talons. The creatures were either silvery in colour, or wearing something metallic. Their movements on occasion seemed to defy gravity with them floating above the ground and appearing in high up places, and they 'walked' with a swaying motion as though wading through water".*

How it all started – Billy Ray Taylor sights disc-shaped object

Billy Ray Taylor of Pennsylvania and his family were visiting the Sutton family of Kentucky. There were a total of eleven people in the house that night, including the children of the two families. As the Sutton farmhouse had no running water, Billy Ray Taylor went outside to the water pump for a drink, at about 7pm, when he noticed unusual, strange lights in the sky to the west, which he described as *"disc-shaped in appearance, and featured lights on its side that had all of the colours of the rainbow."*

He ran back to the house excitedly, telling the others about a flying *'saucer'* but no one believed him, thinking he was mistaken.

Strange noises heard

At about 8pm, the families began hearing strange and unexplained noises outside, followed by the Sutton family dog (which was in the yard outside) barking loudly; it then hid under the house, where it remained until the next day. Going outside a few minutes later with their guns, Billy Ray Taylor and Elmer 'Lucky' Sutton then told of seeing a strange *'creature'* emerge from the nearby trees.

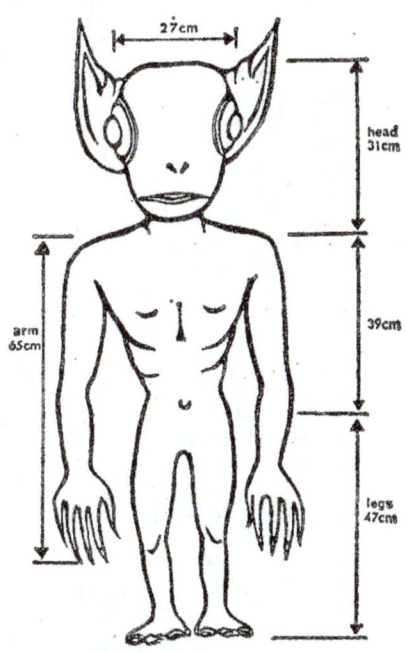

The Kelly-Hopkinsville 'Goblin', redrawn from a sketch released by the United States Air Force, by Pauline Bowen, for the book 'The Humanoids', edited by Charles Bowen, then editor of 'Flying Saucer Review', and published in 1969.

Haunted Skies Volume Ten

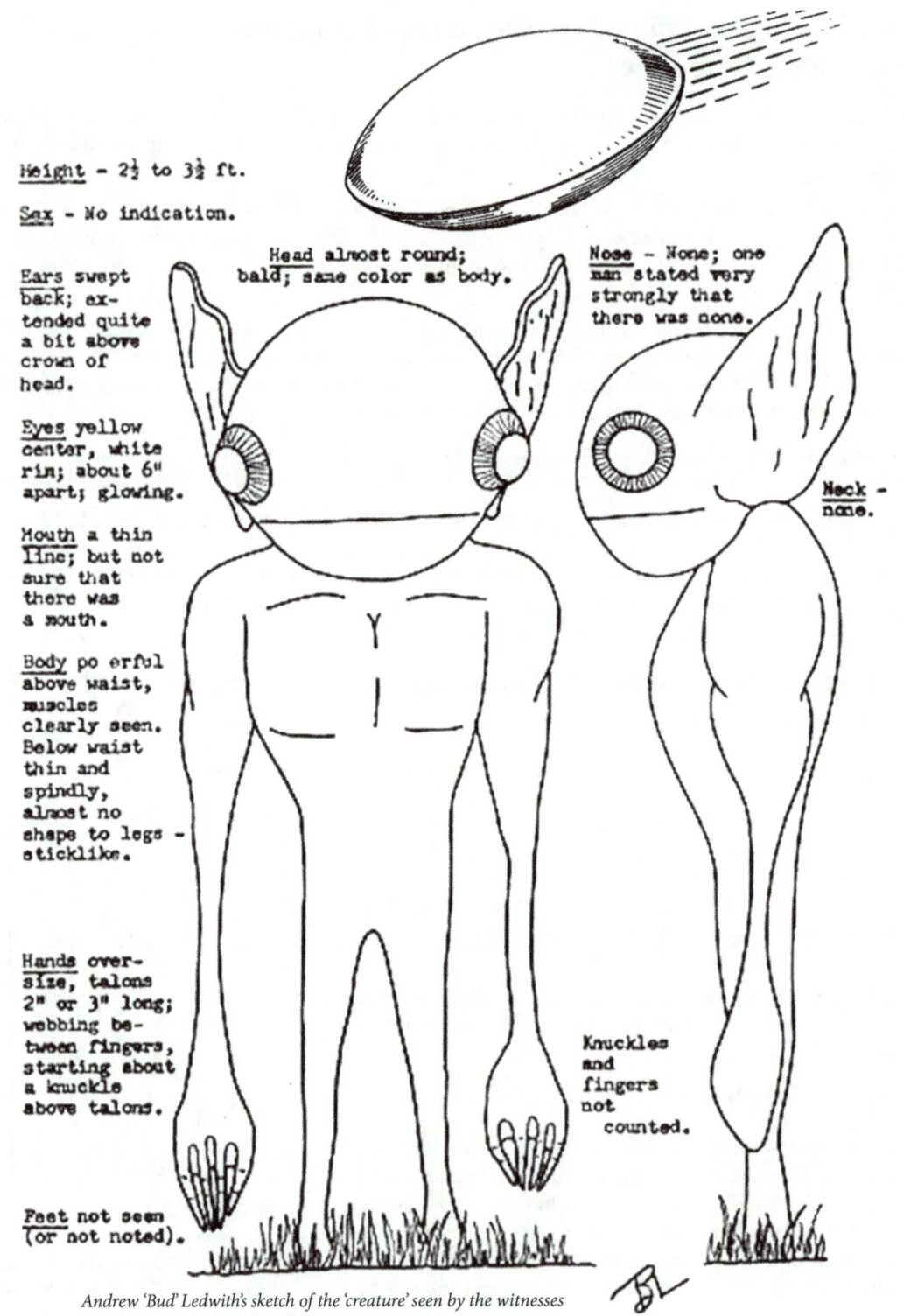

Andrew 'Bud' Ledwith's sketch of the 'creature' seen by the witnesses

Shoot first, ask questions later!

When the *'creature'* approached to within about 20ft, the two men began shooting at it; one using a shotgun, the other man using a .22 rifle. There was a noise *"sounding like bullets being rattled about in a metal drum"*; it then flipped over and fled into the darkness and shadows. Believing they had wounded it, Lucky and Solomon went out to look for it. As the men were stepping from the porch, they saw one of the *'things'* perched on an awning and fired at it, which they claimed knocked it off the roof. This was followed by the rattling noise, although the *'creature'* was apparently unharmed by the weapons. [One speculates if it might have been the sound that caused them agitation, rather than the bullets themselves.]

Lucky and Solomon returned to the house in a disturbed state. Within minutes, Lucky's brother – J.C. Sutton – said that he saw the same *'creature'* (or at least a similar one) peer into a window in the home; J.C. and Solomon shot at it, breaking the window, whereupon it, too, flipped over and fled.

Haunted Skies Volume Ten

The 'creatures' could be heard loudly scurrying about on the roof, and scratching, as though trying to break through. On occasion, when *'hit'* by gunfire, they would float, rather than fall, to the ground.

The siege begins

For the next few hours, the witnesses asserted that the *'creatures'* repeatedly approached the home, either popping up at the doorway or at windows in an almost playful manner, only to be shot at each time they did. The witnesses were unsure as to how many of the *'creatures'* there were; except for one sighting of two at the same time. All other sightings were of only one, although the first story claimed twelve to fifteen. At one point the witnesses shot one of the *'beings'* at nearly point-blank range, and again would insist that the sound resembled bullets, striking a metal bucket. The floating *'creatures'* legs seemed to be nearly useless, and they

Haunted Skies Volume Ten

Haunted Skies Volume Ten

appeared to propel themselves with a curious hip-swaying motion, steering with their arms. Although the *'creatures'* never entered the house, they would pop up at windows and at the doorway, waking up the children in the house to a hysterical frenzy.

Alan Hendry, who was one of a number of people that investigated this matter, reported that *"Mrs Lankford counselled an end to the hostilities",* feeling that the *'creatures'* had never seemed to try harming anyone, nor had they actually entered the house. Between appearances from the *'creatures',* the family tried to temper the children's growing hysteria.

At about 11pm, the Taylor-Sutton family decided to flee the farmhouse in their cars and arrived at the Hopkinsville Police Station, 30 minutes later. Police Chief Russell Greenwell judged the witnesses to have been frightened by something *"beyond reason, not ordinary; these were not the sort of people who normally ran to the police. Something frightened them, something beyond their comprehension."*

At about 11pm, a State highway trooper, near Kelly, independently reported some unusual *"meteor-like objects"* flying overhead, *"with a sound like artillery fire coming directly from them".*

Police officers visit the scene

The families returned to the farmhouse with Sheriff Greenwell, Deputy Sheriff George Batts (Patts?) and twenty officers, who saw for themselves evidence of the struggle and damage to the house, as well as seeing strange lights and hearing noises, although they did not see any sign of the mysterious *'creatures'.* The police left at about 2.15am, and not long afterwards it was claimed the *'creatures'* made their return. Once again, Billy Ray fired at them, breaking another window in the house.

Newspaper/Radio stations coverage

Kentucky New Era published an account of the incident on 22nd August 1955, and claimed 12 to 15 *'little men'* had been seen, when, in fact, the witnesses were unable to say how many were actually observed, but it appears there were at least two. On this date, Andrew 'Bud' Ledwith, of *WHOP* radio, interviewed the seven adult witnesses in two different groups. He judged their tale of the events as consistent, especially in their descriptions of the strange glowing *'beings'.* Ledwith had worked as a professional artist, and sketched the *'creatures'* based on the witnesses' descriptions. These were generally consistent, though the female witnesses insisted that the *'creatures'* had a somewhat huskier build than the male witnesses remembered, and Billy Ray Taylor was alone in insisting that the *'beings'* had antennae.

Ridicule directed at family

Not surprisingly, as time went by, the family became the target of considerable ridicule, especially as public opinion tended to view the story as a hoax and showed only a brief interest in the event. Some residents of the local community, including members of the police department, were sceptical of the Sutton's story and believed that alcohol (possibly moonshine) may have played a part in the incident, although, to date, no evidence was ever found to support this allegation. Others claimed the whole thing was a hoax, after learning some of the witnesses had been employed by a carnival. The farm became a tourist attraction for a brief period, which upset the Suttons, who tried to keep people away by later attempting to charge people an entrance fee to discourage them. Soon they became fed up and refused to have any contact with UFO researchers – apart from, it is said, Isabel Davis of Civilian Saucer Investigation.

Story Of Space-Ship, 12 Little Men Probed Today

Kelly Farmhouse Scene Of Alleged Raid By Strange Crew Last Night; Reports Say Bullets Failed To Affect Visitors

All kinds of investigations were going on today in connection with the bizarre story of how a space-ship carrying 12 to 15 little men landed in the Kelly community early last night and battled occupants of a farmhouse.

Most official of the probes was reportedly being staged by the air force.

More than a dozen state, county, and city officers from Christian and Hopkins counties went to the scene between 11 p.m. and midnight and remained until after 2 a.m. without seeing anything either to prove or disprove the story about the ship and its occupants.

went out of the house to get a bucket of water. He saw what looked like a flying saucer come over the trees and land in a field at a point about a city block behind the house. There was no explosion, only a semi-hissing sound, and the watcher returned to the house with the bucket of water.

A short time later somebody reported some little men with big heads and long arms were approaching the house. The men were described as having huge eyes and hands out of proportion to their small bodies. The visitors were wearing what looked to be metal plate.

It was a monkey!

In 1957, US Air Force Major John E. Albert concluded that the Kelly-Hopkinsville case was the result of the witnesses seeing *"a monkey painted with silver that had escaped from a circus"*, and that Mrs Lankford's imagination had exaggerated the event. This Air Force Officer was on his way from Gracey to Campbell Air Force Base when he heard a radio broadcast at 8am about the incident and decided to go to the scene and interview Lenny Lankford. The explanation lacks substance as there were no bodies of any monkeys found at the scene. Isabel Davis rejected this explanation as not only entirely speculative but absurd, and published a detailed account of her investigation into the matter. Others suggested it was misidentification of a Great Horned Owl!

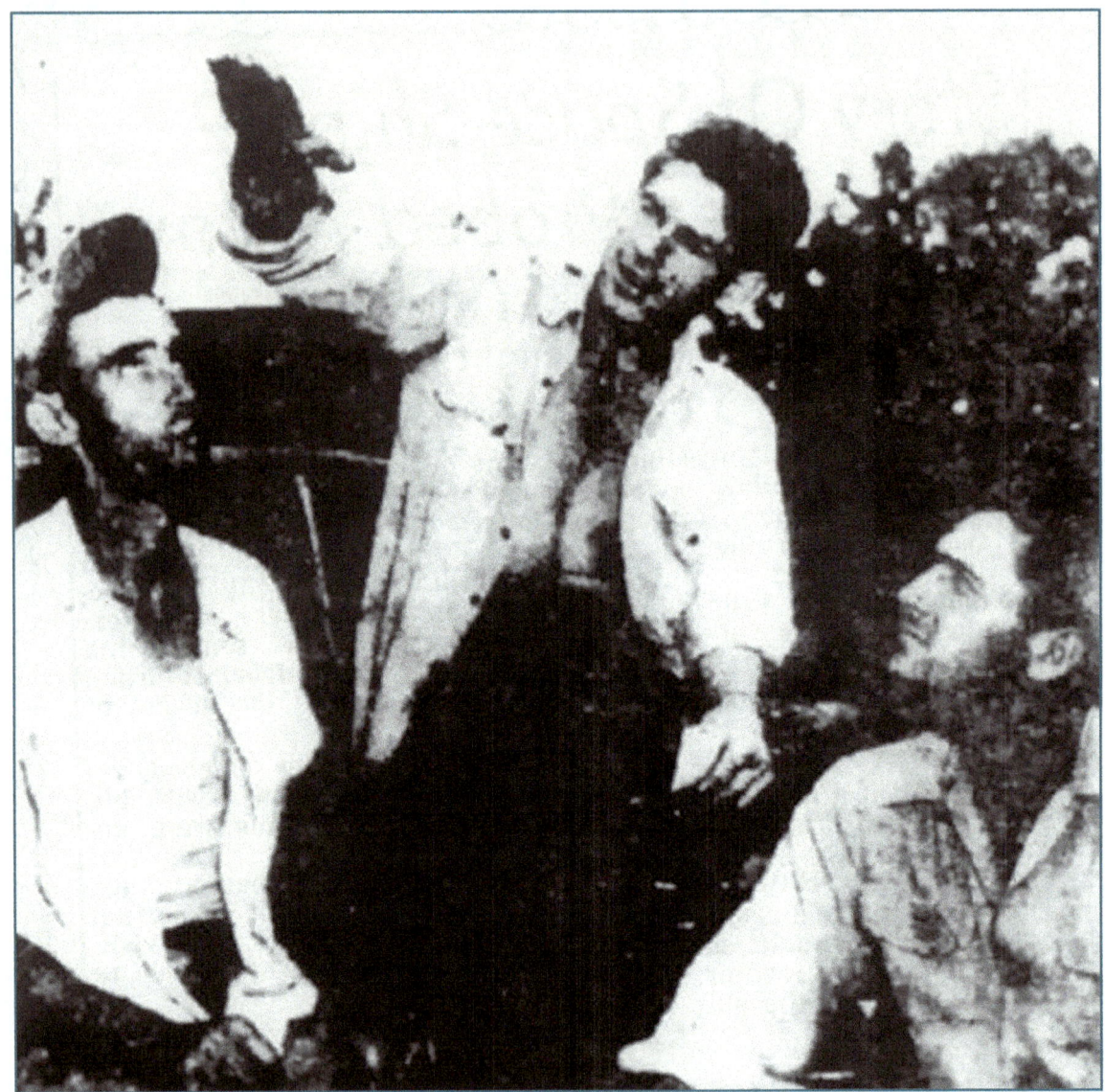

Police investigation

Police interviewed neighbouring farmhouses, whose residents were also distressed, and reported to the police strange lights, strange sounds, and of hearing the gun battle at the Sutton farmstead. Police and photographers who visited the home saw many bullet holes and hundreds of spent shells, and further discovered what appeared to be an odd luminous patch along a fence where one of the beings had been shot, and, in the woods beyond, a green light whose source could not be determined. Though the investigation was inconclusive, investigators did conclude, however, that these people were sincere and sane and that they had no interest in exploiting the case for publicity. The patch sample, although photographed, was never collected and had mysteriously disappeared by noon the next day. In 2002, Lucky Sutton's daughter – Geraldine Hawkins – who believed her father's account, said:

> "It was a serious thing to him. It happened to him. He said it happened to him. He said it wasn't funny. It was an experience he said he would never forget. It was fresh in his mind until the day he died. It was fresh in his mind like it happened yesterday. He never cracked a smile when he told the story, because it happened to him and there wasn't anything funny about it. He got pale and you could see it in his eyes. He was scared to death."

A claim is also made of another 'close encounter' allegedly involving similar entities in another part of the United States, along the *Ohio River*, a week prior to the incidents in Kentucky, of which it is rumoured there were numerous witnesses. Fascinating as this sounded, we were unable to find any confirmatory evidence supporting that version of events. Hopefully we can obtain further information regarding this matter in due course.

With matters such as these, we believe it would be beneficial to examine not only the surrounding area for a clue as to why these *'entities'* manifested, but the backgrounds of the people involved. Is it possible that one of them could have been the trigger for what took place and have experienced strange phenomena before? However, we are at a disadvantage as we only know some of what took place and were never there! Knowing that many photographs were taken of the scene by the police, we emailed the Kentucky State Police in 2014, hoping that they might have retained this file in their Police Museum, and also contacted the local library, wondering if they had a file on this matter. Despite a number of emails and letters sent we never received any reply.

Was it leprechauns or aliens seen in Belfast?

We wondered if there was any connection with an incident that took place some years later, in Belfast, Northern Ireland, when during September 1964, a frenzy of excitement swept over the area. It was claimed a *'leprechaun'* had been sighted in Tamar Street, East Belfast, on or about the 10th September 1964. The fact that the culprit was later identified as six year-old Jimmy Hughes, playing in a derelict house, dressed as Robin Hood, who was chased away by police after fears for his safety, appears to have triggered off, once again, that insatiable 'spark' which ignited the population's imaginations and desire to descend onto the street, causing massive disruption. Ironically, the crowds that gathered there included many adults.

The incident – which involved the attendance of the police and fire service – also attracted the interest of David Bleakley, Labour MP for Victoria, who handed over a petition to Belfast Corporation, demanding action to keep the crowds and children away from the embankment and derelict houses. One senior police officer was quoted as saying, *"a grown man, cold stone sober, insisted to me he had seen a leprechaun!"*

Was it leprechauns or aliens seen in Liverpool?

Oddly, a few weeks later, there was to be a 'repeat performance' in Liverpool. This followed a number of UFO sightings, which were alleged to have fuelled a wave of (what was claimed to be) mass hysteria, on the 1st July 1964. Local newspapers claimed:

> "... thousands of children joined in the hunt, after reports of 'Little Green Men' or leprechauns had been seen near the bowling green, Jubilee Park, Jubilee Drive, Liverpool, east of the city in the Edge Lane district, and that the police were called in to control the crowd."

Coral Lorenzen, APRO Group

Coral Lorenzen was born in Winsconsin. She attended school in Barron and graduated in May 1941. Her interest in the UFO subject began in 1934, when, while aged 9, she saw a hemisphere-shaped object cross the sky in an undulating trajectory. During conservation with the family Doctor – Harry Schlomovitz – she was loaned the books of Charles Fort.

On the 29th September 1943, she married Jim Lorenzen. On the 10th June 1947, she sighted a tiny round object leave the ground and move up into the sky. This was ten days before Kenneth Arnold had his sighting. During the following years, Coral made many contacts with likeminded people. In 1952 she decided to form the APRO Group, with the aim of preserving the history of so many

Jim & Coral Lorenzen

UFO sightings. Coral served as Director until 1964, when Jim took over the role. She then served as secretary-treasurer and member of APRO until 1988. She was the co-author/author of seven books *Flying Saucers – The Startling Evidence of the Invasion from Outer Space* (originally entitled *The Great Flying Saucer Hoax*) (1962, 1966), *The Shadow of the Unknown* (1970), *Flying Saucer Occupants* (1967) (co-author Jim Lorenzen), *UFOs over the Americas* (1968) (co-author Jim Lorenzen), *UFOs – The Whole Story* (1969) (co-author Jim Lorenzen), *Encounters with UFO Occupants* (1976) (co-author Jim Lorenzen), and *Abducted!* (1977) (co-author Jim Lorenzen) – and passed away in 1988.

Jim Lorenzen, APRO

Jim was born in 1922 and was later a professional musician, until inducted into the US Army Corps in 1942 before being discharged in 1945. During that time he served with the Air Transport Command in the China, India, Burma, theatre of operations. He was awarded the Air Medal cluster, A Presidential Unit citation with

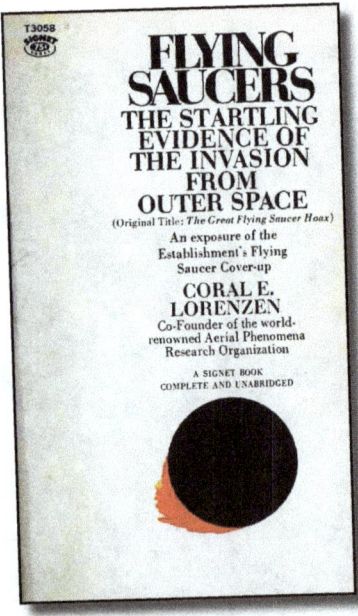

cluster, and the Distinguished Flying Cross with cluster. In 1954, following a number of other jobs, he was employed as chief of electronic maintenance at Holloman Air Force Base, New Mexico. In 1960, he accepted an invitation of senior technical associate at Kitt Peal National Observatory in Tuscon, where he remained until 1967. Since 1964, Jim also served as International Director for APRO. He passed away in 1986.

(Sources: Alan Hendry, *Kelly Hopkinsville (Kentucky) Encounter*, Isabel Davis, New York Civilian Saucer Investigations/Project Blue Book listed the case as a hoax, with no further comment)

USA: 23rd August 1955 – UFO Display over Virginia

At 10.45am, Mr G.M. Park from Arlington, Virginia, watched through his 400x telescope, for 30 minutes, several orange lights moving singly or in groups, circling and stopping through the sky. (**Source: Project Blue Book**)

US fighter jets scramble to intercept UFO

At 12.10pm on the same date, according to Leonard H. Stringfield, editor of *Orbit*, Fighter aircraft from Lockbourne Air Force Base, Ohio, were scrambled to intercept three UFOs, which had been hovering over the control tower. The aircraft climbed to 20,000ft, but the UFOs shot away at incredible speed. Officials at Forestville and Loveland also told of having sighted the erratic behaviour of UFOs on the same day – described as round, brilliant white spheres and discs. [Authors: 'Three' objects reported again! This description dominates our extensive files – whatever the period. They significance of this should be of major importance, bearing in mind that the UFO sightings reported in the 1980s – now referred to as triangular UFOs – have far more in common with earlier reports than we may think.]

Great Britain: 25th August 1955 – At 7.30pm, fifteen UFOs were sighted crossing the sky over Birmingham.

September 1955

USA: 1955 – UFO crash-lands, but precise date not known

At the time of his UFO encounter, in 1955, Colonel Robert Burton Willingham was flying in Cold War training exercises out of Carswell Air Force Base in Texas.

> "I was one of four aircraft assigned to a wing tip watch over a B-47 that left New York and came down at Oklahoma, then down through Archer County, back over and heading to El Paso. We were supposed to fly cover for it. We were flying along when my buddy back there shouted, 'Look at that big star falling!' Whatever it was, we all looked at it I said, 'Are you sure that's a star?' To me it looked

like something else; it was very bight and made a 90° turn at 2,000mph, and I didn't figure it was. I asked the Captain on the B-47 to see where it was going, because we didn't know what it was. He told me to go and have a look. At this time it was right below Langtry, Texas, and leaving some kind of contrail behind it. At this point we were flying at about 35,000ft. It circled around. By the time I descended to investigate further and believed it was going to crash as such, but control of it had been lost in some way.

As I flew over the Rio Grande River *the thing was on the ground, after having bounded a few times over the ground; say, a thousand yards. I didn't see it hit the ground, but it was stopped and was breaking up pretty bad. I made one circle around it, looked it over, and then headed back to my job. I landed at Carswell Air Force Base and decided to make my way back to the crash location, which was about a hundred yards away from the* Rio Grande River, *accompanied by a colleague – Perkins. We flew back down there in a light aircraft and landed about 2-250yds away. I was then approached by a number of armed Spanish soldiers. I put up my hands (at this time the craft was visible) after some conversation with a Spanish Lt., who said he had never seen anything like it before. We walked up to the object and I picked up a piece of it. He later conducted a number of metallurgic tests on the sample at Fort Worth. It was a flat, slightly curved piece of metal, with holes along one end. It looked like stainless steel and had a greyish silver coloration. One side was kind of jagged, as if it had been broken off from a larger piece."*

Familiar with metals because of his father's work as a metallurgist for an oil company, Willingham used a cutting torch to test the strange debris.

"A cutting torch burns anywhere from 3,200 to 3,800° Fahrenheit, and it would make the metal hot, but it wouldn't even start the metal to yield; we tried a cutting torch, grinders, and everything else, but nothing would even touch it."

According to Willingham, the characteristics of the metallic fragment led him to believe the UFO was not earthly in origin.

"You can say I might have seen some kind of missile fly across the sky and crash. You can say that maybe it was some kind of experiment, although I'd never seen anything that looked like that. But, what you cannot say is that the metal I tested with my own hands was anything that was made here on our planet. My daddy started me welding when I was nine years old. I knew my metals. That thing was not anything we had ever seen before."

Because he did not have the proper equipment for more detailed testing of the UFO fragment, Willingham contacted an acquaintance who was connected with a government-contracted metallurgic laboratory in Maryland. Willingham flew the sample to Maryland and turned it over to laboratory technicians there for a detailed analysis of its composition.

"When I got to the lab, I turned it over to one of the workers there, who proceeded to do all the same things I had already done. He tried to cut it, burn it, and so on. Finally, he said, 'Man, this is good stuff.'"

Several days later, Willingham made a phone call from Texas to ask about the specimen he had left at the Maryland laboratory. The person answering the phone told him that they knew of no such specimen, that the person with whom Willingham left the fragment no longer worked there, and that the laboratory was closing down and moving to another location. Willingham made further inquiries about the laboratory and his specimen, until he received a phone call from a superior officer in the military, instructing him to *"stop asking questions and just forget about it"*.

Willingham claims that he then began receiving a series of phone calls from officers in military intelligence, instructing him *"never to speak about what happened down on the border"*. One of the callers – a General in military intelligence – warned him that there would be *'consequences'* if he told anyone about what he saw.

Within a week after his UFO incident, Willingham flew over the UFO crash site and could no longer see any visual evidence that anything at all had ever happened there.

"It looked like they went through every inch of ground with a fine toothcomb."

Colonel Robert Willingham

Several years after his encounter, Willingham received an anonymous letter with a comment regarding the disappeared metallic fragment. According to Willingham, the letter said:

"Remember the metal you left at our lab in Maryland? We have never tested anything like it, ever – before or since."

Willingham believes the unsigned letter came from the laboratory technician.

"I never told anyone – not even my wife, until I told it to a newspaper reporter in 1967."

The brief article was sent by a member of the National Investigations Committee on Aerial Phenomena (NICAP) to NICAP headquarters, where it sat for 10 years before anyone followed up on it. In 1977, NICAP member Todd Zechel contacted Willingham, asked him to file a written affidavit about his sighting, and then arranged for the filming of a documentary for Japanese television. During this same period, the story of the 1947 Roswell UFO incident was also released for the first time, following initial interviews by Stanton Friedman with Jesse Marcel, Sr.

Haunted Skies Volume Ten

Beginning in the 1980s, references to the Willingham case appeared in the writings of several major civilian UFO researchers, including Bruce Maccabee, Kevin D. Randle, Stanton Friedman, and Ryan S. Wood.

In 2007, UFO investigators – Noe Torres and Ruben Uriarte – following up on Zechel's earlier work, contacted Willingham and obtained his permission to write a book about his UFO case. The book, *The Other Roswell: UFO Crash on the Texas-Mexico Border*, written by Torres and Uriarte, as told by Willingham, was published in May 2008, by Roswell Books.com.

Colonel Willingham remained in the Reserve until around 1972, rising to the rank of Colonel. Interestingly, from 1959 to 1963, he served as a UFO investigator for Project Blue Book, assisting other investigators in taking over 2,000 witness testimonies from persons claiming to have seen UFOs.

We wrote to him in 2014, c/o a Veterans Clinic in the States, and sent him Volume 1 of *Haunted Skies*, but we were surprised not to have received any answer, as Noe had told us the Colonel was in ill health.

Bearing in mind the recovery by Colonel Willingham of the mysterious piece of metal, and its subsequent loss, we felt we should once again remind the reader of the piece of metal recovered from a crash landing of a UFO on a farmer's field at Llanilar, Wales, on the 9th January 1983. The field was covered in masses of great shards of metal. Nobody has ever accepted responsibility for the incident. We wrote to the MOD and received this answer:

Haunted Skies Volume Ten

'Dear Mr Hanson,

I am writing concerning your request for information about an incident of metal debris being discovered on farmer's land, near Aberystwyth, on 9th January 1983. Your request has been passed to this department, as we are the focal point with the Ministry of Defence for correspondence regarding UFOs. I have made a search through all the UFO related files we have for that year 1983, and found no documents relating to this alleged incident. Sorry I could not have been more help.

Yours sincerely,
Mrs J. Monk.'

Discrepancy over date

In Volume 1 of *Haunted Skies*, we briefly outlined details relating to this matter, which we had initially believed had taken place in 1950, involving USAF Colonel Robert B. Willingham, who was navigator aboard a F86 Jet, heading south-west, when he saw a UFO crash-land near the Mexican border. However, it appears there is some confusion about the date, according to the witness, who in 2007 declared it had occurred in 1955.

It is obviously of some concern that the correct date for what is, after all, one of the most spectacular UFO crashes of the post-war period (excluding Roswell) is not known.

A more recent photo of Colonel Robert Willingham who witnessed a UFO crash-land on the Texas-Mexico border in 1955

Some years ago we came across this information from what appears now to be a dubious source quote: Colonel Robert Willingham, of the USAF, was a navigator aboard a F94 jet. He said ...

> "A saucer flew right over [us], put down three landing gears, and landed out on the dry lakebed.
>
> [The cameramen] went out there with their cameras toward the UFO. I had chance to hold [the film] up to the window. Good close-up shots. There was no doubt in my mind that it was made someplace other than on this earth. Headquarters wouldn't let us go after it and we played around a little bit. We got to watching how it made 90 degree turns at this high speed and everything. We knew it wasn't a missile of any type. So then, we confirmed it with the radar control station, and they kept following it, and they claimed that it crashed somewhere off between Texas and the Mexico border."

It also nominated the date of the occurrence as the 6th September 1950. We presumed this date was from his original affidavit made in the 1970s, although we have never seen a copy of that document.

According to Wikipedia 2014 in his 1977 NICAP affidavit, Robert Willingham did not give a date for his UFO encounter, which led to confusion among some UFO researchers, who later speculated the event had occurred on 6th December 1950, because on that date the US government issued an alert to its military forces, due to waves of UFOs having been spotted on radar. In addition to this, mention is made of a UFO crash near Del Rio, Texas, in December 1950, which is mentioned in the Eisenhower Briefing Document, part of the controversial Majestic 12 Documents. However, in 2007, Willingham told Torres and Uriarte that he was absolutely certain that his UFO encounter did not take place in 1950.

Now we know that Robert Willingham retired as Colonel, but what was his rank when the incident took place? We cannot seem to find this out either.

If it was this date (which now appears very unlikely) then it took place the same day as the incident involving Farnborough Test Pilot Stan Hubbard who, along with others, witnessed a display of UFO behaviour over the base during that afternoon. Stan was later interviewed by a group of men from the Scientific Intelligence Department, and said:

> "They were very, very specific that I was not to discuss the matter with anybody because it was highly classified."

The fact that the actual date is not known is very unusual but should not cast any doubt on the validity of the testimony given by Colonel Willingham, who is well respected and should be congratulated for having the courage to come forward and tell what he saw.

USA: 9th September 1955 – Mr N. Dawkins from Alcoa, Tennessee, sighted, through binoculars, a brown (almost square) object in the sky, which was seen to move around in a circular motion, for 10-15 minutes. **(Source: Project Blue Book)**

USA: New York, 17th September 1955 – UFOs seen over Titicus Reservoir

During a dark and breezy night, Frank and Eileen Bordes, of The Bronx, were out fishing on Titicus Reservoir, near Bush Pine, New York State.

Eileen was the first to see an iridescent pink mushroom-shaped object rise about 2ft above the water, before disappearing below the surface. She brought this matter to her husband's attention and then asked him to row ashore. When this was done, the couple looked out into the darkness, which was illuminated by twinkling stars. They then noticed a light, followed by two long lights below this, apparently emanating from an elongated object some 15ft long, which was partially submerged, around which appeared a good deal of turbulence. Frank and Eileen rowed along the shore, feeling they were being watched in some way. They also remarked on the curious fact that whenever they headed towards the object(s), it would speed towards them; when they moved back, so did it. (**Source: Dr. Paul Gray**)

October 1955

Great Britain: 18th October 1955 – The Reverend Pitt-Kethley, from West London, was travelling on an Uxbridge train to East Harrow, London, at 4.10pm., when the train was halted by a signal at West Hampstead Viaduct. As he casually looked through the window, he saw a strange craft approaching in the sky, at a height of about 120ft, described as being reddish brown and grey in colour, reminding him of:

> "...a German troop carrier, about the size of a small bus, containing about 30 immobile helmeted figures, with human faces, all apparently dressed in khaki uniforms, some of whom were seated and staring fixedly forward. I was puzzled how such an object, with its low trajectory, could possibly clear London."

New Zealand: 31st October 1955 – An airliner reported having been overtaken by a pulsating light, while over Auckland.

November 1955

USA: 1st November 1955 – Gigantic object seen by astronomer

Frank Edwards – author of *Flying Saucers, Serious Business* – tells of an interview conducted with Frank Halstead, curator at Darling Observatory, Duluth, Minnesota, in 1959, during which Mr Halstead outlined the mysterious sighting of a peculiar straight black line on the floor of the Crater 'Piccolomini. He and his assistant – Raymond Matsuhara – along with 16 other visitors,

Right on Schedule Oct 20-55

Mystery Lights Still Loom Around County

Those right-on-schedule mystery lights in the sky above the western section of the county still are being seen and they're still mysteries.

The eerie phenomena—nature unknown—has caused widespread apprehension in some parts of the western section. Some families have ordered their children to remain indoors after nightfall.

The lights have been observed by many residents of the section in the vicinity of Zion and Buffalo Ridge Roads for several weeks. They invariably dart westward and apparently at high speed.

IT HAS BEEN definitely established that they are not figments of the imagination—too many persons have seen them.

One theory—that they might be jet planes making scheduled test runs or "check" runs for the Jefferson Proving Grounds at Madison, Ind., directly to the west of the area, was pretty well squelched Thursday.

At the proving ground officials said that they have no such scheduled use of aircraft.

James Denning, control tower operator at Lunken Airport, and William Bradshaw, WKRC photographer, were two of those who have seen some lights.

DENNING SAID he was of the opinion that the one light he saw several nights ago was a jet plane. He and Bradshaw turned the telescope of the Cincinnati Astronomical Society on the object and saw light of reddish cast, beneath which was a second, a red light so dim that it could not be seen by the naked eye.

Denning says that this light definitely was not the same light observed by one of his acquaintances.

That man, he said, told how he and a friend had followed a light in their automobile about two months ago, in the Hooven oil refining area.

THE LIGHT was a bright one and it seemed to be travelling slowly at lower than tree top level, the witnesses said. They described it as a white light with a reddish tinge and bigger than the normal aircraft light.

Some of the residents claim that the lights show with almost clock-like regularity on certain evenings. They have been seen, according to all reports, on Mondays and Wednesdays at 9 and 10 p. m.

observed the effect for several hours before bad weather closed in. Mr Halstead confirmed that Frank Manning – an amateur astronomer, from New Orleans – had also observed the phenomena through his 15 inch reflector telescope. In addition, the nearby Tulane Observatory also corroborated the sighting. Mr Halstead also spoke of another sighting which took place on the 1st November 1955, while he and his wife Ann, were travelling on a Union Pacific passenger train.

> *"We were about a hundred miles west of Las Vegas, when my wife called my attention to an object moving just above the mountain range, in the same direction as the train. At first I thought it was a blimp, but as I watched it I realised it could not be, as this thing was 800ft long. It was then joined by another object, which was disc-shaped – very shiny, flat on the bottom, with a low dome on top. They then began to rise upwards, slowly at first, then much faster, and in about 15 seconds disappeared from sight."*

New Zealand: 6th November 1955 – Mr D.W. Paul reported having sighted a long object, showing 3-4 lighted windows, crossing the sky over Avondale, making a swishing noise.

New Zealand: 11th November 1955 – The pilot of an aircraft flying between Wellington and Auckland, at a height of 8,000ft, sighted a *'point of light'* which flew alongside, on a parallel course, before overtaking the aircraft at 850mph.

USA: 17th November 1955 – At St. Louis, Missouri, twelve round, flat objects, silver on top and dark on the bottom, were seen to fly across the sky in a four-deep formation, tipping in pitch and roll, for 45 seconds, at 6.10am, by local resident Mr J.A Mapes.

USA: 20th November 1955 – at 5.20pm over Lake City, Tennessee, Capt. B. G. Denkler and five men of the USAF 663rd AC&W Squadron sighted two oblong, bright orange, semi-transparent objects flying at terrific speed and erratically, toward and away from each other. The sighting was explained away as being a mirage.

New Zealand: 22nd November 1955 – A brilliant pulsating light was reported having overtaken an airliner flying over the Southern Alps.

EVENING STANDARD 7.12.55

MYSTERY EXPLOSION SHAKES SOUTH LONDON

A loud explosion was heard in many areas of South London this afternoon.

Reports of a "loud bang" came from Croydon, Beckenham, Wimbledon, Sutton, Carshalton, Tooting. Some reports said the explosion lasted five seconds.

Shook building

A spokesman at the Croydon Fire Brigade said: "The explosion at about 3.20 this afternoon shook the building, but we received no telephone calls. We have no idea what caused it."

In the Sutton area houses were shaken and windows were broken.

A woman at Wimbledon said: "The explosion shook the block of flats in which I live. The curtains were drawn through the windows as if a bomb had dropped."

A Beckenham man said he thought he saw a large fire. "The explosion was like a wartime rocket," he added.

EXPLOSION

(See Page One)

Air Ministry spokesman said later that there were no aircraft capable of supersonic speed flying in the area. Control centres at the RAF stations at Biggin Hill, North Weald and West Malling also reported that none of their aircraft was in vicinity at the time.

---

*Piccolomini is a prominent lunar impact crater located in the southeastern sector of the Moon. The crater Rothmann lies to the west-southwest, and to the south is Stiborius. The lengthy Rupes Altai begins at the western rim of Piccolomini, curving to the northwest. The crater is named after 16th century Italian Archbishop and astronomer Alessandro Piccolomini. It is 88 kilometers in diameter and 4,500 meters deep. It is from the Upper Imbrian period, 3.8 to 3.2 billion years ago. The crater rim has not been severely worn by crater impacts, and the inner wall possesses wide terraces. These structures have been somewhat smoothed by landslips and erosion, most likely induced by seismic activity. An influx of material has entered across the northern rim, flowing down toward the base. The crater floor is relatively smooth, with only minor hills and impact craters. In the middle is a complex central peak surrounded by lesser mounts. The main peak rises to a height of 2.0 kilometers above the surrounding floor. **(Source: Wikipedia)**

Haunted Skies Volume Ten

USA: 25th November 1955 – at 10:30am over La Veta, Colorado, a dirigible-shaped object – described as having a fat front and tapered tail, luminous green-blue in colour and jellylike in appearance – was sighted overhead in the sky by State Senator S. T. Taylor (**Source: Blue Book**)

January 1956

USA: 31st January 1956 – Was a USAF plane downed by a UFO?

At 2.50pm on this date, Lt. Colonel Joseph Lee Merkel – a member of the 123rd Kentucky Air National Guard – took off from Standiford Field, Louisville, Kentucky, in an F-51D aircraft, with the intention of carrying out a maintenance test flight for a carburettor and propeller change. He climbed to 20,000ft and made contact with Oak Hill Air Defense Command Radar Station. A course was then set for Terre Haute, Indiana, at 3.pm.

As the flight continued, the pilot was contacted by Oak Hill, who told him that the aircraft was fading on their radar scope. Lt. Colonel Merkel replied he had Terre Haute in sight.

3.24pm: Oak Hill received a message from Lt. Colonel Merkel to say he was returning to Louisville, at 34,000ft, climbing to 35,000ft. At this point, the pilot was informed of an aircraft approaching from his right. The pilot replied he did not have this in sight and the 'blip' then faded from the radar scope.

3.35pm: Communication ended between the pilot and Oak Hill – presumably caused by the aircraft crashing onto the farm of Mr Ormel Prince, near Bloomington, Indiana. Mr Prince later told the Aircraft Investigating Officer – Grady Bishop – that he was fairly sure the aircraft had exploded in mid-air! The Official Air Force accident report into the incident left an impression that this was due to oxygen starvation.

In April 1980, Mr B.F. Greene Jnr., of Brookline, Massachusetts, contacted the son – Lee Merkel – who told him the Air Force had given the cause of the accident as malfunction in the oxygen equipment. Lee also recalled of having read in an Indiana newspaper report about a UFO detected on radar, and planes being scrambled to intercept. His father headed towards the object but, sadly, crashed and died. (Source: *FSR*, Volume 32, No. 3, 1987 – Aircraft Accidents and Ufos: *A review of some ufo related aircraft disasters*. T. Scott Crain Jr., State Director for MUFON)

April 1956

Great Britain: 27th April 1956 – At 8pm, Mr Reynolds from Limehouse Lane, Wolverhampton, was studying the sky, looking for a missing pigeon, when he noticed a brilliant silver coloured object heading south-east across the sky, with one accord, *"the whole flock cocked their heads as the object passed over."*

Mr Reynolds shouted for his wife, who came rushing outside. The couple stood watching as it passed overhead, low enough to see that, *"the outer surface was chequered, covered with small dots, like rivets, similar to those seen on a water tank"*, before it was lost from view as it headed into a cloud, making a humming noise.

(Source: Wilfred Daniels, Stafford)

First public showing of UFO film

May 9th 1956 – First public showing of United Artists film *Unidentified Flying Objects*, a Green-Rose production – the world's first feature length documentary on the 'flying saucer' phenomena. It covered the period from the Kenneth Arnold UFO sightings in 1947, the Thomas Mantell incident of 1948, and UFOs seen over Washington in July 1952.

The film also included interviews with Air Force personnel, who had been involved in those incidents.

*In 1952 Clarence Greene saw an object twisting in the sky. He got in contact with the US Air Force information officer, Albert Chop, who was in charge of UFO queries. Chop told Greene about the existence of footage of UFOs. Greene obtained the footage for the documentary.

June 1956

New Zealand: 10th June 1956 – At 9.30pm, Mr Brian Lovelock was walking along the right-hand side of St Leonard's Road, on a cold and wet night, with a strong north-easterly wind blowing, when he saw an object resembling an upturned saucer, with a ball-shaped dome on top, about 200ft off the ground, at an angle of 40°. The object moved slowly eastwards, which pulsated from a dim to bright light as it did so. Suddenly, it shot upwards and disappeared from view.

Australia: 5th/6th July 1956 – A bright red glow, surrounded by a *'flaming halo of light'*, was seen in the sky over Sydney, at 11pm. It eventually disappeared at 11.35pm in a cloud of haze.

At noon, the following day, two brightly-lit, apparently metallic, objects were reported over the same City, at an estimated height of 2,000ft.

August 1956

Great Britain: 14th August 1956 – At 7pm, three orange lights were seen in the sky over Leicester, heading towards the London area, by David Hester and Brenda Wagstaff.

Great Britain: 15th August 1956 – Triangular UFO seen; airplanes scrambled.

An object, resembling an upside-down *'cup and saucer'*, was seen over Barton Power Station, at 5pm.

At 9.30pm, radar operators at RAF Bentwaters and Lakenheath tracked a group of *'dots'* moving in over the East Anglia coast, from the direction of Holland. The *'dots'*, which could also be seen visually, were then 50 miles distant and closing at nearly 5,000mph – well over the speed of sound – but failed to produce any sonic boom.

Radar then picked up a number of other *'blips'*, showing as an irregular group of twelve to fifteen in number, heading north-east at a much slower rate, *"being led by three UFOs, forming a triangular formation"*.

USAF jet scrambled

At 10pm, a United States Air Force jet was scrambled to intercept but returned to base, shortly afterwards, after failing to make contact. Fifty minutes later a UFO, described as *'an oval-shaped white light'*, was seen crossing the sky over RAF Bentwaters, at speed – apparently connected with the report of a similarly described object seen hovering over RAF Lakenheath, for a short time. An RAF Venom Night Fighter aircraft, already on patrol over the Bedford area, was instructed to intercept the UFO. After making airborne radar contact, the object began to zigzag behind the jet; both *'vehicles'* being tracked by ground radar. Despite a number of high-speed manoeuvres, the plane was unable to shake off the UFO until another aircraft appeared. (**Source:** *Flying Saucer Review*, Volume 2, No. 5, Sept/Oct. 1956) (See full account in Volume 1 of *Haunted Skies*)

UFO plotted over London

Great Britain: 30th August 1956 – At 10pm, a UFO was plotted on radar over London. Thirty minutes later, Flight Lieutenant Harry Goldstone, navigator on board a Meteor Mk.XI, was preparing to land at West Malling, Kent, at 2,000ft, after being asked to look out for an unidentified light in the sky that could be seen visually by Ground Control.

> *"The light was a few thousand feet above us, but it didn't have a star's intensity of light. I don't subscribe to 'flying saucers' but I don't know what this light was, nor does anyone else."*

(Source: *Flying Saucer Review*, World Roundup of UFO Sightings and Events)

September 1956

UFO tracked on radar

On 1st September 1956 radar stations in the UK were put on alert, after an unidentified *'blip'* appeared on the screen. Aircraft were scrambled but failed to sight anything, despite flying straight through the plotted location. This was explained away on 3rd September by the Air Ministry, who blamed electrical storms. (Source: *Evening Chronicle*, 3.9.56 – 'Radar image was due to storms')

New Zealand: 3rd September 1956 – Crescent-shaped UFO, seen by pilot

At 6.42pm, Squadron Leader K.B. Smith and Squadron Leader O. Staple were flying a Hastings aircraft at 500ft, and making a landing run at Whenuapai Air Force Base, when a glowing object crossed their flight path, at 6.45pm, in the vicinity of Devonport. The object was in view for about half a minute, before then disappearing northwards.

Squadron Leader Smith:

> *"I first thought it was a jet, but we soon changed our minds when the object revealed its terrific speed. It had a glowing crescent-shaped light in front and a brighter light trailing at the rear, which seemed to pulsate. It was travelling in a*

flat, horizontal trajectory, at an estimated height of 2,000ft. Neither of us has ever seen anything like that previously and it didn't resemble shooting stars or meteors."

They were not the only witnesses. Sergeant T. Cooke and two others, in a vehicle at Whenuapai, saw what they described as a cylindrical object, trailing a pink-blue flame from the rear. Over 60 people between Gisborne and Auckland reported having seen this object passing through the sky that evening. One of them was Captain Harold Hill – then living in Takapuna. At 6.45pm that evening he was exercising his dogs, at Black Rock, when he saw what he first took to be a large passenger aircraft, travelling at an inclination of 45°, heading towards the direction of Milford, showing forward cabin lights tapering away to one or two astern.

"I could not see any navigation lights and realized they would have been clearly seen had it been a conventional aircraft. I expected to hear the roar of engines as it passed overhead, 8-900ft a mile away; there were none. After being in sight for a few seconds, the object disappeared from sight in mid-air. The object bore no resemblance to a comet, meteor, or shooting star. After spending 28 years of my life at sea and witnessing many astronomical phenomena, I can say this with some confidence."

(Source: Interview with K.B. Smith, 11th November 1966, as published in *Harmonic 33*, Captain Bruce Cathie, Sphere Books, 1980)

Bruce Cathie sights UFO

In 1956, Bruce Cathie found himself witnessing further examples of UFO activity. The first took place while driving home. He saw two bright white *'lights',* hovering in the sky east of Onehunga, Auckland, about a quarter of a mile apart, at an estimated height of 3,000ft.

A second sighting occurred while he was a co-pilot on a flight from Auckland to Paraparaumu, at 6pm [Actual date not given] just south of Waverley, at 7,000ft. On this occasion Bruce saw an object at an extremely high altitude in the east and brought the Captain's attention to it. They watched it travel in a curved trajectory from east to west through the sky, across their track, in the vicinity or slightly to the north of Cook Strait.

Bruce:

"It was so large that two streaks, similar to vapour trails, were seen to extend from either side of its pale green disc. About halfway across the Strait, a small object detached itself from the larger body and dropped vertically, until it disappeared from sight. It looked almost as if the main 'disc' were at such a high temperature that a globule had dripped from it. It then disappeared in a flash of light near D'Urville Island."

Calculations made later proved this object had been 1,500-2,000ft in diameter.

New Zealand: 4th September 1956 – At Takutai near Hokitika, a bright cigar-shaped object, showing a rounded top end and tapered base, accompanied by a number of smaller objects, was seen at 10pm.

New Zealand: 5th September 1956 – At 1.30am, Farmer Bert Thompson of Kaponga, was outside, inspecting a sick animal, when he became aware of a hissing sound. Looking upwards he saw a white light, followed by a blue one. The sound increased as the object approached closer, enabling him to see:

"... a turret like glass nose, showing a white light. It had delta-like rounded wings, with a larger glass turret on the middle of its main body, from out of which came the blue light; it also had a tapering tail that I couldn't see clearly."

New Zealand: 12th September 1956 – At Aburiri, a small white object was seen stationary in the sky by hundreds of people.

NATO tracks UFOs on radar

[According to NICAP, UFOs were tracked by NATO radar for over three weeks, during the period from August to September 1956, at speeds between 2,000 and 3,500mph, over the Denmark area.]

Great Britain: 13th September 1956 – At 5pm, Paul Porcher from Flixton, Manchester, was leaving work when he noticed a red object in the sky, framed between the two roofs of the nearby Barton Power Station.

> "It was about 50 yards across, a few hundred feet up in the air, and seemed to have bevelled edges, resembling an upside-down cup and saucer. After about 15 seconds, it moved away, towards Eccles. I don't claim to have seen a 'flying saucer'. I can't say what it was that I saw."

New Zealand: 16th September 1956 – Three cigar-shaped objects seen

A total of eleven people gathered at a house in Dominion Road, Auckland, to view the planet Mars on the 16th September 1965, which was at is closest approach to Earth. They included Mrs P. Vosiliunas, her daughter – Duna, Mrs M.J. Bennett and Mrs Cherie Barton.

After looking through the eyepiece of a pair of 20 x 40 binoculars for a short time, Duna was surprised to see a long, glowing, cigar-shaped object – its light appearing to pass through the colours of the spectrum. Other members of the party confirmed the sighting. At this stage observations were continued using a 2 inch refractor telescope, as efforts to identify it with a 4 inch refractor proved unsuccessful. They were startled to see three similar disc-shaped glowing forms appear, each with a domed top, which emerged out of the main object and hover in a group, briefly, before moving out of sight. A short time later they returned and joined the larger cigar-shaped UFO, which then shot off into space before being lost from view.
(Source: *Harmonic 33*, Bruce Cathie)

Great Britain: 17th September 1956 – At 8.30am, pupils and staff were travelling to school through Glendean (seven miles from Dunoon) when five flat half-circular objects, with aluminum like surfaces, were seen hovering in the sky.

Great Britain: 22nd September 1956 – What lay behind the mysterious appearance of a *'sphere'* seen high in the sky during the afternoon, at Cleethorpes, by thousands of people? It was described as looking like a glass globe, with something inside it, and estimated to be 80ft in diameter. The object, plotted at a height of 51,000ft, remained still in the sky, despite a wind of 40mph at that altitude. A spokesman from RAF Manby told reporters:

> "We have no idea what it was, but it isn't a weather balloon. Two fighter jets were scrambled. By the time they had arrived, the object was nowhere to be seen."

(Source: *Daily Herald*, 23.9.56 – 'They're seeing saucers')

Australia: 24th September 1956 – At 8am, over Crows Nest, Queensland, what looked like a silver-grey bullet-shaped object was seen dropping skywards. It then moved slowly up the slope of a nearby drive, some 10ft off the ground and was described as having some sort of cabin and attachment on the rear.

October 1956

Great Britain: 23rd October 1956 – Retired Squadron Leader Ernest Booker from Lower Hill Road, Rugby, sighted two very bright *'lights'* moving across the sky towards Coventry, at a height of some 1,500ft.

> "The lights could not have been attached to balloons, drifting with the wind, because the wind was blowing in another direction, and they would not have been gliders as they were travelling at a leisurely speed and were brighter than normal aircraft lights. When one changed course, so did the other."

Great Britain: 25th October 1956 – On this evening ex-RAF serviceman Mr Christopher Orton of Stocks Lane, Thurlaston, Rugby, sighted:

> "... two exceptionally bright yellow-orange 'lights', attached fore and aft to something quite out of the ordinary. Not a sound was heard, as the lights moved overhead."

Great Britain: 26th October 1956 – An RAF jet fighter pursued what the pilot thought was a huge flying object, near Coventry, but had to give up the chase when it out-distanced him. The unnamed pilot told of

> "climbing to 25,000ft, when two bright amber 'lights' appeared above me, situated to the front and rear of some very large object, displaying no navigation lights".

(Source: Bob Tibbitts, Coventry UFO Research Group)

December 1956

New Zealand: 28th December 1956 – Triangular formation of UFOs seen

A police officer on duty at Invercargill, between 11pm and midnight, described what he saw:

> "A formation of objects flew over the city, travelling at high speed in an east to west direction. At first they appeared to be a flock of birds, surrounded by a white phosphorescent glow. This formation appeared to be following one particular light which seemed to have control over the remainder of the flight in a triangular formation. The total length of time they were visible would be approximately thirty seconds. A single light travelling from the east was visible to me, and two firemen, for approximately seventy-five seconds. This object circled over South Invercargill, before disappearing into the south-west direction. Ten minutes later, eight lights sped across the sky in the same direction as the previous ones. This formation was also triangular in shape. All lights seen on this night were flying well below the cloud layers."

(Source: Letter to George Fulton from the Chief Inspector of Police/*Harmonic 33*, Bruce Cathie)

[A week later a similar sighting took place over the city]

January 1957

Great Britain: 1st January 1957 – At 3.30pm, a grey ring-shaped object, with defined inner and outer margins, was seen moving northwards across the sky over St. Helens, Lancashire, before shooting upwards and vanishing from sight. At 4.30pm the same day, a glowing orange *'cigar'* was seen in the sky over Staffordshire, by Mrs Jessie Roestenberg, who alerted her next door neighbour – Mrs D. Osbourne. The two women watched as it crossed the sky, heading westwards, leaving a trail twice its length. An RAF jet appeared in the sky and approached the object, which ascended vertically and vanished into the sky. (See Volume 1, *Haunted Skies* for full details of Jessie's other sighting and photographs of Jessie)

New Zealand: 1st January 1957 – At Rissington, 16 miles from Napier, Mrs McEwen sighted a number of huge bright rays of light extending from an object in the sky, *'shaped like a wrapped newspaper'*, during the early hours of the morning.

Great Britain: 3rd January 1957 – Unable to sleep during a stay at the Royal South Hampshire Hospital, Southampton, Mrs I. Hurcoop looked out of the window of the Cowan Ward at 2.20am and saw:

> "... an unusual bright star, moving slowly across the night sky. I shouted for the night duty sister and attendant nurse, who stood watching with me, as the 'star' slowly disappeared below the roof line of the Grimston Ward, followed by the appearance of several more stars, which began an aerial display lasting until 5.30am."

Another witness to strange phenomena during this period was Mr John Hanney.

Jan 57

John Hanney,
16 Woodview Terrace,
Lesmahagow,
Lanarkshire,
Scotland.

9th March, 1969.

Dear Madam,

I am a member of G.U.F.O.R.S. (Glasgow Unidentified Flying Objects Research Society). I would like to describe what I saw on early January 1957.

I was coming home from Bible Class one Sunday. As I was walking up the road leading from village to where I lived (housing scheme situated at the top of a hill) I was star watching when I noticed a very bright star to the north. It was just like any normal bright star. As I moved my head round to observe other stars, the bright star was moving to my amazement. A smaller star appeared alongside it and both were moving rapidly towards me. At the same time, there was a slight strange mist falling. I hurried along to a railway bridge at the top of the hill. When I reached the bridge, they were almost overhead about half a mile approximately above the rooftops of the houses. They stopped directly overhead and I could see a very large black oval shaped object, suddenly there was an orange/red flash and in the light it gave off I saw a small silver oval shaped object descend from the large one. They moved off. There was a faint whirring noise as they did so keeping the same height for about three-quarters of a mile approximately and stopped again. The same thing happened again, orange/red flash, another oval shaped object descended from large one. The large object and the smaller ones moved off and then went out of sight.

I have a few books on flying saucers, one or two by George Adamski, a lot of people think he was a crackpot – why I don't know. Just because we breathe oxygen on this planet, this doesn't mean people from other planets have to breathe oxygen. For example, take those deep sea divers who breathe a mixture of helium and oxygen, but they wouldn't be able to breathe this mixture on the surface unless they were in a pressurized chamber.

What if a space probe from another planet landed on one of our deserts, what information would it send back? – Planet Earth consists of Nothing But Sand. May I wish you all the best with your bulletin.

Yours sincerely,

John Hanney

New Zealand: 6th January 1957 – Mrs McEwen also told of sighting two twinkling golden coloured objects moving slowly across the sky, surrounded by a spectrum of colour.

Great Britain: 21st January 1957 – a fast-moving red glow, looking like *'a large fire, in the sky, with several rays running through it'*, was seen flying across the Bristol area, at 10.30pm and ruining television reception for many viewers, who contacted the BBC after the screens dissolved into wavy patterns and jagged edges between 10 and 10.30pm – followed by reports of an object seen over Downend, Portishead and Clevedon, a few minutes later – lighting up the sky with red light, before moving over Whitchurch. The sighting was explained away by Filton Meteorological Office as likely to be the aurora borealis, although it seems unusual for it to be visible this far south. Mr Ronald Anstee from Fishponds, Bristol, told of a noise like *"a vast armada of heavy bombers, lasting for several hours, making my wife quite ill"*. Was there any connection with the sighting of a large metal *'ball'* or *'disc'*, reported over an army base in the United States on the same day? **(Source: NICAP/Personal interview)**

February 1957

Australia: 21st February 1957 – Mr Kingston, who was living eight miles from Longreach, Queensland, sighted an egg-shaped object in the sky, which he described as being 12ft long and very *'thick'*.

> *"It stopped, and shot off – now about 100 yards away – stopped again, and then disappeared from view."*

USA: 27th February 1957 – At Castle AFB, California, nine objects were tracked by military radar, at 9.45pm, for 24 minutes. Explanation: Mirage.

March 1957

New Zealand: 22nd March 1957 – At 10pm, a violent explosion rocked the Central Police Station and nearby buildings in Wellesley and Rutland Streets, at Auckland. Believing that a safe had been blown, the police conducted a search of the College and offices of the Auckland Education Board. Constable P. Wiseman was one of a number of other officers who witnessed a flash from the upstairs window of the police station, followed by an explosion which was heard as far away as the Auckland Hospital. UFO researcher – George Fulton – contacted the police station and spoke to a sergeant, who was unable to offer any explanation, although he had himself witnessed the phenomenon. **(Source: Mr George Fulton of the Civilian Saucer Investigation)**

USA, California: 23rd March 1957 – UFOs tracked on radar

The first of four UFOs appeared on the radar scope at a civilian airport in the Los Angeles area, at 1.50pm. According to the CAA operator:

> *"It was moving faster than anything I had ever seen; about 40 miles north-west it came to an abrupt halt, and then reversed its course in just a few seconds."*

Five minutes later two more UFOs appeared, also heading in the same direction. These were tracked at a distance of 30 miles in 30 seconds, at 3,600mph, before they disappeared off the scope. A fourth *'target'* appeared and also went off the scope at 3,600mph; by this time some of the objects were at 10,000ft, or lower. Eight members of the NICAP Board of Governors, Rear Admiral Herbert K. Knowles, USN (retired), Colonel Robert B. Emerson, USAR, Dr. Earl Douglass, Frank Edwards, Professor Charles A. Maney, the Reverend Albert Baller, and the Reverend Leon Le Van, confirmed having seen the signed radar report. Explanation: malfunction of equipment!

April 1957

New Zealand: April 1957 – Mr Conrad reported having sighted what looked like 'Angel hair' falling from the sky. The Australian Department of Air was able to put our minds at rest!

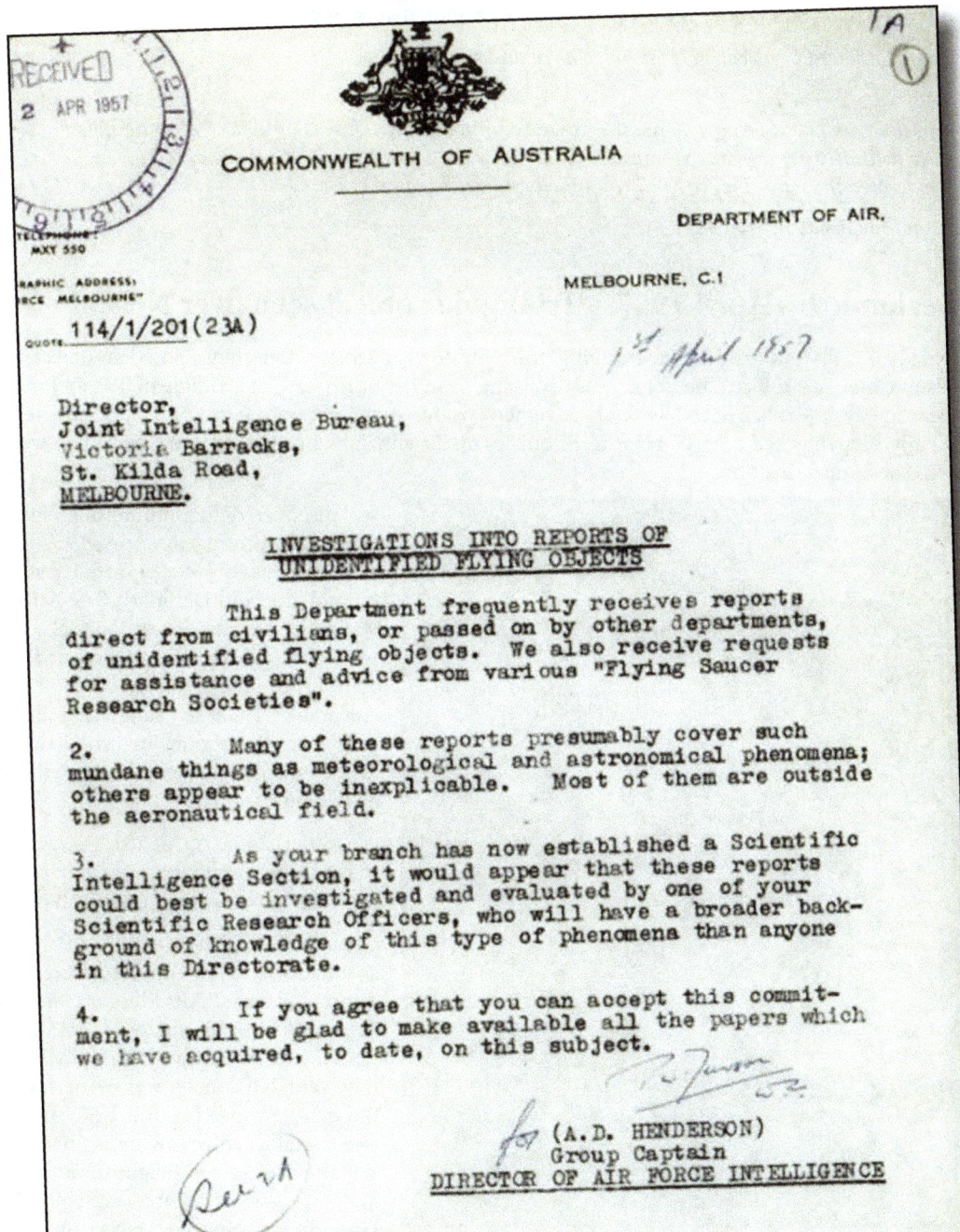

Haunted Skies Volume Ten

Great Britain: 4th April 1957 – During the early morning, radar operators at the Ministry of Supply Bombs Trial Unit, West Freugh, near Stranraer in Scotland, picked up on radar five stationary *'objects'* at 70,000ft – the size of battleships – later explained away by an Air Ministry spokesman as an air balloon, sent up from Aldergrove Airport in Northern Ireland. This hardly seems in character with the attitude of the Base Commander – Wing Commander Whitworth – who was quoted as saying:

"I am not allowed to reveal 'its' position, course and speed."

Adding:

"From the moment of picking 'it' up, it was well within our area. It was an 'object' of some substance – quite definitely not a freak. No mistake could have been made by the Ministry of Supply civilians, who operated the sets – they are fully qualified and experienced officers."

(Source: *Sunday Dispatch*, 7.4.1957)

New Zealand: 9th April 1957 – Triangular object seen over Nelson

At 7.15pm, Mr B Mills and his wife were driving down St. Vincent Street, when they sighted an object to the left of Nelson Chief Post Office. The object was dropping from the north-east, at an angle of 45°, and moving slowly over the bay. It was bright red, with an extremely bright white light on the top right-hand corner, and was unlike anything they had ever seen before. Enquiries made with Tahuana Aerodrome revealed no weather balloons had been up at the time.

Lieutenant-Colonel Petersen, showing a map of Denmark with UFO sightings. Photo © B-T Magazine, Arne Bloche.

We discovered that numerous sightings were made around the April 1957 period of a similar object, reported over the Jutland area and Denmark. The Air Force Station at Skrydstrup was besieged with so many reports they were unable to cope. [The activity continued; on the 20th November 1957, a triangular UFO was seen over Bornholm, in broad daylight, inside which were seen what appeared to be two human figures.]

Australia: 24th April 1957 – A cigar-shaped object, showing an orange flame from the rear, was seen over Melbourne.

Great Britain: 29th April 1957 – At 8.50pm a squadron of Javelin jet aircraft were scrambled from RAF Odiham, Hampshire, in response to anomalous radar returns tracking an object over Orr, St. Margaret's Bay, Kent. No contact was made, owing to the extreme speed of the UFO. However, two metallic objects were sighted in the sky at an estimated height of 30,000ft, by Shanklin, Isle of Wight resident – Mr L Humphreys. (**Source: Declassified MOD documents AIR 20 9994**)

May 1957

Great Britain: Questions asked in the House of Lords

On 15th May 1957, *Major Patrick Wall, MP, asked the Under Secretary of State for AIR, (Charles) Ian. Orr-Ewing OBE CEng MIEE:

Major Patrick Wall, MP

> "How many unidentified objects had been detected over Great Britain this year, as compared with previous years, and whether the object picked-up on radar over the Dover Straits, on the 29th April, has been identified?"

Answer: (At a later date) in 1955-6, they had received 64 reports of unusual aerial phenomena. These had been classified as 26 balloons, 16 meteors, eight aircraft, two planets, three flares, one mock sun, one fireball [sic] and one contrail. The unexplained cases, which all occurred in 1956, were: The navigator of a Vulcan obtained a radar contact for one minute 15 seconds with an invisible object. On 19th March, Lakenheath radar detected a target moving at 2,000-4,000 knots, which then stopped and hovered at a high altitude; a 'Venom' was scrambled to intercept, but saw nothing. It could have been inversion and reflection from the ionosphere ('angels' and 'anaprop'). RAF Wethersfield vectored two interceptors onto a radar target, and one obtained a brief visual contact. No other radars could see it; a member of the Royal Observer Corps reported something with insufficient information to identify it as any particular thing. An object was reported at 12,000ft, which may have been a balloon, described as a round object, emitting rippling waves – like heat shimmer; it was not known what it might have been. In 1957 up to April, there had been 16 reports, classified as one radar fault, two aircraft navigation lights, one meteor, two flares, one private experiment and three newspaper reports (one, the Jersey UFO in the *Daily Sketch* of 6th April, had been admitted to be a fake).

The unexplained cases were:

The 'West Freugh' case, Wigtownshire. On 4th April, a stationary target was observed by the Balmalloch radar to rise vertically from 50,000 to 70,000ft in 10 minutes. The object was automatically plotted by two radars alternately, as it moved off slowly to the north towards a second radar station, 20 miles away. After travelling 20 miles, it made a very sharp turn to the south-east and picked-up speed to 240mph, at 50,000ft. The second radar also picked-up a target in the correct position, which split into four objects at 14,000ft, travelling in line astern, about 4,000yds apart. When the single object passed beyond Balscalloch's range, they also could see these four. The echoes were much larger than normal aircraft; in fact, nearer to those of ships. There were no known aircraft or balloons in the area (in any case they had made sharp turns against the wind) and a passing V-bomber had been correctly tracked at the same time. On 26th March, at †RAF Church Lawford, a target accelerated from rest to 1,400 mph – thought to have been a balloon. A Glasgow boy of ten observed an object at 10,000ft, travelling at 750mph for 15 seconds.

†Diamond-shaped UFO over RAF Church Lawford, in 1951

Authors: One Sunday, in July 1951, RAF Serviceman – Leonard Burrell – sighted a luminous object descending through the sky over the base, at 12.25pm. Approximately 10 minutes later, the object descended low enough for him to see an object between 5-10ft long and 3-6ft wide in the middle. It was silver metallic in appearance,

---

*Major Sir Patrick Henry Bligh Wall, KBE (1981), MC, VRD (14th October 1916-15th May 1998) was a British senior commando in the Royal Marines, during World War II, and later a Conservative politician. He was Member of Parliament for Haltemprice, East Yorkshire, and subsequently for Beverley. He was a leading figure in the Conservative Monday Club, and a parliamentary consultant to the Western Goals Institute. In the last decade of his life, he was President of the British UFO Research Association (BUFORA).

with a very high gloss to its outer surface, and seemed to have been constructed from glass-like material, with a mirror finish. It reminded him of a very large diamond, with finely cut edges. The object was now at its lowest point; about 500ft off the ground and 2-300yds away, appearing to rest for a while, for several seconds, over a group of trees near the school buildings. A short time later, it rose upwards and was gone from sight. Was this another balloon?

Great Britain: 1st May 1957 – At 11.30am ex-Royal Navy Petty Officer Eric Pengilly was delivering mail in the Coverack area of Cornwall, when he sighted a dome-shaped object in the sky, flying slowly from west to east for 10 minutes. When it reached the coast, just north of Manacle Point, it tipped at an angle of 45° and shot upwards at that angle, climbing faster than any jet would have done. It then disappeared from sight.

Eric later received a visit from RAF intelligence officers, who questioned him for a couple of hours on what he had seen. He was not the only one to sight something strange in the sky. Other reports of strange objects, encountered in May 1957, included a landed UFO on the runway at Winkleigh Airfield, Devon. When the witness approached it he was unable to advance further, owing to what appeared to be a force field surrounding it.

Great Britain: 11th May 1957 – A black *'disc'* was seen in the sky over Oxfordshire. (Full details in Volume 1 of *Haunted Skies*)

Great Britain: 13th May 1957 – A mystery *'light'* over Nottingham.

Great Britain: 16th May 1957 – Three UFOs were sighted over Tyneside.

Australia: 19th May 1957 – A large object, showing various colours, manoeuvring in the sky over the State of Victoria, travelling at an estimated speed of 2,000mph, was sighted by thousands of people and reported extensively by local radio and the *BBC*.

Great Britain: 20th May 1957 – A *'flying disc'* shaped object was sighted over Henley-on-Thames, followed by a report of USA pilots scrambled to intercept a *'flying disc'* over Lincolnshire, at 10.48pm on this date. The pilot – Milton Torres – was ordered to open fire on the UFO. (Full details in *Haunted Skies*, Volume 1)

Great Britain: May 1957 – In May 1957, Bill Dillon from Bedfordshire, now settled in Cornwall, still has no difficulty in describing exactly what he saw while a pupil at Ramridge Primary School, Turner Road North, Luton, Bedfordshire, now 56 years ago! The sighting was to have a profound impact on his life – still very evident today, during many

Haunted Skies Volume Ten

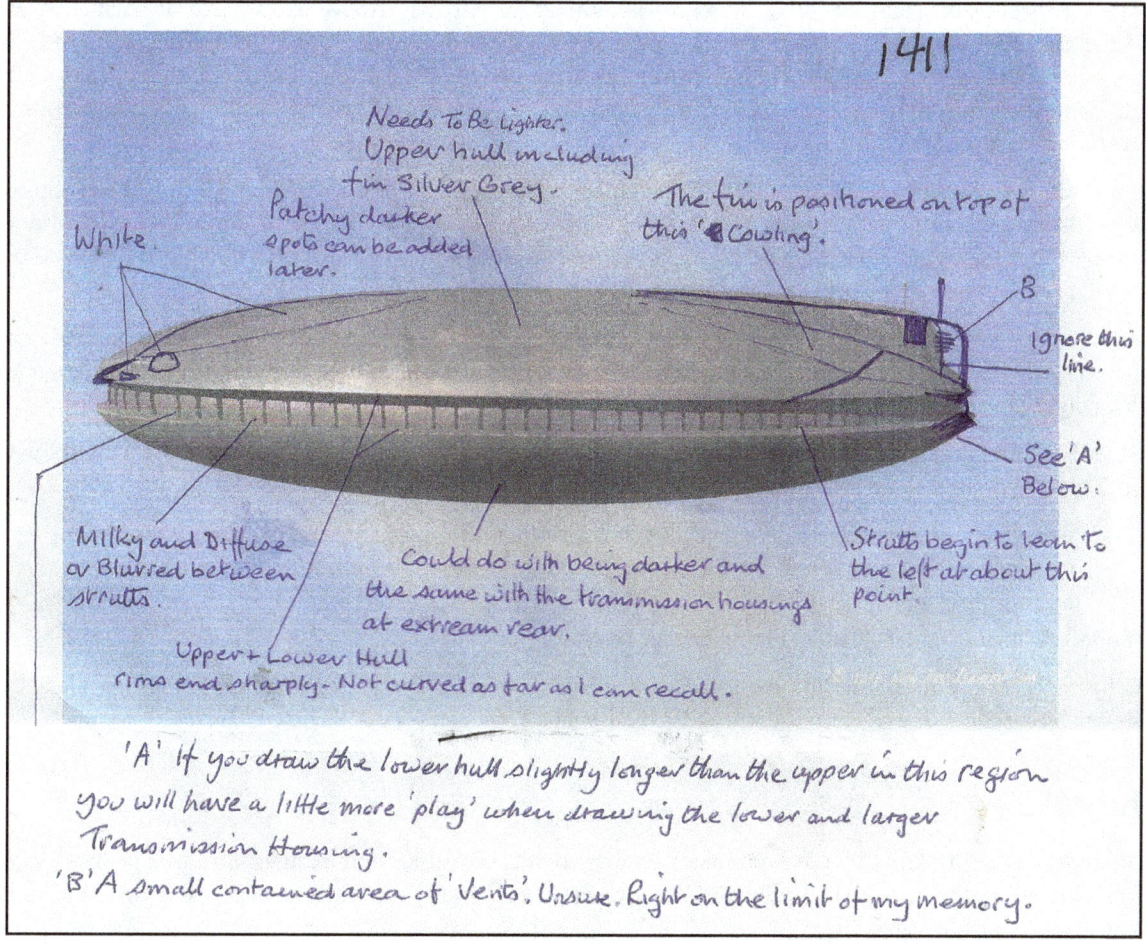

conversations held with him about the matter, bordering on a passionate, almost obsessive desire to recover his original illustrations.

Australia: 20th May 1957 – A brilliant fiery object was reported in the sky over Bass Strait, Victoria.

Great Britain: 26th May 1957 – A yellow cigar-shaped object was seen above the Torpedo factory, at Alexandria, Scotland.

June 1957

Great Britain: June 1957 – Increased UFO activity takes place

Mr Albert Brown was returning home to Long Eaton, Nottingham, at 9.15am on the 14th June, when he sighted an unidentified flying object, resembling an artist's impression of a *'flying saucer'* – aluminium or silver in colour – about 1,000ft in the air, over the road bridge at Chilwell.

Later that day, at 10.30pm, an object was seen zigzagging across the sky over Ilkley, Yorkshire, followed by a green flare-like object – roughly square in shape, with a piece missing at the rear – by Mr Gregg, while visiting Middleton Hospital. (**Source: Mr I. Ibson**)

Haunted Skies Volume Ten

A few days later, on 17th June 1957, Mrs June Watkins from Barnsley, twelve miles north of Sheffield, was at her home address, at 8.20pm, when she saw *'a strange light'* dropping down from the sky, followed by the appearance of a thin golden *'cone.'* Ten minutes later, people at Firth Park, Sheffield, sighted a similar phenomenon. This was to be just the start of a flurry of UFO reports, brought to the attention of the authorities, over the next few days.

On 18th June 1957, Mrs G. Pennells and her daughter, June, sighted a cylindrical, silver-gold coloured object, about half a mile away, with a *'blunt end'*, moving across the sky over Stafford, at 9.15pm. Twenty or thirty minutes later the object, now more orange in colour, reappeared in the sky – this time moving at the speed of a piston-engine aircraft, before slowing down.

At 9.30pm, a silver cylindrical object was seen over Gailey, Staffordshire, by Mr L. Broomhall, following a curved path across the sky, before remaining stationary for a short time and then proceeding on its journey, at a height of between 5-10,000ft and speed of 30-50mph.

At 9.45pm, the same day, Ann Poulton and her boyfriend were out walking near Bee Lane, close to Bushbury Hill, Wolverhampton, when they saw what looked like:

> "...a glowing, saucer-shaped object, heading in a straight line towards Stafford. We don't think it was a plane. It was oval and orange/red in colour. After a few seconds, it gained height and disappeared towards the North".

(Source: Wilfred Daniels, British Flying Saucer Bureau)

Other sightings, contained in Volume 1 of *Haunted Skies*, include a *'flying saucer'* seen on 21st June, a bright silver object seen in the sky on the 25th, and a cigar-shaped object on the 27th June 1957.

July 1957

Australia: 16th/17th July 1957 – A luminous object was reported over Katoomba, at 9.10pm, by a police officer, followed by a sighting, the next day, by Mr T. Brody, who told of seeing a brilliant object circling over the same town. (See opposite page).

Australia: 18th July 1957 – It was reported that two Meteor jets were on standby, after sightings of UFOs were reported over the area.

September 1957

New Zealand: 11th September 1957 – Mrs Bates of Mount Street, Avondale, Auckland, arose at 5.40am. Looking out of the window she saw a brilliantly-lit object, hovering in the western sky. After fetching a pair of 20 x 60 binoculars, she saw:

> "... a golden-red object – larger than the moon – rotating slowly in the early morning half-light. I could see bright rays of light being shone from it. I watched for ten minutes, during which time it banked over to reveal its full circular shape, before it righted itself once again. It had a domed central portion, with a flange around the middle, or horizontal centre line. In the centre of its base was a probe, like a radio antenna, protruding downwards. On top of the domed section protruded four strut-like extensions, with small round objects on the end."

The object then moved away towards the direction of Titirangi, before disappearing into cloud.

The R.A.A.F. had two jet fighters standing by at Richmond last night ready to investigate any unexplained objects in the Blue Mountains sky. Shown making preparations for the stand-by are (from left) Flying Officer R. Allen of Perth and Wing Commander D. D. Hurditch of Inverell. They could have been over Katoomba within five minutes in their Gloster Meteor aircraft.

KATOOMBA UFO CLASSIC *1957 UFOIC*

On the night of July 16, 1957 a bright oval object about half the size of the moon, flew over Katoomba, a mountain resort 66 miles from Sydney. It was sighted by Mr. John Hickey, a businessman, with his wife and son. The craft had two horizontal beams and two narrower ones pointing towards the ground. There was also a smaller light going on and off. The object was bluish in colour and gave off a vapour. It approached with a roar and stopped in mid-air in the north-east, at about 30° above horizon, for six minutes when the sound ceased.

For four consecutive nights the Blue Mountains were the scene of sightings in the sky. The attempt to attribute to the star Canopus a phenomenon such as Hickey's object failed because the object was half the size of the moon and in diametrically opposite portion of the sky from Canopus. It came with a roar similar to that of a jet. There were no helicopters in the locality at the time.

Frank Walford, author, former Mayor of Katoomba and a trained Army expert on maps stated at the time: "The object which I (and hundreds of others) saw was neither a star, planet or meteorite..."

R.A.A.F. jets were alerted. Evening newspapers came out with headlines and street posters "RAAF TO STAND BY – FLYING SAUCER HUNT" and "TOWN AWAITS FLYING SAUCER" photographically reproduced on this page. This made Australia-wide news.

HICKEY'S U.F.O.

Great Britain: September 1957- UFO sighted over Bedfordshire by Peter Drew

P. R. DREW   Telephone LUTON 411892

Bedford Astronomical Supplies

Specialists in short focus refractors, binocular telescopes, and catadioptric systems.

5B OLD BEDFORD ROAD
LUTON
LU2 7NX

March 27, 1981

22 Park Hill,
Ampthill,
Bedford.

Report of "U.F.O." sighting-September 1957

Definition of U.F.O. in this case is that the object was not identified, was airbourne and therefore presumed flying, and having a well defined form, could qualify as being an object.

Location- 10 Irwin Road, Bedford.

Time- aproximately 1900 hours.

Circumstances of sighting.

The writer and two friends were in the garden with two small telescopes waiting for the sky to become dark enough to start astronomical observation. In order to pass the time I proposed that we competed to be the first to see a star appear to the naked eye. The evening was perfectly clear and the Sun , from memory was either just set or obscured by buildings. As I had far more experience astronomically I was sure that I would pick up a star first, and was most surprised to hear one of my companions claim that he could see one. Sure enough, thre was a stell-ar object about the brightness of Venus when seen against a bright sky. The position was just a little south of due east at an elevation of about 25 degrees, a position which I knew was not occupied by a known astronomical object of that brightness.
My first impression was that it could be a bright nova and accordingly turned my telescope on to the object. The telescope was out of focus as we had earlier been idly looking at nearby terrestrial objects. I located the object which appeared as a star out of focus. To my surprise instead of focussing to a stellar point as expected,the object sharpened up to the classic " flying saucer " shape. I naturally exclaimed to this effect to the disbelief of my friends. I let them both have a look which confirmed my description. I immediately suggested that we each made a sketch of what we had seen. Not only did we agree closely, but we observed the same appearance in the other telescope, thereby eliminating possible optical error. We watched the object telescopically for some 7½ minutes during which time the object did not move in the field of the telescope at 64x magnification. Apart from its shape, the most noticeable feature was a thin ray of light shining downwards from some sort of aperture about the colour of a welding arc. When the object finally moved off it seemed to disappear in the direction of the line of sight so swiftly that its perspective contracted to zero almost instantly.
This sighting was not reported to any authority because quite frankly the popular press was full of bogus sightings at that time.

(cont on page 2

Conclusion

The position of the sighting would have placed the object in the vicinity of Cardington Hangers, an area from which weather balloons and associated equipment are frequently released. However I was very well acquainted with the appearance of these items and could not match the report sighting with any of thse. In any case the fact that the "U.F.O." eventually disappeared suddenly, leads me to believe that the sighting was associated with the area.
In the intervening years I have taken a fringe interest in the U.F.O. phenomina, and, coupled to my current increased experience of unusual objects in the sky, I cannot to this day come up with a satisfactory explanation of what we had seen.

Peter R. Drew

Peter R. Drew.

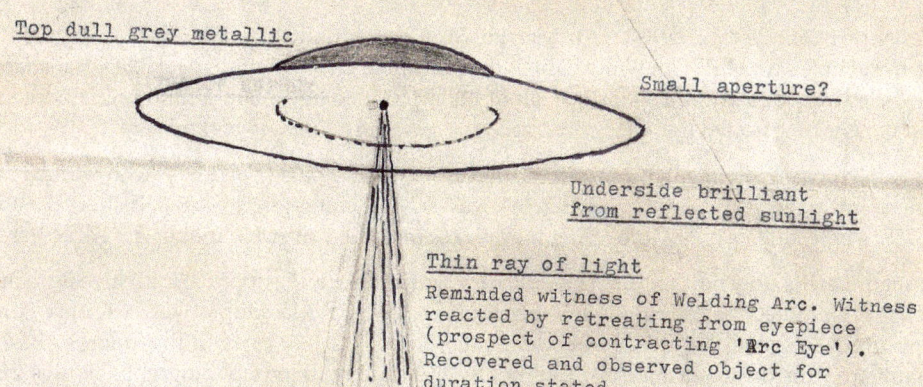

Sketch of object from memory

Top dull grey metallic

Small aperture?

Underside brilliant from reflected sunlight

Thin ray of light
Reminded witness of Welding Arc. Witness reacted by retreating from eyepiece (prospect of contracting 'Arc Eye'). Recovered and observed object for duration stated.

Investigators Notes.

The telescopes being used were both of the astronomical type resulting in an 'inverted image'. Objects 'B'. These secondary objects were observed as the result of 'Sky Sweeping' and were located at an approx half passed one position a short distance away from the primary object.
The witness feels certain that the 'thin ray of light' was directed directly downward and, unlike the primary body, was NOT at a slight inclination relative to the observers.
As far as can be established objects 'A' and 'B' both departed at the same moment. The witness still finds the rapid departure most impressive and expressed a sympathetic attitude when I described the often mentioned charactoristic of UFOs seemingly diminishing 'on the spot'.

UFO appears over Maralinga

During September and October 1957, nuclear weapons test series – codenamed ANTLER – were undertaken at *Maralinga, South Australia, with kilotons range nuclear explosions being detonated on 25th September and 9th October. The site was subject to intense security. During that period the integrity of the facility was challenged in an extraordinary fashion.

Just before dusk, one evening, Royal Air Force Corporal Derek Murray, and some colleagues, were called out of the Maralinga village canteen to witness a UFO, hovering apparently silently over the airfield. The UFO was described as:

> "... a magnificent sight, silver/blue in colour, of a metallic lustre, with a line of windows or portholes along its edge."

Corporal Murray states that the object could be seen so clearly that they could make out what appeared to be plating on the object's surface.

The duty air traffic controller also witnessed the spectacle. He allegedly checked Alice Springs and Edinburgh airfields, who reported that they did not have anything over their areas. No photographs were taken, as the top security status of the area required that all cameras be locked away. These had to be signed in and out when used. After about 15 minutes, as dusk began to fall, the aerial object left swiftly and silently.

October 1957

Australia/America 16th October 1957 – Air Marshal Sir George Jones, Chief of Air Staff (1942) was with his wife, when the couple saw a brilliant white light at the bottom of a shadowy shape – like a transparent balloon – which travelled very quickly and silently, at about 400mph, at some 1,500ft altitude. Sir George was certain it was not a meteor or reflected light. He described it as travelling *"in a purposeful way"*.

On the same day, admittedly many thousands of miles away, Ella Louise Fortune – who worked as a nurse at the Mescalero Indian Reservation, New Mexico – was driving along Highway 54, at about 1.30pm on 16th October 1957, when she saw a UFO hovering motionless in the sky over Holloman Air Force Base.

Ella continued on her journey to the Three Rivers Settlement and stopped the car. She continued her observations of the object before taking one photograph, using Kodachrome with a Kodak Pony 135, at a 1/50th exposure. Ella stated that it was not a lenticular cloud; she had lived in the Tularosa Basin for 20yrs and was familiar with cloud formations. Her hobby was taking colour photographs. It was claimed that mathematicians and analysts employed by Holloman Airbase, who were familiar with current missile and parachute research, were unable to identify the object. (**Source: Coral E. Lorenzen, Director of the *APRO Bulletin*)**

---

*Maralinga and Emu Fields were contaminated with radioactive waste in the 1950s. On 27th September 1956, Operation Buffalo commenced at Maralinga, as Emu Field was found to be too remote a site. The operation consisted of the testing of four fission bombs, codenamed One Tree, Marcoo, Kite and Breakaway. One Tree and Breakaway were exploded from towers; Marcoo was exploded at ground level and Kite was released by a Royal Air Force Vickers Valiant bomber from a height of 30,000ft (9,144m). This was the first launching of a British atomic weapon from an aircraft.

Operation Antler followed in 1957. Antler was designed to test the triggering mechanisms of the weapons. Three tests began in September, codenamed Tadje, Biak and Taranaki. The first two tests were conducted from towers; the last was suspended from balloons. Yields from the weapons were one kiloton, six kilotons and 25 kilotons respectively. The McClelland Royal Commission of 1984–1985 identified significant residual contamination at some sites. British and Australian servicemen were purposely exposed to fallout from the blasts, to study radiological effects. The local Aboriginal people have claimed they were poisoned by the tests and in 1994 the Australian Government reached a compensation settlement with Maralinga Tjarutja of $13.5 million in settlement of all claims in relation to the nuclear testing. Previously, many of these facts were kept from the public. Despite the governments of Australia and the UK paying for two decontamination programs, concerns have been expressed that some areas of the Maralinga test sites are still contaminated 10 years after being declared 'clean'. (**Source: Wikipedia**)

Haunted Skies Volume Ten

Was there any connection with what Sir George and his lady wife had seen?

Sir George Jones, KBE, CB, DFC (18 October 1896-24 August 1992) was a senior commander in the Royal Australian Air Force (RAAF). He rose from private soldier in World War I to Air Marshal in 1948, and served as Chief of the Air Staff from 1942 to 1952, the longest continuous tenure of any RAAF chief. During World War I, Jones saw action as an infantryman in the Gallipoli Campaign of 1915, before transferring to the Australian Flying Corps a year later. Originally a mechanic, he undertook flying training in 1917 and was posted to a fighter squadron in France. He achieved seven victories to become an ace, and was awarded the Distinguished Flying Cross. After a short spell in civilian life following World War I, he joined the newly formed RAAF in 1921, and rose steadily through training and personnel commands prior to World War II. After World War II, Jones had overall responsibility for transforming what was then the world's fourth largest air force into a peacetime service that was also able to meet overseas commitments in Malaya and Korea. Following his retirement from the RAAF, he continued to serve in the aircraft industry and later ran unsuccessfully for political office. He was knighted in 1953.

Sir George Jones, KBE, CB, DFC

Sir George Jones also expressed an interest in unidentified flying objects, having first encountered unexplained aerial phenomena at Warrnambool, Victoria, in 1930. He reported witnessing another UFO in October 1957, but admitted that he was:

> "... loath to talk about it publicly, lest people should think I was either an incompetent witness or getting a little screwy in the head."

In the mid-1960s, he became the patron of the Commonwealth Aerial Phenomena Investigation Organisation and joined the Victorian UFO Research Society. Jones published his autobiography, *From Private to Air Marshal*, in 1988. He was Australia's last surviving World War I Ace when he died in Melbourne on 24th August 1992, at the age of 95.

In 1930, Squadron Leader George Jones was sent to Warrnambool, Victoria, to carry out an investigation into reports of 'mystery aircraft' seen flying over the coast, but was unable to conclude as to what lay behind such reports, despite further sightings of this phenomena over the Pacific, Papua and New Guinea areas, in 1930. In 1931, the RAAF denied any of their aircraft were the explanation for mystery planes reported widely in Tasmania.

In 1965, the former Air Marshall, (now) Sir George Jones, recollected the 1930 affair in an interview published in the *Australian Flying Saucer Review* (UFOIC, Sydney edition, No.8, June 1965, page 18):

> "My first introduction to UFOs was in 1930. At the time I was a Squadron Leader in the Air Force and was sent to Warrnambool because some people down there had seen a formation of what they took to be aircraft flying over the coast. I went there but could not establish what they were. They were not aircraft belonging to us and, as far as I could find out, they were not aircraft belonging to any other powers. The possibility that they might have been a formation of swans or other birds was always there. But the thing was left open – I could not establish what it was."

Bill Chalker had the pleasure of interviewing Sir George about his UFO reminiscences in 1988, when he was 92.

> "I found him to be remarkably lucid in his recollections and certainly would not attribute to him any thoughts of being 'a little screwy in the head'. One only has to read his autobiography, *From Private to Air Marshal*, published in 1988, to realise just how remarkable and impressively credentialed a witness he was!"

Great Britain: 21st /22nd October 1957 – A RAF pilot almost collided with a cigar-shaped object over Gaydon.

The following day a cigar-shaped object, showing a double row of portholes, was seen over West Worthing.

In the same month, Barbara Hall told us of having sighted what she described as *'silver balls'* in the sky, with a clover leaf pattern on them, while out walking in Devon.

November 1957

Great Britain: 2nd November 1957 – At 4pm, Mr I. Andrews of Highlands Road, Andover, was watching a football match at the London Road Ground, when he saw: *"... a dozen circular, disc-shaped objects apparently composed of vapour, resembling dark grey clouds, twisting and turning in the air – like an aircraft performing aerobatics."* (**Source:** *Echo* newspaper, 4.11.1957)

USA: 2nd November 1957 – Interference with motor vehicles, Texas

At 11pm, Levelland, Texas – Police patrolman Fowler was one of four officers who received the first of fifteen phone calls from people reporting having encountered a landed object in the road. Two men, four miles west of the town, noticed a brilliant object approaching the vehicle. As it passed overhead, the headlights went out and the engine died. After the object moved away, the lights and power were restored. At midnight, the officer received another phone call from a driver on the opposite side of the town. He told of coming across an egg-shaped object, about 200ft long, in the middle of the road, followed by the lights and engine failing.

The phenomenon was explained away by Project Blue Book as ball lightning, which was later dismissed by Dr. Allen Hynek. Further enquiries into the matter revealed that the other police officers involved were Sheriff Weir Clem, and his deputy – Pat McCulloch. One of the sightings involved Pedro Saucedo, who was driving along Highway 116 towards Levelland, with his passenger – Joe Salav, when an immense object, showing blue-green lights swept over the truck. Straightaway, the engine and lights died. Frightened, the men jumped out of the truck and watched, in disbelief, as the object settled onto the highway. Both of them later said they heard what sounded like a faint clanking or hammering, and other noises which they interpreted as voices. The red glare given off by the object was so bright that the men were unable to look directly at it. A few minutes later, the dirigible-shaped object, estimated to be 200ft in length, rose up into the night sky and was soon gone.

(Source: *Flying Saucers, Serious Business*, Frank Edwards)

USA: 4th November 1957 – UFO flies over Kirtland Air Force Base

A UFO was seen to fly right-to-left along the east-west runway, and then turn south-west toward the tower, where it then halted near the nuclear weapons storage area for about a minute. The object was reported by CAA tower personnel, Mr R.M. Kaser and Mr E.G. Brink, who were reliable observers, with 23 years of airport control tower experience between them. According to them, the lighted object came down steeply at the east end of a runway, left the flight line, crossed runways, taxiways and unpaved areas, at about a 30° angle, and proceeded south-west towards the control tower, at an altitude of less than 100ft.

Through 7x binoculars, the object appeared to be egg-shaped, having no wings, tail, or fuselage, and was elongated vertically. It appeared to be 15-20ft tall, about the size of an automobile, standing on its nose, and had a single white light at its base. After the UFO left the area it was tracked on surveillance radar, where it exhibited some amazing flight characteristics. The object also came back towards Kirtland, until it took up a position behind an Air Force C-46 that had just taken off. It stayed in position behind the C-46, until they both moved out of radar range. There have been several UFO incidents in and around Kirtland Air Force Base through the years.

(Source: Dr. J. Allen Hynek, James McDonald, Francis Ridge, NICAP)

Elliptical UFO disrupts car engine

At about 1.10pm on the same date, James W. Stokes – a high altitude research engineer of the USAF Missile Development Center, near Alamogordo, reported that he saw an elliptical UFO sweep twice across the highway. The car radio and the engine failed. Stokes claimed that ten other drivers were also on the road, and their engines had also failed. Stokes reported a wave of heat and, later, his face appeared sunburned. This case was explained by the Air Force as a hoax. (**Source:** *Daily News*, Alamogordo, 8th November 1957)

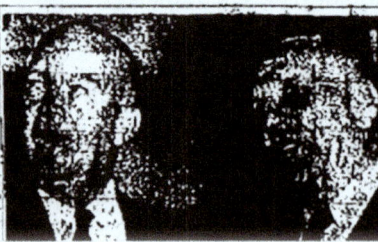

USA: 6th November 1957 – Close encounter with UFO

At 6.30am, Everett Clark (12) – a farm boy of Dante, Texas – got up to let his dog 'Frisky' out. As he did so, he was surprised to see a strange glowing object, resting in a field about 300ft from the house. Thinking he may have been dreaming, he went back into the house. A few minutes later he opened the door and called the dog in, and was taken aback to see several other dogs around the oblong object, barking at two men and two women, dressed normally, who were stood next to it. One of the *'men'* attempted to grab hold of 'Frisky', but the dog growled and backed away. They were conversing in a language which sounded like German. The *'men'* caught one of the other dogs but was forced to let go of it, as the dog snapped at *'him'*.

Clark: *"The four 'people' then walked through the wall of the object – like walking through glass."*

Reporter Carson Brewer, of the *Knoxville News Sentinel*, visited the location and discovered an elongated impression in the ground, 24ft by 5ft. Later that night, Farmer John Trasco of Everittstown, New Jersey, went outside to feed his dog, when he saw a glowing egg-shaped object, hovering above the ground near his barn. John claimed that he was approached by,

> *"... a weird little man, some three and a half feet tall. He had a putty coloured face, with large bulging frog like eyes, dressed in green overalls. He said, 'We are a peaceful people. We don't want any trouble. We just want your dog'. I told him to get the hell out of here. The little man scurried back into the object, which shot off into the evening sky."*

UFO close encounter, California

During the same evening, at Playa Del Rey, California, three motor vehicles stalled along the Vista del Mar highway. The drivers – Richard Kehoe, Ronald Burke and Joe Thomas – got out and saw an egg-shaped object, surrounded by blue haze, sitting on the ground of a nearby beach. Incredibly, they were approached by two *'men'*, who spoke to the party in difficult-to-understand English, described as 5ft 5ins tall, dressed in black leather trousers and light coloured jerseys, whose skin appeared to be yellowish-green. The *'entities'* asked a number of questions, such as *'what time was it, and where were the men going?'* They then left, following which power was restored to their vehicles.

US Coastguard sight UFO

United States cutter Sebago

Haunted Skies Volume Ten

November 1957. USCGC Sebago WPG42. Mobile, Alabama. Left to right: Donald Scheafer LtJG, James Moore RD2, Kenneth Smith QM1, Thomas F. Kirk SN/RD, Wayne Shockley ENS.

At 5.10am on 7th November 1957, Commander Waring of the United States cutter *Sebago* was informed that the ship's radar had picked up an object, which was racing around the cutter. On one occasion it halted in mid-air, before darting ahead at speed. Eleven minutes later, at 5.21am, four men on deck – Donald Scheafer; Quarter Master, Kenneth Smith; Radioman, Thomas Kirk and Ensign, Wayne Schockley – were able to obtain a visual image of the circular object, which was described as shiny and moving at speeds beyond the capabilities of known aircraft. The UFO was explained away as being a piston-engine aircraft!

UFO close encounter, Mississippi

Truck driver Malvin Stevens (48) was driving home, near House, at 7.25am (7th November?), when a large egg-shaped object dropped out of the sky and landed on the highway in front of him. Malvin thought it was a weather balloon, at first.

> "It had a propeller on either end and on top of the object. I got out and was confronted by three people – two men and a woman – all about four and a half feet tall, with pasty white faces. They were dressed in gray suits. They tried to talk to me but I couldn't understand them; one of then tried to shake my hand. They then got back into the object and flew off."

On the same date, according to Project Blue Book, UFOs were sighted at Boerne, Texas, and Radium Springs, New Mexico.
(Sources: APRO [Aerial Phenomena Research Organization] & *UFOs: Operation Trojan Horse*, John A. Keel)

Farewell Laika (Barker) – gone but not forgotten!

Following the success of Sputnik 1, Nikita Khrushchev wanted a spacecraft launched on 7th November 1957, the 40th anniversary of the Bolshevik Revolution – a mission that would repeat the triumph of Sputnik 1, stunning the world with Soviet prowess. The planners settled on an orbital flight with a dog. Soviet rocket engineers had long intended a canine orbit before attempting human spaceflight; since 1951, they had lofted 12 dogs into sub-orbital space on ballistic flights, working gradually toward an orbital mission, possibly some time in 1958. Laika, who was found as a stray, walking the streets of Moscow, died within hours after launch from overheating – possibly caused by a failure of the central R-7 sustainer to separate from the payload. Five months later, after 2,570 orbits, Sputnik 2 disintegrated, along with Laika's remains, during re-entry on 14th April 1958. On 11th April 2008, Russian officials unveiled a monument to Laika.

A small monument in her honour was built near the military research facility, in Moscow, which prepared Laika's flight to space. It features a dog, standing on top of a rocket.

New Zealand: Close encounter with UFO

At 10.40pm on the 7th November 1957, residents of Paeroa – a town about 50 miles south-east of Waiuku – reported having sighted a curious round pink object in the sky, heading from south to west, which took ten minutes to disappear over the horizon.

At 10.43pm, Mr R J. Pollard – a RNZAF flight engineer of No. 5FB Squadron – was returning home to Waiuku, on what was a clear night, with nearly a full moon. As he rounded a bend in the main road he was startled to encounter an object, approximately 50ft above the road, described as:

"... like looking at an electric light bulb. On top was what appeared to be an antenna protruding upwards in a narrow pyramid form, glowing green in colour."

Mr Pollard stopped the car and got out, in order to study the object more closely. As he did so, it seemed to be aware of his presence and rose up in the air to about 100ft, before suddenly diving down to circle the edge of Lake Pukera, at low altitude. It then rose upwards again and stopped in flight, hovering over a nearby sandhill. Mr Pollard drove home and called his wife. The couple then drove as close as they could to the sandhill. Shortly afterwards the object was seen to move southwards down the coast, following the line of sandhills, at an estimated speed of 40 knots. Mr Pollard contacted the Press but they declined to publish his story.

(Source: Mr George Fulton, *Civilian Source Investigation Journal*)

Australia: 8th November 1957 – At 3.30am, four astronomers at the Commonwealth Observatory, Mount Stromco, New South Wales, sighted a bright pink object in the western sky, at high altitude, which was observed for eight minutes.

New Zealand: 16th November 1957 – Mr Lynch was fishing off the rocks at Whatipu, when he sighted a bright yellow object – about half the size of a full moon – moving in a straight line, almost westwards. The object was in sight for about five seconds, before it vanished behind cloud.

USA: Project Blue Book reports a sighting on the 26th November at Robins Air Force Base. This was followed by a UFO sighted on the 30th of November at New Orleans, Louisiana.

Great Britain: Silpho Moor – 'Flying Saucer' found, believed hoax?

On the late evening of 21st November 1957, Frank Hutton, Charles Thomas, and Fred Taylor, were driving up a steep hill on Silpho Moor, when the engine of their car cut out. They then saw a glowing object in the sky, above some trees, which seemed to come down to the ground. Mr Hutton went out with a torch and found an object in the bracken (described as an 18-inch metallic *'saucer'*, weighing 35lb) On the way back to tell the others, he passed a man and woman, but after having told his friends what had transpired, discovered the object was missing from where he had seen it. Incredibly, following enquiries being made, the couple were traced and agreed to sell the object back to Mr Hutton for £10. Mr Hutton then took the *'saucer'* to a Mr Avendel, whom he believed was an authority on *'flying saucers'*. *The Yorkshire Post* carried an article on 9th December 1957, under the headline – "Has Yorkshire got a flying saucer? Mystery object found on Scarborough moors". Other accounts tell of an advert being placed in the newspaper, offering a reward for the object.

Mr Avendel (believed to be a pseudonym) claimed to have returned to the scene and found no impression on the bracken, but some burning. He described a disc-like object, made largely of copper, 18ins in diameter and weighing 35 pounds. There were two scorched vent holes and a shaft running down the middle. Some markings were present on the outside, but not decipherable. The thing was nicknamed 'The Silpho Moor artifact' from the spot of its find, and was eventually prised apart. Within the disc was a *'thin copper book'*, 6ins x 5ins, composed of 17 thin sheets, upon which *'glyphs'* were written or stamped.

Alien message to Earth people!

This book was given to Mr P. Longbottom – a local cafe owner – to translate. This forms part of a much larger translation:

> *'My name is Ulo, and I write this message to you, my friends on the planet of the sun you call Earth. Where I live I will not say. You are a fierce race, and prepare space travel. No one from another planet has ever landed on the Earth and your reports to the contrary are faulty . . . It is impossible to receive radio over far distances, owing to natural waves in space, unless key of several frequencies is used, but we can receive single frequencies from near transmitter-recorder in space vehicles.'*

This is the shortened version, as published in *Flying Saucer Review*. In the November/December edition of the magazine, Scarborough restaurant owner – Philip Longbottom – writes an article relating to the recovery of the object, and tells the reader that Mr Avenall is a local solicitor and actually writes under a pen-name on metaphysics, rather than *'flying saucers'*. He describes how the artifact was opened, and then later carried out a translation from the information contained in the book.

In our opinion, to publish the full extract in this book, which consists of many pages of translation from the entity ULO, with talk encompassing spaceships, alien women's busts, a life span of 138 years, and warning about the destruction caused by atomic bombs, and the lifestyle of an alien race that enjoys listening to the Charleston and 'Les Amour', intermingled with descriptions of how they dress and live, is extreme and bizarre to such a point that we will not publish any more of what we regard as a hoax.

The Teesside UFO Group said that they had the material chemically analyzed by Mr Rush and it was normal terrestrial copper, which had been sealed together using normal solder. Their conclusion was that it was a slightly elaborate hoax.

Authors: We appreciate we cannot prove categorically that this was a hoax but, bearing in mind the circumstances which lay behind its recovery and subsequent translation, in contrast to many other incidents involving recovery of genuine UFO material, regard the whole of this matter with great suspicion; others, of course, may disagree. (**Source:** *FSR* – 'The Silpho Moor Mystery', March/April 1958 / *FSR* – 'Silpho Moor Controversy', July/August 1958 / *FSR* – 'The Silpho Moor Mystery', by Philip Longbottom, November/December 1958)

Great Britain: 27th November – At 4pm, a strange object was seen high in the sky over Southampton Water, drifting towards the direction of Hythe, before disappearing from view. A number of people who saw the object described it as a stubby rigid cross, with solid looking appendages hanging from it. (**Source: Volume 1,** *Haunted Skies*)

USA: 16th December 1957 – Landed UFO, with entities seen

Mrs Mary M. Starr – a resident of Old Saybrook, Connecticut, and a former teacher with a Master's Degree, from Yale – retired to bed, at 10pm, on the night of 15th December. Between 2am and 3am, she was awoken by a *'bright light'* and first thought it was an aircraft in trouble. Looking out she saw:

> "... a cigar-shaped object, brightly lit, with square portholes, hovering just above my clothesline; I could see men inside".

The object, no more than ten feet from the north side of Mrs Starr's home, was approximately 20 to 30ft long and dark grey or black in colour.

It hovered motionless, about 5ft above the ground, between the house and the tool shed. No wings, fins, or other appendages, were seen. Through the object's lighted windows Mrs Starr saw two figures that passed each other, walking in opposite directions.

> "I could see that it [the object] was so shallow that the men could not have been more than three and a half or four feet tall. The occupants' right arms were raised but no hands were visible. They wore a kind of jacket that 'flared out' at the base and their heads were unusual – square or rectangular, red-orange in colour, and with a brighter red 'bulb' in the centre. I thought they might possibly be wearing some kind of helmets."

A third *'being'* came into view from the left. Mrs Starr leaned forward to see more clearly, then the portholes faded and the entire shell of the object began glowing brightly. From the top end, closest to her, there arose a kind of six-inch *'antenna'* that oscillated and sparkled. After five minutes of glowing steadily, the *'antenna'*

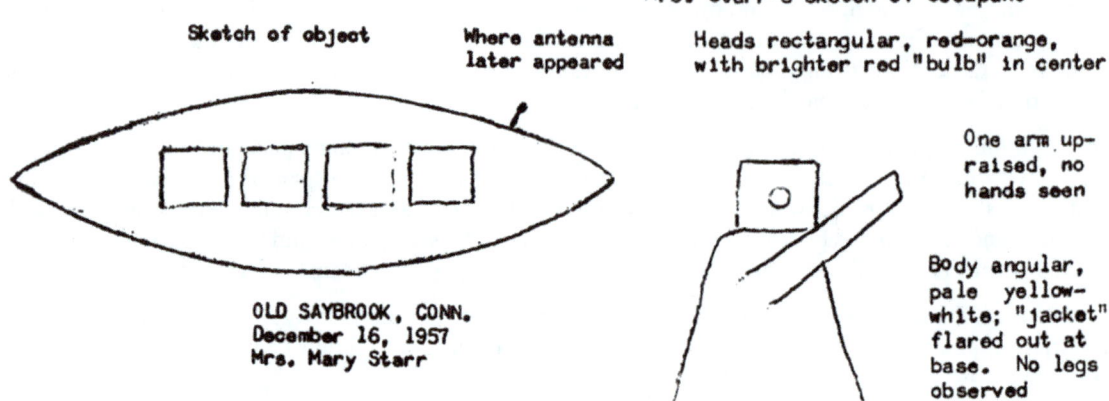

was retracted and the craft began to move. It retraced its original path, gliding smoothly in the direction from which it had apparently arrived. It then made a very sharp right-angle turn, now appearing oval in shape. The hull had changed to a dull grey-blue, and small circular lights now outlined the entire rim. The UFO dipped and undulated, following the contours of a small depression to the north of the witness' house, then tilted sharply and shot up into the sky, at terrific speed, in total silence.

It is of interest to compare the image drawn by Mrs Starr with what was seen by Philip Freeman and his friend, Angela Carter, who were travelling towards Woking, Surrey, in a red Triumph Vitesse, at 12.30am on 13th November 1967 – a cold damp morning. They decided to stop on the side of the road, about two miles from Cranleigh, near Pitch Hill, to demist the windscreen. They left the engine running, with the side lights on. As Philip cleaned the windscreen, he became aware of a very unpleasant odour, as if someone had let off a stink bomb. As he returned to the driver's seat, he was shocked to see:

> ". . . a face, staring in through the nearside passenger window, with no visible features, like eyes or mouth, and what looked like an arm reaching up to the top of the car's hood".

The apparition as sketched by Mr Freeman

Angela saw, from the horrified expression on Philip's face, that something was happening and, without looking around, urged him to drive away.

In the time it took Philip to perform this operation, the *'being'* had apparently moved to the rear of the vehicle. Philip switched on the headlights and started the car, *"seeing the same white face"*, close to the Perspex back window. As he drove away, he had an impression of a dark bell shape, surmounted by two white or luminous parts. He cannot recall seeing any legs. As they recommenced their journey, the smell dissipated.

(Sources: NICAP, Richard Hall & Isabel Davis, Charles Bowen, *Flying Saucer Review*, Jan/Feb.1968, Vol. 14, Page 15-16. 'The Spectre at Winterfold'/*Woking Review*/SIGAP)

A BRAZILIAN FARMERS STORY 1957.

On the 15th December 1957, Adhemar, a young farmer of Ponte Poran Brazil was out ploughing, it was midnight, suddenly Adhemar observed a star like light which approached at great speed from the North, seconds later the light stopped about 300 feet above the field. Adhemar thoroughly alarmed decided to pack up and go home, at that moment the object in the sky swooped down and landed some twenty yards from his tractor. Two "people" emerged from the machine and ran towards him, they grabbed him from behind, as Adhemar struggled, others came from the saucer and finally Adhemar was hustled into the space craft. Inside Adhemar was stripped of his clothes, blood was drawn from his chin by a flexible suction syringe, he was then covered with a plastic material and then moistened all over with a kind of sponge. Adhemar was then left alone for twenty minutes then a girl came into the cabin, she was about 4ft 8ins tall had blonde hair, no eyelashes or eyebrows, she looked "Chinese", she approached Adhemar with open arms, stood near him and waited, perhaps to note his reactions, soon the girl left and Adhemar was given back his clothes, he was then taken outside the saucer, as soon as he was clear of the machine the queer craft suddenly took off in a blinding white light, Adhemar had not been harmed by his encounter.

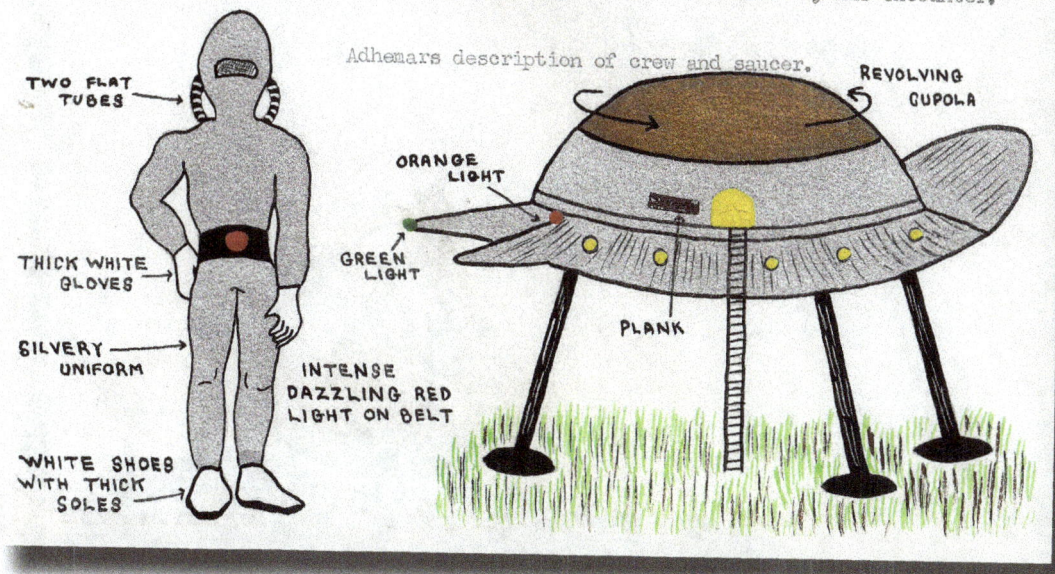

Adhemars description of crew and saucer.

AN INTERSTING BRAZILIAN SIGHTING 1958.

One day in April 1958, a Brazilian jeweller named Senhor Wilson Lustosa was travelling along the beach from the port of Maceio to Parapueira, Wilson was driving along the beautiful beaches of white sand which streatch for miles, as he neared a spot called Saude Wilson noticed several fishermen looking at something that was in the sky above them. Wilson asked the men what they were watching? they said that they had seen a flying saucer, he could see nothing at first, then he heard a humming noise which grew louder and louder, and then he saw something which seemed to fall out of the sky towards him. It was a machine of some sort, about 15 to 20 metres in height, Wilson described the width as "travelling circus" it seemed to be made up of three parts, the upper half was like aluminium, like an inverted bowl, on the top was a small dome which shone as bright as an electric welding arc. The lower part was also a bowl, but dark in colour, around the centre was a band with square portholes, as the machine moved over the water it made a humming sound and the water seemed to boil.

January 1958

Australia: 8th January 1958 – Mr B. Wellstead and four others, from Sydney, New South Wales, sighted a luminous red-yellow object heading northwards. Suddenly, it swung around at 90° and headed eastwards.

Australia: 13th January 1958 – Mr Cecil Manning reported having sighted a huge dome-shaped object in the sky over Casino, New South Wales, at 6.30pm. Also on this date Mr Crittenden, of the same town, was driving his car when the car radio began to suffer heavy interference. He looked up and saw a dome-shaped object, with a long narrow light on the underneath, following his vehicle. The object, which was 50 yards away from the vehicle, continued to follow the car, occasionally swooping down in flight for three miles, until flying away. In the same month, Mr J. Sutherland and another man sighted two very bright golden lights crossing the sky, one behind each other, at 8pm, over Culburra, New South Wales. The objects, which were estimated to be 50ft in diameter, were sighted by two boys from four miles away.

POLICE GO TO THE MARS MAN'S MEETINGS

By RODNEY HALLWORTH

DAILY MAIL 28-1-58

GRAMOPHONE records claiming to bring messages from Jesus and St. Peter in outer space, which have been on sale for 25s. from a recently formed spiritual society in London, are being examined at Scotland Yard.

Three senior police officers have attended meetings at Caxton Hall and have bought blue glass bottles for 1s. each.

These, it is claimed, if filled with tap water and exposed to the sun, can bring "benefit and relief" to sufferers of various ailments from nervous debility to swollen ankles.

The detectives took statements from a number of women who have attended the meetings, organised by the Aetherius Society.

The blooms

The leader of the Aetherius Society is Mr. George King, a slim 38-year-old bachelor, who says he has visited Mars "in a mental state," spoken to the people who live there, and admired the planet's exotic blooms.

The headquarters of the society is a fourth-floor flat in Fulham, S.W. He works there with his secretary, Miss Grace Abercrombie.

Mr. King is editor of the society's magazine *Cosmic Voice*.

Mr. King, relaxed in grey slacks and white pullover, told me last night:

"So far as I'm concerned the whole of Scotland Yard can come and visit me. I have simply nothing to hide. The society's accounts will be published in full at our annual meeting next month.

"I have received many messages from Jesus and the saints. It is correct that a message from St. Peter through my voice is on sale on a gramophone record for 25s. I have sold quite a number.

"The label states quite clearly that it was received while I was in a Yogic trance. I do not claim direct voice.

"Our income comes from various sources. We have several publications at 2s. 6d. each, the records at 25s., and about 300 bottles for water at 1s. each.

"But I must emphasise there was no profit on the bottles. They cost us about a shilling, and sometimes we sold two for 1s. 6d."

DAILY TELEGRAPH 24-1-58

SECRET HEARINGS
Flying Saucer Evidence

Telephone calls flooded the switchboard at the Columbia Broadcasting System H.Q. in New York last night after a speaker on a programme dealing with flying saucers was cut off the air for 15 seconds. This action was taken, it was explained, because Mr. Donald Keyhoe, a retired Air Force major, who believes that flying saucers may come from another planet, departed from his script.

He had started to refer to secret hearings by a Congressional committee. To-day he said: "For the past six months our group has been working with a Senate committee. I was going to say that if they held public hearings with the information we have given them it would have proved the reality of these things and would have caused a sensation."

Mr. George King.

Miss Grace Abercrombie.

Great Britain; 10th January 1958 – An RAF jet was seen passing over Ipsley, Worcestershire, during broad daylight, being followed by a silver *'disc'*, to the surprise of the witness. Later, the same afternoon, three similar objects were seen flying over Studley, Warwickshire a few miles away. (**Source: UFOSIS, Birmingham**)

March 1958

USA: 14th March 1958 – at Healdsburg, California. Mr and Mrs W.F. Cummings, and one other person, watched over a two minutes duration, a 3ft round, black object, which touched the ground before taking off at 8.45am.

Haunted Skies Volume Ten

Australia: 25th March 1958 – At 10pm, two shimmering *'discs'* were seen performing intricate manoeuvres over Woomera, New South Wales, for more than 30 minutes, before they moved away.

(Source: Hervey, *UFOs over the Southern Hemisphere*)

April 1958

USA: 10th April 1958 – At 7.20am, a bright silver teardrop-shaped object was sighted in the sky at 35° elevation, for a few seconds, moving eastwards, by Warren J. Knapp, of the 9th OSI District at Western Kentucky, then reported to Lt. Colonel John B. Woodyard, at Lake Charles USAF Base, the same day.

(Source: National Archives – Declassified documents)

Australia: 14th April 1958 – A large *'mass'* descended from the sky over Sydney Harbour, followed by a loud explosion that shook hundreds of waterfront homes. On the same date at Lynchburg, Virginia, USAF Major D.G. Tilley, was flying a C-47 transport at 1pm, when he sighted a grey-black rectangular object rotating very slowly on its horizontal axis for four seconds. **(Source: Project Blue Book)**

Great Britain: 19th April 1958 – Aircraft from RAF Lakenheath were scrambled to intercept UFOs plotted on the station's radar, ten miles away from the Airbase – later explained away as being due to freak weather conditions.

May 1958

Australia: 2nd May 1958 – At the Caltex Refinery, Kurnell, New South Wales, John Smith reported seeing two 10ft long *'rockets'* flying through the sky, at 1.30am.

> *"They were flying at about 400ft; the first was burning brightly, the second had a long tail of orange flame."*

(Source: Hervey, *UFOs over the Southern Hemisphere*)

Australia: 3rd May 1958 – A reddish-golden object was seen heading in a south-west direction across the night sky, over Chullora, New South Wales, by Mr H. Edwards.

Australia: 6th May 1958 – Mr R. Wilson reported sighting a *'large rocket-shaped object'* rising up into the sky, making a terrific roaring noise, showering orange sparks and smoke as it did so – gone in seconds.

Great Britain: May 1958 – Eric Apter – now in his 70s, from Suffolk, with over forty years experience working with horses outside, was exercising a horse along the main track at Newmarket racecourse, along with 20 other riders, when he saw

> *". . . a silver UFO, darting in and out of small clouds in the sky above us – almost as if playing a bizarre game of 'tag'. We watched it for about 20 minutes, until it left".*

June 1958

Australia: 5th June 1958 – During the afternoon an object, making a loud roaring noise, flew over Marrickville, NSW.

Australia: 6th June 1958 – An unusual light was reported over Sydney, at 8.15pm, which was seen to make a sharp turn in the sky.

USA: UFO sighted over Pueblo, Colorado.

Great Britain: 10th June 1958 – the Under-Secretary of State for Air – Mr Charles Orr-Ewing, was asked:

> "How many instances of unidentified flying objects had been reported during the last 12 months, and what steps were taken to co-ordinate such observations?"

He replied:

> "Reports of 54 unidentified flying objects have been received in the last 12 months. Such co-ordination as is necessary is undertaken by the Air Ministry. Most of the objects turn out to be meteors, balloons, or aircraft. Satellites have also accounted for a number of reports."

USA: 20th June – At Fort Bragg, North Carolina, a silver, circular object – its lower portion seen through a green haze – was sighted hovering in the sky at 11.05pm. It then oscillated slightly, before moving away at great speed.

July 1958

Great Britain: 16th July 1958 – A few minutes before 4pm, Peter Smith (13) – a pupil of Rickmansworth Grammar School, Hertfordshire – situated on a hill close to electric power generators and main railway line – was looking out of the window at an overcast sky, as dark storm clouds gathered.

> "Suddenly, a bright white glowing hat-shaped object appeared in the sky and performed a number of movements, slowing slightly on the downward 'runs', travelling faster than a jet, and disappeared out of sight behind trees."

Other pupils spoke of seeing a yellow band around the centre, with a blurred top and sharply defined base. The following day two silvery *'discs'* were seen over Winchester.

(Source: Gordon Creighton, *Flying Saucer Review***)**

Australia: 19th July 1958 – Between 7.30pm and 8pm, there were several sightings of an object that appeared to be lit by an orange light, over Sydney.

Australia: 20th July 1958 – A bright oval object, half the size of a full moon, showing two horizontal beams of light, with two narrower beams pointing downwards at an angle, and a smaller light flashing on and off on its body, throwing out vapour, was seen over Katoomba, New South Wales, by Mr J. Sen's family and police officers.

August 1958

Great Britain: 20th August 1958 – Gilbert Wilkinson (12) from Crawley, West Sussex, was out roller skating at the back of his house, just after the sun had set, when he saw:

> ". . . a huge, golden-yellow, object shaped like a disc, flash across my field of vision between the houses in the close and gone in two seconds. It was like viewing a bicycle wheel from its side, showing a small flame flowing from the bottom of its circumference. It was larger than a full moon in size, completely silent, showing no condensation trail or sonic boom."

Haunted Skies Volume Ten

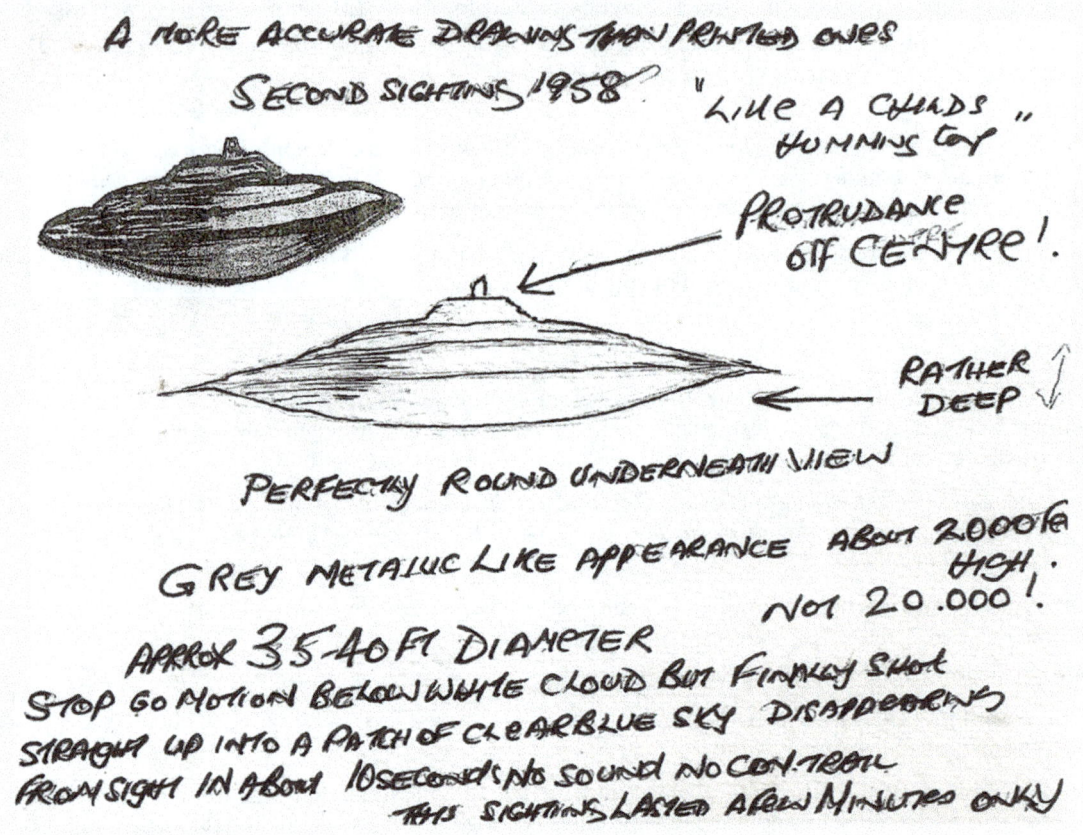

Great Britain: September 1958 – Ron Lucas spoke to us on a number of occasions about what he saw in the same year, over Southampton.

> "I was chatting to a young apprentice at work about, of all things, UFOs. Rather foolishly, I told him we should go outside and have a look, never imagining, in my wildest dreams, that we would see anything. We were astounded to see a saucer-shaped object moving across the sky, under cloud cover, at a height I estimated to be 20,000 ft."

USA: 3rd October 1958 – At 3.10am, caboose (rear of train) crew Cecil Bridge, fireman, and engineer Harry Eckman, aboard a southbound freight train on the Monon Railroad in Clinton County, Indiana, sighted four odd lights crossing the track in front of them. The lights then turned and approached the train, dropping down to 2-300ft, before crossing the length of the train and heading eastwards, in formation. The men alerted the rest of the crew about the incident. Conductor Edward Robinson shone a torch at the objects, which flew away but returned. After manoeuvring around the train for one hour and ten minutes, they headed north-west and disappeared from view. (**Source: NICAP**)

USA: 17th October 1958 – Two flights of 12 separate round amber objects were seen 25 seconds apart, moving at high altitude over the Grand Rapids. They were later explained away as meteors! (**Source:** *The Hynek UFO report*)

December 1958

Australia: 5th December 1958 – At 11.37pm, a white object with a bright blue and red tail was seen over Mildura, Victoria.

The list of consultants and contributors to 'Flying Saucer Review' during 1959

INTERNATIONAL UFO OBSERVER CORPS
1, DOUGHTY STREET, LONDON, W.C.1., ENGLAND

FSR — **1959**

Chief Investigator
The Hon. B. le Poer Trench, Editor, FLYING SAUCER REVIEW

Area Investigators

GREAT BRITAIN
COUNTRY AREAS

Aberdeenshire
Ian Taylor, Esq., 46, Berrywell Gardens, Dyce.
Berkshire
Gerald Newey, Esq., 68, Longworth Avenue, Tilehurst.
Cheshire
M. A. Scott, Esq., 52, Davenport Avenue, Crewe.
Cumberland
Commander B. T. Brewster, D.S.C., R.N.(Retd.), Kilbalyn, Braithwaite, Keswick. Tel. Braithwaite 304.
N. Derbyshire (Bakewell area)
C. Curtis, Esq., 1, New Lumford, Bakewell.
S.E. Derbyshire
G. Fox, Esq., 69, Wyvern Avenue, Long Eaton, Notts.
Essex
D. R. Miller, Esq., 282, Main Road, Gidea Park, Romford, Essex. Tel.: Romford 40740.
Hampshire (Bournemouth, Poole, Parkstone, Lymington and Ringwood Area)
D. A. Cadel, 17, Highland Avenue, Highcliffe-on-Sea.
Hampshire (Portsmouth, Southampton, Fareham and District)
E. H. S. Sears, Esq., 116, Gosport Road, Fareham.
Hertfordshire
Miss Thelma Roberts, 52, Clarence Road, St. Albans.
Lanarkshire
John Potter, Jr., 7, High Overton Street, Netherbarn.
Lancashire
J. Dale, Esq., A.Phs., 2, Belfield Road, Reddish, Stockport, Cheshire. Tel.: East 2815.
Leicestershire
Ellis Porter, Esq., " Rosecot," Glen Road, Oadby.
Lothians, Scotland (East, Mid and West)
J. M. Spark, Esq., White Lodge, West Road, Haddington, East Lothian. Tel. Haddington 2174.
Lothians, Scotland (Edinburgh Area)
E. M. Buchan, Esq., 3, Craighall Crescent, Trinity, Edinburgh, 6.
Norfolk
Peter F. Johnson, Esq., 124, Glebe Road, Norwich.
Nottinghamshire
J. F. G. Rayner, Esq., 13, Needham Road, Arnold.
Pembrokeshire (S. Wales)
Miss A. F. B. Wodehouse, Ivy Tower, Tenby.
Shropshire and N. Wales
J. Gavin Gibbons, Esq., Glan Severn, The Mount, Shrewsbury, Shropshire. Tel. Shrewsbury 2938.
Somerset
Sidney M. Lawton, Esq., Mus.B., A.R.C.O., A.R.C.M., Queen's College, Taunton, Somerset. Tel. Taunton 4391.
Staffordshire
Captain Wilfrid Daniels, 134, Weston Road, Stafford.
Suffolk
Geoffrey St. George Schomberg, Esq., Sweffling Grange, Saxmundham. Tel. Rendham 496.
Surrey (Cheam and Sutton areas)
G. N. P. Stephenson, Esq., 12, Dorset Road, Cheam.
Sussex (Worthing and within 10-mile radius)
Mrs. D. C. Lash, Ellenga, 41, The Glen, West Worthing.
Warwickshire (Part)
D. S. Richards, Esq., 39, School Street, Wolston, Nr. Coventry, Warwickshire.
Warwickshire (Meriden Rural District)
C. G. Turner, Esq., A.I.P.R.E., 115, Water Orton Road, Castle Bromwich, Birmingham. Tel. CAS 3546.

Worcestershire
G. T. Morris, Esq., 67, Wood Lane, Streetly, Nr. Birmingham.
Yorkshire (East Yorkshire)
M. Alexander, Esq., 10, Ingleton Avenue, Kingston-upon-Hull, East Yorks. Tel. 55924.
Yorkshire (West Riding)
Jack Ibson, Esq., 2, Laithe Grove, Wibsey, Bradford, 6. Tel. Bradford 79352.
Yorkshire (Middlesbrough and 30-mile radius)
Dennis Rush, Esq., 96, Russell Street, Middlesbrough.
Yorkshire
Richard N. Whitehead, Esq., 8, Hillside Avenue, Fartown, Huddersfield. Tel. Huddersfield 4670.

LONDON AREA

South London and Surrey
H. P. Godden-Kent, Esq., 205A, Underhill Road, Dulwich, S.E.22. Tel. FORest Hill 1037.
W. G. Burnham, Esq., 30, Altenburg Gardens, S.W.11. Tel. Battersea 6018.
Ealing
Torban Nordal, Esq., 16, Castlebar Park, Ealing, W.5.
Wood Green, Edmonton and Tottenham
J. C. Tuohy, 11, White Hart Lane, Wood Green, N.22.
Crouch End, Alexandra Park, Muswell Hill, Hornsey and Harringay
R. R. Russell, Esq., 58, Lausanne Road, Hornsey, N.8. Tel. Chancery 4411. Exten. 568 (Business).
Hampstead, Highgate, Finchley, Barnet, Mill Hill, Edgware
Dr. B. E. Finch, 851, Finchley Road, N.W.11. SPEedwell 1053.
Teddington, Twickenham and Richmond
J. J. Muller, Esq., 20, Lebanon Park, Twickenham.
Barnes, Mortlake, Sheen
C. A. Heathcote, Esq., 26, Bracken Gardens, Barnes, S.W.13. RIVerside 3918.

OVERSEAS

BELGIUM
Monsieur Lucien A. R. Hostie, Jozef Verbovenlei 2, Deurne-South, Antwerp.

CANADA
De Witt Lee, 136, Florence St., Hamilton, Ontario. Tel.: JA 7-5374.

DENMARK
Danish Interplanetary Society for Contact (D.I.S.C.), 18 Morlenesvej, Holte. Tel. Holte 259.

GHANA
Commander J. O. S. Wilde, R.N. (Retd.), P.O. Box 1115, Accra, Ghana.

JAPAN AND FAR EAST
Far East area
Yusuke J. Matsumura, Isogo P.O. Box 18, Yokohama.
JAPAN AREA
Teizi Ogawa, 775 Kokubunji, Kokubunji-Cho, Tokyo.

PERSIAN GULF
Colin Armstrong, Esq., 16, 5th Street North, Ahmadi, Kuwait, Persian Gulf.

N. RHODESIA (LUANSHYA DISTRICT)
J. Whisken, Esq., 118, F. Avenue, Luanshya, N. Rhodesia.

U.S.A. (STATE OF ILLINOIS)
Paul R. Trent, Esq., 7012 South Garden Lane, Argo, Illinois. Tel. Globe 8-3149.

Haunted Skies Volume Ten

January 1959

George Adamski World Tour

NEW ZEALAND

On 13th January 1959, George Adamski left Los Angeles Airport for the first leg of his world tour. He began by stopping off at Hawaii, where he visited the main island of Oahu – the Nuuanu Pass.

On 17th January, he left for New Zealand and arrived at Whenuapai Airport, in Auckland, where he was met by Henk and Brenda Hinfelaar, and other UFO study group leaders from North Island.

His first lecture took place in Kaikohe, for the Kaikohe Flying Saucer Club. From there he travelled to Auckland Town Hall, where 2,000 people were seated awaiting his arrival, and 700 people outside – such was his popularity.

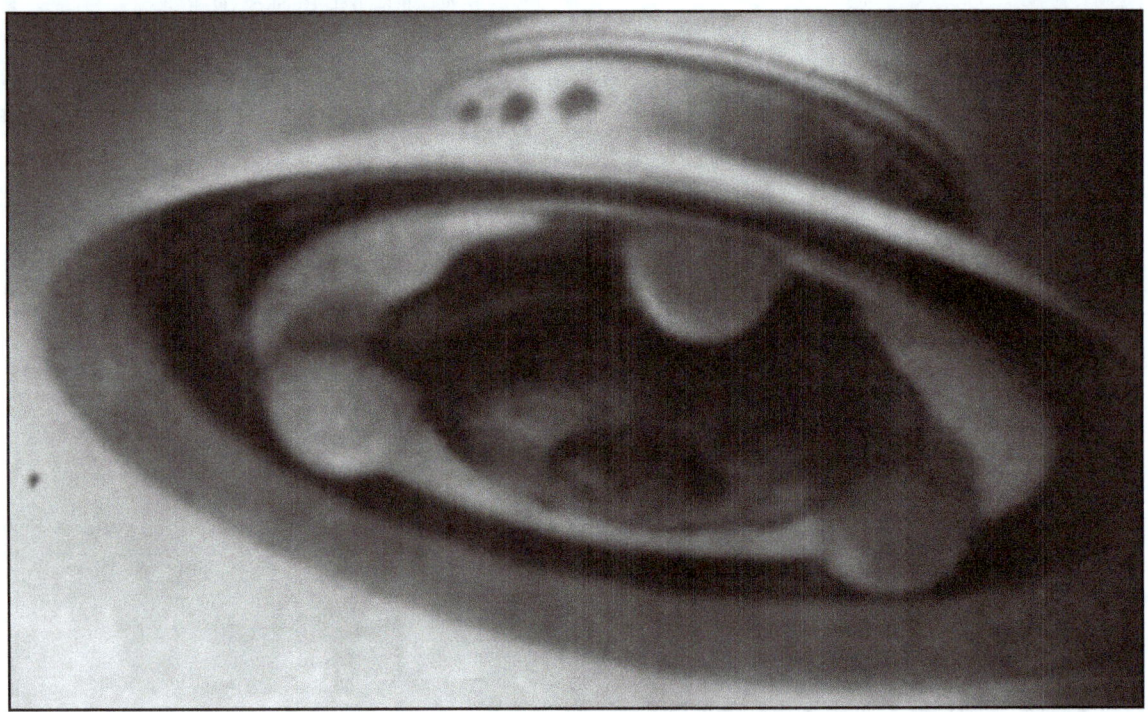

Incredibly, George was invited to speak with the Maori King in the Royal Mahurangi House at Ngaruawahia. Sister Heeni escorted him to the Kings Audience room. While there, six white streaks of light were seen to flash across the sky overhead.

After sampling the delights of a picnic and trip to the Maori village of Whakarewarewa, George left for Napier. When he arrived, he was shown a newspaper article *'Flying Saucers reported over Lake Taupo'*, in which three Rotorua people reported having sighted dozens of *'flying saucers'* high in the sky above the town, after having bid farewell to George.

On 28th January, George lectured to an audience in the town. On 1st February, he addressed the Wellington

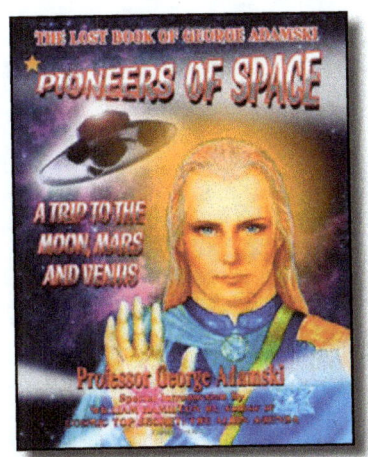

Concert Chamber Town Hall. This was followed by a talk at New Plymouth, during which it was disclosed that a minister and members of the congregation had seen a spaceship.

At Christchurch, he was met by radio personality – Mr 'Happy' Hill – who took some motion pictures and sound recordings.

On Sunday, a final lecture took place at His Majesty's Theatre, Dunedin.

AUSTRALIA

The second leg of the tour was Australia. During the following weeks, George lectured for a UFO group in Sydney. This was followed by a trip to Perth on the 4th February, Adelaide, and then Melbourne. As George was getting ready to leave the city, he was shown a newspaper article in the *Sunday Mail* (28.3.1959) written by John Pinkney – *'Did a Spaceship from an alien planet land this month in South Australia?'* The article spoke of weird multicoloured objects being seen streaking across the sky over Purnong, 91 miles east of Adelaide.

At 2.10am on 13th March, Purnong Landing carrier – Percy Briggs – and Carl Towill – postmaster at Claypans – saw a huge glowing dome-shaped object take-off from a field and rise up into the sky, before shooting upwards at immense speed. We gathered that other witnesses to this phenomena included local nurses.

BRITAIN

In late April 1959, George came to Britain and lectured at Edinburgh, after being invited by Mrs Irene Flucker. He also spoke at Newcastle and met Mr John Leslie Otley – UFO researcher and editor of *ORBIT* magazine. Other places included Manchester, Tunbridge Wells, Bournemouth and London.

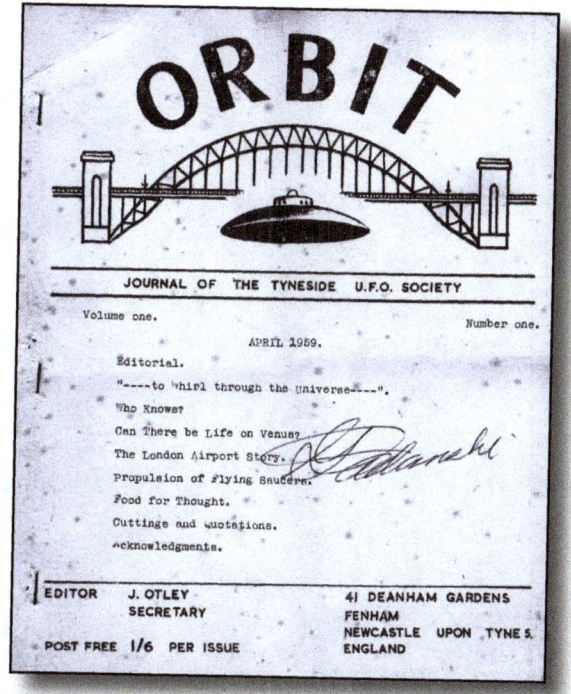

Personally we do not know what to make of George Adamski, who may have been the first of the so-called contactees of the 1950s, bearing in mind he told of having photographed *'ships'* from other planets, met with friendly Nordic alien Space Brothers, and to have even taken trips aboard their vessels. He has been called many things, including philosopher, teacher, student, and *'saucer'* researcher, though his claims were met with scepticism. There are, of course, many that support him and others who do not. His classic photograph of a UFO, taken on 13th December 1952, has attracted much attention. A German scientist – Walther Johannes Riedel – said this photo was a fake, and that the landing struts were light bulbs. We can neither prove nor disprove this was the case. We never met George, so have no views either way.

However, we have met enough people who have seen and described identical objects. Their integrity is not in question. One of the most famous was the incident that took place on the 17th July 1955, involving Margaret Fry. Her drawing is identical to that of George's. This UFO forms a common background to many reports, involving similarly described objects.

Haunted Skies Volume Ten

Jan. 29, 1965

Dear Friend;

Received your letter of the 21st.

First concerning Allingham – a couple of years ago when I was in Europe there was a complete search made for him by Lu Senstock of Switzerland, and as the report stated that he had died, but no place in all of Europe – could there be found any record of his passing on. Which included such record houses in different nations as well as convelescent resorts or sanitoriums – so no one knows whether he passed on or is living quietly some place or was taken away by the Brothers.

Now a little news of the last weeks, things are happening – almost or it will be probably like they were in 1952 after my contact up to 1955. As you know as all the churches know, that the Air Force around the world has been saying there is no such a thing as Flying Saucers, and even when they had appeared over the Capital the Press wouldn't carry the news. They have been appearing over Washington D.C. since 1964 of December 29th. Yet no news in the papers. So I asked the Brothers to let me take some moving pictures in the daytime of Them not too close but close enough – that the forms of the ships may be shown and not just lights. They complied with my request, I at present have ten – twelve minutes of a moving film of them in color – taken in the vacinity of Washington and other places. I still expect to get more. And They maneuvered in such a nature that we cannot do this ourselves. A segment of this film was shown one week before the Inauguration of our President on T.V. in Washington D.C. It really stirred everything up. A number of the Congressmen and Senators want to see a full picture – the Space administration saw a segment of it. Everybody wants to see it. I am leaving for Washington in 2 weeks to show the full film including public lectures. The only people who don't like this film, which I believe they have even better than I have, is the Air Force. For they have been telling the public that there is no such a thing and now we have movie films of Them in public hands. It kind of puts the Air Force on the spot. This film could break the ice in bringing the Truth out as the public demands it. As I intend to go through the nation with it. When I get finished here, the Mexican government asked for the same thing. So it is spreading. Even the critical Press had to say something in its favor which we have on tape. And prior to showing of this film on T.V. 5 space craft were seen the day before, by military and other people around George Washington Monument in Washington D.C. And they had these people including the military compare notes between my films and those ships sighted over the Monument and they all claimed what was sighted was the same as on the film. We have a tape on this. While you U.F.O. researcher's are fueding over minor things – whether you believe something or you don't when things are really happening, which you should place close attention to. Where even governments are shaken up by Their Visitations, so what good is the association. I am wondering sometimes if they are worth the paper they use to write the repeated happenings of years ago, instead of what is happening today. What value are the researcher to the betterment of the world if they wallow in the mud, instead of using God given Intelligence. For everything at one time was considered impossible, that we now have, by the over educated or over egotistical individual. I am wondering, in all of these research groups, what are they searching for – to waste time on nothing but something that took place ten years ago, instead of what is happening at this very moment. The way it looks from here they are messing up, the masses.

There are plans that I might be in Europe, sometime this year, if it works out and I do come, I will have this most valuable film in the world with me to show it to honest – to – god people who are interested in a better world. But experts will have no place – for it is very funny, that some of us in this work from the beginning – are far from being experts, but overnight experts at one time who were diggin ditches – sprung up and now know all the answers to a problem with which the surface has not even been scratched. And are professing to be capable of judging people who have the experience. Some of them would have red faces, if they ever got a view, of the credentials, that I carry – ever since 1952. Given to me to be free to ask even of the highest authority the answers I may be

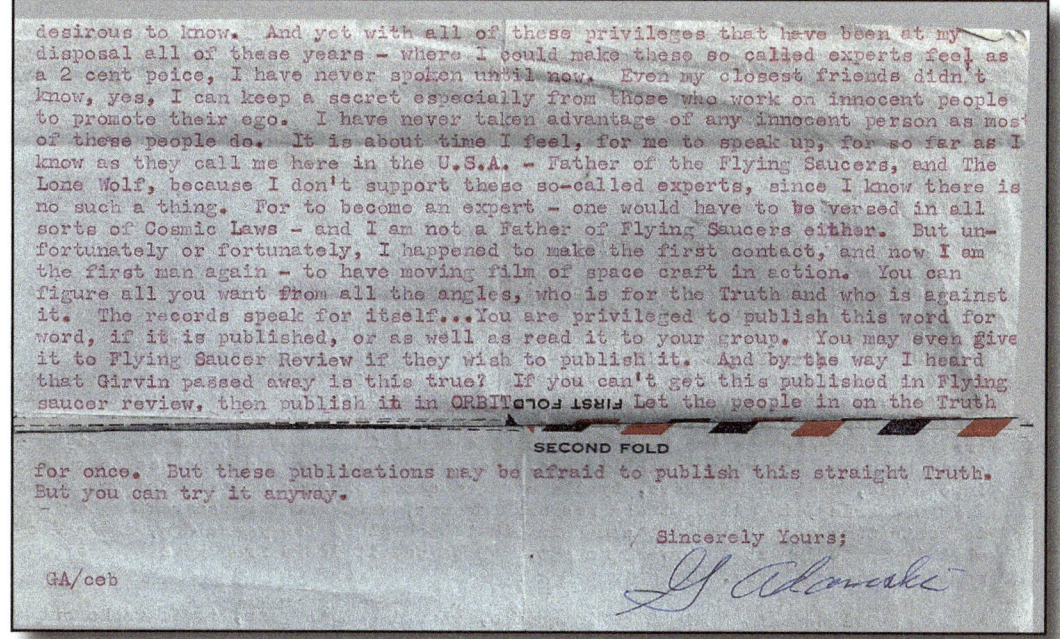

Mrs Rhoda Mills wrote to 'John' Dennis Llewellyn, many years ago. Her letters are interesting as, indeed, is the attached letter from George Adamski, which offer a unique insight into that particular period of UFO activity.

2 King George Road
Minehead
Somerset TA24 5JD

9 February, 1983

Dear

Thank you for your letter, received to-day. I understand the financial problem very well. Life in California is so very different than in England. Because of the climate, more time is spent outdoors for one thing. The tempo is also very different. When we first went to live there at the beginning of the 1950's, California was very beautiful. Miles of orange groves, empty clean beaches, a very small airport for 'prop planes, no smog, no freeways. Then came the aerospace industries. Orange groves were ploughed up to make way for housing tracts for the workers. Then miles of freeways built to get the workers from the tracts to the factories. Then the SMOG. A huge area was dug up to make way for Disneyland.

My husband was a mechanical/electrical engineer and was in 'at the birth' of the new industry. (He designed and developed some of the instruments for the control panel of the capsule which took the first men to the moon - but does not like this mentioned.)

So, we lived in a world of outer space as one might say, which was how we became acquainted with the men I spoke of in my letter.

Now - about George Adamski. First, he told us that it should be pronounced ADamski, as in Adam. Not ADAMski, as pronounced by many people. Several times we chatted with him as we sat outside his little hut on the slopes of Mount Palomar. His sister had a coffee shop (a sort of long wooden hut) and George's 6" telescope was placed on her land. Inside the little hut, George had made a hole in the roof, through which the telescope pointed so he could watch the sky. The other item inside was a small cot for him to lie on.

At this point I will say a little about myself. I will be 72 this month, so in the fifties I was in my forties. I was an executive secretary, and for a time worked at Fox Studios. I knew Marylyn by the way. My point is, that I had to be a quick, alert person to do my job. Not gullible. I believed what George Adamski told us. Sitting talking quietly to him on that mountainside was an extraordinary experience. He was quiet and dignified. With a sort of spiritual quality. I have his books FLYING SAUCERS HAVE LANDED AND SAUCERS FAREWELL. Also INSIDE THE SPACE SHIPS.

I also believed all the others, except one. I believed George Van Tassell, who lived at the airport at Giant Rock. Geo. Hunt Williamson (a brilliant man) Truman Bethurum. The only one I doubted was Dan Fry. I knew him very well because we were in the same study group. He 'hedged' a lot even to us who knew him well. I sort of wondered if he had had a dream as he lay on the sands. But who am I to say. I do know that he got a lot of mileage out of it.

I also have the book ABOARD A FLYING SAUCER by Truman Bethurum, which he autographed for me as we sat chatting while at the Rock.

-2-

I have eleven snaps taken at the Convention at the Rock in the Yucca Valley. I have never heard of the Wells you mention. There was a place nearby called Indian Wells. Several of the snaps are of the Rock. It was huge, with a room inside. It was known as Giant Rock Airport. There is a good picture of Van Tassell, who posed for us. Looking back now, we marvel that we did not constantly take snaps of the things we saw. We just did not think of it because it seemed so ordinary at the time.

Regarding the shapeship we did snap. It would be April of 1954 or 1955 I think. I can't be positive. We were on our way to the yearly Convention, driving along a rough desert track. I should say 'bouncing' along. We were going straight towards the brilliant sun, which in the desert, can be blinding. My husband was gripping the wheel and trying to avoid hazards like clumps of cactus. I was peering ahead, watching out for tumbleweed etc. Suddenly I saw IT. There it was, a huge shapeship, motionless in the sky. I grabbed my husband's arm. "Look up there! Stop the car! Get the camera!" "Be quick before it takes off." "It won't be any use" he said. "The sun will be in the lens." "Nothing will come out." "Try anyway" I insisted. So he stopped and got out. He focussed the camera. The ship had remained quite still. I would be willing to show this picture to anybody, but sorry, I can't let it out of my sight. I saw so many U.F.O's during those years, and this is the only picture I have. That is, the only picture taken by ourselves, so we know it is not a fake.

The shapeship on the beach was at Playa del Rey. A few minutes earlier we had been down to the edge of the water. It goes dark suddenly in California, so while this experience took place it had gone dark and a pale moon had come up. Well, we turned from the sea and set off back towards the car, which we had left at the top of the cliff. The sand was very soft, and after perhaps 100 yards I stopped to empty my shoes. As I hopped around I happened to glance back to the place where we had just been. and was astounded to see this huge spacecraft hovering about 3 ft. above the beach. I shouted to my husband, who was some distance ahead. We walked backway to the clifftop and sat down, never taking out eyes off the ship. I can only guess, but I would think it would be 12 or 14 ft. across. Lights flashed from it. I could see the edge of the tide moving back and forth beneath it, by the light of the moon. After a while a panel slid aside and a brilliant light shone forth, sending a broad beam across the sand. For a few seconds a slim figure appeared and a hand raised slightly, as if in salute. Then the panel closed. We stared and waited. We were afraid to look away, and I don't think we even spoke. Then the lights became much brighter, and then, without a sound, the ship had vanished. We 'came to our senses' as one might say, and it occurred to us to check the time. Forty-fiv minutes since we had turned from the water's edge.

Feel free to ask any questions which may occur to you. We only came here recently. As a matter of fact, our boxes arrived only last week. So we are surrounded by crates. Therefore please ask anyone to write before coming.

Sincerely,

Rhoda Mills

Rhoda Mills

Haunted Skies Volume Ten

Australia: 24th January 1959 – A cigar-shaped object, apparently solid and of metallic appearance, catching the sun, was sighted over Sydney, at 11.30am, by Mr K. Armstrong and G. Montgomery. After hovering for five minutess, it turned at a right angle and flew away at colossal speed, before disappearing from view. Just prior to the sighting, three loud explosions were reported over the city. In the same month at Canberra, New South Wales, Robert Weatherhead, and two others, sighted a bright cigar-shaped luminous cloud, belching flames from the rear. A second object was then seen following behind the first, at an estimated speed of 600mph and a height of 5000ft. (**Source:** Hervey, *UFOs over the Southern Hemisphere*)

February 1959

Great Britain: 23rd February 1959 – Mr George Wild from Honeysuckle Road, Sheffield, was one of a number of people who sighted a *'flying saucer'* hovering 200ft off the ground over the city, at 6.40pm, after experiencing unusual interference on the television sets. The sighting was later explained away by the Commanding Officer, at RAF Norton, who suggested they had seen the Fairey Rotodyne – the world's first vertical take-off Airliner – although this appears unlikely, as the object seen was totally silent. (**Source:** *Sheffield Star/Sheffield Telegraph*, 25.2.59)

USA: 24th February 1959 – Pilots sights UFOs

March 1959

Australia: 15th March, 1959 – Two bright orange *'lights'* were seen heading across the sky over Willoughby, New South Wales, at 9.30pm, by a Mr W. Dietz. These were followed by another two *'lights'*, and yet more *'lights'*, one of which was seen to split away and head southwards.

New Zealand: 22nd March 1959 – A report of a mysterious *'light'*, which was seen to land out to sea off the coast of Wellington, followed by a loud explosion.

Australia: 31st March 1959 – Barry Neale, from Port Elliot, sighted a landed object 100 metres from the road, glowing red and orange, showing a row of portholes, lighting up nearby trees at 11.30pm. He approached it to within 30 metres, when it took off at high speed. We understand checks were carried out with Geiger counters, following an investigation made into the matter, but no trace of radiation was found.

April 1959

USA Washington: 1st April 1959 – Did a UFO bring aircraft down?

At 8.19pm, the pilot of an Air Force C-118 transport plane, from McChord Air Force Base, with a crew of four, was over Orting, Washington, when he radioed:

"We have hit something or something has hit us ... mayday."

The pilot then said he was returning to base, at which point his last words were *"This is it"*.

The aircraft was torn to shreds in a tremendous explosion when it crashed into mountains over the Rhodes Lake area. Two officers and two enlisted men died. Barricades were then set-up around the vicinity. Newsmen, police officers, and the public, were banned from going anywhere near the area. Colonel Robert E. Booth – Commander of the 1705th Air Transport Group – only disclosed a mid-air collision had taken place, but refused to give any further details. An enquiry into the matter by Robert Gribble – then director of the Aerial Phenomena Research Group – revealed, through conversations held with some of those witnesses at the scene, that the aircraft was found smashed to pieces.

Two bodies were recovered from deep in the ground following impact by the aircraft, which was seen to come to earth while in a horizontal position. The fourth body was never found. It was also ascertained that prior to the accident, a number of mystery explosions had shaken the North Seattle area.

At 7.20pm another aerial explosion occurred, causing some damage. At 7.45pm mysterious *'lights'* were seen in the sky and a brilliant glow sighted near the crash area, followed by flashes of light. Mr Gribble learnt, from other witnesses, that none of the four engines of the plane had been running as it passed over their homes.

Parachute-like objects seen

Other witnesses spoke of seeing what resembled two glowing parachute-like objects following the aircraft, and that part of the tail assembly was missing.

At 10pm, further explosions rattled windows over the Seattle area. An anonymous telephone call was made to Mr Gribble, the day after the crash, informing him that UFOs had been tracked on radar. Unfortunately, for whatever reason, the Air Force then decided not to enter into any further discussion about the matter.

The Air Accident Report, later published, attributed the crash to the aircraft being too low and its right wing struck several treetops, causing the wing to burst into flame. The plane lost altitude and flew for another six and three quarters miles before final impact in the Rhoade Lake area, 12 miles east of McChord Airbase, Washington. It appears that this might have been the case. (**Source:** *Flying Saucers Are Hostile*, **Brad Steiger & Joan Whritenour, & T. Scott Crain Jr.,** *FSR*, Volume 32, No. 3, 1987)

USA: 20th April 1959 – Did Dr. Morris Ketchum Jessup commit suicide?

Morris Ketchum Jessup (born 2nd March 1900, died 20th April 1959) had a Master of Science Degree in Astronomy and, though employed at one time as a car-parts salesman and photographer, is probably best remembered for his writings on the UFO subject and his part in the 'Philadelphia Experiment'. He achieved some notoriety with his 1955 book *The Case for the UFO*, in which he argued that unidentified flying objects (UFOs) represented a mysterious subject worthy of further study.

Morris K. Jessup

Morris Jessup speculated that UFOs were *'exploratory craft of solid and nebulous character'*. [Now, over 55 years later, surely one cannot ignore or cast aside any doubts of the presence of a phenomenon which continues to plague us to this present day. For those who remain sceptical, how on earth can they explain the mass of catalogued evidence presented just in this Volume of *Haunted Skies* alone (never mind the other nine volumes) showing the presence of something, or someone, whose influence has shaped the destiny of man in one form or the other?] Morris also associated a connection between ancient monuments and UFOs.

He wrote three further 'flying saucer' books – *UFOs and the Bible, The UFO Annual* (both 1956), and *The Expanding Case for the UFO* (1957).

The latter suggested that transient lunar phenomenon were somehow related to UFOs in the Earth's skies.

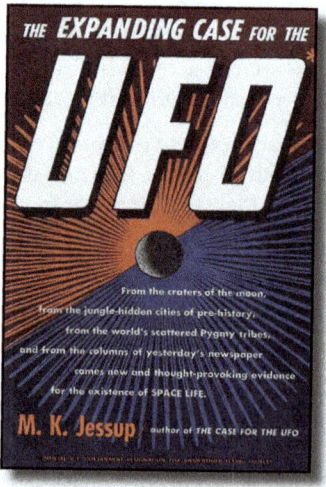

He also believed that anti-gravity and/or electromagnetism was responsible for the observed flight behavior of UFOs. He lamented, both in the book and in the publicity tour that followed, that space flight research was concentrated in the area of rocketry and that little attention was paid to other, theoretical means of flight, which he felt would ultimately be more fruitful. [If the human race possessed the means to replicate the source of UFO energy and able to facilitate the passage of men across the voids of space, then the current methods of sending men to Mars would be obsolete. Is it possible that this is what it is all about? Will we eventually be able to master the mechanisms of UFO flight or will we destroy ourselves long before this? We think most of us know the answer to this question!]

History records that Jessup attempted to make a living writing on the subject of UFOs, but his follow-up books did not sell well and his publisher rejected several other manuscripts. What price would they now fetch?

In 1958 his wife – Rubye – left him, and his friends described him as being somewhat unstable when he travelled to New York. After returning to Florida, he was involved in a serious car accident and was slow to recover, apparently increasing his despondency.

Although some friends claimed that he possibly had been driven to suicide by the 'Allende Case', other friends said that an extremely depressed Jessup had been discussing suicide with his friends for several months before his act. [Who were these friends? We have yet to see any evidence from them either on the internet or in the many hundreds of books that we possess from that era. We don't refute what has been said about his mental state, but would like to see some validity about these claims and, more importantly, the identity of the persons concerned.]

Dr. Manson Valentine

In 1968, Dr. J. Manson Valentine – Archaeologist and Honorary Curator of the Museum of Science in Miami, Florida – encountered a stone pavement off the north-west Coast of North Bimini Island, in the Atlantic Ocean. This ancient pavement was found to be at least 6,000 years old. Made of large flat blocks of limestone, it was named the Bimini Road. He was a personal friend of Morris Jessup and there is little doubt the men shared much in common.

Towards the middle of April 1959 (some accounts give the 19th April 1959), Jessup told Valentine that he had reached what he considered to be some definite conclusions about the series of reactions implied by the 'Philadelphia Experiment' and had prepared a rough draft that he wished to discuss with him. [He was convinced that the Navy, in seeking to create a magnetic cloud for camouflage purposes, in October 1943, had uncovered a potation that could temporarily and, if strong enough, permanently rearrange the molecular structure of people and material so that they would pass into another dimension, with further implications of predictable and, as of yet, uncontrolled teleportation] Dr. Valentine suggested he come around for dinner on the evening of the 20th April 1959.

Dr J. Manson Valentine, preparatory to making a surface dive on underwater stone foundations. Dr Valentine, together with Jacques Mayol and Harold Climo, discovered the Bimini Road in 1968 – the same year in which, by an almost incredible coincidence, Edgar Cayce had prophesised that parts of Atlantis would begin to be rediscovered. Cayce's prophecy was made in 1940, decades before any underwater ruins were suspected to be on the Bahama Banks. Photo courtesy, J.M. Valentine.

Dr. J. Manson Valentine is shown here with his granddaughter. He lived to the age of 92.

Circumstances of his death

At Matheson Hammock Park, South Florida, employee John Goode was carrying out a check of the park, just before closing time, at 6.45pm, to ensure that the area was secure. Entering the south picnic parking area off Cutler Road, he noticed a white Chevy station wagon parked on the side of the lot. John drove by, wondering whether to tell the driver that it was closing time, when he noticed something strange about the rear window – which was rolled down an inch or two, with a hose protruding. His worst fears were realised when he saw the other end was attached to the exhaust pipe and rags were stuffed around it and the opening. He pulled the door open and coughed from the heavy fumes, then held his breath and turned off the ignition.

> "The man was still sat upright, with a backward slump. His eyes stared straight ahead. I knew he was either dead or close to it. I opened the door on the driver's right and then drove to the administration office to summon assistance."

Who was Dr. Harry Reed?

Presumably, Mr Goode then telephoned the police and an ambulance(?) The police, who appeared to be the first on the scene, tried to revive Mr Jessup.

At this point it is claimed a Dr. Harry Reed strolled into the park (though it was after closing time) examined Jessup, then pronounced him dead. Enquiries made later, revealed no trace of Dr. Reed in the Miami telephone book, and none listed in the State licensing records. Who was he – an innocent bystander, or was he connected with the death of Dr Jessup in some way? According to Charles Berlitz, who wrote *Without a Trace*, he quoted Dr. Valentine as saying that he believed:

> "Morris Jessup was still alive when found and that perhaps he was allowed to die; his theories were very advanced and perhaps there were 'influences' that wished to prevent their spreading".

Who was Leon A. Seoul?

The person who identified Jessup's body was Leon A. Seoul, and claimed to be a friend of the family. Unfortunately, none of the family had ever heard of him.

Police Sgt. Obenchain – Homicide officer

> "The job was too professional. I've been on homicide a long time and I feel I can make such a judgment. For example, the ordinary suicide by monoxide poisoning doesn't take the time to wet down all the articles of clothing and to stuff them in the back window to make it more airtight. Most suicides use an ordinary garden hose, but the hose used in Jessup's car was larger in diameter and similar to one on a washing machine. It was not just shoved into the car's exhaust pipe. It was wired on. And all this had been done in broad daylight, just off a well-travelled road, at the height of the rush hour when traffic was leaving the park. The water could hardly have been applied to the rags at the scene, or some second party had removed the evidence. The closest body of water was 200 yards away. There were no containers for carrying water to the car. Jessup's clothes were not wet, yet the rags used for stuffing the window were saturated with water."

Ann Genzlinger – The Jessup Dimension

Mr Gray Barker, author of *They Knew Too Much About Flying Saucers*, was to take an interest in the death of Mr Jessup, following the inevitable claims that the suicide was, in fact, murder. This interest was triggered by a telephone call, received around the 1969 period, from Ann Genzlinger of Miami, Florida, who spoke at some length about Mr Jessup and the manner of his death.

Mr Barker then sent her two books, *The Case for the UFO* and *The Strange Case of Dr. M.K Jessup*. A few days later, Ann contacted him again and voiced the opinion that she believed he had not taken his own life and that if he did, it would have been as a result of some form of mind control. Although this may sound preposterous to the reader, this would not be the last time that people from scientific backgrounds had completely out of character committed suicide – sometimes in the most appalling ways.

Haunted Skies Volume Ten

Medical Examiner's Office

Ann contacted the Medical Examiner's office and was surprised to receive much assistance from the staff and medical examiner – Mr Joseph H. Davis, bearing in mind ordinarily medical records on file were not available to public scrutiny. She was allowed to voice copy the information held on a current file onto tape – this was in 1969, ten years after the death, which seems rather odd and not a little suspicious.

Ann:
> "I know the file was still open because, during my second inspection, I noticed that the information I had given Mr Davis had been added onto the papers."

She was shocked to discover that no post mortem (autopsy) had been performed, and that the body had been donated to the University Of Miami School Of Medicine! This was in violation of *Florida State Code No 406.11, which lists the instances in which autopsies are required. [We have to say that we cannot understand why a post-mortem was never held, as this was a suspicious death – a suicide, with unusual circumstances.

Why did the Medical Examiner's office fail to carry out a post-mortem in defiance of strict guidelines laid down? Clearly this was a serious breach of regulations, with criminal implications – one is bound to wonder on whose instruction was this policy not adhered to?]

If they had conducted a post-mortem, would they have found bruises or injuries on his body consistent with being held down by the offender(s)? [This is presupposing there were any]. Analysis carried out on a blood sample for alcohol and carbon monoxide, revealed alcohol negative, carbon monoxide positive. No tests were made to ascertain the presence of drugs. Ann herself taxed the department about this serious breach of protocol, but was not provided with any explanation. She contacted the FBI, who was helpful with supplying her with various documents pertaining to his death, although the CIA declined to help. Why was there no

---

*Florida State Code (2014) states: A. – Our mission is to determine the cause and manner of death in those deaths that fall under the jurisdiction of the Medical Examiner as set forth in F.S.S. 406.11. Normal office hours are from 8am to 5pm seven (7) days a week. An investigator of the Medical Examiner's Office is available 24 hours a day to accept reports of death that fall within the guidelines of F.S.S. 406.11 and require the initiation of an investigation. An investigator may be reached at 727-582-6800.

B. – The Medical Examiner Act, Chapter 406.11, Florida Statutes, clearly lists the 12 types of death for which we must accept jurisdiction (covered in Section II). Excluded from that list are apparent natural deaths with a Florida licensed attending physician to sign a death certificate. Because these deaths lie outside of those listed, the statute does not require that such deaths be reported prior to release to a funeral home.

C. – Forensic Investigators typically respond to and examine all bodies and surroundings at violent death scenes occurring in Pinellas and Pasco Counties. This also includes apparent or suspected drug overdose deaths. For this reason it is important that the body and/or any items on or near the body not be moved until the arrival of the Medical Examiner Investigator if at all possible. Guns, medications, illicit drugs or drug paraphernalia, or any other wounding objects are included in the items that should not be moved if at all possible. In certain cases, a pathologist may also respond to the scene in addition to the Investigator.

D. – Not all cases referred to the Medical Examiner's Office will be autopsied. In most cases, deaths of a traumatic, suspicious or unnatural nature will be autopsied. This does not, however, include apparent natural deaths. Each case will be examined separately; circumstances of the death reviewed by a medical examiner, and a decision will be made on whether to perform an autopsy. Please do not inform a family that an autopsy will or will not be performed. If the family asks, please tell them to make contact with this office to voice their objection and that it is the decision of the Medical Examiner's Office. If they have questions, give them our phone number and ask them to call us.

E. – Cases are examined or autopsied seven days a week and generally on the day of death or the following day. The medical examiner does not require the permission of next-of-kin to proceed with an autopsy or examination. Death certificates are started by this office and completed by the funeral home making the final arrangements as determined by the family.

F. – An autopsy is an intricate medical procedure often requiring complex laboratory tests and for this reason complete results may not be available for several weeks after the death. Autopsy reports typically take a week or two to complete; however, in cases involving drugs or other complex issues, the autopsy report may not be completed for 30 days or more. This means that the autopsy report may not be immediately available to the family.

G. – The records of the Medical Examiner are public records under Florida Statutes 119. Autopsy reports are sent to the State Attorney and the law enforcement agency investigating the death. Cases under active criminal investigation are not released until the case is closed. Reports are also available upon request to next of kin, attorneys, insurance companies, etc. at no cost but we request a self-addressed envelope stamped with postage for two ounces due to report size. Once finalized, reports are mailed out in any self-addressed envelopes we have received and stored with the file.

note left? Where was the container used to carry the water? Why attract attention by using a larger hose which required wiring onto the exhaust pipe; why park there at all? Who was the second person to examine the body in situ, following the discovery by John Goode?

It is claimed that Sergeant Obenchain took a personal interest in this matter, which is not surprising given the details of the incident. His wife stayed with Rubye for a few days, during which time she learned that telephone calls had been made to Mr Jessup shortly prior to his death that had upset him, although the content of those calls was not established. Mrs Jessup did confirm that she had received telephone calls for Mr Jessup when he was out, but that the receiver was put down on her. It is fair to speculate that while there is no direct evidence to prove that Morris Jessup was murdered, the circumstances surrounding his death are very suspicious to say the least. If the facts presented so far are genuine (which they appear to be) then it is clear that there are many issues which should give rise to concern about the manner of his death.

Was there a flagrant breach of the Medical Examiner's Office to carry out a post-mortem on the body, especially after having taken into account the nature of the police evidence? Or was such an examination at the discretion of the M.E.? This is presupposing that the suspicion felt by the police was brought to their attention?

Great Britain: 23rd April 1959 – George Adamski lectures at Weston-Super-Mare.

May 1959

International Flying Saucer Contact weekend

Over the Whitsun holiday, the first ever International Contact weekend was held throughout the world on the 16-18th May 1959, involving over 50,000 people watching the skies. The Editor of *Flying Saucer Review*, the Honourable Brinsley la Poer Trench, along with a party of friends, was filmed by the *BBC*, while sky watching in Ashdown Forest. (The scene of a report of a UFO having landed some years later). In the same area were a group of people from The Atlanteans. They included Gillian King (29) singer, Henley Thomas (28) actor, Antony Neate (29) accountant, Margot Evans (24) actress, Ronald Simmons (29) accountant, and Miss Jacqueline Murray, actress and writer, President of the group, who claimed they had established telepathic contact with a spaceship!

In Denmark, 36 groups from the Danish UFO organization, SUFOI, took part in the sky watch. Jutland and New Zealand was also well attended.

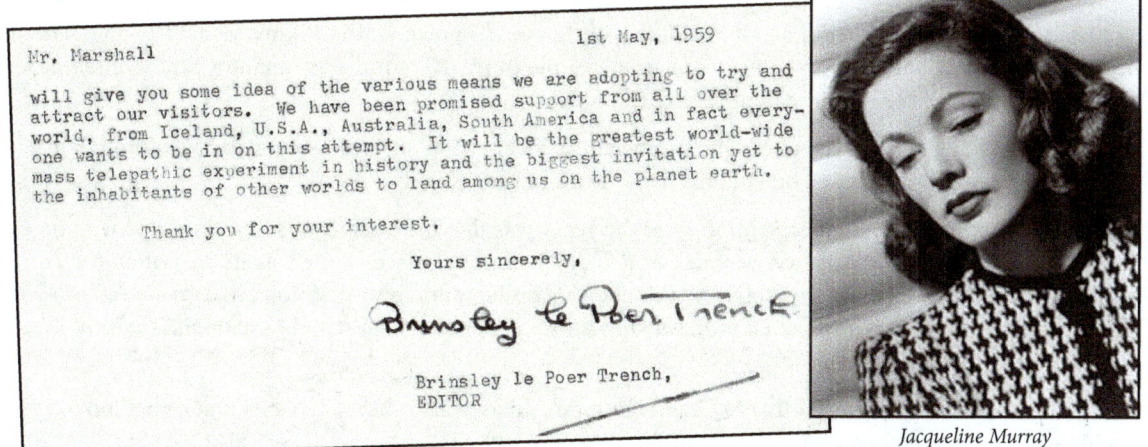

Jacqueline Murray

Haunted Skies Volume Ten

Australia: 17th May 1959 – At 4.30am, three men from Cooktown sighted a circular object some 100 metres away from them.

"It was football-shaped, about 50 metres across, with a band of half-moon windows, issuing vapour."

It is alleged that two of the men who stayed to watch the object suffered severe physical effects, and that one of them died.

Australia: 20th May 1959 – A UFO was sighted over the rocket ranges.

June 1959

USA: 30th June 1959 – United States Commander Mr D. Connolly sighted a gold oblate shaped object, at 8.23pm, in the sky over Patuxent River, Maryland. The object was estimated to be nine times as wide as it was thick, metallic and with sharp edges. It was seen to fly straight and level for 20-30 seconds. (**Source: Project Blue Book**)

Great Britain: – Air Chief Marshall Lord Dowding speaks about UFOs

During a lecture held at the Salisbury Rotary Club in summer 1959, he said:

"The subject is a vast one and the existence of these craft was completely beyond doubt. There have been hundreds of thousands of sightings observed by reputable people, including those in the Royal Observer Corps, and pilots. In the United States, planes had gone in pursuit of the 'saucers' and in one case there had been a collision, which had resulted in the total disintegration of the plane. Radar operators had seen them on their screens; sooner or later these people will make a determined effort to contact people on this Earth."

Did a UFO fire on Captain Mantell's aircraft?

We believe that the Air Chief Marshal is referring to the Captain Thomas Mantell death, in January 1948.

Ironically Thomas had started a small business with his wife, known as the Elkins Mantell Flying School, in Louisville. The couple had two boys – one aged six; the other, 17 months. Poignantly, Mrs Mantell never received the promised telephone call on that date.

We understood that none of the pilots aboard the aircraft were supplied with oxygen masks, although it was claimed Lt. Albert Clements had one but his oxygen was in short supply.

Another rumour, brought to our attention, over the years, was that the aircraft was found riddled with holes, as indeed was the body of Captain Mantell – again, apparently erroneous. Or was it? In *Without a Trace*, written by Charles Berlitz, he also refers to the plane's disintegration and mentions that *"the wreckage was characterised by being peppered with a profusion of very small holes in the aluminum remnants, none of which were larger than a few square inches"*.

According to Blue Book, it is said that Lt. 'Bob' Hammond advised Lt. Albert Clements that he had no oxygen equipment. Both pilots then returned to Standiford Field.

Leonard Stringfield

Leonard Stringfield, who wrote *Situation Red – The UFO Siege* – worked with the Air Defense Command from 1953-1957 in the investigation and reporting of UFO activity, as well as an 'early warning' co-coordinator for the Colorado Project under Dr. Condon. He was a man of great integrity and possessed impeccable credentials. He served in a number of important posts with NICAP, IUFOR, MUFON, and the Center for UFO Studies.

Stringfield wrote:

> *"My informant, preferring anonymity, related that he had talked with Mantell's wing man, who witnessed the UFO incident. The pilot stated that Mantell pursued the UFO because he was the only pilot with an adequate oxygen mask. The pilot also related that he saw a burst of what appeared to be tracer fired from the UFO, which hit the P-51 and caused it to disintegrate in the air! Since the Mantell case, all other military encounters ending in disaster have been hidden from the public."*

Leornard Stringfield was director of Civilian Research, Interplanetary Flying Objects (CRIFO), and published a monthly newsletter, *ORBIT*. In 1957 he became public relations adviser for the civilian UFO group NICAP under the direction of Donald Keyhoe, a friend of his since 1953. From 1967-1969, Stringfield served as an "Early Warning Coordinator" for the Condon Committee. During the 1970s, he wrote a number of books about alleged recoveries of alien spaceships and alien bodies. In 1978, Stringfield served as UFO research adviser to Grenada Prime Minister Sir Eric Gairy. Privately, Stringfield worked as Director of Public Relations and Marketing Services for DuBois Chemicals, a division of Chemed Corporation, Cincinnati. He self-published *"Status Reports"* on alleged UFO *"crash-retrievals"* until his death, on 18th December 1994, after a long battle with lung cancer.

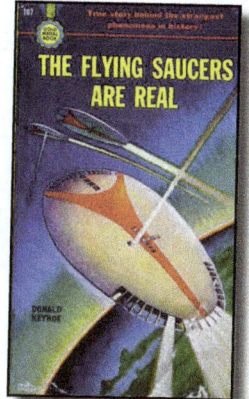

Leonard Stringfield

Desmond Leslie and his engineer informant

This appears in conflict; either he did or he did not have the equipment.

Desmond Leslie disclosed previously that his unnamed engineer informant claimed that some of the radio transmissions from Mantell to the Control Tower were deleted from the original report. Mr T. Scott Crain wrote to Desmond Leslie about this matter, but after not receiving any reply then wrote to Gordon Creighton, at *FSR*, asking him if he could write to Desmond Leslie on his behalf.

Gordon wrote to Desmond in 1984, at his home at Castle Leslie, County Monahan, Ireland, asking him about the identity of the engineer. Gordon received the following letter, on 23rd March 1984:

> *"The engineer's name was Scott. I met him while I was travelling to lecture in America, around 1955/56. We were both tourist class (only £50!) on the Queen Mary – that wonderful ship. I can't recall his first name. He was*

grayish, tall, and middle aged – 40'ish. He claimed to have heard the dialogue, Mantell to the Control Tower, either when in the Tower or from a recording (probably the former, as recordings were thin on the ground in those days). I think he also said that Mantell cried, "It's huge – like the Eiffel Tower!" No need for confidentiality. Scott never asked for it and talked quite openly."

(Source: *FSR*, Volume 29, No. 5, 1984)

July 1959

FLYING SAUCER REVIEW

Vol.5.No.4.   Strike Issue   July-August, 1959

Edited by the Hon. Brinsley le Poer Trench

BEYOND OUR CONTROL

Britain and 'Flying Saucer Review' have been hit by a strike in the printing trade. Consequently, this issue is not in its usual format. We apologise for not having our customary glamorous appearance and hope that the printing dispute will soon be resolved, so that once again we can present your favourite magazine in its proper garb.

PEER ASKS ABOUT LIFE ON PLANETS AND HOUSE OF LORDS ROCKS WITH LAUGHTER

London, June 18 – The House of Lords had a hilarious 15 minutes today – at least the noble lords apparently considered the question of Lord Fraser of Lonsdale (formerly Sir Ian Fraser, the blind M.P.) and the Government answer from Viscount Hailsham.

Lord Fraser asked whether the Government had sought or received any advice "as to the possibility or probability that sentient creatures live in other worlds, and whether any attempts at communication have been considered or foreshadowed"

Lord Hailsham replied that "The Government does not include communications with any possible inhabitants of other worlds among the objects of the United Kingdom space research programme....Certainly, the

U.S. AIR FORCE CHIEF ON COMMUNICATION WITH ADVANCED SPACE RACES

Washington, April 14 (UPI)- Major General Donald J.Keirn Chief of US AF nuclear-engine programme stressed prospect of communicating with other worlds as important reason for establishing a moon base or space station. He said AF had no proof that intelligent beings existed elsewhere, but the UFO reports had "emphasized our innate curiosity." He went on, "it is entirely possible that some of them may have passed through our stage of evolution, and may have already achieved a higher level of social and technological culture than our own".

Government has not sought or received any advice as to whether sentient creatures live in other worlds". (Laughter.)

Dr. Harlow Shapley, former director, Harvard Observatory: "We must now accept it as inevitable....there are other worlds with thinking beings."

.1.

Great Britain: 1959 – Retired Nottinghamshire Police Officer – Philip Holmes, told of a very strange occurrence which happened to him, while attending St. John's Ambulance training course, at *Skegness Minors holiday home, Lincoln.

"One morning, when the camp was surrounded by a heavy fog, known locally as the Haar, I decided to sneak out and have a cigarette. I was stood looking out to sea, close to the waves, when a silver 'sphere', or 'ball', about a metre in diameter, with four metallic prongs, appeared about 20ft away from where I was standing. A few seconds later, a bright blue flash of light shot out of the bottom prong, then it rose rapidly upwards and headed out over the sea, where I soon lost sight of it"

(Source: Personal interview)

13th July 1959 – 'Flying Saucer' lands at Blenheim, New Zealand

New Zealand: 13th July 1959 – At 5.30am Mrs Fredrick Moreland – a nursing aid at Lister Hospital in Old Renwick Road, Blenheim, was on her way to milk the family cows, when she noticed a green glow in the sky. She later told police and a reporter from the *Nelson Evening Mail*:

"There was no moon, so I wondered what it was. I was halfway across the paddock, when two large green things – like eyes or big lamps – appeared above me and then descended towards the ground. I, and the surrounding area, was bathed in green light. I thought I shouldn't be here and made a dive for the other side of the paddock and waited. A saucer-shaped 'glow', with two indented lights

---

*Following a 'UFO sighting' over Gibraltar Point in 2013, Chapel St Leonards man, Eddie Portsmouth, reported that he spotted a mysterious light in the sky when he was cycling to work in the early hours of Friday, October 4th. Eddie says he followed its course for about half an hour as he cycled from Chapel to Summerlands. It seemed to hover for a while over Chapel boating lake at about 2,000ft, in the sky, darting back and forth very quickly, before eventually disappearing. (**Source:** *Skegness Standard,* 17th May 2013)

in the bottom, descended; the air became very warm. Two rows of jets around the middle shot out an orange flame. These appeared to be revolving in opposite directions. The object was about 20-30ft in diameter. The jets stopped and a light came on in the 'dome' or glass roof of the object, which was grayish metal in colour. I could see two 'men' in it, dressed in fairly close-fitting suits of shiny material – like aluminum foil. They were wearing opaque helmets, preventing me from seeing their faces. One of the men stood up and put two hands in front of him, as if leaning downwards. Then he sat down and, after a minute or two, the jets started up. The object began to tilt before shooting up vertically into the clouds, making a soft high-pitched sound."

Mrs Moreland then noticed what smelt like pepper in the air. She then completed the milking before going into the house to awaken her husband – a civilian employee at the Woodburn Station of the RAAF. He telephoned the police, who came to see her, followed by a visit from a representative of the RAAF and a reporter from the local newspaper.

We could not help but contrast this incident with a sighting in January 1959, involving Leonard Hewins, who sighted an object surrounded by blue haze land at Stratford-upon-Avon, inside which were seen four seated occupants. When it took off, he heard what sounded like rushing water. (**Source:** *Strangers From The Skies*, **Brad Steiger/John D. Llewellyn**). (See also Volume 1 of *Haunted Skies* for further information).

Australia: 20th July 1959 – Four glowing objects were reported over Broken Hill, New South Wales, at 10.30pm. (**Source J. Vallee,** *Anatomy of a Phenomenon*)

USA: 10th August 1959 – UFO sighted over Goose Air Force Base, Labrador. (**Source: Blue Book**)

September 1959

USA: 13th September 1959 – A white pear-shaped object, metallic, in appearance showing a trail under it, was sighted at 4pm over Gills Rock, Wisconsin, Bunker Hill Air Force Base, Indiana. It involved at least two control tower operators and the pilot of a Mooney private airplane. The object showed little movement during the three hours observation. An attempted intercept by USAF T-33 jet trainer failed. (**Source: Blue Book**)

USA: 24th September 1959 – 'Flying Disc' seen over Redmond

City policeman Robert Dickerson was on patrol at the edge of town, when he saw a glowing disc like object drop down out of the sky and hover some 200ft off the ground. A few minutes later the object climbed upwards and headed past Redmond Airport, where it once again stopped in mid-air – now hovering in a north-east direction.

Robert contacted Flight Specialist Laverne Wertz at the airport. He and other Federal aviation men went outside to see the object, which had *'tongues of flame'* around the rim. Wertz telexed the Air Force Traffic Control, at Seattle, who told him Air Force jets from Portland were being scrambled and that Air Force Radar at Klamath Falls, Oregon, was tracking the UFO.

At Redmond, the ground observers were still watching the UFO when they heard the roar of jets.

As the planes dived towards the UFO, the flames emanating from it vanished. A fiery exhaust blasted from the bottom of the *'disc'* and it accelerated upwards, at terrific speed – close enough to cause one pilot to frantically move out of its path. Another struggled to control the plane, after being struck by the object's exhaust. Three planes headed-off in pursuit, but were quickly left behind. When the pilots landed, they were ordered not to discuss the incident. The Air Force explained it away as being a routine checkup, following a false radar return. It is claimed that Laverne Wertz checked one of the aircraft with a Geiger counter but that the results of the examination were never released, although it is believed it was no normal reading. The explanation then put forward was that it had been a weather balloon. Unknown to them, copies of the F.A.A logs had been handed to NICAP. When they pressed for further information, they were told it had been Venus!

(Source: *Aliens from Space . . . The Real Story of Unidentified Flying Objects,* Major Donald E. Keyhoe)

USA: 29th September 1959, Buffalo, Texas, Flight 542 crashes – Was it a UFO?

At 10.37pm, Flight 542 – a Braniff Lockheed turbo prop airliner – took off from Houston, Texas, en route to New York, with a crew of 6 and 28 passengers. A short time later the aircraft approached Buffalo, cruising at 15,000ft, at 275 knots.

Major R.O. Braswell was piloting a C-47, at 6,500ft, between Shreveport, Louisiana, and Lufkin, north-east of Buffalo, when he saw:

> "... a thing coloured like a large red fire; it looked like an atomic cloud. It was massive, about 5° above my plane. The base was at an altitude of 12-15,000ft; the top was at 16,000ft."

Billie Guyton of Centerville, Texas, saw an object emerge from the *'glow'*. Teacher Jackie Cox (39), who was driving towards Buffalo, heard:

> "... the noise of a plane, which sounded louder than normal. I then saw a bright light in the sky that spread to cover the entire sky, as if phosphorous or magnesium was burning."

They were not the only ones. Mr William S. Webb, of Buffalo, had just gone to bed. He happened to look outside and see:

> "... a 'ball of fire' that looked like a star shooting across the sky – then I heard a noise like something falling from the sky; it was a whooshing, shrill sound."

Farmer, Richard White, and his wife, had just retired for the night. Richard decided to sleep outside, as it was so hot.

He lay down, watching the late summer stars, when he noticed:

> "... a brilliant light, high in the southern sky. The whole sky seemed to be lit-up like a giant fireball passing overhead, only to be followed by a tremendous explosion, so violent it seemed to shake the ground."

Seconds later, the night was filled with shrill whistles as debris fell through the sky. The airliner had been torn into thousands of fragments. Brannif Vice-President of Operations – Mr R.V. Carleton – told newspaper reporters:

> "Airplane crashes usually leave twenty or thirty major pieces on the ground. I've investigated lots of crashes but never seen one where the plane was so thoroughly demolished, wreckage so widely scattered, and people so horribly mangled. There was nothing which would indicate a fire or bomb aboard the plane."

[The bodies were torn into fragments – some parts of bodies were plastered into tree limbs].

An investigation into the crash revealed that there had been no fire or explosion aboard the plane while in flight, or after it had crashed. Scorch marks were found on glass window ports; the rear of the fuselage showing signs of having been exposed to tremendous exterior heat. The force which had caused the explosion had not come from the inside of the aircraft. Moments after the fireball had disengaged itself from the red cloud, it is

Haunted Skies Volume Ten

said every dog within miles of the Buffalo area began to howl. Whether the accident was caused by a weapon discharged by the UFO or structural failure of the left wing as a result of an un-dampened propeller whirl mode, as put forward by the Air Accident Investigators, is something we shall never know.

(Source: *Flying Saucers Are Hostile*, Brad Steiger and Joan Whritenour)

October 1959

USA: 1st October 1959 – UFOs reported on this date over Telephone Ridge, Oregon. (**Source: Blue Book**)

USA: 6th October 1959 – Military sight UFO over Lincoln Nebraska (**Source: Blue Book**)

Australia: 17th October 1959 – A cigar-shaped object, showing portholes, about 100ft in length, was sighted in the sky over Melbourne, Victoria. At Brunswick, Victoria, on the same date, several silent objects – described as having short wings and copper coloured cylindrical bodies – were seen. A third sighting tells of a number of bright lights seen stationary in the sky over Bulleen, Victoria, between 7.45pm and 8.45pm. (Some accounts give 1960).

USA: 19th October 1959 – Youths fire at UFO!

At 6.15pm, Mark Muza (15), and Harold Moore (14), sighted a circular object – about 4ft in diameter, making a whirring noise – hovering above the ground in a desolate area known as the Big Marsh, at Poquson, Virginia. The object, apparently metallic, was seen to have a dark centre, surrounded by a 6ins wide silvery rim. On seeing the object descend, Muza, who was in possession of a 12ins gauge shotgun, fired three times – the last shot ringing on the *'metal'* when about 50ft above him. The object then went straight upwards, like a spinning top, making noise like a tornado. (**Source:** *Newport Daily Press*, **21st October 1959**)

USA: Oregon, 23rd October 1959 – Boys fire at creature!

USA: November 18th 1959-UFO sighted South of Crystal Springs, Mississippi. (**Source: Blue Book**)

From the card index kept by Kath Smith of the Isle of Wight UFO Society, now sadly passed away, what a delightful and inspirational woman she was.

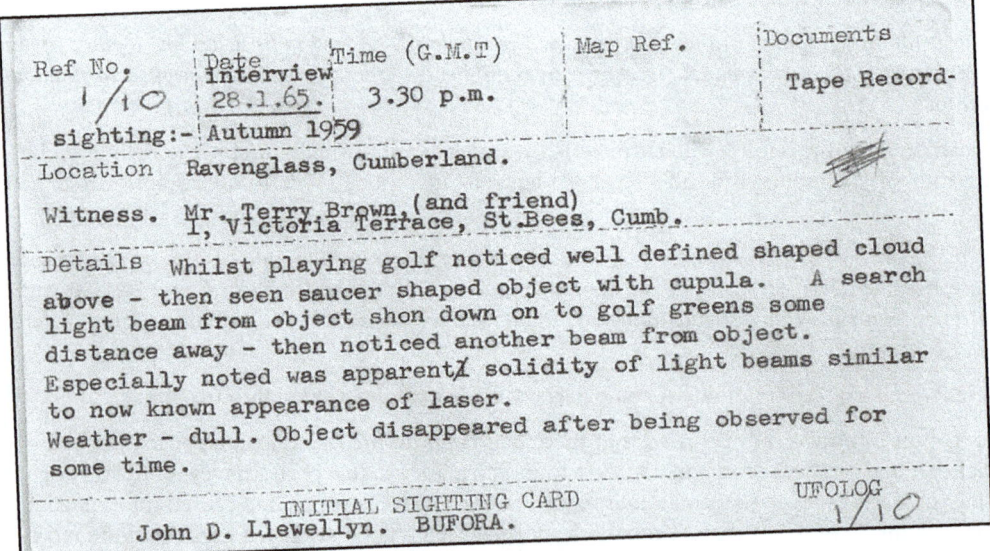

Haunted Skies Volume Ten

January – May 1960

Tasmania: 23rd January 1960 – Twin yellow lights were sighted in the sky over Launceston.

Australia: 1st February 1960 – A bright object, emitting flashes of light, seen over Melbourne, heading in a west to east direction.

Australia: 17th March 1960 – A bright light, resembling a huge candlestick, seen moving slowly through the sky over Waitara, New South Wales. On the same date, a pencil like object – red and gold in colour, similar to a huge candlestick – was seen in the night sky over Forster, 200 miles north of Sydney.

(**Source: Hervey,** *UFOs over the Southern Hemisphere*)

USA: 23rd March 1960 – UFO sighted over Indianapolis, Indiana. (**Source: Blue Book**)

Australia: 26th March 1960 – A spherical silver object was sighted over Canberra.

Australia: 18th May 1960 – A cigar-shaped object was seen in the sky over Melbourne.

June 1960

Australia: 10th June 1960 – Was a UFO involved in a mid-air collision?

A Trans-Australia Airlines (TAA flight 538) from Brisbane, captained by Mr F.C. Pollard – was on approach at night to land at Mackay, Queensland, Australia, with 29 people on board. This included nine passengers, seven adults and nine schoolboys, from Rockhampton Grammar School, who were returning home to Mackay for the Queen's Birthday long weekend.

At 8.17pm, Mackay's air traffic controller – E. W. Miskell – after seeing that fog had rolled in, temporarily closed the Airport. A few minutes later, having come to the spot where he would start descending, Captain Pollard told the tower controller he would take-up a holding position over the airport at 13,000ft (4,000m) in case visibility improved.

At 8.40pm, they reported that they were over the airport and that it was a bright moonlit night, with a completely calm sea, and two approaches were aborted due to a low layer of cloud (presume this was the fog bank?) on the coastline obscuring the sight of the strip on final approach.

By 10pm, the fog was now thinning. Air traffic controller Miskell reported this to VH-TFB, and Captain Pollard said they would begin an approach to the airport. Miskell reported the airport conditions. Pollard acknowledged the transmission. Miskell then telephoned the airport fire service for the latest ground temperature. It was 13° Celsius. Miskell immediately reported this to VH-TFB. This time, there was no acknowledgement. Miskell transmitted again, noting the time was 10.05pm, and again there was no reply. At 10.10pm, Miskell started the procedure for launching a search and rescue operation.

Wreckage found

Five hours after the accident, at about 3am on Saturday, 11th June 1960, a searchlight-equipped motor launch found items of wreckage, including damaged passenger seats, clothing and cabin furnishings, floating on the ocean between Round Top Island and Flat Top Island, five nautical miles due east of Mackay Airport.

Stationary object plotted on radar

It was claimed that a stationary object was plotted twice on the same evening, between 10pm and 11.30pm, by Mackay Meteorological Office, at Queensland. Mr Edward Henry Tindale, then employed as a radar operator,

Haunted Skies Volume Ten

told investigators he had plotted a stationary UFO twice on the same night as when an aircraft had come down.

> "Both plots of the UFO were made in the area where the main wreckage of the airliner was found; the first was 10.30pm, the second at 11.30pm"

It was Trans-Australia Airlines first accident to cause passenger fatalities in the 14 years since the airline was founded. Enquiries, made later, revealed the aircraft departed from Rockhampton, at 7.52pm, and ascended to 13,000ft (4,000m).

A navy survey ship, *HMAS Warrego*, was sent to search for the sunken wreckage and arrived on Sunday, 12th June 1960. At 4.20pm that afternoon, Warrego discovered the major sections of VH-TFB in 40ft (12m) of water, a further four nautical miles (7.4 km) south-west of Round Top Island (or about three nautical miles (5.6km) south-east of Mackay Airport). Salvaging the wreck took another two weeks.

Board of Enquiry convenes

A Board of Accident Inquiry was appointed on 29th July 1960. After allowing the investigators to sift the wreckage, it finally opened on 4th October 1960.

The Board, chaired by Mr Justice Spicer of the Commonwealth Industrial Court, sat for four days in Brisbane and two more in Mackay, before concluding on the 10th November 1960. The inquiry was not able to determine a particular cause for the accident. The aircraft had flown into the ocean for no apparent reason, and so the Board focused on the altimeter. One possibility offered was that the static pressure system or altimeter was malfunctioning and not allowing display of the correct altitude. Another possibility was that the reading of the three-pointer altimeter was misinterpreted. This type of altimeter has individual pointers for thousands, hundreds and tens of feet, and can be difficult to interpret. Errors of 1,000 or 10,000ft were common, as had been outlined by W.F. Grether in a 1949 report for the Journal of Applied Psychology.

As a consequence of this suggestion, three-pointer altimeters were later dropped. If human error were the case, the accident may have simply been the result of a controlled flight into terrain. However, many commentators thought this unlikely, given the long experience of Captain Pollard.

Trans-Australia Airlines Director of Engineering – John L. Watkins, OBE – was intrigued by a mysterious brown glass medicine bottle, discovered in the wreckage of the cockpit. He theorized that one of the schoolchildren on the flight may have been an aviation enthusiast, and had been shown into the cockpit whilst handling a bottle of model aircraft fuel. At some point the bottle's contents may have spilled in the cockpit, the fumes distracting the pilots enough for them to make a mistake and crash.

Frank McMullen – Trans-Australia Airlines Technical Services Engineering Superintendent and F27 Project Engineer – was a member of the team that joined with Department of Civil Aviation officials studying the crash. He formed the view that at the third attempt to land, the crew adopted a low flight path – hoping to keep the airstrip in sight below the cloud layer – but were deceived by the difficulty in assessing height over a glassy sea, and put the left wing tip into the water, turning onto the runway approach. One of the recommendations made by the Board of Accident Inquiry was that passenger-carrying aircraft of the size of the F27 and larger should be equipped with flight data recorders.

The authors would like to pay their respects to those that died and offer our condolences to the relatives of the loved ones, for their loss. There is no proof that a UFO caused this tragedy but the facts should be reported.

Australia: 26th June 1960 – An explosion of lights was observed over Melbourne and Launceston.

Australia: August 1960 – At Belmont, New South Wales, a resident was awoken at 1.30am, by a buzzing noise. He looked out and saw a bright light emanating from a round object. He was then shocked to see a *'being'*, described as about 5ft tall, of average build, wearing a dull olive-green skin-tight suit, helmet, and white or grey footwear. Other sources give the time of 3pm. The man involved went to fetch his son; when he returned there was nothing to be seen.

Australia: 18th August 1960 – A bright flashing object was seen heading east to west over Mullewa.

USA: 23rd August 1960 – UFO sighted over Wichita, Kansas. (**Source: Blue Book**)

USA: 29th August 1960 – UFO sighted over Crete, Illinois. (**Source: Blue Book**)

October 1960

Tasmania: 2nd October 1960 – An illuminated crescent-shaped object was sighted above the southern horizon from Launceston.

Tasmania: 4th October 1960 – UFO Display over Cressy

At about 6.10pm on the 4th October 1960, Church of England Minister – the Reverend Lionel Browning – and his wife, were in their rectory near *Cressy, Tasmania, looking out at a recently formed rainbow, on a

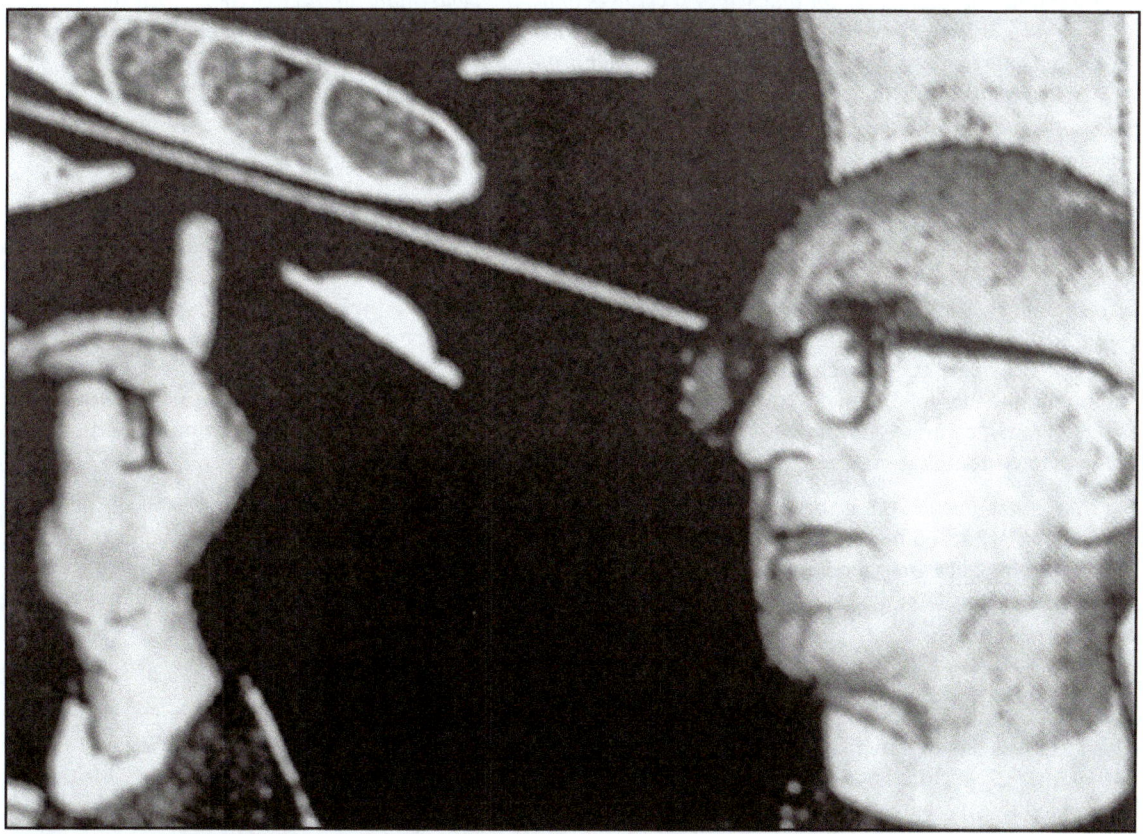

*Cressy is a small country town in the rural Northern Midlands of Tasmania, about 30k south-west of Launceston. The surrounding area is mainly pastoral and relatively flat, although the Western Tiers, some 20k to the south-west, rise to over 1200m. A similar distance to the north-east of the town is Launceston Airport.

cloudy evening, with the sun just setting in the west. To the east a curtain of rain concealed Ben Lomond ridge, extending through the south-east and to their south, when his wife drew his attention to a long cigar-shaped object, which was emerging from a rain squall. He had this to say:

> "The object was dull grey in colour, had four or five vertical dark bands around its circumference, and at regular intervals along its length had what looked like a short aerial array, which projected outwards and upward from the northern facing end of the object. The object seemed to be slightly longer than Viscount Aircraft frequently seen flying in that area and I estimated the object's length at about one hundred feet. The outline of the object was well-defined and was even more so a little later, when it had as a background the tree covered slopes of a rain free area of the hills.
>
> I estimated from landmarks below the object that it was over Panshanger Estate, owned by the Mills family, and probably three to four miles distant.
>
> After emerging from the rain squall, the object moved on an even keel in a northerly direction, at an estimated speed of 60-70mph, and a constant height of about 400ft. The object moved approximately one and a half miles north, also estimated by reference to landmarks below it, and then abruptly stopped. Within seconds, it was joined by five or six small 'saucer like' objects, which had emerged at high speed from the cloud above and behind the cigar-shaped object. The small objects stationed themselves at positions around the cigar-shaped object, at a radius of about one half of a mile (800m) and then, after an interval of several seconds, the cigar-shaped object, accompanied by the smaller objects, abruptly reversed backwards and then disappeared into the rain squall from which it had emerged. The reverse movement was at about the same speed and height as during its outward movement. In all, the cigar-shaped object had been visible for approximately two minutes and the small objects for about one minute."

[No noise was heard throughout the sightings]

In an interview conducted later, by UFO researcher Paul Norman, the Reverend made an interesting comment. He said: *"The smaller objects skipped like stones on water."* Reverend Browning and his wife watched the area for several minutes, after the disappearance of the objects into the rain squall, but there was no reappearance. Reverend Browning then telephoned the Control Tower at Western Junction (Launceston) Airport and reported the sighting. On 9th October 1960, Reverend Browning gave a full report of the sighting to the *Launceston Examiner*. A sketch of the object was superimposed on a photograph taken through their dining room window. The following day, the story was published in the newspaper. Lionel felt the artist's impression depicted fairly accurately the shape, size, and appearance of the objects, but they should have been shown as being below and not above the skyline.

He stated that since making the sighting public, he had received several reports of sightings of unidentified flying objects, and many reports of loud explosions heard, including his own experience which occurred at 9.30pm on the 27th October. Reverend Browning believes the explosions are in some way associated with the UFOs seen by him and his wife, and that prior to this he had been sceptical about reports of such objects, but not now.

Professor James E. McDonald

The case was investigated by the Royal Australian Air Force, and the Victorian UFO Society. In 1967 Prof. James E. McDonald – Senior Physicist in the Department of Meteorology at the University of Arizona – travelled to Australia and interviewed Reverend Browning. TUFOIC published details of the sighting, and other events in the area at that time, in its Annual Report for 1970, with a more complete account in its *Cressy Revisited* publication. The sighting prompted questions in the Australian Parliament and was mentioned in various books and journals, both in Australia and overseas. The meteorological summary for 4th October

Haunted Skies Volume Ten

Mysterious ships in sky

Rev. Lionel Browning, an Anglican minister and Tasmanian Secretary of the World Council of Churches, and Mrs. Browning, observed in Cressy, Tasmania a strange cigar-shaped airship accompanied by five smaller craft at 6.10 p.m. on Tuesday, October 4, 1960.

Pictured is Mr. Browning pointing through the rectory window in the direction of the sighting. The EXAMINER's (Launceston, Tas.) artist has drawn in the objects from the Browning's description and a sketch by Mrs. Browning.

"There was definitely a mother ship and five or six flying saucers," said Rev. Browning. "First we saw a large dull-grey object about 300 feet long. It came at plane-stalling speed and seemed to pause."

Rev. Browning estimated the speed of the ship at less than 50 m.p.h. The object was stationary for about 30 seconds.

"Then out of the clouds above and behind the ship, five or six small discs came shooting at terrific speed." According to the minister they were approximately 30 feet across and flat underneath with a dome on top. The noiseless mother ship had four vertical bands and at the bow there was a moving device like radar or propeller.

describes a small depression over the Central Plateau, with a front extending to the east of Flinders Island. Light to moderate rain was experienced ahead of the front, with rain clearing after 15.00hrs (3pm). However, extensive cloud build-up was associated with the trough along the Western Tiers (south-west of Cressy) during the late afternoon. Thunderstorm activity was reported from areas near the Tiers.

Explained away as moon rise!

In early 1961, the Directorate of Air Force Intelligence explained the case as *"Moon rise associated with meteorological conditions at the time of the sighting"*, which is ridiculous as moon rise took place shortly after 6pm, in an east, south-east direction. Reverend Browning dismissed the RAAFs explanation. The moon, he said, would have been competing with a glorious sunset, whilst the easterly skyline was not visible due to rain covering the Ben Lomond area.

A check reveals that the sun was indeed about to set in the western sky and, if anything, would have been the more likely of the two astronomical bodies to light up the sky. Reverend Browning told Professor McDonald that the sun was illuminating the objects, there being a distinct difference in tone between the dull grey of the larger object and the shiny, metallic luster of the smaller disc-like objects. The moon was just rising, but at the time of the sighting would have been at a mere 6° to the east. In fact, it may have had trouble at that time in being visible over mountains to the east.

Subsequently, Reverend Browning became the patron of the Tasmanian Unidentified Flying Objects Investigation Centre when it was formed in 1965. He remained interested in Tasmanian sightings until his departure from the state in 1990. Reverend Browning travelled to Melbourne soon after the 1960 sightings, to present details of the case to a VUFORS meeting.

(Sources: *Tasmanian UFO Investigation Centre Annual Report*, 1970/*Cressy Revisited* (TUFOIC)/ *Unidentified Aerial Sightings*, RAAF, 1960/*UFOs Over The Southern Hemisphere*, Hervey (1969)/ *FSR*, March 1979, Volume 24, number 5/*Motherships Over Australia*, by Paul Norman/*The Mercury*, Hobart/*The Examiner*, Launceston, 10.10.1960)

5th October 1960 – Thule, Greenland – UFOs spark atomic alert

Was it sheer coincidence that, on the following day, World War Three was averted after a formation of UFOs were picked-up on the radar screens of an early warning station at Thule, Greenland? The objects were plotted heading towards North America, from the direction of the Soviet Union. Within minutes, the red telephones at Strategic Air Command Headquarters in Ohama, Nebraska, were ringing, setting in motion an alert with atomic bomb laden B52s already in the air, awaiting instructions to head for predetermined targets deep within the Soviet Union.

SAC contacted Thule, but received no answer. Had the Base been attacked? Suddenly, the mysterious blips on the radar screen changed course and disappeared. Enquiries made later, revealed an iceberg had severed a submarine cable connecting Thule to the United States. (**Source:** *Operation Trojan Horse*, John A. Keel)

Questions raised in the House of Commons, England

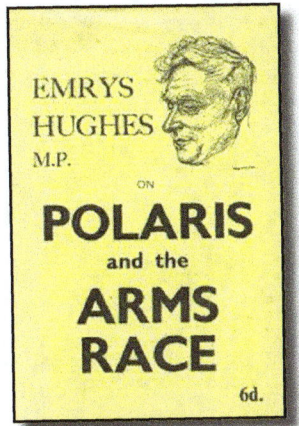

This was a matter which was raised in the House of Commons by MPs Mr Emrys Hughes, Mrs Judith Hart and Mr Stephen Swingler, who demanded an explanation. The Air Force told them that the radar signals had actually bounced off the moon and then been misinterpreted.

We searched Hansard, in 2013, but were unable to locate the necessary information regarding the exchange between the above MPs and a representative from the American Government, although there was considerable discussion about the early warning radar systems 'Blue Streak Rockets', the role of NATO, Vulcan Bombers, and other related items of Defence interest. It was also claimed the story had appeared in the *Guardian* newspaper, Manchester, on the 30th November 1960.

USA: 5th October 1960 – UFO sighted Mount Kisco, New York. (**Source: Blue Book**)

Australia: 13th October 1960 – A mysterious white light was seen in the sky over Mackinda Downs, Queensland, at 45° elevation.

Judith Hart

Australia: 18th October 1960 – A dull grey coloured cigar-shaped object, showing a bright orange rear, was reported over Sydney.

Tasmania: 27th October 1960 – An orange *'ball of light'* was seen hovering in the sky over Cressy, Longford, Tasmania; other sightings told of cigar-shaped objects seen. Explosions were also heard around the same locality at the time of the UFOs appearance. At Poatina, Tasmania, an orange, blue and red, coloured object was seen trailing a cloud of sparks, before exploding in mid-air.

November 1960

Australia: 15th November 1960 – An orange *'ball of light'*, estimated to be 70ft in diameter, was seen moving across the sky, at high altitude, over Hobart.

Tasmania: 27th November 1960 – A strange *'light'* was reported seen in the sky over Poatina. Two days later, on 29th, a blue and green *'light'* was observed rising above the horizon, over Trevallyn.

USA: 27th November 1960 – UFO sighted over Chula Vista, California. (**Source: Blue Book**)

December 1960

Tasmania: 7th December 1960 – A formation of 30-40 objects was sighted heading southwards, over Launceston.

Australia: 25th December 1960 – A mysterious star-like object was seen in the sky over Campbell Town, which took about 20 minutes to cover a quarter of the sky, heading west to east.

Haunted Skies Volume Ten

Cape Canaveral, Florida, USA

Greetings From Sheppard Air Force Base Wichita Falls, Texas

PART 4

1961 – 1962

January 1961

USA: 10th January 1961 – Cape Canaveral, Florida

DURING this morning, following the launch of a US Navy Polaris missile, a *'flying disc-shaped object'* – whose diameter was close to the length of the Polaris – altered its tracking, but did not block the missile firing. The tracking system in operation continued to plot the UFO and later returned to track the Polaris downrange. The diameter of the *'disc'* was approximately 20 to 25ft and about 6-8ft thick at its centre. It was then visually lost to ground observers and primary witness Clark McClelland.

(Source: *True Magazine*, January 1965/NICAP, Fran Ridge/*Flying Saucers, Serious Business*, Frank Edwards)

USA: 10th January 1961 – UFO seen to land at Texas

At 9.12pm on the same day, attorney Mr W.K. Rutledge and his colleague – drilling engineer, Mr George A. Thomas – were flying to Abilene, Texas, from Tulsa, at a height of 6,500ft, when they sighted an odd phenomenon in the sky, about 1500ft above them, which they described as being '*a large, round, luminous craft, surrounded by a brilliant glow*'.

Puzzled, Rutledge flew towards the object in order to obtain a closer look. As he did so, the object began to descend.

At the same time, a number of people on the ground sighted an orange glowing *'craft'* zigzagging across the sky. One of them was the Guthrie King County Sheriff – Dub Holler; another, wife of Knox County Sheriff – Homer Melton.

The object was then seen to land less than ten minutes later by Mr Rutledge, a short distance west of Benjamin. He then radioed Wichita Falls to enquire about any aircraft trouble in the area and was told there weren't any. Mr Rutledge then spoke to Sheriff Melton about the incident, who told him he was assembling a search party, while he continued to circle the object – which was glowing so strongly that it cast light onto the aircraft now flying at 4,000ft. At 10pm, when the searchers were within 100 yards from the object, Rutledge was forced to leave as he was running low on fuel. As he did so, the object shot up into the sky and was lost from view.

Haunted Skies Volume Ten

The next day Rutledge and Thomas made their way back to Benjamin, hoping to discuss the matter further with the Sheriff and newsmen, but were prevented from doing so by Air Force Intelligence Officers from Sheppard Airbase. This seems more like the script from *The Invaders* science-fiction TV series, starring Roy Thinness as 'David Vincent', than reality! In 2014, after emailing a colleague of Roy's who seemed most interested in our work, we sent a copy of *Haunted Skies* to Roy, hoping for, but not receiving, an answer.

(Source: Dan Wilson, McDonald List, NICAP/*Flying Saucers Are Hostile*, Brad Steiger & Joan Whritenour)

February 1961

USA: 5th-7th February 1961 – UFO Display

Numerous reports were made of strange lights, which were seen flashing around in the sky over Maine. Some blinked and moved up and down. Others lit up like a ball of fire, heading at speed over Portland. Unidentified shapes, showing green, yellow, and red lights, were seen to hover over Brunswick – then dart away at unbelievable speed. (**Source:** *Portland Press Herald* editorial, 9th February 1961)

USA: 9th February 1961 – During the early morning, a mysterious flash of blue light lit up the sky south of Cleveland, Ohio. This was followed by a vibration that was strong enough to rock the car of John Lengel, Deputy Sheriff on patrol in Geuga County. The *'flash'* was also seen by two pilots approaching Cleveland Hopkins Airport in their planes, separately. Enquiries made revealed no trace of any satellite launched on that day as being responsible, or in orbit, over the locality.

11th February 1961 – The Brains Trust, Caxton Hall, London

This consisted of a panel of five people, who met to discuss the 'Flying Saucer' subject. They were Reginald Dutta, Director on the board of *Flying Saucer Review*, Desmond Leslie, author, Dr. Bernard Finch, investigator into the widely publicised 'Ring Angels', Leonard Cramp, author, and Eric Smith, researcher in Physics and Fellow of the British Interplanetary Society. One of the questions put to the panel was:

> "Are space people friendly and, if so, what we are doing about it?"

Desmond Leslie replied:

> "There have been few hostile incidents, apart from the Captain Mantell case and the various small incidents which have been cooked up for publicity purposes, and that the space people are just as curious about us as we them at this critical stage in the evolution of mankind."

Leonard Cramp made reference to a sighting recorded in Captain Cook's logbook:

> "Two small clouds approached each other at great speed; there was the sound of gunfire, then a gigantic flash, at which one disappeared."

Following some discussion, the panel agreed that approximately 10% of UFO sightings were caused by temperature inversion, and that many such sightings could be explained away as meteorological in origin.

They were then asked for their opinion on the infra-red photographs taken in the sky by Trevor James Constable, which appeared in his book – *They Live In The Sky*. Reginald Dutta, in answer, believed they were forms that fringed on a fourth dimensional state, while Desmond Leslie felt that the 'gaseous caterpillars' were elementals and it was difficult to draw the line between these and UFO sightings.

USA: 27th February 1961 – UFO display, three UFOs seen

At 10.45pm, a USAF Sergeant at Fort Mead Missile Master Center, Maryland, tracked on radar, for approximately 20 minutes, a cluster of three objects at an altitude of approximately 6,300ft. The objects had the ability to stand still and had a high rate of change of direction. Their speed was tracked at 900 knots, with stops and starts.

USA: 28th February 1961 – Waverley Air Force Base, UFO tracked on radar

At 9.16pm local time, a fast moving object appeared on a Mark X radar of the 788th Radar Squadron, at 245° at a range of 40 miles and on a south-west heading. The object proceeded to a range of 125 miles at 240° – then made a left turn to 230° at 140 miles. The object turned inbound on a heading of 40° and disappeared at a range of 30 miles. Length of observation was 10 minutes. All of the witnesses employed by the Federal Aviation Administration were considered very reliable. (**Source: Dan Wilson, McDonald List**)

March 1961

Great Britain: 2nd March 1961

A mysterious object, projecting beams of light from its base, was seen travelling slowly north-west across the sky, between the horizon and the visible star-line, at 9.15pm. At the same time and date, Barbara Bowyer of Portchester, Hampshire, sighted *"a white top-shaped object, heading across the sky in an east to west direction, over the Portsdown Hill area."* (**Source: Isle of Wight UFO Society**)

April 1961

USA: 11th April 1961 – Cape Canaveral

At 9.57am, an object was picked up on ground radar at speeds between 150 knots to 600 knots. The object orbited six or seven times along an azimuth of 126°, between 10 and 55 miles from the Cape. The length of the observation was 30 minutes. The UFO was picked up prior to launch of test number 1352, a Polaris Missile. [Was there any connection with the January date?] (**Source: Dan Wilson, McDonald List**)

Great Britain: 14th April 1961 – Miss Jacqueline Murray lecture on UFOs!

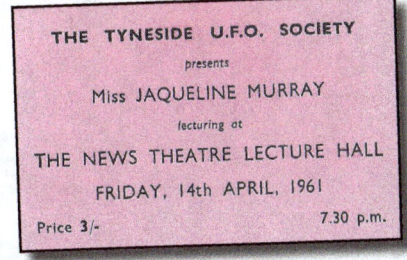

USA: 18th April 1961 – Alien seen at *Eagle River*, Wisconsin
At 11am, local resident Joseph Simonton (60) – a chicken farmer

by occupation, then living four miles from *Eagle River* – heard a whining sound.

On going outside to investigate further, he saw an object – 30ft in diameter, 12ft high, with exhaust pipes around the periphery – descend close to the ground, near his house.

A door or hatch – some 5ft from the ground – opened, allowing him to see three men in the *'machine'*. One of them was about 5ft tall, wearing a black, turtleneck pullover, showing a white band at the belt and black trousers, with a vertical white band along the side, and looking Italian in appearance. He held up what appeared to be a jug, made of the same material as the craft, and then motioned as to indicate that he wanted water.

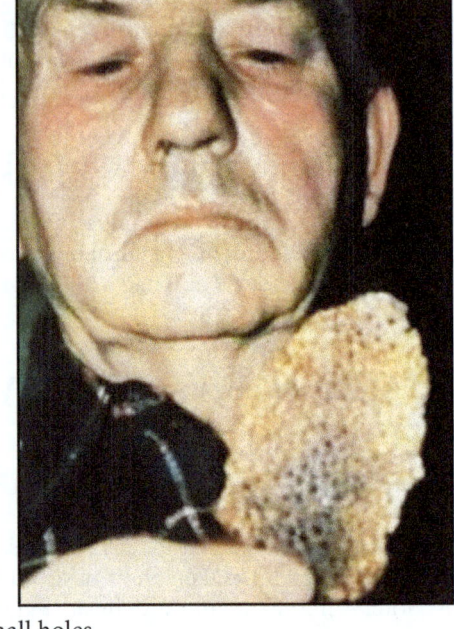

Simonton filled a jug with water and returned it to the man, who gave him three ordinary pancakes. At this stage, Joseph was able to see inside and noticed the interior was black – the colour of wrought iron – and also that several instrument panels were making a slow whining noise, like a generator. A man was frying food on a flameless grill of some sort. Joseph expressed an interest in this food, which was being prepared, and he was handed three small cakes, described as 3ins in diameter, and perforated with small holes.

The object then took off. As it did so, it caused a blast of air to bow nearby pine trees.

Sheriff Schroeder (who had known Joe for 14 years) sent two deputies to the scene, after learning of what had taken place. One of the cakes was sent to Major Donald Keyhoe – Director of NICAP – for analysis. It is claimed that subsequently, following analysis, the pancake contained buckwheat hulls, soybean hulls, wheat,

Haunted Skies Volume Ten

fat bran, and starch. (**Source:** *Milwaukee Journal*, 23/24.4.1961/Jacques Vallée, *Magonia*)

USA/Great Britain: 19th 20th April 1961 – HMS *Maxton* sights object in the west-north-west, at high altitude, emitting a strong green light, at 7.40pm, while en route from Algeria to Palma, Majorca. The following day crew aboard sighted a similar phenomena – this time at 2.50pm, involving an object which was seen flying erratically in the north-north-east direction – thin, at first, and then getting much broader at its leading point as range decreased. Admiralty were unable to explain the sightings.

At 6.20pm, an object at an estimated altitude of 97,000ft was tracked by FPS-6A radar from 791 Radar Squadron (*SAGE), at a bearing of 96°.

The object disappeared one hour and four minutes later, at 10,000ft, on a 95° bearing. In the same month a joint statement by 21 American Scientists, released by NICAP, called for open investigation of UFOs without secrecy, the need for a more thorough investigation. It was also suggested that the Air Force should have a more straightforward information policy, specifically to give out all facts on major UFO sightings.

May 1961

Great Britain: 18th May 1961

At 8pm, a torpedo-shaped object, trailing sparks, was seen flying through the sky over the Midlands and Nottingham areas, by many people.

(**Source:** *Hull Daily Mail*, 15/26th May 1961/*Birmingham Mail*, 13.5.1961/*Notts. Evening News*)

USA: 19th May 1961 – Long Beach, California – Another UFO Display!

At 3.50pm, twelve shiny UFOs were seen manoeuvring erratically over the area and observed moving with an odd fluttering motion. This was followed by two loud sky quakes. (**Source:** NICAP)

USA: 20th May 1961 – Tyndall Air Force Base, Florida – UFO tracked on radar

At 5am four Air security policemen saw a round, rusty-orange coloured object, moving up and down and gaining altitude in the sky over the Drone Launching Area. The target was also picked up on radar, following which a fighter aircraft was scrambled to investigate the object, estimated to be initially moving at 2-4mph and then up to 45mph. [A helicopter had been scrambled, due to the slowness of the object] Air Force GCI (Ground Control Information) radar also tracked the object at a height of between 2,000 and 10,000ft. Total time of observation was approximately one hour and forty minutes. (**Source:** *UFOE*, III, Dan Wilson)

Great Britain: 25th May 1961

Just after 10pm, Shepperton resident – Julia Cardoza (16) – noticed a brilliant point of yellow light in the western sky.

"As it came closer I saw an object, resembling a bowler hat – the top part of which was glowing like

---

*The SAGE radar stations of Air Defence Command (Aerospace Defence Command after 1968) were the military installations operated by USAF squadrons using the 1st automated air defence environment (Semi-Automatic Ground Environment) and networked by the SAGE System, a computer network. (**Wikipedia**)

an electric light bulb, but yellow light. Below it was a dark portion around the edges, of which were what looked like portholes glowing with a green light. I last saw it disappear silently behind rooftops, towards the north-east direction. I estimated it was 20-30ft in size and about 150-200yds away from where I saw it, moving at about 20mph".

(Source: Philip Heselton/*FSR*, 1961, Volume 7, Number 5)

USA: 29th May 1961

Robert Miller and his friend, who preferred to remain anonymous, claimed to have seen and cine-filmed in colour, using a Kodak 8mm, with telephoto lens, a UFO passing through the sky over Newark.

"It was a large white 'ball', as large as the moon with a blue halo, with a larger oblong trail, and travelled in a north to south direction."

Four copies of this film were made and one was sent to NICAP. It appears authentic, as opposed to a hoax – but without far more information, who knows? (**Source:** *UFO Sighter*)

Sequence of three frames, showing change of shape and appearance of two smaller UFOs.

Australia: 31st May 1961 – UFO over Toompang, New South Wales

At midday another UFO sighting, involving smaller craft seen leaving the larger one, was witnessed over Toompang, New South Wales, Australia.

A seven men crew was out marking lambs, when they heard the sound of what they thought was a jet aircraft. One of them, who asked his name be kept confidential, fearing ridicule, looked up and saw an eagle hawk high up in the sky.

"I heard the sound again, but couldn't see any jet. Then I saw this object – it looked like a silver star and seemed to be over Wyalong – it was so high up and stationary. I shouted to the rest of the men to have a look. One man was short-sighted, another couldn't pick up the object, but the remaining four of us watched it on and off for over an hour, possibly two hours. I saw one object leave the first object and go to the left and later two others go to the right, and then come back. The objects I saw leaving the stationary object seemed round. The one I saw leave it on the left came overhead as it went towards Young. I could see it was V-shaped. When I went home I said to my wife, 'Has anything come over the air about anybody seeing things in the sky?' She told me nothing had."

Mr Neville Sheahan, one of the other witnesses, described the large objects as being:

"... round, with a dome on top. The small objects which left it seemed flatter; a tennis ball could have covered the big object. We watched them when we sat down to lunch. About 2pm the sun moved around in that direction and we couldn't see the things anymore against the strong light."

June 1961

USA: 4th June 1961

A cigar-shaped or long elliptical UFO, with a cluster of smaller UFOs, was seen over Blue Ridge Summit, Pennsylvania. First motionless, the smaller objects then streaked across the sky to the large UFO, before vanishing behind trees. (**Source:** NICAP *UFOE*)

Australia: 6th June 1961 – UFO Display over Millaa Millaa

A group of about 60 people watched a silvery-red spherical object, performing what appeared to be aerobatics in the clear sky over Millaa Millaa, Queensland, Australia, for some 90 minutes. By the time an Australian Air Force plane arrived to carry out an investigation, the object had gone from view. Enquiries made with Meteorological Officers, at Cairns, revealed it was unlikely to have been a balloon.

Australia: 13th June 1961 – 'Flying Saucer' over Bethungra

Assistant railway station master – Mr Tom Henshaw, of Junee – was on duty at 3.35pm. He heard what he thought was a low flying aircraft and went outside to have a look.

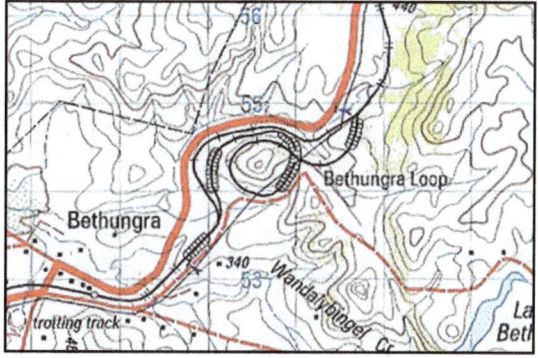

> *"I saw a glowing red object in the sky, travelling towards the Station, at a height just above the telephone wires. As it moved along it created a series of 'whirly winds', sucking up dust in large clouds from the bare land. It was close enough to the wires to tangle them up as it moved past them."*

Three members of a railway gang – Mr George McDonald, Reginald Seymour and Jack Lloyd – also witnessed the object, making a noise like a screaming whistle as it moved through the sky. Suddenly it changed course and disappeared over Cootamundra Hills, some 800ft high. During the same week, sightings of UFOs were reported from Gundagai, Goulburn, Atherton, Tablelands, and Young. (**Source:** *Juneee Southern Cross*, 19.6.1961)

Great Britain: 18th June 1961

A green cigar-shaped object was seen at 10.40pm, heading west to east, over Gateshead. (**Source:** *LUFORO*, Vol. 2, No. 9, September 1961)

Great Britain: 19th June 1961

At Exeter, *"an unidentified flying object"* was reported to have hovered for more than an hour above an airport. Officials said:

> *"We do not know what it is. It was seen on the radar screen and we have had it under observation for some time. We think it is pretty big. It appears to be shining brightly and is about 50,000ft up."*

(**Source:** NICAP)

Haunted Skies Volume Ten

July 1961

Great Britain: 1st July 1961

At 9.30pm a blue-grey bodied object, estimated to be 250ft in length, showing two yellow white lights, was sighted stationary in the sky, approximately at 13,000ft, a few miles from Halstead, in Essex. This was witnessed by at least 20 people. At 9.40pm the object turned northwards, after making a noise like a *'turbo prop'*, before heading northwards in a climbing arc. As it did so, the lights changed to orange-red. One person claimed it had portholes along its side. **(Source: Alan J. Watts, B.Sc. F.R. Met .S)**

USA/Great Britain: 4th & 5th July 1961

Isle of Wight residents – Mrs A.W. Taylor and her mother, Mrs C. Smith – were on the flat roof of Mrs Taylor's house in George Street, Ryde, overlooking the *Solent*, at 12.35am on 4th July 1961, when Mrs Smith saw a row of five *'lights'* in the direction of Seaview. They looked like a ship, except for the fact that it was in the sky.

> *"The object came towards us and stopped at about eye level. It appeared to have a top and base, rather like a hovercraft, and the whole base emitted an orange light. It then disappeared at high speed – faster than any jet plane – in the direction of Seaview, leaving behind it a ring of smoke, which dissolved into a haze of light."*

According to Isle of Wight UFO Society researcher, Mr Leonard Cramp – a world-renowned inventor, aerospace engineer, and author – to whom we had the pleasure of writing on a number of matters, over the years, the two women were sincere and of unimpeachable honesty.

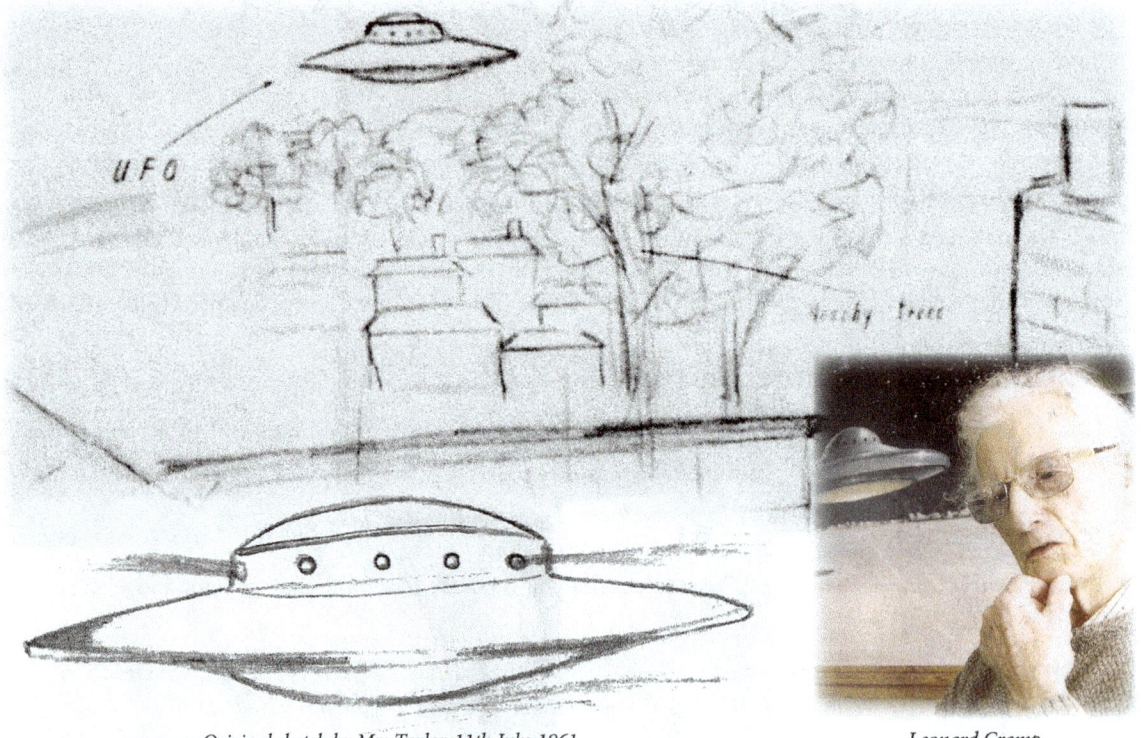

Original sketch by Mrs Taylor, 11th July, 1961   *Leonard Cramp*

At 10.15pm on the same date, this time over Cleveland, USA, a glowing green and white object swooped down at a plane, but stopped suddenly and climbed away at tremendous speed.

Great Britain: 5th/6th July 1961

Several people living in the Ryde area reported having sighted UFOs. They included a Commander Mole, who was later interviewed by *Southern Television* and the local Press. Also on the 5th July 1961 the Cleveland pilot sighted a second similar object, which was also tracked on radar at Cleveland Airport. The following day an object described as resembling a *'flying hovercraft'*, was seen stationary in the sky over the Isle of Wight. (**Source:** *Evening Standard*, **6th July 1961/***Isle of Wight County Press*, **8.7.1961/Leonard Cramp, Isle of Wight UFO Society, 1961**)

USA: 7th July 1961

At 11pm, waitress Nannette Hilley from Copemish, Michigan, saw a large *'ball'* flying slowly through the sky, which split into four after four minutes, descend, and then fly away westwards. (**Source: Don Berliner**)

USA: 11th July 1961 – Springfield, Ohio. Ex-USAF air navigator – Mr G. Scott, his wife, and neighbours, saw a round bright *'light'*, resembling shiny aluminum, pass overhead, at 7.45pm. (**Source: Don Berliner**)

USA: 13th July 1961 – UFO Display over Washington

A strange object, showing beams of light, was seen circling south-west of Mount Rainer, Washington, by many people, including police officers, who described seeing one large *'light'*, surrounded by several smaller ones. The *'lights'* moved up and down and back and forth, for several hours. (**Source:** *Saucer News*, **September 1961**)

USA: 17th July 1961 – At 2am, two civilians in a car being driven along Highway 95, one mile north of Bonny Spring Ranch, near Las Vegas, saw, through the rear-view mirror, a low-flying object that overtook their car, followed by a rush of cold air. It was then seen to stop and circle the vehicle, before flying away and then lost to sight behind the mountains. (**Source: Vallée,** *Magonia*)

USA: 20th July 1961 – UFOs over Texas

At 9am, Trans-Texas Airlines Capt. A.V. Beather, flying a DC-3, saw two very bright white objects straight ahead of aircraft, hovering between 6,000ft and 7,000ft over Bayton, Texas. The objects disappeared on a heading between 65° and 70°, at 10,000ft. following an erratic flight path, travelling much faster than any aircraft. Weather radar showed small non-persistent blips on the scope in the general area of the sighting, south-west of Orange, Texas. These blips were apparently not ground clutter. (**Source: Don Berliner,** *Sparks*, **42 pages of document by Dan Wilson**)

Australia: 27th July 1961 – 'Flying Saucers' over Darwin

At 7.55pm and 8.40pm, a saucer-shaped object, bluish in colour, appeared from the north-west direction, at a height of 1-2,000ft. It was seen to move around in a wide circle across the harbour, before moving southwards. One of the witnesses was Emira Parker of the Esplanade, Darwin, who was at the wharf when it appeared. Mrs Zdenek Hostalek also saw it for about 30 seconds, before it headed away. Ten minutes later, the object was seen over Tennant Creek. Other witnesses to the phenomena included Douglas Clarke, the driver of a train travelling between Larrimah to Darwin, and his fireman.

Douglas:

> *"We saw this big 'ball of fire' coming towards the train from behind. It gave us quite a turn. I've never seen anything like it. I don't believe it was a comet. I don't know what it was."*

[Some accounts give the 27th June 1961] (**Source:** *Australian Flying Saucer Review,* January 1962)

August 1961

Australia: 5th August 1961 – UFOs over Mount Hale

A shearing contractor, aged 37 years, working at Mt. Hale station, situated about 70 miles west of Meekatharra, told of being approached by another man, who came over to the shearing shed and asked him to have a look at two objects in the sky.

> *"The objects were round in shape, bright silver, about 2ft each in diameter – that is from ground level. The objects appeared to be about 8 to 10,000ft – possibly higher. They were travelling at a fast speed and could be kept in sight for only about two minutes. Their course appeared definite, no surface wind. In all 12 objects were sighted, the last being about 9.15am. They appeared to be in pairs. The objects gave off a white substance, which took on various shapes whilst falling to the ground. The white substance was followed and I managed to pick up some of the substance. It was of snow white colour and appeared to be in a fine mesh. It crumbled very easily."*

An interesting account, involving what appears to be the fall of 'Angel hair' – a by-product released during the passage of these objects through the sky. (**Source:** *Flying Saucers Over Australia,* **James Holledge**)

Great Britain: 10th August 1961:

At 9.35pm, Peter Kent and his girlfriend were out cycling at Pulham Market, Norfolk, when they saw:

> *"... two searchlights, pointing downwards in the sky approaching from the west, about 1,000ft high. When some 1,500ft away, there was a blue flash – like electricity fusing – and they disappeared from sight."*

(**Source:** *Eastern Evening News,* 11th August 1961)

USA: 12th August 1961 – Kansas City

At 9pm, College seniors – J. B. Furkenhoff and Tom Phipps – saw a very large oval object, with a fin extending from one edge to the centre, *"like a sledge with lighted car running boards"*, which hovered at 50ft altitude for three to five minutes, then flew straight up and eastwards, disappearing in about five seconds. (Source: Don Berliner)

Great Britain: 15th August 1961

Mr R.G. Clift of Chelston, Torquay, was studying the night sky through binoculars, at 12.15pm, when he sighted

> *"... a saucer-shaped object emitting a faint blue light, which scintillated in the rays of the sun. The upper part, or superstructure, was of a burnished white colour – almost opaque – in strong contrast to the underneath, before it sped away towards the Berry Head direction. Then it accelerated away in a burst of speed and was gone."*

On the same day, a UFO – described as looking like a *"hand mirror, reflecting in the sky"* – was seen heading westwards, in a perfectly straight line, over the coast of Tyneside.

(**Source:** *Herald Express,* 16.8.1961)

"Three pink objects, resembling inverted saucers, visible for only a few seconds", were sighted moving through the sky at an incredible speed over Barrow, Lancashire, during the late evening of 15th August 1961. They were heading in a straight line, north-west to south-east, according to local resident – Mr M. Poland. The sighting attracted the attention of the Meteorological Office, who denied that they were balloons, adding:

"I don't wish to be facetious, but they could have been something from outer space!"

Just to show how one can misidentify earthly objects with something completely out of the normal, was a photograph taken by us some years ago, in the Worcestershire area, as the sun began to drop down. Although we hasten to add this was a 'one off' we don't believe the majority of UFO sightings can be attributed to noctilucent clouds!

(**Source:** *Western Evening News*, exact date not known/*LUFORO Bulletin*, Vol. 2, No's. 11 & 12, November/December 1961)

USA: 17th August 1961 – Stillwater, Minnesota

A 'V' formation of yellowish lights, or V-shaped UFO with body lights, was seen to pass behind trees at low altitude. (**Source:** NICAP *UFOE*, II)

Great Britain: 27th/28th August 1961

At 8pm, Wolverhampton housewife – Mrs Lea and her husband – sighted a long rectangular strip of brilliant light with a *'ring'* at one end.

It was motionless in the north-west part of the sky for half an hour, before it faded away.

(**Source:** *Express & Star*, date not known)

The following day (28th August 1961) at 5.17am, an amateur astronomer, living near the Castlereach Hills, County Antrim, Northern Ireland, noticed three objects moving across the sky; one leading, with the other two behind.

> *"The rear two suddenly accelerated, moving closer to the first one, as if under some sort of control, before disappearing behind the hills."*

Fins on the side

An object, with what looked like *'fins'* on the side, was seen over Wednesbury, one minute later, at 5.18am, by night watchman – George Parr.

As it passed over, one of the *'fins'* fell away. Another witness, Mr Banks Fearon – a resident of West Bromwich – described seeing an object resembling a military shell, showing three lights, with flames shooting from its rear. To his surprise, it returned over the area, a short time later, and appeared to explode in mid-air. Two of the lights then vanished, whilst the other slowly drifted to the ground. (**Source: Personal interviews**)

September 1961

Great Britain: 1st September 1961 – Nottingham

At 10.10pm, Celia Fox was out walking with a friend – Mr J. Berry of Chilwell – when they saw:

> *"... a number of whitish lights, as bright as car headlights, darting about in the sky in all directions – not in formation. There were lots of them visible in the northern part of the sky, between 30° and 70°. We watched for about ten minutes, until they became obliterated from view by gathering clouds approaching from the south".*

(**Source:** *LUFORO Bulletin*, **May/June 1962**)

USA: 2nd September 1961

At Albuquerque, New Mexico, at about 4.50pm, a Mr Ziegler (no other details) saw an object reflecting the sun from its surface, moving erratically west to east across the sky. It stopped and ejected several smaller, silvery objects, about 1/6th the size of the main object, then continued on its flight towards the south-east where it stopped once more and ejected, for the second time, several similar silvery objects, before moving away and climbing to an elevation of 50°, until lost from view. (**Source: Project 1947; McDonald List; FUFOR Index**)

USA: 13th September 1961

At 4am, at Crawfordsville, Indiana, three people sighted an orange-shaped UFO moving across the sky rapidly, in an east to west direction. It then stopped and hovered for five minutes, before accelerating rapidly and disappearing into the distance. (**Source: NICAP *UFOE*, XII**)

USA: 19th September 1961

At 5.22am, North Concord Air Force Station, Vermont, height finder radar tracked an object at an altitude of 62,000ft, 196° distance, 84 miles. The target was the size of a large aircraft and appeared as a normal target. Contact was lost at 199° at 80 miles, going north-west, then south. Length of observation was 18 minutes. The target moved at a low speed on an erratic course. The location of observers was at five miles east of Claremont, New Hampshire. Pease Air Force Base also had an unidentified radar contact at 2.14am. (**Source: Dan Wilson, Vallée,** *Magonia*, **NICAP/*UFOE*, XIV**)

USA: 19th/20th September 1961 – Betty and Barney Hill – Missing time: Three hours

American couple Betty and Barney Hill's account of what happened to them has so many parallels with similar incidents which have been previously outlined by us in the various volumes of *Haunted Skies*. Their encounter with the UFO, and interaction with its occupants, along with information obtained from later sessions of hypnotic regression, is now well-known and has been the subject of an enormous number of articles over the many years, reflecting the public's ongoing curiosity about the event.

Reflections on the UFO phenomena

Over the years we have interviewed many hundreds of people's accounts of UFO activity, some of them going back to the early 1940s.

The reports appear to fall loosely into three categories:

1. What is referred to something unusual seen in the sky, which is generally judged important enough to bring to the attention of either a UFO group or the police; admittedly, some of these incidents – often seen at great height – can be misidentified natural phenomena, or aircraft.

2. Objects seen performing manoeuvres in the sky, which we have termed 'displays of UFO behaviour', followed by the appearance of what are described as 'structured craft' rather than lights. This category also includes reports from motorists, who complain of having been followed by mysterious 'globes of light' - mostly through rural localities, rather than cities.

3. Some motorists allege, later, that they have been abducted, and report instances of missing time; others make no such claims.

These incidents should be of concern to us all.

Is it possible when certain criteria are met, such as distance, severity of 'UFO' exposure, length of time, previous history, and other undetermined factors, that each and every sighting may be the forerunner to an allegation of abduction? This is a frightening scenario. We hope that time will prove we have nothing to fear from interactions with UFOs, but we remain pessimistic.

Our culture seeks to convince us of a vast gulf between the sighting of UFOs in the sky and paranormal events on the ground. In fact, eminent researchers maintain the likelihood of a strong association between the paranormal and UFO phenomena.

People have, and will, continue to claim allegations of what they interpret as an alien abduction, involving being taken against their will by non-human entities and then subjected to complex physical and psychological procedures. Often those reports will speak of a forced medical examination of their reproductive system. Abductees sometimes claim to have been warned against environmental abuse and the dangers of nuclear weapons. While many of these experiences are described as terrifying, some have been viewed as pleasurable or transformative.

Due to the lack of any substantial physical evidence, most scientists and psychiatrists will explain allegations of UFO abduction as deception, suggestibility (fantasy-proneness, false-memory syndrome) personality, sleep phenomena, psychopathology, psychodynamic therapy and other environmental factors. The evidence presented by us so far appears to indicate that on occasion this hypothesis may be flawed.

Dr. John Edward Mack

As reported in the *Harvard University Gazette*, in 1992, Dr. John Edward Mack told of having investigated over 800 claims of abduction and spent countless therapeutic hours with these individuals. He said:

"The majority of abductees do not appear to be deluded, confabulating, lying, self-dramatizing, or suffering from a clear mental illness."

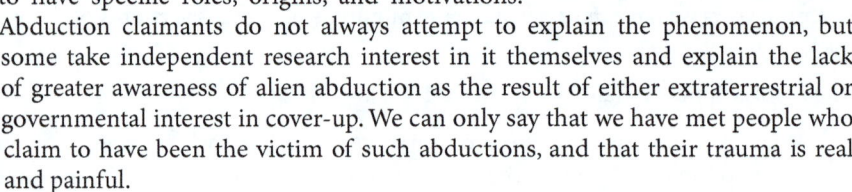

Some abduction reports are quite detailed. An entire subculture has developed around the subject, with support groups and a detailed mythos explaining the reasons for abductions – The various aliens (Greys, Reptilians, 'Nordics' and so on) are said to have specific roles, origins, and motivations.

Abduction claimants do not always attempt to explain the phenomenon, but some take independent research interest in it themselves and explain the lack of greater awareness of alien abduction as the result of either extraterrestrial or governmental interest in cover-up. We can only say that we have met people who claim to have been the victim of such abductions, and that their trauma is real and painful.

There appears to be a misconception that the abduction phenomenon is a fundamentally new one and began with sightings of UFOs back in the 1940s and the realisation, some following 20 years later, that these 'craft' contained occupants. Whilst the reader may have their own opinions about this, we do not believe that the majority of UFO incursions are attributable in extraterrestrial origin, but feel 'they' are indigenous to the home planet – Earth.

The problems arise with determining how long 'they' have been here – where that leaves the human race in the scheme of things we are not sure! Personally we believe they represent a modern chapter in the history book of human presence on this planet, which involved recorded sightings of flying vehicles and creatures which have been seen in the skies, going back many thousands of years. Whilst we cannot prove the abduction process involves alien beings who carry out medical examinations of their human victims, as claimed by so many people worldwide, it is clear that an ongoing process of behaviour in itself completely alien to our normal way of life continues to take place – this should concern us all.

Dr John E. Mack presents the Dalai Lama with a copy of his book 'Abduction – Human Encounters with Aliens', in 1999

Haunted Skies Volume Ten

John G. Fuller – *The Interrupted Journey*

Betty & Barney Hill's widely publicized claim of what appears to be an alien abduction, was later adapted into the best-selling 1966 book *The Interrupted Journey*, by John G. Fuller, and the 1975 television movie *The UFO Incident*. We have to say that we were very impressed with the thorough account outlined by Mr Fuller, contained in his book of 388 pages. In it John tells of meeting psychiatrist Dr. Benjamin Simon, in the mid 1960's, describing him as a man of impressive qualifications and Director of one of the largest State Mental Institutions in Massachusetts. The subject of their conversation were two of his patients, Barney and Betty Hill, who had allowed John – then a reporter for *Look Magazine* – the opportunity to examine their medical reports, which included records and tapes of their experience with a UFO, while in the White Mountains of Hampshire, a few years previously.

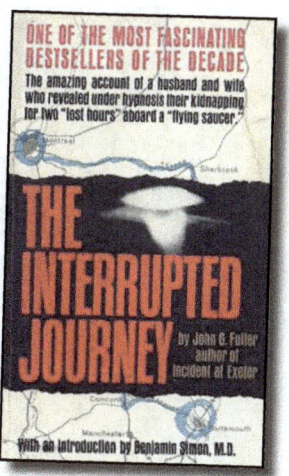

How it all began

At around 10.30pm on 19th September 1961, the couple were driving back to Portsmouth from a vacation in Niagara Falls, Montreal, and Quebec, Canada. There were only a few other cars on the road as they made their way home to New Hampshire's sea coast. Just south of Lancaster, New Hampshire, Betty sighted a bright point of light in the sky that moved from below the moon and the planet Jupiter, upward to the west of the moon.

While Barney continued navigating US Route 3, Betty speculated if she had seen a falling star, but remained puzzled why it moved upwards erratically, like a plane or a satellite, and growing bigger and brighter as it did so. Betty urged Barney to stop the car for a closer look, as well as to walk their dog, 'Delsey'. Barney stopped at a scenic picnic area, just south of Twin Mountain. Worried about the presence of bears, Barney retrieved a pistol that he had concealed in the trunk of the car.

Betty and Barney Hill with their pet dog 'Delsey'

A 'craft' is seen

Betty fetched a pair of binoculars and saw an *'odd-shaped craft'*, flashing multicoloured lights, flying across the face of the moon. Because her sister had confided to her about having a *'flying saucer'* sighting, several years earlier, Betty thought it might be what she was observing.

Through binoculars Barney observed what he fist took to be a commercial airliner, travelling toward Vermont, on its way to Montreal. However, he soon changed his mind, when the *'craft'* rapidly descended towards their direction.

At this point the couple returned to the car and drove toward Franconia, a narrow, mountainous stretch of the road.

Haunted Skies Volume Ten

The Hills continued driving on the isolated road, moving very slowly through Franconia Notch, in order to observe the object as it came even closer. At one point, the object passed above a restaurant and signal tower on top of Cannon Mountain.

It passed over the mountain and came out near the 'Old Man of the Mountain'. Betty said that it was at least one and a half times the length of the granite cliff profile, some 40ft long, and that it seemed to be rotating. The couple watched as the silent, illuminated, 'craft' moved erratically and bounced back and forth in the night sky. As they drove along Route 3, through Franconia Notch, they stated that it seemed to be playing a game of *'cat and mouse'* with them.

UFO descends over highway

Approximately one mile south of Indian Head, the object rapidly descended toward their vehicle, causing Barney to stop directly in the middle of the highway. The massive silent craft, resembling a huge flattened *'disc'*, then hovered approximately 80-100ft above the Hills' 1957 Chevrolet Bel Air and filled the entire field of the windshield [windscreen]; it reminded Barney of a huge pancake.

Suddenly, in an arc like movement, it shifted from its location directly ahead, and rested above the treetops in an adjacent field. Barney pocketed his handgun and walked toward it. The silent enigmatic *'craft'* was huge; maybe 60-80ft in diameter. As he approached it, two red lights at the end of fin-like structures parted from the sides of the *'craft'*, and it tilted toward Barney. Lifting his binoculars to his eyes, he noticed a group of figures – eight or nine of them – that were *"somehow not human"*, moving about with the precision of German officers, described as humanoid forms, wearing glossy black uniforms and black caps.

As the *'craft'* tilted downward and began to descend toward him, one of these strange creatures, who remained at the window, communicated a frightening message telepathically, telling him to *"stay where you are and keep looking"*. Barney had the immediate impression that he was in danger of being plucked from the field. Overcome with fear and with all of the courage that he could muster, he tore the binoculars from his eyes and raced back to the car. Breathless, trembling, and in near hysterics, he told Betty that they needed to get out of there or they were going to be captured.

After arriving home

The couple began to experience odd sensations and impulses they could not readily explain: Betty insisted their luggage be kept near the back door, rather than in the main part of the house. Their watches would never run again. Barney noted that the leather strap for the binoculars was torn, though he could not recall it tearing. The toes of his best dress shoes were inexplicably scraped. Barney says he was compelled to examine his genitals in the bathroom, though he found nothing unusual. They took long showers to remove possible contamination and each drew a picture of what they had observed. Their drawings were strikingly similar. After sleeping for a few hours, Betty awoke and placed

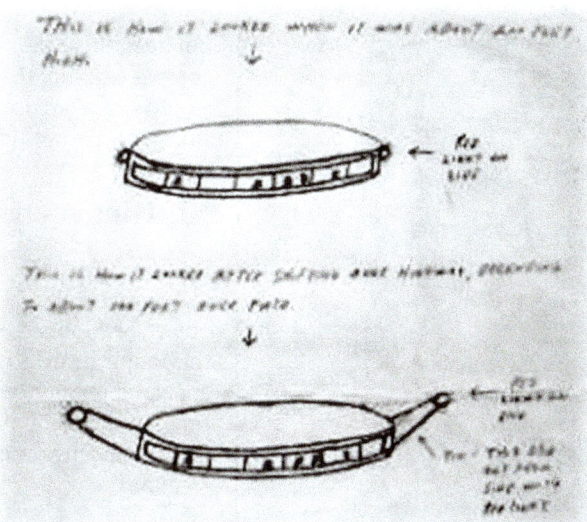

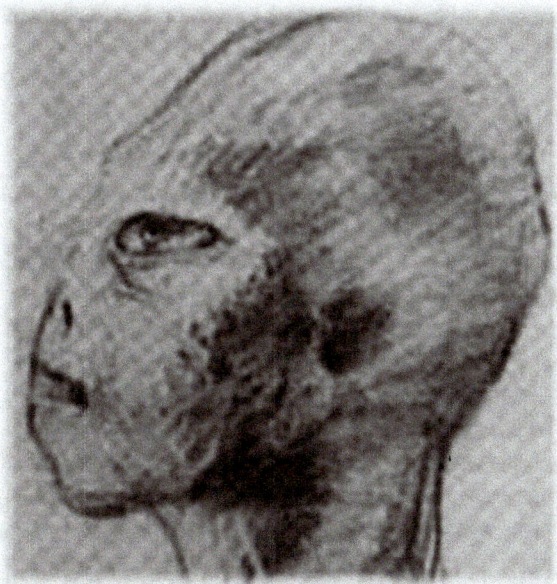

the shoes and clothing she had worn during the drive into her closet, observing that the dress was torn at the hem, zipper and lining. Later, when she retrieved the items from her closet, she noted a pinkish powder on her dress. She hung the dress on her clothes line and the pink powder blew away.

However, the dress was irreparably damaged. She threw it away, but then changed her mind, retrieving the dress and hanging it in her closet. (Over the years, five laboratories have conducted chemical and forensic analyses on the

Haunted Skies Volume Ten

dress.) 'There were shiny, concentric circles on their car's trunk that had not been there the previous day. Betty and Barney experimented with a compass, noting that when they moved it close to the spots, the needle would whirl rapidly. But when they moved it a few inches away from the shiny spots, it would drop down.

Entities seen inside 'craft'

Further details obtained about the incident revealed that after driving away from the scene, at high speed, Barney told Betty to look out for the object. She looked but saw no trace of it, although almost immediately, the couple heard a rhythmic series of beeping or buzzing sounds, which appeared to bounce off the trunk of their vehicle. The car vibrated and a tingling sensation passed through their bodies. Betty touched the metal on the passenger door, expecting to feel an electric shock, but felt only a vibration.

The couple believes the strange sounds were the precursor to the onset of an altered state of consciousness that left their minds dulled, and that a second series of code-like beeping or buzzing sounds returned them to full consciousness. They discovered that they had travelled nearly 35 miles south, but had only vague memories of driving along this section of road. They recalled making a sudden, unplanned turn, encountering a roadblock and observing a fiery orb in the road.

'Could there have been any connection with an incident that took place in France, involving the discovery of *'circles'* found at the scene following a close encounter claim?

Strange sights seen in skies of France

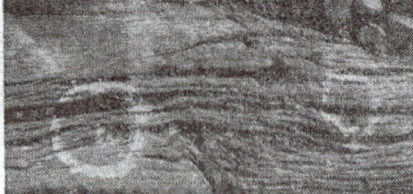

IMAGINATION? Truth?
Millions of Frenchmen seek the answer. From every part of France have come reports of strange machines of all shapes flying through the air.

There have been so many separate accounts of these unexplained spectacles that many people in France are tempted to believe in the existence of the mystery machines.

The most astonishing story of all is told by a French metal worker, Marius Dewilde, who lives in a cottage near the railway line at Quarouble, in Northern France.

Dewilde was in his kitchen one night when he heard his dog howling terribly.

He ran outside and saw two men between the railway lines. He thought they might be burglars or dynamiters and he ran forward, shining his torch.

He was dumbfounded to see that the "men" were only two feet high with their heads encased in a transparent turret. And they had no arms.

A bigger surprise was a Flying Saucer sitting on the rails only 50 yards away.

The little robot men ran towards the saucer. As Dewilde gathered his courage to run after them a ray from the saucer struck him in the face, temporarily paralysing him.

The men entered the saucer through a trap door, and the saucer disappeared in the darkness.

The French Government have been asked to investigate the strange happenings in the skies of France.

MARIUS DEWILDE, who claims to have seen two crew members of the Flying Saucer, points to the exact spot where they stood between the railway lines (above). The picture (right) shows the chalk-like circles left on the wooden sleepers by the mysterious, armless men.

Incident reported to USAF and NICAP

On 21st September, Betty telephoned Pease Air Force Base to report their UFO encounter, though, for fear of being labelled eccentric, she withheld some of the details. On 22nd September, Major Paul W. Henderson telephoned the Hills' for a more detailed interview. Henderson's report, dated 26th September, determined that the Hills' had probably misidentified the planet Jupiter. (This was later changed to 'optical condition', 'inversion' and 'insufficient data') (Report 100-1-61, Air Intelligence Information Record). His report was forwarded to Project Blue Book, the US Air Force's UFO research project. USAF Explanation – Misidentified Jupiter!

Within days of the encounter, Betty borrowed a UFO book from a local library. It had been written by retired Marine Corps Major Donald E. Keyhoe, the head of NICAP, a civilian UFO research group. On 26th September, Betty wrote to Donald Keyhoe relating the full story, including details about the humanoid figures that Barney had observed through binoculars. Betty wrote that she and Barney were considering hypnosis to help recall what had happened.

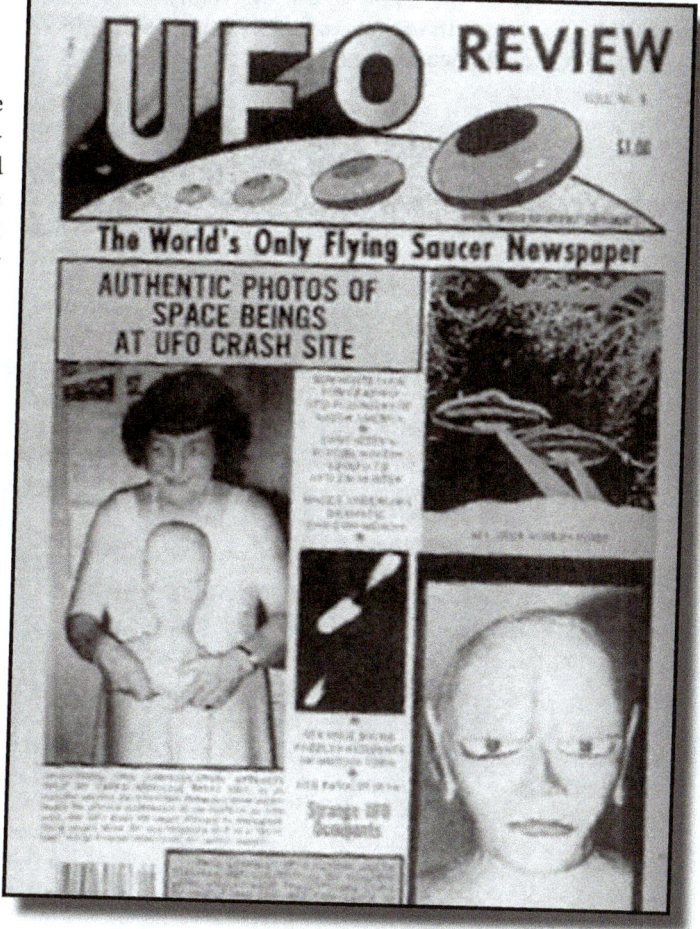

Her letter was eventually passed on to Walter N. Webb – a Boston astronomer and NICAP member – who met Betty and Barny Hill on the 21st October 1961. During a six-hour interview, the couple related all they could remember of the UFO encounter.

Barney pointed out that due to a *'mental blockage'* he was unable to remember some portions of the event, but described in detail what he could remember about the craft and the appearance of the *"somehow not human"* figures aboard it.

Mr Webb was satisfied that their account was a truthful one and had probably occurred exactly as reported, except for some minor inconsistencies to be expected, where human judgement is involved; such as, exact time, length of visibility, apparent sizes of object and occupants, distance and height of object, etc.

Vivid dreams experienced

Ten days after the UFO encounter, Betty began having a series of vivid dreams. They continued for five successive nights. Never in her memory had she recalled dreams in such detail and intensity. However, they

Haunted Skies Volume Ten

stopped abruptly after five nights and never returned again. They occupied her thoughts during the day. When she finally did mention them to Barney, he was sympathetic but not too concerned, and the matter was dropped. Betty did not mention them to Barney again.

In November 1961, Betty began writing down the details of her dreams. In one dream, she and Barney encountered a roadblock and men who surrounded their car. She lost consciousness but struggled to regain it. She then realised that she was being forced by two small men to walk in a forest in the night-time, and of seeing Barney walking behind her, though when she called to him, he seemed to be in a trance or sleepwalking. The men stood about 5ft to 5ft 4ins tall, and wore matching uniforms, with caps similar to those worn by military cadets.

In the dreams, Betty, Barney, and the men, walked up a ramp into a disc-shaped *'craft'* of metallic appearance. Once inside, Barney and Betty were separated. She protested, and was told by a man she called *'the leader'* that if she and Barney were examined together, it would take much longer to conduct the exams. She and Barney were taken to separate rooms. Betty also dreamt that a new man, similar to the others, entered to conduct her exam with *'the leader'*. Betty called this new man *'the examiner'* and said he had a pleasant, calm manner. Though *'the leader'* and *'the examiner'* *spoke to her in English, *'the examiner's'* command of the language seemed imperfect and she had difficulty understanding him. [In Betty's dream they had black hair, normal human eyes, large noses, ears, lips. Under hypnosis however she described them as having bald heads, large wraparound eyes, small ears and almost absent noses. Their skin was a grayish colour.]

Medical examinations take place in the dreams

The examiner told Betty that he would conduct a few tests to note the differences between humans and the craft's occupants. He seated her on a chair, and a bright light was shone on her. The man cut off a lock of Betty's hair. He examined her eyes, ears, mouth, teeth, throat and hands. He saved trimmings from her fingernails. After examining her legs and feet, the man then used a dull knife, similar to a letter opener, to scrape some of her skin onto what resembled cellophane. He then tested her nervous system and he thrust the needle into her navel, which caused Betty agonising pain. However, *'the leader'* waved his hand in front of her eyes and the pain vanished. The examiner left the room and Betty engaged in conversation with *'the leader'*. She picked up a book with rows of strange symbols that *'the leader'* said she could take home with her. She also asked where he was from and he pulled down an instructional map, dotted with stars. In Betty's dream account, the men began escorting the Hills' from the *'ship'* when a disagreement broke out. *'The leader'* then

---

*Under hypnosis, she understood them in English, but their mouths did not move. Occasionally she could see a membrane that would flutter when they spoke to one another in a mmmmmmmmmmmmm sound.

Haunted Skies Volume Ten

informed Betty that she couldn't keep the book, stating that they had decided that the other men did not want her to even remember the encounter. Betty insisted that no matter what they did to her memory, she would one day recall the events. She and Barney were taken to their car, where the leader suggested that they wait to watch the craft's departure. They did so, and then resumed their drive.

Further interviews with couple by NICAP

On 25th November 1961, the Hills' were again interviewed at length by NICAP members – this time by C.D. Jackson and Robert E. Hohmann. Having read Webb's initial report, Jackson and Hohmann had many questions for the Hills'. One of their main questions was about the length of the trip. Neither Webb nor the Hills' had realised that the drive should have taken about four hours, but the couple did not arrive at home until seven hours after their departure. When Hohman and Jackson brought this to the attention of Betty and Barney, the couple was unable to recall almost nothing of the 35 mile journey taken between Indian Head and Ashland.

However, although Betty's recall was somewhat fuller than Barney's, both were able to remember an image of a fiery orb sitting on the ground. Betty and Barney reasoned that it must have been the moon, but Hohmann and Jackson informed them that the moon had set earlier in the evening. The subject of hypnosis was mentioned as a means of unlocking some of the unconscious memories. Barney was apprehensive about hypnosis, but thought it might help Betty put to rest what Barney described as the *'nonsense'* about her dreams.

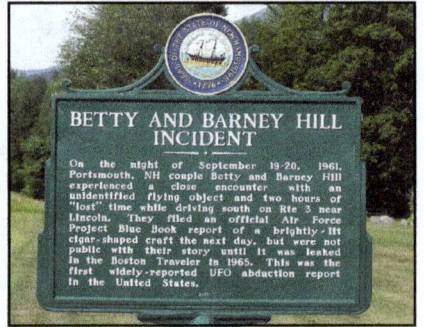

By February 1962, the Hills' were making frequent weekend drives to the White Mountains, hoping that revisiting the site might spark more memories. (This was actually identified in 1965).

Meeting Captain Benjamin H. Swett at the local Church

On 27th November 1962, the Hills' attended a meeting at the parsonage of their church, where the invited guest speaker was Captain Benjamin H. Swett, of Pease Air Force Base , who had recently published a book of his poetry and was known locally for his study into hypnosis.

After he read selections of his poetry, the pastor asked him to discuss his personal interest in hypnosis. After the meeting broke up, the Hills' approached Captain Benjamin Swett privately, and told him what they could remember of their strange encounter. He was particularly interested in the *'missing time'* of the Hills' account. The Hills' asked Swett if he would hypnotize them to recover their memories, but Benjamin Swett said he was not qualified to do that and cautioned them against going to an amateur hypnotist, such as himself.

Capt. Benjamin H. Swett

On 3rd March 1963, the Hills' first publicly discussed the UFO encounter with a group at their church.

On 7th September 1963, Captain Swett gave a formal lecture on hypnosis to a meeting at the Unitarian Church. After the lecture, the Hills' told him that Barney was going to a psychiatrist, Dr. Stephens, whom he liked and trusted. Captain Swett suggested that Barney ask Dr. Stephens about the use of hypnosis in his case. When Barney next met with Dr. Stephens, he asked about hypnosis. Stephens referred the Hills' to Dr. Benjamin Simon of Boston.

Dr. Benjamin Simon

Discussing the incident at a UFO group

On 3rd November 1963, the Hills' spoke informally before an amateur UFO study group – the Two State UFO Study Group in Quincy Center, Massachusetts.

On 14th December 1963, they met Dr. Simon for the first time. Early in their discussions, Simon determined the UFO encounter was causing Barney far more worry and anxiety than he was willing to admit. Though Dr. Simon dismissed the popular extraterrestrial hypothesis as impossible, it seemed obvious to him that the Hills' genuinely thought they had witnessed a UFO with non-human-like occupants, or humanoids. Simon hoped to uncover more about the experience through hypnosis.

Dr. Simon hypnotized Betty and Barney several times. These began on the 4th January and lasted until 6th June 1964. Dr. Simon conducted the sessions on Barney and Betty separately, so they could not overhear one another's recollections. At the end of each session he reinstated amnesia. Barney described the beings as generally similar to Betty's hypnotic, not dream recollection, though he did not know the content of Betty's memories under hypnosis. Dr. Simon had reinstated their amnesia at the end of each session. The beings often stared into his eyes, said Barney, with a terrifying, mesmerizing effect. Under hypnosis, Barney said things like *"Oh, those eyes. They're there in my brain"* (from his first hypnosis session) and *"I was told to close my eyes because I saw two eyes coming close to mine, and I felt like the eyes had pushed into my eyes"* (from his second hypnosis session) and *"All I see are these eyes ... I'm not even afraid that they're not connected to a body. They're just there. They're just up close to me, pressing against my eyes"*. Barney related that he and Betty were taken onto the disc-shaped *'craft'*, where they were separated. He was escorted to a room by three of the beings and told to lie on a small, rectangular table. Unlike Betty, Barney's narrative was fragmented (based upon physical sensations and not observational details) and he continued to keep his eyes closed during this procedure.

Hypnosis sessions begin

Someone felt his spine, and seemed to be counting his vertebrae. While Betty reported extended conversations with the beings in English, Barney said that he heard them speaking in a mumbling language he did not understand. Betty also mentioned this detail. The few times they communicated with him, Barney said it seemed to be *"thought transference"* – at that time, he was unfamiliar with the word *'telepathy'*. Both Betty and Barney stated that they had not observed the beings' mouths moving when they communicated in English with them. He recalled being escorted from the *'ship'*, and taken to his car, which was now near the road rather than in the woods. In a daze, he watched the *'ship'* leave. Barney remembered a light appearing on the road, and he said, *"Oh no, not again"*. He recalled Betty's speculation that the light might have been the moon – though the moon had, in fact, set several hours earlier. He also stated that he attempted to produce the code-like buzzing sounds which seemed to strike the car's trunk a second time, by driving from side to side and stopping and starting the vehicle. His attempt was unsuccessful.

Betty recollects physical examination

Under hypnosis, Betty's account was very similar to the events of her five dreams about the UFO abduction, but there were also notable differences. Her capture and release were different. The technology on the *'craft'* was different. The short *'men'* had a significantly different physical appearance than the ones in her dreams. The sequential order of the abduction event was also different from Betty's dream account. She filled in many details that were not in her dreams and contradicted some of her dream content. It is interesting that Barney's and Betty's memories in hypnotic regression were consistent but contradicted some of the information in Betty's dreams.

Haunted Skies Volume Ten

Betty exhibited considerable emotional distress during her capture and examination. Dr. Simon ended one session early because tears were flowing down her cheeks and she was in considerable agony. Dr. Simon gave Betty the post-hypnotic suggestion that she could sketch a copy of the *'star map'* that she later described as a three-dimensional projection, similar to a hologram. She hesitated, thinking she would be unable to accurately depict the three-dimensional quality of the map she says she saw on the *'ship'*. Eventually, however, she did what Dr. Simon suggested. Although she said the map had many stars, she drew only those that stood out in her memory. Her map consisted of twelve prominent stars, connected by lines, and three lesser ones that formed a distinctive triangle. She said she was told the stars connected by solid lines formed *'trade routes'*, whereas dashed lines were to *'less-travelled stars'*.

Dr. Simon's conclusions

After extensive hypnosis sessions, Dr. Simon concluded that Barney's recall of the UFO encounter was a fantasy, inspired by Betty's dreams. Though Dr. Simon admitted this hypothesis did not explain every aspect of the experience, he thought it was the most plausible and consistent explanation. Barney rejected this idea, noting that while their memories were in some regards interlocking, there were also portions of both their narratives that were unique to each. Barney was now ready to accept that they had been abducted by the occupants of a UFO, though he never embraced it as fully as Betty did.

Though the Hills' and Dr. Simon disagreed about the nature of the case, they all concurred that the hypnosis sessions were effective: the Hills' were no longer tormented by anxiety about the UFO encounter. Afterwards, Dr. Simon wrote an article about the Hills' for the journal *Psychiatric Opinion*, explaining his conclusions that the case was a singular psychological aberration.

Back to normality – but not for long!

The Hills' then went back to their regular lives and, like so many others that we had spoken to, over the years, were willing to discuss the UFO encounter with friends, family, and the occasional UFO researcher, but they made no effort to seek publicity for perhaps understandable reasons.

On 25th October 1965, the *Boston Traveler* (on its front page) asked, "UFO Chiller: Did THEY Seize Couple?", following information from news reporter John H. Luttrell, of the *Boston Herald Evening Traveller*, who had been given an audio tape-recording of the lecture the Hills' had made in Quincy Center. In late 1963 Luttrell learned that the Hills' had undergone hypnosis with Dr. Simon; he also obtained notes from confidential interviews the Hills' had given to UFO investigators. This seems to be an abuse of confidentiality; surely the Hills' should have been pre-warned about this?

John H. Luttrell

We, ourselves, learned of a similar incident which took place a few years ago, involving video tape-recorded interviews, conducted in the 1970s, relating to an allegation of abduction being given to a representative of a company that were planning to produce a film about the UFO encounter and sessions of hypnosis carried out later. The woman witness expressed much anxiety about this and, quite rightfully, felt this was a form of betrayal – never mind the awful possibility of seeing those very private images of herself during the emotive sessions.

On 26th October, the United Press International (UPI) picked up Luttrell's story, and the Hills' earned international attention.

In 1966, writer John G. Fuller secured the cooperation of the Hills' and Dr. Simon, and wrote the book *The Interrupted Journey* about the case.

The book included a copy of Betty's sketch of the *'star map'*. The book was a quick success, and went through several printings.

Incidents involving allegations of abduction, not surprisingly, will and have attracted enumerable allegations made by those sceptics, who in their boundless enthusiasm to convince others that the world is a sterile place, claim that the experience encountered by the couple could be explained away as an hallucination, brought on by the stress of being an interracial couple in the early 1960s! What a load of rubbish!

Star Map drawn

In 1968, amateur astronomer and elementary schoolteacher – Marjorie Fish of Oak Harbor, Ohio – read Fuller's *Interrupted Journey*. She was intrigued by the *'star map'*, and wondered if it might be deciphered to determine which star system the UFO came from. Assuming that one of the fifteen stars on the map must represent the Earth's sun, Starting in 1968, Marjorie constructed 26 three-dimensional models of nearby sun-like stars, using thread and beads, basing stellar distances on those published in the 1969 *Gliese Star Catalogue*. Studying thousands of vantage points over several years, the only one that seemed to match the Hill map was from the viewpoint of the double star system of Zeta Reticuli.

Haunted Skies Volume Ten

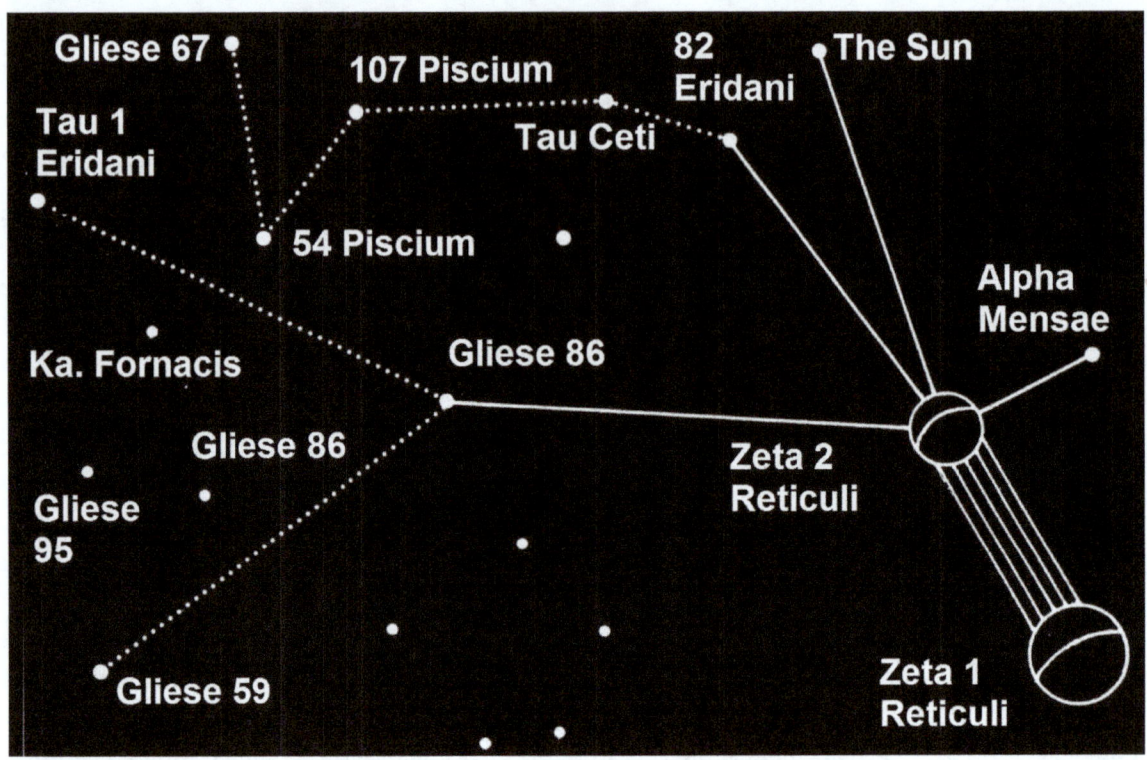

Films and TV

The couple was portrayed by James Earl Jones and Estelle Parsons in the 1975 television movie, adapted by S. Lee Pogostin, *The UFO Incident*, and by Basil Wallace and Lee Garlington in the 1996 television series *Dark Skies*. The Hills' were briefly pictured and discussed in the mini-series *Taken*.

The book *The Chronologies of Babylon 5*, which describes the fictional timeline of the *Babylon 5* universe, states that the couple was abducted by a race called The Strieb.

The encounter was portrayed in a segment on the 12th TV episode of Carl Sagan's mini-series *Cosmos*, 'Encyclopedia Galactica'.

Details of the Hills' case were also used in *The X-Files* episode José Chung's *From Outer Space*. Certain components of the case were depicted in *American Horror Story: Asylum*.

Niece, Kathleen Marden

In 2014, we contacted Kathleen Marden – a well-known and highly respected UFO abduction researcher, author and lecturer, with 23 years experience in the field, and MUFON's International Director of Abduction Research. For ten years Kathleen volunteered as MUFON's Director of Field Investigator Training.

In 2012, she was the recipient of MUFON's 'Researcher of the Year' award. She earned a BA in social work from the University of New Hampshire, in 1971, and participated in graduate studies in education while working as a teacher and education services coordinator. She has had extensive formal training in hypnosis. Her interest in UFOs dates back to 20th September 1961, when (aged 13) her aunt, Betty Hill, phoned her nearby home to report that she and Barney had encountered a *'flying saucer'* in New Hampshire's White Mountains. A primary witness to the evidence of the UFO encounter and the aftermath, Kathleen has intimate knowledge of the Hills' biographical histories, personalities, and the previously unpublished historical files pertaining to their sensational story.

Author of Three Books

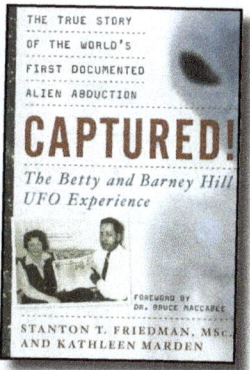

She is the author of three books: *Captured! The Betty and Barney Hill UFO Experience*, *Science Was Wrong*, with nuclear physicist/scientific ufologist Stanton T. Friedman, and *The Alien Abduction Files*, with Denise Stoner (May 2013 release). Her chapter 'UFO Abductions: Fact or Fiction' appears in *UFOs and Aliens: Is There Anybody Out There?* Her articles have been published in the *MUFON UFO Journal*, *Open Minds* magazine and on several websites. Kathy has appeared on television and radio programmes in the US, Canada and the UK, and has lectured throughout the United States. She is recognised as the world's leading expert on the Betty and Barney Hill abduction.

We asked Kathleen about the physical examination carried out on Barney, involving a cup-like device being placed over his genitals, and a sperm sample taken [although he did not experience an orgasm]. Barney also told of his skin being scraped, and samples extracted from his ears and mouth. In addition to this a tube, or cylinder, was then inserted in his anus. Kathleen clarified this was on the hypnosis tapes and is covered in *Captured! The Betty and Barney Hill UFO Experience*.

Kathleen was asked why she decided to write about her aunt's experience. She replied,

> ". . . initially, because I wanted to write my Aunt Betty Hill's biography; this was in the early 1990s. And before I could do that, I asked her to mentor me in everything that she knew about UFOs. In the course of nearly 15 years, she opened all her files to me, including all of the letters that she had received from various researchers and scientists. She also gave me her hypnosis tapes, which I transcribed for comparative analysis. It turned into a UFO book, because the information that I found was just so fascinating. I thought that the truth needed to be told and that there was a great deal of misinformation about the case itself."

Although this incident happened in 1961, now over 50 years ago and thousands of miles away from England, it is clear the same 'intelligence' [if one may refer to it as that] is responsible for numerous other Close Encounters.

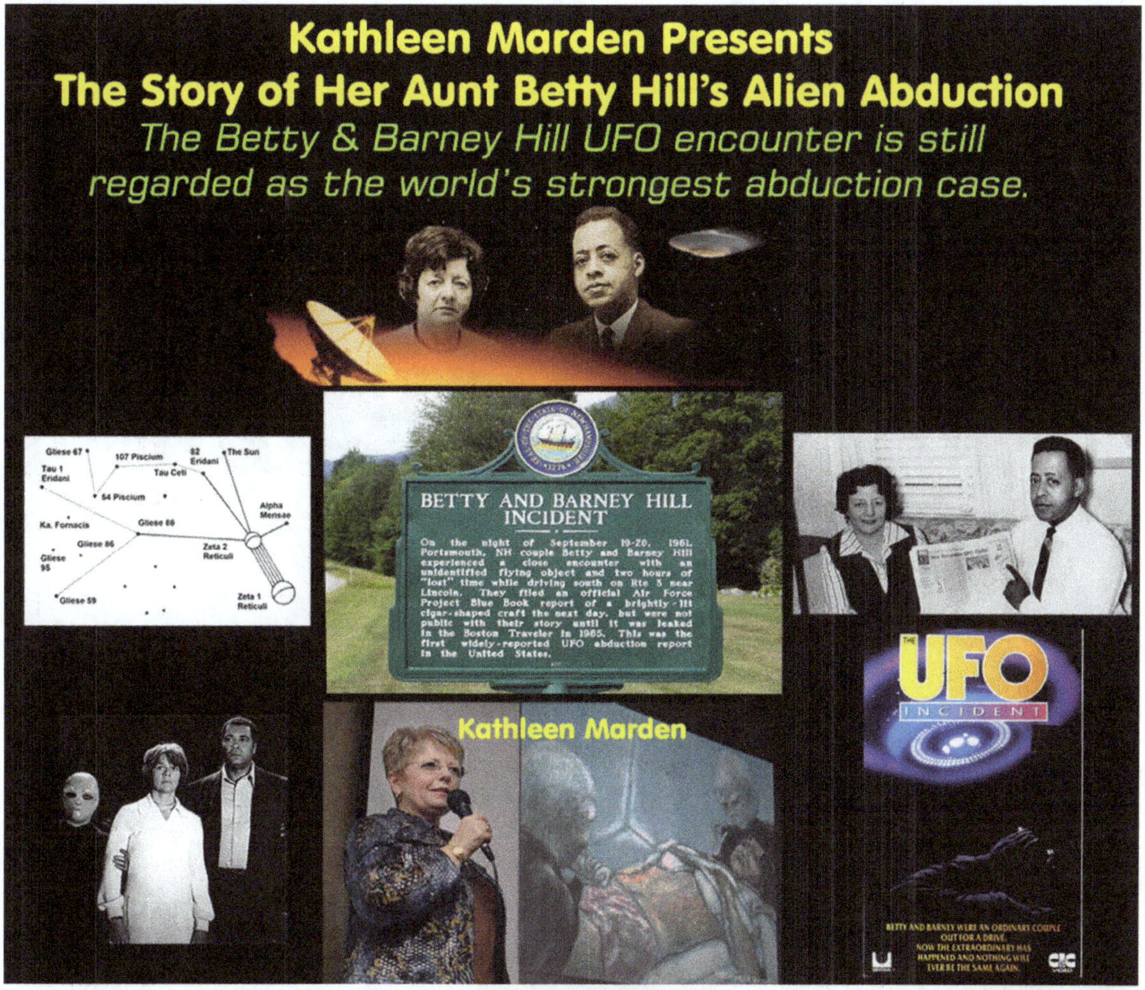

Haunted Skies Volume Ten

Kathleen Marden Presents
The Story of Her Aunt Betty Hill's Alien Abduction
The Betty & Barney Hill UFO encounter is still regarded as the world's strongest abduction case.

How many of these beings exist? Are they few in numbers, or large? Do they perceive us just as strange as we do them? Can they truly manipulate time – a luxury they appear to possess plenty of, if one accepts they are as ancient as man himself? – Likely, bearing in mind that human history on the planet contains many apparent accounts of their presence on the Earth.

It is difficult to accept, in the cold light of day, that the purpose of these abductions is the collection of eggs and sperm from the luckless few who have been ensnared in the web of the 'close encounter' for the creation of genetic engineering, in order to continue a human alien hybrid offspring.

Haunted Skies Volume Ten

Mr and Mrs Barney Hill. Their amazing stories tallied even under hypnosis

AND WERE KIDNAPPED BY CREATURES FROM OUTER SPACE!

Incredible? Fantastic? Preposterous rubbish? OR FACT?

The story started four years ago when Betty and Barney Hill thought they'd had an encounter with a flying saucer — but were too embarrassed and ashamed to talk about it.

But they told a relative. This led to a visit from Walter Webb, a scientific adviser to the American National Investigations Committee on Aerial Phenomena. His report on the Hills concluded:

"It is the opinion of this investigator . . . that they were telling the truth, and the incident occurred exactly as reported, except for some minor uncertainties and technicalities that must be tolerated in any such observation where human judgment is involved.

Honesty

"I was impressed by their intelligence, apparent honesty and obvious desire to get at the facts and to underplay the more sensational aspects of the sighting."

But they were still plagued by a nagging feeling that "something more had occurred." And so they went to the office of Dr. Benjamin Simon, a distinguished Boston psychiatrist and neurologist.

During World War II, Dr. Simon was Chief of Neuropsychiatry and Executive Officer at Mason General Hospital, the American Army's chief psychiatric centre.

He had extensive and remarkable success with hypnosis in the treatment of many psychiatric disorders among military personnel.

Dr. Simon accepted them as patients. During the months that followed, the Hills began—under individual psycho-

w Hampshire Exeter in last year.

several weeks stakingly taping interviews, vercoming the the conservants—and the of the airmen se nearby.

is the most count of mass ver produced.

own words ople tell of of huge craft. are people com- amiliar with of aircraft that base and who be confused. the base Fuller hat radar fixes FO's were com-

Fuller became intrigued by a report of a UFO

shoot at them, they could never be overtaken.

In his most convincing interviews three policemen, one a flying veteran, told of observing a saucer over a one-hour period from 100 yards.

Two other people saw the same craft from different viewpoints.

After investigation, the Pentagon judgment was: "Stars and planets in unusual formation."

This, said Mr. Fuller, was not taken seriously even at the base. After all, pilots, both military and civil, are some of the prime sources of UFO reports.

And two of the policemen wrote to him: "The story put out by the Pentagon was not true. It could not be, because we were the people who saw this, not the Pentagon."

Fuller went to Exeter as a "friendly sceptic," he said. "But I returned feeling that something must be done.

That although fighters had standing orders to

A rare photo taken of Betty Hill with Ralph Hull in 1976 taken at a farm owned by Ignatius Kennedy in Tatamagouche, Nova Scotia.

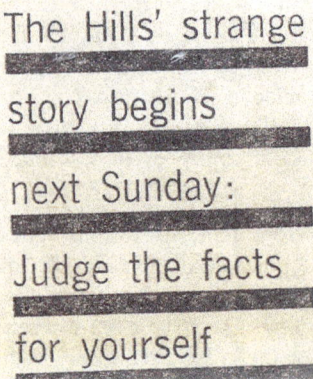

The Hills' strange story begins next Sunday: Judge the facts for yourself

462

Dr. Margaret Mead

Dr. Margaret Mead (1901-1978) – a renowned anthropologist and prolific writer, who produced 44 books and more than 1,000 articles. Her publishing was translated into many languages.

In 1974, she stated:

> *"There are unidentified flying objects; that is, there is a hard core of cases – perhaps 20 to 30 per cent in different studies – for which there is no explanation. We can only imagine what purpose lies behind the activities of these quiet, harmlessly cruising objects that time and again approach the Earth. The most likely explanation, it seems to me, is that they are simply watching what we are up to."*

(Source: Mead, Margaret, *UFOs – Visitors from Outer Space?* **Redbook**, Vol. 143, September 1974)

Margaret:

> *"Do you believe in UFOs? Again and again, over the years, I have been asked this extraordinary question. I think it is a silly question borne from confusion. Belief has to do with matters of faith and nothing to do with the kind of knowledge that is based on scientific inquiry. We should not bracket them with angels and archangels, devils and demons. This is just what we are doing when we ask whether people believe in UFOs. As if their existence was an article of faith. Do people believe in the Sun or Moon, or the changing seasons or the chairs they are sat on?*
>
> *When we want to understand something strange and something previously unknown to anyone, we have to begin with an entirely different set of questions, what is it? How does it work? Are there recurrent regularities? With an open mind, people can then take a hard look at all of the evidence. They can then sift out the vague rumours, the tall tales, the obvious mistakes in judgment, the fanciful embroidery of detail, the hoaxes, and the distortion introduced both by those who are overeager to believe and by those who are determined to discredit everything. Beginning in this way, we can answer the question most people really have in mind. Yes, there are unidentified flying objects. There are phenomena that, even after the most cautious and painstaking investigations, cannot be explained."*

Thanks to the courage of people like Betty and Barney, and countless others, who, often in the face of ridicule and scepticism, just tell it how it was – plain and simple truths, not sensationalist in any way – we should be proud of all of them. Sadly, Barney died of a cerebral haemorrhage on 25th February 1969, at the young age of 46, and Betty Hill died of cancer on 17th October 2004, at the age of 85.

From the Files of *Haunted Skies* – Allegations of alien interaction (1940-1988)

Whether the UFO presence is actually representative of an alien species, indigenous to the planet, or examples of what some people claim to be paranormal or demonic, are questions we cannot answer. All we can say is that our heart goes out to people like Betty and Barney Hill, who, often in the face of anticipated ridicule, just tell how it was. Surely some day soon, people will demand an answer to what lies behind all of this – we all deserve that. We decided the reader should have the opportunity of being able to contrast some of these accounts with that of Betty and Barney, to show that they and many others, worldwide, are not on their own and that at some stage in our history we will begin to take matters like this with far more seriousness than we apparently do.

UK: 1940 – Alien landing – Encounter with aliens and medical examination

Bob Tibbitts – Former Head of the Coventry UFO Research Group – interviewed Cathie Connolly about her UFO experience, which took place in the summer of 1940, on the outskirts of Meriden – a small village, situated near Coventry, in Warwickshire.

Following her encounter with a landed dome-shaped object, while walking through a leafy lane, she saw a number of tall *'men'*, dressed in one-piece garments. These *'men'* had unusually high foreheads, strange eyes, and tanned skin.

Cathie Connolly:

> "A few months later, I was working in the chain room at Reynold Chains, Coventry, examining the metal links, when all of a sudden I became aware of a man next to me, whom I instantly recognised as being similar in description to one of the persons I had seen near the structure. He said, 'It's your war as well. Take me to your King and Queen'. I was stunned. I told him I couldn't do that. The next thing I was aware of was lying on my back in what I took to be a spaceship. I tried to move but couldn't, as I was being held down by a number of strange men who had slits for a mouth, stretching almost to their ears, with cat-like faces and eyes devoid of the white part. One of them said, 'We are not going to hurt you. We just want to know if you are pregnant'."

Bob Tibbitts:

> "I have to admit that when I first heard of what Cathie claimed had happened, all those years ago, it seemed too incredible to believe, especially when she revealed a number of journeys made in the 'craft' (UFO) to places like New York and Rhodesia. However, as time went on, I realised I was dealing with a genuine woman, who firmly believed wholeheartedly in what she had experienced, as opposed to any flight of fanciful imagination."

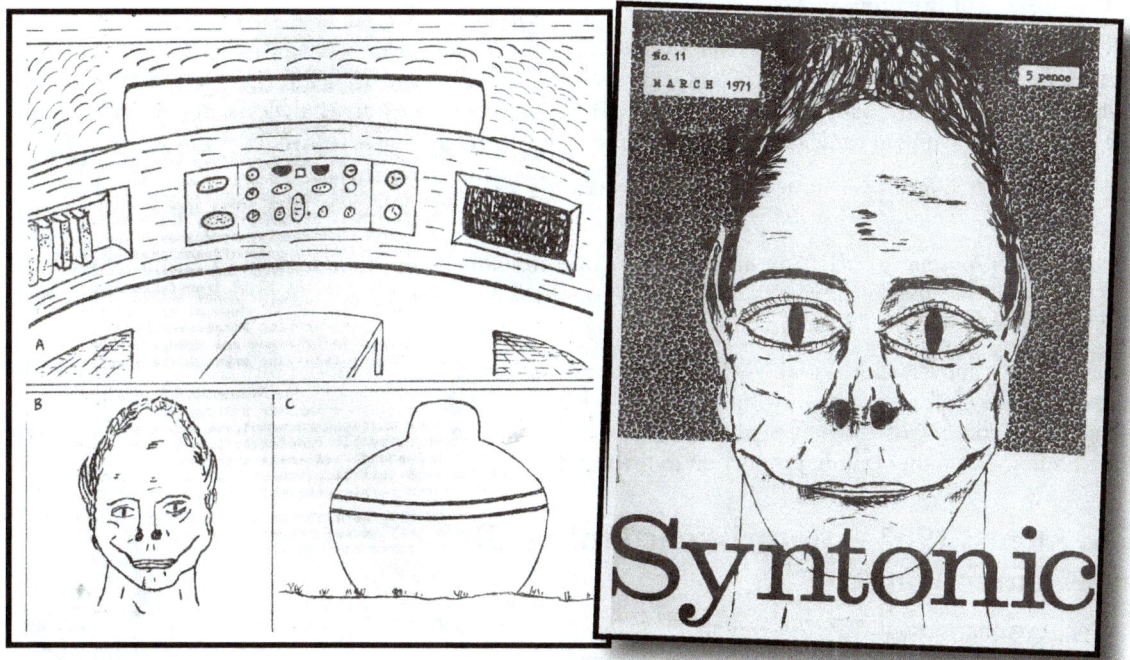

Below: A. "Inside the craft". Impression based on original sketches made by Mrs Connelly. B. Sketch made by Bob Tibbitts from the description given by Mrs Connelly. C. The 'craft' at Meriden. From an original sketch by Mrs Connelly. Right: Cover of the March, 1971 edition of Syntonic, which featured the Cathie Connelly story that began in 1940, at Meriden, near Coventry.

UK: 1941 – 'Horse-like entities' attack girl in home, causing injury

Alison Richards, from Kidderminster, told of what she endured, when aged six and living with her mother, while her father was fighting overseas.

"When Mum went to bed she had to bandage on a metal splint to her leg, as her only way of getting about was to hop. It was always an unwritten rule that if I needed her, perhaps because of sickness, I would always go to her, except for when I had a visit from what I can only describe as 'horse beings', who always entered the room from out of the linen cupboard, next to a window over the stairs, when I would scream and shout for her. By the time my Mum had reached the bedroom they had left via either the window, or the linen cupboard. I kept telling Mum what I had seen. She insisted horses could not physically get into the house, but I knew they were real because, on at least four occasions, they actually hurt me. I would end up with flesh gouged out of my left leg on the shin bone, about the size of a five pence piece. The injuries to my leg (which always happened after the shortest one came into the room) frightened my mother. She thought, to begin with, that I had caught the leg on a loose mattress wire on the bed spring. She and a neighbour thoroughly checked the bed but could find no trace of what was causing these injuries to occur, always in the same place on the shin."

Sadly, Alison died in August 2008.

UK: 4th/5th September 1951 – Alien landing, occupants seen

On the 4th or 5th September 1951 Mrs Shelia Burton, in her late teens, was visiting her parents at Withdean on the outskirts of Brighton, Sussex.

After waking up at 6.30am she went over to the bedroom window, overlooking the long garden, and was peering out over the early morning ground mist. As the sun began to rise, she saw something large and flashing, followed by the landing of a silvery-green, light green, or lime-coloured, dome-shaped craft. Panel-like doors opened and out came three *'men'*, who moved in a straight line across the lawn.

> "They were 5-6ft in height, with bald heads, wearing a dark green khaki one-piece garment, and holding what looked like a 'machine gun device'.

> The 'men' continued walking for about 30ft and then simultaneously began to walk backwards to the craft and re-entered their respective panels, which closed. Red flashing lights restarted and the object shot upwards vertically, and became lost from sight."

During further conversation with UFO researcher Andy Collins, Mrs Burton told him that she estimated the diameter of the craft to be 40ft in width and 25ft in height, and the red flashing lights to be 6-7ft below the apex, equally spaced around the perimeter of the dome. Nothing could be seen of the interior of the craft. Their bodies were rather thin in proportion to their size. (**Source: Personal interviews**)

UK: August 1967 – Motorist encounters UFO – dead circle of skin found on body

Late one evening, in August 1967, Shrewsbury, Shropshire housewife – Bridget Kelly – was on her way home with her husband and three children:

> "We were driving along the road, when we saw what we took to be a shooting star but realised it wasn't falling. It then hurtled towards the ground, as if about to crash, stopped, and hovered in front of us, allowing us to see a glistening silver metallic object, with a bright light flashing on top and a lighted window to one side. The next thing I became aware of was standing outside the front door. We looked up and saw the 'craft' taking off across the rooftops. I had this feeling of sadness that whoever, or whatever, was on it was saying good-bye.

> The following day, I discovered a *curious circle of dead skin on my stomach. If I had told anyone what had happened to us, they would have thought us mad."

In 1992, she had a flashback of the experience and decided to contact the British UFO Research Association, and after discussing the matter with them she agreed to undergo hypnotic regression – after just one session, she became aware of having been the subject of some medical operation performed while aboard the *'craft'*:

> "I could see faces around me, while something was done to my stomach. There was no pain – just faces, with large eyes. They looked like ordinary people, rather than anything alien in image."

She drew a tall muscular man, in a grey jumpsuit, with reddish-golden hair, standing at an instrument panel with a clipboard, who told her his name was *'Aplouff'*.

Mysterious circles found on the body

*According to John G. Fuller, Barney Hill was to tell of the appearance of a number of warts on his groin, forming a perfect circle, which appeared a few weeks after the incident. It may well be that this is coincidental to the ring mark noticed by Bridget, or what appears to be a similar medical anomaly discovered by motorist David McMurray and his wife, Susan, who had a 'close encounter' along the B311 road in Bagshot Heath, Surrey, on the 15th September 1985, involving the sighting of a saucer-shaped object. Shortly after the event David found himself experiencing disturbed sleep, accompanied by memory flashbacks of the UFO incident, and these coincided with memory lapses. He then noticed an outbreak of small red circles, about one and a quarter inch in diameter, on his body. The first one appeared on the side of his neck and lasted for a few hours. As this faded away, another appeared.

Even stranger and worryingly was the fact that red rings, which had previously appeared only on the left-hand side of his body – neck, shoulder, trunk and groin – had repeated themselves during the event, plus 17-22 days on the right-hand side of his body, in a similar pattern. He also became aware that, at odd moments in his mind, he was explaining the function of various mechanical and electrical domestic appliances, such as the electric light switch when in the house, and the mechanism of the car and engine while out driving. The strangest thing of all was a message running through his head almost continuously – 'Epsilon 44L-47L'. (Full details in Volume 9, *Haunted Skies*.)

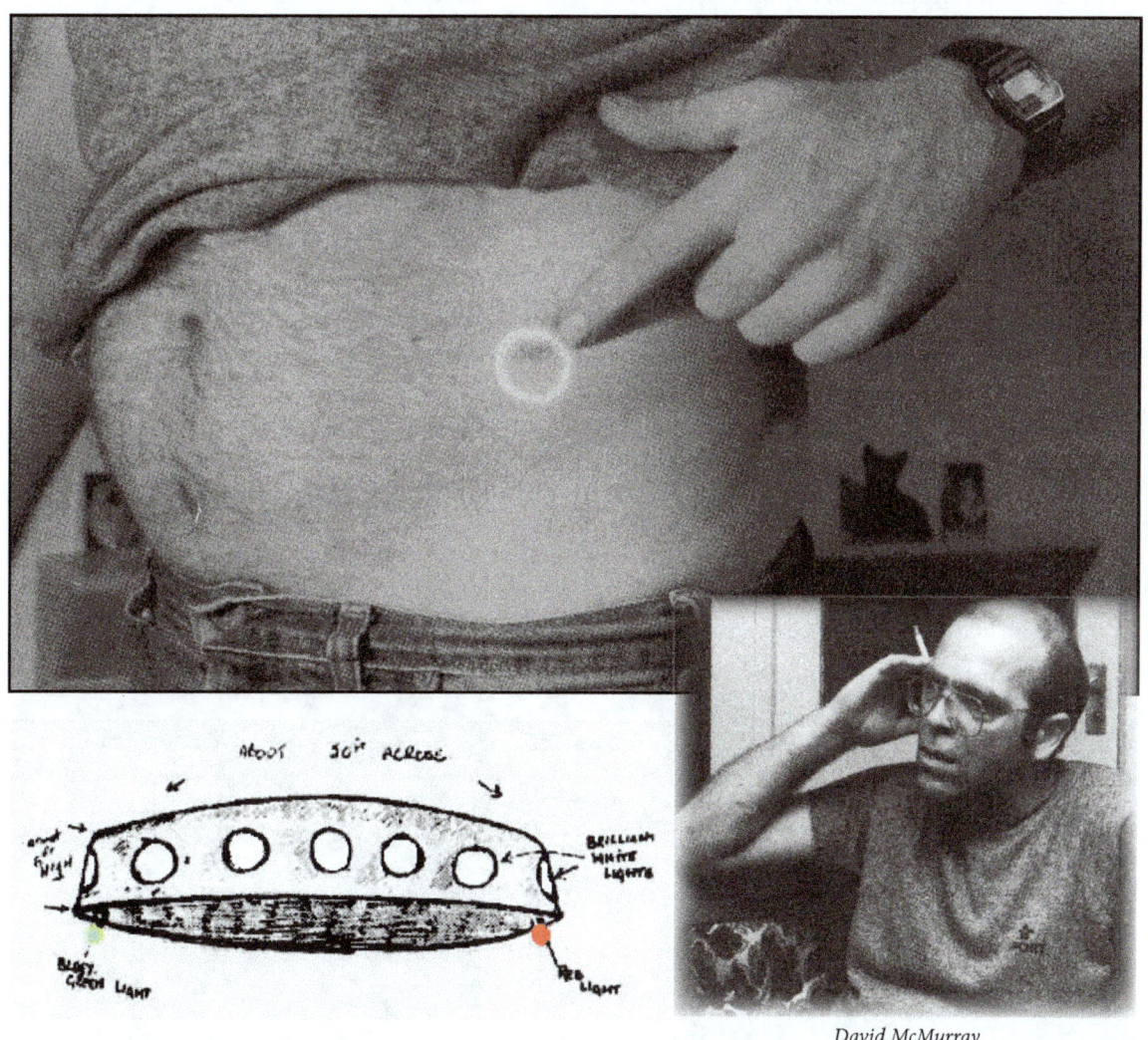

David McMurray

Haunted Skies Volume Ten

In July 1986, Gordon Creighton – editor of *Flying Saucer Review* – received a letter from a retired nurse (then aged 72) living in California, who told him of a very strange and rather disturbing account which had happened on 26th February 1986. In Volume 9 of *Haunted Skies*, we outlined her sightings, which involved the appearance of an object outside her window and of being rendered unconscious by something that came out of the UFO. Following the event she told him:

> *"As the headaches were of concern, I didn't pay much attention to an itchy spot that I found in the left groin area. I eventually became annoyed and curious, because I couldn't feel anything there, so I took a mirror and found a perfect ring or circle – a bit smaller than a 25cent piece – and very red inside the ring. It appeared as though some sort of suction had been applied, for the blood appeared to be just under the surface of the skin. The circle has gradually disappeared after a few months; the itch has gone. The headaches are diminishing in frequency. I kept thinking if these were 'weapons' following the larger craft, what they could do to the nearby Strategic Air Command Base and the aircraft there?"*

(Sources: Close Encounter on Bagshot Heath, Page 2, *FSR*, Volume 31, 1986/*SundayMirror*, 29.9.1985 – 'Our UFO Terror'/*FSR*, Volume 31, No. 6, 1986, Omar Fowler/Gordon Creighton)

UK: 27th February 1968 – Motorist sees 'flying saucer' with occupants, Devon

On the 27th February 1968, Police Constable 285 Herbert Edward Hawkins was on duty at Bridgwater Police Station, when lorry driver Andrew Norman Perry (37) of Adscombe Avenue, Bridgwater, approached him in a clearly agitated condition.

From copies of the original police statements, submitted to the Chief Constable and RAF, he said:

> *"I have seen something, just now, which I never hope to see again."*

PC Hawkins took him into another room and was then told by Mr Perry, that he had seen a *'flying saucer'*, or similar (mushroom-shaped) object, at 6.55pm, on the Crediton side of Winkleigh, in a field with *"five or six 'men', about 4ft in height, stood [sic] near to the object"*.

PC Hawkins:

> *"Perry was clearly suffering from shock, and kept repeating how frightening it had been when he had seen the object and 'men' in the field."*

At this point, PC83 (Acting Police Sergeant) Derek Davis took over the enquiry.

After being given the gist of what had transpired between PC Hawkins and Mr Perry A/Sgt Derek Davis went over to him,

> "... and noticed how terrified he looked. His complexion was white. I went through the report again and was confident, in my opinion, this was not a man who had been drinking and appeared to be a reasonable, unimaginative, person of average intelligence."

The officer then asked Mr Perry if he would be willing to accompany him back to the scene and show him where it had happened. After some perhaps understandable reluctance, Mr Perry then agreed. By the time they reached the location there was nothing to be seen.

UK: 20th November 1968 – Motorist sees 'flying saucer' and occupants

At 5.50pm, Mr & Mrs Milakovic from Hednesford, near Cannock Chase, Staffordshire, were driving home with their small child, past Hanbury Hall, when their attention was caught by a number of rabbits running across the road in front of their car, as if frightened by something, followed by the appearance of a brilliantly-lit object, which rose slowly upwards from the field on their left, passing over the car. Mr Milakovic slammed on the brakes. The family watched, as the UFO headed towards a nearby house, some 100 yards away, where it took up a stationary position above it, appearing to be,

> "... quivering, like a jelly. We felt warm, although this soon passed when the object moved away. It was as big as a house in size and silent. We couldn't see anything on the object rotating, although we did see several figures, 'human' from their silhouettes, walking backwards and forwards across the brilliantly-lit top portion. Occasionally, some of the figures would bend down, as if looking for something in the object below the rim. Except for the three lights and the 'figures', nothing else was visible in the upper part of the craft. The object then began to move away in a series of pulsating, jerky movements, shining with light – so intense, it hurt the eyes to look at if for too long".

Haunted Skies Volume Ten

After details of the incident were later published by the *Wolverhampton Express and Star* newspaper, the family was contacted by Stafford UFO Researcher, Mr Wilfred Daniels, who conducted a search of the area where the incident had taken place. However, he was unable to identify the whereabouts of a distinctive house, seen by the witnesses, prior to the appearance of the UFO, although the absence of this building did not detract what Mr Daniels believed to be a very genuine account.

(Source: Wilfred Daniels/NMH Turner, *FSR, The Milakovic Report,* 1968/*FSR,* Volume 15, No. 1)

USA: 6th January 1976 – UFO encounter, Kentucky – Missing time: One hour 25 minutes

Another extraordinary UFO sighting caught our attention – this time from Kentucky, United States. The 1st February issue of the *Kentucky Advocate*, published at Danville, Kentucky, reported on UFO sightings in that general area. It included a report from Louise Smith (44), Mona Stafford (35) and Elaine Thomas (48), who were driving home to Liberty from a late dinner at The Redwoods Restaurant, located five miles north of Stanford. At a point about one mile south of Stanford, they saw a huge metallic grey, disc-shaped object, with a white glowing dome. A row of red lights rotated around the middle, and underneath were three or four red and yellow lights that burned steadily. A bluish beam of light issued from the base. It then moved across the road to their left, circling behind and above some houses, and then came back to the highway and swung in behind the car, lighting its upside with a bluish light.

Louise Smith initially thought it was a police state trooper, approaching from behind, but realised, almost immediately, that it wasn't. Louise and Mona started to panic. The car began to pull to the left and Louise screamed at Mona to help her control it. The speedometer was registering 85mph and both Mona and Elaine Thomas shouted at Louise to slow down. Louise held her foot in the air to show them, and said:

"I don't have my foot on the accelerator and I can't stop it!"

Mona reached over and grabbed the wheel and they fought the force together. Then, quite suddenly, the women experienced a burning sensation in their eyes and Louise later described an additional pain, which seemed to *"go right through the top of my head! It was almost unbearable"*.

Pulled backwards!

Some force pulled the car backward; as it did so, they felt as if it was going over a series of *'speed bumps'*. Mrs Thomas urged Louise to stop, so that she could get a good look at the object, but Mona and Louise were too terrified. Elaine had only a glimpse of the object as it circled to their left, then around behind her, and was later to comment about the object's beauty.

"I can't describe it", she said, *"I've never seen red that beautiful. I wanted to get out and look at it."*

The women then saw a strange, wide, *'lighted road',* stretching as far as they could see, ahead of them. At the same moment, Mona noted a red light on the instrument panel, which indicated that the engine had stalled, despite the sensation they were moving very fast. A split second later, the women saw a street light ahead and realised that they were coming into Hustonville, a full eight miles beyond, where they had encountered the strange aircraft.

They wondered among themselves how they had reached there so fast, and then became quiet while they proceeded on into Liberty.

When they arrived at Mrs Smith's trailer, they all went inside. Mrs Smith experienced a variety of physiological reactions, including the impressions that her right arm was pinned or fastened; her left leg forced back under her, with pain to the ankle and foot, pressure on the fingers of the left hand – as if they were being forced or squeezed in some way – and a feeling of being examined by four or five short humanoids, who sat around in *'surgical masks'* and *'surgical garments',* while observing her. At one point, she sensed that she was either experiencing out-of-the-body travel, or else she was waiting outside a large room, in which she could view another person – probably a woman – lying on a white bed, or observation table. She perceived a long tunnel or a view of the sky – as if she had been transported to an area inside a large mountain or volcano.

Physical injuries

All three had a red mark on the backs of their necks, measuring about three inches long and one inch wide, with clearly defined edges, giving the appearance of a new burn before it blisters. Louise and Elaine's marks were centrally located between the bases of their skulls and the top of the back, whereas Mona's was located to the left, behind her ear. They could not account for the marks, which disappeared two days later. All three were experiencing burning and tearing of their eyes, but Mona Stafford had a much more severe case of conjunctivitis (an inflammation of the conjunctiva membrane of the eyes). Prior to washing her hands, Louise had taken off her watch and was startled to see that the hands of her watch were moving at an accelerated rate of speed; the minute hand moving at the speed of a second hand, and the hour hand was moving also. Upon experiencing the pain of the water on her hands and face, she forgot about the phenomena of the watch and does not recall when it returned to normal or when she reset it.

Regression

Mrs Thomas relived the UFO experience, her main impression of having been taken away from her two friends, and of being placed in a *'chamber',* with a window on the side. She seemed to recall *'figures'* which moved back and forth in front of the window of the chamber – as if she were being observed. Her impression was that the observers were 4ft tall humanoids, with dark eyes and grey skin. One disturbing aspect of the experience was the memory recall of some kind of contraption or *'covering',* placed around her neck; whenever she tried to speak, or think, the contraption or *'covering'* was tightened, and she experienced a choking sensation during these moments. At first, Mrs Thomas interpreted the memories as indication that she was being choked by hands, or that she was being prevented from calling out to her friends. Later, however, she came to the tentative conclusion that an experiment was being conducted, and the experiment was to learn more about her intellectual and emotional processes. She recalled a *'bullet-shaped'* object, about an inch and one half in diameter, being placed on her left chest; she previously had experienced pain and a red spot at that location.

(Source: MUFON [Mutual UFO Network] investigator, Jerry Black)

Haunted Skies Volume Ten

UK: 16th July 1981 – Motorist encounters UFO – Missing time: 55 minutes

Valerie Walters, Rosemary Hawkins and Vivien Heywood, were returning home from a nightclub at Shrewsbury, along a stretch of the A5, early one morning.

Valerie:

> "I looked out of the front window and saw, slightly to the left of the car and in front of us, the base of a strange 'craft', hovering a couple of hundred feet in the air above, forming a perfect circle, with two red lights in the middle and four very bright yellow/white lights spaced evenly around the inner rim of the outer edge, which illuminated a grey metallic surface in appearance, accompanied by a low buzzing noise coming from it, despite the car engine running. I heard Vivien shout out, 'The car's losing power. There's something wrong with the engine'. I felt disorientated and, looking out of the window, had a notion there was something wrong with the landscape. It seemed different, as if we were travelling along an unfamiliar route. It was like something out of a science fiction film. Rosemary wanted to stop the car to get a closer look. Vivienne refused. She put her foot down hard, but things seemed to go into slow motion. When I looked through the window again, I could see it quite low down in the field next to us, enabling me to see it sideways, when I saw a row of windows and a dome, which lit up the field below it, highlighting a nearby oak tree in its brilliance – then it was higher up in the sky, showing windows, dome, and bottom of the 'craft'. As it went upwards, the white lights dimmed, before it vanished from view. We seemed to have been watching it for only a few minutes, but found ourselves driving past the Shamrock Café, which was only a minute's drive from where we had first seen the UFO."

Hypnotic Regression carried out

> "Following some initial enquiries made into the matter by a UFO organisation, it was suggested that we might like to try hypnotic regression to find out what had happened during the missing time. Our first hypnosis sessions took place in September 1981, when Harry Harris, Norman Collinson, Mike Sacks, and hypnotist – Dr. Joseph Jaffe, were present. In Christmas 1981 another session took place, involving just myself, Harry Harris and Dr. Albert Kellar."

Valerie also spoke of seeing Vivienne staring straight ahead in the car.

> "In the moonlight I saw small human-like creatures, moving towards the car and approaching the passenger door. The door was opened. Rosemary screamed that they were trying to pull her out and was resisting furiously. A black mist enveloped her and she was gone. I remember climbing out of the car. Vivienne was still comatose. I was aware of walking through an open gate into the field, feeling completely bewildered. I felt a pair of hands placed on my shoulders from the rear, and a strong masculine voice said to me 'Don't be afraid'."

Star Map drawn in 1991

On 24th April 1991, the respective parties assembled once again at Harry's house. The two women were taken back to the strange rooms and questioned about the *'tunnels'*, but became

Haunted Skies Volume Ten

Another star map connected with the encounter

very confused and refused to answer any further questions. *Roy Dutton, who was also present, asked the hypnotist if he could speak to them, and was given permission to do so. He told them that he had made a full transcript of the conversations and was puzzled why they were now reluctant to answer the questions. Rosemary replied:

"You haven't asked the right questions."

Roy asked them some questions about a *'star map'* which was mentioned in conversation and handed a pencil and pad to Rosemary, who was then asked to try and draw what she could remember of the map, which she agreed to, and was then awoken. The minutes ticked by, as Rosemary struggled to draw the diagram, but eventually, she finished and handed the map back to Roy. Valerie was asked to do the same. The session then came to a close. (See Volume 8 of *Haunted Skies* for a fuller account of this incident).

*Terrence Roy Dutton was a member of the Special Projects Office, Weapons Research Division of A.V. Roe and Co. Ltd., located at Woodford Airfield, Bramhall, in Cheshire. He believes that the Earth is under surveillance by strange aerial craft. Roy's analysis correlates the time and location of thousands of UFO sightings and compares them with astronomical paths in space around the Earth. After years of analysis, Roy has refined his model and can predict particular locations when a UFO visitation is most likely. In 2011 he published *Programmed Aerospace Monitors of Our Species* by Author House.

Haunted Skies Volume Ten

UK: 27th October 1974 – Motorist encounters UFO, Essex – Missing time: Three hours

John Day (32) and Elaine Day (28) accompanied by their three children, Karen (11) Kevin (10) and Stuart (7) set out from Harold Hill, Essex, at about 9.50pm, anticipating that they would be home within 20 minutes. John drove along Hacton Lane (a mile away from Hornchurch) in his white Vauxhall Victor car, on what was a beautiful clear night – mild and dry, with little traffic about. Karen and Stuart were asleep in the back of the car. Kevin was awake, looking out of the window.

Suddenly, Kevin brought his father's attention to a light he could see above a line of terraced houses, to their left. John and Elaine glanced around and saw an oval-shaped light, bluish iridescent, resembling a large star, about 30° off the horizon, approximately 500 yards away; it seemed to be travelling in a similar direction to their car, in a series of stopping and starting movements.

The time was now 10.10pm. Karen and Stuart remained asleep. John again remarked on the absence of traffic on the road. The *'light'*, was now still about the same distance away – some 500 yards. About half-a-mile east along Park Farm Road, the *'light'* appeared to have changed course to south-easterly, and was now observed heading towards the road at an angle of 50°. As they began to negotiate a right-hand turn, with a block of four terraced houses to their right, they had a terrible feeling that something was wrong, as the sound of the engine and tyres on the road receded into the background – just the radio still playing.

> "In front of us, some 30 yards away, covering the whole road, was a green mist or fog/gas bank, about 9ft high, bordered on the left by bushes, its right-hand part curved to the ground behind a thin line of trees along the verge of the road. Its top was flat; the bottom was touching the ground. The car radio began to crackle and smoke. I pulled the wires out of the back of it and disconnected the appliance – then the lights on the car failed. Everything went black as darkness settled – the 'fog', unlike any fog I had ever seen, engulfed us. The windows were up; Kevin was standing on the floor behind the other two children, who were still asleep. It was 'light' inside the fog and very cold, dead silent. I could feel a tingling sensation – things seemed hazy – then there was a jolt, like the car going over a hump-back bridge, and seconds later the mist or fog was gone. The oddest thing was that I felt I was alone in the car. My next recollection was being aware of driving along the side of White Post Wood, exactly half-a-mile away!"

Sketch based on drawing by John of the 'green mist'

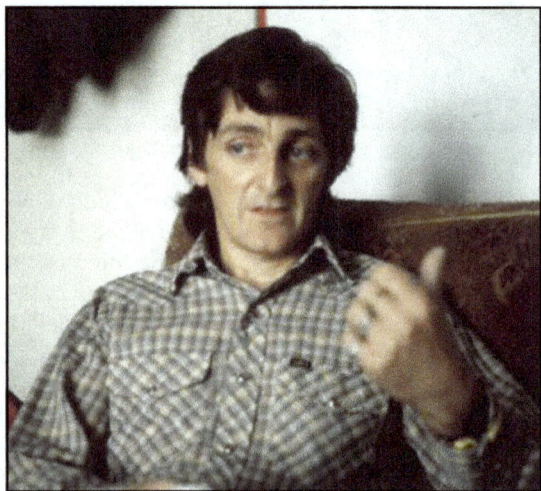

John Day

Haunted Skies Volume Ten

Arriving home

On reaching home John was surprised to discover the time was now 1am. This seemed impossible, as they had expected to have arrived home at 10.20pm, which meant there were three hours of time they were unable to account for. The next day, Elaine telephoned her mother and told her about the incident, but didn't mention about the *'missing time'*. Both John and Elaine felt tired, but all three children went to school as normal. In conversation about the matter, the couple decided that they should try and forget about it.

We were not surprised to hear that, after the event, John was to develop a new found interest in art, craft, and writing poetry. Such changes in behaviour appear common, following UFO close encounters like that described by John and Elaine. In addition, the couple was to complain of physical interruptions to power supply and electrical devices within the family household, together with sightings of strange noises and shapes seen.

Shortly after the encounter, John and Elaine became aware they were being followed, on a number of occasions (individually) by three cars – a small red *'sports'* car, a blue Jaguar, and a large white car (Ford Executive?). The number plates were the British new-style yellow at the front, with white at the rear. All of the vehicles had darkened windows.

In addition, the couple began to have strange recurring dreams, involving *'being operated on'* by small, ugly beings, resembling gnomes.

Hypnotic regressions

John and Elaine also took part in three hypnotic regressions, which took place on 25th September 1977, the 2nd October and 16th October 1977. During those sessions, conducted by Dr. Leonard Wilder – a qualified hypnotherapist and dentist by profession – John described:

> "... tall hooded beings, with pink eyes, wearing one-piece suits, and tables made out of a peculiar substance – not wood or metal. A thick honeycombed bar, apparently made of metal approximately 30ins long, by 10ins wide, was moved over my body, causing a vibrating sensation. I noticed a small *'being'* present, he was clothed in what looked like *'fur'* – but it wasn't fur. He touched my left shoulder and I passed out. When I regained consciousness, I found myself lying on a table, two and-a-half feet wide, a few feet off the ground. The surface of the table was soft and covered with small grey bubbles. Eighteen inches above my head was a *'scan'* type of apparatus, rectangular-shaped, 30-36ins in length, about 3ins. in width, approximately one inch thick, with an underside of honeycombed design, supported by two circular rods, one on each side of me. The device took about one minute to pass over my body, creating a warm, tingling, sensation. I then became aware of three tall entities to my right, and two small, ugly looking ones to the left, referred to as *'examiners'* who were four feet tall – no apparent neck – with large, slanted triangular eyes, light brown nose or beak, a slither for the mouth, pointed, slanted back ears, large hairy hands – four digits on each, with claws or long nails. This *'being'* walked awkwardly, making an occasional guttural chirp"

John asked the tall entities if he could get up. *"Sit there for a while"*, he was told, startled, realising that the words were not spoken, but received telepathically. Shortly afterwards, he was allowed to get up. The *'examiners'* then left the room, at which point he became aware that he was dressed in a one-piece garment, similar to what the tall entities were wearing.

Haunted Skies Volume Ten

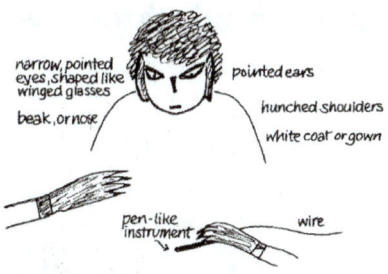

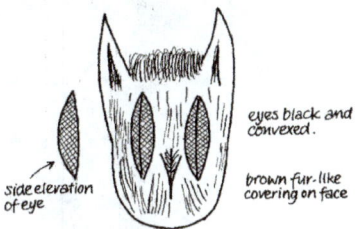

Based on an early attempt by Elaine to draw one of the small entities or 'examiners'.

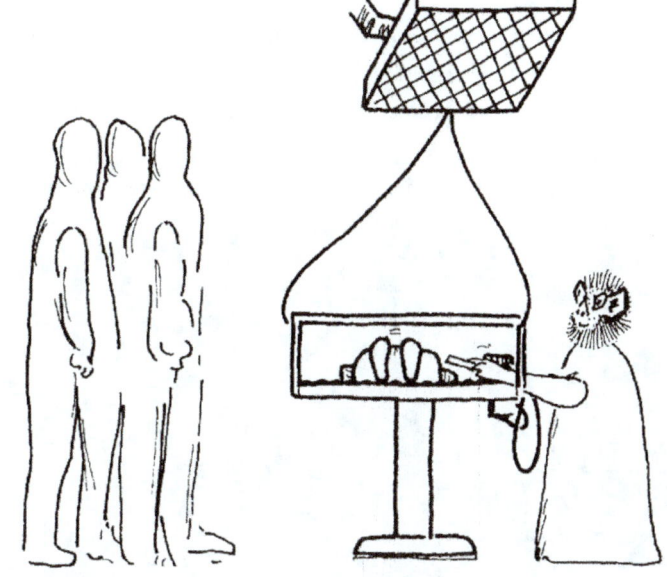

Early impression by John of an 'examiner'.

Right: Based on John's impression of himself on the examining table, while the 'three' watch 'examiner' at work.

"The room was oval-shaped, perhaps 20ft in length, by 12ft in width, and about 7-8ft high – very smooth, like being inside a bubble – the only furniture being the table and two overhead lights."

John described the taller entities to be 6ft. 6ins tall, except the 'leader', who appeared to be 2ins taller.

"They all appeared to be wearing a one-piece suit, made of material resembling lurex or synthetic felt, that even covered their hands and feet. They had two eyes, slightly larger than ours, with pink irises and creamy eyeballs. No nose or mouth was seen, and I speculated whether they were wearing masks. I saw what appeared to be only three fingers on each hand, and their skin looked very pale – almost transparent. They reminded me of a 'bendy toy' or 'blow up doll' when they moved, as they seemed devoid of joints in their arms or legs, yet walked gracefully but with no long strides."

During his entire onboard encounter, the tallest entity was the only *'being'* that John had direct contact with. John asked these beings what they did when they went outside their *'ship'*, and was told that they used a visor – which was shown to him.

We felt this was one of the most detailed accounts we had ever come across, involving considerable conversation between the parties known as the *'Watchers'*, who told John they had formerly inhabited the planet long ago.

We wish John, Sue, and his family, all the best with their new lives.

(Source: Andrew Collins, UFOIN/The Aveley Abduction, *FSR*, Volume 23, No. 6, April 1978/Volume 24, No. 1, *FSR*, June 1978, The Aveley Abduction/Personal interviews, John Day)

Haunted Skies **Volume Ten**

UK: 23rd January 1976 – UFOs over Bolton, Lancashire – family threatened!

At 5.15pm, 'Shelley' from Bolton, Lancashire [her real name is known to us] was walking home, past Rumworth Lodge Reservoir, when she sighted:

> *"…a spinning metallic 'disc', ablaze with lights, flat on the top, with sloping sides, three lights and three legs"*

which swooped over her. As a result of this, she was to complain of crumbled dental fillings, burn marks on her arm and side, nausea and vomiting, and the discovery of a strange purple rash on her neck and shoulders.

On 2nd February 1976 'Shelley's' mother received a telephone call from a man who declined to identify himself, but told her he was *'an investigator of such things'* and asked her whether *'any marks had been left on the girl's body'*. She put the telephone down, declining to discuss the matter with him.

At 7pm the same day, two men arrived at the home address of 'Shelley' and demanded to interview the girl, described as both being aged about 40 years old, wearing crisp black suits – one of them tall and almost blonde. Although the father initially declined to let them in, the men persisted. One of them said, threateningly:

> *"If you do not let us in now, we will come back later and make 'Shelley' speak to us."*

In a subsequent hypnotic regression, performed by Dr. Albert Kellar, from Manchester, 'Shelley' reacted in absolute terror to the visit by the *'two men'* and the Doctor was forced to abandon the treatment because of a dangerous rise in her vital signs. We spoke to Peter Hough, in 2008, about the incident.

> *"Yes – I only ever referred to her as 'Shelley'. Interesting that you have tracked her down after all these years – I last spoke to her in 1988! At the time of the experience (1976?) she was only a 17-year-old receptionist. My feelings still are that this was a genuine example of the phenomenon and exhibited many of the key components; sighting of unusual object, missing time (although no full-blown abduction account), physical effects, subsequent visit by the MIB (verified to me by her parents) and post-experience paranormal abilities. This was at a time when details of the abduction phenomenon was not widely publicised, and therefore it was less likely that they had been fabricated."*

(Source: *Bolton Evening News*, 24.1.1976 – 'Girl spots UFO'/Peter Hough)

UK: 17th March 1978 – Alien seen at nuclear power station – Missing time: 45 minutes

At 11.30pm, Kenneth Edwards (39) – a Service Engineer by occupation – was travelling home to Fernhead, along the Dayton Road, towards Risley, when he noticed, in the glare of the van's headlights, an object on his right-hand side, moving down a short embankment between the AA Relay Station and the University Reactor (part of the Atomic Energy Commission administration centre).

> "As I approached closer, I realised it was a 'figure' stood in the middle of the road, with its 'head' turning towards me, showing two pencil lights for eyes.
>
> I watched as it continued along its journey, before it stopped, brought its hands up to waist height, and then walked straight through a 10ft high security fence."

As a result of his telephone call to Padgate Police, officers arrived at the scene and made a search of the area, along with security guards from the power station – but found nothing, although a gap was discovered in the wire fence close to where the *'figure'* was last seen.

Jenny Randles and Peter Hough later visited Mr Edwards, after his sighting had been made public, when they discovered he was *'unable to account for 45 minutes of lost time. His watch had stopped, and he had sustained sunburn to one of his fingers'*.

Sadly, Mr Edwards passed away four years later, from cancer of the kidney and throat, triggered, some believe, from exposure to the fields of energy that were present – powerful enough to cause severe damage to the transceiver installed in the van, rendering it unusable. Examination of a copy file relating to the incident, sent to us by the Manchester UFO Group (MUFORA), included the original illustration, as drawn by Mr Edwards.

(Source: As above/Tony Pace, BUFORA)

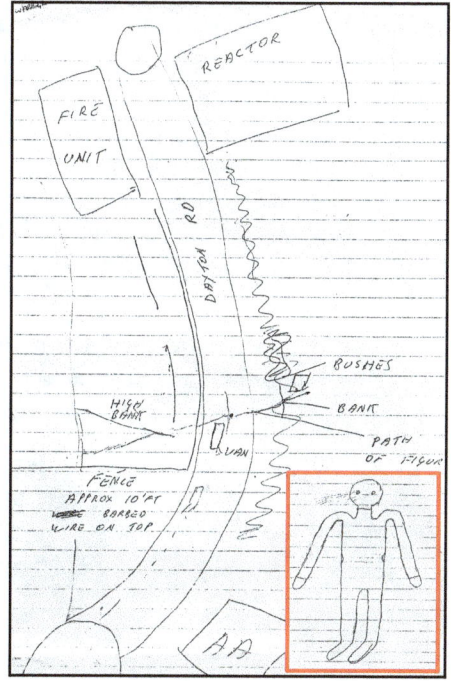

19th June 1978 – The Janos People, allegation of abduction, with missing time

At 1.15am, Michelle Lovis from Elm Green, Hertfordshire, was driving home, after babysitting for a friend, when she noticed that the night sky was a vivid bright yellow, accompanied by a strange noise. After a while, the noise stopped but started up again. Michelle was not the only witness to this unusual phenomenon. Other people also reported having seen the weird glowing sky. The Meteorological Office suggested a possible explanation to be the reflection of aircraft lights in the clouds!

Later, the same day, John and Gloria Mann from Brockworth, Gloucestershire, were to encounter a saucer-shaped craft, while travelling near the Oxfordshire village of Stanford-in-the-Vale. Full details of the family's extraordinary account, involving allegations of alien abduction, accompanied by those now all too familiar traits of UFO behaviour, including missing time, unfamiliar landscape, and strange marks found on their bodies, were later published in a book, entitled: *The Janos People*, by Frank Johnson (Neville Spearman Publishers).

UK: 22nd November 1978 – UFO over Northampton

Schoolteacher Mrs Elsie Oakensen was on her way home from Daventry, on the late afternoon, when she saw a dumb-bell shaped object in the sky. This was followed by the car coming to a stop, and beams of lights falling around her. She remains perplexed by what happened, and the discovery of a strange scar, just behind her knee, and speculates whether she was the subject of an abduction orchestrated by an *'alien'* species, whose presence she believes was benevolent, rather than hostile. (Full details in *Haunted Skies*, Volume 7).

UK: 17th March 1979 – UFO over Hertfordshire, strange star seen

At 7pm on 17th March 1979, Rosina Kirk – a housewife from Puckeridge (seven miles north of Hertford) – and her daughter, were travelling in the back seat of a car being driven by Valerie (her son's girlfriend) along the A10, towards the town, having just passed the 'Foxholes' roundabout in heavy traffic. Mrs Kirk noticed what she thought was a *'star'*, hovering in the sky. Puzzled by its brilliance, she continued to watch it as the car slowly moved along.

> *"It looked like a gigantic ball – nothing like an artificial satellite. Suddenly, what looked like smoke came out and covered it – that faded, and was replaced by four ordinary white lights, set at each point on the outside of the 'globe'. It then began to move northward, passing from my point of view – now rotating in flight. My daughter was also watching it. She screamed, 'Oh, my God, it's coming down on the car'. As it approached, two red lights appeared together on its underside. These were dimmer than the others.*
>
> *As it passed overhead, I saw four protrusions. They looked like legs – short, thin, and black in colour – projecting down from its underside, which also rotated around the object."*

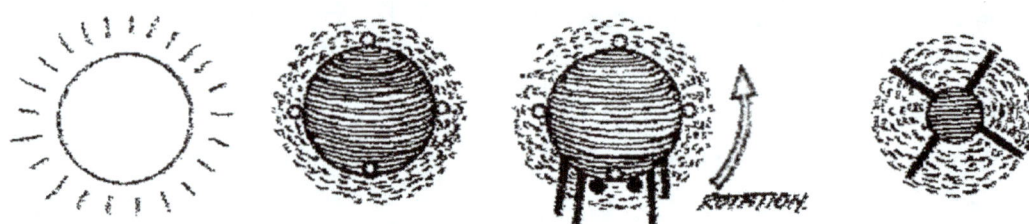

At this point, Mrs Kirk and the other occupants of the vehicle began to feel dizzy, suffering the sort of effect one would have when looking at strobe lights for some period. When they next looked up, it was now receding into the distance – five minutes after they had first seen it.

Feeling that surely somebody else must have seen this object, Mrs Kirk contacted the local newspaper – *Hertfordshire Mercury* – who published her story on the 6th April. As a result of this they established an unnamed family, consisting of two males and two females, also saw what they described as a yellow *'ball'*, which hovered at first, before moving over the road. PC Tony Faulkener interviewed the family, who told him:

> *"A partly obscuring vapour was seen around the object, which showed four red lights and what looked like two 'legs' on its top and bottom. The two passengers in the car felt sick and experienced misty vision. Just before we saw it, the car lights went dim and the music faded from the radio cassette, playing at the time."*

(Source: Police Constable Tony Faulkener, Hertfordshire Constabulary)

UK: 1979 – Close Encounter, near Manchester, missing time: One hour 30 minutes

Lynda Jones (36) was walking along the banks of the *River Mersey* at Didsbury, with her two children, as dusk fell, during summer of 1979, when they noticed:

> "... an oval, pink/red spinning object – like an aircraft on fire – apparently travelling towards us across the sky, at 9pm."

Lynda walked towards it, wondering, "... *if I would be looking in at them and watching what they were doing*", realising the danger they were in, and ran back home with the children. Trevor (Lynda's husband) asked them what was wrong and why the skin around her eyes was red and scaly. Lynda explained what had taken place to Trevor. He asked them to draw, individually, the strange object. When this was done, it was clear that they had all seen the object in the same way, described as:

> "... looking in two parts; the bottom of the object was nothing like what is generally reported as a UFO. The bottom of it looked like the shape of a boat, apparently made of some type of lattice – grey in colour, with small 'round things' all over it. The top part was just light."

Lynda suddenly thought, '*Why is Trevor here? He doesn't normally get home until 10.30 pm.*'

When she looked at the time, she was astounded to discover it was 10.50pm., which meant she was unable to remember why a journey of some 10 minutes (the length of time it took to run back to the house, from the time they saw the object, at 9pm) should have taken so long.

Eventually, Lynda was persuaded to take part in a series of hypnotic regressions, carried out with the assistance of Manchester Solicitor – Harry Harris.

The gist of those sessions, carried out, obtained the following information:

> "I remember the point when we had turned to run from the object. I saw several people running towards it. They looked like men, dressed in long dark coats and wearing trilby hats, holding what looked like satchels, with a strange mist that surrounded them. When they got close to the object, they simply disappeared. Every time I tried to see what was going on, a bright light would shine in my eyes."

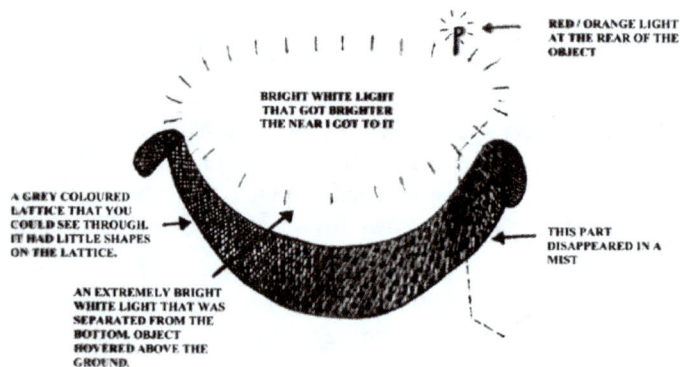

The regression was to also unlock painful and very personal memories, involving medical examination, carried out inside the *'craft'* by *'beings'*, in a similarity of behaviour echoed, countless times over, worldwide. Lynda was to also discover strange marks on her body, which had not been there before the encounter. This was neither the first or last time we were to hear of a sinister individual(s) wearing what was described as a trilby hat, following the sighting of a UFO – ridiculous as it first sounds. Some people believe their odd mannerisms and bizarre clothing suggest they are alien-human hybrids, and that their purpose is to silence UFO witnesses by intimidation, even on occasion after the witness has, through the media, published their account – very much a case of 'locking the stable door after the horse has bolted!'

(Source: Steve Mera, MAPIT (Manchester's Association of Paranormal Investigators & Training/Personal interviews)

Jane – extract from her story over a twelve year period

In July 1987, Jane from Birstall, West Yorkshire, was interviewed on a number of occasions, by UFO Investigators Philip Mantle and Andy Roberts, with regard to what she had experienced over a twelve year period. She was asked to describe the aliens she met. Initially, she could only remember their eyes, which were completely black or blue in colour, and larger than human ones.

> "Their hair was like doll's hair. They were human in appearance, but not quite human. They were about 7ft tall; there were both male and female species of the aliens, although I did not notice any physical extremities as the ones which distinguish male and female humans."

In March, 1987, Jane, who retired to bed late – suddenly awoke to find herself standing in a field, feeling very cold and wet. She then noticed a huge metallic object, hovering over the field. Suddenly, a group of *'figures'* (as many as ten) approached her. The *'figures'* were vaguely humanoid, but for some reason Jane found herself unable to focus on them.

> "One of the *'figures'* had a cloth in his hand and put it over my face. I pretended to be unconscious but they injected me; I blacked out. I acted as if I was asleep, but *'they'* weren't fooled. The next thing I knew was being injected in the arm and then lost consciousness. I was then aware of being on a couch or a table. I was instructed to wash in a type of shower or bath, apparently constructed to hold a human being in shape. My sexual organs were examined. I was then led to a table close to the *'aliens'*, on the top of which was a number of what looked like *'sweets'* displayed. I took one, and was about to eat another, when I was told quite forcibly, by one of the aliens, not to."

UK: 15th February 1995 – UFO, the number '22', and 40 minutes of missing time

In 2013, we interviewed John from rural Gloucestershire.

At 9.45pm he was driving home along the M5 to Newent, having left work at 9.30pm – a regular journey taken over the last seven years – and had covered a distance of nine-and-a-quarter miles, normally taking 15 minutes maximum. He saw a bright *'light'* in what was a starless night, low down in the sky, racing across fields towards his position.

> "I first thought that it must be a helicopter, or aircraft, but once again lost sight of it, due to the side of the road. As I came out of the other side of the bridge, an intense 'light' dropped down onto my car; it wasn't like a searchlight and I could still see the dipped headlights of the car. This light flooded the inside of the car. I looked and saw, with utmost astonishment, a 'craft' pacing my vehicle, at about 50mph. I switched off the radio, put the car in neutral, and pressed the driver's side window down. I put my head out and looked up and saw an intense white 'light', showing a dark circular patch in the middle. Whether this 'patch' was a hole in the underside of the object, which I estimated, to be 80ft above me, and the length of two double-decker buses, I cannot say. Suddenly, I heard a voice in my head, saying 'Pull over and you can get a better look'. I looked along the hard shoulder for a safe place to stop, as told. At this point, as the hard shoulder disappears, due to a small road which runs underneath the motorway, there are warning barriers. Straightway, I heard the voice again – 'Unsafe, Unsafe'. I started to pull over, feeling that my actions were being guided by some form of hypnotic control, rather than my own free will. From the bridge to this point it takes about 20 seconds, during which time the light, 'craft', object – call it what you will – was now positioned above the car and between the rock faces of the opposing motorway lanes. I believe this was the time when I was abducted, as in the blink of an eye – almost like watching a frame jump in a film – I was back again and aware of my surroundings. The car was in 5th gear and I am driving at 50mph; everything seemed normal, when I heard a voice, saying, 'Don't stop now – keep going. There is no traffic either side of the motorway. Keep going'. I remember saying out aloud to myself 'Where's the light?', but it was now all over."

John continued on his journey and then turned off at the Gorsley sign (B4221) for Newent. He stopped the car briefly, when he saw some *'lights'* going down behind a nearby wood, but wasn't sure if this was connected with what he had just experienced. He looked at his watch; it was showing 10.22pm, which meant a short journey normally taking a few minutes had lasted 40 minutes. John noticed the lights of a car, heading away from Gorsley Golf Club. This was the first vehicle he had seen since entering the M50.

He arrived home at 10.35pm, still wondering what had happened to him. After checking the car over for any damage, or injuries caused to him, there were none.

John believes he was medically examined during the abduction process and, over the months and years that followed, experienced flashbacks of what took place, many of which caused him considerable trauma (still noticeable 28 years later).

Pair of eyes

In addition, he began to notice some very bizarre synchronicities in his life. They included the number '22'.

They included:

1. While travelling up the motorway, a stone flew up and smashed his windscreen at 2.22pm.
2. He was driving along the road when a vehicle cut in aggressively in front of him. The number plate showed 22.

Haunted Skies Volume Ten

3. One of the lottery dice '22', used at work for the firm's syndicate, went missing. This was found under the fridge, at home.

4. Templates used at work showed the number 22.

5. During a visit to a shop in Gloucester, to collect a new fridge, he discovered his car had been stolen. The thieves had left another stolen car in its place – its registration number was 22 SKY.

We feel that this may be just a complete coincidence but, if this was the case, what were the chances of the car being abandoned and later found by the police in Battledown Approach, Cheltenham, near where the Circular Forum UFO Group held their meetings!

John does not wish to be regressed, fearing it will confirm his suspicions that an abduction took place.

We wish him well and hope that in time, the painful and very personal memories that he appears to be trying to block out, will fade.

Far more other accounts – past, present and future!

The accounts (as shown above) represent just some of the incidents involving what appears to be alien beings or non-humanoid entities investigated by us, over the years – there are many more. Incredibly, despite a time period of over 20 years, we have still not reached 1990!

Chronological narrative continues ...

USA: 21st September 1961 – Doughnut-shaped UFO seen near Wake Island

Capt. R.F. Griffin was pilot of a BOAC jet, flying at 37,000ft, at about 7am, when the UFO appeared.

> "Suddenly we saw this bright 'ring' in the sky, about 50° up."

The British pilot described the object as round, with sharply outlined edges and a *'very clear hole'* in the centre.

> "It was travelling in our direction, but at far greater speed. There appeared to be reflected light coming down from it. The object went over the horizon in seven minutes."

The confirming Pan-American report was also logged at Honolulu, and the object was witnessed by the watch aboard a US ship, moving at extremely high altitude, heading south-easterly above the North Pacific – gone within 10 minutes.

On 25th September, in a surprising Press statement, the Air Force admitted being flooded with reports of *'flying objects'* near Wake Island. The pilot of a Pan-American Airways plane, about 400 miles south-east of Captain Griffin's sighted what appeared to be the same doughnut-shaped object, moving easterly, about 10° above the horizon.

A few days later, The Soviet Union announced that they had successfully tested a multi-stage carrier rocket over the Pacific (exact date not on record). However, the reported size of the UFO was far too large to be explained away as a rocket payload.

Object seen by *USS Iberville* (North and East of Midway Island)

Second Officer William C. Ash and Captain M.O. Vinson reported the following:

> *"At 1700 GMT (5pm) on 21st September 1961, while in lat. 31° 30' N, long. 175° 30' E, a few minutes before morning twilight, a white opaque mass, about twice the size of a full moon, appeared in the north-west at an elevation of about 20°. It continued to climb toward the zenith and at about an elevation of 40°, the mass opened gradually to appear as a huge halo, with a satellite in the centre, having very nearly the brightness of a first magnitude star. By the time it reached directly above, it had more than doubled in size, before then diminishing as it proceeded to the south-east. As it diminished it continued to decrease in size, but did not appear to shrink into a corona as it had appeared, but rather faded out completely at an elevation of approximately 20°. The entire mass was in view for approximately 8-10 minutes."*

The weather was partly cloudy, wind north-west, force 2, slight sea and small north-west swell, temperatures: dry 74°F, wet 67°F, sea 79°F.

(Sources: George D. Fawcett, *Psychic Observer*, Vol. 3, No. 11, Southern Pines, N.C., November 1962. FAA report to NICAP, *US Navy Oceanographic Office Publication Notice to Mariners Report*)

USA: 27th September 1961

At 7.57am, a radar operator sighted five objects on his scope over the Pacific. Four of the objects were on a heading of 90°; the other object was on a heading of (80°?). All were moving at a high rate of speed, and disappeared into sea clutter. Three minutes later, two objects appeared heading 70° and moved across the scope and also disappeared into sea clutter. The speed of one of the objects was measured at 1,800 knots over a distance of 200 nautical miles. While these two objects were on the scope, a single stationary object appeared. After remaining stationary for approximately two minutes, it moved on a heading of 265°, at 60 knots, and was lost in the sea clutter. (**Source: Dan Wilson, McDonald List**)

USA: 30th September 1961

At around 9.04am, a weather observer at Indian Springs Air Force Base, Nevada, saw objects on a 20 power theodolite, at 133.4° azimuth 55° elevation. The observer first saw one object – white or metallic in colour, round in shape and the size of the head of a pin. Four smaller objects, travelling very fast, came from the first object. The 865th Air (CW) control and Warning Squadron, Las Vegas Air Force Station, tracked a UFO on radar, 45 miles south-east of Nellis Air Force Base. The object was tracked for approximately 45 minutes. (**Source: McDonald List**)

USA: 2nd October 1961

Salt Lake City, Utah – A disc-shaped UFO was seen in the sky and manoeuvred away from investigating aircraft. (**Source: NICAP *UFOE***)

USA: 12th October 1961

Indianapolis, Indiana – A spherical UFO, with a row of pulsating lights, was viewed from many angles by different observers. (**Source: NICAP *UFOE*, XII**)

October 1961

USA: 21st October 1961 – Near Datil, New Mexico

A motorist reports four lights pacing the car, before manoeuvring and shooting away upward into the sky. **(Source: NICAP *UFOE*, II)**

November 1961

USA: 7th November 1961 – Three UFOs tracked on radar

At 1.55am, several employees of the Martin Company and Army personnel from *Arlington Heights, Illinois, observed three unusual radar returns on the long-range radar. Three objects were observed approaching the Chicago area from east-south-east, with 30 seconds separation, at speeds in excess of 4,000 knots. The radar return was very sharp. An attempt was made to determine the altitude of the objects, but their speed was beyond the capability of the equipment. After the sightings, the equipment was tested and found to be in perfect operating order. **(Source: Dan Wilson, McDonald List)**

Great Britain: 9th November 1961

Stratford-upon-Avon UFO researchers Ruby Llewellyn and husband, John 'Dennis' Llewellyn – then living in South Green Drive, Stratford-upon-Avon, watched an intermittently flashing crimson light, moving through the sky over the town, heading in a north-west direction. We had the pleasure of meeting 'Dennis' (as he liked to be called) some years ago, and were impressed with his demeanor and knowledge of the UFO subject.

USA: 21st November 1961

At 7.30pm over Old Town, Florida, Mr C. Locklear and Helen Hatch saw a round, red-orange, object fly straight up into the sky, before fading away. **(Source: Don Berliner)**

USA: 22nd November 1961 – near Grafton, North Dakota

A metallurgist observed a hovering, greyish, cigar-shaped UFO, with *'portholes'*. **(Source: NICAP *UFOE*, VI)**

USA: 23rd November 1961 – over Sioux City, Iowa

At 9.30pm, Mr F. Braunger reported having sighted a bright red *'star'* fly straight and level across the sky. **(Source: Don Berliner)**

Great Britain: 29th November 1961

At 6.15pm, Swansea resident – Alan Williams – saw an object flash across the sky, heading towards Port Talbot.

> *"It was oval-shaped, with two windows at the front – one fully in view; the other, partly. There was a dome on top. It was trailing red flames, which illuminated the object – out of sight in five seconds. It was not an aircraft, as it had no wings or tailfin."*

(Source: *Western Mail*, 22.11.1961/*LUFORO*, Vol. 3, No. 1, Jan/Feb. 1962)

---

*Arlington Heights Air Force Station was a 1960-1969 general surveillance radar station 1.8 miles (2.9 km) south-south-west of Arlington Heights, Illinois.

December 1961

Great Britain: 11th December 1961

At 10am, Mr Aubrey C. Fishel was driving near Bootle, Liverpool, when he saw an elliptical object, with a fluorescent green top, flying through the sky. A similar object was then seen to the right of the first one, leaving a thin trail of black smoke. Aubrey rejected any explanation that it was an aircraft, and was adamant he had seen *'flying saucers'*.

USA: 13th December 1961

At 5.05pm, Mr C.F. Muncy, ex-U.S. Navy pilot, Mr W.J. Myers, and Mr G. Weber, saw a dark, diamond-shaped object, with a bright tip, flying straight and level through the sky, over Washington DC. (**Source: Don Berliner**)

1962

January 1962

Australia: January 1962 – UFO over Delissaville

Crocodile shooter – Mr Roy Moffat – was in his boat, anchored up near the town, when he saw a UFO in the air above him, at a height of about 2,000ft. The object then moved away and appeared to *'buzz'* a Boeing airplane, flying at 30mph over Darwin Airport, at a height of 1,500ft. Roy, who had a camera with him, took some colour photographs of the object, and sent them away for processing. Three days later history was repeated, when Roy sighted another UFO in the sky. On this occasion, due to the camera being set for long distance, the lens failed to capture the UFO.

Mr Moffat's sighting was one of dozens reported to the RAAF and the local newspapers.

(Source: *Australian Flying Saucer Review*, 26.8.1961)

Great Britain: 13th /15th January 1962

Mysterious green fireballs were sighted flying through the sky over Southampton, in Hampshire, and Stow-on the-Wold, Gloucestershire.

On the 15th January 1962, a highly polished object – kingfisher blue in colour and as large as a football, held at arm's length – was seen rotating across the sky over Harwood, Bolton, Lancashire, by Mr H. Kirkham. It was estimated to be moving at hundreds of miles per hour. (**Source:** *Bolton Evening News*)

Was there a connection with the similar phenomena reported throughout the United States, during the late 1940s, and then sporadically over the following years?

Great Britain: 20th January 1962

A green *'ball of fire'* was seen over Stafford, by many people. Police Constable C. Fox and PC Parry saw it descending through the sky, towards Seighford Aerodrome. (**Source:** *Stafford & Mid-Staffordshire Newsletter*, 20.1.1962 – 'Opinions differ on flying object')

February 1962

Great Britain: 9th February 1962 – 'Flying saucer' sighted over Buckinghamshire

At 3.30am, Ronald Wildman (not Wildam as shown on the Internet)! from Luton, Bedfordshire (who was employed as a car delivery driver) was travelling along the A41, Ivinghoe Road, through *Aston Clinton, Buckinghamshire, to deliver a new car, when he noticed *"a large, metallic-looking object, hovering approximately 30ft off the ground, over some nearby trees"*. (Full report in Volume 2 of *Haunted Skies*)

*Over 50 years later strange lights continued to be seen around this locality according to Keith Fensom, *"We were travelling back to a friend's house at 10pm on the 12th of August 2011 when we saw two orange lights in the sky. They were too far apart to be lights on an aircraft wing. They were both travelling in the same direction but in staggered formation, I was wondering what they were, thinking if they were helicopters, but realised they were too high, and suddenly they immediately changed direction at about 90 degrees with no curve just immediate, and one of them went behind a cloud but could be seen faintly through the cloud. We then drove on and looked again but they had gone."* (**Source:** WWW.UK.co.uk)

USA: 12th February 1962

At 8.06am, S/Sgt F. Grover – a crew Chief with 11 years of radar experience, stationed at Winnemucca Air Force Base, Nevada, (658 Radar Squadron) – tracked a large target, at 74,000ft, which disappeared in excess of 96,000ft, after being on the scope for five minutes. (**Source: Dan Wilson, McDonald List**)

USA: 19th February 1962

Three people, driving south on Dauphin Island, Alabama, sighted a red-orange object, about one third of the sun's diameter, in the south direction, at 10° elevation. It was then seen to change shape to football and then cigar shape. They stopped the car and called Dauphin Island AFS radar site, 693rd Radar Squadron, which coincidentally had received a similar report from two USAF airmen, driving north on the toll bridge, who saw it in the West. The object's location was then approximately triangulated at being about 30°16' N, 88° 10' W, distance to civilian observers two to five miles, depending on how far north when first seen, actual size of at least 30ft. No radar contact reported. (**Source: J. Allen Hynek, CUFOS**)

Great Britain: February 1962

Was there any connection between the saucer-shaped object seen by Mr Wildman, and an object picked up on radar during February 1962, by the RAF, who scrambled an aircraft, already on patrol, to investigate the matter further? The incident involved United States Air Force Major George A. Filer (now retired).

The sighting was to trigger-off a lifetime's interest in UFOs. George A. Filer is currently Eastern Director of MUFON (Mutual UFO Network) and Vice President of Sky-watch International (2006). George attempted to intercept a UFO, hovering between Oxford and Stonehenge. (Full details are in Volume 2 of *Haunted Skies*)

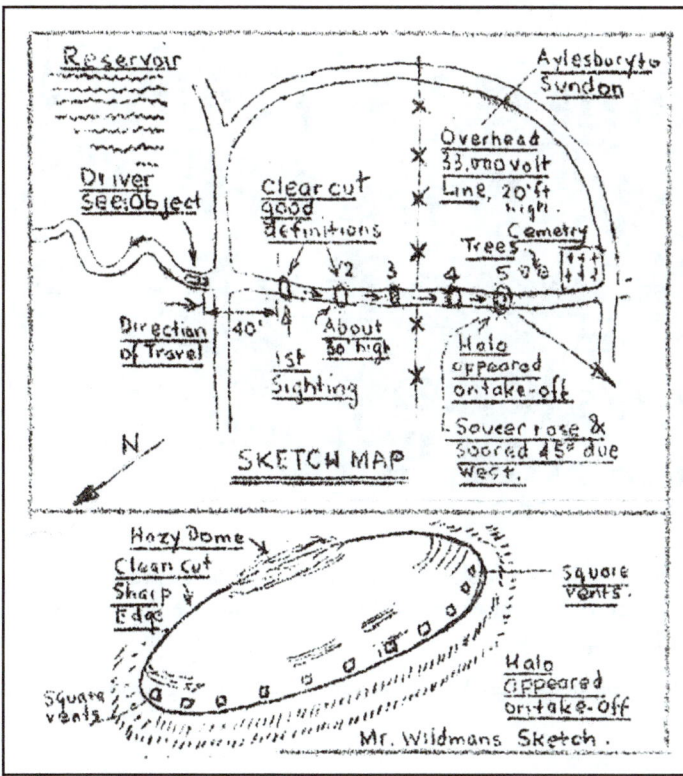

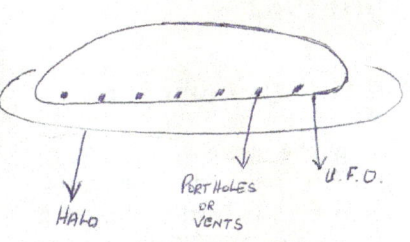

A young George A. Filer

March 1962

USA: 1st March 1962

At 10.35pm over Salem, New York, Mrs L. Doxsey (66) saw a gold-coloured box, moving through the sky on a straight and level trajectory across the horizon. (**Source: Don Berliner**)

USA: 26th March 1962

At 11.40pm, Mrs D. Wheeler and Claudine Milligan from Naperville, Illinois, sighted six to eight *'red balls of light'*, arranged in a rectangular formation, moving across the sky. These changed into two objects, with lights, by the end of sighting. (**Source: Don Berliner**)

Great Britain: 15th-30th April 1962

Nine star-like objects were seen over Tyneside. This included a report by Mrs Betty McKeown of Merkland Farm, Dumfries, on the 27th April 1962, of *"a strange object, flashing with green and red lights, seen sweeping back and forwards"*.

After observing it for over an hour, she called the police. Police Constable John Williamson arrived and watched the object with Mrs McKeown and her husband, John, but was unable to identify it.

April 1962

USA: 18th April 1962

During the evening, a glowing red object crossed the skies of the country in a swathe stretching from Oneida, New York, to Utah – bright enough to light up the streets of Reno, Nevada. It was tracked by Nellis Air Force Base, but disappeared from their radar at 10,000ft. Jet fighters were scrambled from Luke Air Force Base to try and intercept the object, which came down near Eureka, next to a power station, causing the plant to be put out of operation. It then took off, heading westwards, where it was again seen and then lost over Reno, Nevada. Some accounts say it exploded in mid-air. (**Source:** *Las Vegas Sun*, 19.4.1962 – 'Brilliant red explosion flares in Las Vegas sky')

In the same year Alan Shakespeare from Sutton Coldfield, West Midlands, saw something highly unusual and wrote to us about it, in 2002.

> Dear Mr. Hanson and Ms Holloway,
>
> Thank you for your letter of 16th May last. I am indeed the person who saw the saucer in 1962.
>
> Whilst looking from an upstairs window in Mill Street, Sutton Coldfield, I noticed this thing hovering and having the appearance of spinning above the Midland Bank. I must have heard of flying saucers for I immediately knew that was what I was observing. After watching it for several seconds it shot off at incredible speed to a higher altitude possibly over the New Hall area I think it was called Coleshill Road. After several more seconds it shot back to the same area as when I first saw it but quite a bit higher. After several more seconds there it then shot away again in the same direction of New Hall but this time continued until out of sight.
>
> It was certainly a metallic solid object and is the most incredible thing I have ever seen and I feel very privileged to have seen it, although I realise now that many of these things are sighted regularly by people all over the world.
>
> I have since (in recent years) read a few books on the subject and now contribute to Flying Saucer Review, in my opinion an excellent and serious journal on the subject. From what I have read I would believe we are being visited but thanks to my 1962 experience I know.
>
> I trust the above will be of interest to you but if I can help in any other way please do contact me.
>
> Yours sincerely,

Later in same month, NASA Pilot – Joseph Walker – sighted five disc-shaped/cylindrical objects, during a record-breaking attempt flying the X-15 aircraft.

During a lecture on 11th May 1962, at the Second National Conference on the Peaceful Uses of Space Research in Seattle, Washington, Joseph disclosed that one of the mission objectives during his April 1962 flight in the X-15 was to detect and film UFOs at high altitude. During the lecture, Walker showed several photographs to the audience of these UFOs captured on film, although NASA has since only ever made one of these frames public. (**Sources:** *Daily Mail*, 29.4.1962/*LUFORO Bulletin*, May/June 1962/*Daily Telegraph*, 12.5.1962/ *The Calgary Herald*, Friday, 11.5.1962)

NASA Pilot – Joseph Walker

USA: 24th/25th April 1962

Philadelphia, Pennsylvania, was the venue for a number of UFO sightings, involving the appearance of a circular object, with body lights, showing an apparent dome on top and projecting shafts of white light downward from the base. In the centre of the object were seen a rotating row of what appeared to be square *'windows'*. **(Source: NICAP, *UFO Evidence*, XII)**

USA: 28th April 1962

At Fort Worth, Texas, an egg-shaped light was seen crossing the sky – brighter than the Echo 1 satellite.

May 1962

USA: 18th May 1962

At Pompano Beach, Florida, a cigar-shaped UFO, brilliantly-lit below and dark on top, was seen hovering in the sky. A short time later, it sped away. **(Source: NICAP *UFO Evidence*, VII)**

Great Britain: 19th May 1962

At 10pm, a lighted horseshoe-shaped object was seen rising and falling in the sky over Solway Firth, Dumfriesshire – displaying coloured lights around the rim – by amateur astronomer, James McGill.

> *"It was humming, like a vacuum cleaner, as it moved across the sky, forwards and backwards, where it hovered for a while and then flew past Criffell – an 1,800ft hill, on the opposite side of the Estuary – before stopping and hovering over Loch Kinder. It then reversed and moved northwards, passing over the ICI factory at Drungans, where it passed over the River Nith and continued on its journey towards the north-east, where it became lost from view, at 12.15am."*

(Source: *LUFORO Bulletin*, May/June 1962, Volume 11, No. 3)

USA: 20th May 1962

A scientist was one of a number of witnesses who sighted a manoeuvring light source – brilliant blue, changing to yellow – over Defiance, Ohio. **(Source: NICAP, *UFO Evidence*, VI)**

USA: 24th May 1962

At 5.22pm, an object – the size of Venus – was observed by ground and airborne witnesses in the sky over Albuquerque, New Mexico, and also observed on air route traffic surveillance radar. The object was described as round and white during the day, pink at sunset, and dark at night. It was mostly stationary, but with a slight north-east movement during the day – then returned to its original position. The object was observed 20-30° above the horizon at Albuquerque. At Las Vegas, New Mexico the object was observed directly overhead. At Sante Fe, ARTCC personnel watched the object with binoculars. The object was also observed from a KC-135 tanker aircraft, its heading and speed unknown. **(Source: McDonald List)**

Great Britain: 26th May 1962

Captain Gordon Pendleton – a former RAF Officer – was piloting an Aer Lingus 'Viscount' to Brussels, from the UK, at a height of 17,000ft. He and the First Officer – Peter Murray – saw *"a circular object, with protrusion-like antennae – smaller than a 'Viscount' – pass underneath, at 14,000ft, heading across the sky, at 600 knots, 35 miles south-west of Bristol."* (**Source:** *Blackburn Evening Telegraph,* 27.4.62/*Irish Times,* 22.5.62)

On the same day, Mr H.G. Pryor from Truro, Cornwall, sighted *"a silver and black UFO, resembling a stack of coins",* led by a small object, heading across the sea. It was 50ft above the water, at an estimated speed of between 60-70mph.

USA: 26th May 1962

At Westfield, Massachusetts, a round, slightly oval, bright red object, giving off sparks from top and bottom, with a yellowish or white centre, was seen in the sky. (**Source: Air Force Project Blue Book, 1962**)

USA: 27th May 1962

Two triangular UFOs were seen diving and climbing over Palmer, Alaska. (**Source: Project Blue Book, 1962**)

June 1962

USA: 21st -23rd June 1962

At 4am, Lt. Colonel H. King and tail gunner M/Sgt. Roberts were aboard a B-52 bomber over Indianapolis, Indiana, when they saw a bright, star-like object, followed by two similar ones, 10 secondss later.
(**Source: Don Berliner**)

The following day over Columbus, Georgia, between 10.25pm on 22nd June and 3am on 23rd June, a number of people reported at least seven sightings of flying objects over the Columbus area. There were observations of ground-visual, air-visual, and ground-radar. One witness observed three objects passing silently over his house. One sighting, by a qualified pilot, estimated the speed of objects at 300mph. A sighting was made at the Columbus Airport Control Tower. (**Source: Dan Wilson**)

July 1962

Great Britain: 1st July 1962

People living in the Bridlington area sighted several mirages of *"ships, sailing upside-down and part of the Grimsby landscape, 40 miles away"*. A large number of mysterious coloured *'stars'* were also sighted in the sky over Leyburn, the same evening. (**Source:** *Space Bulletin,* **Volume 1, No. 4, Sept.-Oct. 1964/***Northern Echo,* **2.7.1962**)

USA: 7th July 1962

At 9.05pm, a mushroom-shaped object was seen rising in the south and moving north over Albuquerque, New Mexico. When the object reached overhead it turned north-east and flashed, following which seven objects, in an arrowhead formation, came out of the main object. These seven objects travelled east, while the main object travelled to the north-east – six minutes later, the sky was clear. **(Source: Dan Wilson)**

New Zealand: 7th July 1962

According to Mr C.B. Taylor – Scientific leader of the New Zealand Antarctic Cape *Hallet Station:

> "... an object, showing three yellow-white lights – the centre light being midway between the other two and much brighter, which took a few minutes to cross the sky – was seen heading in a south-west to north-east direction, about 35° from the zenith, at 11.10pm. When it reached the northern part of the sky, it emitted a brilliant flash of white light. Seven of the Station's crew sighted the object, which was photographed by the auroral camera."

(Source: *New Zealand Herald*, 13.7.1962/*The Press* – 'A very strange object', 11.7.1962)

USA: 10th July 1962

A disc-shaped UFO, with a rotating dome on the top, was seen to sweep low over a Naval Auxiliary Air Station, at New Iberia, Louisiana. It then slowed over an area of runway and hangar, before climbing out of sight, at a 20 to 30° angle, accelerating rapidly as it did so. **(Source: NICAP,** *UFO Evidence*, **IV)**

USA: 29th/30th July 1962 – Ocean Springs, Mississippi

At 11.20pm, Mr and Mrs M.O. Barton saw a bright cherry-red, diamond-shaped, object fly through the sky in a series of slow, hover, and fast loops of movement. **(Source: Don Berliner)**

USA: 17th July 1962

Test pilot Major Robert White, of Edwards Air Force Base, California, flew the X-15 plane to an altitude of 314,750ft, or 59 miles, to become the first to do so at speeds up to Mach 6. He reported sighting and visually tracking an unidentified object *"for a full five seconds, before it moved away"*.

Two frames of film from the X-15's rear-facing 16mm camera appear to have captured an object (or objects) that seem to match Major White's visual description of the UFO he saw. Major Walker later described these objects as being *"five or six

---

*Hallet Station was a joint American/New Zealand facility, built during the first international Geophysical year 1957-1958. The Station was the first and with the exception of a more recently established joint French-Italian facility, the only international effort in Antarctica. In 1964, a fire destroyed the main scientific laboratory. From that time until abandoned in 1973, the station was manned during the austral summer. The purpose of the station was to provide weather data for the US aircraft, flying between Christchurch and McMurdo. Scientists also researched meteorology, aurora, ionosphere, and seismology.

disc-shaped or cylindrical objects", seen near his aircraft. (Major White passed away on the 17th March 2010). During August 1962, the pilot was interviewed for *Life Magazine*. He said:

> *"There are things out there, absolutely. I have no idea what the objects were that I saw up there. They were very small, flaky, objects. I thought they might be residue from the peroxide fuel that the engine burns. I looked out of the left window and saw what looked like a piece of greyish-white paper, about the size of my hand, about 30-40ft away. Five seconds, later it moved away."*

August 1962

USA: 2nd August 1962 – Several UFO reports were made to Central Airlines agent Fred Jones, at Liberal Airport, who himself went outside at about 8pm, when he saw a bright object hovering over a nearby field – its dazzling light strong enough to light up the runway. Some passengers also witnessed this. They told of seeing three objects, flying above the airport.

At 8.30pm Captain Metzger, who was flying between Wichita and Kansas, saw a brilliant object, heading swiftly through the sky in an east to west direction. Thirty minutes later, after landing and then taking off at Guymon, Oklahoma, Captain Metzger saw an object flying at high altitude. The pilot dismissed any claims that these were meteors. Following this, he was interviewed by a Colonel from Dayton, and a Lt. Colonel at NORAD HQ, Colorado Springs. (**Source:** *UFO Investigator*, Vol. 11, No. 5, NICAP)

USA: 7th August 1962 – Oracle, Arizona – UFO seen over Titan missile silo

This was a matter investigated by Coral and Jim Lorenzen. Unfortunately, the first informant whom they spoke to refused to give his name for publication, for fear of some kind of official reprisal for talking about the incident, but within five weeks the couple were able to obtain corroborating information from two other witnesses – both of whom are known to us but who also asked to remain anonymous. The incident started off with the sighting of a brilliant *'light'* in the sky, at about midnight, which, according to the witness, began to descend directly over the site. The man told another, who came outside to have a look for himself. Before long the object had become so large that both of the men were frightened and went back inside the complex, where they informed Davis-Monthan Air Force Base, at Tucson, by telephone.

```
VZCZCNEA273
FTT3 JAF RUCSAAA0196 0703915-SSSS--RUWMBOA.
ZNY SSSSS
P 17225Z MAR 67
FM SAC
TO RUWMBBA/OOAMA HILL AFB UTAH
INFO RUWBKNA/15AF
RUWMBOA/341SMW MALMSTROM AFB MONT
RUWMBAA/AFFRO BOEING CO SEATTLE WASH
RUWJABA/BSD NORTON AFB CALIF
BT
S-E-C-R-E-T DI 22752 MAR 67.
ACTION: OOAMA (OONCI/OOME-COL DAVENPORT). INFO: 15AF
(OM4C), 341SMW (DCM), BOEING AFFRO (D.J. DOWNEY, MINUTEMAN
ENGINEERING) BSD (ESS, SSQR)
SUBJECT: LOSS OF STRATEGIC ALERT, ECHO FLIGHT, MALSTROM
AFB. (U)
REF: MY SECRET MESSAGE DMTR 02751, 17 MAR 67, SAME SUBJECT.
ALL TEN MISSILES IN ECHO FLIGHT AT MALMSTROM LOST STRAT ALERT WITHIN
TEN SECONDS OF EACH OTHER. THIS INCIDENT OCCURRED AT 0845L ON
16 MARCH 67. AS OF THIS DATE, ALL MISSILES HAVE BEEN RETURNED TO STRAT

PAGE 2 RUCSAAA0196
ALERT WITH NO APPARENT DIFFICULTY. INVESTIGATION AS TO THE CAUSE OF THE
INCIDENT IS BEING CONDUCTED BY MALMSTROM TEAM. TWO FITTS HAVE
BEEN RUN THROUGH TWO MISSILES THUS FAR. NO CONCLUSIONS HAVE BEEN
DRAWN. THERE ARE INDICATIONS THAT BOTH COMPUTERS IN BOTH G&C'S
WERE UPSET MOMENTARILY. CAUSE OF THE UPSET IS NOT KNOWN AT THIS
TIME. ALL OTHER SIGNIFICANT INFORMATION AT THIS TIME IS CONTAINED IN
ABOVE REFERENCED MESSAGE.
FOR OOAMA. THE FACT THAT NO APPARENT REASON FOR THE LOSS OF TEN
MISSILES CAN BE READILY IDENTIFIED IS CAUSE FOR GRAVE CONCERN TO THIS
HEADQUARTERS. WE MUST HAVE AN IN-DEPTH ANALYSIS TO DETERMINE CAUSE
AND CORRECTIVE ACTION AND WE MUST KNOW AS QUICKLY AS POSSIBLE WHAT
THE IMPACT IS TO THE FLEET, IF ANY. REQUEST YOUR RESPONSE BE IN KEEP-
ING WITH THE URGENCY OF THE PROBLEM. WE IN TURN WILL PROVIDE OUR
FULL COOPERATION AND SUPPORT.
FOR OOAMA AND 15AF WE HAVE CONCURRED IN A BOEING REQUEST TO SEND
TWO ENGINEERS, MR. R.E RIGERT AND MR. W. M. DUTTON TO MALMSTROM
TO COLLECT FIRST HAND KNOWLEDGE OF THE PROBLEM FOR POSSIBLE ASSISTANCE
IN LATER ANALYSIS. REQUEST COOPERATION OF ALL CONCERNED TO PROVIDE
THEM ACCESS TO AVAILABLE INFORMATION, I.E., CREW COMMANDERS LOG
ENTRIES, MAINTENANCE FORMS, INTERROGATION OF KNOWLEDGEABLE PEOPLE, ETC.

PAGE 3 RUCSAAA0196
SECURITY CLEARANCES AND DATE AND TIME OF ARRIVAL WILL BE SENT FROM
THE AFFRO BY SEPARATE MESSAGE.
FOR 15AF, OOAMA HAS INDICATED BY TELECON THAT THEY ARE SENDING
ADDITIONAL ENGINEERING SUPPORT. REQUEST YOUR COOPERATION TO INSURE
MAXIMUM RESULTS ARE OBTAINED FROM THIS EFFORT. GP74. BCASMC-67-437
BT
```

CUFON/UFO Reporting & Information Service
P.O. Box 832, Mercer Island, WA 98040, USA
Voice:(206) 721-5035 • Data:(206) 776-0382
jimklotz@prostar.com

Two USAF jet interceptors were scrambled and approached the object, which then took off at a fast speed, heading northwards – out of sight within seconds. The jets circled the area and headed back for the Base. Minutes later, the UFO returned and descended toward the silo, before taking off vertically and finally disappearing from view. It appears that a similar object was seen either the night before or the night after this incident.

[On the 16th of March 1967, all ten missiles lost strategic alert and was the cause of understandable concern)

(Source: Coral and Jim Lorenzen – *UFOs The Whole Story*)

Sketch Based On Interviews With Witnesses Drawn By Dr John Pagano, NICAP Member

Oradell, N J
Sept 15
7 50 p m

September 1962

Great Britain: 8th/9th September 1962

At 6.40pm, Mrs Ellen Jordan from Nelson, Lancashire, happened to glance out of the window across a deep blue sky and see two red objects – like saucers on edge – hovering in the air. Ellen awoke her husband, Ernest, and, while he was getting dressed, went back to the window, where she was just in time to see them swoop down and disappear. (**Source: Personal interview**)

On 9th September 1962, a number of spectators attending the Farnborough Air Show reported having seen a long, silver coloured object, rising upwards into the sky – completely unnoticed by five RAF jets, flying in the near vicinity. (**Source:** *UFOLOG*)

USA: 15th September 1962 – UFO seen over Oradell Reservoir

At 6pm, ex-US Navy electronics officer – J. J. McVicker from Oradell, New York – sighted what looked like two *'silver dollars'*, apparently revolving, as they passed across the sky over West Nyack, New York. At 7.50pm NICAP member Victor Cipolla saw it descending towards Oradell.

At about 7.55pm, five boys reported sighting a disc-shaped object, hovering over the Oradell Reservoir – which touched down on it, before taking off silently at high speed. Later, two other boys said they had seen a very bright *'light'*, moving back and forth over the edge of the reservoir, following which a loud explosion was heard. Other reports told of an object seen with a fin on top and another under it. (**Source:** NICAP, *UFO Evidence*/Jacques Vallée, *Passport to Magonia*)

USA: 18th September 1962

At 4am, two policemen from Westword, New Jersey, sighted over a period of 7-8 seconds, a huge object in the sky, described as round at the top and tapering to a cone – out of view in five seconds. At 4.45am, two Oradell policemen reported seeing a brilliant light in the sky. (**Source:** NICAP, *UFO Evidence*)

USA: 21st September 1962

Four Hawthorne police officers watched a device with two beams, like headlights, hover over a local quarry. Officer George Jediny, in a report to NICAP, said that the UFO – which he sketched as a disc – seemed to revolve. The quarry night watchman – Mr Stocks – said the UFO had appeared the night before. When he drove a jeep to check out the object, it deliberately manoeuvred to keep out of the headlights of the vehicle.

Just after midnight on 24th September, the same or similar flying object was seen over the quarry, by over a dozen Hawthorne police officers and the chief reporter of the *N.J. State Press* – George Della Penta. When a police car spotlight was pointed up at the UFO, it began to move. Before it left, Mr Della Penta shot 18ft of colour film. Later, Oradell police received a letter signed "The Bergenfield Pranksters", purporting to be from some boys, who said they faked the sightings with aluminum-coated model aircraft, supported by helium balloons. This was promptly rejected by the police and newspapers as being responsible for what was seen.

Great Britain: 22nd September 1962 – British UFO Association Conference

On Saturday, 22nd September 1962, people from all over the world made their way to the Kensington Central Library, London, where they were met by Mr G.N.P. Stephenson – Chairman of the London UFO Research Organisation. He began the conference by speaking optimistically about the serious attitude displayed towards the UFO subject and hoped this might lead to greater co-operation between the Government and UFO Societies.

Guest speaker, Mr Leonard G. Cramp – author of *Space, Gravity and the 'Flying Saucer'* – gave a fascinating lecture on the subject.

During the afternoon, Alex Birch (14) from Mosborough, Sheffield, addressed the 200 people audience for four minutes, explaining how he had taken five UFO photographs in May of the same year. The afternoon ended with the showing of a selection of photographs and slides by Dr. G.G. Doel, followed by two short cine films of UFOs, seen over Corpus Christi, Texas, by Ray Stanford.

Alex Birch outside The National Archives office.

BOY STARTS NEW PROBE INTO FLYING SAUCERS

NEWS OF THE WORLD REPORTER

A PHOTOGRAPH taken by a 14-year-old boy has started Air Ministry experts on an investigation into a new flying saucer riddle. The picture, of five mystery objects in the sky, was taken by Alex Birch while he was playing with friends at his home in Moor-crescent, Mosborough, near Sheffield.

He and his father visited the Air Ministry in London, told officers what had happened and showed them the picture.

"They are very keen to get the exact time and date this took place," Mr. Birch said yesterday.

Alex said: "I think it was Sunday, February 25, we saw them. It was either then or March 4.

Looked up

"Three of us, Stewart Dixon, David Brownlow and myself were in the field at the back of our house taking photographs.

"David bent down and picked up a stone to throw. As he got up he saw the shapes in the sky. He shouted to me and we all three looked up

Alex Birch, the boy photographer whose camera captured the flight of mystery objects in the sky.

USA: 28th September 1962

Police from seven counties reported seeing UFOs between 2.30am and 3.30am. Most reports related to three objects seen, which changed colour. (**Source: NICAP,** *UFO Evidence*)

October 1962

USA: 23rd October 1962

At 3pm, Mr O. Christensen from Farmington, Utah, saw a grey and silver *'ball'* in the sky, trailing what looked like twine with two knots attached. *"It then swerved, and climbed away at a 45° angle, making a sound like a flock of ducks."* (**Source: Don Berliner**)

USA: 25th October 1962

A police dispatcher from Delta, Colorado, reported having sighted a round, glowing, object from his office window. A short time later a state patrolman and Cedar Edge Marshal reported having observed two UFOs, *"like an inverted umbrella with a number of bright, tail-like appendages"* in the sky. (**Source: NICAP,** *UFO Evidence*, VII)

November 1962

Great Britain: 6th November 1962

At 8pm, an orange *'light'*, approximately 15ft in diameter, was sighted at an estimated height of 50ft above the ground, close to Portsmouth Harbour, by Mr P. Thorne and his wife.

"It was completely still and remained in the same position for 10 minutes, before disappearing from view."

(**Source: Letter to Kath Smith, Isle of Wight UFO Society**)

USA: 17th November 1962

At 9pm, bright star-like objects were reported in the sky over Tampa, by ex USMC Captain – Mr F Swindale – who told of seeing them hover and bounce in the sky, before fading away. (**Source: Don Berliner**)

USA: 19th November 1962

Three star-like objects were seen hovering in the sky over Tampa, Florida. The witness felt that the objects were under intelligent control at all times. (**Source: Project Blue Book, 1962**)

December 1962

Great Britain: 19th December 1962 – 'Flying Saucer' seen in Cumbria

At 4pm Mr Harold Threkeld was out collecting holly, near the village of Elterwater.

"I saw this huge great thing in the sky, disc-shaped, like an upside-down saucer, hovering about

700ft off the ground. It then came down to about 150ft. After a couple of minutes, it swished away, at tremendous speed, and disappeared in the direction of Wrynose Pass. As it moved away, I was able to see the underneath very clearly. It had three projections, like beer barrels, underneath, and a transparent dome, glowing with blue radiant light, with what looked like tables, or benches, inside. I also saw what looked like spars all around the rim, with slats or fins. I estimated the 'saucer' to be 60ft in diameter."

(**Source: Personal interview**)

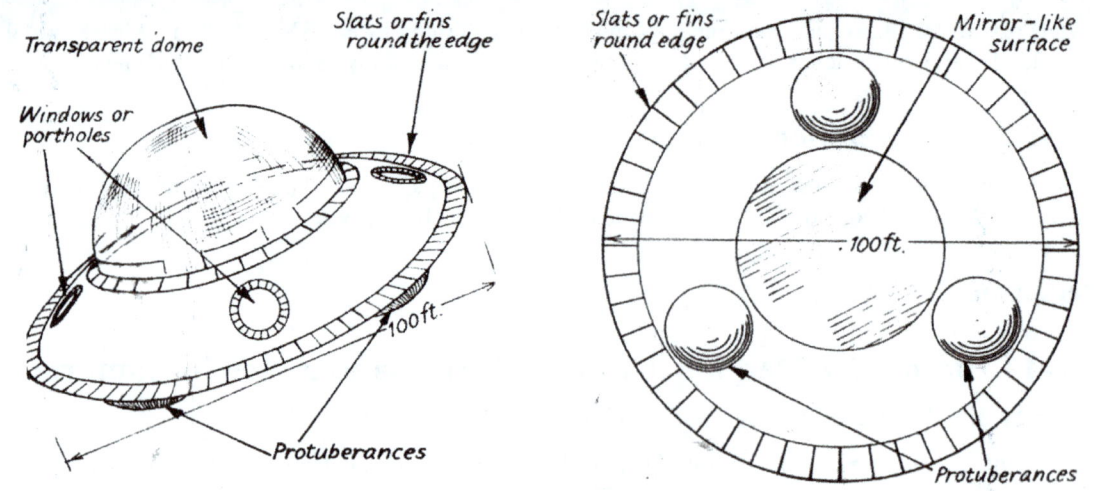

Great Britain: 21st December 1962

At 7.15am, Mr Harold Mayhew of Hempnall, Norfolk, was riding to work when he was stunned to see a peculiar object, hovering silently above a field. It was 500yds from the village, at a distance of some 200yds. He said:

> "It was like a thin bar giving off a faint light, with three bright lights hanging underneath; one at each end, and one in the middle. It was making no sound and moving very slowly. As I cycled past, I got ahead of the object and lost sight of it".

(Source: *ORBIT*, Vol. 4, Number 4/*Eastern Evening News*, 27.12 1962)

UPDATE...

Smoke rings over the West Midlands

The famous Rex Heflin image of a smoke ring, taken at the same time he sighted and captured a flying disc in California, USA, on August 3rd 1965, are not unique in appearance. Here are two other smoke ring cases – one from 1969 and the other 2014.

At 9.10pm on 18th June 1969, Carl Robbins was driving along Charles Road, Bordesley Green, Birmingham, when he noticed a huge *'ring of smoke'* in the sky:

> "... almost a perfect circle, but distorted slightly in the breeze as it slowly rolled over the sky – like a large rubber band. At a very rough estimate, I would say it was about 50ft in diameter. It appeared as a thick ring of black, oily smoke, having some sort of inner core around which it was burning. There were three equally spaced lumps around the ring, which appeared to be burning a little more fiercely than the rest. After about five minutes, the smoke started to burn away from one of these 'lumps' in each direction, towards the next – then the smoke between these last two 'lumps' burned away, leaving a thin ring of what appeared to be smoke or gas. It reminded me of some sort of fuse, burning down.
>
> The thin 'ring' remained for another three or four minutes around the 'lumps' – then the whole lot faded away."

Two photographs were taken within a few minutes of each other and processed by the *Birmingham Post*, who

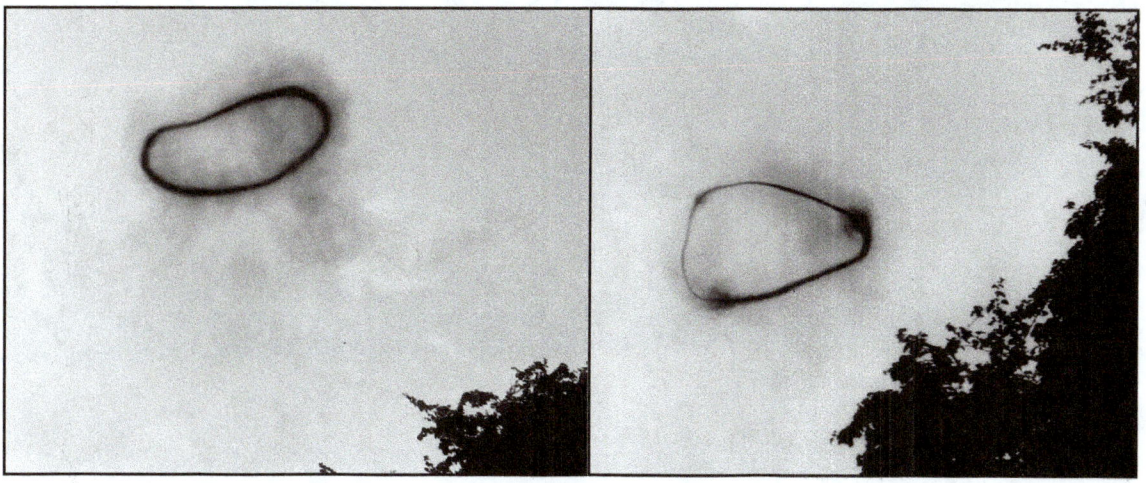

published the photos in its edition of the 19th June 1969. The police attempted to explain away the sighting as a gaggle of black Canadian geese flying in formation, while local resident – Rebecca Harvey – thought it was caused by someone throwing a can of petrol or spirits on a bonfire. **(Source: Bob Tibbitts)**

15th April 2014 – 'Smoke ring' seen over Leamington Spa

Georgina Heap (16) captured this effect on film. Explanations: Swarm of insects, or home-made smoke signal. Warwick Castle spokesman said:

> *"It was our Trebuchet Fireball Spectacular Show – the world's largest firing catapult. We've seen a number of different effects, including the vortex images that have been reported."*

Haunted Skies Volume Ten

In 1965, Rex Heflin took four photographs of a UFO (below). Significantly, the fourth image he took bears more than a striking resemblance with a photograph of what was explained away as a smoke ring taken in Bordesley Green, Birmingham, UK, during 1969, and a more recent photograph captured on camera in Leamington Spa, Warwickshire.

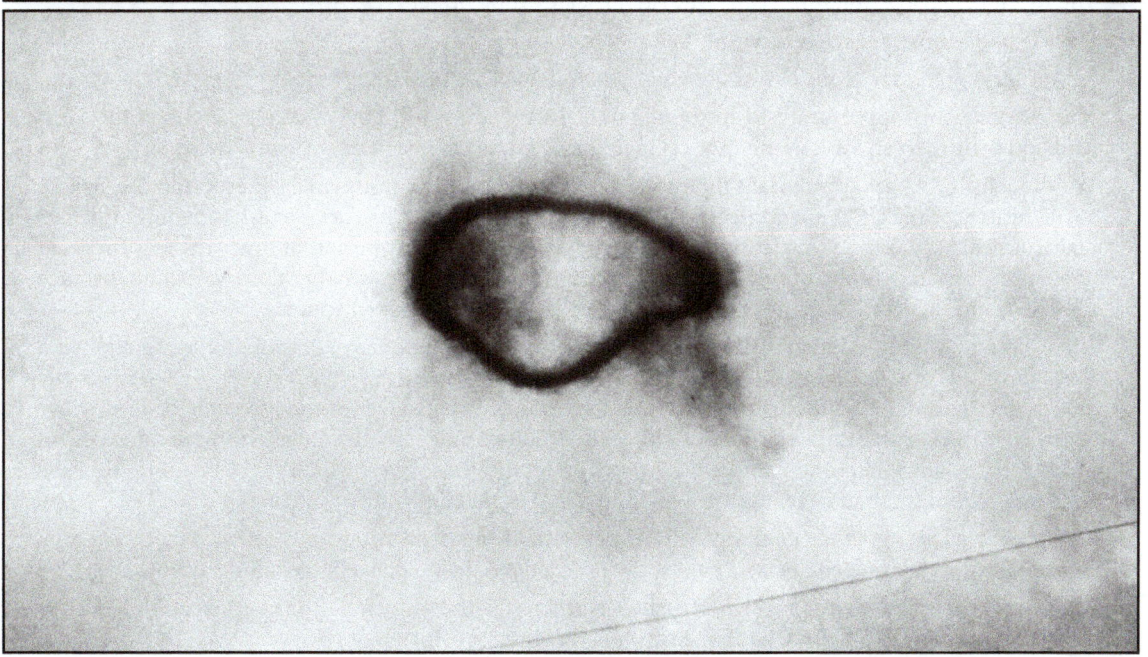

Haunted Skies Volume Ten

Suspicious death of Zygmund Adamski

Mr Burns-Williamson

In Volume 9 of *Haunted Skies* we mentioned we had sent our file pertaining to our investigation into the suspicious death of Zygmund Adamski to Mr Burns-Williamson, Office of the Police and Crime Commissioner for West Yorkshire, hoping for them to conduct 'a cold case review' of the Coroner's file.

This was due to what we felt was new evidence offered to warrant re-examination of the original statements taken by the West Yorkshire Police, which would confirm that (1) the death of this man was in no way linked to UFO activity and (2) while his death may have been due to natural causes, the circumstances in which he was found were highly suspicious and have never been satisfactorily explained. In June 2014 we received an answer, following examination of the file that the West Yorkshire Police judged there were no suspicious circumstances – which we reject, on the grounds of common sense; clearly justice is not going to prevail here!

The Daily Mail & UFOs

The Daily Mail (unusually) published a two-page spread about Alien Abductions, in May 2014, and featured our friends – Hilary Porter and Ken Parsons, of BEAMS.

We wrote to the newspaper, asking if they might at some stage in the future be prepared to allow us the opportunity of letting people know about the *Haunted Skies* series of books, and enclosed Volume 8, by way of recorded delivery (which was subsequently lost in the post). In mid-May we sent another copy of Volume 8 to them along with a letter of introduction, in the post, but have never received any reply

In June 2014 we wrote the following letter to Prime Minister David Cameron and enclosed Volume 1 of *Haunted Skies*.

> The Rt. Hon. David Cameron, Prime Minister, 10, Downing Street, SW1A
>
> Dear Prime Minister David Cameron,
>
> Re: Preserving the social history of the UFO phenomena
>
> May we take this opportunity to introduce ourselves; I am a retired Police Officer from the West Midlands, who served for a number of years in the CID, and my partner is Dawn Holloway.
>
> We thought it was an appropriate time to advise you of our commitment in preserving the British social history of the UFO phenomenon during the 20th Century. It has been a task (ongoing) that has taken us nearly 20 years of in-depth research to cover such a lengthy period of time. This has involved contacting hundreds, if not thousands of people, in order to ascertain whether there was any substance to reports of UFO activity, rather than relying on other unsubstantiated sources.
>
> I first became interested after Police Officers (known to me personally) described having sighted a UFO hovering over a suburb to the south of Birmingham, on 19th January 1995. This was shortly after retiring from the Force. Prior to this, I had no interest whatsoever in the subject and would have regarded claims of sightings of UFOs as either the result of an overactive imagination or an excess of alcohol, especially when one considers that during my police service, which involved 'pounding the beat' on night duty, I had never seen anything unusual in the night sky.
>
> This event was to trigger my curiosity. Surely inexplicable objects – commonly referred to as UFOs or, in past years, 'flying saucers' – was a concept which could have no place in our modern world.
>
> I believed at the time that UFO sightings, however strange initially, would be later explained away as misidentified natural phenomena. Time was to tell a different story!

After having accumulated a large amount of information, together with my partner Dawn Holloway, over the forthcoming years, we contacted various publishers but were unable to find anyone who was willing to help us, despite the proposed submitted synopsis entitled: *UFOs – Chronicle of a Phenomena* being judged extremely interesting.

We decided to write a chronological account of what had taken place, which proved daunting indeed, understanding the complexities involved with recording UFO reports on a day-by-day basis, which required 12 years of intensive research.

2010

In 2010, after unsuccessfully attracting the attention of a publisher, we took advantage of the 'print on demand' facilities now available via the Internet, offered by a Devon based company, who agreed to publish *Haunted Skies*, Volumes 1-6.

2011

In 2011, we felt confident enough to publish *Haunted Skies* ourselves, in order to facilitate the use of colour illustrations, and to increase the pagination of the books from 320 to 600. This was achieved with the publication of Volume 8 (1980), Volume 9 (1981-1986), and Volume 10 (proposed) 1987-1988.

The public still continues to be fascinated by the UFO concept, as can be seen in the plethora of programmes continuing to be shown in TV documentaries – some on the *History Channel*. Unfortunately, their understanding as to what the phenomena is actually about is influenced firstly by the way in which the Media continually sensationalise such accounts (often published alongside tongue-in-cheek comments, calculated to denigrate some puzzling experiences) and is also due to cultural misconceptions about UFOs, and the stigma still attached to the subject.

Admittedly some of the sightings would no doubt fit into the category of celestial objects, such as fireballs or meteorites, which we felt should be included to provide an invaluable source of information to Astronomical Societies, who may have been unaware of this activity.

We are pleased that the MOD has made available many declassified sighting reports through the Public Records Office. However, we would like to point out that the role of the MOD has never been to investigate UFO sightings but to catalogue reports from the public.

We hope that the *Haunted Skies* series of books will complement existing files declassified by the MOD, and provide an excellent reference guide, and are pleased that some Libraries are beginning to stock them.

We accept the possibility that future science may (for all we know) be able to identify UFOs as natural phenomena indigenous to our planet, rather than the popular incursions of extraterrestrials – a scenario continually perpetuated by the Media, purely because stories about 'little green men' and invading aliens will always fire the public's imagination!

This project is funded by ourselves at a heavy financial loss, but we feel passionately that while we cannot offer any explanation as to what these things are, and where they come from, one cannot help but note the commonality of behaviour characteristics associated with the movement of these objects throughout the decades.

We are not asking you for any commitment with regard to any specific statements about UFOs per se, but hope you will at least acknowledge our efforts to ensure that such information is saved, rather than being lost from history itself.

Nobody (to our knowledge) has ever tried to take on such a daunting, immense task, but we feel our efforts will be judged by future students of the UFO subject as providing a most useful research tool.

We enclose an example of our work and hope that you will find the time to eventually read it.

Signed: John Hanson

Haunted Skies Volume Ten

10 DOWNING STREET
LONDON SW1A 2AA
www.gov.uk/Number10

From The Direct Communications Unit

9 June 2014

Mr John Hanson
31 Red Lion Street
Alvechurch
Birmingham
B48 7LG

Dear Mr Hanson

The Prime Minister has asked me to thank you and Ms Dawn Holloway very much for sending him a copy of your book 'Haunted Skies'.

Mr Cameron appreciates your kind thought and you taking the time and trouble to write.

Yours sincerely

Correspondence Officer

Prime Minster Anthony Charles Lynton Blair briefed on UFOs

In 1998 Prime Minister Tony Blair was briefed on the UK's files about UFO sightings, according to newly declassified MOD documents in July 2012. The request came as the Government began to implement the Freedom of Information (FOI) requests.

Some 6,700 pages of UFO documents have been released by the National Archives.

Haunted Skies **Volume Ten**

16th May 2014 – Photograph of triangular UFO taken

We were particularly impressed with some recent UFO photographs, taken by David Bryant – a retired school teacher, and Navy Pilot – who has furnished us spasmodically with some illustrations to be used in our books.

He and Linda, his charming wife, are owners of 'Spacerocks UK' – the UK's only full-time professional meteorite dealership, with a 15 year presence on the Internet. David and Linda both posses Degrees in Astronomy and Biology, and can discuss their inventory with experience, enthusiasm, and knowledge. They supply most of the UK's wholesalers, museums and educational institutions, and are members of the IMCA, and offer a lifetime guarantee with any purchase.

David and Linda, who have also been very helpful with introductions to Astronauts like Buzz Aldrin, Retired General Charlie Duke, and Dr. Edgar Mitchell, at the National Exhibition Centre in Birmingham, are also very interested in photographing rare birds. In May 2014, they went to their local nature reserve (Strumpshaw Fen) to listen for a rare night-calling bird (Spotted Crake). This is what they had to say:

> *"We arrived at Fen Hide, right in the middle of an isolated reed bed, at around 9pm, and spent an hour or so sitting quietly listening to Water Rails, Marsh Harriers, etc. We noticed a light above the horizon to the south-west: this grew brighter, until it was about magnitude five or so. Through binoculars we could see a central bright white light, with a triangle of red, green, and white lights, chasing in an anticlockwise direction. The object moved north and south over the distant reed bed, before suddenly disappearing. We walked back to our car and drove to Brundall, to see if we could hear the Crakes: we had to stop at the railway crossing by the Yare pub and became aware of a square of red and green lights, hanging several hundred feet above the road, at 9.45pm. I got out of the car and took several photos with a 300mm lens, until the crossing gates opened. We drove through and*

Haunted Skies Volume Ten

the object followed us. When we reached the end of the public road and stopped to turn around, the lights suddenly dropped and disappeared behind moored boats in the marina."

David wonders if it could have been a surveillance drone. We cannot say what it was, other than it is identical in description to so many sightings of what has become labelled as appearances of the Triangular UFO.

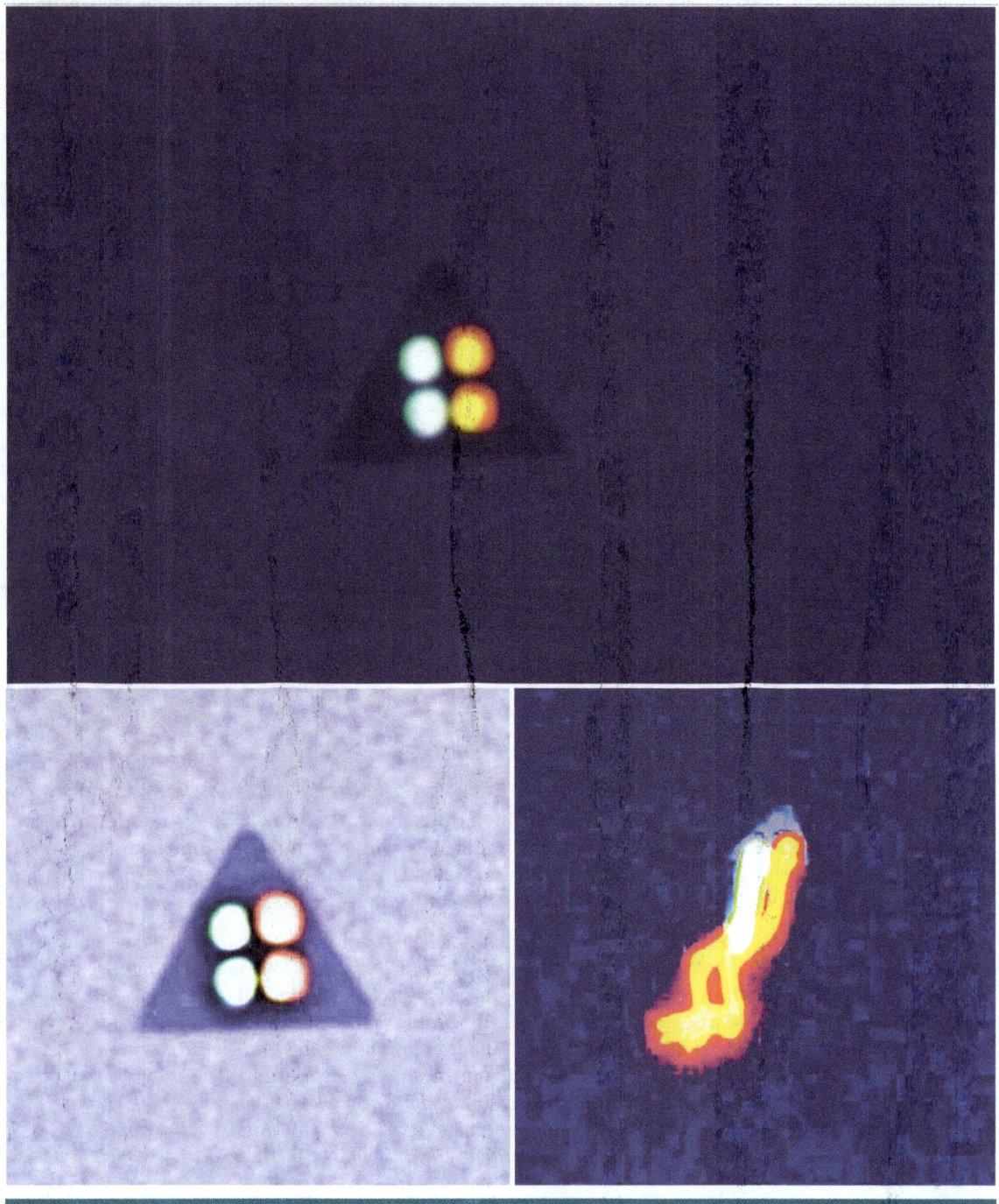

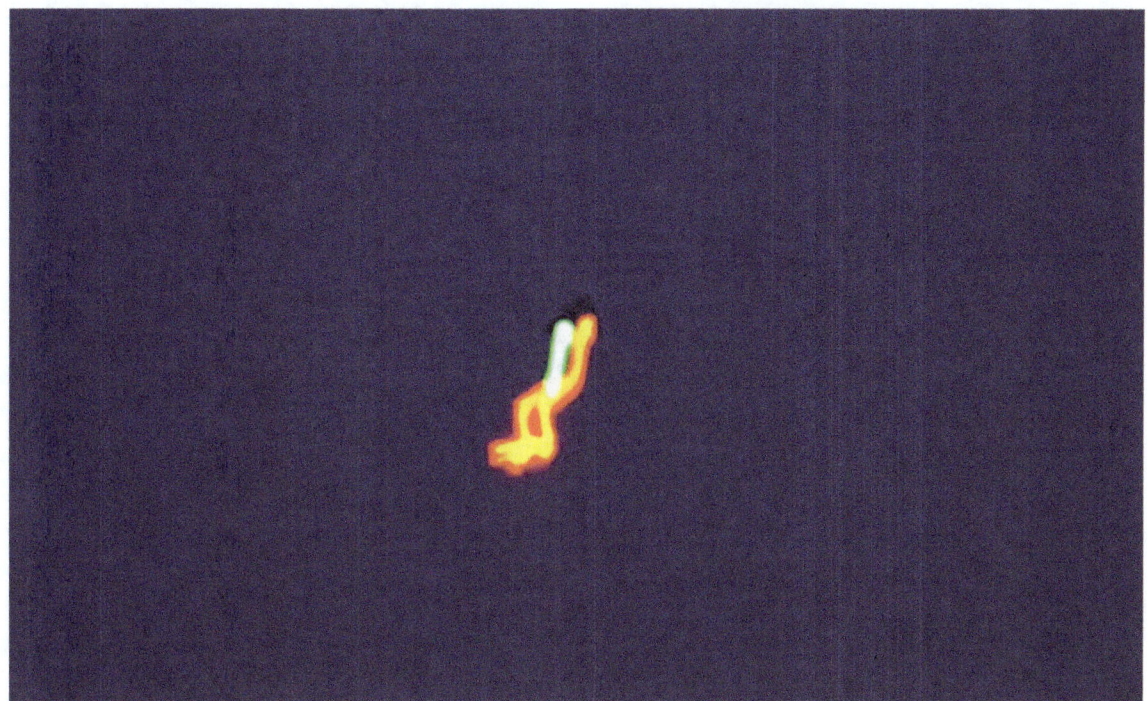

1st October 2012 – Close Encounter with the 'Shadow Soldiers'

Another man that we met during our recent visit to Rendlesham Forest was Felixstowe resident – Derek Savory – who has long been interested in reports of UFO activity and was formerly a member of the UFO group, run by Ron West many years ago.

Derek Savory, seen here with his son Matthew, in Rendlesham Forest

He is a friend of Brenda Butler and regularly accompanies her and other members of the group around the forest. We found him to be an honest, genuine, likeable man. While the version of events which we are going to outline may, to some, sound almost unbelievable, one thing we can be assured of is that they are not fabricated.

Derek has also been a regular guest of Deborah Jane East, who runs a radio station from Virginia, USA, during which he has spoken of the encounter with the 'Shadow Soldiers'. Podcasts of his talk can be found on the internet.

On the 1st October 2012, Derek, his brother – Andrew, and son – Matthew, decided to meet up in the forest at 7.30pm.

After parking their car in the car park, close to the East Gate entrance road, they got out. After chatting to another visitor – Jonathan Marston – the party set off where, at the entrance to Track 12, Jonathan Marston left.

The three men continued their walk on what was a clear night, with a full moon.

Derek:

> "We heard the sound of owls, as if very agitated. [Authors: During our visits we have only ever heard a solitary owl, maybe only a few times if that, over many years attendance.]
>
> It was the first time we had been to the Forest. We carried small torches but no cameras. As I was familiar with the UFO events that had taken place in December 1980, I outlined the incident while walking along Track 12, intending to show them the route taken by Larry Warren, the previous week, who had been accompanied by Paul and Ben Eno, along with Brenda and myself. As we neared where the forest trails split into four, Andrew said he could smell something dreadful – 'evil, like death' was the way he explained it.
>
> We continued walking and took a left, but I soon became disorientated and wondered if we were near the location nominated by Charles Halt as the scene of his 1980 encounter. At this point the temperature dropped sharply and we began to shiver. This was followed by the appearance of four or five monk like figures, about 4-5ft tall, which suddenly appeared and moved as if in concert over to our right.

Shadows appear

> Matthew then pointed out a group of 8-10 human-sized shadows to our left. The oddest thing is we should have run away in fright, but didn't. We stood there and felt, in some way, that we were being protected. I know it's weird, but that is how it happened. Matthew shouted out 'what the bloody hell is that?', and pointed towards what I can only describe as a giant 'figure', 10-15ft tall, standing on the path some 20 yards away. This had long arms, long fingers, and a face – a bit owl-like, reminding me of 'King Raedwald's mask.

> Reality suddenly swept over me. Was I leading my son and brother into danger, especially after Andrew said he was having problems breathing? We stood there discussing what to do, while still surrounded by the entities – whatever they were.

Loud bang is heard

> At this point there was a loud bang, like something had hit a tree. We should have run but stood there, trying to make sense of it all.

Matthew shouted, 'Dad, it's coming towards us', so we moved back about 10 yards and stopped. Andrew asked if we should go back to the car. Once again, there was another loud bang and the tall entity began to head towards us. We realised the futility of trying to stop him and headed quickly away back down Track 12, towards the car park, still accompanied by the 'monk like figures' on one side and the 'shadow soldiers' on the other. There was also a red light which appeared to be following us. As soon as we reached the road the 'beings' vanished, but the red lights were still there at either side. We reached the car park and unlocked the vehicle, allowing some light to come on, and stood there silently, discussing the incredible events that had just taken place, unsure of what to make of it all."

Mathew shouted "Dad, behind you!"

Derek looked to see:

". . . three or four small, silver-blue-grey beings- some 3ft high. Once again, we stood there watching each other, but I didn't feel frightened and was ready to deal with whatever was going to happen next. However, the ground began to shake, as if something was passing underneath, so we jumped into the car and drove away."

Bleeding from the shoulders and missing time discovered

While travelling back, not unnaturally the events that that had just transpired were the subject of much conversation. Andrew complained to his father that when they had first seen the *'giant figure'* he had felt something pressing into his shoulders, and that it winded him. As they reached a lay-by, after leaving the forest, Andrew asked his father to pull in. Derek thought his son was going to be sick. Andrew lifted his coat to reveal a mark on each shoulder, which was bleeding. When they arrived home, Derek examined him and his clothes. There was no sign of any cuts or tears on the clothing that could have been associated with the marks, although there were blood stains on the shirt from the cuts to the skin. It was now 9.55pm.

At this stage Derek realised there was some time missing, as he only lives 40 minutes away, and claims that all of what happened could not have fitted into a time scale of two hours, fifteen minutes.

The following morning, Andrew drove back to Devon. It took him a year before he could discuss the matter again with his brother – such was the trauma experienced by him. Unfortunately, photos taken on Derek's mobile phone of the marks on his brother's shoulders were later mislaid, due to upgrades.

In June 2014 I (John) spoke to Derek at some length about the matter, when he had this to say:

> "After arriving home in great excitement, Andrew opened up his laptop and went onto the internet in an attempt to find something similar, and tapped in the word 'Demon'. The screen went very fuzzy and what sounded like a voice began to talk, as if trying to communicate, although the words were illegible. I shouted 'switch it off' – which he did. When the laptop was opened up again and reconnected with the internet, everything was back to normal."

Monks and shiny beings seen in Rendlesham Forest

Listening to the version of events given by Derek, we could not help but wonder if there was any connection with what Mr Jolly had seen and what Brenda and Dot Street were told, during a visit to see RAF Squadron Leader Donald Moreland, at RAF Woodbridge, on the 18th February 1981.

When they arrived at the base, they were shown into the office. After introductions, Squadron Leader Moreland and his secretary erroneously presumed the two women were from the MOD and that their visit was with regard to an incident on the 31st December 1980. Brenda said, *"No . . . the 27th December"*. The secretary replied: *"The report was for the 31st"*. Brenda and Dot asked Squadron Leader Moreland some questions. He replied: *"There were some lights out there – just a few, and some shiny 'beings' that looked just like angels"*. When he discovered they were not from the MOD, he told them to go.

Mr Jolly – then employed as a rabbit catcher on base (confirmed by Colonel Halt as being employed there) – telephoned Brenda to say he had seen some *'little brown monk figures'* around the bomb dump on Woodbridge Base, whilst out shooting rabbits. This is what he told her:

> "I was driving along to the bomb dump, one night at 11.30pm, when I thought I saw movement in the forest, stopped my jeep, got out, and hid behind a tree and looked through my gun-sight. I saw what I first took to be four children, dressed in monk habits, but thought it strange as I could not see any feet, or faces, and wondered why four children should be playing around at that time of the night.
>
> I telephoned the security guards on base and told them what I had seen. They told me to stay where I was and they would send two security policemen out to meet me. They arrived within 10-15 minutes, and got out of their car with their guns, making a lot of noise. They looked through their sights and started to walk towards the four 'children', who immediately disappeared somewhere behind the bomb dump. When we arrived at the spot, all that was left was a green, sticky, gooey mess. They picked some up and it dematerialised in their hands."

Mr Jolly was then taken to the base security hut and asked to make a statement – which he did. He was then advised not to talk about this to anyone. He did not, until another man, working on base, saw the same thing in a copse of trees – four little *'monk'* figures, watching him. He first thought they were children, dressed-up.

He told the other workmen, but they did not report it to the authorities. After the sighting of the little *'monks'*, Mr Jolly was not allowed to go to the bomb dump area without guards being present.

Brenda:
> "He wasn't the only witness to seeing 'brown monks' in the forest during that period of time. Another man contacted me with a similar story."

© Don Ramkin

Strange figures seen in the forest

On Friday, 31st May 2014, David Bryant and his wife, Linda, met three friends in the East Gate car park at Rendlesham Forest. It was a clear, balmy, evening and the walk along Track 10 was taken slowly to maximise their enjoyment of the Forest's abundant wildlife.

David:
> "An interesting change since our last visit was the addition of red hazard signs to the concrete caps covering the many access shafts that lead downwards to an apparent network of underground tunnels. These have been explored by braver investigators than we and this has obviously caused a reaction from the MOD. Once it was dark, we walked slowly back through the woods, taking video and frequent stills pictures as we went: I use a Pentax DSLR and Linda, a point and click 'Coolpix'. When Linda and I reviewed our photos at home, we found a number of hard-to-explain images. Near the 'Halt Landing Site' (which is soon to be adorned with a fibreglass replica of the Penniston/Burroughs object!) I obtained an intriguing picture that seems to show a figure to the left of the clearing. I attach two crops of this: the first is unadjusted; the second has been improved for contrast and brightness.

'Rædwald (Old English: Rædwald, 'power in counsel'), also rendered as Raedwald or Redwald, was a 7th-century king of East Anglia, a long-lived Anglo-Saxon kingdom which today includes the English counties of Norfolk and Suffolk. He was the son of Tytila of East Anglia and a member of the Wuffingas dynasty (named after his grandfather, Wuffa) who were the first kings of the East Angles.

From around 616, Rædwald was the most powerful of the English kings south of the River Humber. According to Bede he was the fourth ruler to hold imperium over other southern Anglo-Saxon kingdoms: he was referred to in the Anglo-Saxon Chronicle, written centuries after his death, as a bretwalda (an Old English term meaning 'Britain-ruler' or 'wide-ruler'). He was the first king of the East Angles to become a Christian, converting at Æthelberht's court some time before 605, whilst at the same time maintaining a pagan temple. In receiving the faith he helped to ensure the survival of Christianity in East Anglia during the apostasy of the Anglo-Saxon kingdoms of Essex and Kent.

He is generally considered by historians to be the most favoured candidate for the occupant of the Sutton Hoo ship-burial. (a location which we have visited and found to be the source of other strange images and reports of ghostly legions seen.) **(Source: Wikipedia)**

Haunted Skies Volume Ten

Linda had a similar figure (and plenty of the usual orbs!) on one of her photos, taken along Track 10, a few minutes later. We call this 'Lawnmower Man', for obvious reasons! At the time, I was 50 or 60 yards behind Linda, while our companions were 100yds ahead: you can see one of their night vision red torches in the distance. I suppose the most interesting occurrences took place halfway back along Track 10, at a spot where we have had strange experiences in the past. As I was taking a photo, a strong force pushed the lens of my camera downwards; at the same time, I felt something tugging at the hair on the back of my head. Simultaneously, Paul gave a cry as the side of his face was stroked!"

Original photograph taken by David Bryant depicting a 'figure' to the right by a tree. Barely visible in this un-enhanced image.

Haunted Skies Volume Ten

The 'brightened' version of the same photograph. A 'figure' can be seen next to the tree on the left.

Haunted Skies Volume Ten

Further enhancements in order to reveal more detail from the original photograph taken by David Bryant in Rendlesham Forest.

Linda Bryant's photograph taken in Rendlesham Forest at the time David had taken his own shots. This is 'lawnmower man'.

An enlargement of Linda Bryan'ts photograph of 'lawnmower man'.

Charles Halt and Brenda Butler meet up

(John Hanson): I finally met up with Colonel Charles Halt, face-to-face, during a visit made to Woodbridge, Suffolk, at 7pm on Tuesday, 10th June 2014, following his arrival in the United Kingdom for a forthcoming TV documentary. He came into the lounge of the public house and looked around, wondering where I was. I whistled (probably not the best way to acknowledge the presence of a retired Colonel of the USA). He came over and was absolutely delighted to see Brenda Butler, who greeted her old friend with warmth.

Over a glass of *'Speckled Hen'*, we talked very informally. Much was discussed, including a request from Charles Halt that we speak to a representative of the Forestry Commission, on his behalf, with regard to exploring the feasibility of a future film to be produced by Colonel Halt.

This would involve some filming in the United States, followed by (presumably) a re-enactment of the incident, involving Colonel Halt with a promise to donate monies earned through its sales to the Forestry Commission.

He was also handed a copy of Volume 9 of *Haunted Skies* (1981-1986) and later told us that he had read and enjoyed it – especially the information at the back, relating to Brenda.

Are there Portals in Rendlesham Forest?

Brenda wondered, in light of strange things seen down there, whether a portal could exist – though taking into consideration the problems associated with trying to identify the nature and source of something that is clearly on the edge of our peripheral understanding. Charles Halt said he had pondered whether there were portals in the forest through which the anomalous phenomena was coming, but reiterated it was speculative.

In a previous email sent to us some time ago he remarked:

> *"I think your approach is very appropriate. I will tell you I have had so many believable people tell me of strange things that occurred in the area that there may be something to the portal claims. Who knows?"*

It is important to remember that despite the various 'skirmishes' made between him and Brenda, during the investigation by her and others into the incident, which took place in December 1980, he has always remained friendly and has often emailed her over the years in answer to specific questions raised by her relating to an incident now over 34 years ago. It is clear while there are many that would like to spend time with him during his infrequent visits to this country, he always finds time from a busy schedule to see Brenda.

Bearing in mind that he had to prepare for his journey back to the United States, the following day, he bade us goodnight at 9.45pm.

Dear Brenda:

Thank you for updating me on happenings in Rendlesham Forest. I was sorry to hear you received what sounds like radiation burns. I hope you are ok. In several similar cases in the States the victims suffered badly. I suspect you now believe me and the fact that I was not trying to hide anything or part of a cover up. I'm convinced now that certain agencies left me out there to take the heat and look foolish.

I am also convinced that whatever is going on is much more than mind control although that appears to factor for some of the participants. Be careful, as there could be some real danger in what you are doing.

Keep me posted, as your experience sounds so familiar.

Chuck

July 3, 2002

Dear Brenda:

It was good to hear from you. I don't remember telling Georgina I did not want to be contacted. It sounds like you are really on to something. You are seeing and experiencing a lot more than we did. I seriously doubt the military has anything to do with it.

When I went out with the police we went from Bentwaters to Woodbridge (as I remember) by way of the public road (through Eyke) onto Woodbridge and then out the East Gate down the road. We turned right on the Forest service road for a hundred or more feet then left on the dirt road toward the sea. After several hundred yards we turned left on a trail and continued for several hundred feet. From there we went right into the trees toward the fence line. The "landing site" was about 200-300 feet from the fence. Ahead and to the left was the Boast home. Hope this helps.

The marks on the trees in the pictures are much larger than we noted on the infamous night. I also think you have mislocated the site in the picture of a map you sent. The map is not large enough and does not have enough clear references to say for sure. As far as posts. I did not see any and do not remember seeing any at later dates (1989 and when I did the filming).

Have you tried to catch some of the happenings on film? Infrared film?

Good luck- win the lottery and I'll join you for a party at the site.

Chuck

Dear Brenda:

Your wild experiences really sound like something is really heating up at "the East Gate". It's hard enough to believe what happened to us back in 1980 let along what's going on now. I would suggest you try hard to establish a dialog with what ever you've come in contact with. I would be most interested in hearing the results. If you do establish a dialog and I can help, I'm willing.

When I warned you to be careful I was not talking about something beyond us. My concern was that an agency with secretive powers might do something. You be the judge of that. I do know several of the airmen were hypnotized, drugged and threatened.

I have to assume that now you realize that other than when I gave up on your original Sky Crash trio, I have been telling the truth.

Keep in touch and be careful.

Chuck Halt

Dear John and Dawn

I found your letter quite interesting. I was not aware that the former 67th ARRS building had been a mortuary during the Second World War.

Many of our Security Police had seen unexplained things at RAF Woodbridge. Several personally told of seeing "East End Charlie" (as they called him). He appeared to be a World War Two Aviator that wandered near the back gate. One particular event occurred on Guy Fawkes Night in 1981. A large cigar shaped craft silently floated over the airfield and circled the Air Traffic Tower before drifting off.

To the best of my knowledge I did not experience any unusual incidents immediately after the incident. Further, I did not experience any sustained ill effects. I can not speak for the other individuals involved as I'm told that several feel they have sustained lasting health problems.

Hope this helps. Say hello to Brenda for me.

Sincerely,

Charles I. Halt

I thoroughly enjoyed the evening spent with him, and was able to thank him personally for all the help and encouragement he had given us with the production of *Haunted Skies*.

'Flying Saucer' under construction! Hush, hush!

Colonel Halt asked us to speak to Forest Ranger, Nigel Turner – a pleasant, friendly, helpful man – and put forward his proposal. During a subsequent visit to see Nigel, who was accompanied by part-time volunteer – Olivia, we asked if we could photograph the dome-shaped UFO currently under construction, parked incongruously next to forestry vehicles in their car park, but were advised by her that this was not possible, despite procrastinations from Brenda that photographs of the *'flying saucer'* were on the Internet! We honoured our promise not to take any photographs. However, we were later sent a photograph from a third party, who wishes to remain nameless!

Haunted Skies Volume Ten

It is believed that the *'flying saucer'* will be moved into the location (known locally for Colonel Halt's 1980 sighting) to endorse the opening of a new children's playground, in September 2014, by a visiting 'dignitary'.

This area, suitably labelled with posts and alien stickers, forming part of the *Forest UFO Trail* bears little resemblance to how it was originally – (then covered in trees – and not particularly easy to find). Unfortunately, this ultimately leads to confusion and should not be relied on to identify the exact locations (and there are many) of who saw what and where.

Some people naively believe the UFO trails and 'UFO landing sites' forms part of a UFO curriculum, whose aims are to educate the younger mind with the truths of what UFOs represent, but common sense dictates otherwise. One cannot blame the Forestry Commission for using the famous incident that still attracts so much controversy, to promote various organised venues which take place in the Forest.

The photograph below shows Brenda and Derek Savory, standing in an area cleared by the Forestry Commission, just off Track 12 – recently nominated by John Burroughs (2014) as being the scene of his encounter, which was previously unknown to us.

Did John Burroughs take photos of the UFO?

On Page 417 of Volume 8 of *Haunted Skies*, we had enclosed a letter to Dot Street from Lawrence Fawcett, Assistant Director for CAUS (Citizens Against UFO Secrecy) where it mentions that *'John Burroughs took photos of the object when it landed, but the film and camera were confiscated by the OSI'*. As far as we know, apart from Monroe Nevels, who took photos (they were later found to be fogged) the only other person was Jim Penniston. He also says that when later processed they, too, were found to be fogged. We presume this was a mistake.

John Burroughs

Rendlesham Forest has also been the focus of much attention by UFO enthusiast Peter Parish, from Ipswich – a friend of Brenda Butler. Peter has always been intrigued by the suggestion that the trees were damaged during the UFO landing and has discussed this with Georgina Bruni, on many occasions, before her untimely death. Peter has also recorded, through many sketches, various sightings of UFOs that he has shared with Brenda, along with his own humorous viewpoint of the famous events that took place in 1980. Currently (2014) he is recovering from a serious stroke and we wish him a speedy recovery. (Some of these sketches can be seen within this volume of *Haunted Skies*).

Brenda now feels that it is time to put the record straight with regard to the original story being sold to the *News of the World*, taking into consideration that, over the years, there appears to have been a misconception that she was involved in negotiating a contract with this newspaper, after having sold the UFO story and of later receiving a large fee. Whatever fee was paid out and split between the parties involved is a private matter and will stay that way.

*Rendlesham Forest UFO Conference – September, 2014

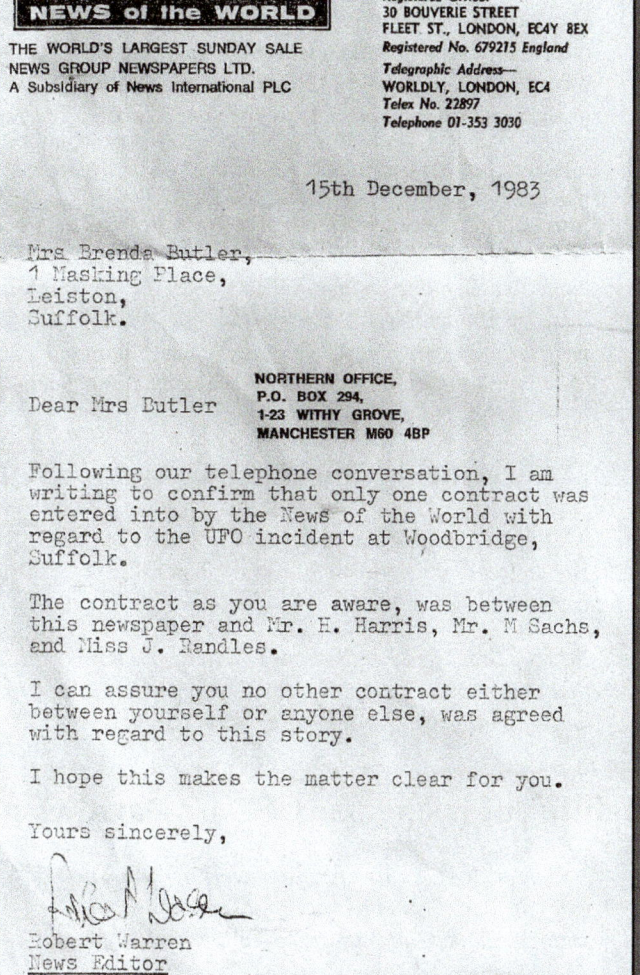

John F. Burroughs, USAF Tech Sgt. (Ret.) is planning to appear at a UFO Conference, to be held at Woodbridge Village Hall on the 20th September 2014, and now claims the following is the answer for what he and others witnessed (in June 2014).

John:

> "As far as I am concerned, the entire (Rendlesham Forest) affair and evidence trail constitutes official Top Secret confirmation that humanity is dealing with intelligence capable of engineering interstellar travel."

John complains of medical effects resulting from his encounter, and is involved in an ongoing campaign to force the authorities to reveal the truth about what happened and to seek justice for the men and women

---

*Mr G. Goodger – The tickets for this forthcoming venue are priced at £20 each. Please add £2 per ticket to cover PayPal fees and postage. Entry is strictly ticket only; tickets will not be available on the door. We accept PayPal, cheques and postal orders. To order tickets using PayPal, please visit: www.spaceportuk.com/events.html

caught up in these incidents, some of whom have suffered adverse physical and psychological effects.

> "I am convinced that the real reason the DOD (US Department of Defense) classified my medical records and attempted to doctor my (USAF) Service Record to show I was not in service at the time, was not to allow the VA (Veterans Administration) to deny me benefits, but to specifically keep the medical information about my condition a classified secret."

On Thursday, 15th May, John F. Burroughs issued a Press release, asserting . . .

> "the UK's Ministry of Defence is using 'bureaucratic double-speak' to claim the MOD has released all of its 'UFO files' to the UK National Archive, while withholding the substantive files under a bureaucratic name change trick so that the truly sensitive UFO files remain hidden under the category Unidentified Aerial Phenomena (UAP). I think given the type of radiation that causes certain biological damage, we're dealing with something exotic, something that serves a purpose that every-day-humans on this Earth have no idea is capable of being done."

MOD declaration about the dangers of UFO radiation

The MOD make the following reference in Page F-4, ANNEX F, "Unidentified Aerial Phenomena in the UK Air Defence Region: Executive Summary, Scientific & Technical Memorandum – No. 55/2/00", Ministry of Defence, December 2000.

> "The well-reported Rendlesham Forest/Bentwaters event is an example where it might be postulated that several observers were probably exposed to Unidentified Aerial Phenomena (UAP) radiation for longer than normal UAP sighting periods."

Sighting of triangular UFO by David Gann – 1981

> "While at RAF Bentwaters and working the east gate at RAF Woodbridge, I observed a black triangle-shaped aircraft fly over the gate after dark. I observed three dim round lights on the underside of the craft. As it went over, there was no sound whatsoever! I was scared by this and was hesitant to call it in to the Law Enforcement desk. Just a moment later, Security in the WSA observed it and called it in over the WSA. At the end of shift I was questioned repeatedly about this. I had no idea something like this was ever seen in the past. I was on temporary duty to Bentwaters. I lived in the visiting airman's quarters. I did not know anyone at Bentwaters, other than the two others – TDY from Vance AFB – that I was with. It seemed to make a lot of people mad that I had also seen this aircraft . . . this was in late October/early November in 1981."

David Gann

Our opinions

It is generally believed that only in certain circumstances has the MOD become involved in any direct 'out in the field' investigations following complaints of UFO activity, brought to their attention by the public, although they have, for obvious reasons, taken much interest in reports involving sightings of humanoid occupants near to landed craft.

With regard to the events that took place at Rendlesham Forest, that still continues to capture the attention of so many people, now over 34 years later, Brenda Butler tells us that there are six specific documents which will never be released into the public domain.

The fact that these documents are being withheld may indicate, in our opinion, that this was an extremely sensitive military operation rather than the landing of an alien craft. If this is the case then the UFO story must form part of an elaborate ruse, engineered to cover up the recovery of something, or someone, belonging to a foreign power.

During the course of the years we have come across many accounts, involving the ill-effects of UFO radiation given off by UFOs – albeit apparently unintentionally rather than any deliberate action. Few of those reports will be found in any MOD archive – if there are, they will remain classified. We know that from our own enquiries there has been occasion when the MOD has sympathised with people who have suffered medical ailments, but they have declined to make any further comment.

Was it a triangular UFO that crash-landed?

Knowing that Lt. Colonel Charles Halt and others described seeing three lights in the sky and what appears to have been a display of UFO behaviour, during their excursion into the forest, one cannot help but wonder if there was any association with reports made of a triangular UFO seen over the airbase.

Whilst this craft may (for all we know) have been an example of Top Secret covert technology, we doubt this could have been the answer for a 'plague' of UFO activity which was witnessed by hundreds of Essex residents, involving the sighting of three lights forming a triangle in the sky, completely silent and stationary in the air, during the later 1980s.

On occasions the witnesses reported seeing one or two of the lights move away and then return later, which surely rules out any flight characteristics associated with man-made aircraft.

Hexagon Satellite was the answer

We spoke at some length with Chris Pennington, who is convinced that the object recovered was a film capsule dropped by a ' 'Big Bird' Hexagon Satellite, after the drogue parachute came adrift. Chris claims that the UFO story was disseminated as part of a contingency plan to camouflage the recovery of this film capsule, and has even brought the matter to the attention of Colonel Halt, who declines to make any comment – which is only to be expected, bearing in mind his obligations to the USA Official Secrets Act and should not be construed either way.

Chris:

> "The satellites were designed to release film canisters in capsules called buckets, which were recovered in mid-air by specially designed aircraft during their parachute descent. They were designed to float

in water for a short period of time, and then sink if the mid-air recovery failed. The early missions operated with a single bucket, but starting with KH-4A two buckets were made available.

H9-16 Mission number 1216 'Big Bird' Hexagon was launched on the 18th June 1980, with a decay orbit date given as the 6th March 1981. Was there a connection with what happened? – I do believe there was and that they have been covering it up for years.

KH-9 HEXAGON Operations

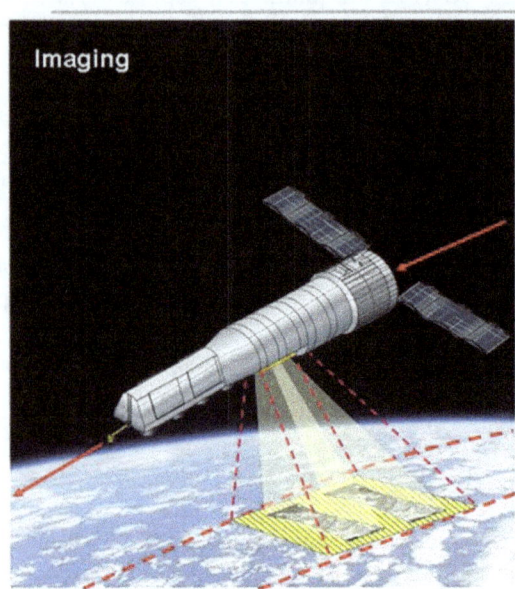
Imaging

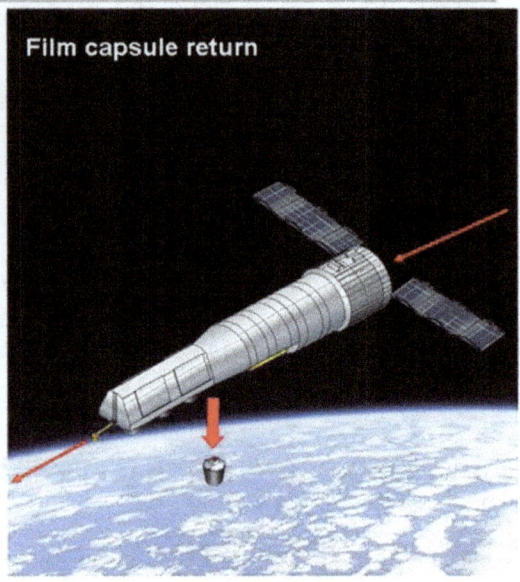
Film capsule return

Around this time the French Air Force had refused to be in NATO; the Americans were thrown out of France. They closed down the USA Airbus in France; when they went to Spain they had to fly around France to get there. At that stage in history France were actually doing exchange postings with the Russian Air Force. If the Russians wanted to get to France, how would they go about it? They could come down from the Baltic, through the Channel, which they were entitled to do because anything over three miles is international airspace. Another route was by Ireland but whatever route, they would have to go past Britain, or the Caspian Sea, by the Med. I believe it was common knowledge that Russian 'Bear' reconnaissance aircraft used to fly close enough to test our responses. I remember, on one occasion, they used to wave at each other. What would happen if one of these 'Bears' had some sort of hydraulic failure and was going to crash into the sea? If this had happened, involving air sea rescue, it would have brought the matter to the attention of the whole world to it. What do you do? ... Let the AC crash into the sea and forget about it, or do you try to rescue the aircrew? Do you say, well, we will give them special dispensation to land, say, Kinross, where we would go over it with a fine toothcomb, or do you land at RAF Bentwaters/Woodbridge, which is three runways wide, surrounded by woodland, repair it, and then let it go out again? Now that's what I think happened.

*KH-9 (Keyhole-9), also known as Hexagon or unofficially as 'Big Bird', was a large reconnaissance satellite to replace the earlier KH-4B Corona satellites. In contrast to earlier models, it was not based on the Agena stage, but on a new manoeuvrable bus called SCS (Satellite Control Section). It featured four return capsules for a much increased lifetime. The McDonnell Douglas manufactured Mk.8 return capsules were of a similar type as in the earlier Corona satellites and were designed to de-orbit a film capsule from space with mid-air recovery of the returning capsule by a specially equipped aircraft. The camera system was built by Perkin-Elmer and consisted of two large panoramic cameras for area surveillance.12 of the 20 satellites featured also a mapping Camera System (MCS) mounted on the forward end with an own smaller Mk.5 return capsule. It was present on missions KH-9 5 to KH-9 16.The lifetime of the satellites increased from 40 days in the beginning to up to 275 days during the final missions.

Secondly what did happen but it didn't come about till later was there was a time when the USA discovered that the photographs which the Russian satellites were taking over Russia were being intercepted; in other words, Russia knew what the USA knew about them! What if the satellite jettisoned the film capsules that fell to Earth by parachute with the film to be picked up?

One of them could have landed in the forest. As for getting material out of the Airbase was concerned, in answer to your question about what level of security was in existence, as long as you showed all the courtesies, there was never any problem getting on and off Base. Nine times out of ten they waved you through. It's when you did things (if you were, sort of, a visitor) they would stop you.

Brenda used to drive in and out of that Base all of the time and with reporters. Nobody ever used to pull them up. I used to go down to the Rod and Gun Club on the Base. One night, we were there all night and weren't allowed off Base because of some sort of 'Red Alert'."

Telephone being tapped

Both Chris and Brenda suspect their domestic telephones were tapped, but appreciate that they cannot prove it. Brenda still believes to this present day that some form of electronic *'eavesdropping'* went on while they were in the forest, as she received two letters from an unidentified *'agency'* containing reproduced conversations held with other parties, while walking through the forest during the investigation.

Brenda Butler and Chris Pennington in jovial mood, displaying a copy of Haunted Skies, *Volume 8, which contains important contributions from them both*

1983 – Strange lights over the forest – Alert on Woodbridge Airbase

In June 2014, Mrs Daria 'Dee' Clayton Tantao of Tampa, Florida, described a highly unusual experience which befell her, sometime in the late summer or early autumn 1983. At the time she was living in Air Force accommodation at RAF Woodridge, with her mother, sister and father, who was stationed at RAF Bentwaters during the last 18 months period of his tour, between January 1981 and January 1984. Prior to that, the family had been living in Ipswich.

Dee:
"During that time on Woodbridge, we lived in the second duplex on Thorn Walk, a road just past the southern-most gate that was located at the intersection of Otley and Heath Road. I am not certain that the woods across from the residence are technically a part of Rendlesham Forest, but this did indeed occur on Base rather than off. unfortunately, I am not sure of the time frame. Sometime in the middle

of night, I awoke to the sound of whistles blowing and men shouting. My father and sister were also awakened, so we all went to the front door to see what was happening. I saw armed, uniformed personnel running alongside military vehicles, lining up along the road directly across from our home. The men ran down the street and into the woods, about 15-20 yards to the south-east of our house."

Softly pulsating lights seen over the forest

"My dad rushed outside to find out what was going on, while my sister and I remained in the doorway of our home. At first I was watching all the commotion, trying to overhear the conversation between my dad and a guy that he had flagged down, but then I became aware of something very much out of place ... Approximately 50 yards further into the woods, I became transfixed by extremely bright lights filtering through the trees that were shining in all directions from one single location – on or near the ground. The lights were like rays or beams, similar to movie marquee lights. They were softly pulsating with glowing green and pinkish and pastel hues, and as bright as a football stadium – they lit up most of the forest within our view, and they were emanating from what I can only describe as a dark sort of shadow, if that makes sense. I recall standing in the doorway completely mesmerized. I only saw this for a few minutes before my father ushered my sister and I back into the house, rather urgently, with orders to gather the family and remain indoors – which is exactly what we did. It seems the noise continued for about another hour, and eventually I went back to sleep.

I remember feeling very frightened. In the morning it was as if nothing ever happened. In the next days and weeks, rumours spread around the base that a UFO had landed."

Neither downed aircraft nor forest fire

"I can attest that it was not a downed aircraft, nor was it a forest fire – there was most definitely no smoke or fire, no emergency vehicles, and no noise for that matter, other than the noise coming from the men and military vehicles. It seems highly unlikely that the Air Force would conduct war games so close to dependent housing in the middle of the night, unless we were under a direct threat of attack, as it was the Cold War era. Because there were so many personnel involved, it stands to reason that there is some official documentation somewhere. Either way, I'm convinced there are many other witnesses or participants out there, besides myself and family, who know something about this – I recall at least 20 to 30 individuals involved, perhaps more. Since there have been no other claims that I know of, I suppose the incident has been classified and the individuals involved have been sworn to secrecy. But if it's true that Colonel Halt made claim to witnessing a second event in 1983, he would be the one to talk to."

Retired Colonel Charles Halt – 22nd June, 2014

"I am familiar with the area. It's now Council Housing. The area across the road from where she lived is private property. I don't ever remember any incident, other than some vehicle accidents. If a UFO landed here with all the witnesses, I would have known about it. We also had a fatality at that location when a GI crossed the road, looking the wrong way, and was hit by a car. It was about that time frame. I suspect that's what it was."

Dee:

"I will ask my dad about the fatal accident, but I can tell you that what I saw was not emergency vehicles or anything reminiscent of that sort of thing. This was definitely a military situation in the middle of the woods, nowhere near the road. In fact, I would estimate 'it' was approximately equidistant from both roads – the one I lived on and the one just off the base. I'm afraid I had some difficulty with the map you sent me. I will try to refine the one I have to make it more readable. I asked our old neighbour what she remembers and she only has a vague memory, but said she will get in touch with another old neighbour who lived on the same road to see if she remembers any details about that night."

PART 5

HAUNTED SKIES – GLIMPSES INTO OTHER REALITIES?

Orbs

WHILST it is generally believed that orbs can be attributed to being out of focus particles of dust, insects, or water droplets, caught in the flash of a digital camera, we should remember that identical images were being caught on 35mm camera long before the digital camera revolution. The fact that people can take hundreds of photographs now, instead of being bound by the constraints of 35mm film and its processing costs then, has, of course, increased the interest in the capture of orbs and its speculated source believed paranormal in nature by some – others maintain they are only dust!

Haunted Skies Volume Ten

On one occasion we saw with our own eyes, close to the East Gate entrance, a diffused milky, mushroom-shaped *'light'*, hovering a couple of feet off the ground. On another occasion we were able to see an *'orb'* astride one of the branches of a nearby tree clearly before taking the photograph, which rules out any camera defects. Whatever the orbs were they have the propensity to move at tremendous speed and were sometimes seen forming what appeared to be tubes of light, snaking across the forest tracks.

Rendlesham Forest apports of stones

It is impossible to offer, in our opinion, any logical explanation for the arrival of the warm stones that fall down onto the forest floor in Rendlesham Forest. It is a phenomenon that we have experienced personally on at least three occasions, during visits there and we remain baffled as to how this occurs and for what reason? In Volume 8 of *Haunted Skies* we discussed this matter and can only presume that logically, they are being levitated up into the air by some unknown force, and the energy created causes the increase in temperature.

Michael Oram – Does It Rain In Other Dimensions?

We also had the pleasure, once more, of talking to Michael Oram – who lives in the Cumbria area. Mike's interest in the UFO subject goes back to the halcyon days of Warminster when, in the 1970s, he was a regular visitor to Cradle Hill during a 'wave' of UFO activity that occurred there. Michael has also published the following books: *Does It Rain In Other Dimensions?* by Mike Oram, *Alien Interface* by Mike Oram & Fran Pickering, *The Zen Of Ben* by Mike Oram & John Pickering, *The Strange World Of Jimmy Hayes* by Mike Oram.

Mike:

> "When I went for a walk through Rendlesham Forest, one night, with Brenda Butler, an odd thing happened. At one point she told me that this is where stones fall through the air and land with quite a thump and quite close, but she had never been hit by them.
>
> Shortly after this, a stone brushed my hair, and landed with a thump on the ground. Brenda, who was walking a short way in front of me, immediately shouted 'stone!' It was near my feet and I picked it up. It was very warm indeed, and this is something that Brenda had mentioned beforehand. When I arrived back in Cumbria, a few days later, we put the stone under John's microscope that is linked to the computer, when images of a strange 'wire' were seen that is somehow connected inside the stone. I did send this to a scientist friend of mine, who showed it to a couple of colleagues, who commented they had not seen anything like it before."

Author, Mike Oram from Cumbria, who had come to visit former skywatcher John Rowston, with Dawn Holloway, August 27th, 2011 at Cradle Hill, Warminster.

Haunted Skies Volume Ten

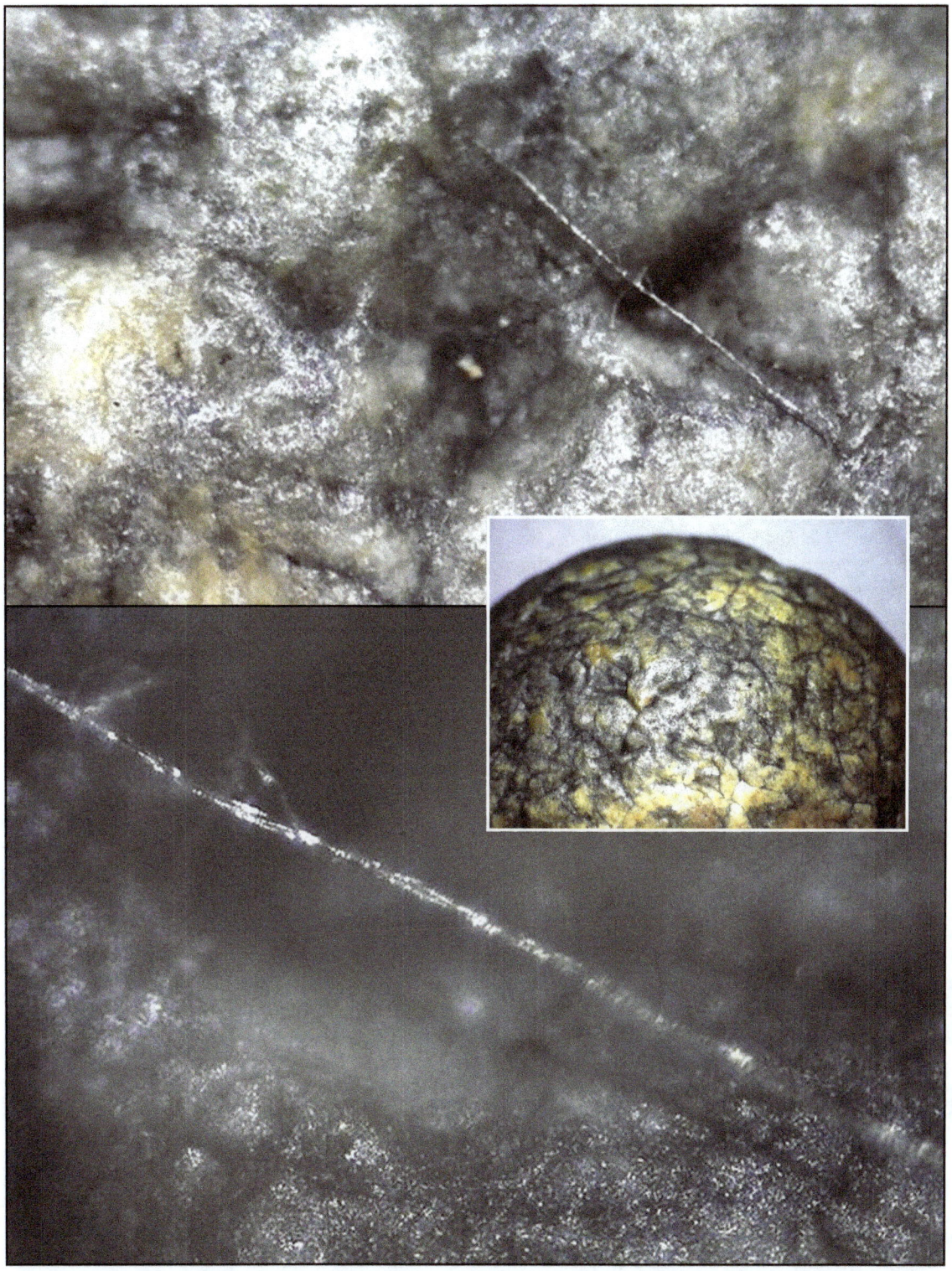

Communicating with the orbs

February 2011

Mike:

"In February of 2011, I received a telepathic image to take my small compact camera out into the garden. I was told where to stand and took a shot. I was amazed to see the image that I captured. Looking at the height of the wire fence, this 'being' was around 30ft in height. You can see the legs are straddled over the wire fence and also the parting of the head, which is similar to the cover of my book. The image of the cover on my book is not completely correct. When I had a regression with Delores Cannon and came into contact with these intelligences, I explained that the head parted into two halves and was swept back. I said under regression that it reminded me of a French nun, from the old days. I thought this was what I was seeing, until Delores guided me to look more closely and observe. I then found myself in a completely different place, I was three hours under regression and it involved hybrid children."

May 2011

"On 5th May 2011, the day before my 60th birthday, I was typing on my computer, around 10pm at night, when I suddenly received a telepathic message to take my large digital medium format camera outside onto my balcony. I was also instructed to fix the more powerful external flashgun to the top. My balcony looks out over a field and that is where I pointed the camera and shot the first image. I looked back at this first shot and was amazed to see a whole host of what I termed 'shooting orbs' coming out of the ground and shooting skyward. I took 15 shots and then all became still and returned to normal.

On the 7th May, I was working at the computer at about the same time, when once again I received the same telepathic message. My camera was still resting on the kitchen top and I quickly grabbed it and rushed out onto the balcony.

I began shooting into the field and captured another 45 images and, as before, this strange experience stopped. While I was capturing these images, I received another message telling me that this was a form of consciousness and was leaving the earth plane due to changes in its vibration and I was to witness this."

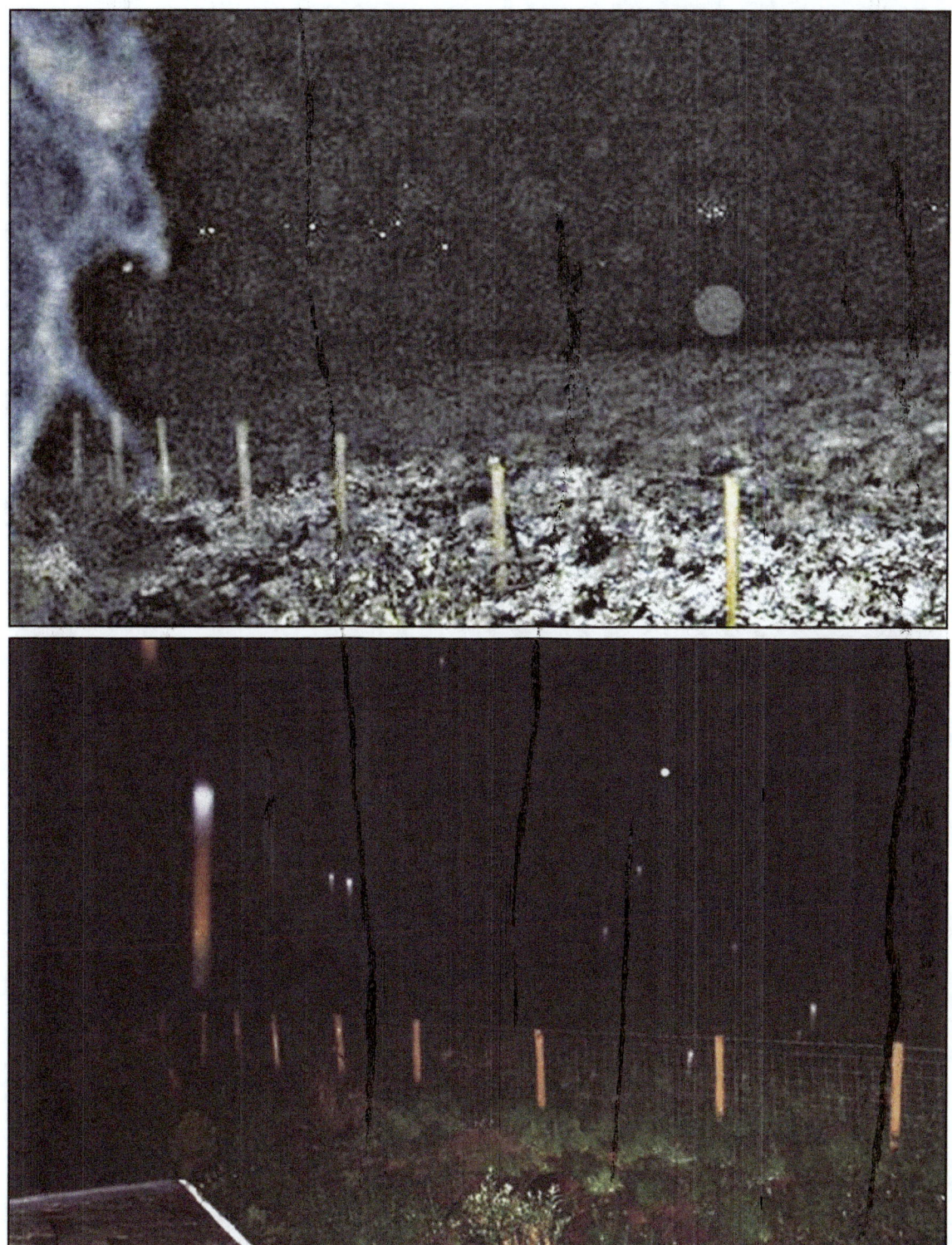

Haunted Skies Volume Ten

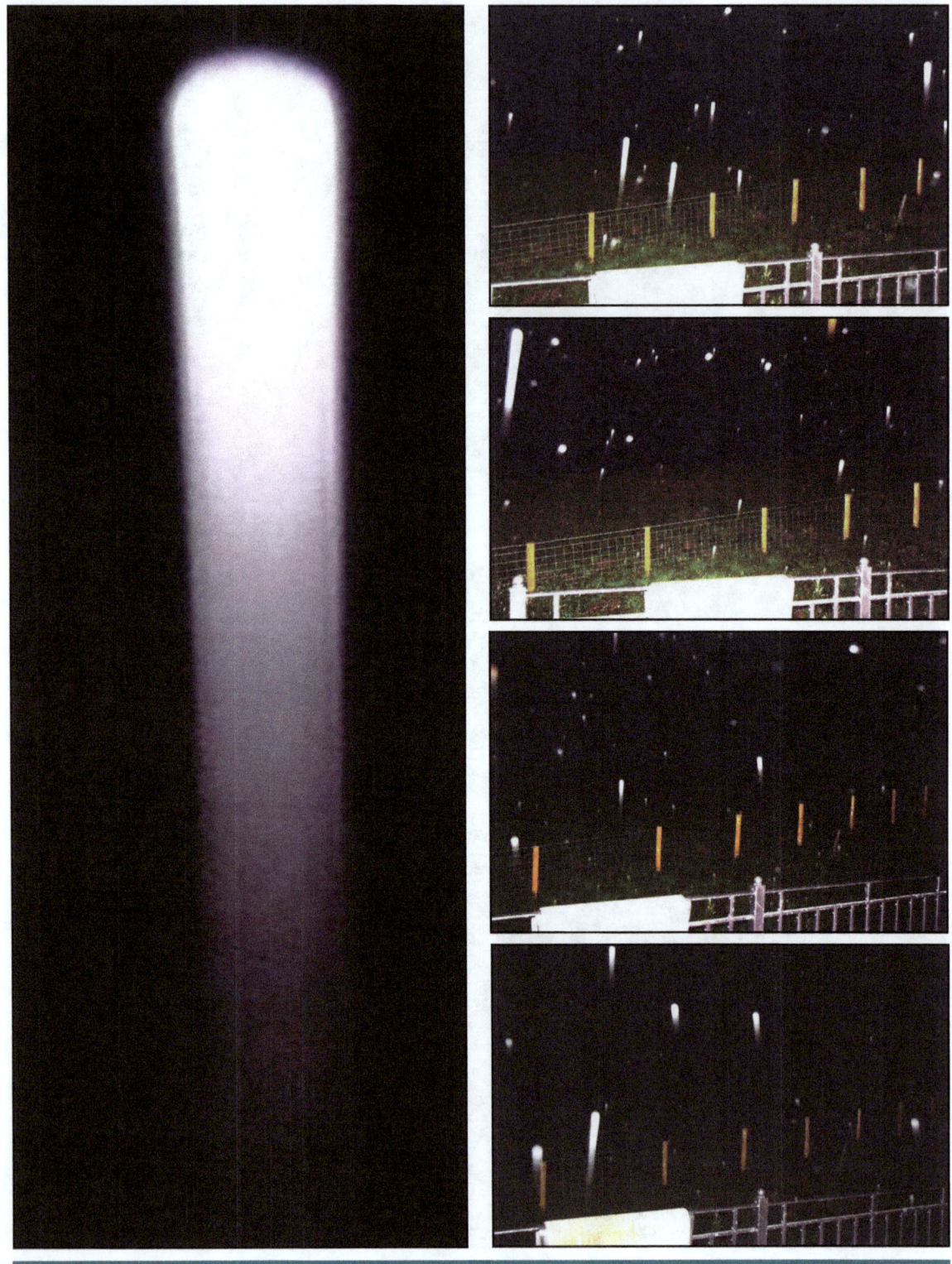

Vortexes and ghostly mists – discussed in the 1990's!

Generally speaking, common sense and scepticism from those who have not spent a great deal of time 'out in the field' seeks to convince us that objects such as tiny bits of dust, or insects, can also appear out of focus in paranormal photos. In addition to this, another frequent offender is the camera strap. Some years ago, around the mid-1990s, we discussed this in detail with a Dr. Vernon Harrison, who was a photographic specialist with ASSAP (The Association for the Scientific Study of Anomalous Phenomena).

A number of strange photographs, showing what we referred to as *'a spiral of light'* being caught in the camera lens were sent to him for comparison purposes. He was able to show that there was a distinct difference between the out-of-focus shot of the camera strap and something occurring a few feet away from the camera lens. We also discussed the differences in black *'spirals'* – this was long before orbs were referred to.

Bearing in mind the following thought-provoking photographs taken from around the Rendlesham Forest, Suffolk area, during a number of years, by people such as Brenda Butler, Peter Parish, Beverley Plumridge, Derek Savory and ourselves, it is clear that something peculiar is taking place.

Haunted Skies Volume Ten

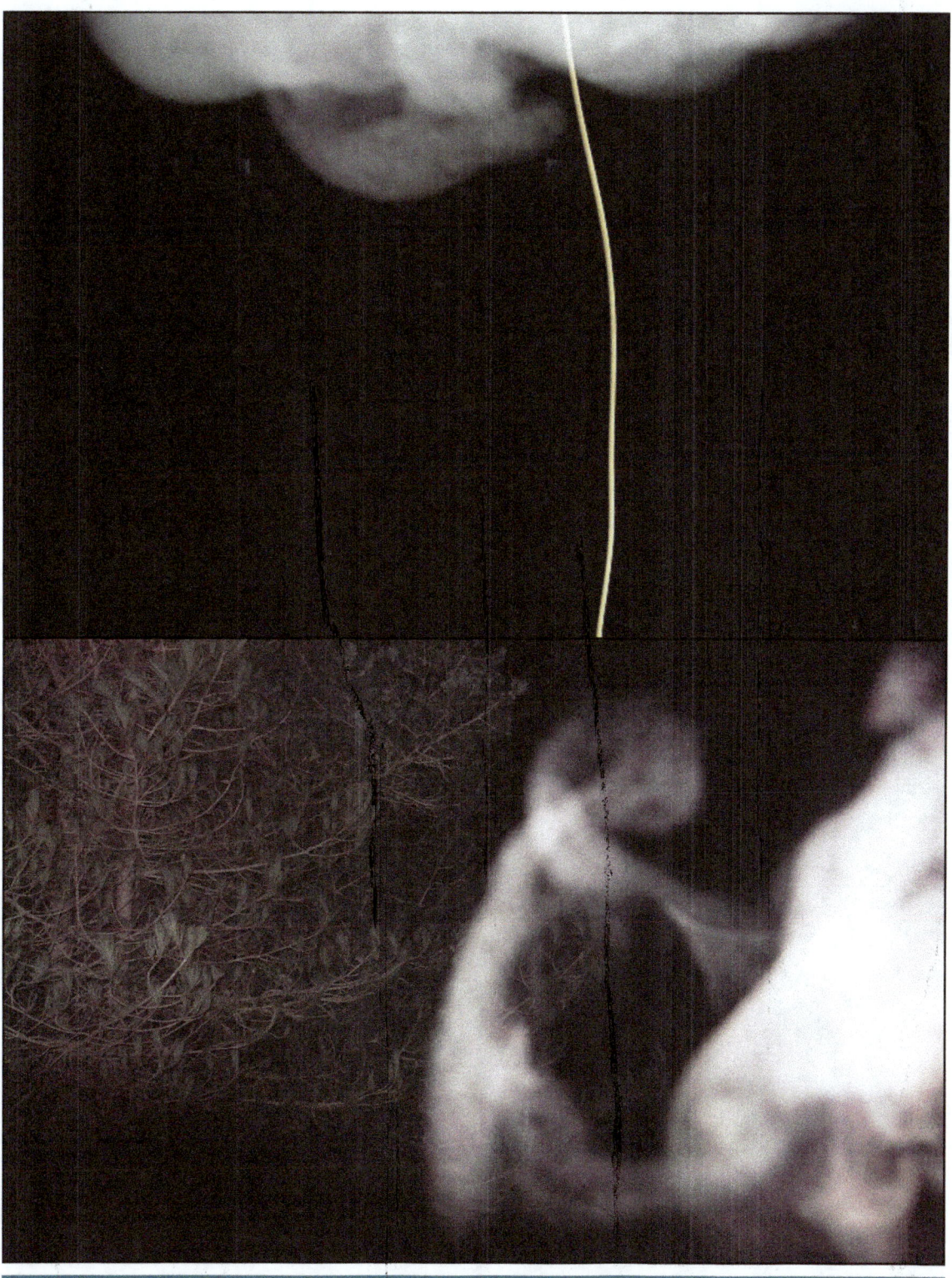

Haunted Skies Volume Ten

Haunted Skies Volume Ten

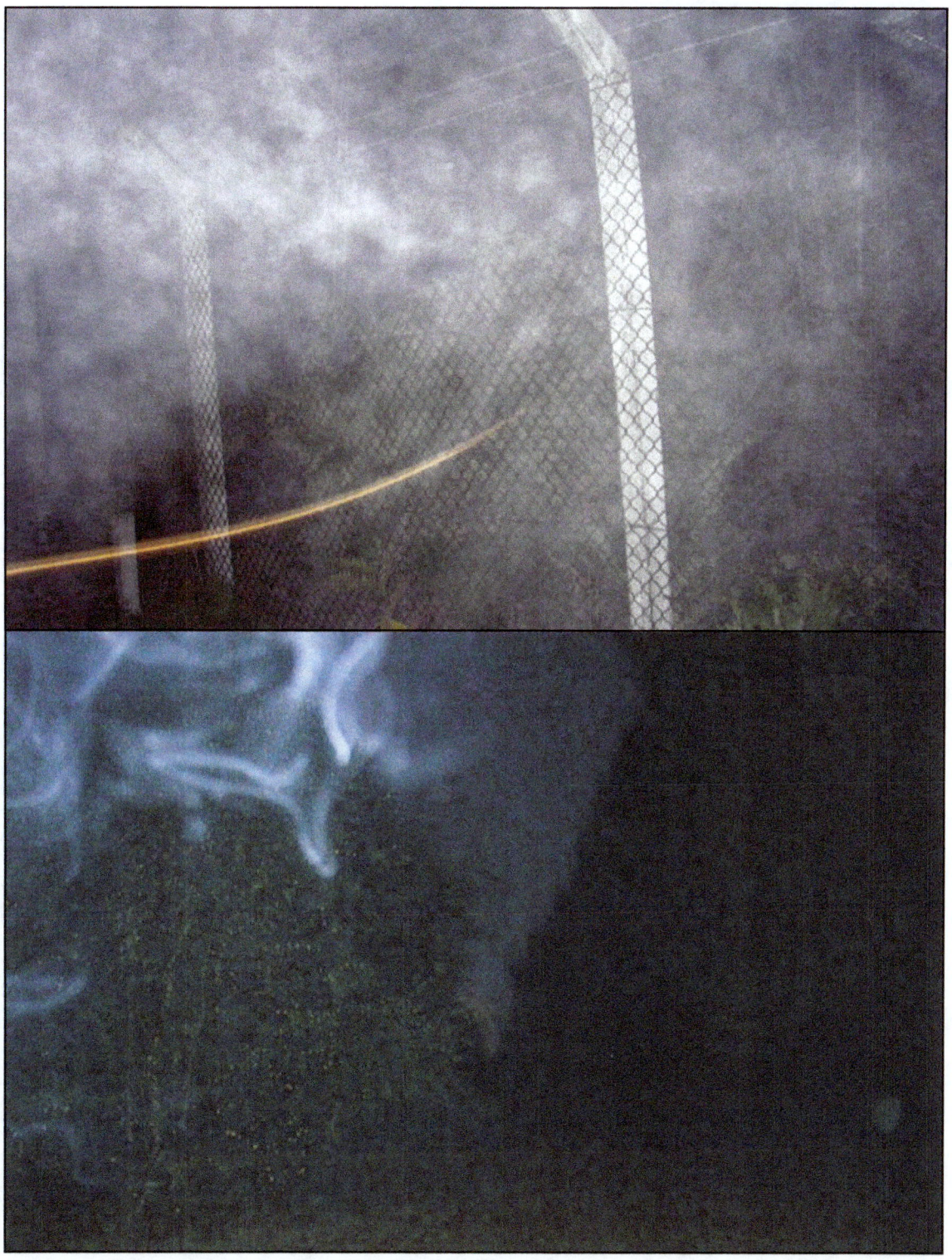

Haunted Skies Volume Ten

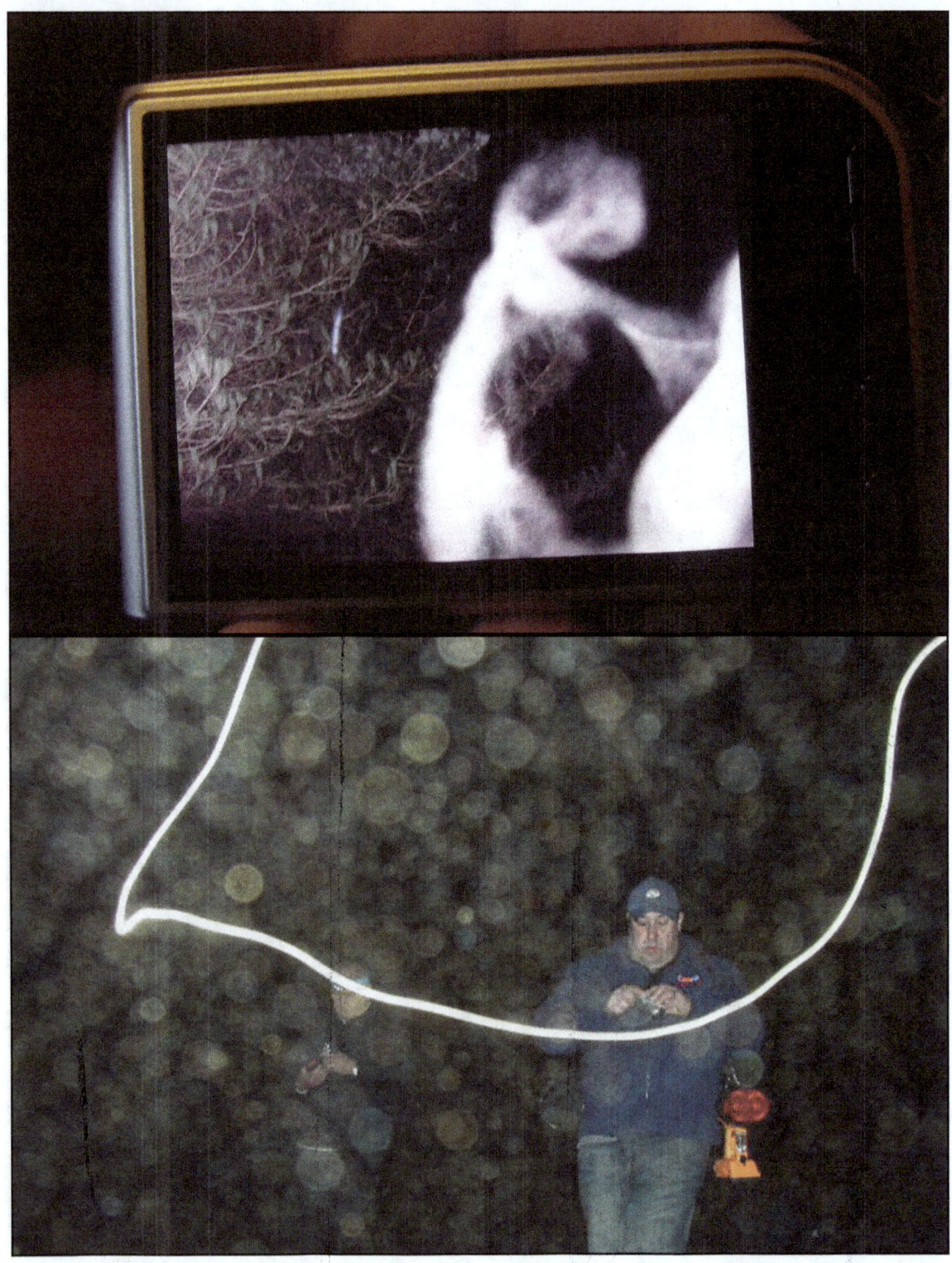

Haunted Skies Volume Ten

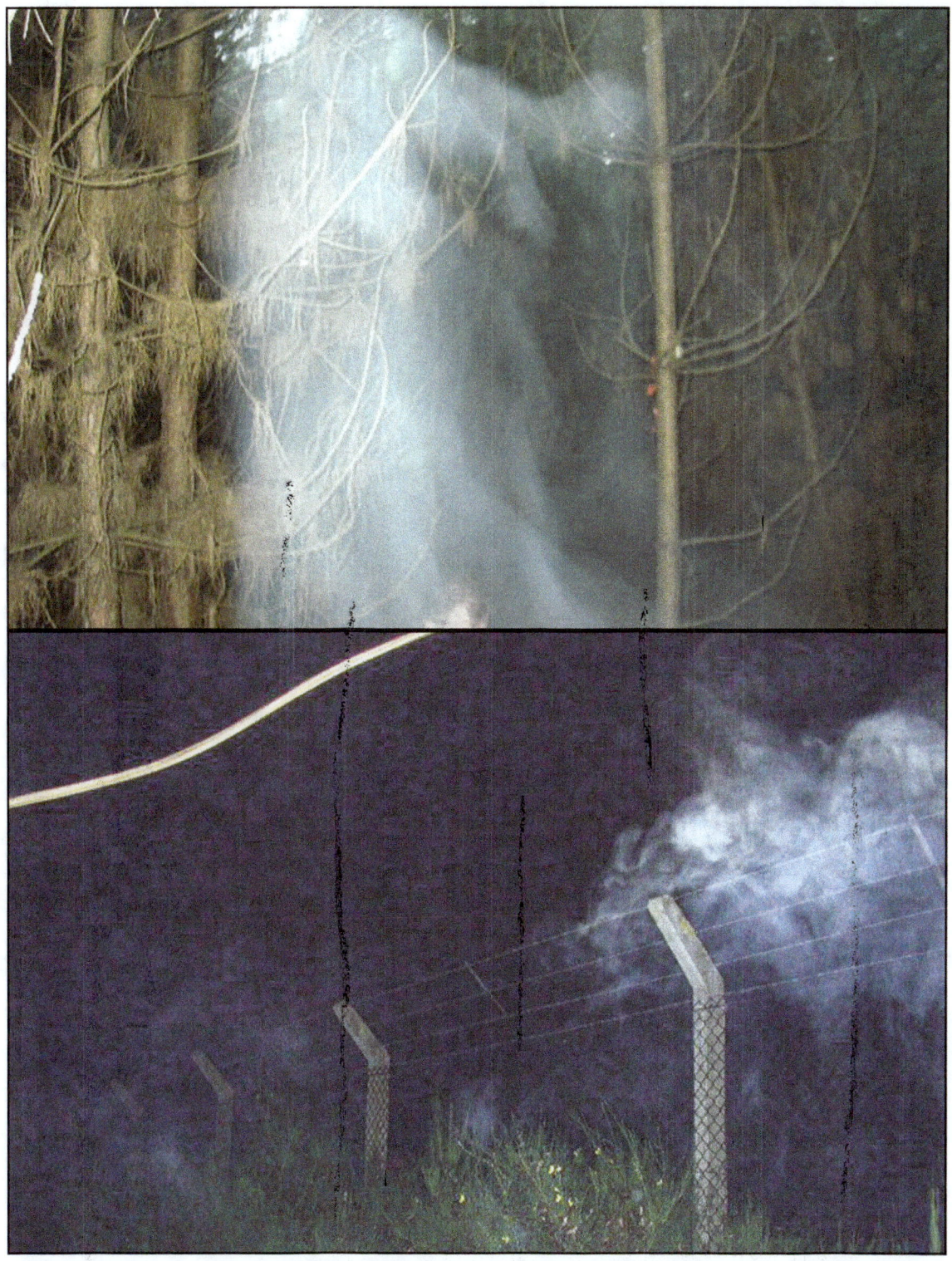

Haunted Skies Volume Ten

Haunted Skies Volume Ten

The Portals of Sedona, Arizona, USA

In 1997, another book which influenced our view of the world was *Merging Dimensions – The opening Portals of Sedona* (ISBN 0-9622748-4-4) written by Tom Dongo and Linda Bradshaw. This records a fascinating journey of self-enlightenment taken by the couple, during a 'wave' of UFO/paranormal activity, which occurred in the Sedona area at their individual ranches in 1993.

We contacted Tom Dongo and spoke to him at the time but lost touch as the years slipped away, although we never forgot the spectacular photographs taken by him and *Robert Meyer, a psychic and tourist guide from Sedona. Ironically although we travelled to the United States and visited Sedona some years ago, we never met face to face!

The Bradshaw Ranch

The ranch is named after its owners, Bob and Linda Bradshaw, and contains 90 acres. The Bradshaw homestead was featured on the television show – *Sightings*. Over 400 movies were made on the ranch, including *Stay Away Joe*, featuring Elvis Presley. The ranch was featured in *Marlboro* advertisements and *Playboy Magazine*. The ranch offers many adventures for tourists: horseback riding, western dinners, dancing, a petting zoo of western animals, such as a buffalo and pot bellied pig, historic wagon rides, walking trails, cattle drives, western museum, an old western saloon, and an Indian village.

Tom Dongo

*Robert Meyer is a teacher/master of Reiki and a student of Sacred Geometry and Ancient Wisdom. He was guided in the 1990s to Sedona. His pictures have been published in *Time Magazine*, *Sedona Journal of Emergence*, *The Shining Light 11 & 111*, and *Merging Dimensions*. He is intuitively guided to aim his camera and snap the shutter.

Haunted Skies Volume Ten

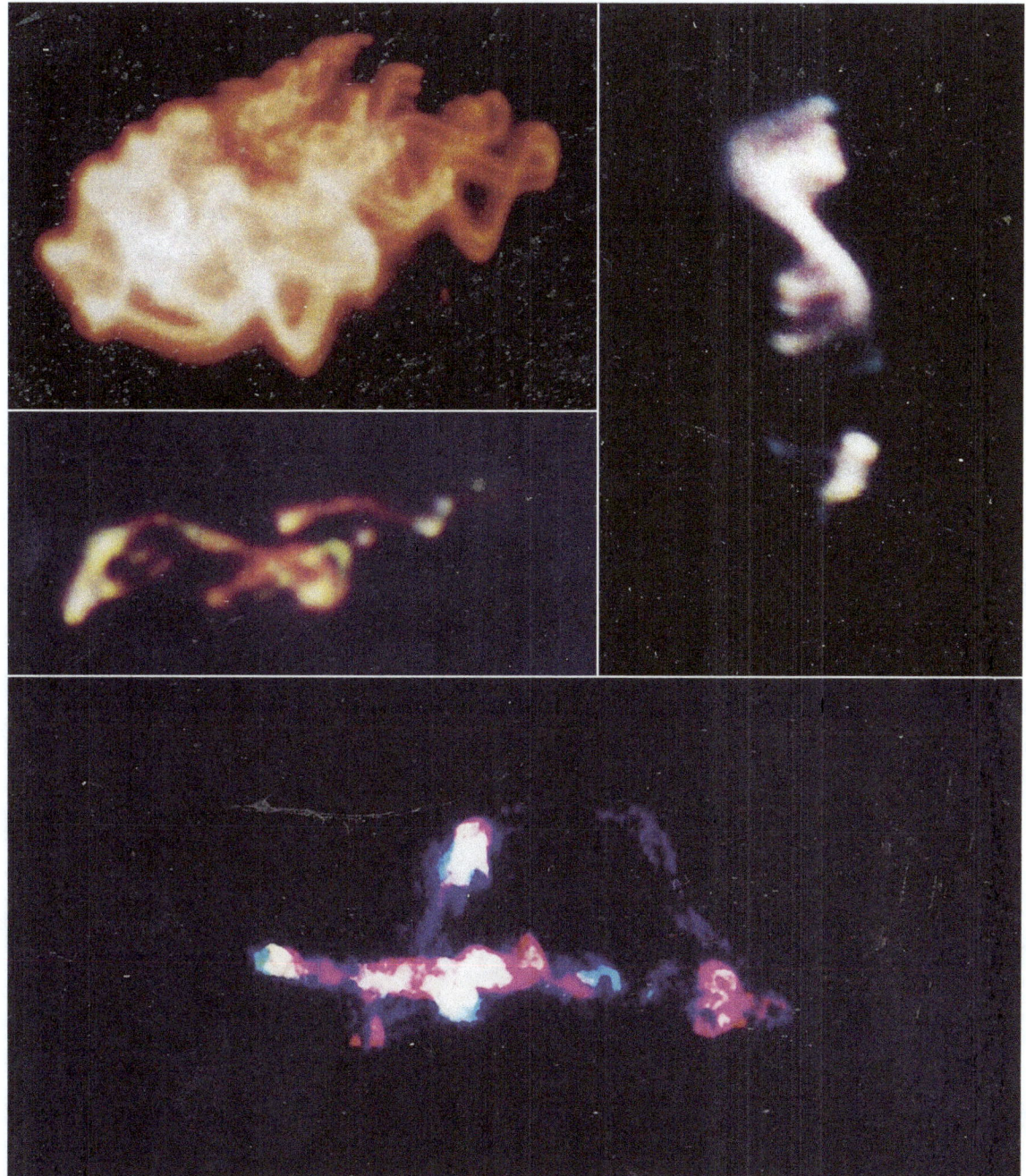

Pulsating lights and levitating trucks

We learnt of mysterious *'globes of pulsating light'* seen hovering a few feet off the ground, captured on 35mm film, using a Kodak 365 camera. (When later processed by the film laboratory, the relevant frames appeared to have been deliberately removed from the roll of film).

Haunted Skies Volume Ten

A truck being levitated up and down in the air – photographs taken at the time show a cloud of intense white energy near the vehicle.

Square lights were seen in the sky – photographs taken show a very different landscape. Are we looking into another world?

Livestock being found wedged in trees by branches so thick that they had to be cut with a handsaw.

Strange growths that appeared almost overnight seen on dogs and horses, which were believed to be tumours. Examination carried out by the vet, revealed no rational explanation for their presence.

Mysterious footprints – 16-17ins long, by 8ins wide, showing five toes – found in the ground. Was this 'Bigfoot'? These were found near a set of smaller ones, suggesting an offspring.

'Bigfoot'

According to Linda, her son saw what he described as a female 'Bigfoot', solid white in appearance, who seemed friendly rather than hostile. Suffice to say, he ran away. Tom and Linda tell of recovering long white hair near the prints, and of seeing what they believed was further sightings of the *'creature'* who is looked upon almost affectionately by the couple and named 'Big Girl'.

'Bigfoot' print in soft sand. ©Linda Bradshaw

Haunted Skies Volume Ten

'Bigfoot' print. ©Linda Bradshaw

Animal Mutilations

Mares with their manes found torn off had been reported and an animal, described as resembling a cross between a cat and a horse and 4ft in height had been seen.

Orbs seen in great numbers

Black helicopters seen

The couple also reported the presence of black unmarked helicopters seen flying around their locality, carrying what appeared to be missiles underneath them, and a number of white vehicles – many of them without license plates. From some of the encounters with the occupants of these vehicles, it is clear that this represented some form of harassment carried out by people who were not, in all probability, police.

Is this a being from another dimension?

An extraordinary attempt, using a thousand photographs, was carried out by Linda and Tom to try and capture, on camera, what appears to be a male person, approximately just over 5ft in height – this humanoid has a bony bump or ridge on either side of his forehead. He is dressed in what appears to be a jumper, or trousers – to all intent a human being, although clearly that is not what he is. We do not know where he comes

Haunted Skies Volume Ten

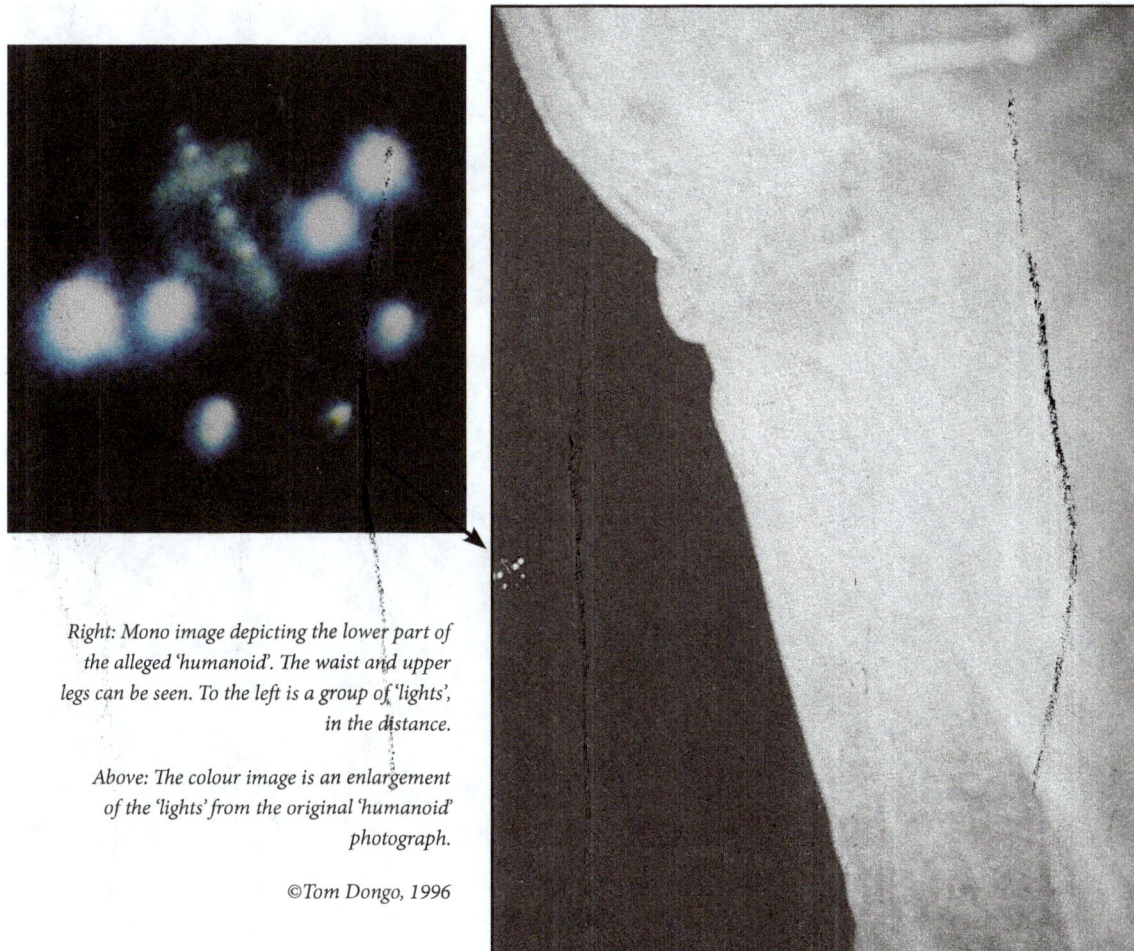

Right: Mono image depicting the lower part of the alleged 'humanoid'. The waist and upper legs can be seen. To the left is a group of 'lights', in the distance.

Above: The colour image is an enlargement of the 'lights' from the original 'humanoid' photograph.

©Tom Dongo, 1996

from, but it may well be on a completely different plain of existence to us – frightening in its implication but exhilarating in its discovery.

Is this a UFO?

In the background photo of the *'man'* can be seen what appears to be a UFO in the distance.

The photographs of orbs taken by the couple, some of them streaking in flight, appear to be identical to the ones taken by Brenda and her colleagues, during their visits to Rendlesham Forest, Suffolk, and those captured in Yorkshire.

In more recent years

This suggests that whatever they are and wherever they come from, they are far more widespread than we may ever know. If, in fact, they live alongside us, what lives alongside them and ad infinitum? – Now that is frightening to consider!

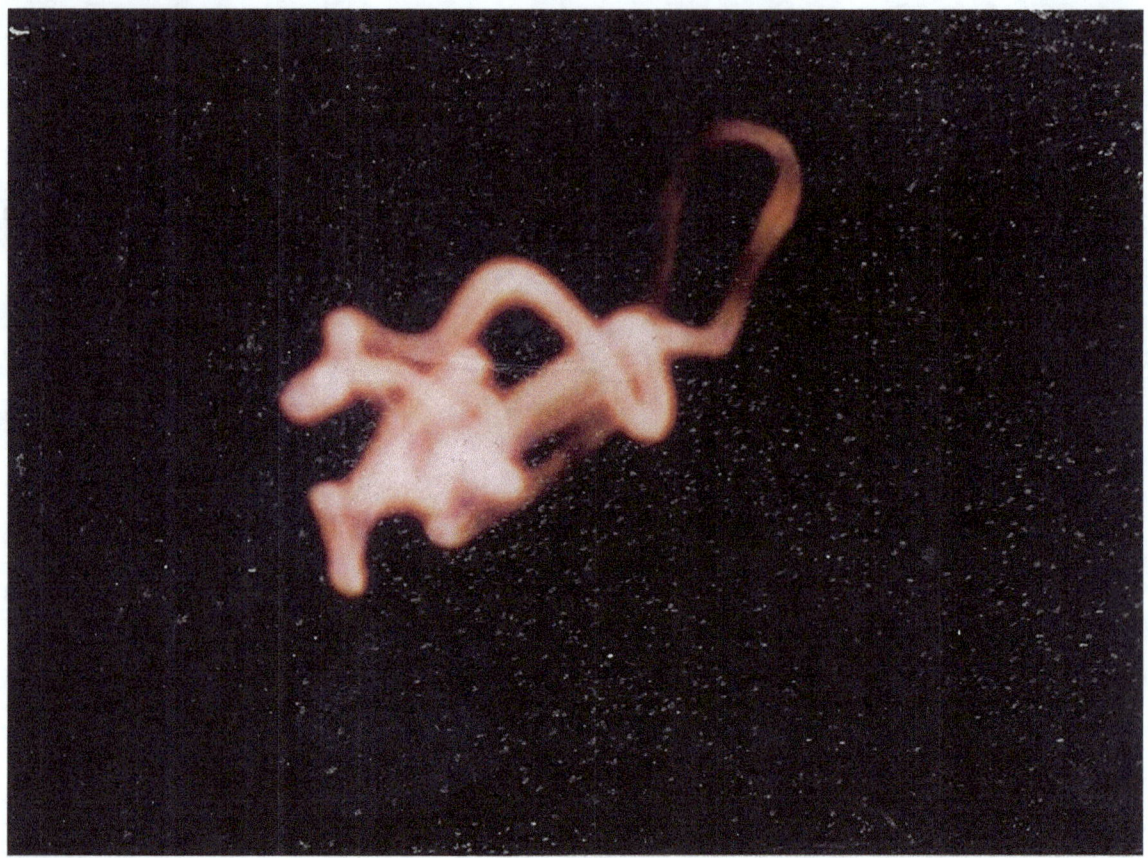

In 2011, it was claimed that the US Forest Service had continued to cut allotments at the ranch belonging to Bob Bradshaw and by the mid-1990s the taxes on their operations grew to an unmanageable amount. John Bradshaw took over the ranch and promoted it as an adventure destination for tourists – offering horseback riding, jeep tours and dinner dances. The Arizona weather and spectacular rock formations of the area provided additional inspiration, but the 90-plus acre site was soon purchased by the US Federal Government and is today managed by the US Forest Service. The entrance gates to what was the Bradshaw ranch are securely chained and there are large signs advising the public *'Property of the US Government — Trespassers will be prosecuted to the furthest extent of the law!'*

Tom Dongo is now recognised as one of America's leading authorities on UFO/Paranormal research. He has authored eight books on these topics and has made over 36 TV appearances on National television. He has spent the last 21 years in Sedona, Arizona – known as the premier UFO 'Hot Spot'; Tom offers both private and group tours throughout the area, and a Skywatch Tour, where people can experience UFO sightings for themselves. It is interesting to note that Tom believes the portals represent exit or entrance points into another dimension and he says that:

> *". . . around the world are a number of these anomalies developing, or just being discovered. In my opinion there are probably hundreds of these anomalies spread around the globe. Many of these 'zones' are located in regions of high magnetic or electromagnetic activity."*

Tom refers to three portals known by him in the Sedona area. One is believed to be two square miles in size, the second three square miles, with a third approximately 30ft in height and a 100ft in length and width.

He says:

> "These anomalies have been known to vanish if too much human pressure is focused on them. On May 22nd 1995, one of the portal areas was sprayed with a strong chemical smell. This took place late at night from either a helicopter or aircraft. On another occasion a sample of the sprayed material was analyzed and found to contain an unknown biological agent."

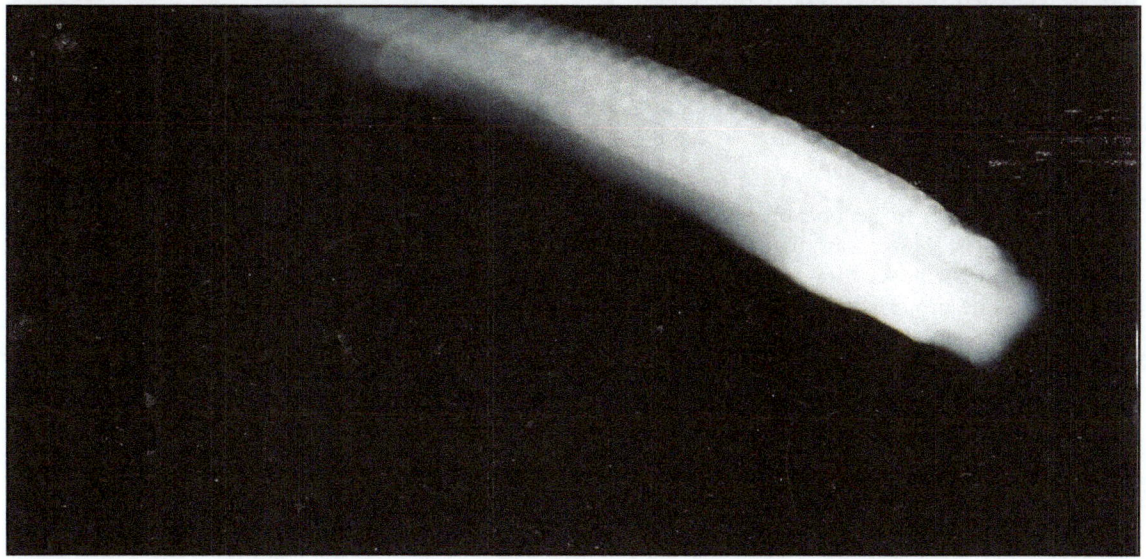

Haunted Skies Volume Ten

Communication with the orbs

In September 1997, orbs appeared to Rob and others at a retreat centre in Southern California. Rob set up his videotape equipment to film them. They were seen to slow down and stop in front of the video equipment. He communicated with them telepathically. Rob asked that they stop in front of him; the orbs did as requested. Rob then asked that they circle his friend; which they did.

At Lay Dute Canyon on 14th May 1998, following a sky watch composed of Rob and 10 other people, the orbs appeared in large numbers and circled the group.

While driving back to Sedona on a remote dirt road, Robert Meyer saw lights coming from Doe Mountain. As they moved closer to the lights the group saw pulsating UFOs, consisting of many colours.

He stopped the vehicle and jumped out. Robert then walked up the road towards the UFO and sent three short flashes from his torch/flashlight, to establish communication with the UFOs. This was followed by three short bursts and then three long bursts.

UFOs & Light Energy over Sedona

Photographed by UFO researcher Robert Meyer in December 1995. This beautiful pattern appeared in the skies above Sedona. It is one of hundreds of UFO photos he has captured while exploring the high frequency energies of Sedona's sacred red rock canyons.
Each picture is unique in color and design. Often there is special meaning in the configuration of the colors and shapes - Some are ancient Hebrew letters, some appear to be symbols and others have been interpreted by Native Americans to be signs and messages to mankind from those who inhabit the relms beyond earth.

May this photograph touch your heart and spark your spirit
Robert B. Meyer © 1995
PO BOX 10781 - Sedona, AZ 86339

Celestial Light Creations

P.O. Box 10781
Sedona, AZ 86339

Haunted Skies Volume Ten

The craft sent back three flashes of coloured lights. This action continued for 40 minutes. Members of the group followed and saw colours of yellow, blue and green, and what appeared to be *'beings'* in the vicinity. The group sent flashing bursts of light and the *'beings'* returned coloured lights. They kept this up for 15 minutes. The orbs appear as octagons and basketball globes. The lights take many shapes and pulsate in different colours. The orbs hover, perform acrobatic manoeuvres, and change shapes. Meyer believes the orbs originate in other dimensions and manifest in the physical world.

2009 – Mysterious being seen in Sedona

The 2009 *MUFON Journal* reports the sighting of a *'creature'*, seen running in broad daylight in uptown Sedona, on July 10th 2009, described as being about 5ft 8ins tall, with light brown skin all over, wearing human apparel. Unfortunately its face was not seen by the three witnesses, due to the angle of its movement. It is said that one man who reported the matter claimed it was not human, as no human could run at this speed. However, at one point the entity stopped in a parking lot and turned to face the witness, who said:

> *"Its eyes were larger than human beings and black. It then ran away and disappeared seconds later."*

We contacted Donna Carbone of the Las Vegas branch of MUFON, and asked her if she could obtain further details regarding this incident.

She replied:

> *"In case you weren't aware, two other sighting reports from the Prescott Valley were reported that they thought might be connected with the case."*

We also emailed the local newspapers in Sedona, hoping to discover if they had knowledge of this matter, but have not received any reply.

Attacked by what or who?

Paranormal Investigator 'Paul Dale Roberts of HPI (Haunted & Paranormal Investigations International) told of receiving a telephone call from a man identified as Rudy on the organisation's hotline number.

Haunted Skies Volume Ten

Rudy:

> "I just want to get your opinion on something, or maybe you know something about this. I went to Sedona, Arizona, with my wife. One night while I was up there, I was attacked by something invisible. I felt like something was shooting me with quills. My body had red botch marks all over. I felt like I was attacked by an invisible porcupine. My wife saw the red marks. One mark even looked like it was bleeding. I was in extreme pain for a while. The very next day, the red marks were gone. I have no idea what attacked me. I was hit by quill attacks. I've never been hit by a porcupine, but I can imagine that is how it would feel and I got hit twice."

Rudy then told Paul that he thought he had seen a 7ft '*shadow figure*' move between some rocks after the attack, although his wife was unable to confirm this.

2014 – Linda Bradshaw – *Dimensional Journey: Encounters and Teachings*

We were pleased to find that Linda Bradshaw (neé Ball) was still involved in the chosen subject. Her book, *Dimensional Journey: Encounters and Teachings*, is currently available on Amazon.com.

In this book, Linda openly talks about her experiences on Bradshaw Ranch and even shares the spiritual guidance she received from her messengers during that time. In the years that have passed since her extraordinary experiences, amidst the red rocks around Sedona, Linda has come to realise that:

> "Yes, there are high-energy spots on this Earth that provide phenomena, but there is also another energy spot that creates this setting and that is us – humankind. We, as humans, continually evolve, creating a higher energy within ourselves. This works as a conduit for those who wish to observe another aspect of life within the cosmos. This path we call life is filled with many wonderful experiences if we only realise how capable we really are; in other words, we all are capable of embarking on our very own dimensional journey."

Paul Dale Roberts and his partner, Shannon McCabe of H.P.I. International (Haunted & Paranormal Investigations, International) have also published a number of books relating to investigations carried out by their organisation. Paul was born on 17th January 1955, in Fresno, California, and now holds an Associate Degree in Criminology. Between the periods 1973 to 1976 he served with the US Army's DST (Drug Suppression Team) CID (Criminal Investigation Division) in Germany, working in narcotics. From 1979 to 1986 Paul served in the US Army's Military Intelligence, holding a Top Secret SBI (Special Background Investigation) clearance as an Intelligence Analyst. Paul is also a professional dancer, and has appeared in films like Roller Boogie, *and* Skatetown USA. *He was nominated in the* Guinness Book of Records *for disco dancing a total of 205 hours. In 2004 he became a paranormal investigator, by then already having investigated a prolific number of incidents brought to his attention, from which he later wrote (and continues to do so) many paranormal articles for the media. He is in constant demand on TV and podcasts. They include investigations carried out at the Skinwalker Ranch in Utah, looking for Natalee Holloway's ghost in Aruba, UFOs, and 'Bigfoot' at Mount Shasta, UFOs and USOs at Monterey Bay, Area 51, and Guatemala City.*

Kim Carslberg – Magic of Sedona

Another company that specialises in arranging tours of the Sedona area is Kim Carlsberg, of Sedona UFO Sky Tours. She is a graduate of the Art Center College of Design, Pasadena, California, in commercial photography. Kim's career as an advertising and portrait photographer has covered all aspects of the entertainment and music industries.

Kim has been commissioned to photograph the most noted celebrities in private sittings, from rock stars to presidents. Her work has appeared in hundreds of publications worldwide, including *Rolling Stone*, *TV Guide* and *Time*. She worked for five years as an exclusive photographer on the TV series *Baywatch*, which brought her the honour of being the first woman accepted into the Hollywood Camera Union, IATSE (International Alliance of Theatrical State Employees).

She claims that on a typical tour, which lasts 90 minutes, the sky watchers will hope to see between five and hundreds of UFOs moving across the night sky, followed by a visit to the ET Encounter Diner, situated at 1655 West Highway, West Sedona.

Haunted Skies Volume Ten

According to the website:

Kim:

"One of our most popular daytime Sedona UFO Sky Tours locations is the famous Bradshaw Ranch. The mysterious Bradshaw Ranch, located deep in forest land, which was confiscated by the US Government by eminent domain because it houses one of the most powerful inter-dimensional portals, perhaps on Earth. It is the subject of many books about countless sightings of UFOs, ETs, 'Big Foot', and many other extraordinary inter-dimensional beings. The raw beauty of the area, and the enchanting vortices and portal energies are reasons enough to venture to the ranch's borders. No other tour company dares to venture to the ranch. Tour is approximately three to four hours."

Kim has also written three books. Her first was *Beyond My Wildest Dreams, diary of a UFO abductee*, written nearly 20 years ago.

Sedona is a city that straddles the county line between Coconino and Yavapai counties in the northern Verde Valley region of the State of Arizona. As of the 2010 census, its population was 10,031. Sedona's main attraction is its array of red sandstone formations. The formations appear to glow in brilliant orange and red when illuminated by the rising or setting sun. The red rocks form a popular backdrop for many activities, ranging from spiritual pursuits to the hundreds of hiking and mountain biking trails. Sedona was named after Sedona Arabella Miller Schnebly (1877-1950), the wife of Theodore Carlton Schnebly, the city's first postmaster, who was celebrated for her hospitality and industriousness.

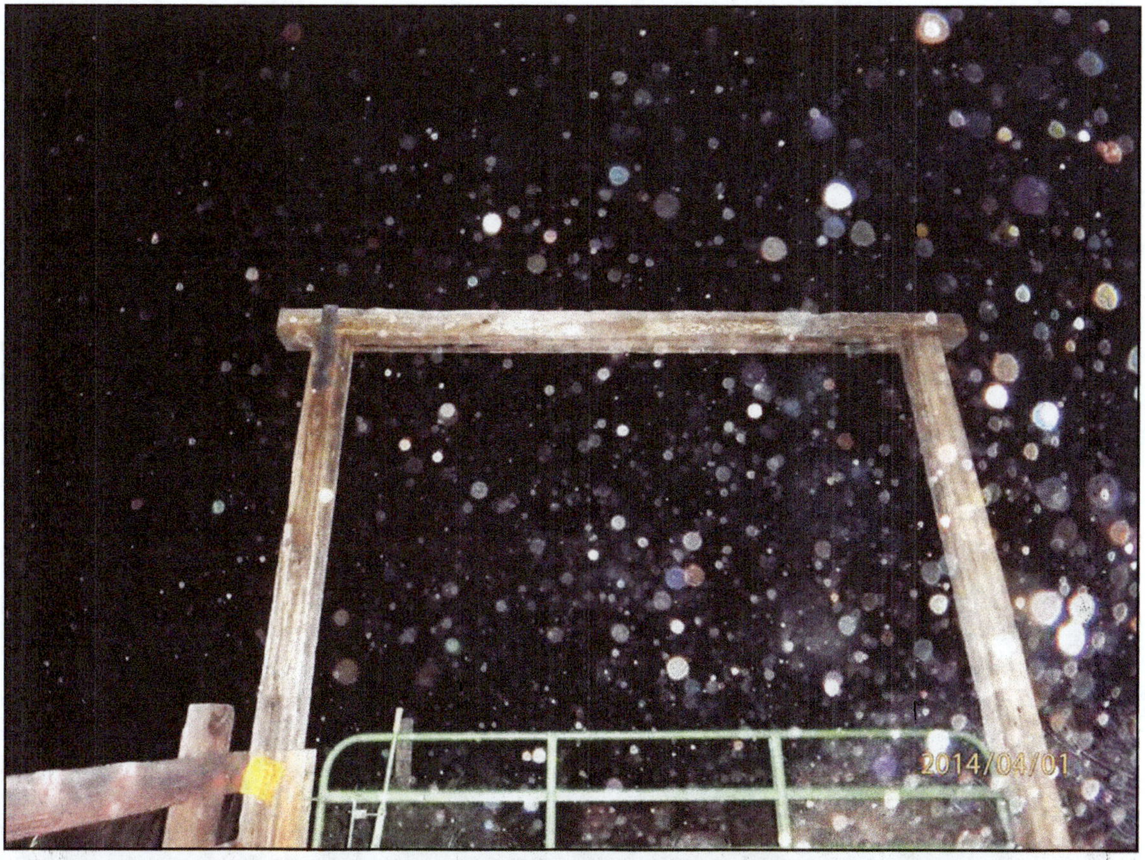
2014/04/01

RED
PLANET
DINER

CONTACT
CARDS
An
Extraterrestrial
Divination
System
KIM CARLSBERG
DARRYL ANKA

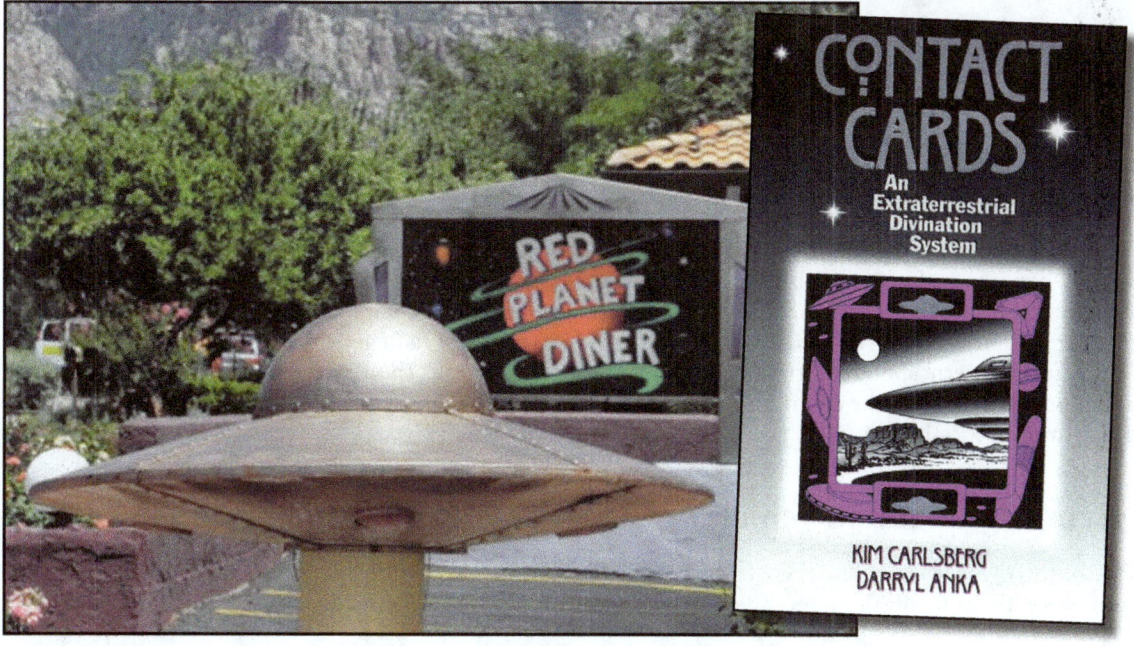

Haunted Skies Volume Ten

The Portals at Uintah Basin, Utah

We couldn't help but ponder whether there was any connection between the mysterious mists, orbs, and sightings of strange figures seen in and around Rendlesham Forest Suffolk, with incidents of high strangeness reported from the 'Skinwalker Ranch', Uintah County, Utah, in 1994.

The 480-acre ranch lies just south of Fort Duchesne in Uintah County, and has became the focus of attention for UFOs and bizarre paranormal activity. Terry and Gwen Sherman and their two teenage children, who were living there, witnessed many strange happenings and still find it difficult to accept it as reality, wondering if it was something to do with a top secret project.

Those sightings included regular appearances of three apparently separate types of UFOs, described as a small box-like craft, with a white light, a 40ft long object, and a huge ship – the size of several football fields. In addition, strange airborne lights were seen – some of which appeared to emerge from orange or circular *'doorways'*, which opened up in the sky, and three circles of flattened grass – each about 8ft across, in a triangular pattern, about 30ft from each other – were discovered. These were approximately 3ft wide and a foot or two deep, with the dirt in the centre, perfectly flattened, and strange impressions were found in the soil at another location.

'Flying lights' follow vehicle

One of the *'flying lights'* followed Gwen's car on her way home from work, one night, and while out in one of the fields with the family dogs, Terry heard male voices speaking an unfamiliar language. The voices seemed to

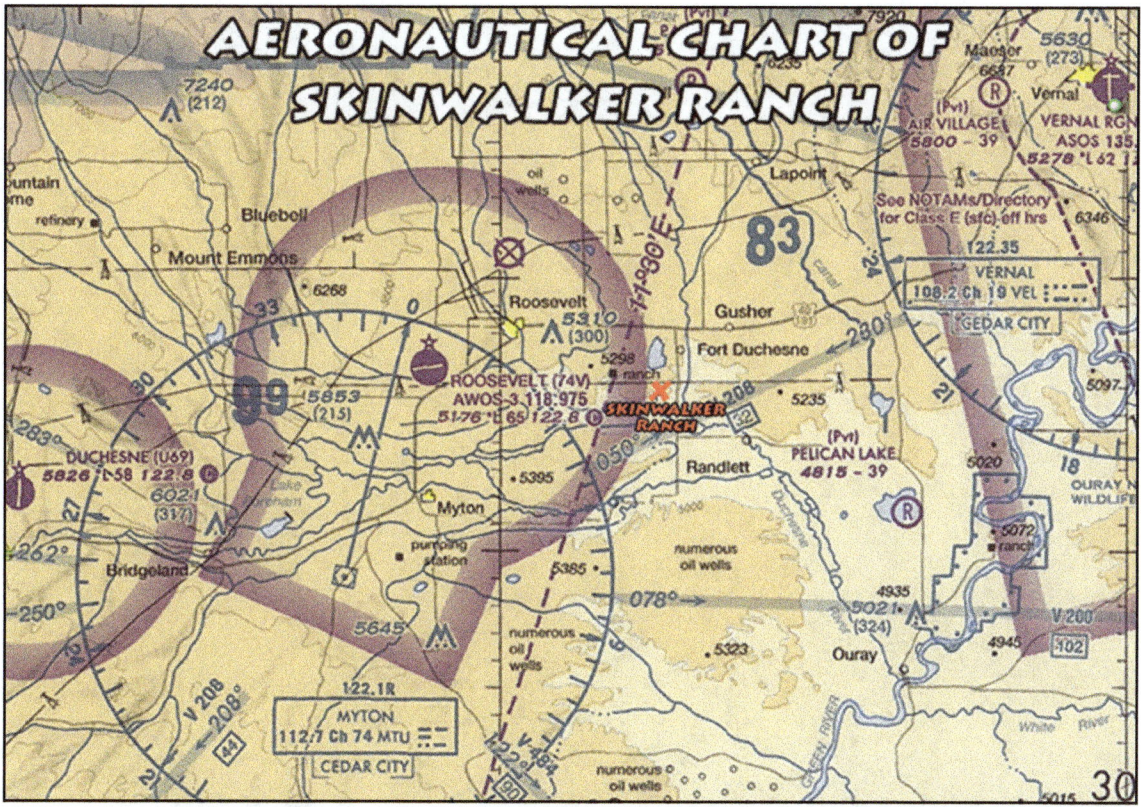

be about 25ft above him, but Terry couldn't see a thing. The dogs were frantic. They barked and growled, before running off to the ranch house. It was of interest to find an image (there weren't many) on the *Skinwalker.org* website, which appears to have similarities with what was photographed by Linda Bryant in Rendesham Forest.

50 years of strange happenings

It is claimed the bizarre events which have occurred at the remote Utah ranch, ranging from the perplexing to the wholly terrifying, have been happening for the last 50 years. This wouldn't be surprising – one senses a much longer time period.

Incredible accounts, found on the internet, tell of vanishing and mutilated cattle, unidentified flying objects, and the appearance of huge creatures, invisible objects emitting magnetic fields, with the power to spark a cattle stampede, and *'flying orbs of light',* with dazzling manoeuvrability and lethal consequences. Further claims tell of three dogs being vaporized by apparently intelligently-guided flying blue orbs (which we regard as dubious) and objects disappearing but reappearing later in other locations.

Late 1800s – Bottle Hollow Lake

It is also alleged that there is a connection with the manifestations and strange phenomena recorded on the ranch and mysterious creatures seen swimming in Bottle Lake – originally a ravine used by soldiers, returning home to their fort, to throw their empty whisky bottles into following an evening out at Fort Duchesne. So many bottles were thrown in that it eventually earned the name Bottle Hollow. Bottle Hollow is now covered

Haunted Skies Volume Ten

Above: Image from the Skinwalker.org *website depicting strange forms. Compare this to the image on the right taken by Linda Bryant in Rendlesham Forest (p516/7)*

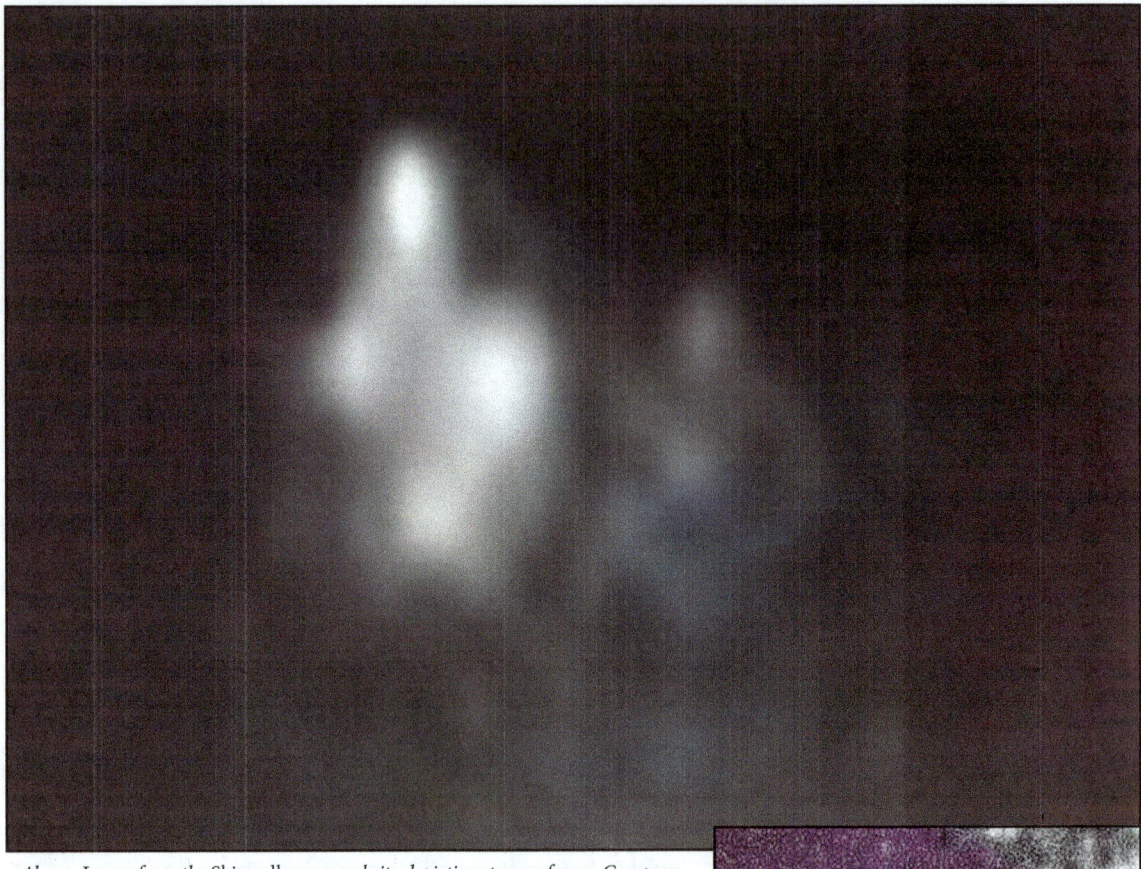

mostly by water from the reservoir. In the late 1800s, Congress designated seven thousand acres of the Ute land as public domain, and inadvertently exempted that acreage from any official control or law enforcement.

In 1970 a reservoir was built, covering about 420 acres, making Bottle Hollow one of a kind – a premiere resort built on an Indian reservation.

The motel and convention center at Bottle Hollow was built with federal money to help the Northern Ute Tribe with economic diversity and provide jobs for tribal members. The resort was an attractive oasis in the eastern Utah desert. A sparkling swimming pool was the perfect site for fashion shows in the early 1980s. In the summer, Bottle Hollow Resort was also home to a popular local community dinner theatre and numerous high school reunions. The dramatic decline of the oil boom in the Uintah Basin in the late 1980s also brought the eventual abandonment of the Bottle Hollow Holiday Resort by the Ute Tribe.

Serpents seen in the lake

The Utes believe that the lake is inhabited by several large aquatic snakes, with the first serpent sightings dating back just after the area was filled as a reservoir. Eyewitnesses claim that, on occasion, they have seen things crawling around from the marina all the way down to the end of the reservoir. There are also accounts of strange lights entering and leaving the water.

Bottle Hollow Lake

1950s to the present day

Another person who was to take a keen interest in the events which took place around that locality was Joseph Junior Hicks – a retired junior high school teacher from Roosevelt. He has investigated more than 400 UFO sightings in the Uintah Basin since the early 1950s. Reports of UFOs during that time have numbered in the thousands, according to Hicks, and some have been associated with cattle mutilations.

Hicks:

> "At least half-a-dozen eyewitnesses have told me they saw living beings in the windows, or portholes of UFOs. The number of UFO sightings which took place at the Sherman ranch is extraordinary for their number, duration and quality, but what they've witnessed is hardly unusual for the Uintah Basin."

(See: *The Utah UFO Display: A Scientist Brings Reason and Logic to Over 400 UFO Sighting in Utah's Uintah Basin*: Authors: Frank B. Salisbury, Joseph Junior Hicks.)

> "I'd estimate over 10 per cent of the population of the Uintah Basin has seen something. I think what's happening is we are being visited by beings from another world, or some other place. I think primarily its research and exploration."

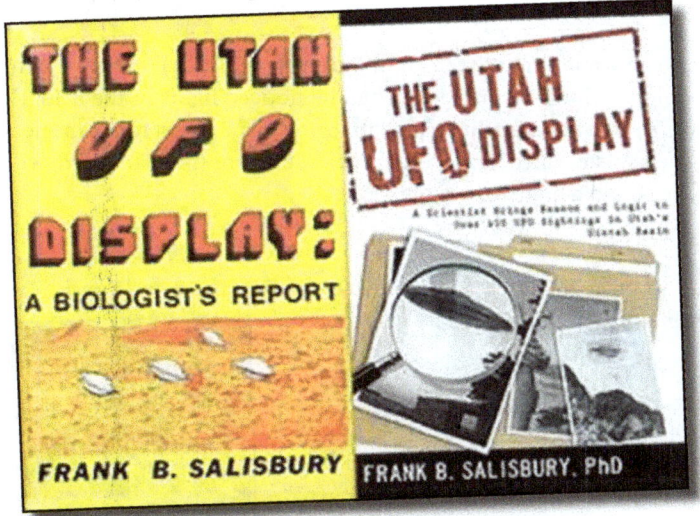

Frank B. Salisbury, Joseph Junior Hicks.

1964 – Paul Pedersen close encounter

In 1964, Paul Pedersen was leaving a neighbour's Emigration Canyon home, early one morning, when he noticed a huge oval-shaped craft in the sky above him. *"It drifted over and down, and then hovered above the driveway"*,

Pedersen said:

> "As it stood still, people inside came to the portholes and looked out at me. That kind of unnerved me, because it was so dark I knew I couldn't be seen by human eyes ... They looked just like people. They were silhouetted against this green light in the background."

Pedersen then received a telepathic message from the *'beings'*. They asked if he'd like to come with them. It was one individual's voice.

He said:

> "I didn't say anything but answered by thinking. My thought was that I can't leave; I have a wife and two children who depend on me.
>
> Their response was 'That's OK', and the craft just hovered above the trees and went over the mountain behind me."

1993 – UFO landing. Who were the occupants?

Bill Lyons – a Mutual UFO Network investigator in Iron County – remains intrigued by a February 1993 incident, in which a man and woman saw a dozen UFOs near Hurricane, including an egg-shaped craft, with telephone pole-size landing gear and a large hot dog-shaped craft. After the sightings, the couple surveyed the ground nearby and found a trail of small three-toed footprints in the snow. Other markings indicated a tail might have been dragging behind whatever made the prints. *"The thing that struck me about this sighting was its depth and the copious amounts of information. There was just so much detail to it."* The woman, who lives in Kanab, confirmed the sighting in an interview with the *Deseret News* but did not want her name published.

1995 – Strange lights seen

In April 1995, Terry Sherman – then owner of the Sherman Ranch (now Skinwalker Ranch) – was carrying out a check on a cow that was calving in a field south of the property, when he noticed lights in the field. He assumed they belonged to recreation vehicles or maybe kids from a neighbouring farm riding four-wheelers. He then realised this was unlikely, as the ranch was isolated, and lying three miles from the main road, with access prohibited due to being cut off by a creek and a huge rock ridge.

His wife Gwen told of seeing:

> "... what looked like headlights, a little way away from a craft – a red glowing thing, about an 18-inch circle; it just lit up the whole side of the mountain, like broad daylight."

UFO flashed on and off – Was it communicating?

In the months that followed, the Sherman family saw a myriad of lights and flying objects, including more than a dozen on one evening. Sightings generally occurred during a new moon and often when the sky was overcast or stormy. In May, during a thunderstorm, Terry and his son were travelling west along the ranch road, when they saw a lighted object duck behind the rock ridge, as if avoiding them. Moments later they managed to quietly, without detection, creep up on the object. Before it could hide again, they stood and waved their arms at it. The light flashed on and off three times, as if signalling them, and then disappeared.

Haunted Skies Volume Ten

George Knapp at the Skinwalker Ranch gate

1996/1997 – The National Institute for Discovery Science

We were fascinated to read of the work carried out by Scientist researchers from the National Institute for Discovery Science into the numerous complaints of high strangeness over a two-year period, involving cattle disappearances, manifestations of a shape-shifting entity the Ute Indians called a *'skinwalker'*, floating blue orbs of light, cattle mutilations, a giant wolf that seemed unaffected by bullets, and a sinister, hyena-like creature.

Millionaire buys Utah UFO ranch

FORT DUCHESNE, Utah (AP) — The search for answers to one of science's greatest questions has led millionaire Robert M. Bigelow to an isolated cattle ranch in the heart of eastern Utah's Uintah Basin.

Here, far from the bright lights of his native Las Vegas, the real estate magnate hopes his team of scientists can unearth the roots of UFO folklore prevalent in this region since the 1950s.

Bigelow, easily the most prominent American financier in the paranormal research field, is convinced there is something to the weird stories told by the family of Terry Sherman.

Last July, the Shermans broke years of silence and went public with bizarre tales of strange lights and UFOs on their 480-acre ranch.

Sherman said he and other members of his family had seen lights emerging from circular "doorways" that seemed to appear in mid-air, had three cows strangely mutilated and several others disappear. The rancher also reported unusual impressions in the soil and circles of flattened grass in a pasture.

The Shermans' story appeared in the Deseret News and on a national radio broadcast. Several weeks later, Bigelow met with the Shermans and negotiated to buy the ranch for about $200,000.

The Sherman family has relocated to a smaller ranch 15 miles away — far removed, they hope, from the disturbing occurrences they endured for 18 months.

Bigelow has erected an observation building and moved in a pair of scientists and a veterinarian. He has someone on the property 24 hours a day, recording anything out of the ordinary.

Officially, the research is being conducted by the National Institute for Discovery Science which Bigelow formed last October. Among the scientists involved is John B. Alexander, former director of non-lethal weapons testing at Los Alamos National Laboratories in New Mexico.

"Our approach is to do good, high-quality research using a standard scientific approach and do what we can to get hard data," Alexander said from the institute's Las Vegas offices. "One of the missions of the institute is to make information widely available."

Bigelow himself declined an interview. Alexander would not provide details of how or why the research is being conducted.

Sherman, now employed by Bigelow to maintain the ranch, said he can no longer discuss the activity because of a nondisclosure agreement Bigelow had him sign.

Haunted Skies Volume Ten

The group was funded by billionaire Las Vegas businessman *Robert Bigelow, of Bigelow Aerospace. Robert had this to say, during an interview by the *New York Times*:

> "I've been a researcher and student of UFOs for many, many, years."

Mr Bigelow also said:

> "Anybody that does research, if people bother to do quality research, comes away absolutely convinced. You don't have to have personal encounters. People have been killed. People have been hurt. It's more than observational kind of data."

Bigelow is in the process of building a space port in New Mexico. According to his website:

> "Bigelow Aerospace is dedicated to developing next-generation crewed space complexes to revolutionize space commerce and open up the final frontier to all of humanity. At Bigelow Aerospace, we're building the future today!"

(Source: *New York Times*)

Robert Bigelow

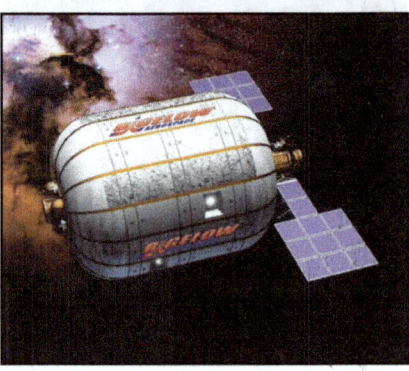

George Knapp

Dr. Kelleher documented investigations made into the incidents in his book with George Knapp, *Hunt for the Skinwalker*. We emailed George in Las Vegas, hoping to discover more about this particular case and ascertain the nature of the extent of scientific and photographic evidence obtained during investigations carried out at the ranch, but never received a reply.

Throughout 1996 and 1997, the N.I.D.S. team spent hundreds of days on the property, mostly at night; it is alleged they encountered dozens of strange phenomena.

1st May 1997 – New Mexico animal found dead

Although we do not know the exact location, we learned that representatives of the N.I.D.S. team were told about this matter on the 3rd May, following which it was estimated the Hereford/Charolais Bull had expired approximately four days prior to examination.

Enquiries made revealed that a *'green light'* had been seen flying around the sky on the evening when this fatality had occurred.

---

*Bigelow Aerospace is an American space technology start-up company, based in North Las Vegas, Nevada, that is pioneering work on expandable space station modules. Bigelow Aerospace was founded by Robert Bigelow, in 1998, financed through his ownership of the hotel chain Budget Suites of America. By 2013, Bigelow had invested US$250 million in the company. Bigelow has stated, on multiple occasions, that he is prepared to fund Bigelow Aerospace with about US$500 million through 2015, in order to achieve launch of full-scale hardware. Bigelow is pioneering a new market in a flexible and configurable set of space habitats. Moreover, industry observers have noted that Bigelow is demonstrating audacity to pioneer such a market "in a capital-intensive, highly-regulated industry like spaceflight".

Examination of the scene

The ground around the area had been disturbed, as though something had caused local turbulence, as cow-pats and other debris were overturned. It was presumed that indentations discovered in the ground 150ft away and 5-6 inches in depth had been made by a heavy mechanical object.

Bearing in mind no presence of other impressions or marks leading up to the locality, such as a vehicle might have expected to have left; it was thought the culprit had been airborne.

Post-mortem examination of the bull

The tongue was missing, having been cut out from the root. The right eye was missing and on the right-hand side of the neck a smooth one inch in diameter hole was found. A five inch diameter hole was found deep in the neck tissue. The margins of this hole appeared to be charred and a yellow powdery substance was found in and around the hole. There was severe haemorrhaging. The penis and testicles had been removed internally through the rear of the animal, as the scrotum was intact. The yellow powder was also seen near the scrotum area. The anus was missing, but there was some evidence of scavenger activity in that location. [The yellow powder had also been seen at other unexplained cases of animal mutilation.]

15th October 1998 – North-East Utah, animal found dead

A Hereford cow, three months pregnant, was found by its owner lying on its front, with the front legs tucked in and rear legs splayed (similar to the animal at New Mexico). It was of interest to learn that sixteen other animals, which were found deceased in suspicious circumstances in the Utah Basin, were found lying in a north-south axis with the head pointing north.

Post-mortem examination of the cow

Examination of the animal revealed the following:

The left eye was missing; a neat edged half-an-inch diameter disc of periorbital tissue completely around the left eye socket had been cut out with a sharp instrument down to the bone.

The left ear had been cut off by the use of a non-surgical instrument (confirmed by post-mortem).

The heart was devoid of blood and the internal muscle structure was shredded.

Enlarged uterus but no sign of recent abortion present!

Blood tests confirmed recent pregnancy and that the foetus had been removed by some unknown means close to or at the time of death.

Lung emphysema, involving grossly enlarged air sacs with the presence of a small half inch diameter hole found in hide near brisket area.

Conclusions

Bacteriology, virology, and toxicology tests carried out, along with analysis using a scanning electron microscope, revealed:

1. Abnormal levels of potassium chloride in the cow's arterial blood compared to abdominal blood, indicating that this chemical was used to kill the animal

2. Low levels of copper and Vitamin A in the liver.
3. Thousands of apparently crystalline unidentified white yellow small amorphic (lacking any definite shape) structures embedded through the heart.
4. Unidentified blue speckled gel-like substance found around the left eye, ear, lips of the vulva, and the anal area.

David Cayton

In 2014, we discussed these matters with David Cayton, who is one of the United Kingdom's leading authorities on animal mutilations. Another is Shropshire based UFO researcher, Phil Hoyle.

David told us, during conversation about the N.I.D.S. and the Skinwalker ranch, that the late Graham Birdsall had been to a conference at Laughlin, Nevada, some years ago, and had written a letter introducing himself and his *UFO Magazine*, hoping to take the opportunity to interview Robert Bigelow. It appears that the letter was never answered. Enquiries made later at the address given to Graham, where Robert Bigelow allegedly lived, proved unsuccessful; there was no such address.

David Cayton

We tried to contact Mr Bigelow via his website, Bigelow Aerospace, 1899, W. Brooks Avenue North Las Vegas which claims...

> "... since 1999 our mission has been to provide affordable options for spaceflight to national Space agencies and corporate clients. In 2006 and 2007 we launched our orbiting prototypes Genesis 1 and 11. Using our patented expandable habitats, our plan is to greatly exceed the useable space of the International Space Station at a fraction of the cost by developing our next generation of spacecraft"

...but found there were no email contact details – only a business address. This seemed odd, understanding a man of his considerable wealth and standing within the community, although a postal address was given.

Graham Birdsall

$37Million dollars – Anybody fancy a trip?

Flight costs for anybody wishing to visit the Bigelow Alpha Station were quoted as being either $26.25 million, or $36.75 million. A little 'digging' revealed a contact email address for that purpose!

19th October 1998 – Animal mutilation, Northampton

David also told us about an incident that happened at a farm belonging to John, when he and Peter – a pest control worker, working on the farm that day – accompanied by a stockman, found two sheep dead with unusual identical wounds on their body. This matter was reported to him after David had placed an advert in the *Farmers Weekly,* in April 1998.

1. Both sheep had their sexual organs neatly excised.
2. The rectums were cored out, leaving 4in. diameter holes, with internal digestive organs removed from the same entry points.
3. No blood or staining was seen around those orifices, or on the fleece or on the ground.

MAFF arrive!

The following day, an 'R' registered BMW car arrived at the farm. Two men got out and showed green ID cards endorsed with MAFF (Ministry of Agriculture, Fisheries and Food). They informed the farm stockman that they had come to collect the two dead sheep. He thought this had been previously arranged by the framer, who was away at the time, and loaded the animals into the boot of the BMW. When John (the farmer) arrived back, he was understandably indignant that the animals had been taken away without his knowledge. He was also dismayed to discover the stockman had not taken a note of the two men's names.

John contacted his brother, a Police Chief Inspector with the Oxfordshire Constabulary, and asked him to contact MAFF and complain about the covert way in which this had been handled. When the officer did this, he was initially told that they had no knowledge of any of their employees being sent to the farm. When pressed, a senior official came to the phone and admitted they had collected the bodies of the sheep, and advised the officer *"it was not a police matter"*, adding that the farmer would be compensated. After the officer told him that at this stage he was now investigating a report of theft of the animals, he was again advised not to pursue the allegation. A short time later, the officer was advised by a senior officer to drop the case.

David has wondered how it was that MAFF heard about this incident, as the only people who knew about it never contacted the police or the authorities about this matter. Curiously it was revealed that four nights before the sheep were found, a *'bright light'* was seen over the field where the sheep were kept, at 8.30pm. Twenty minutes later, two dark coloured helicopters were seen.

David:

> *"A possible explanation might have been that a UFO was tracked on radar, following which helicopters were scrambled to investigate.*
>
> *It would have taken a few days to identify the location."*

David Cayton is to be congratulated for his commitment to seeking some answers to what is, after all, a frightening phenomenon involving attacks on livestock that go back many years. To suggest that these injuries are being caused by predatory animals is not worthy of consideration. We wonder if wild animals are also being targeted. If they are being mutilated and killed by an unknown agency, then what stops this intelligence if one can apply such terminology to something or someone we are still unable to comprehend, from targeting human beings?

These are harrowing accounts. We accept our current inability to be able to stop those responsible for an ongoing agenda of animal mutilations, which may go back Centuries. It is likely that, contrary to speculation, any human assessment of what these things are and where they come from may be badly flawed. Is this representative of an advanced, superior alien intelligence or reflex? While we appear to be unable to stop *'them'* mutilating animals, does this necessarily mean those responsible are superior or more advanced than us? Is it possible they have no comprehension of us as a race but through an unknown deliberate or accidental process enter our plane of existence when needs must?

24th March 1978 – New Mexico

A cursory look at other reported mutilations reveals an incident brought to the attention of the New Mexico police and the FBI, when an 11-month-old cross Hereford-Charolais bull, belonging to Mr Manuel Gomez of Dulce, New Mexico, was found mutilated on 24th March 1978. It displayed 'classic' mutilation signs, including the removal of the rectum and sex organs with what appeared to be *'a sharp and precise instrument'* and its internal organs were found to be inconsistent with a normal cause of death, followed by predation. *"Both the liver and the heart were white and mushy; they had the texture and consistency of peanut butter",* said Gabriel L. Veldez, of the New Mexico Police.

Samples sent to Los Alamos Scientific Laboratory

The animal's heart, as well as bone and muscle samples, was sent to the Los Alamos Scientific Laboratory for microscopic and bacteriological studies, while samples from the animal's liver were sent to two separate private laboratories.

Clostridium bacteria found

Los Alamos detected the presence of naturally occurring clostridium bacteria in the heart, but was unable to reach any conclusions because of the possibility that the bacteria represented post-mortem contamination. They did not directly investigate the heart's unusual colour or texture.

Samples from the animal's liver were found to be completely devoid of copper and to contain four times the normal level of zinc, potassium and phosphorus. The scientists performing the analysis were unable to explain these anomalies.

Blood samples taken at the scene were reported to be *"light pink in colour and did not clot after several days"*, while the animal's hide was found to be unusually brittle for a fresh death (the animal was estimated to have been dead for five hours) and the flesh underneath was found to be discoloured.

None of the laboratories were able to report any firm conclusions on the cause of the blood or tissue damage. At the time, it was suggested that a burst of radiation may have been used to kill the animal, blowing apart its red blood cells in the process. This hypothesis was later discarded, as subsequent reports from the Los Alamos Scientific Laboratory later confirmed the presence of anticoagulants in samples from other cows mutilated in the region.

Are sea mammals being mutilated? By David Cayton

> *"It would seem a reasonable premise, since practically all other warm-blooded, land-based animals have been found suffering from very similar types of injury wounds, so why not sea mammals too? Various species of seal seem to be the most affected, simply maybe because they are the most prolific around our shores. For the past three years or so, I have been in touch with an RSPCA veterinary specialist, based in Norfolk, East Anglia, who has carried out post-mortem investigations upon eleven or more seals, exhibiting unusual but similar external injuries. These mostly occurred from late 2009 to late 2010.*

Multi seal decapitations

> *At this point, it is pertinent to acquaint you with an astonishing case of multi-seal decapitations on adjacent Orkney Isle beaches, in the winter of 1991-92. This was reported by retired Police Sgt. Tony*

Dodd, initially, in an issue of the old Quest International UFO Magazine, *and later in his book, 'Alien Investigator', published in 1999.*

This intriguing case, involving over 30 seals, demonstrates that these attacks upon sea mammals are not unheard of. The SSPCA, police and local vets, in Orkney, were all baffled. All the seals were surgically decapitated with some very sharp non-serrated instrument, cleanly, cutting through the narrow gap in between the vertebrae BUT without any sign of blade damage to the bone!

As is often the case, none of the heads were recovered. The veterinary surgeon, who carried out the post-mortems, remarked to Tony Dodd, "We cannot guess what killed these animals but whatever it was, had knowledge of seal anatomy"! There was an absence of blood on the sand even though there was a total blood loss, so how could this precision decapitation, over 30 times, have been done at sea? There was no evidence of these 'operations' having being carried out on the beach."

As vet Steve Bexton recently pointed out to me, seal skin and blubber is very hard to cut into, even on a mortuary slab! Furthermore, just consider this, what would the odds be of hacking a head off with JUST ONE clean blow, not just once but on over 30 seals and then each time, hit the precise narrow gap in each vertebrae without damage?

Remember, the bone structure would be completely invisible to the eye! Of course each animal would ALSO have to be completely inert, to even attempt this impossible task. How would one approach them all on the beach in the first place?

Sea birds found decapitated

Within weeks of these seal deaths, large numbers of decapitated sea birds were found on the shores of the Orkney and Shetland Islands. Again, like the seals, the heads were never found.

I contacted the police officer investigating the deaths, Inspector Mike Brown and the Blakeney Point Warden, David Wood, for information. Inspector Brown was very helpful and informed me that a number of the seals, 13, had been sent for post-mortem examination by a RSPCA Centre near Kings Lynn, but at least one of these had been transported to the DEFRA Regional Veterinary Laboratory in Bury-St.-Edmunds.

The cover-up continues…

Annoyingly, within a short space of time, Inspector Brown informed me that he could not liaise further with me because the MMO (Marine Management Organisation) had been 'appointed' to 'take over' all investigations into the seal deaths! I ascertained that the MMO is an arm of DEFRA! Perhaps belatedly, they had an inkling of what was responsible for the seal injuries and were keen to keep control of information of the situation and thus 'manage' any future incidents?

We have experienced other animal mutilation cases, where the police have closed off communications and denied us copies of post-mortem reports and their photographs, after initial agreement to co-operate! I strongly suspect that they are subsequently 'instructed' to do this by some 'higher government' department? Prior to this, both Insp. Brown and Claire Graves, the Press Officer for the National Trust, kindly furnished me with numerous photographs.

Between July and August, the numbers of seal deaths rose to over seventy-five (including the Scottish cases)! I made contact with the Norfolk based RSPCA veterinary officer, who had carried out autopsies on eleven of the seals.

Haunted Skies Volume Ten

Steve Bexton, was also puzzled about the unusual spiralling cuts and could only speculate what type of cutting mechanism had been capable of slicing with a continuous action and with very great force! He established that all the seals were in good health prior to death BUT had been alive when the unknown 'machinery' caused the wound! He found that the 'device' which made the huge cut (but not with a sharp edge) made it in one uninterrupted motion, starting under the left chin, pealing rearwards with a great shearing force into the blubber!

The Seal Mammal Research Unit (SMRU) The Unit was formed in 1978 from two other organisations, both part of the NERC (Natural Environment Research Council) which was incorporated into the University of St. Andrews in 1996. A Royal Charter requires the NERC to supply Government about the management of seals in the U.K. This is a central role for the SMRU! They established and agreed the same modus operandi as RSPCA Vet, Steve Bexton.

There were also one or two cases reported from the Strangford Lough, just by the east coast of Northern Ireland. These U.K seal deaths follow on from the earlier rash of 2008 incidents, with the same spiral cuts, found around Sable Island, Nova Scotia, and St Lawrence River estuary, Canada.

Arctic shark was responsible!

I had watched previously a Channel 5 screened documentary film ('The Seal Rippers') which attempted to show evidence that the perpetrator was the Arctic Green Shark.

Our SMRU and Norfolk Vet, Steve Bexton, had viewed this film and strongly disagreed with the production conclusions. I discovered their collective opinions, when I asked whether these sharks could have been responsible for the UK seal injuries. They were 100% certain that they could not inflict these types of wounds as a predator and went on to point out that this species of shark do not visit our shallow and warm waters off the coasts of Britain.

Speculation as to why seals are being targeted?

Over past years, after viewing all these differing seal mortalities, I ponder the reason and need for removing heads, blubber, skin and other organs? Assuming for a moment that advanced alien species ARE responsible? My thoughts turn to consider pollution aspects.

For a long time, when I first started to seriously investigate the mutilation of land-based animals in 1997, I believed that the ET's were monitoring the health of the animals by testing the organs and blood for pollution contaminants, which would then be indicative of the level of dangerous substances on our planet's surface; such as radioactive 'fallout' from nuclear industrial accidents, poison's from farming pesticides, chemical applications to soil and plants, etc. These would all have more impact on our farm stock, which live in the open and are constantly consuming pasture grasses etc, which then pass through their digestive systems. Data from analysis of brain, tongue, liver, blood and digestive tract, would then provide a means of evaluating the general health of planet Earth and, particularly, its human population who then eat lamb and beef, etc."

Sometimes it takes courage to tell it how it is and that is what David Cayton does. Thank goodness there are people like him.

August 1997 – Humanoid seen

It is said that at 2am on a day during this month, seen with the benefit of infra-red technology, a 6ft tall, black, heavily muscled humanoid, crawled through some kind of *'door'* about 4ft above the ground, and vanished into the night. Another observer only saw a weird light, without the benefit of infra-red technology. Colm Kelleher spent hundreds of days and nights on the Skinwalker property, conducting research into these matters.

Colm A. Kelleher, Ph.D. – is a biochemist, with a 15 year research career in cell and molecular biology. Following his Ph.D. in biochemistry from the University of Dublin, Trinity College, in 1983, Kelleher worked at the Ontario Cancer Institute, the Terry Fox Cancer Research Laboratory, and the National Jewish Center for Immunology and Respiratory Medicine.

Colm A. Kelleher, PhD and George Knapp (right)

For the past eight years he has worked as project manager and team leader at a private research institute, using forensic science methodology to unravel scientific anomalies. Biochemist Kelleher tells the story of the team's experiences on the ranch as *"an ambitious if unconventional example of what science is supposed to do…explore the unknown."*

George Knapp is Nevada's best-known journalist. For 20-plus years, he has served as anchor, chief investigative reporter, and commentator for KLAS TV, the CBS affiliate in Las Vegas. He is a six-time Emmy winner, has earned the AP's Mark Twain Award for news writing seven times, and twice was given the Edward R. Murrow Award for Investigative Reporting. His reporting on Nevada's infamous Area 51 military base was selected by UPI as Best Individual Achievement by a Reporter in 1989. He also writes an award-winning weekly column for a Las Vegas newspaper.

Colonel John Alexander – Top Secret clearance

We were surprised to learn that retired Army Colonel John Alexander (who is known to us) was part of the group of researchers and scientists who investigated reports of cattle mutilations and other strange occurrences at Skinwalker Ranch, located south-east of Ballard, Utah, previously known locally as the Sherman Ranch. For years, stories of cattle mutilations, sightings of UFOs, Orbs and 'Bigfoot', among other paranormal events, have been reported as happening on this ranch land.

He is the author of *UFOs: Myths, Conspiracies and Realities*, which can be purchased on Amazon.com

John Alexander was a former serviceman with top secret clearance, who created Advanced Theoretical Physics – a group of top-level government officials and scientists brought together to study UFO reports.

John:

> "There is an assumption made in the UFO community – and the general population – that UFOs are secret and all the information is automatically classified. This is not true."

He was previously in charge of Special Forces 'A' Teams in Vietnam and Thailand, in the 1960s. As a program manager for Los Alamos National Laboratory, he conducted non-lethal warfare briefings for the White House staff, National Security Council, members of Congress and senior defense officials.

Nick Pope:

> "John Alexander is the real deal. He doesn't just talk the talk – he's walked the walk. Here's a man with a top secret security clearance who researched the UFO phenomenon and discussed it at the highest levels, in the shadowy world of military and intelligence which he's inhabited for decades. Forget everything you think you know about UFOs – this insider's account exposes the reality, and it's a reality that will come as a big surprise. Packed with top grade information, insightful analysis and fascinating anecdotes, Alexander's interesting and controversial book sets the gold standard for titles on this subject."

John, in an interview conducted by Aleixandre Rojas for *Open Minds* production, said:

> "The events that took place there were real and tangible, rather than any urban myths of folklore. What you have to understand is that one should take things into the right context here, although the events were mystifying and terrifying. According to some that witnessed them, most of the time on the ranch, it was business as usual – the everyday running of the property. Nobody was injured, to my knowledge, although I understand there were reports of cattle being affected. As part of the surveillance we had a bank of video cameras, set on platforms, monitoring each other. On one occasion the tape stopped. An examination of the cameras revealed that Duck tape fixed to one of them had been removed, so had the PVC clamps. In addition, a 3ft chunk had been cut out of the earth wire. When this occurred there were cattle milling around the pole, at the time, but it was clear they were not the cause of what happened. Examination of the film showed the interferences occurred between the second and third frame of film. People ask me what I think the cause of these paranormal happenings is, attributed by some as being either extraterrestrial or anomalous phenomena, indigenous to our planet. The truth of the matter is that I don't know, purely because there is not solid evidence to substantiate any individual hypothesis."

Cows found mutilated

The Sherman family, not unnaturally in the circumstances, speculated as to whether there was a link between the sightings and the death or disappearance of seven cows, four of which disappeared without a trace; three others were found dead and partially mutilated.

Terry Sherman:

> "You talk to a lot of people around here that at one time or another have seen something they can't explain. There have been a lot of cattle mutilations, and many weren't reported. Several (ranchers) told me that when they had (mutilation), they called the authorities and the authorities couldn't do anything, so it was just a waste of time and effort."

It is alleged that enquiries carried out with the Uintah County Sheriff's Department revealed the department has not received reports of UFOs or cattle mutilations in recent memory. Sheriff Ralph Stansfield, in nearby Duchesne County, said he is unaware of any UFOs or mutilations being reported in the past 18 months.

Soon after the sightings began, the Shermans' found one of their cows dead in a field. It had a peculiar hole in the centre of its left eyeball but was otherwise untouched with no trace of blood. There was no evidence of predators, footprints, or tyre tracks. A strange, chemical-like, odour was present. Later, another dead cow was found with a similar hole in its left eye and a 6-inch hole, only about an inch deep, carved out of its rectum. The same chemical smell was noticeable.

Cows began to disappear

Terry also told of the mysterious disappearance of some of the cows. One appeared to have been lifted from the snow where it stood. The cow's hoof prints led into the field, but the prints stopped at the edge of the field near some trees. The area where the cow apparently took its last steps was surrounded by a circle of broken twigs and branches. Above, Terry noticed the tops of the trees appeared to have been cut off. He said:

> "If its snow, it's hard for a 1,200 or 1,400-pound animal to just walk off without leaving tracks, or to stop and walk backwards completely and never miss their tracks; it was just gone. It was very bizarre."

The last of the three dead cows was found in January, in a clump of trees at the edge of the same field. The cow, which had been seen alive by the Shermans' son, just five minutes earlier, had a 6-inch wide, 18-inch deep hole cored out of its rectum and extending into the body cavity. There was no blood on the cow, or the snow, and the same chemical odour was apparent. There was a circle of twigs around the fallen cow and the tops of the trees appeared severed.

Following on from the book, *The Hunt for the Skinwalker*, we were pleased to discover that Ryan Patrick Burns, who is a researcher of the UFO paranormal activity around the Utah area, has spent considerable time conducting his own investigations into reports of glowing *'balls of light'*, time distortions, strange creatures and government secrets, which have been published in his book, entitled *Skinwalker & Beyond*.

Ryan Patrick Burns

Aliens are invading!

Unfortunately, the media are constantly on the lookout for the more zany and sensational stories to sell their products. Whilst many of the incidents which occurred there are unexplainable by current science, we should exercise great care when it comes to examining events involving incredible allegations which can be found on the internet, relating to what took place – now many years ago.

It is said Dr. Eric Davis, who is the author of what some allege to be a controversial paper, *Teleportation Physics* study, as commissioned by the Air Force Research Study, and Christopher 'Kit' Green (a former CIA official) were also members of the N.I.D.S. team, and that it is alleged Dr. Eric Davis was the target of a telepathic attack on him while at the ranch. Incredibly it was also suggested on the internet that a scientist from San Francisco – Dr. Jack Sarfatti – claims he was told by reliable sources that there was:

> "... actually an invasion of aliens on Bigelow's Skinwalker Ranch in Utah, and he claims a number of Bigelow's men were either killed or injured by the ET's."

Statements like these are calculated to stir the imagination and raise great curiosity, but to put it bluntly does not make a great deal of sense. We are sure that if the intelligence behind the phenomena wanted to *'invade'*, there isn't a great deal we could do about it. Apart from that, *'they'* have been here for a long time, so why precipitate action now? – Not forgetting there is no proof (as far as we know) to corroborate this event as having happened.

Dr. Davis was team leader of the N.I. D.S. (which terminated in October 2004) between 1999 and 2001. During one interview, he said:

> *"There were multiple voices that spoke in unison telepathically. The voices were monotone males, with a very terse threatening tone. Four senses were in their control – so there was no odour, sound, smell, or touch, and overall body motion was frozen (as in the muscles that would not respond). Afterwards, when completely freed from this event — after the dark shadow disappeared — there was no lingering or residual odours, sounds, etc., in the immediate environment – more like an intelligence, giving a warning to the staff by announcing its presence and that they (the staff) were being watched by this presence. Demonic possessions are not short lived, nor as benign as this, and they always have a religious context."*

Our opinion

The manifestations which 'spilled out' at the ranch owned by the Sherman family undoubtedly share similarities with other geographic points around the World. The late Bruce Cathie, who wrote *Harmonic, 33,695 & 288* books, established the existence of an invisible worldwide electromagnetic grid on the surface of the planet on which nuclear power stations and other facilities are mathematically sited.

What should concern us all, are the claims made of animals being mutilated. If, in fact, such mutilations and disappearances are being orchestrated by an unidentified intelligence for their own agenda, then presumably the degree of that intelligence is able to differentiate between humans and animals. Heaven help us if it can't!

In 2005 the incidents which occurred around the Utah area was the subject of further newspaper speculation.

County News 1st December 2005
Is there a "Bermuda Triangle" in Utah?

By Allen Norman

Is the U.S. government hiding something we don't know about the nature of the disappearances that have been occurring in Utah? The residents have witnessed their belongings vanish and never see them again. The government refuses to recognize this and does not maintain an official stand on it.

Since the 1960s, the mystery has continued to attract attention. When you dig deeper into most cases, though, they're much less mysterious. Either they were never in the area to begin with, they were actually found, or there's a reasonable explanation for their disappearance.

There have been many bizarre incidents in Utah. At Big Creek witnesses claimed to have heard dogs barking and children shouting when neither dogs nor children were present.

In the Canyon Crest area, a parked vehicle rolled down a slope into the canyon more than one hundred feet below, killing nine people, including a young boy whose body has never been found. At least five other known fatalities have also occurred on this pass.

There have been nine cattle mutilations in Utah this year The bodies horribly mutilated as if with surgical precision - eyes removed, innards gone, the skin grotesquely peeled away. The predator, or predators, have left no footprints to reveal their identities and no blood stains on the earth to speak to the slaughter.

In some mutilation cases, the cows entire insides appear to have vanished. A horse was found skinned, its tongue, lips and anus had been removed. Strangely, no bullets were found which leads to the possibility that the horse might have been stabbed.

But Utah seems to have a special affinity for these strange events. In 1966, the very first animal mutilation, the strange killing of a horse known as Thunder occurred. Thunder's strange death lead the way to recent mutilations, with no evidence to be found.

Many ranchers believe that aliens are behind these mutilations and extraterrestrials are still offered up today as an explanation for these bizarre events. Skeptics counter that the attacks are caused by predator animals (despite the lack of tracks) and insects. They have no explanation as to why the carcasses of only certain animals show these strange effects or why ranchers, who presumably are familiar with a variety of cattle death, find these specific deaths to be out of the ordinary.

The residents of southwestern Utah experienced an intense, unimaginable bright flash of light which lit the area brighter than daylight for 2-3 seconds. At the same time, people from all across western Utah began calling the UFO hotlines reporting their sightings of an unidentified object trav-

Photo/R. Rogers
Numerous accounts have been reported all over Utah since the 1960s of people observing unusual activity.

elling overhead. Most reported a hovering ball of light.

A crowd of 12 stargazers were shocked when a mysterious UFO was spotted hovering in the sky in rural Utah. Eyewitnesses recall it hovering for half an hour in the clear night sky on Saturday. The witnesses describe the object as moving extremely slowly, not like a plane. The unidentified flying objects lit up the otherwise clear night sky on Saturday. Nobody knows where it came from and nobody saw it land anywhere.

A ranch in the Uintah Basin region is rich in UFO sightings, hauntings and bizarre happenings. The boom in UFO sightings is recent months, observed during both day and nighttime hours is not an isolated incident. Numerous accounts have been reported all over the US of people observing unusual activity. In the stable there has been reported activity such as strange knockings, apparitions, and people reporting the feeling of being touched.

A cluster of paranormal activity has been reported an another ranch in Colorado. Witnesses report sightings of strange humanoid entities and UFOs. The US government is interested in the site because of since the incredible and strange phenomena that has been reported. Reports of mysterious balls of light and a supposed active inter-dimensional portal.

Another highly active location at a ranch in Colorado has been a focus of many paranormal researchers. Strange orange light orbs have been reported to have been spotted, and two horses appeared one morning with strange and unusual markings on them. Researchers feel that the paranormal activity is a mix of both intelligent entities as well as residual paranormal impressions in the environment.

Strange lights that appear bright and then fade away and Unexplained fireballs that streak through darkened skies. During the 1960s numerous UFOs were sighted as well as reports. The objects seen most frequently there are the "ball of light" type UFOs rather than those that resemble metallic craft.

Unexplained cattle mutilations are thought to be related to the alien abduction phenomenon. The mutilations are reported in the vicinity of reported abductions and UFO sightings with bizarre and gruesome reports attached to them.

More on the orbs!

In July 2014, we purchased retired Colonel John Alexander's book: *UFOs, myths, conspiracies and realties*, which included about five pages of information relating to the events that had taken place at the Gorman/Sherman Ranch.

In that book there is the following reference with regard to the incident (which we viewed with some suspicion) of claims made that three dogs at the ranch had been vaporised by a cluster of orbs!

John:
> *"Three of the owner's dogs were observed snapping at the orbs as they floated through the eastern part of the ranch, close to where they lived. The orbs seemed to tease the dogs and led them into a nearby pasture. The dogs never returned to the house. When the owner searched for the dogs, the following day, all he found were grease spots on the ground – which he took to be the remains of the dogs. Fearing that his teenage sons might provoke the orbs, he decided to vacate the premises and sell up."*

This makes fascinating reading. However, surely such a monumental claim would have been the subject of intense investigation by members of the N.I.D.S. and scrutiny by their scientific colleagues? One would hope an examination was made of the ground where the grease spots were found, and samples taken for analysis in order to determine DNA.

Where are the photographs of the scene? Who took what, when, where, and how? We cannot even contact Robert Bigelow by email.

Personally, we doubt the orbs were responsible for the malicious attack on the dogs. If they were, it's a first! As for the dogs, it is likely they ran away – clearly frightened by something, or someone, and were not found.

We discussed this with Brenda Butler, who was keen to point out that she regarded it highly unlikely that orbs could deliberately injure animals. She said:

> *"I have seen Mason snapping at the orbs and, on occasion, apparently chasing them through the forest. I have been walking through the forest for over 30 years, with hundreds of people and many dogs, but never heard or witnessed anything untoward that might be associated to the appearance of the orbs and peculiar images seen and also captured on camera."*

Wolf-like creature

Another report tells of a weird wolf-like creature that manifested from inside a portal, which appeared in August 1997, when two trained researchers sighted a moving dark shape – described as a *humanoid creature* – that was seen to move off into the darkness. On another occasion a wolf-like creature – friendly enough to be petted – approached the ranch in broad daylight. It then proceeded to attempt to abduct a calf, at which point the landowner struck it with a heavy pole to deter it from doing this. When this failed, six bullets from a .44 Magnum were discharged into the animal's (believed heart) – again to no avail. A high powered rifle was then emptied into the animal, causing pieces to fly off. Once again a number of pertinent, valid questions should be asked, the most important being whether any analysis was carried out on the flesh left behind? We accept that, for all we know, this information may have been published – but where?

With regard to the image (as shown) we have tried to contact the copyright holder, without success, so we apologise in advance and will acknowledge copyright when the artist is identified.

Images from beyond our spectrum

During the 1990s, we were intrigued by the *'streaks of light'* and mysterious images shown in Cyril Permutt's book – *Photographing The Spirit World: Images From Beyond The Spectrum* (Harper Collins, USA, 1989, ISBN: 0850307627) – presented as examples of spirit photographs, some of which were taken at religious festivals. Cyril Permutt was a professional photographer, who was very familiar in the use of photography and camera applications.

Spirit Photography

Many of the fascinating photographs shown in this book are alleged to be images of deceased relatives, or figures materialising next to the subject, whose facial features are sharply defined.

His book provides us with a unique experience to see for ourselves many thought-provoking examples of what is referred to as spirit photography, although he asks the reader to take into consideration photographic defects or lens aberrations which may or may not be the answer.

Cyril describes the various techniques required for securing paranormal psychic photography of this kind and points out that the best results were obtained with infra-red. In his opinion, the images *"represent only a few of the large number of attested and authenticated supernormal photographs which I have selected from my files, which prove conclusively that there is more to life than we perceive with our gross physical senses and which show photographic processes can capture the images of other dimensions and times."*

There are examples of ectoplasm – a thick white mist in varying shapes, out of which hands and faces begin to materialise; in other instances, it is seen to form from out of the body of the medium.

An ectoplasmic *'rod'* is shown during a séance, as photographed by Dr. Crawford. A photo is shown of what is referred to as *'ectoplasmic lights'*, which obliterate the body of the person being photographed. [Authors: We have seen examples of this during recent years].

One's own intuition is to wonder if some of them are double images, or deliberately fabricated, but we recognise the dangers of forming any conclusions without specialised knowledge of the chosen subject. Generally speaking, little comparisons could be made with the images of orbs, swirling mists, and humanoid shapes that characterised photos taken in Rendlesham Forest, Suffolk, and those shown in Cyril's book, however intriguing they are, but common sense dictates that whatever label we put on them the source is the same.

During the design and typesetting preparation of this book by Bob Tibbitts – a seasoned UFO veteran, whose research began during the late 1960s, and having seen for himself many strange images – some apparently humanoid, others not, he asks:

> *"If they represent a presence or glimpse of intelligences from a parallel plane of existence or part of a 'multi-universe', it seems odd that 'their' habitat appears to align conveniently with ours. Why are they observed the 'right way up' and many facing towards us, revealing features that are humanoid in shape? As 'space' has no orientation, you would expect these things to appear in a more haphazard way – yet they are presented to us in a way that corresponds with our familiar environment. It is almost as though we have created these apparitions ourselves so that they 'fit' our way of sensing things! Rather like a 'tulpa' – the Tibetan term to describe a 'thought form' that momentarily materialises in the observer's plane of existence and if powerful enough, can be seen by others.*
>
> *It has been theorised that the human mind participates collectively at building the world in which we live – assuming this to be true, I wonder if, given 'favourable' conditions, we sometimes screw it all up and the result is the strange array of apparitions that tweaks our curiosity and feeds our fears. There are so many questions and presently, only a few hints at answers.*
>
> *This may appear as a trite and somewhat shallow appraisal to the experiencer, who may be exposed to this strange phenomenon when standing alone in the dark somewhere, while having it impact upon them as a totally personal manifestation.*
>
> *More disturbing is the often reported physical interaction during the episode and the 'loss' of time and sense of 'purpose' felt, that often leads to a change of lifestyle – for better or worse.*
>
> *Perhaps the collective human mind presents itself with these mysteries so that by trying to understand them, each individual facet of that 'mind' is led eventually to fulfilment."*

Despite huge advancements in modern science and medicine, allowing us to peer even further into the cosmos, with talk of a manned expedition to Mars, the concept of personal survival after death still continues to elude us. Is this one of the reasons why it also fascinates us?

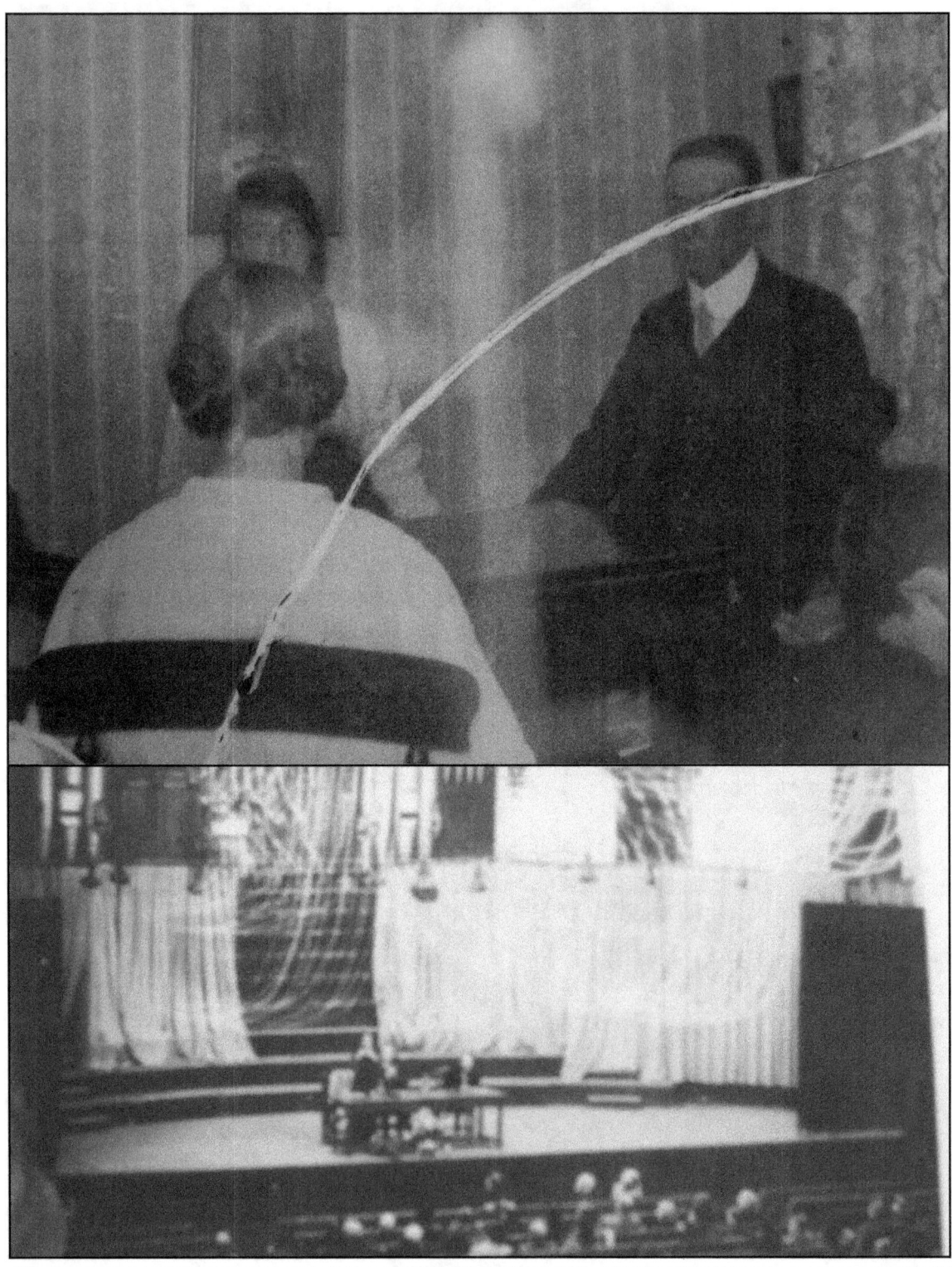

If we knew the answer to what lies outside the realm of our plain of existence, would we be so keen to continue living in this one?

In July 2014, we were pleased to enter into communication with Cyril's son – psychic and medium, Philip Permutt – who founded ISIS Crystals in 1992, which has a reputation as being one of the largest and most successful crystal shops in the UK with its integral healing centre.

Philip has been practicing as a crystal healer and teacher ever since, and is the author of the internationally acclaimed best sellers: *The Crystal Healer, The Little Book of Crystal Tips & Cures,* and *The Complete Guide to Crystal Chakra Healing.* His latest book and card set, *The Crystal Tarot,* has just been published. He has recorded many meditations and workshop CDs, including *Crystal workshop* and the *Little Meditation Album.*

Philip has lectured on crystals and crystal healing and has a Degree in Applied Biology, from London University. In addition to his busy schedule, he writes a regular column – 'Phil's Crystal Clinic' in *Take a Break's Fate & Fortune* – and his many articles have been published in magazines, electronically, and in journals.

He has appeared on radio both in the UK and USA.

Further examples of mysterious images captured on camera

We would first also like to bring the reader's attention to similar phenomena captured in the Cumbria area by Katie Hall and John Pickering, a very pleasant and professional couple, who published the findings of their research in *Beyond Photography* ('O' Books, John Hunt publishing, 2006).

In June 2014 we contacted Katie, who told us that they were intending to publish a new book later this year, entitled *Orbs & Beyond* ('O' Books). We also enjoyed an in-depth conversation with John, whose interest in the UFO subject goes back to the 1950s.

Although the private location of where this phenomenon took place is known, John and Katie have asked us not to divulge where this is because of fears their privacy would be breached by other researchers who may wish to carry out their own investigations.

Katie:

> "It began with the sudden appearance of strange, tiny, twinkling lights in an old haunted cottage. At that time neither of us was aware of the other's existence – but all the decisions we were each making were drawing us together.
>
> Even before the coming of all the strange phenomena related in our book, I had began to call one part of the garden, the 'Faerie Dell', simply because of the ash tree which grew there in a circle of Alkanet. To me it always felt like an enchanted place, which later proved to be just the case. The tiny, briefly visible lights that I was already familiar with, now began to appear on our photographs as orbs and vortices. So began our incredible four year journey into another aspect of reality. We have been fortunate to catch a glimpse of the mystery of life and to share our thoughts and experiences with others. Luminosities and light-forms not only gave us the photographs, they provided us an alternative perspective from which to view a larger reality."

John:

> "During the four years of our experiences with the light-forms, we seemed at times to be living in two realities at once: we were enchanted by the phenomena we were photographing; its existence had captivated our attention; and yet in the 'real' world it could not have come along at a worse time. We desperately needed to totally concentrate our energies on making a living, and on selling the children's books we had spent the last three years creating, but instead much of our waking thoughts were now taken up with the mystery of orbs and light-forms. We now had some incredible photos and we just had to try and make sense of it all. We felt almost impelled to write down our experiences. We had to research what was happening here in a wider context and so our book was born!"

Haunted Skies Volume Ten

The couple were kind enough to send us the following spectacular images:

1. This shows the same (or similar) apparition photographed from 2006 to 2010 – notice the similarities in the structure of the entity.
2. These look like a "spaceman" and a floating "alien".
3. Over 12ft tall entity caught roaming through our woodland.
4. Interesting "light-form".
5. "Valentino" photographed on Valentine's Day by a friend living locally who, having read our book, then started photographing similar images.
6. A visiting psychic sensed a wolf presence in the woods; a minute or so later I took this image of Katie showing a "wolf-like" image.
7. Images from a series of shots taken of "light rods" that travelled across our garden.
8. Brief photo introduction to an interactive phenomenon.

Original images

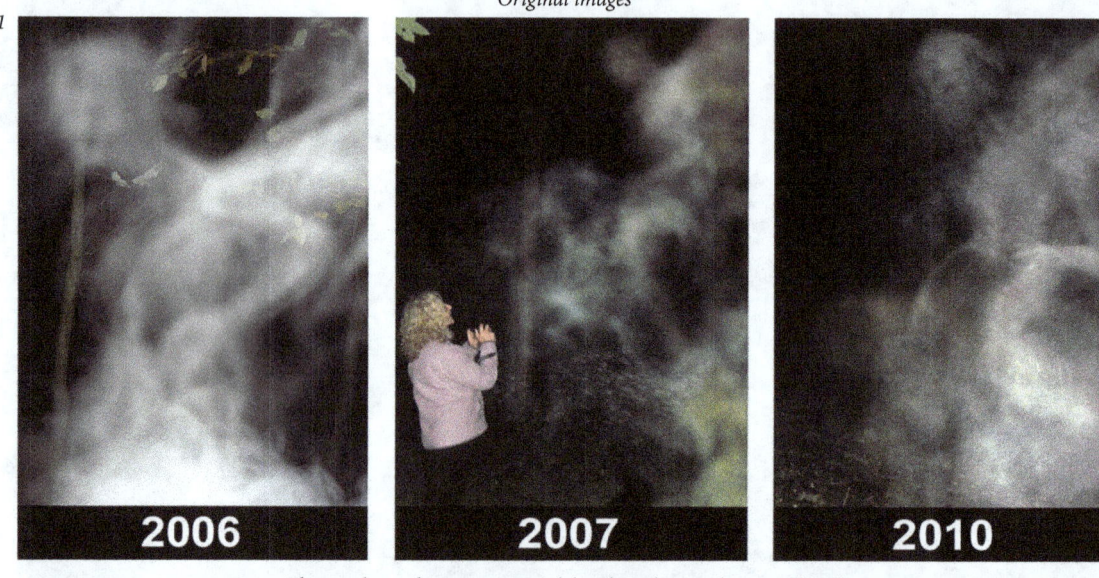

Photo-enhanced images using Adobe Photoshop unsharp mask tool

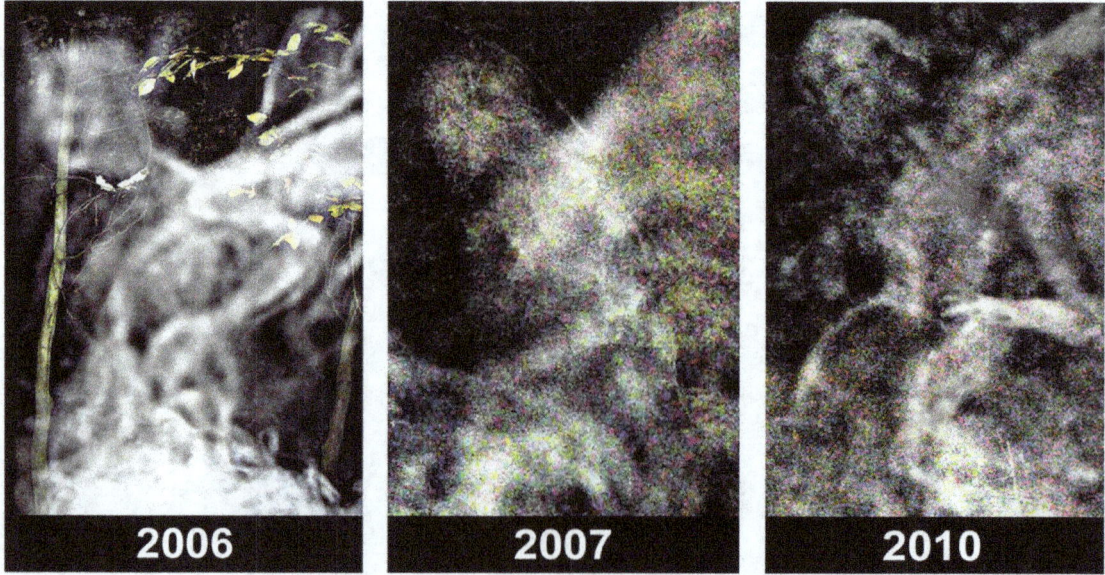

All images copyright © Katie Hall & John Pickering 2007/2014

Haunted Skies Volume Ten

© *Katie Hall & John Pickering 2007/2014*

Haunted Skies Volume Ten

© Katie Hall & John Pickering 2007/2014

© Sara Saunders 2008

Haunted Skies Volume Ten

© Katie Hall & John Pickering 2007/2014

Light rods. Three original photos

Light rods. Slightly enhanced and enlarged images

'Beyond Photography' – An interactive phenomenon

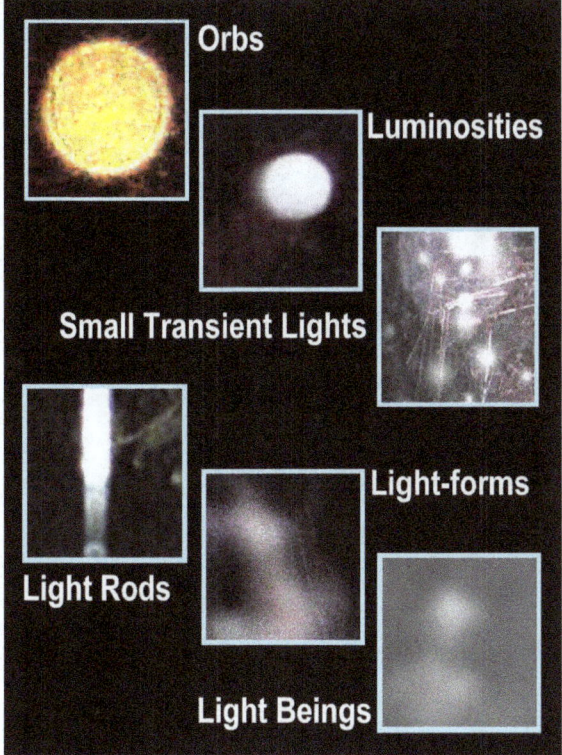

Photographed since the year 2000 by Katie Hall & John Pickering

John:

> "Please mention that all the terms we use in our books and presentations re orbs etc. are descriptive – not definitive and that I always stress that we are all on a learning curve here – in spite of those who claim to know all the answers."

Anomaly captured on camera in December 2013, near Stratford-upon-Avon, England

At Christmas 2013, we experienced for ourselves examples of an unusual image, captured on digital camera, during a visit to a quiet church near Stratford-upon-Avon, Warwickshire. We took half a dozen photographs late at night, after visiting the local church, which was the subject of some interest in more recent years, when the bell tower clock began to chime at 3pm one afternoon, while it was being cleaned and laid out on the nearby lawn!

Haunted Skies Volume Ten

The truth of the matter is that nobody can prove what and where these anomalies (including UFOs) are from, but they exist and probably have been with us for a long time, given that throughout history the number of recorded encounters with apparitions, ghosts or spirits, have shaped the course of human history on this planet.

Dedications

Police Constable Gavin Carlton, murdered in 1988

We would like to pay our respects to family and colleagues, who gathered in December 2013 to mark the 25th anniversary of the murder of a Coventry Police Officer, who was shot when confronting bank robbers in December 1987.

A service was conducted in Torrington Avenue, Tile Hill, in memory of PC Gavin Carlton, 29, who was shot six days before Christmas in 1988.

He followed the robbers, but when they shot his car he mounted the pavement and got stuck on a bollard. As he tried to reverse and escape, he was shot at point blank range.

Every year a memorial event is held on the spot where PC Carlton was killed, but this year a large number of police officers – including West Midlands Police Chief Constable, Chris Sims, and West Midlands Police and Crime Commissioner Bob Jones attended. It was a very poignant ceremony. The Chief Constable said the day PC Carlton died was *"one of the darkest in the history of West Midlands Police"*.

Death of Police Crime Commissioner Bob Jones

Condolences are also offered to the family of West Midlands Police Commissioner Mr Bob Jones, who passed away in July 2014.

Deputy Police and Crime Commissioner Yvonne Mosquito said:

> "This is a huge loss to the West Midlands and to policing. Bob was a dear friend and a deeply committed public servant. All our thoughts are with Bob's wife Sarah and his family at this sad time. Bob was a great supporter of things local to WV11 and was active in the area most recently with the campaign to save the Ashmore Pub - He was a good man who will be missed."

Haunted Skies Volume Ten

Coming soon ... Volume 11, of *Haunted Skies* – 1989-1990

This covers the period 1989-1990 and shows, once again, heavy UFO activity reported in the sky over the Essex area of the UK.

In this book we will now also include UFO reports from Canada, in addition to Australia, New Zealand and the USA, embracing the period between 1962 and, hopefully, the late 1970s – thanks to the assistance of Ralph Hull, shown here. He is another regular visitor to Rendlesham Forest, Suffolk, who has carried out investigations into reported Canadian UFO activity from some years ago.

We have written to Paul Helyer, the ex-Canadian Defence Minster, who has promised to support our work and will discuss his view on the alien presence in this forthcoming book.

Paul's book *Light at the end of the Tunnel – A survival plan for the Human Species* sets out in stark and unvarnished terms most of the world's major problems. The human species is heading for extinction unless we change our attitudes and actions with urgency appropriate to impending disaster.

December 20 2013

Mr. John Hanson
31 Red Lion St.
Alvechurch B48 7LG
England

Dear John Hanson:

This will acknowledge and thank you for your book *Haunted Skies: The Encyclopaedia of British UFOs, Volume 5 1972-1974* which just arrived safely.

Your timing is perfect as I am just reviewing the UFO section of my latest book.

You say you are always looking for endorsements to use on the back of your books and that Dr. Edgar Mitchell and Colonel Charles Halt have both cooperated and Stanley Friedman has promised a foreword. I know each of these gentlemen and have great respect for each one. I just met Jesse Marcel Junior briefly before he passed away. There is no reason why you can't add my name to the list for a brief endorsement to use as you please. I'm extremely busy for the next month or two so it would be good if there is no particular rush. If there is you can always send me a two or three liner to take a look at and amend if considered necessary.

With warmest best wishes for Christmas and the New Year.

Yours sincerely,

Paul Hellyer

INDEX
Denotes Researcher

A

Abbot, Graham – 233
Abraham, Raymond – 211
Acey, Mary – 100
Acocks, Joan – 175
Acocks, Michael – 175
Adamski, George – 404, 407
Adjakdel, Henry – 178
Aerial Phenomena Research Group – 411
Aetherius Society – 13
AFRICA: *Hind, Cynthia – 134
Albert, John – 355
Aldridge, Peter – 200, 208
Ali, Azhar – 100
Alker, Lynda – 123
Allen, W. – 324
Anders, Derrick – 106
Andrews, I. – 389
Angel hair – 195
Anstee, Ronald – 376
Aplouff (alleged alien being) – 466
Appelzoller, David – 276
Apter Eric – 400
Argent, Anna – 238
Armstrong, Irene – 153
Armstrong, Jean – 162
Armstrong, K. – 410
Armstrong, Leslie – 162
Arnold, Kenneth – 274, 369
Arnold, Ross – 300
Asbridge, Steven – 58

Ash, William C. – 485
Aspden, Sally – 144
Astronomy Magazine -11
AU: *Auchetti, John – 263
AU: *Chalker, Bill – 263, 388
AU: *Cilia, Larraine – 263
AU: *Frola, Diane & Robert
AU: *Judy Magee – 263
AU: *McNamara, Dominic – 263
AU: *Norman, Paul – 263, 428
AU: Adelaide – 405
AU: Alice Springs – 325, 326
AU: Atherton – 439
AU: Auckland – 325
AU: Auckland Town Hall – 404
AU: Australian Flying Saucer Bureau – 237
AU: Australian Flying Saucer Club – 327
AU: Australian Flying Saucer Review – 388
AU: Australian National Airways – 322
AU: Australian UFO Research Network – 263
AU: Ballarat, Victoria – 323
AU: Bass Strait – 265, 268, 381
AU: Basterfield, Keith – 263
AU: Belmont, New South Wales – 427
AU: Black Rock, Victoria – 320
AU: Bonbeach, Victoria – 324
AU: Botany Bay – 330
AU: Bowral, New South Wales – 308
AU: Box Hill – 322
AU: Brighton Golf Links, Victoria – 325
AU: British Astronomical Association – 322
AU: Brunswick, Victoria – 424

Haunted Skies Volume Ten

AU: Bulleen, Victoria – 424
AU: Caltex Refinery, New South Wales – 400
AU: Canberra – 425
AU: Canberra, New South Wales – 309, 410
AU: Carnegie, Melbourne – 323
AU: Casino, New South Wales – 399
AU: Caulfield Victoria, Melbourne – 317
AU: Chullora, New South Wales – 400
AU: Claypans – 405
AU: Commonwealth Observatory, New South Wales – 392
AU: Cooktown – 418
AU: Cootamundra Hills – 439
AU: Crows Nest, Queensland – 373
AU: Culburra, New South Wales – 399
AU: Dandedong Road – 323, 329
AU: Darwin – 441
AU: Darwin Airport – 487
AU: Delissaville – 487
AU: Disclosure Australia – 264
AU: East Kew, Melbourne – 320
AU: East Malvern – 324
AU: Elba Island – 324
AU: Ferndale, New South Wales – 267
AU: Flemington, North West Melbourne – 323
AU: Forster – 425
AU: Geelong, Victoria – 315, 326
AU: Gippsland Lakes, Victoria – 323
AU: Goulburn, New South Wales – 333, 439
AU: Graceville – 315
AU: Gundagai – 439
AU: Hamilton Flying Saucer Investigation Society – 327
AU: Hamilton, Victoria – 324
AU: Hampton Beach, Victoria – 322
AU: Hanging Rock, Victoria – 321
AU: Harts Range – 325
AU: HMAS Warrego – 426
AU: Jones, Air Marshal, Sir George – 386
AU: Junee – 439
AU: Katoomba, New South Wales – 382, 401
AU: Kissimmee Highway – 340
AU: Launceston, Australia – 425, 427
AU: Lismore, New South Wales – 318

AU: Mackay Meteorological Office – 425
AU: Mackay, Queensland – 425
AU: Mackinda Downs, Queensland – 431
AU: Maffra, Victoria – 269
AU: Manby Ferry – 339
AU: Maralinga – 386
AU: Marrickville – 400
AU: Meekatharra – 442
AU: Melbourne Airport – 341
AU: Melbourne – 308, 309, 314, 322, 327, 329, 330, 337, 340, 405, 424, 425
AU: Mena Murtie Station, Wilcannia – 337
AU: Mildura, Victoria – 402
AU: Millaa Millaa – 439
AU: Montmorency, Victoria – 330
AU: Moola Boola Station – 341
AU: Moora – 267
AU: Moorabin – 326
AU: Mount Gambier – 324
AU: Mount Hale – 442
AU: Mullewa – 427
AU: Nambour, Queensland – 267
AU: New South Wales – 309, 310
AU: Newcastle – 405
AU: North Melbourne railway yard – 323
AU: Nowra Radar – 333
AU: Parramatta, New South Wales – 309
AU: Pascoe Vale State School, Victoria – 330
AU: Perth – 405
AU: Purnong – 405
AU: Queanbeyan, New South Wales – 330
AU: Queensland – 329
AU: Rockhampton Airport, Queensland – 316
AU: Rockhampton Grammar School – 425
AU: Sadler W.J., Flight Lieutenant – 309
AU: Sale – 325
AU: Shepparton, Victoria – 327
AU: St. Kildar beach, Melbourne – 325
AU: Sydney Harbour – 400
AU: Sydney, New South Wales – 309, 370, 330, 399, 400, 401, 410, 431, 504
AU: Tablelands – 439
AU: Tennant Creek – 441
AU: Texas, New South Wales – 325

AU: Tintinarra – 343
AU: Toompang, New South Wales – 438
AU: Victoria – 329, 322
AU: Victorian UFO Society – 428
AU: Waitara, New South Wales – 425
AU: Warrnambool, Victoria – 388
AU: West Footscray, Victoria – 322
AU: West Freugh Wigtownshire – 379
AU: Willoughby, New South Wales – 411
AU: Wollongong – 309
AU: Wonthaggi, Victoria – 333, 334
AU: Woomera, New South Wales – 268, 400
AU: Wyalong – 438
AU: Young – 439
Aubry, Christine – 13
Avendel, Mr. – 393
Avern, Captain – 267

B

Baca, Harold – 277
Bailey, Cecil – 232
Bailey, Eric – 215
Baker, Shirley – 212
Ballard, Eileen – 174
Banks, Jane – 232
Bansial, Kyme – 205
Barham, Ian – 56
Barker, Douglas, Captain – 320
Barron, Ray – 109
Barton, Cherie – 373
Bates, Nicholas – 15
BBC – 328, 376
BBC Radio Essex – 234
BBC, South Yorkshire website – 45
Beacon, Colin – 326
Beard, Peter & Angie – 22
Bellamy, Barry – 146
Belton, Sylvia – 205
Bennett, M.J. – 373
Bentham, Sylvester – 294
Bentley, H. – 162
Bibby, Nelson – 233
Birmingham Evening Mail – 15
Bishop, Grady – 368

Blair, Lesley – 77
Blake, Gordon – 116
Blake, Thomas – 330
Bleakley, David (MP) – 357
Blythe, William – 192
BOAC Comet Jet airliner – 324
Board of Accident Inquiry – 426
Bobberly, Ben – 283
Boles, Charles – 301
Bolton, A. – 240
Boniface, Barbara – 230
Boniface, Bernard – 230
Boniface, Brian – 230
Booker, Ernest – 373
Boon, Mr. and Mrs. – 31
Boone, Tim – 207
Booth, Joy – 235
Booth, Kelly – 235
Booth, W., Captain – 324
Boston Traveller – 457
Bowen, Mrs. – 163
Bowers, Marian – 199
Bowyer, Barbara – 435
Boyle, John – 322
BP Chemical Plant – 332
Bradbury, N.E. – 305
Braddow, Ivan – 82
Brannan, Margaret – 139
Brannon, Irene – 301
Brannon, Paul – 301
Braunger, F. – 486
Braxton Democrat – 313
Breedon, Richard – 101
Brewer, Carson – 391
Bridge, Cecil – 402
Briggs, Percy – 405
Brink, E.G. – 389
British Airways – 11
British Astronomical Association – 11, 12, 113, 162, 229
Broderick, Raymond – 20
Brooke, Florence – 295
Brooke, Graham – 44
Brooke, Nigel – 44

Haunted Skies Volume Ten

Brookes, Steven – 41
Brooks, Heidi – 215
Broomhall, L. – 382
Brown, A. – 324
Brown, Albert – 381
Brown, Raymond – 130
Browne, Janette – 329
Brussels – 493
Buashton, Audrey – 225
Buckley, Lt. – 301
Burke, Ronald – 391
Burnage, Malcolm – 145
Burnett, Derek – 190
Burnett, G. – 330
Burnett, Norma – 190
Burnett, Y. – 199
Burrell, Leonard – 379
Burton, Sarah – 235
Burton, Shelia – 466
Butler, François – 151
Butterworth, Alan – 129

BOOKS

Abducted! Jim & Coral E. Lorenzen – 358
Breakthrough, Whitley Strieber – 16
Captured! The Betty and Barney Hill UFO Experience, Kathleen Marden and Stanton T. Friedman
Circular Evidence, Colin Andrews & Pat Delgado – 182
Communion, Whitley Strieber – 15
Cosmic Top Secret, Jon King (UFO Researcher) – 89
Encounters with UFO occupants, Jim & Coral E. Lorenzen – 358
Flying Saucer Occupants, Jim & Coral E. Lorenzen – 358
Flying Saucers – The Startling Evidence of the Invasion from Outer Space, Coral E. Lorenzen – 358
Flying Saucers Are Hostile, Brad Steiger and Joan Whritenour – 424
Flying Saucers, Serious Business, Frank Edwards – 286, 366
Harmonic 288, Bruce Cathie – 263
Harmonic 33, Bruce Cathie – 263
Harmonic 695, Bruce Cathie – 263
Inexplicable Sky, Arthur Constance – 342
Ivanhoe, Sir Walter Scott – 39
Project Blue Book, Brad Steiger – 290
Science Was Wrong, Kathleen Marden and Stanton T. Friedman -358
Situation Red – The UFO Siege, Leonard Stringfield – 419
The Alien Abduction Files, Denise Stoner & Kathleen Marden – 358
The Case for the UFO, Morris K. Jessup – 414
The Chronologies of Babylon 5, Babylon5scripts.com – 459
The Communion Letters, Whitley Strieber – 17
The Grays, Whitley Strieber – 17
The Interrupted Journey, John G. Fuller – 457
The Interrupted Journey, John G. Fuller – 447
The Janos People, Frank Johnson – 479
The Riddle of the Flying Saucers, Gerald Heard – 286
The Roswell Incident, Charles Berlitz and William Moore – 273
The Secret School, Whitley Strieber – 16
The Shadow of the Unknown, A.J. French – 358
The Strange Case of Dr. M.K. Jessup, Gray Barker – 414
They Live in the Sky, Trevor James Constable – 435
Transformation, Whitley Strieber – 16
UFOs – Operation Trojan Horse, John A. Keel – 265
UFOs over America, Jim & Coral E. Lorenzen – 358
UFOs, the whole story, Jim & Coral E. Lorenzen – 358
Who Are They? Margaret Fry – 326

C

Cadden, Mathew – 117
Cade, Simon – 117
Cadman, Gillian – 210, 240
Cain, Paul – 218
Caliendo, Ann – 211
Callander, C. – 341
Callow, Sidney – 316
CAN: Grand Falls, Newfoundland, Canada – 283
Cannon, A.D., Dr. – 294
Capes, Edith – 326
Cardoza, Julia – 437
Carleton, R.V. – 423
Carter, Angela – 396
Carter, Horace – 201

Carter, Patricia – 201
Casey, Richard, Federal Minister – 327
Cash, Bill (MP) – 175
Cavalieri, James – 280
Chafer, Mrs. – 211
Chelu, Sue – 225
Chesney, John – 236
Childs, Lisa – 129
Christensen, O. – 499
Cipolla, Victor – 498
Clark, Fred – 121
Clarke, Joe – 148
Clarke, R. – 138
Clarke, Rita – 211
Clarke, Ronald – 160
Clarke, Sarah – 242
Clements, Jennifer – 28
Clift, R.G. – 442
Cobain, R. – 325
Colby, J. – 110
Colby, Mark – 110
Cole, John F. – 277
Colin, Anthony – 11
Collins, Margaret – 212
Connolly, Cathie – 464
Considine, Daniel – 47
Contact – 333
Cook, Gina – 239
Cook, Kevin – 232
Cook, Linda – 161
Cook, Robert – 143
Cook, Steven – 161
Cooke, Sergeant, T. – 372
Cooke, T. – 372
Cooley, Frank – 278
Coomber, Sidney & Nancy – 17
Copleton, Wendy – 37
Coretti, Elda – 145
Cowe, Deborah – 177
Cowell, Valerie – 211
Cox, Jackie – 423
Coyne, Brenda -74
Cragg, Carol – 137
Crater Piccolomini – 366

Craven Heifer Public House – 121
Cropper, Pat – 91
Crow, Paul – 221
Cubbage, Donald – 342
Cummings, W.F., Mr. and Mrs. – 399

D
Danley, J.F. 'Fleck' – 277
Davidson, Alan – 122
Davies, Shaun – 235
Davis, Joseph, H. – 416
Davis, Ross – 234
Dawn, G. – 148
Day, Elaine – 474
Day, John – 474
Dean, Nick – 341
Delancey, Albert – 282
Delaney, Steven – 173
Deleur, Eva – 221
Denmark – 373, 378
Dennis, Glenn - 271
Dickinson, Joanne – 228
Dietz,W. – 411
Dimbleby, Mrs. – 144
Dobbs, W.C. – 276
Dodd, Michael – 143
Doherty, John – 37
Dott, George – 342
Douglass, Earl – 376
Downer, Alec – 327
Doxsey, L. – 490
Doyle, Dempsey – 342
Drane, Kellie – 230
Drolin, Sara – 212
Drummond, Brian – 148
DuBois Chemicals – 419
Dynn, F., Captain – 276

E
Eakins, Horace, Colonel – 294
Eaves, Esther – 204
Eaves, Rueben – 204
Eckman, Harry – 402
Edington, James – 228
Edmund, Harry – 233

Haunted Skies Volume Ten

Edwards Kenneth – 479
Edwards, George – 144
Edwards, H. – 400
Elliot, W. – 323
Ellis, James – 102
Elliston, Terrence – 205
Elmore, Charles – 340
Ely, Steve – 192
Emerson, Robert, Colonel – 376
Emmerson, Pauline – 149
Encyclopaedia Galactica – 459
Epsilon 44L, alleged alien planet 47L – 467
Espina, Robert – 301
Estrada, Ramon – 327
Evans, Allison – 101
Evans, Margot – 417
Evans, William – 196
Everett, Donald – 162

F

Fairbairn, Emma – 239
Farthing, Hayley – 129
Fearon, Banks – 444
Federal Division of Angas – 327
Fellow of the British Interplanetary Society – 435
Ferguson, Donald – 282
Fielding, Arthur – 67
Film: Communion – 17
Film: Dark Skies – 458
Findlay, Andrew – 119
Firminger, Norman – 162
Firminger, Sharon – 162
Fishel, Aubrey, C. – 487
Fisher, A. – 216
Fisher, Bailey, G. – 312
Fitt, Diana – 238
Fleming, Peter – 169, 232
Fletcher, Peter, Captain – 317
Flight 542, Braniff Lockheed turbo prop airliner – 423
Floyd, Loretta – 269
Flucker, Irene – 405
Flying Saucer Club – 340
Flying Saucer News – 328
Flying Saucer Review – 468

Ford, Gordon – 70
Ford, Roger – 70
Foreman, David – 32
Fortune, Ella, Louise – 386
Foster, J.B. – 269, 272
Fox, Celia – 444
Frapple, Nigel – 328
Fraser, Lindsay – 230
Freeman, Mary – 181
Freeman, Philip – 396
Freeman, Roger (MOD) – 175
Frenhoff, Robert – 332
Friedlien, Winifred – 233
Fritz, Irene – 301
Fudge, Betty – 157
Fuller, John, G. – 466
Fulton, H.H. – 327
Furkenhoff, J.B. – 442

G

Garlington, Lee – 458
George, Sonia – 236
Geppart, Mr. – 309
Germany – 171, 325
Ghost Rockets – 262
Gibbs, Ellen – 66
Gilberston, Alan – 20
Gilbert, Ken – 323
Gilbert, Selena – 159
Gindelle, Harry – 342
Ginty, John – 340
Glossop, Caroline – 141
Goldthorpe, David – 41
Goode, John – 413
Goodge, Ronald – 205
Goodwin, Josie – 58
Goodwin, Tony – 58
Goreham, P. – 326
Gould, Dawn – 316
Goulding, Bill – 217
Goulding, Mabel – 217
Green Fireballs – 262, 343
Greene, B.F., Jnr. – 368
Greenman, Phyllis – 222

Gribble, Robert – 411
Griffin, R.F., Captain – 484
Grimme, David – 169
Ground Saucer Watch – 23
Grover, F., Sgt. – 489
Gunn, Lisa – 210
Guyton, Billie – 423
Gwent – 129
Gwinnnett – 188

H

Habberley, Carla – 240
Habberley, Grace – 240
Hall, Barbara – 388
Halstead, Frank – 366
Hancock, Jane – 152, 192
Hangar 84 – 272
Hanger 27 – 325
Harding, Terrence – 236
Harran, John – 199
Harrington, David – 223
Harrington, Patricia – 223
Harris, Harry – 472, 481
Hart, Judith, MP – 431
Hatch, Helen – 486
Hawes, Leon – 242
Hawkes, Kerry – 230
Hawkins, County Commissioner – 284
Hawkins, Rosemary – 472
Heale, Brian – 163
Heap, Georgina – 502
Heath, Toby – 212
Heinrichs, A. – 322
Helliwell, R. – 142
Hendry, Alan – 354
Henley Thomas – 417
Henshaw, Tom – 439
Herring, Joseph – 161
Heseltine, Gary (PRUFOS) – 124
Hester, David – 370
Hewer, J. – 129
Hewitt, P. – 225
Heywood, Vivien – 472
Higginson, Gary – 75

Hildebrand, Peter – 299, 301
Hildreth, Donald (OSI) – 295
Hill, Barney – 445, 466
Hill, Betty – 446
Hill, Harold – 330
Hill, Harold, Captain – 372
Hill, John – 234
Hill, Mathew – 95
Hilley, Nannette – 441
Hinfelaar, Henk & Brenda – 404
Hislop, Bill & Joan – 30
Hodgson, Robert – 144
Hoff, K.C. – 278
Hohman, Robert, E. – 454
Holden, Allan – 28
Hollinger, Margaret – 212
Hollis, Anne – 130
Holloway, Marshall – 305
Holmes, John – 41
Holmes, Mr. – 32
Holmes, Philip – 421
Hood, Max – 276
Hook, M. – 100
Hooper, Keith – 314
Hope, D. – 221
Hopkinsville Goblin – 349
Hortrop, George – 332
Hostalek, Zdenek – 441
House of Commons – 431
Howard, Clare – 205
Howarth, Gary – 90
Howarth, John – 317
Howe, Carol – 222
Hoyle, Mr. – 133
Huffer, Charles – 151
Hughes, Emrys, (MP) – 431
Hulton, J.B. – 316
Humphrey, Vivienne – 234
Hurcoop, I. – 375
Hurn, Gerry – 142
Hutton, Frank – 392, 393
Hyde, Dean – 143
Hyter, Anne & Philip – 20

Haunted Skies Volume Ten

I

International Contact UK weekend – 417
Isgrig, David – 301
ITV – The Time, The Place – 120, 132

J

Jackman, John – 283
Jackson, Allan – 330
Jackson, C.D. – 454
Jackson, J. – 238
Jackson, Kenneth – 171
Jackson, Paul – 263
Jackson, Susan – 132
Jarrold, E.R. – 327
Jensen, L.D. – 294
Jerrams, Mrs. – 322
Jessop, Julie – 228
Jessop, Keith, Petty Officer – 334
Jessop, Mrs. – 164
Jessup, Rubye – 412, 417
Johnson, Chris – 199
Johnson, Dave – 283
Johnson, Edward – 110
Johnson, Jeanette – 329
Johnson, Manuel – 294
Johnson, Mark – 217
Johnson, Sheila – 200
Johnson, Walter – 278
Johnson, William – 157
Jones, B.L., Captain – 315
Jones, David – 124
Jones, Eric – 333
Jones, James, Earl – 458
Jones, Lesley – 238
Jones, Neil – 192
Jones, Ray – 163
Jordan, Ellen – 497
Jordan, Ernest – 497
Journal, Psychiatric Opinion – 457
Juncar, Christine – 101
Jupiter – 451
Jutland – 378

K

Kacherle, Douglas – 282
Kamiya, Glen – 128
Karamastos, X. – 323
Karer, Sylvia – 235
Karim, Simon – 216
Kaser, R.M. – 389
Kehoe, Richard – 391
Keller, Richard – 268
Kelly, Bridget – 466
Kennedy, John C. – 283
Kennedy, Lucy – 242
Kenny, Stephen – 74
Kent, Peter – 442
Kerr, T. – 330
Kethley-Pitt, Reverend – 366
Killick, Susan – 132
King, Captain – 341
King, Gillian – 417
Kirk, Rosina – 480
Kirk, Thomas – 392
Kirkham, H. – 487
Knapp, Dianne – 148
Knight, Alice – 277
Knight, Valerie – 196
Knowles, Herbert, Admiral – 376
Knowles, J. – 236
Knutson, Harry – 342
Knutt, Ralph – 40
Krieger, LeRoy – 280
Kzamme, Morris – 282

L

Lander, Michael – 220
Lang, Leonard – 301
Lankford, Lenny – 355
Lankford, Mrs. – 354
Large, Frank – 160
Lavelle, Patrick – 33
Lawless, Patrick B. – 301
Lee, Elsa (YUFOS) – 120
Lee, Mike (Constant Security) – 41
Lee, Mr. – 115
Leidy, A.R., Mr. – 283

Lemon, Eugene 'Gene' - 312
Lemon, R.L, First Officer - 317
Lewis, Christopher - 30
Life Magazine - 495
Lindsay, Sharon - 63
Littleton, Arthur (Special Agent) - 301
Lloyd, Jack - 439
Lloyd, Marie - 215
Lobo, Isabel - 135
Locklear, C. - 486
Longbottom, Philip - 393, 395
Longbottom, Toby - 217
Lovelock, Brian - 370
Lovett, Jim - 124
Lovis, Michelle - 479
Ludlam, Jose - 124
Luttrell, John, H. - 457
Lutze, I., Miss - 323

M

Maddex, John - 221
Magdalena - 277
Maltais, Vern - 277
Maney, Charles, Professor - 376
Manley, John - 305
Mann, Gloria - 479
Mann, John - 479
Manning, Cecil - 399
Manning, Frank - 367
Manning, Mr. - 267
Mansfield UFO Society - 130
Mantell, Thomas, Captain - 320, 369, 435
Maori King - 404
Mapleton, S. - 211
Marjorie Lees Health Centre, Oldham - 124
Marlow, Jane - 233
Marsden, Jane - 110
Martin, M.L. - 314
Mason, A. - 242
Mason, Peter - 201
Mathews, Bill - 216
Matsuhara, Raymond - 366
May, Edward - 312
May, Fred - 312

May, Kathleen - 312
Mayhew, Harold - 501
McClelland, Clark - 433
McCoy, David and Jaclyn - 66
McDaniels, Elma - 294
McDonald, D.R. - 323
McDonald, George - 439
McDonald, John - 192
McDonaldson, Annette - 113
McDonaldson, Clare - 113
McGette, Gaither - 349
McGill, James - 492
McKay, J. - 314
McKeown, Betty - 490
McMullen, Frank - 426
McMurray, David - 46
McMurray, Susan - 46
McNulty, Maurice - 342
McQuillan, Dora - 230
McWilliams, Geoff - 117
Mead, Margaret - 463
Medical Examiner - 416
Meegan, Robert - 280
Mehrman, J.N. - 283
Melville, Barbara - 232
Merchant, Madeleine - 285, 286
Meredith, Kevin - 30
Metcalfe, Eugene - 342
Miah, Mohammed (fatal accident) - 47
Milakovic, Mr. and Mrs. - 469
Miles, Howard - 12
Millar, Martin - 34
Millard, Stephen - 132
Miller, Robert - 438
Milligan, Claudine - 490
Mills, B. - 378
Mills, Sara - 215
Miskell, E.W. (Air traffic controller) - 425
Mitchell, David - 182
Mitchell, Mark - 325
Moffat, Roy - 487
Mole, Commander - 441
Montgomery, G. - 410
Moor, Owen - 318

Haunted Skies Volume Ten

Moore, Harold – 424
Moore, William – 277
Moran, Bill – 115
Moreland, Fredrick – 421
Morgan, Elmo – 305
Morgan, Jack – 264
Morgan, Owen – 100
Morris, Cornelia – 178
Morrow, Marty – 279
Moss, C. – 233
Mottram, Sam and June – 50
Mountain Rescue Team – 39
Mountner, Steven – 208
Mower, Pete – 342
Much loved dog: 'Bailey'
Much loved dog: 'Angie' – 182
Much loved dog: 'Delsey' – 447
Much loved dog: 'Laika' – 392
Muir, Shirley – 195
Muka, Joseph – 284
Mumford, Brenda – 157
Munn, Frank, Mr. and Mrs. – 276
Murphy, Rose – 309
Murray, M.C., Squadron Leader – 309
Murray, Peter – 493
Murray, Sylvia – 200
Muza, Mark – 424
Myers, Walter – 102

N

Nash, Fredrick – 295
NATO Exercise 'Clean Hunter' – 90
Nauman, Gerald, E., S/Sgt – 281
Naylor, Malcolm – 189
Neale, Barry – 411
Neate, Antony – 417
Nelson Evening Mail – 421
Nelson, Einar – 294
Neuberger, Sidney – 305
New Guinea – 388
Newberry, Maureen – 223
Newman, Monika – 197
Niagara Falls, Montreal – 447
NICAP – 265, 362, 451

Nicoll, Denis – 230
Nielson, Cliff – 302
Nihen, John – 284
Nolan, Rachael – 37
Nuclear weapons test series – codenamed ANTLER – 386
Nunley, Neil – 312

NEW ZEALAND
NZ: Auckland – 373
NZ: Karori – 315
NZ: Ngaruawahia – 404
NZ: *Cathie, Leonard, Bruce – 311, 372
NZ: 5FB Squadron – 392
NZ: Aburiri – 373
NZ: Achilles Point – 344
NZ: Avondale, Auckland – 382
NZ: Christchurch – 314, 315, 405
NZ: Civilian Saucer Investigation Group – 327
NZ: Cook Strait – 372
NZ: Dunedin – 405
NZ: Dunoon – 316
NZ: Gisbourne – 314
NZ: Greymouth, New Zealand – 340, 344
NZ: Hallet Station – 494
NZ: Hastings – 316
NZ: Henderson Valley, Auckland – 315
NZ: House of Representatives – 327
NZ: Inchbonnie – 340
NZ: Invercargill – 314, 327
NZ: Kaikohe Flying Saucer Club – 404
NZ: Kaponga – 372
NZ: Kumara – 344
NZ: Kyeburn – 314
NZ: Lake Pukera – 392
NZ: Lake Taupo – 404
NZ: Lister Hospital, Blenheim – 421
NZ: Manukau Harbour – 311
NZ: Mosgie – 315
NZ: Mount Roskill Bowling Club – 341
NZ: Napier – 314, 404
NZ: National Airways – 311
NZ: Nelson – 378
NZ: Nelson Bay – 326
NZ: Nelson Chief Post Office – 378

NZ: New Plymouth – 332
NZ: New Zealand – 263, 404
NZ: New Zealand Antarctic Cape – 494
NZ: Onehunga, Auckland – 372
NZ: Ongaonga – 315
NZ: Otumoetai – 316
NZ: Paeroa – 393
NZ: Palmerstone North – 314, 316
NZ: Paporoa Park – 315
NZ: Paraparaumu – 372
NZ: Plimmerton – 314
NZ: Prime Minister – 327
NZ: Rangito Island – 344
NZ: Rissington – 374
NZ: River Ngunguru – 315
NZ: Shepparton – 327
NZ: Sockburn – 315
NZ: Southern Alps – 340
NZ: Squadron Leader, K.B. Smith – 371
NZ: Squadron Leader, O. Staple – 371
NZ: Tahuana Aerodrome – 378
NZ: Takutai – 372
NZ: Tauranga – 316
NZ: Titirangi – 382
NZ: Waikato – 316
NZ: Waipahi – 314
NZ: Wellington – 325, 411
NZ: Whakarewarewa – 404
NZ: Whangarei – 315
NZ: Whenuapai Air Force Base – 311, 333, 371
NZ: Whenuapai Airport – 404

O

O'Brien, Carole – 215
O'Brien, Paul – 213
O'Donnell, Vivienne – 110
O'Farrell, J.A., Lt. – 333
Oetinger, Leon – 276
Operation 'High Dive' – 271
ORBIT Magazine (UK) – 405
ORBIT Magazine (USA) – 419
Orton, Christopher – 374
Osborne, David – 232
Osborne, Pamela – 235

Osborne, Thelma – 232
Osbourne, D. – 374
Otley, John, Leslie – 405
Overden, Sandra – 168
Owers, Eddy – 158
Owers, Molly – 158
Oxley, Elsie – 141

P

Paddle Steamer, Patna – 267
Palmer, Jeffrey – 205
Palmer, Ray – 274
Pan American Airways – 283
Park, G. – 359
Parker, Emira – 441
Parr, A.J. – 323
Parr, George – 444
Parson, Estelle – 458
Paul, D. – 367
Pearson, Clive – 74
Pell, Colin – 195
Pelle, S.A., Major – 341
Pengelly, Eric – 380
Pennells, G. – 382
Pennells, June – 382
Perkins, Michael – 62
Perry, Andrew, Norman – 468, 469
Persian Gulf – 267
Petersen, Frank – 302
Peterson, Jason – 213
Petre, Allan – 115
Petsche, John – 276
Phelps-Dodge Corporation – 276
Phillimore, H. – 213
Phipps, Tom – 442
Piddington, J.H., Dr. – 308
Pindar, Pauline – 101
Pinkney, John – 405
Pinto, Simplicio, Captain – 134
Pitman, Ken – 71
Pizzey, John – 199
Pogostin, S. Lee – 458
Point Clear Holiday Park – 233

Haunted Skies Volume Ten

POLICE (UK)

Police (UK) *Chief Inspector, Norman Collinson – 472

Police (UK) Chief Constable, Devon and Cornwall – 468

Police (UK) Chief Constable, John Stalker – 113

Police (UK) Chief Inspector, Brian Smith – 74

Police (UK) Chief Inspector, Chris Partridge – 148

Police (UK) Chief Inspector, Sumner – 48

Police (UK) Chief Superintendent, South Yorkshire Police – 122

Police (UK) Constable, Alan Godfrey – 95

Police (UK) Constable, C. Fox – 488

Police (UK) Constable, Chris Evans – 124

Police (UK) Constable, Douglas – 63

Police (UK) Constable, Herbert Edward Hawkins – 468, 469

Police (UK) Constable, Ian Walmsley – 124

Police (UK) Constable, John Boam – 125

Police (UK) Constable, John Hughes – 159

Police (UK) Constable, John Williamson – 490

Police (UK) Constable, Michael Howell – 139

Police (UK) Constable, Parry – 488

Police (UK) Constable, Peter Smith – 159

Police (UK) Constable, Philip Hutchings – 18

Police (UK) Constable, Richard Ellis – 40, 42, 43

Police (UK) Constable, Stanley Osbourne – 63

Police (UK) Constable, Susan Jackson – 124, 126

Police (UK) Constable, Tony Faulkner – 480

Police (UK) Constable, Trent Davis – 15

Police (UK) Constable, Victor Briggs – 347

Police (UK) Derbyshire – 39

Police (UK) Detective Sergeant, Paul Jackson – 347

Police (UK) Ecclesfield – 129, 132

Police (UK) Inspector, David Tingle – 121

Police (UK) Inspector, Roger Clarke – 138

Police (UK) Sergeant, Andrew Noble – 50

Police (UK) Sergeant, Chris Thompson – 121

Police (UK) Sergeant, Derek Davis – 468, 469

Police (UK) Sergeant, Farrell – 48

Police (UK) Sergeant, Sidney Earnshaw – 159

Police (UK) Sergeant, Steve Godwin – 138

Police (UK) Sergeant, Stuart Griffiths – 139

Police (UK) Sergeant, Tony Dodd – 121,154

Police (UK) Special Constable, John Beet – 40, 42, 43

Police (UK) Staffordshire – 174

Police (UK) Station, Chesterfield – 120

Police (UK) Station, Holmfirth – 74

Police (UK) Station, Padgate – 479

Police (UK) Station, Woodseats, Sheffield – 121

Police (UK) Superintendent, Ecclesfield Division – 40

Police Review – 60

POLICE (USA)/Law Enforcement

Police (USA) Patrolman A.T. Austad, – 278

Police (USA) Chief, Russell Greenwell – 354

Police (USA) Constable, Eric Kearsay – 283

Police (USA) Deputy Sheriff, Batts – 354

Police (USA) Deputy Sheriff, Clarence McKay – 278

Police (USA) Deputy Sheriff, Fred Krives – 278

Police (USA) Deputy Sheriff, John Lengel – 435

Police (USA) Deputy Sheriff, McCulloch – 389

Police (USA) Dickerson Robert – 422

Police (USA) Hopkinsville – 354

Police (USA) Kentucky – 357

Police (USA) Officer, Earl J. Patterson – 278

Police (USA) Officer, George Jediny – 498

Police (USA) Officer, Walter A. Lissy – 278

Police (USA) Oregon Highway, Patrol Sgt. Claude – 278

Police (USA) Patrolman, Fowler – 389

Police (USA) Patrolman, John W. Huggins – 301

Police (USA) Patrolman, Paul Early – 301

Police (USA) Police Sgt., Obenchain – 414, 417

Police (USA) Robert Ellis – 278

Police (USA) Sheriff, Dub Holler – 433

Police (USA) Sheriff, Frank Narramore – 342

Police (USA) Sheriff, Homer Melton – 433

Police (USA) Sheriff, Robert Carr – 313

Police (USA) Sheriff, Schroeder – 436

Police (USA) Sheriff, Weir Clem – 389

Police (USA) FBI Agent Leonard, J. Nulty – 302

Pollard, F.C. – 425

Pollard, R J. – 392

Porcher, Paul – 373

Port, Elliot – 411

Potter, Joyce – 32

Poulton, Ann – 382

Prahn, K.A. (Harbor Patrol Captain) – 278

President, Dwight D. Eisenhower – 325
President, George Bush – 151
Preston, Rose – 192
Prime Minister, Sir Eric Gairy – 419
Prime Minister, Tony Blair – 49
Prince, Ormel – 368
Proctor, Floyd – 269
Pryor, H.G. – 493
Pueblo, Colorado – 400
Purdon, Martin – 129
Purdue, Ted – 282

Q

Quebec, Canada – 447
Quigley, Eric – 168

R

Radio Lincoln – 100
Radio London – 23
Radio Medway – 234
Radio Viking – 100
RAF
RAF: Norton – 410
RAF: 604 County of Middlesex Squadron – 335
RAF: Alconbury – 41, 149, 174,
RAF: Bentwaters – 370, 371
RAF: Boulmer – 19
RAF: Brize Norton – 174,
RAF: *Air Chief Marshall, Lord Dowding – 340, 418
RAF: *Flight Lt. James Salandin (MBE) – 320, 335, 337
RAF: *Flight Lt. Stanley Hubbard – 306
RAF: Church Lawford – 379
RAF: Farnborough – 306
RAF: Flight Lieutenant, Harry Goldstone – 371
RAF: Gaydon – 388
RAF: Humphrey Taylor-Scott – 70
RAF: Lakenheath – 370, 371, 400
RAF: Little Rissington – 314
RAF: Manby – 373
RAF: Marham – 314
RAF: Murray, Derek – 386
RAF: North Weald, Essex – 335
RAF: Odiham, Hampshire – 378
RAF: Rhoose – 332

RAF: Scientific Intelligence Department – 308
RAF: Squadron Leader, Ernie Dunsford – 145
RAF: Squadron Leader, Graham Davis – 71, 72
RAF: Squadron Leader, Pike – 71
RAF: St. Athan – 332
RAF: Topcliffe – 320
RAF: Under Secretary of State, Charles I. Orr-Ewing – 379
RAF: West Malling – 371
RAF: Wethersfield – 379
RAF: Wing Commander, Whitworth – 378
RAF: Winkleigh Airfield, Devon – 379
Ramplin, Malcolm – 168
Randle, Kevin, D. – 363
Randles, Jenny – 77, 94, 95, 479
Rawlings, A. – 222
Rawlings, Reginald – 114
Read, Dennis – 32
Readymarcher, Philip – 100
Redbrook Colliery – 118
Redfearn Glass – 164
Redmond, Mary – 110
Reed, Harry, Dr. – 414
Reed, Maurice – 47
Reeve, Philip – 213
Reines, Fred – 305
Reynolds, Harry – 164
Reynolds, Mr. -369
Rhodes, J. – 115
Rhodesia – 464
Rickard, Sergeant, D. – 301
Rickmansworth Grammar School, Hertfordshire – 401
Riedel, Walther, Johannes – 405
Rimmer, Mrs. – 334
Robbins, Carl – 501
Roberts, Clark – 240
Roberts, Denise – 228
Roberts, Keith – 263
Roberts, Richard, Mr. – 34
Robertson, J.W. – 267
Robinson, Edward – 402
Robinson, J. – 314
Robinson, Mark & Jean – 19

Haunted Skies Volume Ten

Robson, Darryl – 121
Robson, Mrs. – 116
Rock Springs – 342
Rockford, Illinois – 343
Rodgers, Keith – 225
Rodwell, Mary – 263
Rogers Dry Lake – 282
Rogers, Dorothy – 77
Rogers, Elizabeth – 119
Rogers, Maynard – 299
Rogers, Michael – 77
Rolls Royce Fuels – 30
Rolphindy, Mr. – 234
Rose, Gina – 233
Roswell Books – 363
Roswell, New Mexico – 269, 276, 277
Rotherham – 144
Round Top Island – 426
Roundhay Park, Leeds – 180
Royal Air Force Intelligence Officers – 94
Royal Aircraft Establishment – 142
Royal Greenwich Observatory – 159
Royal Observer Corps – 316, 379
Royal South Hampshire Hospital – 375
Royal, T.R.H. – 268
Rugeley – 155
Russell, Pauline – 114
Russian Hinterland – 11
Rutledge, W.K. – 433
Ryan Bryan Francis – 323

S

Sage, Linda – 164
Salav, Joe – 389
Salisbury Rotary Club – 418
Sampson, Marion – 207
Sampson, Stan – 207
Samuel Fox Steelworks – 46
Sanders, Jean – 296
Sanders, Lloyd – 296
Saucedo, Pedro – 389
Savage, Mark – 142
Sayer, Peter – 235
Sayer, Susan – 235
Scarfe, Michael – 232
Schlomovitz, Harry, Dr. – 358
Schockley, Wayne – 392
Scott, G. – 441
Scott, Jannette, Marie – 281
Scott, Len – 340
Scrivener, Reverend – 144
Scrives, Heidi – 215
Sears, Fred – 302
Self, Janet – 162
Sensenbaugher, R.F., Dr. – 276
Seoul, Leon, A. – 414
Seymour, Elizabeth – 234
Seymour, Reginald – 439
Sfeir, Zena – 110
Shakespeare, Alan – 490
Shaver, Ronnie – 312
Shea, Captain – 299
Sheahan, Neville – 438
Shepherd, Joanne – 137
Sherwood Forest, Nottingham – 62
Simcox, Paul – 62
Simmons, Ronald – 417
Simon, Benjamin, Dr. – 447, 454, 455, 456
Simonton, Joseph – 435
Simpson, George – 263
Simpson, Judy and David – 44
Singleton, Jim, Dr. – 95
Skegness Minors holiday home, Lincoln – 421
Skipper, G.S. – 299
Slinger, Cecil – 204
Slinger, Susan – 204
Smith, Barry – 200
Smith, C. – 440
Smith, David – 192
Smith, Donna (CSI) – 313
Smith, Emil, Captain – 279
Smith, Eric – 435
Smith, Ian – 130
Smith, John – 400
Smith, Kath (Isle of Wight UFO Society) – 65, 424
Smith, Keneth – 392
Smith, Louise – 470
Smith, Mr. – 222

Smith, Mrs. – 222
Smith, Peter – 401
Smith, Steve – 200
Smith, Ted – 326
Smith, Valerie – 90
Smith, William (CSI) – 313
Snowdon, Margaret – 195
Sorenson, Bill – 342
Soviet Union – 484
Spang Chalfont Company – 301
Spencer, Edith – 195
Spencer, Philip (pseudonym) – 93
Spicer, Justice – 426
Spooner, Caroline – 233
Sputnik 1 – 392
Sradomski, Charles – 301
St. Petersburg, Russia – 267
Stacey, Geraldine – 205
Stafford, Mona – 470
Stahl, Mr. (OSI Special Agent) – 298
Starkey, Leslie – 47
Starr, Mary, M. – 395
Stephens, M. – 221
Stephenson, H. – 100
Stevens, Malvin – 392
Stewert, Lee, A. – 313
Stokes, James, W. – 389
Stone, Fred – 327
Storer, Eileen – 238
Strickland, Mr. and Mrs. – 180
Suckling, G. – 239
Suddards, Ernest – 346
Suddards, Ray – 346
Sugden, J. – 58
Sullivan, John – 278
Sullivan, Paul – 204
Sullivan, T. – 195
Sunderland, A. – 222
Sutherby, John – 210
Sutherland, J. – 399
Sutherst, Peter – 93
Sutton family – 349
Sutton, 'Lucky' Elmer – 349
Swift, Harold – 132

Swift, Janet – 132
Swindale, F. – 499
Swingler, Stephen, MP – 431
Swinnels, Mr. – 139
Symonds, Alan – 215

T

Tame, Mark – 217
Tasmania: *Browning, Lionel, Reverend – 427, 428, 429
Tasmania: Ben Lomond Ridge – 428
Tasmania: Campbell Town – 431
Tasmania: Cressy – 427, 431
Tasmania: Elizabeth Town – 329
Tasmania: Hobart – 431
Tasmania: Launceston – 431
Tasmania: Panshanger Estate – 428
Tasmania: Poatina – 431
Tasmanian UFO Investigation Centre – 263
Tasmanian Unidentified Flying Objects Investigation Centre – 430
Taylor, A.W. – 440
Taylor, Billy, Ray – 349
Taylor, C.B. – 494
Taylor, Fred – 392
Taylor, Griffith – 339
Taylor, John – 100
Taylor, June – 10
Taylor, Sandra – 60
Taylor, Terrence – 180
Teasdale, John – 175
Teller, Edward – 305
Temple, Jean – 204
Templestowe Brickworks – 320
Thatcher, Robert – 296
The Atlanteans – 417
The Brains Trust, Caxton Hall, London – 435
The Yorkshire Post – 393
Thomas Rush
Thomas, Albert – 310
Thomas, Carol – 153
Thomas, Charles – 392
Thomas, Elaine – 470
Thomas, A., George – 433
Thomas, Helen – 153

Haunted Skies Volume Ten

Thomas, Joe – 391
Thompson, Bert – 372
Thompson, Cyril – 295
Thorne, P. – 499
Thorneycroft, Geoffrey – 120
Thorneycroft, Stephanie – 120
Three Rivers Settlement – 386
Threkeld, Harold – 499
Thule, Greenland – 430
Tidey, Fred – 198
Tilbrook, Doreen – 114
Tindale, Edward, Henry (Radar operator) – 425
Tintown, Arizona – 276
Todd, Alan – 192
Tolouse, Joseph, H. – 298
Topham, Peter – 202
Topham, Rebecca – 202
Towill, Carl – 405
Trans-Australian Airways – 316
Trasco, John – 391
Trent, Ernest – 198
Treul, M. – 267
Triggs, Chris – 120
Trivedi, Kamslesh – 235
Trueman, L. – 222
Tudge, Edna – 179
Tummon, Adrian – 129
Tunbridge Wells – 405
Tutt Hill – 202
Twaites, Danny – 188
Twaites, Gerald – 188
Twaites, Sue – 188
Twyman, Brian – 221
Tyneside – 379

U

UFO and Paranormal Research Society of Australia – 263
UFO Reality Magazine – 89
UFO Today Magazine – 274
UK: Isle of Wight UFO Society – 424
UK: Stanford-in-the-Vale – 479
UK: Swansea – 486
UK: A10 road – 480
UK: A13 road – 212
UK: A41 road, Aston Clinton – 488
UK: A453 road, Bassetts Pole – 220
UK: A5 road – 188
UK: A5 road – 472
UK: A61 road, Derbyshire – 31
UK: AA Relay Station – 479
UK: Abbots Bromley, Staffordshire – 58
UK: Air Ministry, Deputy Director of Intelligence – 306, 318, 378
UK: Aldeburgh Golf Club – 56
UK: Aldridge Ambulance Station – 74
UK: Andover – 389
UK: Annesley Hall – 84
UK: Ashdown Forest – 417
UK: Avebury Stone Circle – 181
UK: B311, Bagshot Heath, Surrey – 467
UK: Bagshot – 119
UK: Balmalloch Radar – 379
UK: Barnsley Hospital – 50
UK: Barnsley, Yorkshire – 22, 133, 164, 165, 166
UK: Barrow, Lancashire – 443
UK: Barton Power Station – 370, 373
UK: Basildon – 66, 201, 210, 213
UK: Basildon Fire Station – 67
UK: Beccles, Norfolk – 318
UK: Bellinas Chocolate Shop – 168
UK: Belper, Derby – 31
UK: Bexleyheath, Kent – 326
UK: Big Moor, Derbyshire – 39
UK: Billericay – 216
UK: Birdwell – 133
UK: Birstall – 482
UK: Bishopstone, Wiltshire – 17
UK: Blewbury, Oxfordshire – 158
UK: Bolsover Castle – 28
UK: Bolton, Lancashire – 487
UK: Bootle, Liverpool – 487
UK: Bordesley Green, Birmingham – 501
UK: Bournemouth – 405
UK: Box Hill, Surrey – 148
UK: Bridge Place, Manchester – 149
UK: Bridgewater – 46
UK: Bridlington – 493
UK: Brighton, Sussex – 466

UK: Brindley Visitors' Centre – 90
UK: Bristol – 376
UK: Bristol Channel – 332
UK: Brockworth, Gloucestershire – 479
UK: Buckinghamshire – 488
UK: BUFORA – 113, 171, 228, 333, 466
UK: Bury St. Edmunds – 152
UK: Bushbury Hill, Wolverhampton – 382
UK: Camberwell – 322
UK: Cannock Chase – 173, 77, 175
UK: Canvey Island – 118, 192, 199, 210, 211, 235
UK: Castle Vale, Birmingham – 153
UK: Channon, Paul (Transport Minister) – 47
UK: Chelsea Football Club – 113
UK: Chelston, Torquay – 442
UK: Cheltenham – 333, 484
UK: Chester Zoo – 171
UK: Chesterfield – 120
UK: Chichester – 341
UK: Chilwell, Nottingham – 381
UK: Circular Forum UFO Group – 484
UK: Clacton-on-Sea – 233
UK: Cleethorpes – 373
UK: Clevedon – 376
UK: Cliftonville, Kent – 10
UK: Colchester – 145, 189
UK: Colchester Army Barracks – 221
UK: Constant Security – 41
UK: Corby – 34
UK: Coventry UFO Research Group – 464
UK: Crakemarsh, Uttoxeter – 34
UK: Crawley, West Sussex – 401
UK: Crediton – 468
UK: Croydon & District Writers' Circle – 144
UK: Daniels, David (alleged Reptilian) – 198
UK: Dartford Tunnel – 212
UK: Derby – 28
UK: Derek Jameson Show – 113
UK: Didsbury – 481
UK: Dragon Models – 163
UK: East Anglia coast – 370
UK: East Harrow – 366
UK: Eaton Wood – 34
UK: Ecclesfield – 137

UK: Edinburgh – 405
UK: Elterwater – 499
UK: Emley Moor TV Mast – 91, 146
UK: Exeter – 439
UK: Exmouth, Devon – 318
UK: Fairey Rotodyne – 410
UK: Farnborough Air Show – 497
UK: Filton Meteorological Officer – 376
UK: Firths Mill, Brighouse – 58
UK: Fishponds, Bristol – 376
UK: Flixton, Manchester – 373
UK: Flouch Inn – 58
UK: Flying Saucer Review – 333, 395, 417
UK: Forest of Dean – 188
UK: Fortune of War Public House – 200
UK: Foulness Island – 20, 114, 218
UK: Gailey, Staffordshire – 382
UK: GCHQ, Cheltenham (transmission mast) – 15
UK: George Inn – 20
UK: Gifford Hall Farmhouse, Wiltshire – 19
UK: Goldings, Hereford – 129
UK: Green fireballs – 487
UK: Gwynedd – 144
UK: Hadleigh Castle – 66, 235
UK: Halfpenny Green Airport, Bobbington – 92
UK: Halstead, Essex – 440
UK: Harold Hill, Essex – 474
UK: Haughton – 173
UK: Havengore Bridge, Essex – 114
UK: Haverhill – 169
UK: Heathrow Airport – 211
UK: Hednesford – 469
UK: Hempnall, Norfolk – 501
UK: HMS Maxton – 437
UK: Houghton, South Yorkshire – 60
UK: Howden Moors – 146
UK: Hunshelf, Sheffield – 39
UK: Hyndburn Sky watchers – 20
UK: ICI factory – 492
UK: Ilkley Moor – 93
UK: Ilkley, Yorkshire – 381
UK: Ipsley, Worcestershire – 399
UK: Ipswich Museum – 56
UK: Isle of Wight – 440

Haunted Skies Volume Ten

UK: Kegworth – 28
UK: Kensington Central Library, London – 498
UK: Kettering, Northants – 22
UK: Kidderminster – 465
UK: Ladygate Woods – 169
UK: Langsett Hill – 58
UK: Leamington Spa – 502
UK: Leckhampton Hill, Cheltenham – 15
UK: Leigh-on-Sea – 66
UK: Limekiln Fields – 28
UK: Little Boltons, Kensington, London – 110
UK: Liverpool – 357
UK: Llanilar, Wales – 363
UK: Loch Kinder – 492
UK: London – 405
UK: London Airport – 216
UK: London UFO Research Organisation – 498
UK: Lowestoft – 316, 326
UK: Luton, Bedfordshire – 153
UK: M25 Motorway – 212
UK: M40 Motorway – 233
UK: M5 Motorway – 483
UK: Manchester – 46, 58, 124, 405
UK: Manchester Airport – 37
UK: Mansfield, Nottinghamshire – 78, 192
UK: Marland – 37
UK: Marsden Inn – 192
UK: McMahon, William (Minister for Air) – 327, 334
UK: Melplash Court, Bridport, Dorset – 316
UK: Meltham, West Yorkshire – 90
UK: Menston – 93
UK: Meriden – 464
UK: Merkland Farm, Dumfries – 490
UK: Meteorological Office – 443
UK: Mexborough – 103
UK: Ministry of Defence – 176, 177
UK: Ministry of Supply, West Freugh – 378
UK: Mitchell's Fold Stone Circle – 35, 36
UK: Nelson, Lancashire – 497
UK: Newark – 438
UK: Newcastle – 10, 19
UK: Newent – 483
UK: Newton Abbot, Cornwall – 58

UK: Normanby Park Steelworks – 161
UK: Norwich – 326
UK: Nottingham – 444
UK: Nottinghamshire Fire Service – 86
UK: Oldham – 123
UK: Oliver's Public House – 133
UK: Orr, St. Margaret's Bay, Kent – 378
UK: Oswestry – 132
UK: Peacehaven – 70
UK: Pearoyd Bridge – 41, 42, 45
UK: Pearoyd Farm – 47
UK: Pendleton, Gordon, Captain – 493
UK: Pentland Hills – 177
UK: Pinxton, Derbyshire – 30
UK: Pitsea – 236
UK: Portchester – 435
UK: Portishead – 376
UK: Portsdown Hill – 20, 435
UK: Portsmouth Harbour – 499
UK: Puckeridge – 480
UK: Pulham Market, Norfolk – 442
UK: Ramridge Primary School – 380
UK: Rayleigh, Essex – 37, 163, 225, 235
UK: Rhoose Point – 332
UK: Risley – 479
UK: River Crouch – 200
UK: River Derwent, Derbyshire – 32
UK: River Don – 39
UK: River Humber – 100
UK: River Mersey – 481
UK: River Thames – 204
UK: Rumworth Lodge Reservoir – 478
UK: Ryde – 440, 441
UK: Sandwell Valley Archaeological Project – 75
UK: Seighford Aerodrome – 488
UK: Shanklin, Isle of Wight – 378
UK: Shardlow Steel Works – 126
UK: Sheffield – 410
UK: Sheffield Forum, WWW – 44
UK: Sheffield Society for Researching into the Paranormal – 40
UK: Sheffield Star – 40, 43, 54
UK: Shrewsbury – 472
UK: Silbury Hill – 182

Haunted Skies Volume Ten

UK: Silkstone Colliery – 103
UK: Silpho Moor – 392
UK: Sizewell beach – 217
UK: Solent – 440
UK: Solway Firth, Dumfriesshire – 492
UK: South Woodham, Essex – 128
UK: South Yorkshire UFO Society – 130
UK: Southampton Water – 395
UK: Southampton – 402
UK: Southend – 195, 213, 225
UK: Southend Airport – 195, 210
UK: Southend Pier – 162
UK: Southern Television – 441
UK: Spellar, John (Transport Minister) – 49
UK: St. Albans, Hertfordshire – 119
UK: St. Helens, Lancashire – 334
UK: St. Joseph's Junior School, Lancashire – 67
UK: Stafford – 382
UK: Staffordshire UFO Group – 175
UK: Stannington, near Sheffield – 141
UK: Stocksbridge – 39, 40, 53
UK: Stocksbridge Bypass – 45, 48
UK: Stonehenge, Wiltshire – 18
UK: Studley, Warwickshire – 399
UK: Surrey Hills – 316
UK: Sutton Coldfield – 62, 318
UK: Swan Pool, Sandwell – 75
UK: Thames Estuary – 217
UK: Truro, Cornwall – 493
UK: Tyneside – 490
UK: University Reactor – 479
UK: Waldershelf – 39
UK: Wallasey Marshes – 160
UK: Walsall – 138, 152
UK: Waterbeach, Cambridgeshire - 320
UK: Wednesbury – 444
UK: Weedon – 228
UK: West Bromwich – 444
UK: West Kennett Long Barrow – 185, 186
UK: West Worthing – 388
UK: Westbourne Park, Derby – 33
UK: Westcliff – 217, 221, 223, 228
UK: Wigan, Lancashire – 330
UK: Wincaton, Somerset – 328

UK: Winchester – 401
UK: Winterbourne Monkton – 181
UK: Winterbourne Stoke – 71
UK: Wivenhoe – 232
UK: Woking, Surrey – 396
UK: Wolverhampton – 369
UK: Wombwell – 133
UK: Woodlands Caravan Park – 228
UK: Wrynose Pass-500
UK: Yeadon Airport – 33
UK: *Birdsall, Graham – 109, 122, 175
UK: *Birdsall, Mark – 109, 122
UK: *Clancarty, Lord – 332, 325
UK: *Clarke, David, Dr. – 34, 40, 122, 126, 144
UK: *Colins, Andrew- 466
UK: *Cramp, G., Leonard – 435, 440, 498
UK: *Allen, Graham – 173, 175
UK: *Andrews, Colin – 71, 72, 182, 184, 188
UK: *Antony, Gary – 100
UK: *Bainbridge, Martin – 235
UK: *Barclay, David – 195
UK: *Beglin, Dominic – 80
UK: *Birch, Alex – 498
UK: *Butler, Brenda – 57, 150, 204, 215, 217
UK: *Constance, Arthur – 342, 343
UK: *Creighton, Gordon – 10, 106, 119, 148, 325, 468
UK: *Daniels, Wilfred – 470
UK: *Delgado, Pat – 182
UK: *Dillon, Bill – 380
UK: *Duffy, Nick – 77
UK: *Dutta, Reginald – 435, 436
UK: *Dutton, Roy – 473
UK: *Emmerson, Andrew – 80, 86
UK: *Finch, Bernard, Dr. – 434
UK: *Fry, Margaret – 345, 405
UK: *Good, Timothy – 60, 144, 153, 179
UK: *Goodwin, Dominic – 58
UK: *Hanson, John – 116
UK: *Hanson, Mick – 119, 121, 126
UK: *Hill, Harold – 11
UK: *Holloway, Dawn – 36
UK: *Hope, Sally – 35
UK: *Hough, Peter – 95, 478, 479
UK: *Hurley, John (UFOSIS) – 57, 154, 155

Haunted Skies Volume Ten

UK: *Jaffe, Joseph, Dr. – 472
UK: *Jones, Lynda – 481
UK: *Keller, Albert, Dr. – 472, 478
UK: *King, George – 13
UK: *King, Jon (Editor, UFO Reality) – 89
UK: *La Poer Trench, Brinsley, – 417
UK: *Ledwith, 'Budd', Andrew – 354
UK: *Leslie, Desmond – 291, 293, 325, 435
UK: *Llewellyn, John, 'Dennis'– 407, 486
UK: *Llewellyn, Ruby – 486
UK: *Lucas, Ron – 402
UK: *Mantle, – 23, 33, 118, 100, 274, 482
UK: *Meaden, Terrence, Dr. – 187
UK: *Moore, Patrick – 113
UK: *Morris, Eric – 178, 206
UK: *Murray, Jacqueline – 417, 435
UK: *Newman, Derek – 203, 213
UK: *Oakensen, Elsie – 228, 480
UK: Oakensen, Teri – 228
UK: *Pitt, Stan – 20
UK: *Plunkett, E.L., Captain – 328
UK: *Richards, Alison – 465
UK: *Roberts, Andy – 34, 74, 118, 163, 482
UK: *Roestenberg, Jessie – 334, 339, 374
UK: *Rondeau, Julie – 169, 232
UK: *Roper, Cliff – 65
UK: *Sacks, Mike – 472
UK: *Sampson, Derek – 265
UK: *Spoor, David – 215
UK: *Stephenson, G.N.P. – 498
UK: *Taylor, Busty – 102, 187
UK: *Tibbitts, Bob – 464, 585
UK: *Tomlinson, Arthur – 95
UK: *Townshend, Robert – 260
UK: *Walmsley, Andy – 134
UK: *Walters, D. – 222
UK: *Walters, Valerie – 472
UK: *West, Arnold – 171
UK: *West, Ron – 15, 114, 149, 150, 162, 189,195,197, 199, 206, 208, 216, 215, 221, 222, 240
UK: *Westwood, Margaret (UFOSIS) – 57
Ulo, alleged alien – 393
United Airlines – 279
United Artists film: Unidentified Flying Objects – 369

University of Miami School of Medicine – 416
University of Pennsylvania – 277
Unmatjera aborigines – 308
Upton, Mr. and Mrs. – 133
Uriarte, Ruben – 363
Urie, A.C. – 284
Urie, Billy – 284
Urie, Keith – 284
USA: Adams (Pilot) – 306
USA: *Condon, Dr. – 419
USA: *Edwards, Frank – 366, 376
USA: *Berlitz, Charles – 277, 418
USA: *Fish, Marjorie – 457
USA: *Friedman, Stanton, T. – 270, 272, 362
USA: *Genzlinger, Ann – 414
USA: *Hynek, Allen, Dr. – 334, 389
USA: *Jessup, Ketchum, Morris – 412
USA: *Keel, John – 265
USA: *Keyhoe, Donald – 419
USA: *La Paz, Lincoln, Dr. – 283, 298, 368, 390
USA: *Lorenzen, Coral, E. – 358, 495
USA: *Lorenzen, Jim – 358, 495
USA: *Maccabee, Leonard, Bruce – 363
USA: *Mack, Edward, John, Dr. – 446
USA: *Maloret, Nick – 20
USA: *Marden, Kathleen, BA – 459
USA: *McDonald, Professor James – 428
USA: *Mead, Margaret, Dr. – 463
USA: *Mills, Rhoda – 407
USA: *Stanford, Ray – 498
USA: *Strieber, Whitley – 15, 16
USA: *Stringfield, Leonard, H. – 359, 419
USA: *Torres, Noe – 363
USA: 'Old Man of the Mountain' – 448
USA: Alamogordo, New Mexico – 276
USA: Albuquerque, New Mexico – 276, 297, 279, 298, 300, 310, 444, 492, 493
USA: Ambridge, Pennsylvania – 301
USA: Anderson (Pilot) – 306
USA: APRO (Aerial Phenomena Research Organization) – 358
USA: Argonne National Laboratories – 280
USA: Arlington, Virginia – 359
USA: Army: Fort. Bragg, North Carolina – 401

USA: Bandelier National Monument – 299
USA: Benjamin – 435
USA: Big Marsh, Poquson, Virginia – 424
USA: Biscayne Bay – 340
USA: Bloomington, Indiana – 368
USA: Blue Ridge Summit, Pennsylvania – 439
USA: Boerne, Texas – 392
USA: Boise Municipal Airport – 299
USA: Boise, Idaho – 284, 299
USA: Bonny Spring Ranch, Las Vegas – 441
USA: Brazel, Betty – 269
USA: Brazel, Vernon – 269
USA: Brazel, William – 269
USA: Buckley, Colorado – 280
USA: Butlers Bay, Idaho – 278
USA: Cannon Mountain – 448
USA: Cape Canaveral – 435
USA: Castro's Ranch – 284
USA: Central Airlines – 495
USA: Chula Vista, California – 431
USA: Civilian Research, Interplanetary Flying Objects – 419
USA: Civilian Saucer Investigation – 313
USA: Claremont, New Hampshire – 444
USA: Clarksburg Hospital – 309, 313
USA: Cleveland, Ohio – 435, 441
USA: Cochise, New Mexico – 339
USA: Colorado Project – 419
USA: Columbus, Georgia – 493
USA: Connolly, D., Commander – 418
USA: Copemiah, Michigan – 441
USA: Crawfordsville, Indiana – 444
USA: Crete, Illinois – 427
USA: Darling Observatory, Minnesota – 366
USA: Datil, New Mexico – 486
USA: Dauphin Island, Alabama – 489
USA: Davis, Isabel (Civilian Saucer Investigation) – 354
USA: Dayton, Ohio – 320
USA: Defiance, Ohio – 492
USA: Detchmendy, E., Captain – 276
USA: Doolittle, T.A. (Pilot) – 300
USA: Eagle River, Wisconsin – 435
USA: Elmendorf Air Base – 283

USA: Eureka – 490
USA: Everittstown, New Jersey – 391
USA: Fargo – 294, 296
USA: Farmington, Utah – 499
USA: Forestville – 360
USA: Fort Knox – 286
USA: Fort Mead Missile Master Center – 435
USA: Fort Sumner, New Mexico – 283
USA: Fort Worth, Texas – 492
USA: Franconia Notch – 448
USA: Grand Rapids – 402
USA: Guthrie King County – 433
USA: Hanford Atomic Power Plant – 302
USA: Harvard University Gazette – 446
USA: Hawaii – 404
USA: Healdsburg, California – 399
USA: Heflin, Rex – 501
USA: Highway 116 – 389
USA: Highway 54 – 386
USA: Highway 80E – 300
USA: Hopkinsville, Kentucky – 349
USA: Indian Head – 448
USA: Indiana – 295
USA: Indianapolis – 425, 485, 493
USA: Joseph Walker (NASA Pilot) – 491
USA: Kansas City – 442, 495
USA: Kelly, Kentucky – 349
USA: Kentucky New Era – 354
USA: Kentucky State Police – 286
USA: Knox Glass Bottling Company – 300
USA: Knoxville News Sentinel – 391
USA: Lake City, Tennessee – 367
USA: Lake Pontchartrain – 302
USA: Lake Washington – 283
USA: Lakeland, Florida – 280, 340
USA: Lancaster, New Hampshire – 447
USA: Las Vegas – 298
USA: Levelland, Texas – 389
USA: Liberal Airport – 495
USA: Liberty – 470
USA: Lloyd, Van, Captain – 298
USA: Long Beach, California – 437
USA: Los Alamos – 300
USA: Los Alamos Ranch – 306

Haunted Skies Volume Ten

USA: Los Angeles – 357
USA: Louisville, 267
USA: Loveland – 360
USA: Lynchburg, Virginia – 400
USA: Maine – 435
USA: Manhattan Project – 298
USA: Matheson Hammock Park, South Florida – 413
USA: Memphis, Tennessee – 305
USA: Mescalero Indian Reservation, New Mexico – 386
USA: Meteorology Department – 428
USA: Metzger, Captain – 495
USA: Mojave, Califonia – 281, 344
USA: Monon Railroad, Indiana – 402
USA: Montgomery – 293
USA: Mount Kisco, New York – 431
USA: Mount Rainer, Washington – 441
USA: Mount Timpango, Utah – 342
USA: Mountains of Hampshire – 447
USA: Museum of Science Miami – 413
USA: Naperville, Illinois – 490
USA: Narragansett, Rhode Island – 268
USA: National Guard's 116th Fighter Group – 278
USA: Naval Centre for Study of Cosmic Rays – 290
USA: Naval Station Pascoe, Washington – 269
USA: Neef (OSI Special Agent) – 298
USA: New Orleans – 302
USA: New Orleans, Louisiana – 392
USA: New York – 332, 464
USA: North Dakota National Guard – 294
USA: Oak Harbor, Ohio – 457
USA: Ocean Springs, Mississippi – 494
USA: Office of the United States Secretary of the Air Force – 271
USA: Old Saybrook, Connecticut – 395
USA: Oldtown, Florida – 486
USA: Oradell Reservoir – 497
USA: Oradell, New York – 497
USA: Oregon – 278
USA: Orlando Municipal Airport – 301
USA: Palm Springs – 325
USA: Palmer, Alaska – 493
USA: Paris, Illinois – 342

USA: Patuxent River, Maryland – 418
USA: Peaceful Uses of Space Research, Seattle – 491
USA: Pearl Harbour, Hawaii – 282
USA: Pearl River swamp – 300
USA: Peoria Airport – 309
USA: Philadelphia, Pennsylvania – 492
USA: Phoenix, Arizona – 276
USA: Plains of San Agustin – 277
USA: Playa Del Rey, California – 391
USA: Point Eagle, Utah – 299
USA: Pompano Beach, Florida – 492
USA: Portland Oregon Journal Building – 278
USA: Portland, Milwaukee – 278
USA: Pound's Field – 341
USA: Radium Springs – 392
USA: Redmond Airport – 422
USA: Reno, Nevada – 490
USA: Rhoade Lake – 412
USA: Rio Grande River – 361
USA: Roswell Army Air Field - 269, 270
USA: Route 3 – 447
USA: Salem, New York – 490
USA: Salmon Dam – 284
USA: Salt Lake City – 295, 342, 302, 485
USA: San Diego – 277
USA: San Miguel, New Mexico – 276
USA: Sand Point Naval Air Station, Washington – 283
USA: Sandia Base – 298
USA: Santa Fe, New Mexico – 300
USA: Santa Rosa Naval Auxiliary Station – 278
USA: Santa, Catalina Channel – 344
USA: Scheafer Donald – 392
USA: Shreveport, Louisiana – 280
USA: Silver City, New Mexico – 276
USA: Sioux City, Iowa – 486
USA: Six Mile Mountain – 276
USA: Socorro – 277
USA: South Brooksville, Maine – 277
USA: South Florida – 340
USA: Spokane Army Air Base – 278
USA: Springfield, Ohio – 441
USA: Squantum Naval Air Station, Massachusetts – 284

USA: St. Louis, Missouri – 367
USA: Stanford – 470
USA: Steven Schiff (New Mexico Congressman) – 272
USA: Studebaker Corporation – 295
USA: Tampa – 499
USA: Tampa Municipal Airport – 301
USA: Telephone Ridge, Oregon – 424
USA: The Bergenfield Pranksters – 498
USA: The Redwoods Restaurant – 470
USA: Tulane Observatory – 367
USA: Turner, Colonel – 276
USA: Tuscon, Arizona – 341
USA: Twin Mountain – 447
USA: Valley Centre, California – 340
USA: Vaughn, New Mexico – 285
USA: Washington – 278
USA: West Nyack, New York – 497
USA: Westfield, Massachusetts – 493
USA: WHOP Radio – 354
USA: Wichita, Kansas – 427, 495
USA: Willoughby, Ohio – 346
USA: Willow Springs, Illinois – 280
USA: Winter Park, Florida – 301
USAF Locations
USAF: Standiford Field, Louisville, Kentucky – 286
USAF: 318th Fighter Interceptor Squadron – 295
USAF: 663rd AC&W Squadron – 367
USAF: 693rd Radar Squadron – 489
USAF: 91st Fighter Squadron, RAF Bentwaters – 328
USAF: Air Force Radar, Klamath Falls, Oregon – 422
USAF: Air Force Traffic Control, Seattle – 422
USAF: Blanchard, William, Colonel – 272, 273
USAF: Booth, Robert, E., Colonel – 411
USAF: Braswell, R.O., Major – 423
USAF: Browning, A.B., Major – 280
USAF: Bunker Hill Air Force Base, Indiana – 422
USAF: Campbell Air Force Base – 355
USAF: Carswell Air Force Base – 360
USAF: Castle Air Force Base – 376
USAF: Childs, Clarence, S. (Pilot) – 293
USAF: Clarby, Lt. David – 328
USAF: Clements, Pilot – 286

USAF: Craig Major General – 286
USAF: Davis-Monthan Air Force Base – 495
USAF: Denkler, B.G., Captain – 367
USAF: Eckes Jnr., Lt. Harry Joseph – 328
USAF: Edwards Air Force Base – 282, 494, 495
USAF: Ford, Major Edward – 300
USAF: Gilkey, Signa, Colonel – 282
USAF: Godman Field, Kentucky – 286
USAF: Godsoe, William A., Major – 305
USAF: Gorman, George (Pilot) – 294
USAF: Groseclose, Captain (Technical Intelligence Adviser) – 305
USAF: Hammond (Pilot) – 286
USAF: Hayes, William, P., Colonel – 285
USAF: Henderson, W. Paul, Major – 451
USAF: Hickam Field Air Force Base, Hawaii – 280
USAF: Hix, Guy, Colonel – 286
USAF: Holloman Air Force Base – 386
USAF: Homer, William, Morris, Major – 295
USAF: Howley, Daniel, Major – 342
USAF: Indian Springs Air Force Base, Nevada – 485
USAF: Jackson Air Force Base – 300
USAF: Jackson, L. Robert, Chief – 277
USAF: King, H., Lt. Colonel – 493
USAF: Kirtland Air Force Base – 297, 298, 306, 389
USAF: Kunzman, Lt. – 296
USAF: Lake Charles Base – 400
USAF: Lockbourne Air Force Base – 359
USAF: Luke Air Force Base – 490
USAF: Mandlekorn, Richard, Commander, Sandia Base – 305
USAF: Mantell, Thomas, Captain – 286, 418
USAF: Marcel, Jesse, Major – 269
USAF: McChord Air Force Base, Washington – 295, 411
USAF: McHenry, Joseph, J., 1st Lt. – 281
USAF: Merkel, Joseph, Lee, Lt. Colonel – 368
USAF: Missile Development Center, Alamogordo – 389
USAF: Moses Lake Air Force Base – 302
USAF: Muroc Airbase – 325
USAF: Muroc Army Air Field – 280, 281, 282
USAF: Nellis Air Force Base – 485, 490
USAF: NORAD HQ – 495
USAF: North Concord Air Force Station – 444

USAF: Oak Hill Defense Air Command – 368
USAF: Pease Air Force Base – 444, 451, 454
USAF: Pelham, Captain (16th District, OSI) – 302
USAF: Personnel
USAF: Philips, C., Major – 390
USAF: Powell, Roland, D. (Pilot Ensign) – 269
USAF: Project Blue Book – 262, 263, 389, 392, 451
USAF: Project Bluewater – 264
USAF: Project Grudge – 262, 305
USAF: Project Mogul – 271, 272
USAF: Project Sign – 262
USAF: Ramey, Roger, General – 270, 272
USAF: Rankin, Richard (Pilot) – 268
USAF: Roberts, M/Sgt. – 493
USAF: Robins Air Force Base – 392
USAF: Ruvolo, Joseph, T/Sgt. – 281
USAF: Scott, Kenneth, Captain – 328
USAF: Sheppard Airbase – 435
USAF: Shoop, Richard, Major – 282
USAF: Smith, Lt. (Technical Intelligence Adviser) – 305
USAF: Sneider, B., Captain – 301
USAF: Stapleton Airfield – 302
USAF: Strapp, John, Captain – 282
USAF: Strategic Air Command Headquarters, Nebraska – 430
USAF: Swett, Benjamin, H., Captain – 454
USAF: Tilley, D.G., Major – 400
USAF: Torres, Milton, (Pilot) – 380
USAF: Travis Air Force Base, California – 280
USAF: Tyherd, William, H., Captain – 284
USAF: Tyndall Air Force Base, Florida – 437
USAF: Ward, Stewart – 284
USAF: Waverley Air Force Base – 435
USAF: Welesgoe, Richard, Sgt. – 301
USAF: White Sands Missile Range – 276
USAF: White, Robert, Major – 494
USAF: Whitted, John, B. (Pilot) – 293
USAF: Wilcox, George, B., Major – 276
USAF: Willingham, Robert, Burton, Colonel – 360, 362
USAF: Winnemucca Base, Nevada – 489
USAF: Wise, C., Jowell, Major
USAF: Woodyard, B., John, Lt. Colonel – 400

USAF: Wright Field – 282
USAF: Wright Patterson Air Force Base, Dayton, Ohio – 300, 301
USAF: Wynn, Major – 305
USAF: X-15 aircraft – 491
USAF: Perry, Colonel (Auxiliary) – 283
USAF: *Filer, A., George, Major – 489
USAF: *Keyhoe, Donald, Major – 436, 451
USMC: Cain, Rayner – 279
USN: Commander Waring – 392
USN: Cutter Sebago – 392
USN: Naval Auxiliary Air Station – 494
USS: Iberville – 485

V

Valentich, Frederick – 265
Valentine, Dr. J. Manson – 413
Valor Magazine – 325
Vancouver – 278
Victorian Fish Café – 323
Vinson, Captain M.O – 485
Vosiliunas, Duna – 373
Vosiliunas, P. – 373

W

Wagstaff, Brenda – 370
Wake Island – 484
Wall, Patrick, Major (MP) – 379
Wall, Julie - 37
Wallace, Anthony – 180
Wallace, Basil – 458
Wallace, Donna – 217, 240
Wallace, Kevin – 217
Wallace, Kevin – 240
Wallis, Eric – 232
Walsh, Peter – 339
Walter, Haut – 270, 272
Ward, R. – 235
Wardrobe, Danny – 92
Warner, Steven – 204
Warren J. Knapp (9th OSI District) – 400
Watkins, John, L. (OBE) – 426
Watkins, June – 382
Watson, Basil – 233
Watson, Denise – 137

Watson, Doris – 233
Watson, Marian – 91
Watson, Roy – 239
Weatherhead, Robert – 410
Webb, Peter – 211
Webb, Walter, N. – 451
Webb, William S. – 423
Webley, Rosetta – 119
Welling, Geoffrey – 200
Wells, Frank – 222
Wellstead, B. – 399
Wentworth, Mr. and Mrs. – 105
Werner, Charles – 298
Wertz, Laverne (Flight Specialist) – 422
West Midlands Ghost Club – 77
West, Mike – 78, 79, 80
Weston, Keith – 337
Wheatcroft, David – 120
White Horse Public House – 239
White House Public House, Kegworth – 28
White Lion Public House – 77
White, David – 158
White, Harold – 301
White, Richard – 423
Whitehead, John – 232
Wikipedia – 186, 187
Wild, Dianne – 152
Wild, George – 410
Wilder, Leonard, Dr. – 476
Wildman, Ronald – 488
Wilkinson, Gilbert – 401
Willacy, Elaine – 175
Willett, John – 211
William, Baker – 277
Williams, Alan – 486
Williams, Bernard – 296
Williams, Brian – 233

Williams, Jean – 109
Williams, S.R. – 9
Williams, Shaun – 118
Willis, Jacques – 342
Willis, Robert – 342
Wilmot, Dan – 276
Wilmot, Mr. and Mrs. – 277
Wilson, Corporal – 301
Wilson, R. – 400
Wilson, William, Inspector – 299
Windle, Mark – 90
Wise, Philip – 57
Women's Land Army – 316
Wood, Ryan, S. – 363
Woodbridge, Leslie – 92
Woodruff, J.E. – 283
Woody, William – 280
Woof, Jean – 213
Wooley, Ivan, Captain – 322
Wootten, Mike – 113
Worne, Scott – 128
Wray, Peter – 66
Wright, M. – 132

X
X-Files episode, José Chung's From Outer Space – 459

Y
Yates, Veronica – 152
Yorkshire UFO Society – 23, 114
YUFOS – 153

Z
Zechel, Tod – 362
Zeta Reticuli – 457
Zolm, C.J., Dr. – 276

Haunted Skies **Volume Ten**

COPYRIGHT/PERMISSIONS

Front Cover – ©Robert Townshend, 2014

Page 4 – Photo of Nick and Elizabeth Pope, ©John Hanson, 2012

Page 5 – Photo of Bailey ©John Hanson, 2013

Page 5 – Photo of Charles Halt, ©Disclosure Project 2012

Page 6 – Photo of 'Boo' and 'Yoda', ©David Sankey, 2013

Page 12 – Image of Aircraft, ©Steven Franklin, 2013

Page 13 – ©www.internet, 2014

Page 15 – Photo, ©Trent Davies

Page 16 – Photo, ©Whitley Streiber, 2014

Page 18 – Photo of J. Randles, ©BUFORA, 2013

Page 21/22 – Sketch, ©Philip Hayter, 1987

Page 23-26 – Photos, ©Philip Mantle, 2012

Page 35 – Photo, ©Sally Hope, 2014

Page 36 – Photo, ©Sally Hope, 2014

Page 36 – Photo, ©John Hanson, 2013

Page 40 – Photo, ©John Hanson, 2013

Page 42 – Photo, ©John Hanson, 2013

Page 42 – Image, ©Steven Franklin, 2013

Page 44 – ©www.internet, 2014

Page 51-53 – ©West Yorkshire Police, 2013

Page 55 – Photos, ©John Hanson, 2013

Page 56 – Photo, ©Colchester & Ipswich Museum, 2013

Page 57 – Photo, ©www.internet, 2014

Page 58 – ©Dr. David Clarke, 1987

Page 59 – Image, ©John Hanson, 2014

Page 62 – Photo, ©www.internet, 2014

Page 63 – Image, ©David Sankey, 2006

Page 64 – Sketch, ©Andy Roberts, Dr. David Clarke, 1987

Page 65 – Sketch, ©Cliff Roper, 1987

Page 65 – Image, ©David Sankey, 2006

Page 66 & 67 – ©Ron West, 1987

Page 68/69 – ©John Hanson, 2012

Page 71 – ©www.internet, 2014

Page 71/72 – Photo, ©Colin Andrews, 1987

Page 75/76 – Images, ©Robert Townshend, 2014

Page 78 – ©Mike Rogers, 1987

Page 79 – Image, ©Robert Townshend, 2014

Page 80/83 – Photo, ©Dominic Beglin, 1989

Page 83-85 – Images, ©Robert Townshend, 2014

Page 88 – ©Jon King, UFO Reality

Page 89 – Photo, ©Dominic Beglin

Page 93 – Photos, ©Peter Hough, 2014

Page 103 – Photos, ©Colin Andrews, 2013

Page 106 – Image, ©Robert Townshend

Page 107 – ©www.internet, 2014

Page 108 – Image, ©Robert Townshend, 2014

Page 111 – ©Zena Sfair, 1988

Page 113-114 – ©www.internet, 2014

Page 120 – Image, ©Stephanie Thorneycroft, 1988

Page 122 – ©David Bryant, 2013

Page 126 – Photo, ©www.internet, 2014

Page 127 – Images, ©Dr. David Clarke, 1988

Page 128 – Images, ©Robert Townshend, 2014

Page 129 – Image, ©www. Educating Humanity, 2014

Page 132 – Image, ©Steven Franklin, 2014

Page 133 – Image, ©John Hanson, 2014

Page 135-137 – Images, ©Steven Franklin, 2014

Page 141 – Image, ©John Hanson, 2014

Page 142 – Image, ©Dr. David Clarke, 1988

Page 147 – Stills, ©Gordon Creighton, 1988

Page 149 – Image, ©Steven Franklin, 2013

Page 149 – Photo, ©Pauline Emerson, 2014

Page 155 – Photo, ©Tony Dodd, 1989

Page 160-163 – ©Ron West Archives, 2014

Page 166 – Image, ©Andy Roberts, 1988

Page 168 – Photo, ©www.internet, 2014

Page 170 – Photo, ©Ron West, 1988

Page 171/172 – Arnold West, ©BUFORA, 1988

Page 173 – Photo, ©Dawn Holloway

Page 183-186 – Photos, ©Colin Andrews & Pat Delgado

Page 191 – ©Ron West Archives, 2014

Page 192 ©www.internet, 2014

Page 193 – Photo, ©Colin Andrews

Page 195 – ©www.internet, 2014

Page 196-200 – Images, ©Ron West Archives, 2014

Page 202-217 – Images, ©Ron West Archives, 2014

Page 218-219 – ©www.internet, 2014

Page 223-225 – ©Ron West Archives, 2014

Page 228-244 – ©Ron West Archives, 2104

Page 246-259 – ©Ron West Archives, 2014

Page 260 – Image, ©Robert Townshend, 2014

Page 261 – Image, ©David Sankey, 2006

Page 262 – ©www.internet, 2014

Page 264 – Photos, ©PRSA (Larraine Cilia and Dominic McNamara)

Page 265 – Photo, ©Greg Bishop, 2014

Page 266 – Image, ©Derek Samson, 1988

Page 269/270/273 – Photos, ©Philip Mantle, 2014

Page 274 – ©www.internet, 2014

Page 275 – ©Derek Samson, 1988

Page 279/281 – Photos, ©www internet, 2014

Page 285 – ©www.internet, 2014

Page 289 – ©Derek Samson, 1988

Page 298 – ©Mrs La Paz, 1948

Page 307 – Image, ©Steven Franklin, 2014

Page 307 – Photo, ©Omar Fowler

Page 307 – Photo, ©Stanley Hubbard

Page 311/312 – ©www.internet, 2014

Page 317 – ©www.internet, 2014

Page 319 – Image – Not identified

Page 321 – Image, ©Steven Franklin, 2014

Page 325 – Image, ©Wayne Mason, 2013

Page 334 – Photo, ©John Hanson

Page 335 – Image, ©David Sankey, 2006

Page 336 – Images, ©Steven Franklin, 2014

Page 337 – Photo, ©John Hanson

Page 344 – Photo, ©John Hanson

Page 345-347 – Image, ©David Sankey, 2006

Page 350 – Image, ©www.internet, 2014

Page 351-353/357 – Images, ©Wayne Mason, 2014

Page 356 – Image, ©www.internet, 2014

Haunted Skies Volume Ten

Page 359 – ©APRO Bulletin

Page 360 – ©Robert Townshend, 2014

Page 362-363 – Images, ©Steven Franklin, 2014

Page 363 – Photo, ©Gary Rowe

Page 364/369/370/372/378 – ©www.internet, 2014

Page 389/381 – Image/Photo, ©Bill Dillon, 1957/1977

Page 384/385 – ©Peter Drew, 1957

Page 388 – Image, ©David Sankey, 2006

Page 391/392 – ©www.internet, 2014

Page 397/398 – Image, ©Derek Samson, 1988

Page 401 – Image, ©David Sankey, 2009

Page 402 – Image, ©Ron Lucas, 1958

Page 404 – ©www.internet, 2014

Page 406/407/408/409 – ©John Hanson, 2014

Page 413 – ©www.internet, 2014

Page 241 – Image, ©David Sankey, 2006

Page 424 – ©John 'Dennis' Llewellyn

Page 427/429/430/431– ©www.internet, 2014

Page 432 – ©Wikipedia, 2014

Page 436 – ©www.internet, 2014

Page 440 – ©Leonard Cramp

Page 443 – ©John Hanson, 2006

Page 446-447 – ©www.internet, 2014

Page 453 – ©Wayne Mason, 2014

Page 456-460 – ©www.internet, 2014

Page 464 – ©David Sankey, 2003

Page 465 – ©Bob Tibbitts, 2014

Page 465 – ©David Sankey, 2003

Page 467 – ©Omar Fowler

Page 468 – ©John Hanson

Page 469 – ©David Sankey, 2003

Page 472 – ©Val Walters, 2014

Page 473 – ©David Sankey, 2006

Page 475 – ©Wayne Mason, 2010

Page 478 – ©David Bryant, 2010

Page 480 – ©Rosina Kirk, 1979

Page 481 – ©David Sankey, 2006/Lynda Jones

Page 482 – ©MAPIT, Steven Mera

Page 484 – ©Wikipedia, 2014

Page 487 – ©Wikipedia, 2014

Page 488 – ©Wayne Mason, 2011

Page 489 – Sketch, ©Ron Wildman, 1962

Page 491-495 – ©Wikipedia, 2014

Page 496 – ©CUFON, 1967

Page 498 – ©Alex Birch

Page 500 – ©David Sankey, 2006

Page 500 – ©Harold Threkeld, 1962

Page 501 – ©Carl Robbins, 1969

Page 502 – ©Georgina Heap, 2014

Page 503 – ©Rex Hefflin, 1965

Page 504 – ©Wikipedia, 2014

Page 507/508 – ©David Bryant, 2014

Page 509 – ©Derek Savory, 2014

Page 510 – ©Wikiepdia, 2014

Page 511 – ©Steven Franklin, 2014

Page 513 – ©Brenda Butler

Page 514-517 – ©Linda Bryant, 2014

Page 518 – ©John Hanson, 2014

Page 522 – ©Derek Savory, 2014

Page 523 – ©Brenda Butler, 1983

Page 524 – ©David Gann, 2014

Page 526/527 – ©www.internet, 2014

Page 527 – ©John Hanson, 2014

Page 528 – ©Brenda Butler, 2014

Page 530 – ©Katie Hall/John Pickering, 2014

Page 531-532 – ©Brenda Butler, 2014

Page 534 – ©John Hanson, 2010

Page 535-538 – ©Mike Oram, 2014

Page 539-551 – ©Brenda Butler, 2014

Page 552 – ©Tom Dongo, 1996

Page 553 – ©Robert Meyer, 1996

Page 553/554/555 – ©Linda Bradshaw & Tom Dongo, 1996

Page 555 – ©Robert Meyer

Page 556/557 – ©Tom Dongo, 1996

Page 558 – ©Robert Meyer, 1996

Page 559 – ©Tom Dongo & Linda Bradshaw, 1996

Page 560 – ©Robert Meyer

Page 561 – ©John Hanson

Page 562 – ©Dale Roberts, 2014

Page 562/563/564 – ©Kim Carlsberg, 2014

Page 565-571 – ©www.internet, 2014

Page 573 – ©Richard D. Hall

Page 574 – ©David Cayton, 2014

Page 578 – ©www.internet, 2014

Page 580 – ©Ryan Patrick Burns, 2014

Page 583 – ©Brenda Butler, 2006

Page 585 – ©Philip Permutt

Page 586 – ©Cyril Permutt

Page 587 – ©Philip Permutt

Page 592 – ©Sara Saunders, 2008

Page 589-595 – ©John Pickering/Katie Hall

Page 595 – ©John Hanson, 'Derek' the dog

Page 596/597/598 – ©John Hanson, 2013

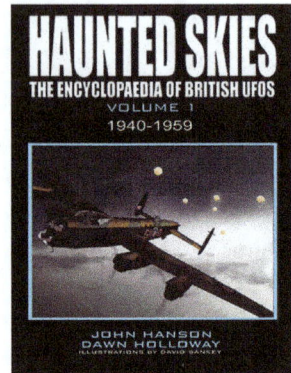

Volume 1 of *Haunted Skies* **1940-1959** *(Foreword by Timothy Good)*

We present sightings from the Second Word War. They include many reports from allied pilots, who describe seeing unidentified flying objects, while on bombing missions over Germany. Some pilots we interviewed told of being ordered to intercept a UFO; one pilot was even ordered to open fire! In addition to these are reports of early close encounters, involving allegations of abduction experiences.

Another report tells of strange 'beings' seen outside an RAF Base. We also outline a spectacular sighting, in 1957, that took place in Bedfordshire, which appears identical to that seen over Oregon by employees of the Ames Research Laboratory, San Francisco. There are also numerous reports of 'saucer', 'diamond' and 'cigar-shaped' objects seen during these years.

Volume 2 of *Haunted Skies* **1960-1965** *(Foreword by Jenny Randles)*

We re-investigated what may well be one of the earliest events, involving mysterious crop circles discovered in June 1960, at Poplar Farm, Evenlode. A 'V'-shaped UFO over Gloucestershire, and an example of a early 'Flying Triangle' over Tyneside in early September 1960. This type of object attracted much media interest in the early 1980s, following attempts by the Belgium Air Force to intercept what became labelled as 'Triangular' UFOs. This book contains many reports of saucer-shaped objects, and their occasional effect on motor vehicles. We also, wherever possible, include numerous personal letters and interviews with some of the researchers. We should not forget the early magazines, such as UFOLOG, produced by members of the (now defunct) Isle of Wight UFO Society.

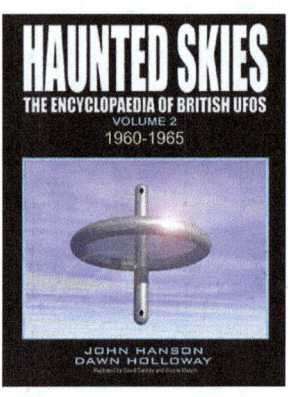

Volume 3 of *Haunted Skies* **1966-1967** *(Foreword by Nick Redfern)*

This was two years before manned landings took place on the Moon. In October 1967, there was a veritable 'wave' of UFO sightings which took place in the UK, involving cross-shaped objects, reported from Northumberland to the South Coast, with additional reports from Ireland and the Channel islands. (The police in the USA also reported sightings of 'Flying Crosses'). The sightings took place at various times, mostly during the evening or early morning hours, and involved an object which was manoeuvrable, silent – and at times – apparently flying at a low altitude. Attempts were made by the police and various authorities to explain away the sightings as Venus, based on the fact that the planet was bright in the sky during this period, which is clearly, in the majority of sightings, not the answer.

Volume 4 of *Haunted Skies* **1968-1971** *(Foreword by Philip Mantle)*

This book begins with a personal reference to Budd Hopkins, by USA researcher – Peter Robbins.

We outline a close encounter from Crediton, in Devon, which was brought to the attention of the police. Further police sightings of UFOs have been tracked down from Derbyshire, and a police chase through Kent. Multiple UFO sightings occur over the Staffordshire area, which are brought to the attention of the MOD. UFO researchers – Tony Pace and Roger Stanway – travel to London to discuss the incidents with the MOD. Close encounters at Warminster are also covered. A domed object at Bristol and further UFO landings are covered. They include a chilling account from a schoolteacher, living near Stratford-upon-Avon, and a 'flying triangle' seen over Birmingham.

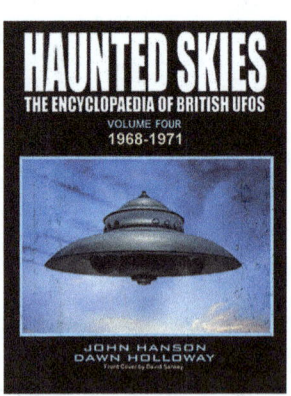

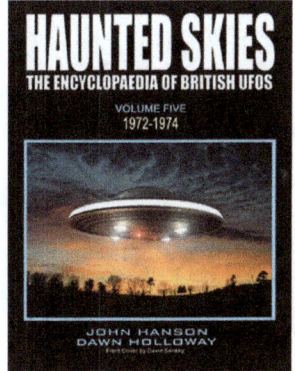

Volume 5 of *Haunted Skies* 1972-1975 *(Foreword by Matt Lyons, Chairman of BUFORA)*

Further examples of UFO activity at Warminster, involving classic 'sky watches' from such locations as Cradle Hill, was the focus of worldwide attention during this period. In addition to this are reports of mysterious footsteps heard. A visit from the 'Men in Black', and other amazing stories, form just a tiny part of some amazing material collected by us, over the years, during personal interviews with the people concerned. UFO fleets are seen over Reading, and a landed saucer-shaped object is seen at Lancashire.

A UFO, containing aliens, is seen at close range over Worcestershire. A local councillor also described seeing what he believes was an alien spaceship, with occupants. There is also an investigation into the famous Berwyn Mountain incident, when it was alleged, by some, that a 'craft' had landed.

Volume 6 of *Haunted Skies* 1976-1977 Jubilee edition *(Foreword by Kevin Goodman)*

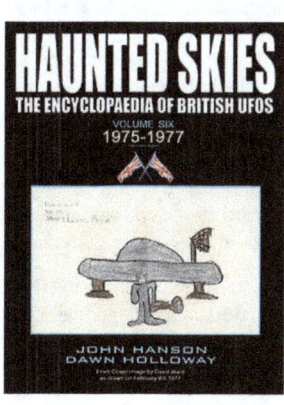

Strange globes of light, seen moving in formations of three (often referred to as triangular in overall shape). Warminster, Wiltshire – reports of mysterious black shadows, flying globes of light and a triangular-shaped UFO seen over Cleeve Hill, near Cheltenham by police officers. There is also an investigation into a number of reported landings of alien craft around the Dyfed area, in February 1977. We present some original illustrations, drawn by children at the local school (which will be reproduced in colour, in a later edition of Haunted Skies). A triangular UFO is seen over Stoke-on-Trent. Comprehensive details were also obtained, regarding Winchester woman, Joyce Bowles – who was to report many encounters with UFOs and their alien occupants.

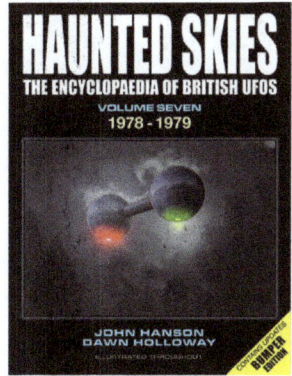

Volume 7 of *Haunted Skies* 1978-1979 *(Foreword by David Bryant)*

The famous debate into UFOs, held at the United Nations, is covered. A UFO landing at Rowley Regis, West Midlands – involving housewife Jean Hingley – labelled by the Press as the 'Mince Pie Martian' case. Many original sketches and additional information supporting her claims are offered. Another classic UFO sighting is re-investigated, following interviews held with Elsie Oakensen – a housewife from the Daventry area – who sighted a dumb-bell shaped UFO while on the way home from work. Thanks to Dan Goring, editor of EarthLink we were able to include a large number of previously unpublished sighting reports from Essex and London. We also include a close encounter from Didsbury, Manchester involving Lynda Jones, who is known personally to us.

Volume 8 of *Haunted Skies* 1980 *(Foreword by Philip Mantle)*

This book covers the period of just one year and is now, for the first time in the *Haunted Skies* series of books, published in colour. Unfortunately, due to the increase in pagination and the use of colour, the price has been raised, but still represents extremely good value. The first part of the book covers the period from January to November 1980. This includes numerous reports of UFO sightings and encounters. In addition to this, we outline our investigation into the Zigmund Adamski death, and the UFO sighting involving Todmorden Police Constable Alan Godfrey. In the second part, which covers December 1980, we present a comprehensive overview of the events that took place in Rendlesham Forest, thanks to the assistance of retired Colonel Charles Halt and long-standing UFO researcher, Brenda Butler.

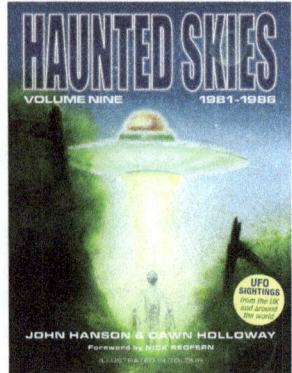

Volume 9 of *Haunted Skies* 1981-1986 *(Foreword by Nick Redfern)*
450 pages, some in colour

The authors point out that the majority of the information contained within the *Haunted Skies* series of books will not be found in declassified UFO files, catalogued in the Public Records Office, Kew, London.

This book contains:

UFO sightings over RAF Woodbridge, Suffolk – the scene of much interest during the previous month; a landed UFO at South Yorkshire; UFOs seen over Kent – harrowing close encounters between UFOs and motorists are outlined. These include a report from three women, driving home along the A5 in rural Shropshire (UK), which can be contrasted with a similar allegation made by three women from Kentucky, USA. A close encounter over the M50 Motorway, Gloucestershire; a couple from Hampshire tell of their roadside encounter – which left the husband with some strange marks on his body; a man out fishing, in Aldershot – who was approached by aliens; mysterious apports of stones that occurred, over a number of years, at Birmingham, West Midlands, involving the police – who staked out the locality in a bid to catch the offender. In addition to this, falls of coins and stones in other parts of the world are also outlined.

Although primarily covering British UFO sightings – wherever space permits (always in short supply) – we now include other forgotten worldwide cases of interest, brought to the attention of the reader. One such incident tells of a triangular UFO, seen over Arizona; another of a UFO sighted by a Russian astronaut.

A bizarre story involving David Daniels, who approached a number of prominent worldwide UFO researchers during the early 1980s – he alleged he was from the Pleiades and claimed to be able to metamorphosise from a human body to a reptilian. While it is difficult to believe rationally that this could be true, the authors tell of visits made to influential people, such as the head of the MOD, and The Lord Hill-Norton. Fact is stranger than fiction!

DISCLAIMER

In respect of the above images, which include sketches, photographs and personal memorabilia, obtained over many years' research, we have tried our utmost to identify exactly who individual copyright lies with.

Should we have got it wrong, we unreservedly apologise and will credit the copyright in *Haunted Skies* Volume 11.

With regard to the many hundreds of anomalous photographs taken by Brenda Butler and her colleagues, during visits to Rendlesham Forest over the years, we have copyrighted them to Brenda at this stage. Should anybody wish to draw our attention to individual copyright, we will be pleased to put the record straight in *Haunted Skies* Volume 11.

Thanks also go to Robert Townshend for his hand-painted images, which he has submitted for use in this Volume, and to Andrew Collins for his excellent investigation into the John Day case. Sadly, we have lost touch with John – hopefully he will contact us in due course.

These books have cost us a great deal of money to produce, but we strongly believe that this information forms part of our social history and rightful heritage. It should therefore be preserved, despite the ridicule still aimed at the subject by the media. *All previous titles – pictured above – are currently available.*

If anyone is willing to assist us with the preparation of any illustrations, it would be much appreciated. We can be contacted by letter at **31, Red Lion St, Alvechurch, Worcestershire B48 7LG**, by telephone **0121 445 0340**, or email: **johndawn1@sky.com**

For those that may wish to consider publishing their own books or magazines, our typesetter, Bob Tibbitts, is available to offer his design, layout and typesetting services – producing a final press-ready pdf file which can then be used for professional printing. He can be contacted on email: **isetcdart@tiscali.co.uk**

SAJID JAVID MP

HOUSE OF COMMONS
LONDON SW1A 0AA

Mr Hanson, Ms Holloway
31 Red Lion Street
Alvechurch
B48 7LG

8th August 2014

Dear Mr Hanson and Ms Holloway

Thank you very much for coming along to my public forum in Alvechurch last night. I was very sorry to hear of the problems you've had in getting copies of your books to me.

I will certainly read through 'Haunted Skies' with interest.

Please do keep in touch if ever I can be of assistance in the future, and thank you again for the kind thought of sending these to me.

Yours sincerely

S. Javid

Tel: 020 7219 7027 • Email: sajid.javid.mp@parliament.uk
www.sajidjavid.com

www.ingramcontent.com/pod-product-compliance
Lightning Source LLC
Chambersburg PA
CBHW060502300426
44112CB00017B/2523